ANNA PAVLOVA
Her Life and Art

KEITH MONEY

ANNA PAVLOVA

Her Life and Art

ALFRED A. KNOPF

New York   1982

Library of Congress Cataloging in Publication Data
Money, Keith.
Anna Pavlova, her life and art.
Includes index.
1. Pavlova, Anna, 1881–1931.
2. Ballet dancers—Russian S.F.S.R.—Biography.
I. Title.
GV1785.P3M66   792.8'2'0924   [B]   81–47502
ISBN 0-394-42786-6   AACR2

Manufactured in the United States of America
First Edition

FRONTISPIECE PHOTOGRAPH:
In the Dance of the Hours, from *La Gioconda*, c.1915.

for Frederick Ashton

CONTENTS

ACKNOWLEDGMENTS

If writing a book seems at times impossible, then thanking all the people who tried to make that work possible is no easier task. When first she knew that I was working on this book, that indefatigable researcher Nesta Macdonald immediately boxed and despatched to me a very big collection of photocopied newspaper clippings on my subject, at a stroke saving me much time and expense by not having to cover the same ground; such selflessness is beyond praise. I was immensely fortunate in obtaining the services of Celia Pinnell as a translator. She worked month after month, painstakingly, with the most meager incentive. Nothing was too much trouble. Her transcriptions from the Tsar's Yearbooks would make an entire book in themselves. In addition, she worked through the British Library's Slavonic newspaper section, struggling with countless copies of *Novoye Vremya* and the like, dating from the turn of the century. Half this book would be an empty shell without her labors.

I received nothing but kindness and immense goodwill from collaborators of Pavlova herself. It was of inestimable value to be able to consult with people who had danced in her company before the First World War; Linda Lindovska, Winifred Edwards, Madge Abercrombie, and Muriel Stuart share an ebulliance and verve that is to be wondered at. Apart from endless patience, they all made material freely available to me without the slightest demur. (Indeed, Miss Stuart allowed me to rummage in one of her cupboards while she searched another, looking for a parcel that had not been untied for sixty years. We found it.) Harry Mills put at my disposal all the material collected by himself and by his late wife, Hilda Butsova; he was kindness itself. In addition I was able to read a draft of an unpublished memoir by Butsova. For other details it was helpful to speak with Vicente Celli, and with Giovanni Bagarotti.

Tamara Finch worked at translating Russian books for me, and suggested others; her labors were offered, and accepted, without any recompense. Judith Reyn Stroux produced valuable material for me in Vienna. Jenny Craven brought me material from Russia; Dalal Achcar sent notes from Rio de Janeiro. My good friend Doris Langley Moore explained interesting details about Pavlova's dresses. Violette Verdy was my very responsive entrée to the Bibliothèque of the Paris Opéra. When I was at the Bancroft Library in San Francisco I was shown every possible consideration. At the Museum of London, Jasmin Cannon Bell displayed a patience, and expended energy on my behalf, that was way beyond the call of duty. Janis Conner, curator of the Malvina Hoffman Estate, gave me total access to material. Others who responded to requests were Russell Hartley in San Francisco and Parmenia Migel Ekstrom in New York. Claire de Robilant sent me clippings relating to South America, and confirmed several dates; Mrs. Alexander Tcherepnin gave me documents to read; Lynn Garafola was helpful with information about Hubert Stowitts.

It is difficult to imagine any serious attempt at ballet scholarship coming to fruition without the Library of the Performing Arts at Lincoln Center in New York. The Dance Collection, presided over with such geniality by Genevieve Oswald, is truly indispensable to one's task. Henry Wisneski helped me there on innumerable occasions, often suggesting items I might otherwise have overlooked, and no library could have been more tolerant. It was Monty Arnold who remembered the vital Robinson Locke scrapbooks in the Theatre Collection. Norman Crider's Ballet Shop on Broadway in New York is a mecca where enthusiasts will always find treasures. I was allowed to record a number of them, and indeed Toby Leibovitz was able to put me on the trail of items already dispersed from the shop. I am particularly grateful to Rosemary Winckley, to Starr Danias and Douglas Wassell, to Tilly Abbe and Phyllis Kennedy, and to Genna Smakov, for rare prints from their collections. Also of help to the cause were Bryce Cobain, librarian at the Royal Academy of Dancing, and Audrey Harman, archivist of the Royal Ballet School.

Joan Dempsey carried the burden of having to type the first half of this manuscript—more than once, and often from my haphazard dictation; her loyalty was always supportive in the most tiresome phases of a task that seemed never-ending. Ruth Dwornik in Norfolk was unfailingly helpful in matters of photography and lent me her darkroom facilities at outrageous hours of the day and night. In New York, Ellen McNeilly gave me the keys to her darkroom and left me a free rein, and Sharon Wagner was a loyal helper in many of these darkroom labors.

Clues to Pavlova came in countless conversations with people in the world of dance, among whom I would mention Sir Frederick Ashton, Dame Ninette de Valois, Felia Doubrovska, and Ruth Page. It is always cheering when people who are busy writing their own books readily take time off to respond to queries by others; shining examples in this regard are Mary Clarke and Richard Buckle. The friends who have tolerated the overflow of madness know who they are, but Fred and Joan Baekeland in New York have given me an address for weeks at a time, and my saintly agent, Anne Harrel, must have "Pavlova" deeply etched into her much-carved-upon heart. She has been unswerving in her belief that the task should reach fruition, no matter how dark the nights.

Robert Gottlieb's commitment to these "impossible" books is unique in its energy, and his team at Knopf are a remarkable band by any standards; somehow they make a book like this "happen." But a great deal happens simply because Bob Gottlieb spends hours at a time tackling details in consort with his authors; weekends and weekdays blur when he is closely involved. It was Eva Resnikova who bore the brunt of me and my manuscript, and I only hope the toil has not blunted her relish for such seemingly appalling tasks, for she can produce an inspired devil's advocacy on occasion. And finally, Dorothy Schmiderer's design talent brought order out of chaos, and Ellen McNeilly devoted endless energy to the production stages of all these labors.

ABOUT THE ILLUSTRATIONS

The pictures in this book have been culled from a multitude of sources, but it would be invidious not to make special mention of two major repositories of Pavlova photographs: the Dance Collection of the Library of the Performing Arts at Lincoln Center in New York, and the Museum of London collection. Both provided a large number of pictures, and the task would have been immeasurably harder without them. For every picture that appears in this book, I must have examined at least a dozen others, and there are probably hundreds more that I have not seen. If Pavlova seems to have had little life beyond dancing, then a lot of that "spare" time was given over to photographers. Was there ever a more cooperative star?

Of the material that I unearthed, much was in a parlous state after half a century of casual handling. Even major collections seldom have the finances to allow for everything to be stored on film, and it was disheartening to see things at the point of no return: newspaper clippings were brown with age and crumbling, photographs were fading or oxidizing, albums were disintegrating, and silverfish and bad glue were often hastening the end. But amid all the wreckage the image was still triumphant, and to make a choice was often frustrating; by rights they should all be seen. Faced with twelve different portraits by Eugene Hutchinson of Pavlova as the Dumb Girl of Portici, I could only dither and then, finally, point to *one*. They were all beautiful.

In many instances I have rephotographed originals and then made new prints, trying to correct any fading or tonal deficiencies. Damaged areas were then reconstituted by hand. I must have done this with 1,500 photographs—from which the final selection was made—and I would not wish to embark on such a job again. The administrators of two major collections overruled policy and allowed me to work directly from their own negatives, a concession for which I am grateful. As late as April 1981 I was still crawling around on the floor photographing ancient relics that had previously escaped the net.

There is a limit to the amount of repair one can effect, and in some of the pictures in this book the image triumphs over the shortcomings of its conveyance. As an instance, pictures by the White Studios in New York, from before the First World War, are—as seen in this book—photographs of photographs of photographs. White would take his excellent studies with a plate camera, and then he would fix an assembly of 10 x 12 prints to his studio wall with strips of tape and upholstery pins. In the corner of each picture (often thirty or more) he would nail a piece of card with an identifying numeral. From the far side of his studio he would then photograph the wall of pictures, and when the resulting photograph was turned into a 10 x 12 print, that would become his order sheet. These fading relics exist today, glued to buckling black linen pages which have started to impress their own pattern onto what is left of the images; over a span of seventy years the prints still show the disfiguring reflected light that bounced off the uneven glazed surfaces in the studio that first day. I then come along and photograph everything again, with the result that some of the pictures (the *Valse Caprice* of 1911 is an example) are now reproduced with a 600 percent enlargement of the original—that is to say, the old *intermediate* image. Of course, all the shortcomings and the decay are evident, yet they are somehow surpassed by the pictures' intrinsic value. Many other photographs have come from newspapers and magazines of Pavlova's era. Some of these were printed in gravure, but others were in coarsely screened letterpress with indifferent inking, sometimes pale sepia, or even mauve. At least my intervening photography has allowed a chance to improve upon the source material, by increasing the contrast or the range of tone. For that reason, some of the pictures actually look better here than they did to contemporary readers when they were first reproduced.

Other pictures presented other problems. Even apart from the endless, and often quite funny, miscaptioning of photographs in highly respectable sources (perhaps nothing can match the errors in Magriel's monograph), there remain images of Pavlova in ballet poses that I, at least, still cannot identify—although background details and points of costuming often help one to make a likely guess. It does not help that the exigencies of touring ballet could make Pavlova on occasion use costume A for ballet B, or pose in bits of costumes for ballets A and B in a pose from ballet C.

We must also accept that certain photographs were either poorly posed to begin with or subsequently cropped badly—by the photographer, the printer, or some early editor. Any dance image in this book that lacks a toe or a finger (or worse) has been deformed by a hand previous to mine. Similarly, early hands—quite frequently Pavlova's own—are responsible for all-too-visible retouching on many of the dance photographs, although there are here a number of pictures with undoctored feet and waistlines; and our age has learned to accept that *les pointes* do not necessarily have *des pointes!*

And finally, with a model as photogenic as Anna Pavlova, almost every picture seemed worthy of being printed full-page; but such a decision would have necessitated drastically reducing the number of pictures—or trebling the number of pages in this book. I can only hope that the balance achieved seems right—of dance images and personal pictures, of early period and late, of large and small. Photographs always illuminate a biographical subject, but in the case of Anna Pavlova, they are a vital part of any attempt to document her life and her art.

INTRODUCTION

There are some names that loom so large and imperishable in one's life that they are ikons, safely international, and to find oneself involved with one is a bewildering affair indeed. Scratching away at a daubed monument, looking for hints of original color—one needs to excuse oneself for treading where so many others have trodden, for exhausting the ground still further. It seems an intrusion.

I knew the *name* Pavlova as a child. Growing up in New Zealand, the country that produced the meringue cake which carries her name, was sufficient to ensure that, at least. Though a helping of Pavlova cake seldom came my way, it was strange and wonderful when it did: all that shattered meringue, and thick cream, and wierdly transparent green slices of Chinese gooseberry! And a hint of passionfruit—that was the trick. There was always the odd seed, hard and elusive. Only now do I understand that no chef could have struck a better balance for the subject of his homage: a delicate and fragile thing, cool yet faintly exotic in appearance. An attempt to take it apart leaves one with a disconcerting collapse of the whole. The slivers of meringue are like ice floes on the Neva; the passionfruit leaves a haunting aftertaste. It is vivid, and yet . . . what was the shape?

Years after my greed for Pavlova cake subsided there came a vague realization that the name represented something else: a touchstone for dancing, for theatrical excitement. Why did every ballerina have to present her art upon a stage already shadowed by this woman? Was she a talisman or an avenging ghost? One day in the early sixties, in a room full of cheerful chatter, my eyes strayed to a glass-fronted cabinet of books. I opened one of the doors and took out a volume; it was illustrated with numerous sepia plates. From nowhere, the owner of the book was at my side. "Isn't she beautiful? I'm sure no one else could *ever* look like that." Since this remark was made by Margot Fonteyn, it made me realize that each generation seeks and finds its own idols.

Two years later, I was asked to do a book on Anna Pavlova. I refused. Several years later, the same suggestion was made. Again I refused. Four years after that, the suggestion was put to me again. I was beginning to feel that the name would not go away. It lurked there, very blurred, but frighteningly large, like a grotesque shadow cast by a small lamp. At a time when I was talking to Robert Gottlieb of Knopf in New York (in retrospect, about everything *but* Pavlova) I was aware of something: that I was ducking away from a shadow while he was focusing on a concept.

He thought I should exorcize the shadow, and he was prepared to encourage the exorcism. He kept all his numerous misgivings to himself and proceeded on his agile way among the crags and pinnacles of the publishing world. Somewhere in the deep ravines, I was left to face the enormity of such rashness.

For a year I merely read related material, and it soon became apparent that no sequential document of Pavlova's life existed, although related memoirs abounded, some enormously self-serving, others less so. The books directly about Pavlova tended to dissect her, examining different aspects of her in isolation from the whole. After a lifetime in the company of Anna Pavlova, Victor Dandré had produced a book that was utterly devoted, very detailed, and ultimately like the Taj Mahal: a monument symbolizing an ideal. It seemed to me that I should commit myself to the orderly progress of a paper chase. If clues led me to a dead end, I would go back until I found the main trail again; I would plunge in at the beginning, and try and emerge at the end. It proved engulfing: the existing books were revealed as outcrops of a vast substructure, veins of ore that ran in all directions, seemingly without end, twisting and turning and doubling back on themselves, layer upon layer. After five years I am still unearthing caches of related material; only now, my capacity for surprise is somewhat reduced. And here I have halted; I must lay out the evidence. In doing so, I know something of the feelings of the Don as he faced up to the looming shape on the plains of La Mancha and—at the very moment when the giant came into focus—found himself upended. The quarry is more diverse, bigger, stronger, more surprising, and, yes, more human than any single thing has a right to be. But even if we cannot capture the creature, we must try and mark her passing; her phenomenal energy alone would deserve a monument.

In a span of twenty years, Anna Pavlova managed to be observed closely by millions of people around the world. Unlike a movie star with hundreds of alter egos spawned across different prosceniums at one and the same time, Pavlova could not tell her tale but that she drew fresh breath each time she told it. For her there could be only one stage at any one time; but there were—literally—thousands of them, and she graced them all. She was constantly expending her physical resources at a fever pitch, and just as constantly she managed to renew them. She did it in the great capitals of the world and she did it, with the same degree of energy, in provincial towns and grim seaports.

Pavlova often turned her back on security and on adulation from people in high office, so we know that she was promoting something more than just herself. She was really selling Art, as a faith, and she was careful not to get too deeply enmeshed in the semantics of its exact nature. She longed to find beauty in the world and to distill its essence. If, in the process, she came across cruelty and ugliness, then she did not flinch; she merely set about finding an antidote, and her laboratory for this happened to be the stage. She was lucky in having a medium of expression that vaulted language barriers, but within its confines she had a very precise, difficult, and esoteric language of her own to contend with: the language of nineteenth-century classical ballet. She had been painstakingly schooled in it—all her early life had been entirely governed by a desire to master its strange complexities—yet she was one of the first to join in the expansive reforms that swept in with the new century. So, contrary to popular myth, she was not a reactionary at heart. She did things her own way, recognizing her boundaries; and if others later raced on more daringly, she respected their right to do so, while reserving her own right to avoid what seemed to her to be excessive modernity. Two-thirds of the way through her life, she was sometimes thought to be old-fashioned—but it was in the way that a genuine Chippendale chair is old-fashioned: expressive, timeless in quality, and always being copied.

History is so often a matter of interpretation—legend made plausible. From the moment of her untimely death Pavlova was swept along, a fugitive occupant in some phantom troika harnessed to Gossip, Apocrypha, and Hearsay. True, she wrote her message in the waters; but it was a powerful message, and we seem to have been cavalier about recording its author's achievements. She was in her time the most famous dancer in the world; and for all the extraordinary numbers of people who actually saw her dance, there were countless others who knew her name and what she stood for. She also happened to have been Russian, yet the late Natalia Roslavleva, an indefatigable researcher of Russian ballet history, could write in a letter: "Nothing much is known about Pavlova; she was never really talked about." The eminent Soviet ballet historian Vera Krasovskaya, in her book about Pavlova, felt the need to employ a *belles-lettres* fantasy. Yet she did turn to contemporary newspaper accounts for information, and in this way uncovered much about the vital first ten years of dancing—years that had all but evaporated in the mists surrounding the legend.

When Pavlova died, it was headline news around the world, but even in that first week the facts were becoming clouded: in Paris, a Russian-language magazine printed the wrong day in the caption for a cover picture. We can forgive the memorial card for her funeral that gave her age discreetly wrong; they were printing what they had been told. But printing her first name wrong? To take another instance from that same week: her partner of thirteen years, Alexandre Volinine, when asked how they came to work together, replied:

In 1910 Diaghilev took me to London in the Russian Ballet along with Nijinsky and Lydia Lopokova. At the same time Pavlova and Mordkin were dancing for Charles Frohman at the Globe Theatre. A year later Mordkin was ill, and Gatti-Casazza took Pavlova and me to the Metropolitan Opera.

It is hardly giving things away to say that in Volinine's statement there is only one correct fact—Mordkin was ill—and even that is not in its correct context.

Memoirs play strange tricks with facts. Victor Dandré, Pavlova's husband (who failed to provide legal title to that relationship after Pavlova's death), wrote a book that was devotedly detailed, and yet he describes with apparent firsthand knowledge a London season during which, in fact, he was in St. Petersburg—and under arrest. Pavlova's last words on this earth have become almost as famous as the costume she was asking to be prepared, and yet there are reports, written within hours, none of which mentions those words (which she may very well have murmured), but which do mention a phrase even more haunting.

Even the facts of her birth are obscured. For the date, we can take an entry in the registry book of the St. Petersburg Military Hospital, which gives us 1881 and January 31 (February 12 new style). In the catalogue of a 1956 exhibition it was said that a birth certificate giving 1882 was in the Constance Paget-Fredericks Memorial Collection in California; there is now no trace of such a document. When Anna Pavlova became widely known in St. Petersburg society, there was speculation about her background. Was she really the daughter of reserve soldier Matvey Pavlov? She seemed to have the look of a well-bred Jewish girl. Pavlova, in 1910, was telling reporters that she had been born in St. Petersburg, that her father was a minor official who had died when she was only two, and that as a result she and her mother had lived in straitened circumstances, relying on a small pension. When Pavlova was a ballet student, it was noticed that she disliked her friends addressing her as "Anna Matveyevna," which was the normal patronymic for a daughter of Matvey Pavlov. The girl seems to have instilled an understanding that a polite fiction, "Anna Pavlovna," was more acceptable to her. (This confused the administration; in records of the company one can tell which writer knew Pavlova well, and which one didn't; she was A.P. Pavlova to some, and A.M. Pavlova to others.) This ambiguity certainly suggests illegitimacy, and the likeliness of her Jewish blood compounded a social stigma. In St. Petersburg at that time such ancestry carried a hidden threat of potential banishment from principal residential districts—if the government took it into its head to enforce its own statutes.

In the Leningrad State Theatre Archives there is a document in the form of an official pass issued to the mother of Anna Pavlova on October 10, 1899, stating that Lyubov Feodorovna Pavlova, from the village of Bor in the province of Tversk, and wife of reserve soldier Matvey Pavlov, is discharged into towns and cities of the Russian Empire. Discharged? The word *uvol* is employed in the decree. It was probably a bad choice of word by some minor clerk; however, it has a stern connotation: the equivalent of being dismissed, or even expelled. Lyubov Pavlova is listed as being married, with a daughter, Anna, by a first marriage. The inference is that Matvey Pavlov, in 1899 at least, was still living. This was a time when wives of peasants did not have the right to leave their husbands without their permission, and a husband had an automatic right to bring a wife home by force, should he so wish. The document makes it clear that Anna is not Matvey's offspring, but it cannot be regarded as evidence that an earlier marriage ever took place. The mother's profession is given as washerwoman, her faith Orthodox, and her age forty. This would mean that she had her child when she was about twenty-two. Lyubov's pass was valid for one year. At the time it was made out, the new season at the Maryinsky—with the new graduate, Anna Pavlova—had been under way for a month, so the daughter at least had a salary of sorts to contribute to a joint dwelling. From one account we know that Pavlova's mother was in St. Petersburg in 1900; yet by the autumn of that year Anna was said to have in her employ a personal maid. This makes one wonder if the mother's pass was not renewed in October. It is difficult to imagine the mother and the maid both catering to a young dancer's needs, and one does have to remember that the world of ballet in St. Petersburg almost dictated that personable young dancers received (and considered) the attentions of ad-mirers. A modestly conventional mother could only have cramped this style, unlike a maid, who would be circumspect in such matters and whose salary in any event would probably come from her mistress's admirer.

Either Matvey Pavlov was content to be abandoned by his wife in October 1899, or he had already done the abandoning. We know that Pavlova acquired from her mother all the out-ward trappings of Orthodoxy: ikons (particularly of the Virgin), the festival of Christmas, and sanctuary in the sign of the cross; but she seems also to have acquired a clear knowledge of a Jewish background. The intensity of the mother's cloak of Orthodoxy is not surprising in the light of Russian anti-Semitism, but the daughter seems to have absorbed the Scriptural teachings as well as a dichotomy of background. She absorbed it, and she also concealed part of it. A member of a wealthy Jewish banking family, Poliakoff, has been reported as saying once that he was the half-brother of Anna Pavlova. If this points to a liaison between Anna's mother and Lazar Poliakoff, we might assume that Lyubov was in that family's employ. Even if Anna's natural father was of reasonable means, the financial support for the poignant outcome of the union appears to have been minimal. Perhaps it was the support that "died" after two years.

Victor Dandré fills in details of Pavlova's early years. The baby had been born two months premature, and she was such a frail mite that she was christened without delay—on February 3 (o.s.), Saint Anne's Day. She was kept wrapped in wool swaddling, but one might guess that her survival had as much to do with the will of her spirit. Dandré said that the child was removed to the care of a grandmother in Ligovo, "in order to improve the health of the little girl." This summer resort, 50 miles from St. Petersburg, may have been less prone to waterway miasmas, but it can hardly be considered a climate's divide away from the city. One imag-

ines the young mother was simply unable to care for the child adequately, having to return to work. In her own fragmentary memoir, first published in 1912, Pavlova displays a deep romantic attachment for her grandmother's cottage and its surroundings, yet she never specifies that it was Ligovo; and though Dandré says that it was there that the local teacher instructed her in Russian and Scripture, Pavlova herself implies that the visits to "the country" were only summer expeditions, when their own belongings had to be transported in a van from the city. It was not a case of the grandmother having died, because Pavlova mentioned her as being alive at the time of an interview toward the end of 1910. The implication is that their frugality of life was such that there was no spare furniture in the cottage. Dandré published a photograph of a dacha of three or four rooms, with an auxiliary lean-to, but it was certainly not isolated; there were adjacent buildings on the same road, behind a picket fence and a screen of birch trees.

We know for certain that the single most important event in the whole of Anna Pavlova's life took place in the city, and we should learn of it in her own words:

> When I was eight years old, I heard that we were to celebrate Christmas by going to see a performance at the Maryinsky Theatre. I had never yet been to the theatre, and I plied my mother with questions in order to find out what kind of show it was that we were going to see. She replied by telling me the story of "The Sleeping Beauty"—a favorite of mine among all fairy tales, and one which she had already told me countless times. When we started for the Maryinsky Theatre, the snow was brightly shining in the reflected light of street lamps and shop windows. Our sleigh was noiselessly speeding along the hard surface, and I felt unspeakably happy, seated beside my mother, her arm tenderly enclosing my waist. "You are going to enter fairyland," she said, as we were being whirled across the darkness towards the theatre, the mysterious unknown. . . .
>
> As soon as the orchestra began to play, I became very grave and attentive, eagerly listening, moved for the first time in my life by the call of Beauty. But when the curtain rose, displaying the golden hall of a wonderful palace, I could not withhold a shout of delight, and I remember hiding my face in my hands when the old hag appeared on the stage in her car driven by rats. In the second act a swarm of youths and maidens appeared, and danced a most delightful waltz. "How would you like to dance this?" asked my mother with a smile. "Oh," I replied, "I should prefer to dance as the pretty lady does who plays the part of the Princess. One day, I shall be the Princess, and dance upon the stage of this very theatre."

But of course. Anyway, it makes a charming scene, even if one wonders how Aurora's entrance came to precede the waltz. The important thing is the sunburst in the child's mind; it is quite likely that she had never heard an orchestra play before, and the impact must have been staggering, given that she was already eight years old. We are left to consider how the mother's house-keeping budget encompassed the price of two seats in the Tsar's theatre, and whether the sophisticated entertainment was sug-gested, and paid for, by an interested well-wisher. The result of this Christmas outing was that the child pestered her mother

ABOVE At six years of age.

OPPOSITE At nine, presumably
with her mother.

BELOW At about eleven.

until she was taken for an interview at the Ballet School. There they were told that Anna would have to complete her tenth year before she could audition. For two frustrating years she seems to have skipped about the woods at Ligovo, waiting for the all-important tenth birthday. Like many an only child, she was very dependent on her own resources, and she had the time to observe natural things without distraction, since there was often no one to talk to. At these times she expressed herself in movement; it was her medium.

A photograph of the little Anna at about six years of age shows an alert child, fully engaged with the camera's presence. She is composed rather than posed, with legs crossed in a naturally elegant manner. Her bonnet and parasol may have been studio props, but she is dressed prettily, and though obviously a fine-boned child, she looks perfectly healthy. Three years later she has acquired a solemn and introverted expression; it is something more than the stillness required by a slow photographic exposure. It seems to be the mother who appears alongside her. But the child's expression is not simply a reaction against the adult's presence; it seems more a look of contained rebellion against the confinement of the static pose she has been made to adopt. There is no communication with the camera—more a resentment at its intrusion. This is not a child with any intention of winning friends. The bangs of earlier years have gone, and the auburn hair is brushed back severely, revealing an almost unnaturally high hairline. Another picture, about three years on, suggests that there had been some attempt to alter this trend; the hair has been cut, and the natural slight wave has sprung into life. There are signs, too, of bleaching from the summer sun, but already the hair is pulled back again, in a manner that suggests the discipline of a school. The expression is proud and the manner detached, and only the natural upturn to the corners of the mouth avoids a look of sullenness. But the eyes are lifted much more, and though the turn of the head still dismisses the camera, the gaze seems to be leveled at some distant horizon beyond the confines of the studio. Her ears have been pierced, and she is wearing earrings designed like a snowdrop cupped around a pearl. They are still in evidence eight or nine years later—but the young Anna has a locket and a brooch, as well as a surfeit of bows. She is dressed to impress.

At the time of her tenth birthday, the child achieved a return visit to the Ballet School, and though there were doubts expressed about her physique, she gave enough hint of promise that the examiners were won over. Her acceptance at the academy can only have been a boon to the hard-working, hard-pressed mother; the school removed at a stroke all financial responsibilities for the girl. Pavlova wrote in 1912:

> Every Sunday my mother came to see me; and I used to spend all my holidays with her. During the summer we always lived in the country. We grew so fond of our little holiday cottage, that even now we have not the heart to give it up in favour of some more comfortable abode. And I am writing these pages on a table upon the verandah, amidst surroundings which I love because every feature reminds me of the days of my childhood.

Among her classmates, the young Anna (at left of birdcage) displays
what is very probably her first professional smile for the camera.

So the early years would seem to have been reasonably happy ones, despite the inherent loneliness of her situation.

As a student, Pavlova was talented and also different. She looked thin by the standards of the day, and in an effort to remedy this she swallowed the regulation issues of castor oil with less fuss than any of her fellows. For such an apparently slight creature she had strong hips and thighs and a thorax that was not particularly waisted, so that the body, though immensely supple, flowed "all of a piece." Her thin ankles and exceptionally arched insteps gave an illusory brittleness to her figure, while the setting of the head on a very clearly defined neck contributed to this suggestion of frailty. It was a body that fooled the Maryinsky selectors, and it went on fooling observers. Her muscles were steely; she was actually a racing machine, a hare.

Pavlova's story is one of will power and dedication underpinning an unwavering belief. Her natural talent, the curious poetry of her body, was so outstanding that nobody could ignore it, even though the idiosyncrasies were disquieting to some. By the time she was eighteen or nineteen she seems to have begun to

realize that a camera might be friendly toward her, that she could conspire with it; she has sensed that she can contact an audience through the lens. The moods swing from the flirtatious to the contemplative, and whereas the childhood photographs tend to shut out the observer, the subsequent ones seem to imply that Pavlova is now prepared to share even the somber moods. In many hundreds of photographs, there is a talent for communing with the camera so rare in its consistency that today she could have become a top fashion model. She wore clothes with a faultless understanding of their potential. On her, any hat seemed a desirable model. Under it, the face was a mysterious confluence of planes and angles. It is difficult for us to realize that this exotic quality was at that time considered disturbing, at odds with the reigning ideals of feminine charm. She suffered from being thought "not beautiful," and this attitude, frequently expressed, seems to have contributed to a certain defensiveness in her character.

Her temperament was a churning mixture of things, volatile and timid. She never acquired the artificiality that could conceal

6

her shifts in emotion, the roller-coaster swings from gaiety to melancholy, which seems in her case to have been something more than "Russian" temperament. The pattern of her moods would today arouse a suspicion that she was a manic-depressive. In an interview in 1910 she put the emphasis on the melancholic side of her nature: "I was born in St. Petersburg—on a rainy day. You know, it almost always rains in St. Petersburg. There is a certain gloom and sadness in the atmosphere of the Russian capital, and I have breathed the air of St. Petersburg so long that I have become infected with sadness."

The adult Pavlova could behave like a child, giving vent to her feelings quite openly, and her inability to channel these currents and divert them into a more acceptable lagoon of social manner made many people wary of her; to them she appeared "difficult." If she felt at ease with someone, she could be the epitome of friendly warmth, but she often seemed hypersensitive and tense, like some forest creature forever alert to signals. She processed stimuli instantaneously and did not block the counter-reaction; this often led to sudden tears, flushes of anger, or merry explosions of joy. The fact that she did not learn to process these emotions in the usual manner may actually have helped her stage personality, because the sincerity of her feeling transferred itself readily to an audience. She had good native intelligence and deep humanity, but she did not have an intellect based upon being well-read, and as a result she suffered a lack of communication in the company of those who had this learning. With them she sometimes retreated into shallow coquetry, not because she was superficial but because she needed an armor.

Pavlova had a rare affinity with birds. In many ways she was like a bird herself in her day-to-day deportment: quick, darting hand movements, a straight-legged walk, and swift turns and inclinations of the head when the dark brown eyes focused brightly or were suddenly averted if she wanted to shield her own reaction. Her voice was birdlike too—a high chirrup. She had that waxy pallor so often associated with dancers, but hers was a skin that took the sun well if given a chance. Notwithstanding the propensity of photographic retouchers in an era that smoothed away all signs of strain, Pavlova's neck did have a natural soft cushioning unusual in dancers. In the latter part of her career her weight fluctuated slightly, according to stresses, climate, and physiological changes, but the costumes she wore were either of the draped variety or tutus so elaborate by present-day standards that it was the extremities—the amazing feet and ankles, and the arms with their wonderful plastique—that claimed the attention. In the latter part of her career, after visiting the Orient, her stage make-up became heavier and more stylized: a whitened mask with great triangles of eyes shaded in violet, and lips of deepest crimson that took on a strangely sardonic cast when she acknowledged applause.

Relationships were difficult for Pavlova: a mixture of loyalty, dependence, and trust that sometimes fractured because she could not always take into account the stresses that her own unnatural and fragmented life placed upon others. She sought and found a surrogate father, one whose adoration was so secure that she could fight furiously against it, knowing that she would be forgiven. She was brought up in an age, and a setting, that taught girls that sexual activity was an obligation, something to be faced up to, and there were signs that she never entirely overcame this indoctrination. In the Ballet School this was by the example of elders, some of whom seemed to owe their advancement to the care with which they picked an admirer. Pavlova was not of a mercenary inclination; nor was she prone to fall in love easily—though she certainly knew what romantic love could be. The lack of it through much of her life seems to have cast a shadow over her spirit. She never had a child, and this too was felt by her to be in the nature of a penalty.

How to chart the course of such a strange and unremitting odyssey? Pavlova's voyages were global, and the effect she had on the history of dancing is incalculable. She took places by stealth or by storm; either way, they never forgot she had been there. In each audience there was usually one person who felt, at the end of the evening, that his life was going on an entirely different and previously unimagined course. Such people were converts. In the age of the airplane, can we begin to imagine traveling over 400,000 miles by train and steamer?

There came a point in Pavlova's career at which world events finally played a decisive hand in the direction of her aims. Previously she had brushed through the edges of conflict and carried on, but the conflagration was finally too great. We can see Pavlova's caravan falter, and then, like some pioneer group realizing that its old base is irretrievably gone, move off again, knowing that the act of living is in the moving, not in the arriving at some new home or in the thought that the progression is finally curving back to hallowed territory.

This book too changes at that point. Because Pavlova survived by carrying with her such secure, even unshakable, traditions, I have thought it vital to try first to discover her surroundings and the influences that formed her. Even if her progress seems now to have been meteoric, that is because so much detail has been pared away subsequently. She did not leap center-stage at one bound and dismiss all rivals. She was surrounded by talent of varying order, some of it exceptional, and unless we understand something of that conjunction, we cannot measure her true strength. Pavlova is often presented as some disembodied head of thistledown, skimming along above rougher pasture as if she had never come from that base. This is quite wrong. She grew out of a dense and competitive field, and she flowered in much the same way as her fellows.

After the psychological juncture in her career—which was arrived at in 1917—the progression became a sort of divine madness, and the reality of what was going on can at best be suggested. One hopes that by then, a determined reader will understand the full implication behind the mere mention of a country or a brutally stark itinerary, and know that Pavlova's energy never faltered. She was a missionary for her art and she served it faithfully, above everything and everyone.

Павлова II я

An early postcard, c.1901, issued for Petersburg ballet enthusiasts.

ANNA PAVLOVA
Her Life and Art

September in St. Petersburg: a beginning as well as a dying. Contrary to the season of nature, a sap of energy was stirring in parts of the city. Society, in its fine plumage, was returning from the enervating drift of high summer, settling once more into its privileged roosts. Amid the more purposeful traffic of commerce, the carriages of the aristocracy and of government officialdom moved in their steady way, back and forth across the bridges and along the flanks of the equally leisurely river. Caught up once more in an amiable round of small nothings, the occupants were seen—though they were unseeing. About them, the lower echelons of bankers and merchants and nameless functionaries promenaded, their only distinguishing feature the self-importance that cloaked them all. Like returning flocks of a half-forgotten species, more and more they were to be observed on the smarter concourses, and in the vicinities of the several Imperial Theatres. But just beyond one of these great theatres there was a silent and shadowy precinct, where the dour stucco-and-stone façade gave no clue to the complex rites it concealed.

Here, behind the Alexandrinsky Theatre, the street seemed almost of another city, so divorced was it from the theatre-going throng beyond the far end of the cul-de-sac. In the precinct, known as Theatre Street, the smooth cobbles seldom echoed to footfall or carriage wheel. One flank was always in shadow; the sun never brightened the heavy wooden doors or the series of big arched windows. Then (as now) they masked entirely any glimpse of the young bodies that were ultimately to be displayed for the avidity of those seeking diversion during the long winter ahead. In the courtyard—the outer sanctum of yet more sacred inner recesses—a privileged spectator might, with luck or an Imperial pass, have seen and heard something of a monastic order, the daily ritual precise and unchanging. At eight, a sonorous bell striking, then more silence, with the endless rows of sashed windows blankly unseeing. But soon enough one door to the inner courtyard would be flung open by a woman in a long, severe dress, her voice intoning instructions—or, more likely, reprimands—toward the impenetrable interior gloom. And then, at another word, a flutter of activity. Life! And pretty life. Moving into the fresh morning air, a procession of girls: first, girls with a slow steadiness of step, betraying seniority; then another group, scarcely distinguishable from the first—these were the intermediates. But the spring of step in the third group gave hints of extreme youth. These girls were dressed in brown—plain, un-

adorned, earth-colored brown. But this drab procession was also part of the privileged minority in the sprawling, elegant, alluring city of St. Petersburg. The students of the Imperial Ballet School were on their way to prayers, before breakfast.

The straight backs and the neat grooming, the precise steps and a hierarchy of color in workday costume, all denoted the raw material of a dedicated regime, one exerted with iron discipline yet followed with willing self-sacrifice. This form of sacrifice had one objective: a chance to appear in the auditorium of the Maryinsky, freshest and most exquisite of the city's Imperial Theatres. There, these same girls—unrecognizable in pale muslins, satins, and swags of false pearls—displayed their physical graces in a demure yet overtly alluring manner. Their job was to entertain an audience that was always remarkably quick to register boredom. The style of presentation was confined within a battery of mannered poses and dance sequences, yet the personal warmth and the humanity of the best of them managed to shine through—indeed the rich and indolent male members of the audience found their roving eyes glazing if they did not discover certain qualities to set one girl or another apart from her fellows. And there was plenty of choice, for despite chaperoning and closed carriages carefully screening the entrance to the stage door, it was possible, with assiduous attention and persistence, to exchange false pearls for real ones and win a decorative young clientele for the late-night salons. Senior girls, in particular, knew that each night the audience contained potential benefactors, from the giddy height of Imperial patronage on down through the ranks, and all of it radiating from the crested box that encompassed the very heartbeat of the theatre and its attendant school. This audience had been accustomed, through generations, to admire, pamper, and select as from a tray of the newest Fabergé baubles. The Imperial School was, after all, an esteemed hothouse of talent, in every sense of the word, and its audience was used to taking grandeur and excess in its stride.

There were colorful precedents. It had been in the old Bolshoi Theatre, on a site opposite the Maryinsky, that the celebrated Romantic ballerina Marie Taglioni had made her Russian debut (forty years earlier than the time that now concerns us), and she had earned an acclaim that had kept her there, comfortably ensconced in the affections of high society, for several years. Though plain of feature and mild-mannered, she provoked the etiquette of the day to be thrown to the winds in ways both graceful and outrageous. The ladies of her audience actually

ABOVE In school uniform.

BELOW The young graduate.

clapped, and—astonishingly for the time—a bouquet of flowers was presented on the stage. When the dancer returned to France and her remaining household effects were auctioned, a pair of her ballet slippers fetched 200 roubles. The purchaser of these astonishingly expensive mementos then indulged in the gastronomic caprice of cooking them at a banquet for fellow balletomanes. The sad remnants were consumed in a suitably disguising sauce, but they were, in any event, slight silken morsels by comparison with today's more indigestible affairs. Such a flamboyant audience had the power, as well as the appetite, to demand the daintiest of morsels, on the stage and off.* If tastes strayed from the feminine, there were boys in the back row. All of the students had families eager and apprehensive for the success of their "privileged one" and for the crumbs of advancement that might fall from higher tables.

That ballet could hold a favored place alongside opera was due in no small measure to Tsar Nicolas I's personal energy. He had given the lead, for his passions were divided almost exclusively between soldiering and dancing. He was reasonably inept at deploying the one and more than a little heavy-handed when interfering in the other, but his interest (as well as his huge financial disbursements) was well intentioned; and if he accomplished nothing else, he certainly set the seal of approval upon aristocratic soldiers taking more than a passing interest in dancers (of whatever humble origin), so that by the end of the century, the Tsarevich Nicolas II's much-flaunted love affair with the ballerina Mathilde Kchessinskaya came to be one of the few full-blooded displays of self-assertion in an otherwise undistinguished apprenticeship.

For the girls, if not the boys, the possibility that all that monastic servitude being exacted behind those imprisoning walls of Theatre Street might, with luck or application, actually enable the young cohorts to blossom into chatelaines, with social power and relative economic security, was not entirely missed. It was an understandable goal for the times. Only a handful felt that they must be loyal and true servants to what they did within their enclosed order, that their master was, and could only be, the Dance itself. Even among the younger girls, in their camouflage of brown cashmere, there were some who knew already that this was the case; they knew it inwardly, if not intellectually, and who knows what their prayers included as they knelt before the ikon and its flickering light in the hour before breakfast? Their prayers might well have included perpetual thanks that they were there at all, for no matter how firm and exacting their confinement might seem, it was in every way a haven of certainty and calm compared with the alternatives of their varying backgrounds. In the country at large nothing was certain, for rich or poor. Above a disintegrating social order there hovered the Imperial eagle, rapidly tarnishing beyond recall, but with wings still sheltering a

---

* The other side of its nature was equally extreme. When the St. Petersburg dancer Yelena Andreyanova attempted to win Moscow, someone threw a handsomely wrapped gift to the stage at the conclusion of the ballerina's principal variation. She picked it up eagerly and opened it on the spot, only to stagger back at the sight of a dead cat. To the tail was attached a label reading "First Dancer."

carefully prescribed life and with talons still able to defend its hereditary perch. But the sinews that held it there were weakening by the hour. So much was clear to any alert onlooker in the last years of the nineteenth century, when even the most immediate future appeared occluded; yet there were, equally apparent, oases of calm that appeared immutable.

Such a one sheltered the young horde at the Imperial Ballet School. This particular oasis resembled nothing so much as a prized stable—not surprisingly, since stables and their pampered inmates had always been the most protected bastion of a social power. The Ballet School's inmates had arrived there by a process of selection that, if it could not dictate the actual breeding, did the next best thing and selected only stock that conformed to a minutely assessed template of physical aptitude. Upon bone and muscle of determinable form there could be imposed order and acceptable response; upon the mind that governed this interaction there could be embossed a careful program of further responses. With careful husbandry, grinding training, and, not least, a softly lit framework for its ultimate display, this assemblage could take to the boards with self-centered assurance, secure in the knowledge that it gave what was wanted and wanted precisely that which was to be given back: protection.

The protection at the Ballet School took many forms. Health was guarded in a way almost unknown in the land at large. A general education was assured, safeguarding the recipients from the possibility of any totally menial future, should they fall from the embracing Imperial arm. There was a screening-off from the uglier realities of day-to-day living experienced by the greater populace. There was the protection of a discipline, in all matters relating to the School, which allowed for no self-exploration along the more frightening corridors of adolescent liberty. There was the hand of the Orthodox Church raised benignly over bowed young heads; there were saints, teachers, close friends, senior idols, mother figures, and father figures. And there was the Tsar himself: resonant, warmly alive, and smelling of cigars. For any ten-year-old girl, whether her mother was a land inheritor or a laundress, there were worse places she could be.

The father figure whose hands shaped, almost literally, the destinies of all these tender young aspirants was the ballet master and doyen of the company, Marius Petipa, still a powerhouse of inventive energy even in his seventies. It was his choreographic constructions, wrought in intricate detail and epic proportions, that gave the company its hallmark and its stature. He, too, was a protector—of artistic standards. This was the more surprising, considering the pressures that were put upon him. His priority was to appease the restless and powerful audience that controlled, however indirectly, the fates of everyone connected with the Imperial School, from the governing board of directors down to the youngest students. Any prolonged discontent from the auditorium would soon travel along the arteries of command, causing recriminatory spasms behind the scenes. Everybody seemed to have a vested interest in maintaining the status quo.

Marius Petipa

They were nervous of any form of experimentation; if a recipe worked, there was no cause to vary the ingredients. Vast numbers of people had an interlocking reliance upon each other; seamstresses upon designers, designers upon stagehands, stagehands upon foremen, foremen upon ministry officials, and those officials, in turn, upon an ascending series of influential offices that led, ultimately, to the Imperial antechamber itself. Experimentation was smothered almost as soon as the thought took wing. Grievances were contained and isolated. It was a life system that worked, to the extent that the components reacted by intuition or rote, mindlessly obedient to signals.

Petipa had a far-reaching view of his own position in this enclave. He knew how to appease his masters as well as his servants, and in the process he went some way toward appeasing his own basic artistic instincts, which had always been of a marked sensibility. With his brother Lucien he had performed as a young dancer in Paris under the direction of his father; and although Lucien seemed to get the starring male roles, Marius's curious combination of self-effacing partnering and touching ardor of execution did not go unnoticed. When he went to Russia, seeking a trail of advancement away from the highly competitive European capitals, he took with him this central belief in the "theatre" that could be inherent in dance performances, and when finally he came to be entrusted with the construction of ballets, he remained mindful of this aspect. The steps

Mathilde Kchessinskaya in
La Fille Mal Gardée.

were pre-eminent, and every bar of music seemed to embrace some fresh difficulty; but within this confine there were pauses in which a gesture or the turn of a head could lend color to the characterization. Elsewhere, key moments in the story line of the ballet became carefully structured incidents, integrated in the dance pattern (though never blurred), with every unit on the stage placed to give such a moment maximum focus.

All this was sugaring the pill for the audience, which expected first and foremost to be sated with a sumptuous spectacle. The rule for the components of such a display was immutable: decoration upon decoration. The scenery flats were never just flat but were encrusted with a confectioner's abandon: trellises, baroque piping, swags, clusters—all were employed as an adjunct to the scene painter's basic skill. The costumes were intricate creations that could bear the closest scrutiny, with their frills, tucks, and furbelows, minutely stitched, and the materials of the highest quality. These, too, were decorated, with panels of Brussels lace or Genoa velvet cut into intricate patterns; they were scarcely visible from a few yards, but the wearer felt transformed, stepping from serge and alpaca into these exquisite creations. She had the distinctive texture of silk moiré and ermine within her scrutiny; it felt right, which meant that the illusion was based on a strange sort of reality. Even the *diamanté* decorations were of a quality to match those on the finest dress in the auditorium.

When it came to the actual steps in the ballet, here too there was an almost baroque frenzy. Countless feet scissored and stabbed in unison, hands flashed, heads nodded on a musical accent. And as a counterpoint to this, soloists did trickier things:

they managed two movements within the span of one from the ensemble—and smiled as well. It seemed impossible that dramatic tension could arise from this physical encrustation, yet Petipa contrived time and again to make the audience lean forward a little, or even gasp. At these moments, when a mortal lover fell from some bow shot or a heroine came to harm, Petipa provided some small chance for his best dancers, so that their personal eloquence held sway. Then, they were in charge of the audience and not its plaything. It was a small enough reward, considering the grinding discipline, but it was enough. Senior dancers invariably took matters into their own hands when it came to duets or solo variations, interpolating at these junctures some idiosyncratic flourish that best showed off their particular technical skill. Established partners were in collusion with the orchestral conductor, who took his time from the dancers on the stage in the hope that he could reach the end of the music at the same moment that the dancers finished moving. Any discrepancy reflected poorly on him and his fellows, for the ballerina was queen.

The baroque mannerisms of these dancers took ten years to perfect. They were the accretions that emerged over and above the unremitting work exacted in the classroom, the "tricks" picked up by observation—with luck, before the fateful day of graduation, when the students were at last taken from their cage and left to flutter from their trainers' hands like precious birds. And when they graduated to their new environment, they found it awesome. They had experienced it from time to time as children, cavorting in crowd scenes, standing as pages in some Court spectacle, or skipping around as lotus buds; but from the time of graduation, the stage of the Maryinsky suddenly became like a sacred temple, ready to exact some fearsome propitiation. The audience was impartial, interested, and expectant, but it was also demanding. It continued to be a form of judge and jury, and there was no appeal.

The annual graduation performance for the St. Petersburg students was held in the spring of each year, not in the Maryinsky itself but in the Mikhailovsky Theatre, where the evening performance was watched with interest by a packed house. A jury, composed of academy staff and selected critics, sat in the best seats, accompanied by the directors of the School; and everyone else in the theatre was rather conscious of these adjudicators busily making notes and awarding marks. The spring of 1899 was even more cold and wet than normal, as if the seasons were reluctant to advance toward a new century; but on April 11* the excellence of the students inside the Mikhailovsky inspired confidence. Among the girls that night were several of promise; yet one student drew attention from the moment she appeared. The critic Valerian Svetlov was on the jury that evening, and he, at least, gave this girl the highest possible marks.

---

* All dates in the Russian section are Old Style, that is, thirteen days behind the Gregorian calendar, and twelve days behind prior to 1900.

She was listed as "Pavlova 2" to distinguish her from an earlier graduate, Varvara Pavlova, who was no relation to the younger girl, who was Anna.

Pavlova 2 had already caught the eye of an influential member of the Duma, or municipal council, who sat on the boards of various charities. Victor Dandré took a strong interest in the work of the Imperial Theatre in St. Petersburg and discussed its affairs with writers and critics similarly interested. He was descended from a French family of minor aristocratic lineage—a background echoed in his Italyansky Street apartment, which was full of French antiques and pictures. It was a bachelor establishment, ruled by an aged housekeeper. On the night of the graduation in 1899, Dandré took with him his nephew Michel Barroy, who was only fifteen but already something of a "balletomaniac," as keen ballet-goers liked to refer to themselves. While the critics made notes about the graduation students (performing in *The Imaginary Dryads* and *Clorinda, Queen of the Mountain Fairies*), Dandré was pointing out the thin young girl called Pavlova as the dancer who appealed to him most. Michel liked her too. It was natural to choose a favorite; Victor Dandré had probably had Pavlova pointed out to him as a student of promise by one of the teachers. There was always considerable interest in the "stable," and although it did not all remain on an exalted intellectual level, the teachers suffered this sort of attention to their protégées for the sake of the genuine artistic admiration that also emerged. The majority of the Maryinsky audience was in any case almost a sort of club, consisting of people with one unifying and obsessive interest which drew them back to regular seats on regular evenings.

The teacher Pavel Gerdt had already discerned Pavlova's qualities as a student. She excelled in all the departments he emphasized: softly rounded port de bras, a harmonious line, movement motivated by intellectual response, rather than executed by rote. Gerdt wanted any dramatic expression to be contained within the dance span as opposed to disruptive punctuations, and Pavlova accommodated this approach with an apparently natural ease. On the minus side, it was noticed that she had certain technical deficiencies, even though she had come through the class of Ekaterina Vazem, a dancer of steely technical efficiency. Vazem had given up dancing in 1884, but she stayed at the school as a teacher of the intermediate classes, inheriting the pupil Pavlova 2 from Alexander Oblakov's junior class. Oblakov was another in the chain of teachers in whom reposed a vast amount of practical stage experience: he had been one of the original four princely suitors in the first production of *The Sleeping Beauty* in 1890 (Gerdt, as usual, getting the male lead), and he had created the role of Benno alongside Gerdt's Siegfried in the 1895 St. Petersburg production of *Swan Lake*. Added to this roster of teachers was Yevgenia Sokolova, who had retired from dancing in 1886 after twenty years of distinguished performing and creating many roles, including a scintillating Queen of the Night opposite Vazem's Queen of the Day in Petipa's *Night and Day* in 1883. The inheritance of roles, and the coaching that accompanied their direct transference, provided a sustaining background of tradition and example that was invaluable for a student. The framework thus acquired acted as a safety net that could be relied upon if all else failed; but the knowledge of its general soundness also gave a student the confidence to seek within a role certain personal inflections and resonances. As a result, he or she could take risks, as Vazem had done by taking on dramatic roles that were not her natural forte and experimenting with big jumps when she was best known as a *terre à terre* dancer. Individuality was not considered suspect; on the contrary, it was viewed as an asset, along with the more prosaic virtues of a strong back and feet, good turn-out, and a pretty face. Rather singularly, Anna Pavlova had shortcomings in all these departments. Her back was immensely supple, but this did not help her in taxing *enchaînements* which required sustained strength from head to toe. She had a marked lack of turn-out in the hip joints, and her legs, though strong, were uncommonly fine-boned. Her feet were a paradox. They were extraordinarily pretty in pointe work because of the high and pronounced natural arch, but the toes were long, especially the big toe, which projected farther than its fellows and thus had to take the entire weight of the body in balance. Her face and upper torso lacked the desirable cushioning of the day.

Pavlova was lucky in her teachers, particularly Gerdt, who saw that her innate qualities far outweighed her weaknesses. He urged her not to strain after difficult technical feats when she could create as great an effect by employing other means. For the graduation performance of *The Imaginary Dryads*, Gerdt followed an accepted custom and interpolated a variation from another ballet in order to show Pavlova's qualities to best effect. This variation, from *The Vestal Virgin*, contained movements which were soft and lyrical, but also gave Pavlova the opportunity to display a strong dramatic tone; people thought her "unusual," and it was this strange quality—most particularly her nonconformist line—that fascinated the young Barroy as well as his uncle. The eighteen-year-old dancer seemed to them exceptionally slim and supple compared with her fellows. Her face was certainly not conventionally pretty, but it was striking: fine bones, dark eyes set beneath a deep forehead, and a mobile mouth that turned up in the corners in a slightly elfin manner. She tended to disguise a high hairline with fluffy bangs at the temples. There was an effervescence about her movement, and in the ballet about the nymphs and dryads she acted the part of a peasant lass with beguiling naturalness. Her flirting with a young lad showed a necessary quality of innocence, and when performing a dance with the imaginary dryads, her simplicity of manner proved a delight; she charmed the audience without apparent effort.

When they left the Mikhailovsky that night, onlookers thought the appearances of Pavlova 2 to be the most vivid of the evening. Although the press made no mention of her, when the examination results were posted it was clear that she had impressed the jury: it was announced that Pavlova 2 had been designated a coryphée for her entrance into the Imperial Ballet in the coming autumn. This was a form of instant promotion, with the directors taking the unusual step of by-passing the ranks of

ABOVE As Flora in *The Awakening of Flora*.
OPPOSITE As Princess Florine in *The Sleeping Beauty*.

the corps de ballet in charting a course for this student. They posted her directly to the group of dancers who often performed in threes or fours. In this category, Pavlova would be watched by the public from the start as an individual performer; it was a responsibility as well as an accolade.

She would never have to bear the frustration of containment and anonymity, but she would never have the "safe" feeling of being in the ranks, either.

On April 21, for the corps de ballet's benefit,* there was another viewing of a production seen on April 10, the night before the graduation performance. Gerdt had made new variations for his four best pupils; these dances were then interpolated into the pas de quatre from an old ballet called *Trilby*, and this pas de quatre was in turn inserted into *The Cavalry Halt*. (The latter, with *Coppélia*, made up the program.) The ubiquitous critic "General" Bezobrazov, writing about the benefit, said in the gossipy *Petersburg Gazette* that Lyubov Petipa and Anna Pavlova showed good schooling and that their *ballon* was exceptional. The *New Times* merely noted that "four pupils [although graduates, they were not gazetted to the company until June 1] of the Dramatic Academy appeared in *The Cavalry Halt*: Pavlova, Makarova, Petipa, and Belinskaya." Such were Anna Pavlova's first press notices. She did not have to wait long before seeing her name in print again. At the end of the season Gerdt interpolated a pas de six into *La Fille Mal Gardée*, and this time Pavlova was singled out as a dancer who was graceful, soft, and feminine—a natural dancer who had the full potential for a classical soloist.

This admired coryphée made her company debut at the Maryinsky on September 19, 1899, dancing a pas de trois in *La Fille Mal Gardée* with Stanislava Belinskaya and Georgi Kyaksht. She was back in the same part the following month, but this time she had Mikhail Fokine in the boy's role. He was a bright young dancer, barely more than a graduate himself, and yet he had already staged a shortened version of this comic ballet when the School's administration, impressed by his organizing ability and his instinctive grasp of sound dance structure, allowed him a free hand with a student production. At this time he often found himself paired with Anna Pavlova for double work in class.

Petipa, like Gerdt, felt that Pavlova had undoubted talent, and that with careful nurturing she would uphold the high traditions of the Maryinsky. For a School production in 1898 he had revived a short work known as *The Two Stars*. It was full of ponderously contrived tableaux, but it had the virtue of two technically demanding showcase roles. These had been made for

Ekaterina Vazem and Alexandra Vergina in 1871, and now Petipa had to find two pupils who were equal to the demands of the roles. For one of the Stars he selected Belinskaya, a strong technician from the class of Enrico Cecchetti. Here was another teacher with a remarkable performing background: in the first production of *The Sleeping Beauty* he had mimed the evil fairy Carabosse to tremendous effect, and then astonished the audience by emerging in the final act as the Blue Bird, displaying a dazzling technical skill derived from his Italian training. Though he continued to appear on the stage, he had a great gift for teaching, and his pupils became noted for their strength. In casting the other Star, Petipa did a surprising thing: he passed over several more likely candidates and chose the delicate Anna Pavlova, who was not in Cecchetti's class and who certainly lacked the technical assurance of Belinskaya. Mikhail Fokine, who earned the leading boy's role of Adonis, noticed that Pavlova danced well and tried hard, but he did not consider her the most promising of the girls he was dancing with at that time. Petipa risked censure by casting a dancer junior to both Belinskaya and his own daughter, Lyubov; but the possible advantages of such a move were worth a few tantrums, and it was plain that his curiosity about the girl was that of an aged creative force receiving fresh impetus.

When Petipa was nearing what is believed to have been his seventy-ninth birthday in 1900 (he may have been even older), he was still in absolute power at the Maryinsky; but the shadow of retirement was inexorably creeping over his shoulder, cast there as much as anything by the evolution of taste, which was beginning to tire of formula ballets. It was not that Petipa's energies were anything less than extraordinary. The previous four years had seen the usual outpourings: in 1896, the year of Tsar Nicolas's coronation, alone he had managed to produce the charming if inconsequential one-act ballet *The Cavalry Halt; The Pearl*, a centerpiece for the coronation festivities in Moscow; and a full-evening work, *Bluebeard*. In addition, Petipa had begun discussions with Alexander Glazunov—then thirty years old and on a tide of great acclaim as a possible true heir of Tchaikovsky—about his writing a full-length ballet score to adorn a libretto concerning a virtuous Middle Ages heroine called Raymonda. The author was a lady novelist by the name of Pashkova, and her mélange of a plot, with whiter-than-white Crusader knights, Moorish villains, and ghostly emanations, was so airily conceived as to need almost superhuman talents in the collaborators if the ballet were to provide an evening of intelligible entertainment. Glazunov worked for two years in close concert with Petipa; the result was a masterpiece in which the composer's glorious symphonic score was underpinned by choreography of the greatest possible felicity, so that the story line barely mattered. The first performance, on January 7, 1898, was a triumph.

A change in the directorship of the Imperial Theatres the following year brought in Prince Volkonsky, a young progres-

---

sive, the author of books on expressive gesture, who still tempered this advanced thought with a deep awareness of the abiding merits of the Master's best choreography. He could see the predicament of the great man: knowing no other life but the ballet and unable to promote a change in that way of life; being the true progenitor of the very school that was now by-passing him; artistically drained by the task of producing three- and four-act ballets, but fearful that only the big works would justify his position. Ironically, Perrot's *La Esmeralda,* from 1844, with its Pugni score, endless scenes, and creaking plot based on Victor Hugo's panoramic vision of Notre Dame, was being revived so that prima ballerina assoluta Mathilde Kchessinskaya might repeat an earlier success. Like many of the old ballets, it managed to incorporate livestock into the cast; in this case it was Esmeralda's goat. He was a pet of the ballerina's and except when *Esmeralda* came into the repertoire lived in the garden of her dacha at Strelna.

Kchessinskaya represented one side of the division that was slowly becoming apparent in 1900: safe traditional virtues of sound technique harnessed to proven formulae. On the other side a restless, questing spirit was emerging in the younger students; they showed an interest in the Romantic era and a closer identification with dramatic motive. The changing tide is neatly summed up in a review for the ballerina who stood second to Kchessinskaya. The popular Olga Preobrajenskaya was making her first attempt at the role of Giselle, and one critic gave a particular clue as to where there might be a likely new contender for the role. The *New Times* reported on December 29, 1899, about the previous day's performance:

> Mme Preobrajenskaya made her debut in the leading role of Giselle today. Recently we saw Mme Grimaldi, whose miming scenes were particularly impressive. The part of Giselle, however, is not suited to the endearing talents of Preobrajenskaya, who not only has little miming ability but lacks ethereality. An ethereal quality is absolutely essential to this role, although Mme Grimaldi hardly qualified in this respect. Nevertheless, Preobrajenskaya had a great success which she earned by the faultless execution of the dances, from the technical point of view, and by her appropriately noble air; but again, there was nothing of the ethereal. . . .
>
> Today there was a one-act ballet, *Marko-Bomba,* in which, among others, Mme Pavlova 2, graceful, ethereal, and elegant, danced delightfully. The ballet has made a fortunate acquisition in the person of this very young but unusually gifted dancer, who has come to the fore in such a short time.

"Short time" was a bit of an understatement: Pavlova had been a full-fledged member of the company for four months.

In addition to dancing Giselle, Preobrajenskaya also took the role of Myrtha, Queen of the Wilis, during Grimaldi's first performance of the title role on September 5. The roles of the two leading Wilis, Moyna and Zulme, had been entrusted to Egorova and Pavlova, and the latter's slightness and delicacy of manner seemed entirely apposite for the specter of a young virgin in a Gothic fantasy. But she was equally capable of suggesting a quite earthy and vivacious nature, as when she played one of the

Mathilde Kchessinskaya wearing her own jewelry in the title role of *Camargo.*

friends of Fleur de Lys (Preobrajenskaya) in *Esmeralda.* This was more in keeping with the student who was often observed after a day's serious work strutting around the classroom mimicking various ballerinas or improvising rather fantastic dances, as the mood took her. Kchessinskaya had the title role in *Esmeralda;* it was "her" ballet. When *The Sleeping Beauty* came back into the repertoire that autumn with Kchessinskaya in her customary role of Aurora, Pavlova was given the small part of the Fairy Candide, which she danced for the first time on October 5.

Pierina Legnani, the Italian ballerina who had performed as a guest artist in St. Petersburg every year since 1893, was giving her farewell performances at the beginning of 1900. Legnani represented an almost perfect example of the old and the new incorporated in one performer. She maintained the tough virtuosity of her Italian schooling, which bravura had earned her initial success with Russian audiences; but during the ten years of her dominance at the Maryinsky she gradually incorporated into her performances some hint of the current French-Russian tradition, with its softer, more expressive approach. When *Swan Lake* was reshaped by Petipa and his assistant Lev Ivanov in 1895 (it had had a disastrous premiere in Moscow eighteen years before), the

role of Odile, with its pyrotechnics, suited Legnani; but as Odette she really astonished, investing the Ivanov choreography with beautiful avian grace notes. Three years later in *Raymonda* she showed a delicacy and lightness that did much to disguise her homely features and short, sturdy body. The two ballerinas who followed Legnani in the role both learned much from the way she had coped with the varying demands of this long ballet packed with pure dance. Moscow's promising young ballerina Ekaterina Geltzer came to St. Petersburg to study, and Preobrajenskaya of the home team was advancing to the forefront. Both had marked successes in *Raymonda* and demonstrated a range that would have been unlikely ten years earlier. It was this rapidly expanding vocabulary that became the fuel for younger students looking on; they were fired by example and the inherent possibilities as yet unexplored. There were potentially brilliant students ready to perform in public: Egorova, Sedova, and Pavlova 2 were all considered worthy of mention from among the new dancers taken into the Maryinsky in 1898 and 1899. Then there was Vaganova from the 1897 class, and Trefilova from 1895, both of whom received particular attention. If anything was lacking, it was similar adventurousness in choreographic expression. The official records of all the activities in the Imperial Theatres were published in the form of Yearbooks, with several volumes devoted to each year. For the 1899–1900 season the publication, when it finally appeared, was unexpectedly lavish. There were many colored illustrations, such as those showing the architectural details of the Alexandrinsky Theatre in an article by Alexandre Benois. He was the painter and stage designer whose erudition about the history of European painting and allied arts made him a magnet for such as Konstantin Somov, Dmitri Filosofov, and Léon Bakst. Another of his group was Filosofov's cousin Sergei Diaghilev, not yet thirty.

Diaghilev came from a well-to-do and cultured background in Perm. He had enrolled at the Conservatoire in St. Petersburg in 1890, while at the same time placating his family by studying law at the University, where one of his associates was Victor Dandré. In time it could be seen that Diaghilev's talents lay not in musicology but in an organizing capacity for promoting the arts in general. He had a voracious appetite for acquired knowledge in these areas, and his long-term aim was a position of authority within the Imperial Theatres. The first step toward this goal came in 1899, when Volkonsky offered Diaghilev the position of a special missions official, which also brought him the editorship of the Yearbook. It was not untypical that under its new controller the 1899–1900 edition had production costs that went above the allocation by more than 10,000 roubles. There was a scandal, but the quality of the product was never questioned. Apart from Benois's work it contained designs by Bakst and Somov, and detailed listings of productions taking place on the dramatic stage, as well as opera and ballet—fifty-five performances of twenty-six ballets given in St. Petersburg that season.

Everything was subsidized by the Tsar's revenues, and the high standards were justly acclaimed by foreign visitors; however, Volkonsky, the director, was still rather shocked by the archaic attitudes that existed within the organization of the Maryinsky, and by the power held by individual dancers who used social connections as a reinforcement for artistic advance. Ballerinas saw nothing wrong in "playing" to the boxes that contained their friends and admirers, and they often showed little or no regard for the thematic action of the works they adorned. The opera ballets struck Volkonsky as embarrassments; when *Tannhäuser* was produced shortly after he assumed his post, he provoked a row by eliminating one of Petipa's ballets in the first act (yet another bacchanal) after seeing it at the dress rehearsal.

Although it was too late to do anything about Petipa's general approach—and there seemed no one to replace him—Volkonsky did institute mime classes, to be run by Gerdt; but he too had devoted his life to projecting a certain type of image, and it was not likely that a youngster would be encouraged to do anything other than mimic his teacher. Nobody dared to interfere with the work of Christian Johanssen, the most revered teacher within the company, who carried with him an unbroken link with the great European traditions: his early training had been with August Bournonville in Copenhagen, who in turn sprang from the Classical French school dominated by the teaching of Vestris. Johanssen had been an immaculate dancer, strong in all departments, with an unusual combination of marked elevation and a facility for turns; but his real interest lay in teaching. He had the ability to extract the most important elements of all the earlier phases of his training, as well as the best of everything he had encountered after arriving in Russia, which he then incorporated into a cohesive program that was vital and individual. Johanssen was well into his eighties when the graduation pupils of 1899 were allocated to their various *classes de perfection;* among those put into his class was Pavlova 2. While analyzing the weaknesses of her technique at that stage and seeking answers to them, he understood that her poor turn-out did not detract from her line, and he was careful not to destroy her confidence by trying to alter what was in fact a mild idiosyncrasy. Most of all he sought to encourage in Pavlova stamina, so that her delicate frame would appear light, as distinct from frail.

Petipa, who often looked in on Johanssen's classes (where he picked up ideas for sequences of steps), kept an eye on the girl too, and he was sufficiently encouraged by what he saw to cast her in the new ballets he was making for the smaller Hermitage Theatre. Anna Pavlova found herself working once again with the boy of whom everyone spoke, the "most promising" young Mikhail Fokine. She liked dancing with him; he was handsome and had an eager, romantic nature, and most of the young girl students seemed to have singled him out as worthy of their daydreams. There was a rush to peep at him practicing whenever the coast was clear between the students' rooms and the artists' studio. (He, in turn, had actually noticed one of the girls—the daughter of the senior performer and teacher Platon Karsavin.)

Fokine chafed at the few opportunities there were for him to appear on stage. He was dispirited by the system of inherited roles, which invariably left him in the second or third cast, getting a performance only when someone was ill or injured: once

ABOVE & OPPOSITE As Zulme in *Giselle*.

roles were allocated, they were jealously guarded by the original casts. But after Fokine began partnering Pavlova 2 more regularly in studio double work, the effect pleased Petipa, and they were given minor chances within several of the Maryinsky productions. These appearances would be in the nature of a short pas de deux interpolated into the body of the main work, and the dancers would perform whatever it was they had most recently perfected in the classroom, usually with an entirely disparate piece of music. Fokine became quite exhilarated on these occasions, but Pavlova was nervous and only overcame her insecurity by drawing on her natural performing temperament, which sustained her with a sort of febrile intensity and wild courage, like a young horse that faces up to a fence without any real knowledge of how it will get to the other side. She made mistakes, but there was no special pleading needed; she had a quality that dismissed faults from the memory almost before they had registered. She had, too, a way of seizing the moment with an intuitive sense of theatre. In the autumn of 1898, as a student performer making her first appearance at the Maryinsky in a responsible role, she caught her foot against the lip of the prompter's box and came down with her back to the audience during the Pas des Almées in the second act of *Daughter of the Pharaoh*. Undaunted, she got up gracefully and curtseyed to the audience—a form of apology

Sergei Legat as Damis in
The Trials of Damis.

Mikhail Fokine as Colin in
La Fille Mal Gardée.

Pavlova as Hoarfrost in
Les Saisons.

which turned a mistake into something infinitely appealing, imprinting itself in the memory so that people discussed it afterward more than they discussed the entire number. When Pavlova continued classes with Sokolova after her graduation, it was this aspect of never letting up during a performance that her teacher stressed—that curtain calls, for example, had to be crafted as carefully as every step of the dance itself, so that an illusion was sustained and the audience returned to reality only gradually. Pavlova learned to test the tension of an audience as if it were a fine fiddle, each night strung a little differently. She was able to divine the pitch that was needed at any given time.

Pavlova emerged into the spotlight of the Maryinsky at a time when the first stirrings of change were in the air, for it was becoming clear that Petipa's reign was drawing to its end. Volkonsky, seeking a way to ease the old man's predicament, suggested that he might care to mount one or two works for the prestigious little Hermitage Theatre, the exclusive domain of royalty, ministers, and specially invited guests. The nature of the setting meant that no elaborate production was required, and the works were expected to be glorified divertissements, of no undue length. The theatre was connected to the main Hermitage building by a gallery built on a bridge spanning a canal off the Neva, and the distinguished guests emerged into a charming semicircular auditorium decorated in the Italian manner, with tiered seating like a lecture room. The exclusiveness of the engagement encouraged Petipa to renew his successful collaboration with Glazunov, albeit on a smaller scale, in one-act entertainments. Petipa was already working with Drigo on *Les Millions d'Arlequin*; with Glazunov he elected to do *Les Saisons* and also *The*

Trials of Damis. The latter work (also known as *Les Ruses d'Amour)* was presented during Legnani's benefit night on January 23, 1900.* That same evening there was a rare performance of *The Pearl*, and Pavlova was among the string of coryphées in the Dance of the Pearls.

Les Saisons, as a microcosm of Petipa's era, is worth examining in detail for a last glimpse of the style that had dominated ballet in Russia for as long as anyone at that time could remember. It showed a great choreographer composing without strain, with the services of a first-rate composer; and for the dancers it represented a mingling of the older members with the new. Glazunov's brief for *Les Saisons* had been to provide music for four main tableaux, beginning with Winter, so that Spring, Summer, and Autumn followed, with short linking passages.

After a musical introduction, the curtain rose to show a *danseur* in the guise of Winter, with his attendants dressed as the attributes of his reign: Frost, Ice, Hail, and Snow. Each sprite was given a solo dance. Frost began with a light-hearted polonaise; then Ice came forward with a slower dance; Hail followed with a hammering little scherzo from the oboes; and finally Snow waltzed around in a swirling, drifting pattern. After this, two gnomes emerged to kindle a fire, which finally drove Winter from the stage. His four sprites followed him and the lights dimmed for the first transformation; when the lights came up

---

* In the Yearbook cast lists for *The Trials of Damis*, Pavlova seems to have appeared as a character called Litz, but there is no distinction made between Pavlova 1 and Pavlova 2. Nevertheless, Pavlova 1 is mentioned as dancing in the Courante and the Sarabande elsewhere in the ballet. The first performance had taken place in the Hermitage on January 17.

again, the stage was seen to be banked with flowers for the entrance of Spring, with attendant dancers in the guise of flowers and birds. Zephyr was on hand too, and all grouped themselves around Spring as he entreated them to dance. There were sections for a group of Roses, and one for a Bird in which Glazunov had cleverly caught the sweeping glide of a swallow; but then the soft swoon of the music suggested approaching Summer, and the scene changed again. The third tableau represented a cornfield, and the corps de ballet, with sprays of corn decorating their dresses, swayed to and fro, as if in a warm breeze. Cornflowers and Poppies ran through the ranks and joined together for a waltz; but gradually the heat of summer overcame them, and they subsided. Naiads then came on carrying long veils representing water, which was eagerly sought by the flowers. There was also a solo variation for a Head of Corn done to a clarinet solo, followed by a coda for the ensemble. Pan pipes were heard, and all the dancers paused, listening. The pipes were heard a second time, and then a horde of Fauns and Satyrs invaded the stage, whirling around the Head of Corn, which they threatened to carry off, while the flowers sought to interpose themselves in the mêlée. Finally Zephyr stepped in, and the interlopers were banished into the ground by the use of trap doors in the stage.

The tableau changed, and a vineyard was revealed, with maidens, dressed as Bacchantes, pursued by young men. The seasons made their reappearance one by one to the accompaniment of musical variants of their original themes, and then there was a beautifully composed adagio for the God and Goddess of the Harvest. (This was for Maria Petipa, Marius's daughter, and Pavel Gerdt. Maria, a big lady in every respect, sported a dress swagged with bunches of grapes and numerous bobbing apples, all at hip level. Even her shoulder straps were bunches of grapes, and there was a great deal more fruit on her head. Gerdt had grapes in a vine-leaf wreath about his head, and his costume sprouted huge quilted and embroidered sleeves cut off at the elbows. He was fifty-six, Maria forty-two. Both had to perform with small brass cymbals strapped to the backs of their hands.)

After the pas de deux there was a further brief chance for the ensemble to join in the bacchanal before a deluge of autumn leaves put a stop to the dancing. The scene was plunged in darkness; then at the back of the stage an Apotheosis was revealed showing the constellations circling the earth. Thus ended *Les Saisons* at the Hermitage on February 7, 1900; and it was considered a pretty enough confection to merit transferring to the larger Maryinsky Theatre. It seemed the old man was not quite finished after all. *Les Saisons* employed a lot of young dancers, and Anna Pavlova had been entrusted with the little Hoarfrost variation at the beginning of the ballet.

Georg Kotschubei was a student at the Emperor Alexander College in the year that Anna Pavlova graduated. His father had the title of Prince, with a permanent box at the Maryinsky, and Georg grew up in the ambience of the theatre, with many opportunities to see the opera and ballet, which he grew to love. When he became a young man about town, it was natural that he should wish to take parties of his university friends to the theatre; and since the ballet was his greatest love, he applied for a permanent box for all dance evenings. Eventually, after many persuasive letters and the pulling of strings, Georg and his friends obtained their prize: Box 26 on the *belle étage*. This box was very near the stage and was considered to lend social distinction, being directly opposite the Imperial box and flanking the front row of the orchestra, where the seats were all allocated on the hereditary principle to members of the aristocracy or to ministers of state. The box of the great Kchessinskaya herself was directly below that of the young men. There could hardly have been a more satisfied quartet than Kotschubei, Zachrevsky, Schatilov, and Raevsky.

On the evening of Kchessinskaya's benefit performance, February 13, 1900, the audience was naturally eager to see who was in the dancer's box, and that quarter of the house was the object of much attention. Kchessinskaya's benefit was taking place after ten years' performing instead of the customary twenty; it was a signal honor for the only dancer with the title of prima ballerina assoluta. Of course, it was much more than that. It signified what the whole audience knew—that Mathilde was the holder of other titles no less important, the principal one being Former Mistress to the Tsar. Hers was a giddy career, the prima facie reason for younger dancers concluding that an admirer was obligatory for a satisfactory career on the stage. Kchessinskaya had talent, and she worked hard; but from a younger dancer's point of view, there was no proof that these attributes would have availed her if she had not deployed herself toward the future Tsar Nicolas.

The Imperial family joined in the fun on Kchessinskaya's benefit night, like good sports and old friends; and after the second act of *Les Millions d'Arlequin,* with Mathilde as Columbine, the curtains were opened and the diamond-studded audience was able to see manifest one little lady's power to charm. For half an hour attendants trailed back and forth across the footlights, struggling with sixty-three vast baskets of flowers, until the stage was a single huge bower and the audience was reeling from the scent. After an intermission, the evening continued with a performance of *Les Saisons.* During the final curtain calls on this benefit evening, Kchessinskaya, with a display of magnanimity calculated to please the crowd, turned to look for the dancer who had been loudly applauded by the audience after her solo, the Frost variation. It was Anna Pavlova, and Kchessinskaya took her by the hand and advanced her to the footlights for a special cheer. Young Kotschubei, from his vantage point just above the stage, saw the girl's eyes lit with a feverish happiness. She had also appeared earlier that evening in several sections of *Les Millions d'Arlequin,* including the Serenade, the Lovers' Meeting, and the Reconciliation of Pierrot and Pierrette.

Using contacts within the theatre, Kotschubei found out Pavlova's home address, and he called on her the very next evening as soon as he was free from his studies. It was a daring act for an etiquette-conscious son of the nobility, and he did not know what to expect or what he was going to say. But if the grand

With Fokine in *Les Millions d'Arlequin:*
(above) the Lovers' Meeting; (below) the Serenade.

Kchessinskaya had admirers, then so did the young Pavlova. Kotschubei found her living with her mother in a tiny apartment, through the inner court of a building on the unfashionable Kolomenskaya Street, and in these simple surroundings she impressed him as much as she had in the ballet the night before. To Georg she seemed totally lacking in affectation, and the quality of movement remained off the stage; everything was done in a gentle way. But there was a strong spark of vitality as well, and when she spoke of her aims, her voice rose excitedly and her eyes betrayed a determination that bordered on fanaticism, particularly when she spoke of the great traditions of ballet and the pioneering work done by Taglioni.

Kotschubei and Pavlova established a friendship during this first meeting, with its long and excited discussion about art. Georg noticed that Pavlova's mother called her Niura, the peasant diminutive of Anna, and it was as "little Niura" that she became known to Georg and his friends. They made a jolly crowd, with outings in a troika, or singing at gypsy parties; and Anna, for the first time, had a taste of the light-hearted side of life that had been so lacking in her restricted and lonely background. Georg and his friends knew little of Pavlova's history; her mother, a domestic soul who looked prematurely aged, with grey hair tied in a peasant bun, was shy of the smart young men and remained in the background, and Anna never discussed her father beyond mentioning that he was dead.

Despite the touches of freedom and the excitement of a certain amount of social life, young graduates needed to work almost continuously in special classes, for each new role on stage presented a fresh set of technical problems. Apart from Zulme in *Giselle,* Pavlova's first role of any real importance had been Aurora, the second lead in *The Awakening of Flora.* At the start of the new season in the autumn of 1900, Petipa moved her up to the title role, which she first danced on September 10. She was seen to be very nervous and was clearly having trouble with her technique, despite the steadying influence of Gerdt, who was on stage with her in his role of Apollo. Fokine had the role of Mercury that night.[*] The start of any new season at the Maryinsky invariably won a great deal of attention from the aficionados of the ballet world, and Petipa doubtless provoked storms of protest from his family when he took the role of Flora away from his own daughter, who had danced it the previous April. Yet Pavlova had zephyr freshness that could bring Flora alive as some enchanting goddess of the antique world, and her delicate grace was so appropriate to the role that Petipa cannot have had any qualms about his decision. Bezobrazov, writing for the *Petersburg Gazette,* described Pavlova as "light and graceful," and when he spotted her in the polka of *Bluebeard* a week later, he commented that she danced with "verve." The "General" was always careful to give encouragement if he felt there was a sign of real talent, and his views were respected within the company. His ideal at the time was Lyubov Roslavleva, an outstanding Mos-

---

[*] In his memoirs, Fokine errs in stating that he took the role of Apollo when Pavlova first danced Flora. He took over the role at subsequent performances.

cow ballerina whom he described as "the best and most talented." She was a dancer with a seamless quality of movement and a strong dramatic sense, and since she was often invited to give guest appearances in St. Petersburg, it would be surprising if the young Pavlova did not watch her with more than passing interest.

If Roslavleva was a model for a young performer of Pavlova's style, it was equally clear that such achievements could not easily be emulated. Although Pavlova had an inborn performer's temperament, the basic vocabulary for its expression still caused her trouble. The first whiff of criticism from the public came from Svetlov, writing in the *Evening Courier* on November 7. He said that in the Grand Pas de Corbeilles in *Esmeralda* Pavlova danced "with a lack of confidence and without animation." This was not a case of unfamiliarity with the work, since she had been in the same ballet the year before, during the benefit performance for the character dancer N. S. Aistov. The criticism must have been a shock for a dancer who had been described by the *New Times,* only weeks before, as "one of the more graceful and light of our ballet artists." This praise had come in a review of the Petipa ballet *Le Roi Candaule** on September 24. In this Pavlova had been given the taxing Pas de Diane (a pas de deux with an attendant character dancer as well), and on this occasion the *New Times* thought it "exquisitely danced" by Pavlova, though her fright at its difficulties must have been extreme. Most dancers thought it a trial.

Legnani, the ballerina who had done so much to encourage technical feats on the stage, was by the turn of the century making her farewells to the Maryinsky. Her benefit performance came on January 28, 1901, when she took the title role in a long Petipa ballet called *Camargo,* based on the life of the revered eighteenth-century Belgian dancer. Petipa's ballet (one of two he made on this theme) centered on the love and intrigue that surrounded Marie Camargo and her sister Madeleine, and the determination of Marie to become a court dancer, leaving her sister to pursue an honorable and far less scandalous future in wedlock. As in the Lancret painting of the famous dancer, the costume for Marie was a long hooped skirt, with panels divided by sprigs of wildflowers. Petipa's long-time assistant Ivanov had been responsible for revivals of *Camargo* and may well have contributed the pas de trois in which Pavlova appeared with Fokine and Georgi Kyaksht. On January 28 Pavlova also danced a "Snow" variation for the first time. (This may have been an interpolation from *Les Saisons,* but her costume certainly had the flavor of eighteenth-century court life and must have been made for *Camargo.*) A week later there was a benefit for Maria Petipa. She had escaped compulsory retirement by carving a niche for herself in character roles, and her benefit was honoring a rare twenty-five years' span of service. The evening included the one-act Saint-Léon ballet *Markitantka (La Vivandière)* as revised by Ivanov. Maria played the canteen keeper of the title, and

* Court etiquette (particularly at the Hermitage) demanded these French titles; this ballet was usually known as *Tsar Kandavl.*

With Fokine: (above) the Polonaise in *Les Millions d'Arlequin;* (below) *Camargo.*

The Awakening of Flora:
Fokine as Mercury (left) and as Apollo (below),
with Pavlova as Flora. Léon Bakst painted in
the backgrounds when the photographs were used
in the Imperial Theatres Yearbook, as seen
in these "before" and "after" versions.

OPPOSITE Pavlova as Flora.

As Snow in *Camargo*.

Mikhail Fokine found himself coping with five girls in the pas de six, one of whom was the nervous Anna, who did not win as much praise as some of her contemporaries.

A storm of intrigue erupted in April. Kchessinskaya, who had taken over the role of Marie Camargo from Legnani, refused to wear the costume—probably because of her diminutive stature. Instead she appeared in a short tutu, with a great many of her diamonds as well, and this insensitivity to the ballet's style outraged the director. As was customary for an offense against company rules, Volkonsky gazetted a fine for the ballerina's misdemeanor, but in doing so he failed to take into account the fact that Mathilde had just formed an intimate alliance with another Grand Duke—Andrei, a younger cousin of her previous paramour the Grand Duke Sergei, and seven years her junior. With some Grand Ducal encouragement, the Tsar soon remitted the fine. This rebuff to his authority placed Volkonsky in an impossible position, and with his power made to seem so hollow he was left with no alternative but to resign, which he did on June 7.

His place was filled by Vladimir Teliakovsky, the director of the Moscow office, who now found himself in the controlling position in St. Petersburg as titular head of the Imperial Theatres. Curiously, he was a retired cavalry colonel who had managed during his military life to maintain a strong interest in the arts, with particular attention to the composition and theory of music. When he was younger he had played piano duets with the famous director of the Moscow Conservatoire, Nicolas Rubinstein; so the bright young men—such as Diaghilev—who hastened to assume that they were dealing with a man of no culture made the mistake of judging their man by superficialities. Teliakovsky also knew all about political intrigue and had no intention of letting Diaghilev get the upper hand on the administrative front. He bided his time, secure in the knowledge that many of the most important Court posts were held by military colleagues with whom he could establish an easy rapport.

In the spring of 1901 Pavlova had been given one opportunity to play Gulnare in *Le Corsaire*; only the heroine, Medora, had a bigger share of the stage action. Plescheyev noted in one of his critiques that Pavlova was arousing the admiration of the public, and that her moving, expressive face was full of animation. He went on to predict that she would be more successful than the Italian ballerinas, who tended to "mar their art with excessive virtuosity." There was talk that Zambelli would be invited from Paris for the next season.

When the Maryinsky company returned from its summer recess, the bulletin board was fuller than usual. Legnani's name was of course no longer in contention for leading roles; and, rather surprisingly, Mathilde Kchessinskaya's name was not featured either. Word soon got about that she had departed for a journey through Italy with the Grand Duke Andrei. Carlotta Zambelli was to fill the gap, and the Milan-trained dancer was listed for *Coppélia*, *Paquita*, and *Giselle*. Other snippets of information included the news that Pavlova 2 had been promoted from coryphée to demi-soloiste. *Giselle* was coming back into the repertoire as a vehicle for Zambelli, and Cecchetti was listed to coach the visiting ballerina in the title role. Much of Marius Petipa's own career had been bound up with *Giselle*, from the moment when his brother had danced the male lead in the first performance of the work in Paris in June 1841.

When finally Zambelli arrived, the critics turned sharp eyes upon her supposedly supreme technique. Those who championed Kchessinskaya against all rivals observed that the star of the Paris Opéra did fouettés en attitude on demi-pointe. By contrast to this dismissive quibbling, Svetlov's review of Zambelli was almost entirely favorable. The visitor was partnered by Nicolas Legat. Julie Sedova was cast as Myrtha, and Pavlova and Lyubov Egorova, as before, were Zulme and Moyna, the soloist Wilis of Act Two.

Pavlova's generation had ample opportunity to observe Zambelli's work as she prepared for the test of facing a St. Petersburg audience. There was further interest in the appearances of Moscow's Ekaterina Geltzer, who performed in St. Petersburg during September and October 1901. She danced Raymonda first and then Nikiya in *La Bayadère* a week before Zambelli's first *Giselle* in Russia. Geltzer displayed tremendous confidence and the openness of presentation that St. Petersburg associated with the other city's exemplars—the "Moscow manner." Geltzer's performance of *La Bayadère* was another in which Pavlova had a chance to appear in a solo spot, in the variations in Act Three. Petipa was about to make a startling decision about future casting in this ballet of his—the "pearl of the repertoire" in the eyes of many critics.

The season proved to be a vital one for Pavlova. She had the chance to work with the company's leading ballerinas, and also those from Moscow and Paris; but though by the end of the season she had made an advance that even her most fervent admirers could not have prophesied, the beginning of the season did not look to be an auspicious start for her. To Preobrajenskaya's Isora in *Bluebeard* she played Anna, Isora's sister, and progressed quickly from this role to appearances as Venus in the last act of this ballet, when she had to perform a full pas de deux with Mikhail Oboukhov in his role as Mars. But when Bezobrazov wrote about her performance as Venus, his general view was that she could, *if she wanted*, be better than several of the ranking ballerinas. The tenor of his article suggested that she was not committed to her work. This view was at odds with the feverish intensity of her talk about the idolized Taglioni, and yet it was a view propounded on more than one occasion—a case in which because a lot was expected, an exceptionally precise yardstick was being applied.

Pavlova was among Swanilda's friends in Zambelli's performances of *Coppélia*, and when Kchessinskaya appeared as Esmeralda, Pavlova and Pikhlankovo played the friends of Preobrajenskaya's Fleur de Lys. Pavlova also danced Henrietta in *Raymonda* during this season. These "friends" were useful roles, for they were on stage for much of the evening.

The Maryinsky's constantly changing repertoire of full-length

ABOVE Possibly as Henrietta in *Raymonda,* though the fleurs-de-lis on the bodice suggest one of the Princess's friends in *La Esmeralda.*

BELOW Possibly as Gulnare in *Le Corsaire.*

ABOVE With Julie Sedova.
BELOW With Alfred Bekefi.

ballets gave numerous chances to young dancers who needed to "feel" the stage and to test their ability to project. The secondary roles, with their lightly sketched characterizations, still required judgment and performing skill, but they were bathed in the reflected light of the star role and thus did not provoke a paralysis of nerves in the executants.

In November, when Zambelli danced the role of Paquita, Pavlova and Sedova were teamed with Nicolas Legat in a showcase pas de trois. Legat was a secure performer who knew how to present his ballerinas with calm assurance. He and Pavlova were already rehearsing Ivanov's *The Magic Flute*, in which they had been assigned the leading roles of Lise and Luke. The choice of this ballet for a revival was questionable, as it was hardly representative of Ivanov's best work; a light-hearted romp with an undue proportion of pantomimic gesture, it had a familiar plot of a peasant girl loved by a local lad, who has somehow to prevent her being married off to a suitably rich but senile Marquis. The Good Fairy provides young Luke with a magic flute so that he can create havoc, with everyone forced to continue dancing for as long as the flute is played.

Ivanov was busy at this time with more choreography. He and Gerdt had been deputed by Petipa to reconstruct a two-act ballet that would give chances to many of the younger members of the company, and the choice of music was Delibes's *Sylvia*, which had only been used previously in St. Petersburg in truncated form.* In its new version it was scheduled for a premiere that coincided with the benefit night allocated to Olga Preobrajenskaya, on December 2. There was an interlude called The Sacred Grove, in which Pavlova was given the role of the principal Naiad, dancing with Fokine and Georgi Kyaksht. Fokine's character was Sylvana; Kyaksht capered about as an old satyr; and the corps de ballet was provided by students of the Ballet School. One of these was Tamara Karsavina, who had a part in the Marche and Cortège of Bacchus. Elsewhere in the new work a pas d'action involved Preobrajenskaya, as Sylvia, with Pavlova, Trefilova, and Egorova, the three girls most consistently used in soloist roles. Act Three of *The Sleeping Beauty* concluded the evening, with Pavlova making her debut as Princess Florine in the Blue Bird pas de deux. The event was marred by the persistence of noisy claques directed against Mathilde Kchessinskaya, who was dancing Princess Aurora, though Mathilde viewed such behavior as nothing more than an amusing challenge.

Sylvia was thought worthy of five scheduled performances, matched that season only by *Cavalry Halt* and *Nutcracker*, but Ivanov, the creator of so much choreographic wealth, was spent. His work as an unsung alter-ego to Petipa had left him with failing health and very little public recognition of his major contribution to ballet. It was a typical irony that one of his own works should be put back into the repertoire after a long absence, with the credit clearly given to him, when before so much had been shuffled about under the banner of Petipa's all-reaching

---

* Diaghilev's involvement in the early stages of this new production had precipitated a squabble with the directorate and his subsequent dismissal from the Imperial Theatres.

As Lise in *The Magic Flute*:
(left) with Giuseppina Cecchetti and Stanislav Gillert.

name. This had to do with the administrative importance of the role of ballet master more than with any particular egocentricity of Petipa's; it was the fate of creative assistants. Perrot had been in a similar situation in connection with Coralli's receiving credit for the first production of *Giselle*. But with Petipa's own days numbered, and Ivanov's name and the value of his work starting to cast their own light again, there came the news of Ivanov's sudden death on December 11. The authorities seemed hardly aware of the fact that ballet had sustained a great loss, for his passing was noted in the journals in an almost cursory manner. When the news was conveyed to Johannsen, the old man was reported to have roared with laughter and then to have said, "His debts must have killed him!" A week later Pavlova found herself on stage performing for the first time in Ivanov's rollicking *Magic Flute*. The dancers must have had very mixed emotions on such an occasion, but their comic timing produced gales of laughter in the audience, and even this lightweight fare made Ivanov's legacy to the company apparent, within the shadow cast by Petipa.

Though the old master himself was obviously satisfied with Pavlova's potential and viewed her as a major new talent, Johannsen was not abashed at giving his own views on some of the younger dancers, and he was inveigled into print on the subject. In the *Petersburg Gazette* on January 1, 1902, he was quoted as saying—clearly for publication—"As a purely classical dancer, Pavlova promises much, but I would advise this young dancer to look upon her art in a more profound manner. She lacks application." Pavlova's limited turn-out and the softened port de bras she had acquired from Gerdt's classes were anathema to Johannsen; he considered her personal style to have become "Romantic untidyness." This public admonishment may have been unpleasant medicine, but it was better than being thought of as not worth a cure, and it acted too as a kind of spotlight: whatever Pavlova did, she did it in the full knowledge that it was being observed acutely. As with all waywardly brilliant children, she aroused conflicting emotions in the same breast. Bezobrazov would comment testily that she appeared to be quite unconcerned about the incorrect positions of her feet, and that her constant dancing with slightly bent knees was ugly; and then, almost within hours, he would feel impelled to write that she had a unique quality that could not be copied. Petipa forebore public comment; instead he gave her more and more roles. She also had a variety of partners: Fokine, as the most efficient student from her near contemporaries, continued to work with her; others were Oboukhov (already giving classes as well as dancing), Georgi Kyaksht, Nicolas Legat, Gorduvoy, and Andrianov, who danced a leszhinka with her in Glinka's opera *Russlan and Ludmilla*. Pavlova was also in the ballet section of Weber's opera *Der Freischütz*, which had an interpolation of the same composer's "Invitation to the Dance," with its cheerful waltz rhythms. There were four dance couples used in this opera, and the casting was frequently Preobrajenskaya, Trefilova, Sedova, and Pavlova, partnered by Gerdt, the Legat brothers, and the Hungarian char-

acter dancer Alfred Bekefi. When the Legats thought this opera was being performed too frequently, they enlivened the routine one night by making themselves up to be indistinguishable from Bekefi. There were delighted shouts of "Bekefi!" from the audience, but when he stepped forward, the Legats echoed his every move, causing hilarious confusion. The administration was not amused.

After the fourth performance of *Sylvia*, on December 30, there was a slight let-up in the schedule of ballets that needed revision, and the dancers had time to prepare for an adventurous undertaking of their own devising. Without help from the senior administration, they put together an evening's entertainment which was given in the Pavlov Hall on Trinity Street on January 18. The novelty of the evening was the fact that two plays were performed: Krukskov's comedy *Capital Aces* and Chekhov's *The Bear*. For the latter, the cast of three was drawn from artists of the ballet company, who also performed in the divertissements in the final part of the program. The hall was packed, and the evening went with a swing. The representative of the *Stock Exchange Register* observed an actress who did not need ballet shoes to make a dramatic point:

> Miss Anna Pavlova performed the quite difficult role of the widow with great success and with a lot of fire; she had a deep understanding of the part—it was clear that it was well assimilated in her mind. She proved to be very animated as an actress and managed to put a great deal of "fire" into her opposite number, Mr. Bulgakov, who was playing The Man Next Door [presumably Smirnov, the debt collector]. The pistols scene was particularly well done, and at the end there were many curtain calls.

In the final part of the program, the small orchestra launched into a polka of Fokine's devising which the program called *Folichon*. The young choreographer had Pavlova as his partner; she was dressed in a yellow silk dress of the Directoire period, and he was in velvet breeches, with a jabot and lace cuffs. The audience thought the piece charming, and at the end there was a storm of applause, which broke out afresh after the two dancers repeated the number. Pavlova's confidence in the young Fokine's ingenuity was from this moment unshakable.

Because Petipa saw in Anna Pavlova qualities that set her apart from her fellows, he determined in the time left to him to set one more star shining in the Maryinsky firmament. He may have been smarting from the way Kchessinskaya had drifted with the current then running strongly against him, and he would have been only human in wanting to see a ballerina whom he had in effect raised to her position made to realize that his power did not end with her but was independent. He knew that if he could find a ballerina capable of the demands of *La Bayadère* that ballerina would automatically have the attention of all St. Petersburg. Though Pavlova 2 was only a demi-soloiste, Petipa was

As one of the Pasha's captives in Rubinstein's opera *The Demon*.

clearly prepared to take risks at this point in his career. If the girl could rise to the technical demands of Act Three, the other acts, and in particular the dramatic pathos of Act Two, were well within her range, even at this stage of her development. Part of Pavlova's armor was a willingness to take risks—at least calculated ones, when she knew that victory was not an impossibility, provided she harness her will power, her acquired learning, and the essential belief in the rightness of her own course. With *La Bayadère* she knew the magnitude of the challenge, but she also knew that she had the faith of its creator.

Kchessinskaya returned from her Italian jaunt with the Grand Duke Andrei to learn that "her" role was being rehearsed by another.* If she was nettled by the thought of being usurped, it was not her only problem: she was also pregnant. However, she was still determined to take the principal role in the new production of *Don Quixote*, scheduled for Johanssen's benefit night on January 20, 1902. The five-act Petipa version of *Don Quixote* had first been produced in Moscow, before being altered and enlarged for St. Petersburg in 1871. It remained popular for thirty years, but toward the end of 1901 there had been much talk about a production of the same ballet by the young

* In her memoirs, written very many years later, Kchessinskaya is at pains to point out that the decision was hers, that she was instrumental in Pavlova's getting the role of Nikiya, and that she gave the girl special coaching in her own studio.

Moscow ballet master Alexander Gorsky. He had been one of Petipa's own pupils and had gone to Moscow to study the Stepanov notation system, with the job of reviving certain Maryinsky ballets for the other company. Given permission to introduce any changes he thought suitable, Gorsky set to with a will and virtually remade Petipa's ballet, introducing many daring innovations based on his belief in true dramatic motivation. At this stage of his career he understood straight theatrical drama more than he understood balletic theatre; like all bright students, he was temporarily impatient with his master. The freshness of work going on at the Moscow Art Theatre, at the Maly, and at the Mamontov Opera (where vital young talent gained wing through private, as opposed to Imperial, subsidy) spurred Gorsky to effect changes at the moribund Bolshoi Theatre, where the auditorium was usually two-thirds empty on the Wednesdays and Sundays when ballet was given.

In Gorsky's version of *Don Quixote* (the ballet's title was actually *Don Quixote of La Mancha*), the rigid corps de ballet routines of Petipa were melded into crowd scenes, which were now richly studded with cameos of market life. Even the designer, Konstantin Korovine, had instructions to keep to absolute historical accuracy in the costumes and architectural settings; there were to be none of the usual confections that tended to banish centuries and frontiers into a never-never world known only to ballet and opera. Gorsky wanted a time and a place; he wanted realism in some measure. The Moscow dancers were happy with this approach, but it earned much criticism elsewhere. Gorsky, who

Javotte: (below) with Fokine.

looked like a hippie of his day, with a long, straggling beard and dangling Oriental moustache, was constantly on the defensive. He made a speech to the company, saying: "There are many people in the ballet profession who love art not for art's sake but because *they* take part in it. Do these people bring any good? Do they develop art and forward it? Alas, of course they don't. Everything they do is done for their own benefit. They have no concern for the meaning of art, for its roots." Fokine would have cheered if he had heard it. Moscow labeled the production "decadent," but that did not stop St. Petersburg from importing it, and Petipa was in no position to argue against something that was ostensibly his work; still, the newspapers were preparing everyone for the worst: "Just how decadent it is, and what that influence will have on the ballet, can only be seen at the benefit."

Mathilde duly took on the energetic role of Kitry without onlookers becoming aware of her condition; and Pavlova won the role of the fan seller, Juanita, which gave her a minuet to be danced with Kchessinskaya. She also won a showcase pas de deux with Georgi Kyaksht. Although Kchessinskaya was willing to join the "new order" without much of a backward glance toward Petipa, most of the company remained intensely loyal to the old man, and there was some high feeling behind the scenes. In the event, *Don Quixote* was not considered a success. Diaghilev and his artist friends seized on a chance to needle the Teliakovsky regime, and they gave the new production a drubbing in their magazine, *Mir Iskusstva* (The World of Art). "Gorsky's new version was vitiated by the abhorrent lack of organization that is typical of amateur performances. His 'novelties' consisted of making crowds on the stage bustle and move about fitfully and aimlessly," wrote Benois. He was in a vitriolic mood and did not spare Petipa's feelings, either, for he went on to say, "*Don Quixote* has never been an adornment to the Imperial stage; now it has become something unworthy of it and almost disreputable."

The production had also caused trouble in the workshops. Korovine had been entrusted, along with Alexander Golovine, with the job of designing a revival of Anton Rubinstein's four-act opera *The Demon,* which had been scheduled for a command performance on the night of Saturday, January 23; but the dress rehearsals were pre-empted by the new ballet production, and the scenery was scarcely ready. After a fever of indecision it was decided (with the Tsar's approval) to transfer the whole production to the Conservatoire, where it eventually found an audience on the Sunday night—there being presubscribed ballet already filling the Maryinsky that evening. *The Demon* could not be seen at the Maryinsky until a month later. At the Conservatoire performance, the visual aspects of the opera caused some derision; the dancers were said to be dressed in yellow, with green and black "stains," which made them appear "like spotted toads." The production itself "could have gone smoother, and probably will," but Pavlova and Trefilova earned themselves a mention as captives of the Pasha. The following evening Pavlova was at the Hermitage, making her debut as Pierrette, the second lead in *Les Millions d'Arlequin,* a role that had been Preobrajenskaya's. This was a notable advance for the younger dancer.

Possibly as Nikiya in *La Bayadère*, c.1903.

Although Petipa was hanging on at the Maryinsky, which was the very core of his life, Cecchetti became dismayed at the way the seniors were being pressured, and over a relatively minor matter, he stood upon his dignity with the management, to the point where he was cornered into resigning. No olive branch was proffered, and he had quickly to accept a post in Warsaw as principal teacher and ballet master. The Maryinsky management smoothly brushed over the matter and allocated one of the four performances of *Don Quixote* as Cecchetti's farewell benefit; this was on January 27. He had been with the company for fifteen years. He went on stage and gave a lugubrious account of Sancho Panza, as memorable as it was endearing. Pavlova danced Juanita again, as well as the showcase pas de deux in the last act, with Kyaksht. Cecchetti excelled too in travesti roles, and before he left St. Petersburg he was given one

last chance to demonstrate this, when *Javotte* came back into the Maryinsky repertoire on February 17. His star pupil Preobrajenskaya had the title role, and Cecchetti played the part of her mother. There was a pretty pas d'ensemble called Dance of the Rivals, which seemed very apt when Pavlova, Sedova, Egorova, and Trefilova all appeared in it together.

Meanwhile, Petipa's plans for these "rivals" had been slowly filtering out, and the *New Times* had revealed on February 10 that Pavlova was to be given the lead in a Friday matinee performance of *La Bayadère* on February 22, and that Julie Sedova was to have the chance to play Medora in *Le Corsaire* at a matinee the following day. "These tryout presentations are always worth seeing," the newspaper stated, "and are of interest to all lovers of ballet." The article went on to suggest that it would not hurt to give Egorova a similar chance. As it happened,

Sedova duly went on in *Le Corsaire*, but Pavlova was replaced in *La Bayadère* by Geltzer, who was in St. Petersburg to dance *Raymonda*. As there was no publicity surrounding this sudden change of plan, the normal assumption would have been that Pavlova had become ill or been injured; yet she was mentioned as playing a secondary role in Sedova's *Corsaire*, and ten days earlier she had played Henrietta to Geltzer's *Raymonda*.

Vera Trefilova in the Danse
Manu in *La Bayadère*.

It is entirely possible that Geltzer's admirers had agitated for a further chance to see her. Such factions could be extraordinarily powerful in their lobbying efforts, and a junior soloist would be no match for that sort of pressure. Then too, Kchessinskaya was a good friend of Geltzer's, always traveling to Moscow for her benefit performances, and she would be unlikely to press the claims of the young Pavlova. And while the general public was still unaware of any reason for Kchessinskaya to retire from the limelight, there could only have been feverish gossip at one of her roles being annexed by a youngster. It was hardly in Mathilde's own interest for Nikiya to be danced by a St. Petersburg dancer—and such a young one at that—until she herself was demonstrably away "on leave." This occurred in March, when she could no longer conceal her condition. The Lent break gave time for Kchessinskaya's roles to be redistributed among the other ballerinas. Preobrajenskaya was the one who appeared

most often in the listings, but *La Bayadère* provoked controversy. Petipa stuck to his guns and scheduled Pavlova for an important evening performance toward the end of the season. The *Petersburg Gazette* thought the casting a brave gesture by Petipa, and it pointed out the anomaly of the situation, with Pavlova's name lost among many others on the *affiche*, not given the prominence that the role of Nikiya normally merited. It read simply: "*La Bayadère*, with Gerdt," although in the small print Pavlova was clearly being announced for the role of Nikiya. The *Gazette* continued in its usual provocative tone, pointing out that this ballet was "the pearl of the repertoire," and that in giving the lead to a demi-soloiste Petipa had offended a lot of other dancers; Pavlova was, it pointed out, "the one known as 'La Petite Pavlova,' only in her third season."

*L*a Bayadère had heart as well as panoply, and the principal dancer was given numerous chances to establish a compelling identity. Act One, set outside a looming Hindu temple, showed Nikiya to be within the power of the Chief Brahmin, for whom she danced reluctantly, submissive by virtue of her lot as a temple dancer, yet preserving her dignity with suppliant gestures—the classic victim. Nikiya had a mysterious lover, Solor, who came to her in a secret assignation by the temple; but the Brahmin observed them together. Nikiya was summoned to the Rajah's palace by his daughter, Gamzatti (who is betrothed to Solor), because the princess was anxious to see the bayadère who sought to claim him for herself, for the Brahmin had revealed Nikiya's secret. Nikiya was then suddenly confronted with a portrait of the princess's future husband, and recognized him as Solor. She was appalled at the suggestion that she must relinquish him. A violent quarrel took place, before the temple dancer was expelled from the palace.

Act Two of *La Bayadère* was one of Petipa's masterful assemblies, with great crowds employed on the stage. There was color and spectacle, with blackamoors wafting ostrich feather fans, slaves bearing great baskets of flowers or shouldering long spears, dancing girls with parrots on their wrists, hunters toting the body of a tiger bound to a pole, the Rajah carried high in a ceremonial chair, and his daughter following in a curtained palanquin. Finally the warrior Solor entered atop an elephant, surrounded by countless more slaves, soldiers, and young Arab attendants. The Preobrajensky Regiment was called in to supply dozens of tall porters.* The presentation was no more relevant to India than a willow-pattern plate reflected everyday China.

The celebrations for the impending wedding of Gamzatti and Solor were the excuse for a massive display of divertissements. Apart from a showcase pas de deux for the fiancés, there was the Danse Manu, in which the audience usually had the chance to observe some fresh new talent from the ranks of the junior

_____
*For serious soldiers, they spent an inordinate amount of time on the stage; in *Le Corsaire* serried ranks of them moved about under huge bolts of cloth to simulate a stormy sea.

La Bayadère

ABOVE As a soloist bayadère in Act One (left);
as Nikiya in Act One (center) and Act Two (right).

BELOW As one of the principal Shades
in Act Three (The Kingdom of the Shades).

soloists. Petipa had arranged the dance as a light-hearted episode between a girl balancing a pitcher of water on her head and two children trying to persuade her to give them a drink. It was designed as a part of the general festive color and abandon of the celebration, and its playfulness contributed to the impact of the pathos that was to follow. These vignettes, as constructed by Petipa, all served to maintain interest in the general spectacle, and they provided a cunning counterpoint for the great set pieces of dance with which they were interposed.

But Petipa reserved the chief dramatic impact for the ballerina playing Nikiya. At the height of the festive scene she entered the palace, commanded by the Rajah to dance at the celebration. As the girl in the blue cloak emerged before the crowd, she betrayed a feverish intensity; the sight of her caused Solor to avert his gaze. This gesture, compounded of pain and guilt, was one of those moments when Petipa gave his characters the chance for some real theatre, and it was unfailingly taken with gratitude. Gerdt could make of it a movement that focused all eyes.

Nikiya's cloak was removed. She knew she must dance, but she found the burden of the command intolerable in the circumstances. She looked to the throne with a beseeching expression. Solor again turned away, and Nikiya began torturously to summon her skills. As she danced, her despair was evident. Though she perfected the steps of the dance, there was a sense of agony in every gesture, and her vulnerability had the entire audience in sympathy. At the climax of this pathetic dance, a servant carried to Nikiya a basket of rare flowers. To Nikiya, it seemed a gift from Solor, but the princess watched maliciously. Suddenly, the bayadère sensed that the basket in some way concealed her fate, and her dance became frenzied. Finally she appeared resigned, and, almost in a trance, she plucked a flower from within the basket. Moments later her body stiffened as she held up a handful of blossoms. A small snake was seen to slither onto her shoulder. The assembly gasped; Gamzatti smiled triumphantly; Solor was aghast. The Brahmin, who still lusted after Nikiya, then came forward with the offer of a secret antidote for the snake's bite. But Nikiya refused the potion which he held before her, and instead chose death. Her arms reached up in a final gesture of pleading and despair, and as Solor supported her, she collapsed, lifeless. Her spirit (played by a surrogate ballerina) was then seen as an apparition rising to the peaks of the distant Himalayas.

The third act showed Solor, heartbroken, seeking the consolation of the spells of temple fakirs. In a dream he hallucinated with such intensity that everything seemed real and vivid.[*] He had entered the Kingdom of the Shades, and in a glorious white vision of purity and eternal calm, he glimpsed Nikiya once more. This scene of pure dance structure was justly considered to be the pinnacle of a superb ballet, which ended with the apocalyptic destruction of the palace during the wedding celebrations, in which Solor had been haunted by the ghost of Nikiya.

_____

[*] Opium was the cause of the dream in the original libretto, but this had been toned down by the turn of the century.

Pavlova danced the role of Nikiya for the first time on April 28, 1902. She was everything that Petipa had hoped for, and more; with her telling mime she projected the ballet's pivotal theme of pure, inflexible love to such effect that all the great set pieces of dancing and the pas d'action became for the first time facets of a single blazing gem, rather than a string of pretty fragments. The ballet fans cheered their latest heroine; Petipa's gamble had succeeded.

Toward the end of the 1901–02 season, a piece of pure luck came Petipa's way. Teliakovsky, eager for innovation, brought from Milan not a ballerina this time but a ballet master, one Cesare Coppini. He had been commissioned to reproduce the ballet *La Source*, to Delibes's score, and he was given several months in which to do it. Those months were to underline the poverty of foreign choreography and make Petipa's slightest work seem a masterpiece.

Although Pavlova could look back on the 1901–02 season as one of accomplishment and advance, Fokine, who partnered her often, was somewhat grudging about her talent; he still did not think she was the most promising of the soloists. The younger girls admired her unreservedly; in their minds she was a ballerina—by accomplishment if not by rank—and they treated her with some deference, which was returned by her with a certain air of condescension to her juniors. Tamara Karsavina (the girl who had caught Fokine's eye) was in an interpolated pas de deux in the last act of *Javotte* on May 1. The girl scored a hit with the audience, and Pavlova, who was also dancing that night, nodded to her as she went by on her way to the dressing rooms, and then commented, "An ovation, my child"—a factual observation about the audience's behavior, getting her over the problem of being encouraging about the actual dancing. This apparent fear of being overtaken by younger talents was irrational in view of Pavlova's own distinctive qualities, but then these were the things she could judge least; the qualitative assessments were based on technical skills and the level of audience reaction, both of which could be measured in the Maryinsky. It was almost as if the dancers never left school at all, but went through a perpetual form of graduation, with the same audience sitting in judgment.

During that summer, Maria Petipa got as far as the Opéra-Comique in Paris, where she presented Russian character dances with Sergei Legat. He was a gifted dancer, twelve years junior to Maria; but this was no encumbrance to their starting an affair. Liaisons were open, as regular and as unremarkable as the horse trams rumbling up and down the Nevsky Prospekt; they came and they went. Some went short distances, others longer; some destinations were glamorous staging posts, others were cul-de-sacs. Anna Pavlova was now being seen rather often with the stage manager of the Maryinsky—not a particularly influential escort, except that his uncle happened to be the director of the Imperial Theatres. If stagehands were adept at moving scenery, it was quite possible that the stage manager was equally adept at moving his uncle in some way. It was a tangled world where influence led through the corridors of court life like Ariadne's silken thread.

From time to time the Tsar presented entertainments at one or another of his country palaces, particularly in the summer months. In May 1902 the choice was Tsarskoe Selo, fifteen miles south of the city, for a performance before the French President. Lyubov Roslavleva was brought from Moscow to help out during Kchessinskaya's absence; she danced as the Tsar Maiden in one act of Gorsky's reworking of Saint-Léon's *The Little Humpbacked Horse*. Pavlova, as one of the Nereids, would have had further opportunity to observe this respected dancer—the one whom Bezobrazov had declared to be "the best dancer in Russia."

A further gala performance was given at the rural palace of Peterhof on August 19, and included the second scene of Act One of *Swan Lake*, with Roslavleva as Odette, and Act One of *Don Quixote*, with Kchessinskaya making a reappearance after the birth of her son, to show that motherhood was no impediment to a continuing stage career. Among the younger dancers, Pavlova again appeared as Juanita to Kchessinskaya's Kitry. Though Anna probably had her eye on Roslavleva, most of the younger dancers strove to emulate the casual brilliance they observed in someone like Kchessinskaya.

Pavlova often found herself paired with Fokine, and they worked well together. When she was about to do a pirouette, she would whisper prudently to her partner not to forget the push, in case she should end on a half turn. Because she was good at pirouettes, she popped them into the choreography whenever there seemed to be a suitable moment; despite the whispering there did not seem to be any preparation, so quickly did she whirl into them. Fokine liked doing jumps best. The two dancers improvised well together, with an eye on the conductor to see how he was doing, and Pavlova whispering to Fokine how much music she thought was left. She did not seem to trust her dreamer of a partner, and it was important to finish with the music. Fokine was now plagued with stage fright a lot of the time, but once the performance was over, his questing mind gave the impression of a youth whose thoughts did stray. At rehearsals he would corner Pavlova, who was a sympathetic listener, and away he would go, on subjects that had never crossed her mind. Why did the Ballet School have no lessons in art and the history of the theatre? There was not even any history of ballet or dance in general! Why are you doing all those pirouettes? Why do I do the same jumps all the time? Is all this necessary? *What does it all mean?* It meant that they would have to work harder so that Fokine would not forget to push at the end of the pirouettes, that is what it meant. Pavlova would drag Fokine back onto the floor, in the hope that the next pirouette would be better.

Despite Fokine's grumbles, there was a great deal of work for him and his young partner. Toward the end of August, when the

ABOVE Lyubov Roslavleva

BELOW Part of the program for the ballet gala given at Tsarskoe Selo in May 1902. Contrary to suggestions that Ivanov never received full credit for his work in *Swan Lake*, here he was given clear credit, with Petipa, for this part of the ballet.

Deuxième acte

du ballet:

Le Lac des Cygnes.

Danses et mise-en-scène composés par M-r M. Petipa, Soliste de Sa Majesté l'Empereur, et par M-r L. Ivanow. Musique de M-r P. Tchaikovsky. Décors par M-r A. Golovine.

PERSONNAGES:

La Princesse	M-me Cecchetti.
Le Prince Siegfried, son fils	M-r Guerdt.
Von Rothbart, mauvais génie	M-r Boulgakow.
Odille, sa fille	M-lle O. Préobrajenskaïa.
Le maître des cérémonies	M-r Solianikow.
Un héraut	M-r Ivanow 2.

Seigneurs, Grandes dames, Pages, Laquais etc.

1) Valse des fiancées: M-lles Astafiewa, Leonowa 1, Konetskaïa, Petipa 2, Maholina, Kouskowa et M-r Guerdt.
2) Pas espagnol: M-lles Pavlowa 2, Feodorowa, M-rs Chiriaew et Koslow.
3) Pas de trois: M-lles Sedowa, Karsavina et M-r Fokine.
4) Danse Vénitienne: M-lle Tréfilowa et M-r S. Legat.
5) Pas Hongrois: M-lle Petipa 1 et M-r Bekkefy.
6) Mazurka: M-lles Bakerkina 1, Pavlowa 1, Vassiliewa, Slanjowa; M-rs Kchessinsky 2, Voronkow 1, Koussow et Loukianow.
7) Pas d'action: M-lle O. Préobrajenskaïa; M-rs Guerdt, Oboukhow et Boulgakow.

Solo de violon exécuté par M-r Kruger.

Solo de célesta exécuté par M-r Gribene.

Chef d'orchestre M-r R. Drigo.

ABOVE In the Ural Cossacks dance
in *The Little Humpbacked Horse*.

BELOW Tamara Karsavina as
the Page in *Fiammetta*.

company reassembled for the opening of the season at the Maryinsky on the first Sunday of September, Karsavina, as a graduate, was placed in class with the group of soloists that contained Trefilova, Sedova, and Pavlova. They were all appearing on the opening night of the season in *The Nutcracker*, with Preobrajenskaya as the Sugar Plum Fairy. Three nights later, Pavlova had the leads in *The Magic Flute* and *The Awakening of Flora*. Among the senior ballerinas, Geltzer shared the early part of the season with Preobrajenskaya, and Grimaldi also came from Moscow, for a performance of *Le Corsaire*. When *The Little Humpbacked Horse* went into the repertoire, Pavlova appeared in the Ural Cossacks' dance, and her vivacity surprised those who had seen her principally in more delicately classical figures. That season she was dancing the Fairy of the Canaries in *The Sleeping Beauty*, Gulnare in *Le Corsaire*, Anna in *Bluebeard*, and Henrietta in *Raymonda*. She was also at this time acquiring the basic groundwork for her debut in the leading role in *Giselle*. As Zulme, Pavlova's appearance and soft style suggested to Petipa a vanished era of dance. Her suitability for this old Romantic favorite seemed unquestionable, and her success as Nikiya in *La Bayadère* helped to convince him that the time was now right. Rehearsals often stretched far into the night.

I t has been seen that senior students and graduates were used to practicing a pas de deux of their own choosing and then performing it as an interpolation within the context of a greater work being given in the theatre. The additions mostly passed without undue notice, other than the mention that so-and-so had performed, and although the dancers' names went into the program, there was not always any information about the authorship of the piece they appeared in. Thus the evening of September 22, 1902, held a significance that could not be divined by those present. *Graziella*, an old Saint-Léon ballet to music by Pugni, which had been reconstructed by Ivanov, was being given, with Trefilova and Nicolas Legat in the leading roles, and, unremarkably, there was an interpolated pas de deux. It was performed by Anna Pavlova and Alfred Bekefi. There was no indication of who had devised the steps, but the music was by Chopin, orchestrated by Glazunov.*

Pavlova's second performance as Nikiya was given three days after *Graziella*. Meanwhile, she continued to rehearse for her debut as Giselle. With *La Bayadère* Pavlova mastered the technical detail as it was laid down, and acquired added interpretive color as she progressed. *Giselle* was quite another problem. It had

---

*There are no more details in the Yearbook for the 1902–03 season, yet one must speculate that Fokine, even at this early stage, had not only made another work for Pavlova (following his frolicsome number at the Trinity Street hall) but had also started experimenting with Chopin pieces, though the first fruits of this concept have always been associated with the initial version of *Chopiniana* five years later. Or had someone, such as Kulichevskaya, spotted the potential of Chopin for dance? Svetlov, in his 1922 book on Pavlova, said that mention should be made of her pas de deux in *Graziella*, but he did not elaborate further. It should be noted that any reader of *The Times* of London (readily available in St. Petersburg) could have learned of Isadora Duncan's dancing to Chopin at the New Gallery in July 1900.

been in the repertoire only spasmodically, with long gaps between one production and the next, and in every instance the ballet had been reworked considerably for the principal exponent, so that there was no clearly defined shape or tradition. Zambelli had been encouraged to interpolate passages that flattered her own particular strengths, and Petipa had not interfered with Cecchetti during this process; it was the accepted way of working at the time.

Giselle had maintained almost as long a career in St. Petersburg as it had in Paris, having been mounted in Russia only eighteen months after its premiere at the Opéra in June 1841. When Perrot, the co-producer with Coralli of the original ballet (and, in fact, its real choreographer) arrived in St. Petersburg to work with Fanny Elssler in 1848, he began changing the ballet in many details, so that her first act was triumphant at the expense of the second, which was thought not to suit her. Two years later, Perrot took the whole ballet apart and began again, when Grisi, his former lover as well as his original Giselle, arrived in St. Petersburg on her Russian tour. Choreographer and dancer worked together closely and were no doubt a little disheartened to find that their combined efforts did not entirely satisfy the critics, who remembered a sharper technical attack from Andreyanova's performances and thought that Grisi, for all her reputation in the role, could have made more of Giselle's inner state and relied less on superficial affectations of tragedy. Martha Muravieva, a hard-working little ballerina of great skills who had been nurtured by Petipa's predecessor, Saint-Léon, made her debut at the Paris Opéra in an 1863 revival of Giselle. Muravieva carried Russian dancing skills into the French capital at a remarkably early stage; she went back there a year later, which could not have happened if her first visit had been anything but a success.[*]

Petipa had followed all these developments during his own reign in St. Petersburg, and Giselle in particular was part of his background—to such an extent that it was almost like one of his own ballets. In fact, when Perrot was working with Grisi in 1850, he had Petipa beside him, since Petipa was technically the producer; and it was Petipa the producer who made certain modifications in the dance of the Wilis in Act Two. He did so again, more distinctively, when the ballet was revived in 1884, while Minkus fiddled about with parts of Adam's score. Now, in 1902, with time running out, Petipa began molding Giselle around the fresh talent of Anna Pavlova. It was an image of a vanished Romantic style that Petipa was determined to put on the stage; to this end he worked ceaselessly with Pavlova, re-examining every aspect of the role.[**] Pavlova had the examples of three other

ballerinas in the role—Grimaldi, Zambelli, and Preobrajenskaya—but during these performances she had always to be on stage herself in Act Two and had thus not been able to view the performances in a detached manner. She was nevertheless aided by the incomparable background of continuity that supported her: at one moment Petipa would be guiding her in some passage from Giselle, one of the most demanding tests in the ballet canon, and only hours later she might find herself in the humble role of a nereid in The Little Humpbacked Horse, the old ballet of Saint-Léon, who had influenced Petipa considerably when the latter was working under his guidance.

Petipa had been constructing works for the Imperial Theatres for fifty years now, and the event was to be celebrated in February 1903 at a special gala performance. Ever since Teliakovsky's accession to the role of director, it had been made clear that this milestone would not be ignored, and Petipa had been mulling over the anniversary work. It was going to be new and vivid and reflect all the wonders that Petipa had strewn across the Imperial stages. It was to be called The Magic Mirror.

Coppini's La Source finally appeared at the benefit night of the corps de ballet on December 8. The corps may have deserved better, but everyone seemed to realize that this was the chance to show the true strength of Maestro Petipa—by revealing the poverty of his would-be replacements. The only pity was that several months of rehearsals had been necessary before such an obvious point could be proved. The main weight fell on Preobrajenskaya, who had the lead; but everyone else was also involved, and Pavlova had the part of a fairy called Ephemerida. La Source had a total of thirty-one dances; number 3 was an apparition fantastique for Pavlova, and number 29 a set of variations, of which the first went to Lydia Kyaksht, the second to Karsavina, the third to Pavlova, and the fourth to Trefilova. The whole ballet was considered a disaster, and an outmoded one at that.

If the audiences had been indulgent and docile over The Magic Flute, the dancers found a frightening change by the time the other bit of magic apparatus, The Magic Mirror, put itself on show. The libretto was a curious amalgam of Pushkin and Grimm, which had been put together, according to the program, by Petipa and a mysterious "Mr. . . . ." Arseny Koreschenko had composed a score, and this looked on the face of it to be a promising innovation, coming from one of Tchaikovsky's most ardent disciples. There were designs by Alexander Golovine, the avant-garde landscapist from Moscow who, along with Konstantin Korovine, had designed the recent revival of The Demon, and

[*] Touring by Russian ballerinas was unusual, but it was not totally remarkable. Lydia Geiten toured the provinces of her own country in the summer of 1894 with shortened versions of several well-known ballets, including Giselle, and she could claim to have danced in London at Covent Garden as far back as 1887, which was three years before she appeared in St. Petersburg, on leave from her Moscow base. And there was Lydia Nelidova, daughter of a domiciled British manufacturer, who demonstrated her Moscow training on the stage of the Empire Theatre in London in 1890.

[**] One can only speculate as to how much Petipa entirely rebuilt the role around Pavlova.

An article in The Ladies' Home Journal in 1924, purportedly written by the ballerina but probably dressed up from a series of interviews and "approved" by her, included the following: "But subtly, in those fine points that really make an interpretation, my eighty-five-year-old master, as keen and quick and despotic as the day he took the reins from Saint-Léon, flung tradition to the bleak Russian winds. The interpretation of Giselle that I fashioned under his tutelage was as remote from the one he built with Taglioni more than half a century before as the earth is from the stars." Pavlova seemed convinced that Taglioni had danced the role of Giselle; she often made the slip in interviews.

As the Spanish Doll in *The Fairy Doll*.

whose employment was another sign of fresh thinking in St. Petersburg. Kchessinskaya took the role of the Princess, and Petipa found room for both of his daughters in the work, as well as for Pavlova and Sedova, who played attendants to the Princess. Oboukhov and Fokine attended the Prince, who was played by Sergei Legat. Kchessinskaya's brother played the part of a Polish Magnate, but mysterious ellipses were prevalent in the program: the leading Gnome was listed as "Pupil . . . ."

Teliakovsky's reforming zeal seemed to have struck a judicious balance between the old and the new, and he viewed the clamor for seats with understandable satisfaction. The gala took place on February 9, 1903, and the Imperial family turned out in full force, with the Dowager Empress accompanying her son and daughter-in-law. Their presence in the Imperial box might normally have lent to the occasion a restraining dignity, but Teliakovsky's reformations had included a lessening of subscribers' nights at the ballet, and many of the seats were now being filled by a newer, less hidebound, and certainly more volatile audience from the middle classes. These were people who were seeing things with a fresh eye and who brought with them no comfortable assumptions. By the end of the first scene of *The Magic Mirror* there was an ominous feeling of discontent coming from the audience, and as the work progressed, this discontent began to manifest itself audibly. Far from being an anticlimax, the evening was growing rapidly into a scandal, with ribald comments multiplying into a buzz of dissatisfaction during the intermission. Long before the

end of the ballet some people were shouting "Curtain!" and by the time the curtains did close, they closed on an era.

There were no gracious invitations to the Imperial box; the gilded auditorium emptied, and the dancers trailed back to their dressing rooms. It was difficult to absorb the fact that the evening which had begun with such high hopes had ended as a disaster. Even if some of the dissatisfaction had been aimed at the unfamiliar décor and music, there could be no disguising the fact that there was a certain poverty of real invention in the choreography, and that the mixture of old elements with new was injudicious.

There was no doubt that there was a desperate need for new choreographers, and Petipa himself had actively encouraged the management's attempt to seek fresh talents. Fokine had shown a marked interest in choreography, but there was no precedent for so young a dancer having opportunities and facilities for creating ballets within the framework of the Imperial Theatres. Even when the Legat brothers were given the chance to try their hands at an entertainment at the Hermitage, the whole venture was treated as something of an indulgence. The work they wanted to put on was *The Fairy Doll*, a new version of *Die Puppenfee*, an old Viennese ballet with music by Josef Bayer, to which the Legats added bits by Drigo and Rubinstein. As the ballet was to be launched at the Hermitage, with its select audience, there was less at stake than there would have been at the Maryinsky. Kchessinskaya was not so enamored of budding young choreographers as she was eager to appear before royalty in the Hermitage; she took the role of the Fairy Doll, and Bakst designed her a flattering costume in shades of pink. The toy shop itself was set in the Gestinny Dvor, circa 1830, and through the window of the shop could be seen people promenading against a representation of the Nevsky Prospekt. The brothers gave themselves the roles of two Pierrots, and there was also a lively variation for Pavlova as a Spanish Doll, in which guise she wore a dress of layered flounces decorated with carnation velvet ribbons. The choreography gave her lots of pirouettes, runs, and tricky pointe work, and she had to manage a fan and castanets as well. She coped with everything: she was vivacious, used her body in a very pliant "Spanish" way, and almost stole the show.

The Fairy Doll was given together with one act of *Paquita* and also Ivanov's *The Magic Flute* on February 7, and if the behavior of the audience at the Hermitage was any yardstick, the new ballet was the biggest success. This was not altogether unexpected, since the work had been under construction in one way or another for more than a year, and there had been several chances to assess the worth of its various components. Kchessinskaya's presence ensured that there would be a multitude of out-of-season flowers at the premiere: a great number of bouquets and floral wreaths were passed across the orchestra pit, and from among this tribute Kchessinskaya plucked a few roses and handed them to Pavlova, who took a solo call, bowing to Kchessinskaya as well as to the audience. This was the sort of enthusiastic end to an evening that should by rights have occurred the week before at *The Magic Mirror*, but instead of the applause being for a work by the Master, it was for a work by two of his pupils. This sign of royal approval seems to have been all the management was waiting for in its determination to bring Petipa's reign to an end. The very next day came a bombshell: it was announced that Petipa's contract with the Imperial Theatres would not be renewed when the company reassembled on September 1. It was small comfort that his salary was to be continued in his retirement; the manner of his dismissal could not have come about in a more painful way, and all the dancers became aware that soon they would be without the father figure who had shaped their very existence. With a brutally cool eye for passing events, the *Stock Exchange Register* gave the news, informing its readers that "the ballet company will have to get used to a new ballet master, A. Gorsky. He will stage his own versions of *The Little Humpbacked Horse* and *Swan Lake*. He stages both ballets entirely differently and in a much more original manner."

And yet Petipa's little works for the Hermitage, *The Trials of Damis* and *Les Saisons*, had transferred happily to the Maryinsky, and the former had been thought worthy of coupling with Berlioz's *Les Troyens à Carthage* for a gala on January 24: on this occasion, the Watteau-inspired confection showed Lyubov Petipa as La Contessa, Olga Preobrajenskaya as Isabelle, and Sergei Legat as Damis. Even more interesting to ardent ballet-goers was the line-up for the *troupe ambulante*, four couples simulating

marionettes as an entertainment at a *fête champêtre*: the program listed Karsavina first, partnered by Theodore Koslov, and had Pavlova paired with Georgi Kyaksht at the end. These dancers were all performing Petipa's works with distinct success at the very time he was fired. Fokine was particularly upset; he had progressed from being buried in the male corps of *The Trials of Damis* to a leading role in a new ballet, and yet he was not going to get the chance to perform it: the newest of Petipa's confections for the Hermitage series was canceled along with the Master's contract to the Imperial Theatres. The ballet was to have been *The Romance of the Rosebud*, with Preobrajenskaya as the flower of the title and Fokine in the principal male role, Moth. Since the dancers thought this new work looked to be every bit as promising as *Les Saisons* and *The Trials of Damis* the management may have nipped this particular bud to their own detriment. It certainly needed the vast resources of Petipa's earlier works to sustain constant changes of program.

The Master's looming departure was a particular blow for Anna Pavlova. At a crucial moment she was losing teachers who were vital to her, and none more so than Petipa himself, for he had already scheduled her debut in *Giselle* for the end of April. Though he would still be present to guide her up to that all-important night, he would not be able to foster her advance thereafter, and Pavlova knew that there might very well be a reaction against favored Petipa pupils, particularly those who might be regarded as usurpers of senior ballerinas' positions. There was a pressing need for Pavlova to be seen as a technically accomplished performer as well as an intuitive interpreter of roles, and it was the steps themselves that had most often been her weakness. At rehearsals of *Le Roi Candaule* she was seen to be lacking in strength; her breathing was deficient, and there was some serious doubt as to whether she would be able to complete her principal variation, which needed to be far more precise. She appeared in the ballet as the goddess Diana, surrounded by nymphs. The scene was built around a cleverly conceived pas de trois—or rather a pas de deux between Diana and Endymion in which a Satyr intervened—whose complexity revealed itself to executants the more they became acquainted with its possibilities. Pavlova had always looked very decorative in the role, with a silver sickle moon highlighting her dark hair, but many of Diana's steps were executed with a hunting bow held in one hand, which always increased the problems.

On this particular night, Leopold Auer was conducting with spirit. The music of Pugni was marvelously suggestive of the hunting theme, with its volley of horns and the muted strings cleverly hinting at flights of arrows. Pavlova loved the role, and she acquitted herself well; but alert onlookers were of the opinion that she had survived the test by an application of extreme will power, not because she had any real command of her technique. It was the sort of complaint often leveled against her, now that her obvious artistry as a performer had focused a weight of attention upon her out of all proportion to that which would normally center upon a dancer of her years.

Sokolova continued her valuable work, taking over as ballet

mistress after Johanssen died, but there were notable gaps in the ranks of teachers Pavlova would normally have turned to for extra tuition: Cecchetti had been the exemplar for the Italian school, and he too was gone. Despite his approaching banishment from the School, Petipa remained a living presence in St. Petersburg, and Pavlova often visited him, seeking advice about her interpretations of various of his ballets. His position with the company was a courtesy one; he was listed on the programs, which saved the management's corporate face, but he was actually to be denied access to the institution itself after September 1903, and discourtesy was the basic element of official behavior toward him. He lingered on, a tethered giant.

Rehearsing for *Giselle*, Pavlova knew that European traditions were based on sound technical accomplishment; despite the tailoring that Petipa had effected for her in the role, nothing could disguise the fact that a suggestion of an ethereal spirit could only be conveyed by a total command of the bodily instrument; one could not rely solely on dramatic fervor.

To get a demi-soloiste onto the stage of the Maryinsky in a principal ballerina role, as Petipa had done with Pavlova in *La Bayadère*, had taken a great deal of maneuvering, and Pavlova had needed many assets over and above her own skill and courage. Fighting her battle for her then had been a formidable array: Petipa, with his great power not quite vitiated; the critic Svetlov, whose admiration was of a nature not altogether professionally detached, and who was greatly involved in her day-to-day welfare; and the Maryinsky's stage manager, putting in a good word with his uncle, Teliakovsky. Pavlova had seized her opportunity in time-honored fashion and had really made her name; but a year later there were conditions of considerably increased stress, principally due to the knowledge that her great mentor was now "under sentence." On the evening of April 30, 1903, Pavlova had to go on stage in a role that she knew could not possibly have come her way for years had not Petipa demonstrated his complete faith in her abilities. Added to this responsibility was a terrifyingly critical audience that included several of the most famous of her immediate predecessors in the role, notably her teacher Sokolova, as well as Varvara Nikitina and Henrietta Grimaldi.

It was not so much a breath of fresh air that Pavlova brought to the stage in *Giselle* that night, but rather a hint of mists and wood violets and a spectral physical grace that was almost disturbing in its singularity. She had the power to project—the one quality that could be encouraged but never entirely taught. As one critic wrote: "She is in absolute command of her own beauty, which is lit up with every flame that arises from her soul, to burn bright with every one of her movements, with every flash of her inspiration." Nicolas Legat partnered her with tact, and if Pavlova's reading of her role was at times tentative—a lightly brushed sketch with some shadowy and undefined areas—it suited her youth and technical immaturity. Her performance delighted most of the audience, and the upper reaches of the house shouted

their approval. Overnight she acquired a group of followers who became known as the "*Pavlovtzi*," and from then on there was a faction that, in time, would rival the crowd pulling for Kchessinskaya, whose admirers followed her from city to city in droves. At the end of the performance, Pavlova received a silver-gilt wreath and a mass of floral tributes.

The all-important notices for this first effort in *Giselle* were mixed, as might have been expected. Plescheyev in the *Petersburg Gazette* thought that Pavlova's Giselle had the soul of a butterfly, that she did not die in any physical sense but rather her earthly figure merely faded away. But a day after this heartening reaction, Svetlov provided a more guarded appraisal in the *Stock Exchange Register* when he wrote that though her general approach was poetically apt, her mime did not wholly satisfy the audience during the first act; he felt that the varying facets of the character as Pavlova depicted them were not integrated sufficiently to suggest a single plausible character, though there was no question of her rightness for the role of the ghostly Giselle in the second act. This detached view may have betokened a shift in their personal friendship; however, she could not expect to be judged by any standard but the highest, and Svetlov may have been protecting himself from any accusations of personal interest. The critics always expected the Peasant Pas de Deux in Act One to be a highlight. The *New Times* noted that as performed by Karsavina and Fokine it "lacked energy," although Fokine "did not dance badly," and of Giselle herself: "Pavlova had a great, and in all respects a well-earned, ovation, particularly in the last act, when, as it seemed, scarcely touching the ground, she floated in the air." *The Awakening of Flora* had been given before *Giselle*, and in it Julie Sedova was said to have "successfully replaced Mme Pavlova."

In later writings Svetlov said that *Giselle's* tragic ending "enabled the two great impersonators of the title part, Grisi and Pavlova, to stamp that part with their respective individualities." And there was perspicacity in the remark that Pavlova, "with the convincing power of genius, gave the signal for that reversion to the older forms of the art of dancing which is today universal." Pavlova did interpret the "older forms" with life-giving sincerity, and it took Petipa to understand that she could do so. Svetlov, perhaps unwittingly, gave the old man his due, when he wrote later:

Every detail, to the most minute, cooperates in its one general effect, tends with forceful directness—the apparent result of unconscious inspiration, toward an intuitive resurrection of the true Giselle. And Pavlova's innermost idiosyncracies, which seem to have been created and combined precisely in view of *Giselle*, make that resurrection most convincing. They afford her endless possibilities for her impersonation.

Svetlov certainly encouraged Pavlova to think of *Giselle* in a very proprietorial way while she was part of the regime of the Maryinsky, where senior ballerinas fought to retain roles once they were allocated to them. She was to cling to this role throughout her life. Pavlova put some element of her soul into each of her roles; they were her life—a little portion of the *real* her, as distinct from the vague cipher who had to act out the role of "ballerina" between the more full-blooded embodiments on the stage—but *Giselle* was something more: to Pavlova it was her direct link with her heritage.

The Imperial Ballet, in its perpetual quest for refinement and technical excellence, had made itself a center where roving foreign influences put themselves to the test. Some were judged to be lacking in merit and were quickly discarded; others, notably Pierina Legnani, were acclaimed and were readily taken into the Tsar's ballet as permanent guest artists with first call on the most important performances.

With the example of Italian technical attack before it, the Russian schooling proved to have a depth of confidence in its own merits that allowed for experimentation in a way that a less secure establishment could not have risked. The traffic was not all one-way, either; the visiting Italians, though lacking the more lyrical grace that came easily to the younger Russians, soon modified their own style in order to achieve a maximum success with the sophisticated and critical Russian audiences. In this way they rapidly acquired a new following. Taglioni had achieved this difficult transition by purveying a wistful Romanticism; years later, Legnani astonished her critics with a prodigious display of the newest Italian trick, the fouetté. A sequence of these whipped turns—at the time outside the Russian vocabulary—was in itself enough to set the seal on a performance in *Swan Lake* that may well have contributed little else to an understanding of the deeper allegorical fabric of the ballet. Overnight, young Russians were practicing fouettés relentlessly, and Kchessinskaya, with her compact little body, was one of the first to master them. Gerdt noticed the young Pavlova practicing this step, and he was worried that the stress would prove too much for such a delicate instep. He tried to assure Pavlova that her qualities were of a marked and individual nature and did not require overt "tricks" to achieve an effect; but she was not altogether convinced and was often observed trying to increase her command of Italian-inspired technique.[*]

With the summer vacation due, Pavlova felt for the first time that it was no longer a reprieve from work, when the joy of life at the country cottage could weave its spell. She and Vera Trefilova made the bold decision to travel to Milan in order to study with the noted Caterina Beretta at La Scala. The trip constituted something of an adventure, since it involved a great deal of rail travel, with numerous changes and stopovers. Neither girl had ever been farther afield than Moscow, let alone anywhere

---

[*] Pavlova seems to have mastered the fouetté. Though she seldom did them in public performances once she had left the Maryinsky, there are reports of her demonstrating them in rehearsals in later years. More than one observer has reported seeing her do a sequence of sixty-four. She disapproved of them nevertheless. When she had her own company and caught one of the girls attempting them, she said sternly, "You want to do fouetté correctly, I show you," then launched into a perfect sequence. At the end she swept on a shawl and stalked out of the room, with no further comment.

ABOVE Unidentified role.
BELOW As Diana in *Le Roi Candaule*.

ABOVE & BELOW *Giselle*, Act One—the mad scene.
OPPOSITE *Giselle*, Act Two.

beyond their national boundaries; but they arrived safely in Milan.

They discovered the famous ballerina to be a dumpy little lady in her sixties, with no vestige of the physical grace that must once have sustained her. She lived in a tiny apartment at the top of a building on the Via dei Tre Alberghi, surrounded by faded and rather sad mementos of her stage life. She held her classes in a practice room at La Scala, to which she was conducted by her servant, Marcella, who fussed about her continuously, wrapping her in a vast rug or chafing her feet if the weather was cold. From this cocoon came a series of commands and imprecations; sometimes the odd word of approval also found its way into the incessant rhythms of her tapping stick. Everything the girls did was within a meticulously defined template; there was absolutely no room for any individual nuance when correctness verged on exactitude.

Beretta's aim was to increase a dancer's endurance, and during the class there was no period of rest; the girls' bodies were kept continually at a degree of tension that made correct breathing a priority. The whole experience was more rigorous, more relentless, than anything the Russian girls had experienced in St. Petersburg. They began to understand how it was that the Italian stars showed such reserves of stamina, as well as technical efficiency; but it was hard for everyone, and the Italian girls in the class were heard frequently to call on the Madonna during moments of stress. Pavlova and Trefilova endured and survived, and when they got back to St. Petersburg safely they had been away more than three months. It was noticed when the season got under way that the techniques of both girls showed considerable improvement in the range of accomplishments and the strength displayed in execution. Indeed, this example set a goal for even younger dancers, and Milan became a priority for anyone with ambition.

The new season at the Maryinsky was in the nature of a new era; on the first day of September 1903, Petipa was no longer present as father figure, and the young Gorsky could not help appearing a very light-weight replacement. Added to this change of command, the death of Johanssen had left a tremendous gap on the teaching side, though Nicolas Legat was endeavoring to re-create the old man's style in classes that he conducted. The Legat brothers found themselves increasingly in demand, not only as dancers with an added ability to give classes, but also as budding choreographers. The management discovered—all too late—that Gorsky could cope only with one production at a time, whereas the ousted Petipa had usually managed to juggle three or four simultaneously; and since the performances that had been started with such success at the Hermitage were expected to continue, there was suddenly a crucial need for small but brilliant entertainments.

Pavlova's intensive work with her teachers allowed her to give good technical accounts of those roles that had been entrusted to her after Petipa's departure, and her progress continued to be

Giselle: (above) Act One, (below) Act Two.

something more than the normal development of an averagely trained dancer; with Pavlova there was almost a headlong rush into prominence. When she danced her second *Giselle,* on October 15, 1903, she was described by Svetlov as "a great artist who has an inborn, natural artistic individuality." The *New Times* recognized Pavlova's affinity for an older style:

> Giselle danced by Pavlova 2 is almost the finest role of this gifted dancer, who is the very embodiment of a Wili. Mme Pavlova in her appearance reminded one of the dancers of the first half of the last century as portrayed in old prints. Her performance evoked a certain tender Romanticism; there was a suggestion of something far removed from contemporary ballet. It must be admitted that M. I. Petipa's arrangement of this ballet faultlessly preserved its original style without the slightest concession to any novelty. Mme Pavlova understood how to interpret the spirit of this extravagant fantasy and preserve its mood to the end. Some of her poses cried out for reproduction in an etching. Giselle is certainly Pavlova's most finished creation, giving promise that in her there is the unfolding of exceptional talent.

This generous appraisal may have precipitated Pavlova's promotion to first soloist for the 1903–04 season. However, her arrival in that rather heady group did not altogether excuse her from playing relatively minor parts, like the role of Ramzé in Petipa's *Daughter of the Pharaoh.* (Ramzé was one of ballet's numerous "favorite slaves"; in this instance she was attached to Aspicia, the principal female character.) Pavlova's opportunities in leading roles were awarded sparingly, but she seemed to have understood the adage that "there are no small parts, only small players." Nothing suggested that she was being held back by any form of lobbying, and her other contemporaries had to be given equal chances. Actually, there were two fewer contenders for roles that season: Lydia Kyaksht and her brother Georgi had decided to transfer to Moscow.

On October 19, when Preobrajenskaya took the lead in a performance of *Bluebeard,* onlookers could compare the talents of several leading soloists, with Pavlova, Egorova, and Trefilova all in secondary roles. The company was scrupulous about the distribution of performances, and even leading roles were now coming the way of the younger dancers: Egorova was given *The Enchanted Forest* and, a bit later, *The Blue Dahlia,* while Trefilova got Ivanov's *The Haarlem Tulip,* and *Coppélia.* Preobrajenskaya danced Raymonda for the first time and was given first consideration in most things, until Kchessinskaya returned in November from her usual long summer sabbatical. She then claimed the plums, including two performances of *Daughter of the Pharaoh* on November 23 and January 7, when Pavlova again took the "slave" role.

All these ballerinas and budding ballerinas needed an individual repertoire of roles that would suit their personal style and at the same time appeal to a fussy audience. This continual need underlined the debt that the company owed Petipa and Ivanov, for the older works continued to serve as the backbone of every program, and even the derided *Magic Mirror* was given another performance during Christmas week in a benefit night for the

The Naiad and the Fisherman: (left) with Georgi Kyaksht.

corps de ballet, when all the principal ballerinas appeared in it. The ballet had been somewhat amended since its first unhappy performance, and a packed house was happy to pay high prices to see it again. Its length was still excessive, and there was doubt that it could survive in the permanent repertoire, but by now the many good sections were recognized as being entirely apposite to Koreschenko's vivid new score. It was felt by critics that in several set pieces Petipa had entirely succeeded, even judged by his own best standards. On this particular night the corps de ballet subscribed to a silver wreath for the great man, and it was handed over to him by Pavlova and Trefilova on behalf of the corps. "Mr. Petipa may have aged, but he can still say, 'The Petersburg ballet—it is I,'" declared the *New Times.*

Pavlova was given the lead in a far more historic revival on December 7, 1903. This was *The Naiad and the Fisherman,* a three-act work that had first been seen in St. Petersburg under the title of *Undine* at the old Bolshoi Theatre in January 1851. Then, it had been mounted by its creator, Jules Perrot, whose able assistant in the task had been the young Marius Petipa, never slow to learn from Perrot's sure grasp of thematic development and plot sense. The ballet had been launched with a glittering cast that included Perrot himself and the ballerinas Andreyanova and Grisi. This was the sort of historical precedent that appealed to Anna Pavlova, and the image of a water sprite was ideal for this much-praised interpreter of elementals.

When Pavlova appeared as Undine on her first night, she had Sergei Legat playing Matteo the fisherman, and there were many other notable names surrounding her. The core of the work was actually contemporaneous with *Giselle* and had been seen in London at His Majesty's Theatre in the summer of 1843, when it was thought to be

> one of the most beautiful productions that any stage ever boasted of. The ballet of *Ondine,* everybody by this time knows, is founded on la Motte Fouqué's fanciful and interesting story of *Undine,* but does not adhere very faithfully to its original. Never mind; narration must give way to impersonation, particularly when we see such a "step-revealing goddess" as Cerrito in the principal character. Her dancing in the *pas de l'ombre* is in the highest degree beautiful, and inclines us to agree more than ever with the old Greek assertion that "dancing is silent poetry." Nothing can be more enchanting than Cerrito's innocent surprise when she first sees her shadow, and thinks (or makes you believe she thinks it) to be something tangible, and "lovely in outline as herself."

This review in the *Illustrated London News* was readily available to the earnest, learned historians of St. Petersburg, who were always eager to impress upon others their view that tradition was a stern taskmaster and that a theatrical event in the Russian capital was necessarily a synthesis of knowledge gleaned throughout Europe. Pavlova, who believed strongly in any suggestion of a "sacred flame" being handed down from generation to generation, took her place in the chain of command, and in the third act she enchanted onlookers in the shadow dance.

It is startling that a ballet as successful as Petipa's 1877 *La Bayadère* did not find its way onto Moscow's Bolshoi stage until 1904. When it did, on January 25, it was at a benefit night for Lyubov Roslavleva, who was essaying the leading role. Petipa's views were no longer of account, it seems. Gorsky now "staged" the work; Solor was danced by Mikhail Mordkin, and there was a Moscow dancer in the cast named Evgenia Anna Pavlova. The St. Petersburg management sent along a group of soloists, who appeared in divertissements at the end of the evening, among them the Pas de Diane, in which Pavlova 2 was supported by Gorsky and Georgi Kyaksht, recently transferred to Moscow. The evening must have been a severe test for Pavlova: not only for the technical difficulties of the Diana role, but also because she already felt a possessive pride in the role of Nikiya.

On the night following the Moscow premiere, Tsar Nicolas, returning from the theatre in St. Petersburg, was handed a telegram from Admiral Alexeiev, Commander in Chief in the Far East. The contents were of stunning import for Russia: Japanese destroyers had made a sudden attack on the Russian squadron anchored in the outer harbor of Port Arthur, and three battleships and five cruisers had been torpedoed. Nicolas wrote in his diary: "May God come to our aid." The following morning, great crowds surged through St. Petersburg as the news spread. They sang hymns, waved banners and religious talismans, and massed themselves outside the Winter Palace, hoping to encourage the diffident and depressed occupier. Such a tremor on the eastern seaboard seemed to be nothing more than a nudge to patriotic consciousness, and the loss of Port Arthur was, at this stage, inconceivable. Some hint of the seriousness of the situation was not really evident for several weeks, but by April 24 the ballet students were being asked to repeat their graduation performance in order to raise funds for sick and wounded members of the army who were "on active service." There were many thousands.

Pavlova finished the season as she had begun it, with a curious mixture of roles large and small: an appearance as the Fairy of the Canaries in *The Sleeping Beauty* followed one week later by the title role in *Paquita*. In the midst of a big article, the *New Times* considered this debut:

The ballet performed on Sunday, May 2, proved to be the most interesting spectacle of the spring season. Several times recently I have been moved to comment on the outstanding progress of Mme Pavlova 2, so happily endowed with dancing talent. Last night, appearing in the ballet *Paquita* and taking the leading role of a ballerina, she fully justified my expectations. This dancer, supple as a reed, ethereal, and graceful—if she did not altogether drive them out of their minds, did at least subjugate and win over those ever-hostile critics, who accepted her with kindness and enthusiasm. Mme Pavlova 2 achieved yesterday evening's triumph not only by reason of her talent, but also by her long and arduous work which included a period of training with an Italian professor of dance.

Mme Pavlova 2 performed the first act in a somewhat pallid manner as regards her acting; she was in a state of agitation. And how could she not be agitated, when on the success—or lack of it—depended, to a certain degree, the future career of the young dancer? But the dancing came to her rescue and, suddenly, entirely captured the attention of the audience. In the second act, consisting of the drama rather than the dance, Mme Pavlova 2, whose Spanish costume suited her admirably, was excellent, and the third act gave her opportunity for a decisive display of her great abilities. Mme Pavlova in the *grand pas* not only held first place while leading a dozen or so of the best dancers; she was also supreme in regard to execution. The variation to the harp was a delight, not only for its grace and aesthetic quality, but also for its vulnerability. Such did the young dancer appear to the public, as one who—more than the rest of her colleagues—has a right to, if not the title, at least the roles of a ballerina. The difference is that a ballerina, however competent she may be, is not satisfied with only a few performances. I think that the management will appreciate the new Paquita as much as the audience did yesterday.

The harp variation had been given to Pavlova by Petipa, who had persuaded Drigo to compose new music for it, as well as for another number, later in the ballet. There were enthusiastic encores, by which the audience made known its feelings about Petipa as much as his protégée.

When the 1904 season got under way, Pavlova was not seen on stage until the fourth week in October. Again, it was the writer for the *New Times* who focused his attention on her, and again it concerned *Paquita*: " . . . a lissome, elegant Spanish girl, passionate, and with a most expressive countenance. Such a Paquita was Pavlova 2, who has been absent from the Maryinsky scene for some months, and who was dancing yesterday for the first time this season."

The anonymous writer (probably Plescheyev) betrays some private knowledge. Pavlova had finished the spring season in style, and to an outside observer nothing would seem greatly amiss if a ballerina (in all but title) entered the new season a trifle late; such tardiness was the hallmark of rank. We can deduce that Pavlova's energies had taken her farther afield in the Russian Empire.* In the autumn review of *Paquita,* the *New Times* underlined its earlier accolade:

> Among the younger generation of dancers she is the most talented, with an instinctive artistic feeling for rhythm and tempo. Never, in her dancing or acting, can one discern any trace of the inartistic. The style of Pavlova 2 has an astonishingly noble quality rather in keeping with the Old School, untouched by any abruptness. This artist dances with an innate loveliness, sweetness, and temperament, and there is an ethereal quality about her movements which illuminates the real significance of her dances. Mme Pavlova 2 is wholly original. Here is a personality which charms not only the connoisseur of ballet, but every member of the audience.

This sort of enthusiasm was certainly not distributed uncritically; the male dancers, with the exception of Kchessinski, were thought to be cold and lethargic, the antithesis of "Spanish." Pavlova's partner was Fokine, and he seems to have been in more of a muddle than usual:

To have entrusted M. Fokine with the role of the ballerina's cavalier was premature. He almost destroyed Pavlova. I do not think that M. Petipa would have allowed this, but his voice is now rarely heard in ballet circles. And what a pity. He should be listened to; the negligence of directors is too frequently apparent. I would mention the mazurka of the ballet pupils in *Paquita*. Petipa presented it admirably. In general, in *Paquita* there can be seen the hand of a great master; the pulse has a healthy beat. It would be a pity if it were to falter.

Notwithstanding a general unease about the drift in ballet management, the expected number of performances took place on the Maryinsky stage. The ballet had talent in great depth. Pavlova was watched eagerly; her knack of taking on varying choreographic "color" and shading her style to suit the image was much commented upon. For instance, in *Paquita* she produced embellishments that gave every appearance of genuine Spanish folk dancing, rather than the superficial clichés that were more usually paraded. Though her back was considered weak in severely classical pieces, in the dances that proliferated throughout *Paquita* its pliant grace was a distinct advantage which she employed to effect. Her "Spanish" poses may have been phony, but they were performed with such conviction and evident enjoyment that they seemed valid. In the purely classical canon, her footwork was improving all the time, and her aerial qualities were no less marked. She was able to perform clearly defined entrechats and other beats, and at the same time keep a soft, expansive quality in her overall dancing, so that, for instance, her cabrioles were high and unhurried. Onlookers were beginning to

---

* The absence seems to have been for *Giselle* in Warsaw.

Karsavina as Medora in *Le Corsaire*.

notice her ability to convey a musical impulse with each particle of her body; everything danced: her head and her eyes, her hands and her fingers. The poet S. A. Andreyevsky thought her dancing resembled the vibrating flight of tone from the string of a harp. Her acting was no less vivid, and in the tavern scene in *Paquita* she displayed the knack of integrating the mime element into the general thread of the dancing, so that one flowed naturally to and from the other. This interweave created a distinct impression in terms of style, and it gained strength by being focused through Pavlova's own intriguing personality; the components were subtly blended, yet the general effect was powerful.

These qualities might have suggested a matchless talent, but it was surrounded on all sides by the competitive skills of others. Many people felt that Trefilova was being groomed for a premier position among the ballerinas; she had, in this autumn season, the responsibility of the lead in a lengthy new ballet being created by Alexander Shirayev, the assistant ballet master. Trying to help fill the gap left by Petipa, who was his inspiration, Shirayev began crafting a rustic potpourri which was to be given on his own benefit night. The linchpin of the plot was a wayside inn, through which coursed a steady flow of unlikely traveling companions. Three couples in quick succession arrived from Spain, Italy, and Poland; and Pavlova and Fokine were cast as the Spanish pair, Carmen and Rodrigo. The ballet was given the title *At the Crossroads,* and it had a serviceable score by Armsheimer. Trefilova had the leading role, as she did in *Graziella* and *Coppélia,* and she followed Kchessinskaya as the Fairy Doll in the Legat brothers' ballet.

After performing in *Paquita,* Pavlova contracted influenza, and the management considered she would be unwise to attempt her second scheduled appearance that season, which was for *Giselle* on November 3. But Pavlova would have none of their advice; she was determined to go on, and she signed a paper which released the directors from any responsibility should her going on stage have some deleterious effect on her health. Grimaldi had performed *Giselle* only four weeks earlier, and Pavlova must have been desperate to re-establish her own imprint on the work as soon as she had the opportunity; her only other performance in this ballet was scheduled for November 17, and a year could go by before she would have another chance to appear in the work that many people already considered her finest achievement. The management's concern for her health was well founded in their eyes, since her school reports had made constant reference to her being of a nervous disposition, anemic and needing extra rest. The object of these prognoses, on the other hand, confounded the doctors by being unbelievably tenacious, always ready to work longer and harder than any of her colleagues. Nor did she succumb. Her anxiety to perform was something more than normal; even when rehearsing she would, whenever possible, work on the stage of the Maryinsky itself, and she would often do a class there as well, if the stagehands were not actually using the boards. Her apartment was a considerable carriage ride from the theatre, so there was an inducement to utilize her time to the maximum. When she arrived one day to discover that she had left her practice clothes behind, she draped herself in two towels from the dressing rooms and worked in those, unmindful of the stagehands' coarse interest in the sight. Nothing mattered but the pursuit of excellence. The paradox was that as she improved and gained artistic stature, so the chances for her to appear necessarily dwindled, since it was less becoming for her to dance insignificant parts. From one season to the next—1902–03 to 1903–04—she slumped from forty-six appearances in twenty-one ballets to twenty-five appearances in thirteen ballets. She had to make every one tell.

A major acquisition for Pavlova at the end of 1904 was the leading role of Medora in the five-act ballet *Le Corsaire,* which she performed three times during the season, taking over on December 5; she was following in the steps of Julie Sedova, who had performed it on September 19. Medora was the Byronic heroine par excellence—an exotic Romantic—and Pavlova had the qualities to give her life on the stage. The capricious, fey, and otherworldly nature was underpinned with a strength of purpose; Medora was the one weak link in the pirate's otherwise invincible armor. Pavlova had the invincible Gerdt on stage as Conrad, the corsair, and he seemed an embodiment of Byron's untrammeled hero; his looks and bearing had a dash about them that belied his sixty years. Svetlov thought that Pavlova was unquestionably the finest exponent of the role of Medora, able to qualify the more lurid aspects of the libretto, such as the cavern scene, where she gave certain movements a more subtle reading than her predecessors had done. Pavlova had performed the secondary role of Gulnare on a sufficient number of occasions to have reached some conclusions about the general shape of the ballet, and she was able to invest Medora with a touching quality.

Technically, this was a role ideally suited to Pavlova's new-found assurance. She could be aerial, and suggest virtuosity, but she never lost the quality of expansiveness in her pursuit of precision. Svetlov wrote:

> All the requisite qualities are displayed by her from the outset to the finish, from the flying leaps when she enters to the various passages in the *Finesse d'Amour*, in which she asserts coquettish grace in countless delightful ways. In the pas de deux her renversés, at the end of which she gracefully falls to her knees, are pure marvels. The same may be said of that variation of hers founded upon the fouettés *en diagonale*, a step technically more difficult but far more beautiful than the ordinary fouetté. And there is in *Le Corsaire* another passage worthy of notice, one that constitutes a charming *tableau de genre,* with Pavlova in male attire: the Little Corsair, a dance devoid of complications but one that calls for discriminating and refined taste.

Pavlova's slight build suited the youth's tunic, and her appearance was equivocal and strangely memorable. At the end of this particular scene, Pavlova, as Medora, had to seize a megaphone and mime the shouting of nautical commands. "All her dances and mimed speeches are very good; each moment makes one long to be able to sketch a record of her outline. Nothing is over-sweet, it is all so completely natural, as, for example, when the artist goes on pointe along a garland of roses laid down before her. The 'Pavlova applause' did not die down all night." Another critic declared: "Surely Byron, even when he was penning his work, never dreamed up quite as perfect a Greek as this!" As a most poignant compliment, Plescheyev compared Pavlova to a great exemplar of the role, Roslavleva, whose recent death was on the minds of many. Eleven days earlier, in Switzerland, she had died as a result of complications following surgery. She was thirty.

During Pavlova's performance there had been noticed in certain parts of the house an energetic encouragement from the "*Pavlovtzi.*" A thrumming sound would begin (which was the enthusiasts stamping their feet in quick time), and then an entire bloc would break into persistent applause. During one of the intermissions, Andreyevsky commented to Plescheyev on the fervor of this special "Pavlova applause." Such was the success of the evening that at the end, the crowd not only showered Pavlova with tributes but called loudly for the choreographer of such a beautiful vehicle of expression. If Petipa was in the auditorium that night, he did not reveal himself. (The *New Times* reported: "He is rarely a guest there nowadays. One can only deplore this.")

A week later came Shirayev's benefit night and the first performance of his *At the Crossroads.* Elsewhere on the same program was a performance of the second act of Montplaisir's old ballet *Brahma,* about an Indian god expelled from paradise; in this Kchessinskaya took Virginia Zucchi's original role of Padmana. Mathilde was in fine dancing trim; her "farewell" benefit performance, which had taken place the previous February,

seems to have been a euphemism for a respite and a bolstering of finances rather than any serious intention to quit the stage.

Although Pavlova had not been given a great deal to do in Shirayev's ballet, she must have been hoping for some degree of praise, particularly after the warmth of the reception accorded her Medora in *Le Corsaire;* but in the *New Times* the day after the premiere, there was no mention of her performance in *At the Crossroads,* and the rest of the column was devoted to a rave review of Kchessinskaya's performance in *Brahma.* The next day the *New Times* returned to the subject of Shirayev's benefit night, and Pavlova would have been shocked to read: "I pass over Mme Pavlova, who danced the Spanish Dance—which was badly choreographed—languidly and without skill. Mme Pavlova's talent did not find its expression here." The critic ended his report with a reprise of the delights of Kchessinskaya: "We have no one else who can do with such perfection what she does in the *grand pas d'action.*"

The much-publicized Isadora Duncan arrived in St. Petersburg from Berlin this same Sunday, December 12; and as it was a gala night at the ballet, the American dancer was doubtless invited to one of the boxes. Everyone in theatre society was interested in "Little Barefoot," and though Duncan herself viewed the Russian capital as the seat of reactionary conservatism in dance, she was caught up in that circle and was treated to its hospitality. Shirayev's evening could only have confirmed her

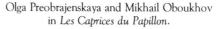

Olga Preobrajenskaya and Mikhail Oboukhov
in *Les Caprices du Papillon.*

Isadora Duncan

worst views about classical ballet being a circumscribed medium for dance expression, but she noted the extraordinary skill of its best exemplars. Her own debut took place the following day in a charity performance, and since *Aida* was playing at the Maryinsky, many of the dancers crowded into the Hall of Nobles. Fokine was there with Pavlova and Karsavina. The music for the evening was all Chopin: mazurkas, polonaises, and waltzes. Far from finding Duncan's art outrageous, the audience was quickly charmed and ultimately fascinated. Fokine and Pavlova reacted as to a fellow spirit. Duncan accepted an invitation to dine at Pavlova's apartment and there found herself surrounded by invigorating artistic talents that were a marked contrast to the starched company she encountered when Kchessinskaya took her to a Grand Ducal supper. Diaghilev was at Pavlova's supper, as were Benois, Bakst, and Fokine. It was a lively session, and Duncan encountered a good deal of advanced thought springing from the more radical members of St. Petersburg theatrical life.

For the New Year festivities in 1905 there had been a plan to hold a concert in the Army and Navy Assembly Hall to honor the "heroes" of Port Arthur. Maria Petipa, Olga Preobrajenskaya, and Anna Pavlova were announced for the dance sec-

tion of the evening, which was to conclude with a ball, during which Kchessinskaya was to join the ballerinas in selling champagne, programs, and flowers. It was an attempt to stir nationalistic patriotism and to inculcate some sympathy for the army; but any such latent goodwill was snuffed out in one cataclysmic moment of misjudgment when bullets ripped into the crowd on fateful "Bloody Sunday." At that moment, the last vestiges of respect and faith linking the monarchy with the people were finally swept away.

Although January 9, 1905, provided the most obvious signs that the country was headed toward a total breakdown, a social front prevailed, and Preobrajenskaya was dancing in her benefit that same night. She had reached *Les Caprices du Papillon*, the revision of an act from *Le Roi Candaule*, and the last of the three ballets on the program, when a *frisson* swept through the audience. A rumor was quickly spreading: it was said that more violence had broken out in the city and that a mob was making its way toward the Maryinsky, having already burst into the Alexandrinsky and disrupted the performance there. Preobrajenskaya and the rest of the company danced on, supported by the orchestra, but within a few minutes they were faced with an empty auditorium. When the curtains finally came down there was a frantic scramble by the artists, who were anxious to get out of the theatre as quickly as possible. The students who had taken part in the performance were hustled into their big closed wagons and driven away at top speed, but senior dancers leaving the building a little later were surprised and relieved to find the streets deserted by all but an icy and snow-laden wind.

Despite the unabated descent into open anarchy, Maryinsky performances were unaffected. Kchessinskaya, that living symbol of Imperial favor, could be seen in *La Fille Mal Gardée*, *Fiammetta*, and *The Little Humpbacked Horse*, and on January 26 she was designated an Honored Artist of the Imperial Theatres. This was the benign side of Tsarist power, which was otherwise being employed in increasingly strong-armed tactics in most civil areas, provoking in return an equal degree of force. One of the casualties was the Grand Duke Sergei, who was blown up by a bomb tossed at him as he left his Moscow apartment. Nevertheless in St. Petersburg Kchessinskaya, without a tremor, carried on dancing for her public; in February she took the lead in the two-hundred-and-seventh performance of *Daughter of the Pharaoh*. With her was the venerable Gerdt, showing no signs of his age as he strode around as the Pharaoh. In writing about this corps de ballet benefit, a contributor to the journal *Theatre and Art* took a wider view of the current state of the ballet and tried to encapsulate the qualities that most distinguished each of the leading ballerinas at the Maryinsky. Kchessinskaya was said to express the best elements of technique allied to good mime; Preobrajenskaya was thought to be the epitome of a charming coquette; Trefilova had the quality of a simple and unaffected soul; and Pavlova made light of the laws of gravity. All this dancing talent was not given vivid new choreographic expression. The second half of the 1904–05 season betrayed the lack of fresh invention since Petipa's departure; his works were being revived right and left: *The Blue Dahlia* for Egorova, *The Pearl* for Vaganova, *Graziella* for Trefilova, and *A Parisian Market*, which was reconstructed by the teacher Klavdia Kulichevskaya for the students' performance. Pavlova made eight appearances in opera ballets, including the Fandango in *Carmen*, but her ballet performances were very restricted, consisting of only thirteen performances in six ballets. When she appeared in the third act of *Paquita* at the very end of the season, she had not performed for two months, which suggests a serious illness or injury, possibly presaged by her uncharacteristically listless display in *At the Crossroads*.

Easter Sunday 1905 was marked by the destruction by a mob of six hundred houses in the town of Kishinev in the province of Bessarabia, and by the time the police deigned to intervene at the end of the second day of pillage, forty-five Jews had been murdered. A deep-seated anti-Semitism was flourishing, with most of Russia's five million Jews being the object of an endemic distrust. The disaster of Russia's surrender of Port Arthur provoked strikes everywhere, and in St. Petersburg a small element of unrest at the giant Putilov steelworks erupted overnight into a major display of civil disobedience, with angry workers from other companies all joining in to make a united gesture of discontent. Even the navy produced a rash of mutinies among the ships in the Baltic and Black Sea fleets. Where Nicolas's diary had in the past recorded sweet nothings about his amiable routine as an army officer and his light-hearted pursuit of Kchessinskaya, now his entries struck a more disillusioned tone: "It makes me sick to read the news: strikes in schools and factories, murdered policemen, Cossacks, riots. But the Ministers, instead of acting with quick decision, only assemble in council like a lot of frightened hens and cackle about providing united ministerial action."

Notwithstanding the severe discipline of the Ballet School, the management found itself less certain of its power to control. Factions were forming within the company. There was no obvious reason why dancers should be more receptive than singers to the social undercurrents of a city's life, but they were—and to this day the distinction seems to hold. In St. Petersburg many of the dancers were progressives; some attended the University or the Conservatoire and were thus closely informed about general student reaction. Their alertness found no counterpart in the opera, which remained detached and complacent. Widespread unrest in the country was not concealed; the front pages of newspapers ran columns of brief items relating provincial disturbances, set out for the reader almost like football results.

Pavlova and Fokine took a particular interest in the latest developments, and at a meeting of the dancers, after the Tsar's army had fired into the crowds gathering in the streets, Pavlova made a forthright speech in which she poured scorn on an army that saw innocent workers as the enemy.

Despite the tension and elements of fear, it was in many ways a time of genuine excitement. Fokine was about to begin rehearsals for his first full-length ballet, *Acis and Galatea,* for the 1905

graduation performance, and he had already announced some startling innovations with his plan to produce everything in a classical "Greek" style, which he was absorbing by studying countless books in the public library; however, the School's directorate took a suspicious view of the young dancer's ideas and forced him to postpone the premiere of the ballet until he was ready to compose a work more in keeping with traditional format. By employing compromise, Fokine eventually got the new work on stage for the graduation performance in April, but he was only biding his time with the management. One of the Fauns was doing his acrobatic tumbling with tremendous enjoyment in a little solo that singled him out from his fellows; inquirers discovered that his name was Vaslav Nijinsky.

Exactly one month after the Maryinsky season closed, events of a calamitous nature occurred on the high seas, when the Russian fleet encountered Admiral Togo's squadron blocking the Strait of Tsushima, between Japan and Korea. Admiral Rozhdestvensky had been in command of eight battleships; all were destroyed, as were seven of his twelve cruisers and six of his nine destroyers. Nothing like it had been seen since Nelson engaged the French fleet off Cape St. Vincent.

On September 4, the 1905–06 Maryinsky season opened with Pavlova performing Nikiya in *La Bayadère*. A sight of this interpretation was much sought by connoisseurs of the ballet, since Pavlova, though highly praised in the work, had not appeared in it since the previous October. Then Gerdt had partnered her, but now she had Sergei Legat as Solor, with Gerdt taking over the more strictly character role of the Rajah. Gerdt also appeared in *The Little Humpbacked Horse* a week later, with Trefilova in the principal ballerina's role of the Tsar Maiden, hitherto thought to be the prerogative of Kchessinskaya. Preobrajenskaya was given another chance at the title role in *Raymonda* on September 25, and in this performance Pavlova took on the subsidiary role of Henrietta. Gerdt played the part of the villain, while that of the hero fell once more to Sergei Legat, who was winning a spate of important roles at this time. The policy was to give all the younger members of the company testing roles, and each in turn got a chance. Sedova was given another opportunity to play Medora in *Le Corsaire*, while Karsavina won the lead in *Graziella* on October 2. This was followed on the same evening by *Coppélia* with Trefilova dancing Swanilda and Pavlova in the Work variation in the third act. When Trefilova danced Aurora in *The Sleeping Beauty* on October 30, Pavlova made a brief appearance as the Fairy Candide in the first act, while in Act Three she danced the Blue Bird pas de deux as well as an additional interpolated pas de deux.

There were tremendous outside distractions at this particular time: all the signs of major unrest, with a sequence of strikes beginning to paralyze many of the essential services within St. Petersburg. The weather in October was bitter, and an early onslaught of sleet blanketed the city, aggravating conditions still further. Trains had stopped running, the ships at the quays were no longer being unloaded, and factories were closing. Food supplies had disappeared in many areas and electric power was dwindling, with most of the hospitals and schools forced to close as a result; general fear and confusion were compounded by the absence of newspapers, so that every form of rumor took wing. Crowds surged through the streets, with orations taking place on street corners and red flags hanging from many balconies and upper windows. In the countryside beyond St. Petersburg, the peasants were sabotaging many of the estates: removing cattle in the darkness of night and crippling those they left behind, and in many instances setting fire to the principal houses.

At the School, the Drama day students who crossed the city returned with stories of pickets and minor confrontations. Quite junior members were infected with reforming zeal and passed numerous resolutions echoing those heard outside. Dancers in the company had their own complaints and claims against the management, and they decided to meet to discuss the numerous points. The real foment came from a small faction, among whose members were Josef Kchessinski (Mathilde's brother), Fokine, and Pavlova—the last two lent their apartments for meetings. At Fokine's address there was a constant coming and going, and visitors risked the disapproval of the porter of that block; it was a time when the informer was beginning to flourish. The dancers conferred constantly at late meetings, lit by petrol lamps after the electricity supply had ceased. A draft petition was drawn up in which were clarified the various injustices that the dancers wished to have set right. There were the usual complaints about overwork, with a demand for a further free day each week; some categories of dancers were considered to be underpaid; and there was a strong feeling that they should be able to choose their own company managers, as they believed—justifiably—that appointments stemming from the director could never represent the dancers' best interests. Most notably, they wanted Marius Petipa reinstated; and they raised the name of Alexander Shirayev, who had fallen foul of Teliakovsky over the matter of revising some of Petipa's ballets. Shirayev had worked as the old man's assistant and knew that his works should not be tampered with; he refused to have a hand in any alterations. This loyalty was rewarded with a request for Shirayev's resignation.

On October 14, Teliakovsky gave permission for the dancers to hold a meeting at the main rehearsal hall on the following day, a Saturday. At this first meeting, which went on for six hours, all the demands were discussed and voted upon, a petition was drawn up, and twelve delegates were selected. It was a democratic group: although Fokine and Pavlova featured among the delegates, its president was a corps de ballet dancer who also studied at the University. Not only had Teliakovsky allowed this meeting, but he seemed also to be totally aware of its nature; in fact, during the meeting Fokine went so far as to single out Nicolas Sergeyev, the principal régisseur, as being the directorate's spy. Sergeyev was certainly responsible for much wavering of intent during these troubled days, making effective insinuations that the management was even considering disbanding the troupe if the unrest continued. Undeterred, the delegates requested a meeting with Teliakovsky, and he agreed to receive them at 11:15 a.m. the following day. But when the delegates arrived on Sunday morning, they found the incumbent absent and were received instead by Deputy Manager Viuch, who listened with a pained expression on his face while the chief delegate voiced their requests. At the conclusion of the meeting, the deputy gave a dry bow, clicked his heels, and remarked that the resolution of the troupe would be handed over to the director "on his return from Moscow."*

Ten days earlier, the students of the Conservatoire had pressed for a reduction of the traditional subscription lists to the Imperial Theatres, which seemed a sound enough idea. The dancers had subsequently felt safe in leaking two of their own principal concerns to the outside world: they wanted to get a mutual benefit fund established and they wanted the School curriculum to include a broader program in the humanities. (In this respect, an editorial in *Theatre and Art* was later to suggest that the dancers were more intelligent than the administration, who were described as being "about as bright as cavalry chiefs.") Teliakovsky's regime most certainly lacked flexibility, and the tenor of military-style discipline was all too evident in the schools of the Imperial Theatres; however, its latest rebuff to the dancers probably masked a fever of indecision. The director must have known that the publication of an Imperial manifesto was imminent, and may have been playing for time in order to know whether or not to take a hard line. Though the manifesto was approved the next day (Monday, October 17), its publication could not take place until the following morning, and in those crucial hours before its appearance, there was space for tragedy.

Though Monday was a nonworking day for the Company, all the dancers congregated in the School buildings. There had been two hundred and twenty-five signatories to their petition (which suggests that the meeting had included students and technical staff as well), and Teliakovsky knew that this was no tempest in a teacup; yet when the delegates now made a further request to see him, they were told that he was "busy." Meanwhile, a notice appeared on the Company bulletin board inviting signatures from those dancers who wished to show loyalty to the adminis-

* For my account of these events, I have relied principally on contemporary exposés published in the *New Times* and in *Theatre and Art*. Other sources that refer to these turbulent days vary in their detail. Karsavina, in her memoirs *Theatre Street*, supplies Krupensky, the assistant director, in place of Viuch and attributes to him the remark suggesting that Teliakovsky was in Moscow. Teliakovsky's diary has an entry for October 15 recording that boys from the Ballet School had assembled, without permission, in order to discuss their needs. Karsavina gives the location for a further meeting as the Alexandrinsky Theatre. She offers a vivid account of how the dancers went there in order to seek solidarity with the actors, whose intention it was to strike. The evening was, according to Karsavina, an anticlimax, with the dancers remaining in a room backstage and the performance continuing without interruption. Natalia Roslavleva, in her *Era of the Russian Ballet*, includes a meeting taking place on the stage of the Alexandrinsky, complete with the arrival of policemen, who were, we are to believe, defied—though no source is offered for this stirring anecdote. Karsavina refers only to an attempted strike that failed, involving dancers in an opera matinee. This would be the occasion when senior students went on stage in place of the dancers and were warmly applauded. Their success did not go unnoticed by the Company.

tration. Dark hints were disseminated—mostly by Sergeyev—to the effect that all those who refused to sign would "catch it." One of the cleverest threats concerned pensions: it was suggested that in the event of the Company's closing, only those dancers with a minimum of ten years' service could hope to receive a pension. This created panic. It was already public gossip that a certain male dancer had succumbed to a nervous breakdown and had been taken directly to an insane asylum, that another was also sick, and that most of the ballerinas showed distinct signs of nervous disorder. Among the men, this was certainly true of Sergei Legat. He had always been acutely involved in the radical group, and his beliefs had led him to attend general workers' meetings in the city. His liaison with Maria Petipa was a complication: she represented the traditionalist faction in the company, and because of her own spells of freedom, leading troupes abroad with displays of national dancing, she was less inclined to be linked with any developments that could jeopardize the established administration.

When the signatures were counted on the management's counterpetition it was seen that there were only sixty-eight abstentions, the most notable of them being Preobrajenskaya. Maria Petipa was furious that Sergei Legat's name was missing, and she attempted to persuade him to add it to the list. For much of the night the distraught Sergei raged and raved, feeling that he might become a traitor to a cause in which he genuinely believed. By the early hours of the morning, he appeared to have become genuinely deranged, and some time before dawn he suddenly rushed into the dining room, shouting, "The theatre officials are coming!" Seizing a cheese knife, he attempted to slice his own throat, but Maria, with a struggle, managed to get the knife away from him. Thus thwarted, Legat rushed next to the bedroom, and before he could be stopped he used his razor in place of the cheese knife, with horrible effect. He was dead within minutes.

Hours later, the new freedoms contained within the Imperial manifesto became known. Though the major part of it concerned the State's intention of beginning the almost impossible task of retreating into a semiconstitutional monarchy—while at the same time attempting to retain its traditional seat of true power—from the dancers' standpoint the most important section was the one that stated a concession to "the firm principles of civil freedoms on the basis of the sanctity of the individual and the freedoms of speech, assembly, and association." On that Tuesday evening the dancers' delegates were exercising that freedom in Fokine's apartment when the news was brought to them of Sergei Legat's death. It had a shattering effect. They were already under severe pressure from the campaign of dissension being fomented within their own ranks, and the Imperial manifesto had to some extent taken the wind out of their sails; but this ghastly dénouement to their uprising galvanized a further meeting of all the abstainers. At this assembly, the radicals decided that it was a certain Monakhov who had acted as a turncoat, and Pavlova denounced him as a blackguard before bursting into tears. When the truth of her assertion became generally obvious, Kchessinski

Caricature of Pavlova by the Legat brothers.

slapped the man's face—an action that got him suspended when the victim rushed a complaint to the director's office.

Legat's funeral provided the most somber note of a deeply troubled week. Teliakovsky noticed with disapproval that Pavlova was remaining to the fore as a nonconformist; at the service she would not allow any other floral tribute to obscure the banner of the Company's wreath, and she was constantly rearranging the ribbons in order to draw attention to the inscription, which read: "To the first victim, at the dawn of the freedom of Art, from the newly united Ballet Company." Legat was described as "The Irreplaceable" on another banner, which *Theatre and Art* later suggested, in a cruelly dismissive tone, was hardly accurate.[*]

On Wednesday, October 19, the dancers very naturally declined to appear in the scheduled opera performance at the Maryinsky. The following morning Teliakovsky summoned the delegates, ostensibly to reply to their petition. He began by pointing out that their refusal to give the performance was an act

---

[*] *Theatre and Art* had been willfully engaged in the creation of fuel for the fire. In August, it had gossiped that Kchessinskaya's new house on Petrovska Side had cost 500,000 roubles; then it noted that all the artists of the Imperial Theatres had decided to give 1 percent of each month's salary to sufferers from the famine, until the harvest twelve months hence. It also observed that the Prefect of the City declared it permissible for all stage workers to meet in order to organize their own affairs; it then carried the *Gazette's* rumor that starting in 1907, all artists of the Imperial Theatres whose yearly salary exceeded 5,000 roubles would be forbidden to accept extra engagements in private theatres. This was a huge salary; at the time, 1 rouble purchased a gross of eggs.

of flagrant insubordination that would have provoked very serious consequences had there not been an amnesty incorporated into the Tsar's manifesto. He concluded by describing the troupe as merely misguided and deserving of exoneration. Pavlova and Fokine in particular were infuriated by this smooth dismissal of their aims, and they began preparing a letter for the Court Minister, Count Fredericks, in which one of the first aims was to achieve the reinstatement of Josef Kchessinski. This proposal was anathema to Teliakovsky, who let it be known that he would resign if the Court Minister relented. Kchessinski's sister, with her royal connections, elected to stay clear of the whole imbroglio, and noting her silence, the minister felt safe in dismissing the appeal. But before he had drafted his reply, the *New Times* came out with the first public information surrounding Legat's suicide. It was a real broadside: "Such a swamp has been revealed in the theatrical administration, such a bureaucratic quagmire, that the extinction of the young artist's life seems in comparison no more than the snuffing out of a little flame, victim of the rottenness of the whole system." The paper then detailed all the events leading up to the suicide, concluding:

And what was all this about, this frightful drama? And for what reason? The crumbling structure of an unreformed bureaucracy has claimed yet another victim and swept it under its rug. It will remain a black mark on the conscience of the theatrical administration, on the whole system of red tape in its dealings with others, in its lies and its shameless browbeating. Poor Legat. What a frightful end to the life of he who smiled at us from the boards and from the mocking cartoons of his clever pen.

This fusillade of admonishment, publicly delivered, was sorely needed moral support for the die-hards in the ballet reform group. Surely the dancers could not go on stage, smiling sweetly, after that? Pavlova took the lead and gave notice that she was refusing to appear in *La Source* that evening. This spirited reaction galvanized many of the dancers, and a sufficient number supported Pavlova that the management was forced to replace the ballet with a performance of the opera *Eugene Onegin*. Senior students were put on stage in the dance sections, and though Teliakovsky was furious at having to make this change, he stayed his hand in an attempt to defuse the situation; there were already signs that the opera chorus was beginning to catch the zeal of the dancers. It was left to Count Fredericks to apply the brake. He pointed out—correctly—that the ballet troupe owed its existence to the personal dispensation of the Tsar, who might not be able to continue his support in difficult times. The Ministry recognized the commission from the Ballet Company, but it rejected the appeal to have Kchessinski reinstated, in view of his aggressively radical behavior. (The chief object of Kchessinski's aggression, Monakhov, was at this point diplomatically awarded a "vacation" for six months.) The Court Minister added a warning to Pavlova: further trouble would put her own position at risk. In many ways the Ministry was being remarkably lenient toward her, and it is a measure of her importance as a dancer that they were so loath to provoke the loss of her services. The revolt ran

out of steam very swiftly. A week later, Pavlova and Fokine were back on stage, performing the Blue Bird pas de deux in *The Sleeping Beauty*. The policy of "divide and conquer" had worked for the administration, and Sergeyev, for one, was headed for a higher role in the School administration.

Pavlova's part in all of this must have seemed baffling to anyone who thought that the position of ballerina at the Maryinsky was a sinecure to be guarded at all costs. But to Pavlova, all authority represented the stable society of which she was not, by upbringing, a part. She was still the daughter of a washerwoman, so that in speaking out she was not risking any position in society, nor was she compromising numerous relatives; many of the other dancers were less vocal in their support of reform because of family ties. Nevertheless, she always set the Tsar above the malfunctioning of his government; all royalty, to her, was of the "divine right" order.

One of the few successes associated with the dancers' petition was the reinstatement of Shirayev, who was made general *répétiteur* as of September 1. In mid-November, when the city's strikes had abated, he revived *The Haarlem Tulip*, with Trefilova in the leading role. But on December 4 she was dancing Pavlova's old role of Juanita in *Don Quixote* while Pavlova played Kitry for the first time, with Gerdt as Gamache and Preobrajenskaya as the Street Dancer. (As a senior ranking ballerina, Preobrajenskaya was unusual in her willingness to take cameo roles when a younger dancer performed the leading role. Pavlova was to follow this precedent.) The part of Kitry called for long passages of pure dance without the usual sections of mime; Gorsky seemed more intent on telling the actual story through the by-play of the attendant characters. He left the ballerina to express herself in a series of technical essays, varied in their demands but with a cumulative effect. It was a big role, and one that, like Princess Aurora, allowed for no weaknesses. It was not a part that would have fallen to Pavlova had there not been a new confidence about her control of technique.

Four nights later, Riccardo Drigo was given a benefit night for twenty-five years' staunch musical service to the Company, which put on three ballets to celebrate this event. Ivanov's *The Enchanted Forest* started the evening, with Pavlova taking the lead as the peasant girl Ilka, and causing some brief excitement by ending a variation with an entrechat sept. *Les Millions d'Arlequin* with Preobrajenskaya was next, and this was followed by a revival of Tarnovskova's ballet *The Talisman*, reconstructed for the occasion by Sergeyev. This Oriental fantasy was swarming with maharajahs and their feminine distractions, including Pavlova, Karsavina, and Egorova as nautch girls. Preobrajenskaya appeared in the guise of a European lass named Ella, and Fokine and Oboukhov struck curious poses as a pair of Hindu dancers.

For the twenty-fifth anniversary benefit night of Konstantin Kuvakin—who was noted as a painter quite apart from his career on the stage—the Moscow management arranged that Anna Pavlova should appear there on January 15 in Gorsky's new

As Kitry in *Don Quixote*

ABOVE As Vint-Anta in the Moscow production of *Daughter of the Pharaoh*.

OPPOSITE As Aspicia in the original, St. Petersburg production of *Daughter of the Pharaoh*.

version of *Daughter of the Pharaoh*. This was a distinct honor, but it entailed much extra work for the dancer, since she had to disregard the Petipa choreography she was working on at the Maryinsky. Some of the changes seemed merely arbitrary: the heroine's name was changed from Aspicia to Vint-Anta, daughter of Ramses II. Gorsky's Moscow production was muddled, with passages of supposed "realism" that were in effect grossly stylized in the manner of wall paintings. The scenery, which included a Karnak-type temple, dwarfed the ranks of dancers spread across the sprawling Bolshoi stage. There were often two hundred or more people in the big set numbers, but Pavlova still managed to focus attention on herself, and the morning after her appearance she was able to bask in the fact that Moscow had taken to her Vint-Anta wholeheartedly.

Pavlova was high-spirited and friendly; her gaiety was such that the usual jealousy between Moscow and St. Petersburg dancers quickly changed—on the men's side, at least—to open adoration. The critics particularly liked her scene in the fisherman's hut, when the Pharaoh's daughter recalled the adventures that had overtaken her and Ta-Hor* during their flight from the Nubian king, played by Kuvakin. Ta-Hor was danced by Mikhail Mordkin, now much in favor in Moscow. With the curious convention of the theatre, he had begun his association with this ballet by playing, in his extreme youth, the aged Nubian king, but now he was in a part more befitting his years. It was conventional too that the leading dancers exchange gifts and good wishes before the performance, and Mordkin kept the ribbon that had entwined the wreath of flowers Pavlova gave him.

In Moscow she encountered Cecchetti, whom she had not seen since he had left St. Petersburg in 1902 after the directorial changes. He was much interested in seeing this highly praised product of his old school. After a performance, Pavlova took Cecchetti back to the house where she was staying and asked him to give her a frank and detailed opinion of her progress. Cecchetti remarked on her obvious qualities, but he commented also on the weaknesses that were still apparent in her technique, especially those caused by the relative lack of strength in her back—a fault Pavlova had been striving to correct, without noticeable success. She knew the progress Preobrajenskaya had made under Cecchetti's tutelage in St. Petersburg, and it seemed a logical step for him somehow to be involved in her own further training. Pavlova was sufficiently persuasive for Cecchetti to risk agreeing to return to St. Petersburg, ostensibly to give Pavlova private lessons but with the hope of ultimately re-establishing himself there, if only as a private tutor. The fact that Cecchetti was to all intents and purposes entirely dependent on Pavlova for financial support suggests another of the vast changes in the life style of "little Niura." It was not Grand Ducal largesse, but it was way beyond the salary of any soloist.

---

* There was a poverty of invention concerning "Egyptian" names; Fokine later used this name for a female slave. In this production, and in Petipa's, the character is an Englishman who dreams he becomes Ta-Hor and saves the Pharaoh's daughter, etc. His traveling companion was called, with dazzling originality, John Bull!

Daughter of the Pharaoh, Moscow:

ABOVE (left) With the Pharaoh; (center) with Mikhail Mordkin as Ta-Hor in the Dance of the Cymbals; (right) with Mordkin as the Englishman.
BELOW (left) As the mummy of Princess Vint-Anta; (right) as the Princess.

Pavlova's St. Petersburg debut as Aspicia coincided with the benefit night for Alfred Bekefi on January 29. It was actually a farewell, for though there was no elaboration of the fact, Bekefi was yet another member of the Imperial Ballet who had managed to fall foul of its administration, which had somehow extracted a resignation from the dancer. The benefit was thus something of a hasty arrangement, and the already scheduled performance of *Daughter of the Pharaoh* saw Bekefi in the rather thankless part of the Nubian king, since Gerdt was playing the Pharaoh and Nicolas Legat had the part of Ta-Hor. Oboukhov and Karsavina played the Fisherman and his Wife. All the dancers were very fond of Bekefi and wished to honor him in their own way, and Preobrajenskaya once more took a secondary role, that of the favorite slave, Ramzé. Pavlova had the problem of adjusting to the St. Petersburg production only a few days after appearing in Gorsky's production in Moscow.* But the evening was certainly popular with the crowd; a poster went up three days before, stating that all seats had been sold. This had not been the case when Kchessinskaya had last performed the work.

Only a fortnight lay between Bekefi's benefit night and that of the evergreen Pavel Gerdt, celebrating forty-five years of service to the Imperial Theatres. Though male dancers traditionally had far longer careers than their female counterparts (due in part to the convention that allowed heroes to step aside from any embarrassing exertions, which were then carried out by a younger performer), Gerdt's continuing presence was remarkable, and his benefit night became a genuine tribute to someone who still retained his place on stage with absolute authority. His first benefit had been back in 1871, a night he had shared with the ballerinas Ekaterina Vazem and Alexandra Vergina. At the 1906 benefit, which was the last performance in the Maryinsky before the traditional closing for Lent, Pavlova appeared with her teacher and sometime partner in scenes from *La Bayadère*. Gerdt then danced in *Javotte* with Preobrajenskaya, and after the first scene of this ballet Sergeyev spoke on the dancers' behalf and made the presentation of a gift. Following Gerdt's benefit, Pavlova—mindful of the hard work that would confront her when Cecchetti arrived back in St. Petersburg—traveled back to Milan during the Lenten break to refresh her grasp of Italian schooling.

---

* A number of references in ballet literature place the student Nijinsky in a performance of *Don Giovanni* at the Maryinsky during this week. His appearance in the opera was first mentioned by Romola Nijinsky in her 1933 book *Nijinsky*; the latest reference comes in Bronislava Nijinska's memoirs, published in 1981. (Although details vary between sources, not one of them specifies that this program, celebrating the 150th anniversary of Mozart's birth, gave only three scenes from the opera, after a performance of the *Requiem*.) The program was first presented on January 18, and at the second performance (January 24) Pavlova is said to have replaced Trefilova as Nijinsky's partner in a Legat pas de huit called—with no great originality—*Roses and Butterflies*. In later life Trefilova is said to have spoken of dancing in this program. Interestingly, the Yearbook's list of 52 dancers for the ballet section on January 18 does not include Trefilova's name—nor, for that matter, Nijinsky's. Pavlova's Yearbook entry for 1905-06 has no opera listing at all, but has 22 ballets. The second performance came within the week that spanned two very important debuts for Pavlova, in Moscow and St. Petersburg. It seems strange to me that a leading ballerina should risk blunting the impact of her big night by dancing with a student, tucked into a pas de huit within an opera scene, when it was not even the first night of that program.

Daughter of the Pharaoh, Moscow: the Princess and Ta-Hor (Mordkin) disguised as Assyrians. Vint-Anta has just been delivered from the Nile.

Pavlova and Mordkin, in *Daughter of the Pharaoh* costumes, demonstrating their ability to draw a bow behind the head.

For all its glittering Imperial image, St. Petersburg contained the seeds of the newly developed political awareness at all levels of class distinction, and the dancers, with their own swiftly developing social consciences, were always eager to involve themselves in charity performances that aided underprivileged sections of the society. As a bonus, these performances afforded them opportunities to exercise more artistic control. For the annual performance in support of the Greblovsky School, in 1906 the dancers elected to approach Mikhail Fokine with a request that he choreograph a ballet for the evening. In view of the part Fokine had played in the dissent during 1905, the request was a particularly useful prop for his reinstatement with the influential ballet followers, particularly Alexander Krupensky, the assistant director, who had betrayed a marked suspicion of the young dancer and his crusading activities.

Fokine settled on one act from a full-length ballet score by Anton Rubinstein, who was something of a musical hero in Russia. *La Vigne* was composed in 1883 but had never been produced in Russia. It had a simple story line with plenty of opportunity for a succession of dance variations representing the spirits of different types of wine, which emerged from barrels opened in quick succession by a group of revelers who had supposedly broken into the cellar of a rich household. Maria Petipa was still to the fore with her penchant for national dances suiting her rather stately figure, and Fokine allocated her a czardas representing the gutsy Hungarian wine Tokay. Lydia Kyaksht bubbled along as champagne, Karsavina represented another beverage, and Fokine put himself in a pas de deux with Anna Pavlova. The choreographer had shown particular ingenuity in his use of the ubiquitous trap door for special effects: in this instance, Lydia Kyaksht began a series of turns just as it rose into position, so that she appeared to be burgeoning forth like a foaming head of champagne.

In the audience that night of April 8 was Marius Petipa himself. After the performance, the old man—suffering the indignity of not being allowed to pass the stage door—sent his calling card through to Fokine, and the budding choreographer was thrilled to see what Petipa had written across the back of it: "*Cher camarade Fokine, Enchanté de vos compositions. Continuez vous deviendrez un bon maître de ballet. Tout à vous.*" It was an important voice in Fokine's defense; the press damned the youthful effort with very faint praise. Also given that evening was the second act of *Coppélia* and various divertissements, in one of which Pavlova confirmed the worst fears of the new regime by leading a cakewalk—a fatal lack of dignity in the management's view, though it amused the audience greatly.

One night later came another Fokine enterprise, this time presented under the umbrella of special performances by the students of the Ballet School. April 9 provided an evening full of eager young talent, bolstered by some junior members of the company. Fokine had unearthed Petipa's production of *A Midsummer Night's Dream* and had been given permission to revise the groupings and principal variations, though the basic structure of the original work was to be retained. The Mendelssohn music was used, but Fokine introduced some new dances: Glinka's *Valse-Fantaisie,* and *Flight of the Butterflies,* a pas de deux to Chopin. This was danced by Elena Smirnova and Vaslav Nijinsky as the centerpiece of the ballet, and there were new costumes by Bakst. Nijinsky's sister, Bronislava, was in the ballet's Andante section, as a rose. There was also an exciting dance called *The Battle of the Elves and Bats.*

After the intermission, Nijinsky took his first leading role: Langruf in *The Gardener Prince,* a ballet in one act based on Hans Christian Andersen's story "The Swineherd." Kulichevskaya arranged the ballet to music by Davidov, and she transferred the action to France at the time of Louis XVI. There were numerous dances, designed to show off as many of the pupils as possible. At one point there was a Marche for the prince's envoys, ending with a presentation of gifts; one page came forward with a delicate child dressed as a rare and costly rose, and the bloom was listed in the program as Spessivtseva. In the center of the ballet, just after a beautiful waltz in which the entire cast carried polychrome lanterns, Nijinsky and Ludmilla Schollar danced an adagio pas de deux. Then, for a spectacular climax, the usual interpolated pas were introduced. Smirnova and Nijinska were among the five dancers in a Butterfly dance (from *Le Roi Candaule*); then Schollar and Nijinsky danced the famous Pas de Diane from the same ballet, to bring the performance to a close. Drigo had conducted for the young dancers, and the evening was a tremendous success, even though Nijinsky had lacerated his hands from the encrustations of fake jewelry on the costume used by Schollar in this final pas de deux, which was notorious for its technical difficulties and numerous supported pirouettes. (It was this pas de deux that often had Pavlova at full stretch.) At the end of the 1905–06 season Pavlova danced *La Bayadère* at the Maryinsky, while her chief rival from her own group, Trefilova, closed the season with her debut in *Swan Lake,* dancing both Odette and Odile. (Younger dancers were normally only given one or the other to start with.) When the promotions were announced for the Imperial Theatres, Anna Pavlova, despite the odium attached to her name during the period of the strikes, found that she was officially forgiven and promoted to ballerina, with an accompanying rise in salary to 3,000 roubles a year.

During the summer break Pavlova once again traveled to Milan to study with Caterina Beretta, and she seems also to have paid her first visit to London. The quality horses fascinated her most, but she must also have noted that ballet was relegated to music halls as a variety element with no great standard of execution. Equally evident, though, was the fact that it was well paid; there were obviously numerous openings for skilled dancers.

Now that Pavlova was officially a ballerina, her new status demanded a fitting base. As a soloist she had lived in modest circumstances on Torgovaya Street and for shorter periods of time at other austere addresses. Now she took a large apartment in a newly constructed building on the Anglisky Prospekt. It was

In her St. Petersburg drawing room, c. 1908–09. The photograph on the table was taken in Berlin in May 1908.

not a very fetching address by the standards of St. Petersburg society (even though Nicolas, as Tsarevich, had installed Kchessinskaya at Number 18 during their liaison), but a variety of artists and radical writers lived in the neighborhood (Diaghilev was around the corner) and it was therefore more interesting than a drearily aristocratic enclave. Prior to this move, Pavlova had taken her daily classes either in Sokolova's studio, or at the Ballet School, or in the Maryinsky itself. Now she had the chance to incorporate into her new apartment a private studio, in what otherwise would have been a spacious salon designed for entertaining on a large scale. The room had a high ceiling with fine plaster work and decorations in the Adam manner. Other rooms had nice deep windows, and whether she was influenced by Dandré or not, much of the furniture in the apartment was in the French manner and of good quality.

Between Pavlova and Dandré there seemed to have grown a tremendous bond of adoration, rather than an ardent love. The relationship had the complication of Dandré's awe of Pavlova's artistic talents, while she had already cast him in the role of her missing father. Years later, Pavlova confided to Natalia Trouhanova that Dandré had provided this apartment, and she also said that around this time she had been willing to marry him but that he considered she might be tempted to let her dancing slip, so he urged her on in her professional career, unencumbered by domestic commitments. Pavlova saw this as a rejection, and she determined not to be put in this position again. She formulated a theory that accommodated this situation, so that eventually she was able to write:

To answer another question that has often been put to me: Why I don't marry. That comes about simply as a result of the fact that a true female artist must be consumed in her art, just like a nun. She

Carmen:
(above) Preobrajenskaya in the Olé;
(below) Pavlova in the Fandango.

does not have the right to lead such a life as would seem desirable to most women. She cannot burden herself with concerns about her family and her house, and cannot ask from life the quiet family happiness that is granted to other women. That is *my* opinion!

To the rest of St. Petersburg, Pavlova was that unremarkable thing: a handsomely housed lady of the stage, which implied that she was an expensive mistress as well. With her natural simplicity and marked generosity, Pavlova was at times unnecessarily hurt by conventional attitudes toward her situation. On one occasion, two young graduates were sent to her studio to rehearse a dance, and at the end of the session Pavlova pointed to a trunk full of ballet shoes and told the girls to help themselves, and that her carriage could then take them home. The girls prudishly declined both offers because Pavlova was a "kept woman."

Pavlova opened the 1906–07 season with *La Bayadère*, partnered by Pavel Gerdt. Despite his age, he was required to dance almost every performance, and within one month he appeared with Pavlova in the Ural Cossacks dance in *The Little Humpbacked Horse*, in *Don Quixote*, in *Paquita*, and in *Giselle* (as the woodsman)—all this quite apart from partnering Trefilova and Egorova in their ballets. Gerdt's presence lent a sense of continuity to the performances, and despite his own protestations about his advancing years, there was no sign that the management contemplated an end to his dancing services. Gerdt was also kept busy overseeing the revivals of a string of full-length Petipa ballets, which were the mainstay of the Maryinsky; many of them might otherwise have been used more sparingly had Petipa's absence not created such a void of new choreography. Even Coppini's lamentable *La Source* was pressed back into service.

In December the Company was required to put on its annual benefit night for the corps de ballet, and there was by then a real scramble for any sort of novelty. Sergeyev had assiduously acquired a mastery of the recently perfected system of notation originated by Vladimir Stepanov, and had notated the revival of Petipa's *The Itinerant Dancing Girl* two years earlier. He was able to reproduce this, while Nicolas Legat created a new work, *Puss in Boots*, remarkable for providing a role for every female dancer of note in the company except for Kchessinskaya and Pavlova, who both came on later in the evening. But the death of Sergei Legat had left far-reaching effects, and Nicolas was quite unable to re-create the unforced charm of *The Fairy Doll*. His lone efforts to provide a sound dance structure in *Puss in Boots* ended in a hopeless ballet. Kchessinskaya tried to lift spirits at the end of the evening by making a rare appearance as Raymonda, and in the same ballet Pavlova performed the Panaderos; but the event as a whole had demonstrated no artistic advancement, and it was clear that the company's hopes now centered almost exclusively on Fokine. For the Society for the Prevention of Cruelty to Children's charity performance in two months' time, Fokine was requested to provide the entire evening's entertainment.

Three nights after the subfusc evening of the corps de ballet benefit, Karsavina was seen for the first time in one of Kchessinskaya's favorite ballets, *The Little Humpbacked Horse;* it was a sign that the young dancer had definitely been accepted into the first rank, reinforcing the judgment of five years earlier, when she had been placed in the special classes containing Pavlova, Trefilova, Egorova, and Sedova. Now she had come of age as a dancer. The girls were all given important roles at this time, and each in her own way was considered a first among equals. Petipa's favorites had been Preobrajenskaya and Pavlova, but there was now an absence of such paternal ranking, and, apart from Kchessinskaya, the ballerinas did not hold rank to be all-important. Preobrajenskaya would sometimes play Mercedes in *Don Quixote* when Pavlova was playing Kitry; Pavlova would be Princess Florine in *The Sleeping Beauty* on a night when Trefilova was Princess Aurora, and Trefilova would take one of the solo roles when Pavlova was dancing Nikiya in *La Bayadère.* And when Kchessinskaya took the title role in Act Two of *Fiammetta* on January 7, 1907, the public had the added bonus of seeing Pavlova as Amour. But since rank did not avail one, it was not good enough merely to get a big role; one had to be seen to do it in a manner that vanquished rivals, of whom there were many. There was a great deal of flattering comment about Trefilova at this time, and she must have seemed something of a front runner in the ballerinas' race. This display of talent helped in some measure to disguise the fact that one young choreographer, no matter how brilliant a prospect, could not be milked for new productions in the manner of his great predecessor.

By January 1907, Fokine was hard at work preparing his big night for the S.P.C.C., and Glazunov's jubilee celebration on January 28 had to rely on revivals. The company performed *The Trials of Damis* followed by *Les Saisons,* which Nicolas Legat now attempted to revise with alterations that did nothing to improve what had always been a charmingly antiquated confection, even in 1900 when the ballet had been first produced. There were some interesting cast changes: Vaganova danced the Frost variation, which had been created by Pavlova, while Pavlova herself now appeared as the Bacchante in an updated revision of the pas de deux originally danced by Maria Petipa and Pavel Gerdt. Andrianov played Bacchus opposite Pavlova.

Special evenings were a recurring problem, and their organizers were constantly seeking novelties to attract an audience already sated with ballet. Victor Dandré held an honorary post on the board of the S.P.C.C., and as Pavlova had been a staunch advocate of Fokine's talent ever since their student days, it was hardly surprising that Dandré went to him concerning the charity performance to be staged for the Society. But when Dandré requested a full evening's work, Fokine apparently lacked the confidence to tackle a single three-act ballet and chose instead to provide two shorter works: an interpretation of the novel *Quo Vadis?* in two acts followed by a series of divertissements to music by Chopin.

Fokine's renewed interest in the orchestrations of Chopin brought him, at last, into direct contact with Glazunov, and he discovered in the composer a firm ally. Glazunov, after his early success with Petipa, had maintained his interest in ballet, and now that he was the director of the Conservatoire, his support carried particular weight. Certainly Glazunov's sympathetic treatment of Chopin appealed to Fokine far more than did Shtcherbashev's mundane score for the *Quo Vadis?* work, which Fokine was calling *Eunice.* Fokine's problem was that he was not in a sufficiently powerful position to commission new music and had instead to rely on existing scores, which he found in the library of the Imperial Theatres, where they had been filed after brief service for various Court entertainments.

The music had dictated Fokine's approach to *Eunice.* It was crammed with waltzes, but he attempted to disguise this by rearranging the sequences so as to relate the music to a dramatic theme, though he had to fall back on the device of an "entertainment," this one given by Petronius Arbiter; it gave Fokine a chance to experiment with his concepts of the antique. He was at pains to differentiate between the styles commonly associated with Roman, Greek, and Egyptian civilizations as portrayed in the books and artifacts in the museums in St. Petersburg, and he placed particular emphasis on the torque and sinuousness evident in the figures of certain archaic friezes.

Pavlova probably demonstrated some of Gorsky's efforts in that direction. She must have been the placating intermediary between Fokine, with his wild ideas, and the archconservative Dandré, answerable to a stuffy committee. But even Fokine was a conservative compared to the magnificent nonconformist then in town: Isadora Duncan was back in St. Petersburg, giving performances that caused dismay in a few staid quarters; but by now she had won many devoted followers and other observers full of curiosity. Fokine was recharged with all the fervor that had marked his initial response to Duncan, when her work had seemed to confirm so many of his own feelings about dance; and Pavlova too remained deeply interested in Duncan's art and openly expressed her interest, making a point of attending several performances despite a busy schedule. The plastique of Duncan's arms continued to make the strongest impression.

Kchessinskaya agreed to take the lead in *Eunice*—a sign that she had spotted from whom the new influences were emerging and that she was determined that they should not pass her by. Fokine gave her several difficult variations as the slave girl Eunice, and at one point she was required to execute a dance in and out of eight swords fixed to the floor with their blades pointing upward. Pavlova was not given anything more dangerous than seven veils which she had to discard, not as Salome but as a slave named Acté. Fokine arranged the veils in such a way as not to encumber Pavlova's slight build, and the removal of each one was designed to focus attention to a different part of her body; but the young choreographer seemed loath to make anything entirely straightforward for the dancers, and his puckish sense of humor found plenty of outlets, in particular a dance in which he required two slaves to execute their steps while balancing on a

Nijinsky and Pavlova in *Chopiniana*. (These photographs are of the 1908 revised version.)

sheepskin bag supposedly full of wine. This exercise brought them swiftly to their knees on several occasions. There were also slaves juggling with wreaths, and others careering about with dangerously real flaming torches; the Maryinsky stage management, with its policy of novelty and expense being of no object, had to find a chemical formula that would prevent the combustible from setting the floorcloth alight. While the management was prepared to countenance live flames, it drew the line at bare knees and feet, which were considered too inflammatory. The dancers were required to wear tights, on which the forbidden physical attributes were carefully simulated in paint.

After the first dress rehearsal, word spread that the ballet was aiming to outrage, and prior to its first performance, planned for February 10, Fokine was summoned before Bezobrazov, who counseled a slower reform; he suggested that the corps de ballet should take any risks, leaving their ballerinas clothed in convention and their classical tutus. Fokine declined to accept this advice. Bezobrazov, to his credit, wasted no time in admitting that he had enjoyed the performance once he had seen it in its completed state, and his pleasure seemed to be echoed by the audience.

The Chopin work was not without its alarums; here too tradition was being tampered with, not least by Glazunov in daring to transcribe for orchestra acknowledged masterpieces created for a solo instrument. His temerity was the result of a deep admiration for the basic strength and flexibility of the compositions, and he wanted them to gain a wider usage in the concert hall. With his sympathetic approach and his innate brilliance in orchestration, Glazunov ensured that no real harm came to Chopin's basic intent. There was particular daring in harnessing the Etude in C-sharp minor to the Waltz in the same key, by way of an introduction. This waltz went to Pavlova and Oboukhov. Fokine's guiding aim in creating it was to evoke a mood, and he saw the piece as a chance to further the Romantic image that Pavlova sustained so well in *Giselle* and that had been glimpsed so tantalizingly in the uncredited pas de deux to Chopin interpolated into *Graziella* four years earlier. The music had, in a way, come full circle: Chopin had said that he had more than once received his inspiration from the dancing of Taglioni.

As was the case with most of these charity performances, the costumes were a potpourri culled from the wardrobe department, with minor new additions. Oboukhov wore a Bakst design from *The Fairy Doll,* but for Pavlova Bakst sketched a full-skirted costume in the manner of Taglioni. Their waltz mirrored the soft outlines of the costumes: there was to be no technical strain, no bravura, no awareness of the audience; it was to exist strictly within its own time and space, with the dancers totally absorbed in their dreamlike sequence.

This interlude was at some variance with the rest of the ballet, which reverted to traditional excuses for displays of handsome dancing. The opening was an ensemble in which Polish ballroom dancers executed a polonaise, before cumbersome machinery was employed to transform the setting into a mountain fastness in Majorca, where the figure of a distracted Chopin was discovered seated at a piano, while being assailed from all sides by hallucinatory monks. The sinister Waldemos brethren, in deathly make-up, wafted around the frantically miming pianist while thunder sheets rumbled and artificial lightning rent the stage. This intended nightmare was gradually dispelled by the influence of a Muse, who soothingly encouraged "Chopin" (Alexis Bulgakov) to render a nocturne, once the storm had abated. The Waltz followed, with no apparent link to the next section: a rustic wedding scene full of the usual theatrical complications and "will she, won't she?" excitements as the heroine waited to be rescued from the fate of a loveless marriage. Sedova was the bride, Sergei Grigoriev was her unsuitable old suitor, and Gerdt was her "young" admirer. Finally, with a disregard for anything that had gone before, the scene changed to reveal sunny Italy. Mount Vesuvius belched smoke over a glittering Bay of Naples, and a horde of brightly dressed Neapolitans passed the time of day in a tarantella; this included Fokine's young bride, Vera. Her husband's work was at odds with his own edict that ballet should have dramatic cohesion, but he was careful to follow the dictates of the music with the moods of the individual sections. *Chopiniana,* as the piece was named, had come within an ace of being an "abstract ballet," and Pavlova's instinctive rightness in the Waltz held the key to future possibilities in this direction.

The search for suitable music became a constant factor in Fokine's new role as choreographer, and he continued to hunt through the libraries for little-used scores, and to attend concerts in the hope of hearing some relatively neglected piece. It was in this way that he discovered the Tcherepnin score for *Le Pavillon d'Armide,* which had been commissioned by the directorate some years earlier and then not used. Fokine met Nicolas Tcherepnin, who was only a few years his senior, and the two discussed the possibility of getting the ballet mounted. It seemed to them that the best chance was for the composer to redraft a suite from the score, allowing Fokine to construct a small, manageable work for one of the student recitals. As a result of using Benois's libretto and subsequently his designs, Fokine found himself an accepted member of that circle of guiding lights from *The World of Art.* Despite these heady acquaintances, Fokine was still expected to get his ballets onto the stage without incurring major costs in costumes or décor (quite apart from the strictures on new music), and he was reduced to scrounging around the wardrobes for existing remnants. The shortened version of *Le Pavillon d'Armide* was finally presented on April 15, 1907, by a group of graduating students, under the title *The Animated Gobelin,* a reference to the Théophile Gautier story of a peopled tapestry that comes to life.

To Fokine's astonishment, Krupensky, who had always been so suspicious of him, now embraced him warmly and showered him with compliments. From this moment one of the major barriers to Fokine's progress as an officially recognized choreographer for the Maryinsky appeared to fall away, and the bemused Fokine found himself asked to mount the ballet for the company, for the coming autumn.

The 1906–07 season ended on April 29 with a mixed bill. There was one act of *Le Corsaire, The Trials of Damis, Les Saisons* with Pavlova as the Bacchante, and *The Enchanted Forest* with Vaslav Nijinsky, still officially a student, taking Fokine's place as the Genie of the Forest opposite Lyubov Egorova. Two weeks earlier Nijinsky had danced a variety of items at his graduation performance, including the Lightning variation from Petipa's ill-fated *Magic Mirror.* Kchessinskaya had congratulated the boy and informed him that she would be pleased to have him as one of her partners. Nijinsky was swept up into the inner circle that summer when he danced with Kchessinskaya at Krasnoe Selo, the military camp outside St. Petersburg used for summer maneuvers; he gained an immediate position within the company that no amount of brilliant dancing could have won so quickly. Certainly Fokine encountered no managerial opposition when he chose Nijinsky for roles over more senior male dancers.

Though the simmerings of discontent had settled by the time of the 1906–07 season, a shift in the Moscow-St. Petersburg balance was more discernible. Teliakovsky was voicing an idea that the Moscow School should be cut out altogether (there had been only ten graduates for 1906). He wanted to transfer his administrative offices to Moscow, and turn the St. Petersburg offices into a residence. He also thought the ballet company was too big; he claimed that by reducing the number of students slightly, there could be an effective saving of 100,000 roubles a year. This slightly dismissive attitude to Moscow may have been a contributory factor in the decision to allow a group of young St. Petersburg dancers to manage themselves in an early summer season there. They would be without senior supervision and entirely responsible for their own repertory and casting. It was not the sort of risk the St. Petersburg directorate would have taken a few years earlier, but now the tide of Maryinsky confidence was running strongly. Fokine was chosen to direct the troupe. The tour would commence in Moscow's Hermitage Theatre on May 18 and continue through to July 13. Pavlova was to be the ballerina for the early weeks, before handing over her responsibilities to Trefilova for the rest of the season.

After the Maryinsky closed at the end of April, Pavlova and Fokine had a fortnight in which to sort out their principal roles, including parts that were new to them. At the end of each day, Victor Dandré would arrive to collect Pavlova, and if the weather was fine they would all take an evening drive in Dandré's new motorcar. On such evenings young Michel Barroy sometimes joined his uncle for the ride. He was now a member of the Lancers' regiment stationed at Peterhof, an easy trip from the city. One night he attended an all-star benefit concert of the Nobility Circle, where he encountered Fokine, anxious as ever for new stimuli. One of the items was a "melodeclamation" by the dramatic actor Hodotoff; he strode on stage with an accompanist, who played a short piano introduction before the actor launched into Konstantin Balmont's poem "The Dying Swan," which began with the lines, "The lake's asleep, no ripples stir its waters . . ." and finished with the description of the wounded bird returning to die among the reeds of its home ground. Barroy was reminded of a tableau he had witnessed some days before on one of the drives around the outskirts of St. Petersburg. It was in the area of shoreline known as The Islands, near sunset. As they approached one of the small lakes that dotted the area, Pavlova saw a swan close to the bank and asked that the car be stopped; she had with her the remains of the sandwiches she had taken to the rehearsal earlier, and she took them to the water's edge to entice the bird. Fokine was struck by the sight and he grabbed Michel's arm as he pointed out the striking grace of the young dancer, dressed all in white, reaching out to the exquisite bird.

Apart from the visit to Moscow for Roslavleva's benefit night, this trip was Fokine's and Pavlova's first taste of traveling with a company, but besides Egorova, the female dancers, though gifted soloists, had no real experience in leading roles; of them Vil, Schollar, and Lopokhova were the best. The men were stronger; they included Mikhail Oboukhov, Alexander Shirayev, and Adolph Bolm. The corps de ballet comprised twelve girls and eight boys, and the whole party had a jolly send-off from St. Petersburg, with a crowd of well-wishers seeing the smartly dressed dancers to the train, where they occupied an entire carriage. At the other end, however, they seemed less important. The Moscow Hermitage had several auditoriums with various entertainments, even including other ballets: on opening night the St. Petersburg dancers were in the Concert Parisien, while a Cecchetti ballet, *The Bird Vendor*, was playing in the Bouffe. The repertoire of the Maryinsky group included *The Magic Flute, The Cavalry Halt, Paquita, Coppélia, Les Caprices du Papillon,* and *La Fille Mal Gardée* and Pavlova danced in all of them. Some of the ballets were grouped with dramatic sections employing local talent. The director of the Hermitage complex had an eclectic policy, and patrons expected variety; the St. Petersburg dancers had been preceded by the Theatre of Geisha.

Fokine seems to have viewed this time as an ideal one in which to experiment; these performances were considered "summer stock" by the critics, and very little news of the troupe crept into the press. Most of the dancers managed to sample a number of extramural activities in Moscow, but Pavlova, with so many extra rehearsals, seldom left the vicinity of the theatre; she had to be content with snatching a few moments' rest in the surrounding gardens. Fokine was reviving *Eunice*, and, unbeknown to the officials in St. Petersburg, he was also reshaping *The Animated Gobelin*, which was presented on May 25 as "scenes and dances from a new ballet, *Armida's Pavilion*, music by Tcherepnin." The significance of this ballet landmark was not evident at the time, but it was to change the lives of almost everyone who took part in it. As a reward for her hard work, Pavlova was given a Moscow benefit on June 2. She danced Liza, the heroine of *La*

Fille Mal Gardée, and it marked the first time she had essayed the role since joining the Imperial Theatres.* The role of Liza was one of Kchessinskaya's most successful; she was always endearingly pert and bubbly as the country lass prescribed by a well-meaning but mercenary mother; Pavlova was no less successful, adding a natural, impish humor to the filigree lightness of her dancing. She was able to make the steps themselves seem witty.

This initial taste of touring, away from the restrictive controls of the Maryinsky offices, seems to have fired Pavlova with an incentive to go on seeking out new audiences, in the way that Taglioni, her spiritual idol, had done. In a fragmentary memoir five years later, Pavlova wrote at one point, in speaking of her travels, "My first tour began with Riga, in 1907. . . . I arrived with a company, and we performed two ballets at the opera house."

There is a poverty of information about this Riga visit, but it may well have been a part of the same Maryinsky "package," traveling back to St. Petersburg by a roundabout route in the summer. A presentation ribbon exists, with the inscription "A. P. Pavlova. From your friends. Riga, 26 February 1908." It is quite conceivable that she returned for a second visit, the following winter; the sentiments on the ribbon suggest familiarity between Pavlova and her audience. Both Dandré and Bolm support this view in later writings. Whatever the exact truth of the matter, Pavlova passed a personal frontier in 1907 quite apart from any other. She acquired an ineradicable desire to take her dancing outside Russia.

Notwithstanding Dandré's paternal presence in her life, Pavlova seems to have struck up a romance with the young Adolph Bolm at this time. A number of clues indicate that Pavlova got as far as London in the summer of 1907, and she seems to have made attempts to secure an engagement there. Dandré was her official escort at this juncture, and yet Bolm joined them in a London hotel. (He may well have had to stay on in Moscow and complete the season with Fokine, Trefilova et al.) Bolm highlighted a hurtful little episode in which Pavlova was distressed and rebuffed by a brash London production manager who had no knowledge of her, or her credentials for performing. She was expected to turn up with her tights and audition like the other girls. "At that time," Bolm later wrote, "Western Europe knew nothing whatever about Russian Ballet or Pavlova." On the latter point he was correct; but Roslavleva had danced in Monte Carlo, and Trouhanova, another Moscow dancer, had appeared in music hall in Paris. And there were even earlier precedents. But for Pavlova it was a temporary setback, and she must have left

* In 1931 Svetlov wrote: "Already at the age of fourteen—says one of her fellow pupils—she made an appearance on the stage in a school performance with M. M. Fokine. The ballet was *La Fille Mal Gardée.*" We know from Fokine's memoirs that as a student, he danced Colin in this ballet, and though he does not specify the fact, it seems likely that Anna Pavlova partnered him then. She must have watched it on many occasions thereafter. (Liza and Colin were the names given to the lovers in Ivanov's reconstruction of the old Dauberval classic.) The Moscow performances of *Coppélia* and *Les Caprices du Papillon* were certainly "firsts" for Pavlova.

London with a sense of frustration, knowing that—for the time being, at any rate—Adeline Genée would remain the undisputed Queen of the Toe Slipper in London's gaudy theatre world.

When Pavlova arrived back at the Maryinsky in the autumn of 1907 she had been in London (presumably) and Paris, and she knew at least something of the great divide between the sequestered Maryinsky and the raucously commercial and competitive state of theatre in those other cities. If she was not entirely deterred, she certainly had something to think about: nobody could quite explain English music hall, for instance, unless he had seen it for himself. At the Maryinsky, the program suggested a friendly rivalry between Trefilova and Pavlova, and Sedova too. But when Kchessinskaya came back to the attack—earlier than usual, on October 7—Pavlova and Trefilova had to be content with secondary roles in *Daughter of the Pharaoh*; they played, respectively, Ramzé and the Fisherman's Wife. At this time Kchessinskaya was learning the role of Princess Elga in *The Gardener Prince* in order to increase the repertory available to herself and Vaslav Nijinsky. Ludmilla Schollar, the young girl who had first danced the role with Nijinsky, had to teach it to Kchessinskaya and must have viewed the result rather wistfully. On October 14, Pavlova got another chance to dance the role of Giselle. Though she convinced the public more and more that she was its ideal interpreter, she could hardly acquire total confidence in the role, since she never got more than two performances of it a year, and in 1907, *Giselle* was scheduled only once. Preobrajenskaya danced *The Trials of Damis* on the same night as Pavlova's *Giselle,* and three nights later she danced Mercedes to Pavlova's Kitry in *Don Quixote*; there was little chance of the younger dancer seizing an evening unconditionally. *The Gardener Prince* was given on October 28 together with *La Fille Mal Gardée,* and Kchessinskaya danced in both ballets. She was Princess Elga in *The Gardener Prince,* and Karsavina and Kyaksht were in it too, but the audience seemed unimpressed, though the *New Times* thought it "a rather charming piece." It was not rescheduled.*

Maria Petipa had been on leave for a year, and her maturity at last caught up with her; she had escaped the axe longer than most. Her farewell benefit was scheduled for November 11; it marked thirty years of service to the Imperial Ballet. For this special evening she came back to dance the Panaderos and a mazurka from *Raymonda* and a character dance from *The Little Humpbacked Horse*. Preobrajenskaya played Raymonda, and the other principal ladies paid their respects with small items at the conclusion of the evening. Kchessinskaya, Trefilova, and Pavlova each had something new to show the audience. Kulichevskaya's pas de deux for Kchessinskaya and Nijinsky used a nocturne and a waltz by Chopin; Nicolas Legat danced a pas de deux of his own devising with Trefilova; and Pavlova and Fokine danced *Pas des Papillons,* to Chopin's Waltz No. 6 in D-flat major. Such a

feverishly brief little number must have made a good contrast to the nocturne. One imagines Fokine throwing it together in scarcely more than a minute.

In meetings with Teliakovsky, Fokine argued as persuasively as he could for the full score of *Le Pavillon d'Armide* to be used in his expansion of the ballet for the Maryinsky, and he also put forward the name of the original librettist, Alexandre Benois, as designer. Though Teliakovsky viewed the whole Diaghilev circle with considerable mistrust, he acceded to the latter request; presumably he had heard favorable reports from the Moscow tryout in May. When Fokine came to examine the libretto in detail, he concluded that there was unnecessary padding, and following his instinct for condensing ballets, he suggested that the full work could be adequately presented within the span of one act with three scene changes. Benois was deeply pained by the suggestions of cuts, which ran directly counter to his own views; he considered that one-act ballets were first cousins to music-hall entertainments. But a commission from the Imperial Theatres was important to him, so he began the work of enlarging his designs, aided by cohorts of scenery painters in the theatre workshops. They were striving to create the atmosphere of the court of Louis XIV (though, with the extravagance of the day, the period of Louis XV was embraced as well), and it was Fokine's first experience in creating a ballet for which the decorative element was freshly designed in every detail, rather than consisting of castoffs. There was even entirely new music, as Tcherepnin needed to score several extra pieces for changes in the libretto. Benois was concerned that the work should adhere to the traditional format for ballets of the time, particularly as he had envisaged the story in terms of a fanciful, episodic work full of tableaux and mimic gesture. His general sympathy and undoubted artistic credentials enabled him to exert a restraining influence over Fokine in such a manner as to ease any frustrations the choreographer may have felt about outmoded styles.

Fokine's task in this instance was strictly defined, and the creation of dance steps was his only real concern, though he could not help darting around the various workshops to inspect the technical aspects of the production. These included a flock of mechanical sheep, which were tested in the director's office, where they stalked across the carpet. If Krupensky was amused by the sheep parading in his office, he was dismayed that Benois had no intention of being included in their number; the designer had lively views of his own about the rightness of certain elements, and despite his mild and scholarly appearance, he had a surprisingly firm way when differences arose. When a sudden frost entered the atmosphere between the management and the creative side, principally because of some misunderstandings and imagined slights, the shifting allegiances had a deleterious effect on the completion of the ballet. Once more the theatre was buzzing with factions: Diaghilev, watching a rehearsal, suddenly found himself escorted from the auditorium by theatre guards.

---

*In her memoirs, Nijinska errs when she suggests that Schollar was still dancing Elga at the October performance.

Le Pavillon d'Armide:
(above) with Nijinsky.

Kchessinskaya, who had seemed ready to welcome the new dawn of choreography and who had been given the lead in this ballet, as she had in *Eunice,* now sought to remove herself from the production, and Fokine and Benois were sitting in the theatre trying to assess the import of this latest disaster when help flew in, in the form of Pavlova. She had been taking a close interest in the progress of her friends' work and was well aware of all the political machinations surrounding it; her own absence from the role (which she had already danced in Moscow) was due partly to the fact that she was rehearsing a big new Legat ballet, and partly to prevailing political maneuvering, which decreed that favored elements had to be kept happy at the expense of nonconformists. Pavlova was always at a disadvantage against the influential retinue that surrounded Kchessinskaya and furthered her every move, but Mathilde's sudden abdication of an obviously important role presented Pavlova with a perfect opening, and the whole situation appealed to her curious delight in tilting at authority. She had the knowledge that the general crowd would support her as a performer, and she was deeply committed to Fokine's aims. Pavlova soon persuaded her friends that she could pick up the role of Armide (actually Madeleine, who counterfeits the image of Armide) in the time left. But their troubles were still not over: Gerdt had to be cajoled into staying, and the final dress rehearsal was chaotic, the dancers having to familiarize themselves with many strange props and exotic costumes. At this point Fokine asked for another dress rehearsal, which would have delayed the opening night, but the management was not inclined to allow him any more leeway—a view not unreasonable in the circumstances of the schedule.

It was unfortunate that the directors conspired at this time to create such a no man's land between themselves and the artists, so that there was no common ground for compromise and expediency. Everybody took up extreme positions as a matter of course. Benois immediately called in the aid of his particular circle, getting Bakst's brother, the columnist Isaiah Rosenberg, to air the problem in the *Petersburg Gazette.* Rosenberg was not looking for a head-on confrontation with the Imperial Theatres and saw to it that Benois put his own name to the article, which laid bare all the niggling events that had hampered the creation of their work. Within an hour of the newspaper's appearance on the streets, there was the making of a scandal, with many prominent people expressing outrage on behalf of the creators. The management was quickly forced to concede the round, and *Le Pavillon* won an extra week's grace.

During this time all the unwieldy details were harnessed within the greater pattern of the ballet, with Pavlova given the necessary time to perfect her principal variation, including a lot of stage business with a long scarf, which in the earlier rehearsals had tended to catch under her pointes. The brilliant young Nijinsky (having by now graduated and joined the company) had been given the role of a favored slave in order to introduce his idiosyncratic skills into the ballet. Though his role had nothing to do with the ballerina other than to offer support in moments of her variations, which were in effect solo dances, Pavlova and

Nijinsky were both asked to take their costumes to the photographer's studio and pose for pictures recording the production.

The management had one final sting in its tail: it scheduled the Fokine-Benois ballet on a night when *Swan Lake* was also being given, so that the curtain did not go up on *Le Pavillon d'Armide* until after midnight. But the chequered career of its making had been so fully aired in public that there was tremendous curiosity. At one o'clock the curtains came down to a wave of enthusiastic applause from the audience. Admirers had made sure that there were plenty of expensive floral tributes ready to be sent on stage, and Pavlova, relieved and delighted, found herself the principal recipient. Choreographer, designer, and composer were guided to the footlights in order to receive their own dues, and Benois, suddenly shy and rather overcome by the moment, had his confusion compounded when Pavlova kissed him in front of the delighted Maryinsky audience. If the management had sought to divide the new order, then it had failed, and instead these young artists acquired a new degree of confidence in their own individual talents—a confidence which had first blossomed with the challenge of dancing for the Muscovites earlier that year.

When the Opera choir asked Pavlova to appear in a charity performance at the Maryinsky on December 22 on behalf of poor mothers and newborn babies, she readily agreed and asked Fokine to choreograph something new for her. He had been practicing a mandolin transcription of some pieces from Saint-Saëns's *Carnival of the Animals* and was perfecting a rendition of "The Swan" with a fellow dancer accompanying him on the piano. In a mood of sudden enthusiasm, he went with Pavlova to her studio and began to shape the imagery of a swan, moving about as he hummed the music, with Pavlova stepping behind him. Then she tried a sequence on her own, and he made modifications in her arms and carriage. He was aiming to suggest the gliding of a swan on water, and to this end he gave Pavlova an almost unbroken series of bourrées, leaving her arms to express the futile efforts of the creature whose wing beats could no longer carry it clear of the lake's surface. Pavlova understood precisely the mood of the piece, melancholic and resigned, yet containing the last dying fire of a spirit that had known untrammeled freedom. As with all their work together, the two dancers progressed in an easy way that was not exactly improvisatory but more the result of an intuitive accord between them. Fokine had to give but the merest hint of the image in his mind for Pavlova to take that thought and flesh it out with an ineffable physical signature. The dance was completed in under half an

The Swan (studio portrait taken in New York in 1910).

hour, and for Pavlova it proved to be an instant success.[*]

For the same charity performance, Fokine had created for Karsavina *Assyrian Dances*, to music of Arensky, and this was received with equal enthusiasm. Fokine's romance with Karsavina had come to an end some years earlier; under pressure from her mother, she had declined to marry him. In 1905 he married Vera Antonova, a 1904 graduate who specialized in character dancing. Thereafter he had continued his professional association with Karsavina, displaying an impeccable impartiality but never addressing a word to her on matters other than work.

While *Le Pavillon d'Armide* had been attracting so much drama and publicity, a far larger work was being quietly put together by Nicolas Legat, who was now ballet master. Evidently undeterred by the cool reception accorded his *Puss in Boots* a year earlier, Legat had begun work after the summer recess on a ballet in no fewer than five acts, to be given its premiere at the benefit for the corps de ballet on December 16. He had taken as his theme S. T. Aksakov's story "The Little Red

[*] For a dance whose image is possibly the most ubiquitous in the history of ballet, the exact provenance of *The Swan* is intriguingly uncertain. Fokine, in his memoirs, gives the year as 1905 and the theatre as the Hall of Nobles. (He used the word "schoolmate" to describe his piano accompanist of the time, but one must assume that he means a fellow dancer from the Ballet School, not that they were still students.) Nijinska, in her memoirs, accepts Fokine's date and goes further: she suggests that, but for illness, Vaslav Nijinsky would have performed with Pavlova a pas de deux from *Swan Lake* at the 1907 charity gala, and that the substitution of the Saint-Saëns piece was a last-minute necessity. However, Vera Krasovskaya turned up a poster clearly listing *The Swan* for December 22, 1907. Though Nijinska ties in the sudden illness of her brother with this charity performance, his unexpected absence from a December 16 premiere was mentioned in the newspapers a day later. (Nijinska wrote: "I knew he had been bothered by a lingering cold ever since he returned from Moscow. . . . ") But records show that Nijinsky did not go to Moscow until January. Michel Barroy's memory of Pavlova feeding the swan at The Islands was dated by him as 1907 (when recalled years later), but this could have been prompted by the date in Dandré's book: "1907 or 1908." Barroy would have been just as involved with the group in 1905, when, indeed, the piece may have been tried in the Hall of Nobles.

Flower"; Marzhetsky supplied the libretto, F. A. Hartmann the music, and Korovine the scenery and costumes. This mixture of disparate talents was vaguely reminiscent of *The Magic Mirror*. Strangely, the very Russianness of Aksakov's story was adulterated by giving the ballet a Venetian setting, with the three daughters of the rich merchant becoming Annunciata, Flaminia, and Angelica. Determined to use the best talent available, Legat gave the roles of the three sisters to Pavlova, Preobrajenskaya, and Trefilova, and for Kchessinskaya he made a cameo, known as the Reverie. Gerdt was the automatic choice for the merchant, and Bulgakov played the Wizard. Fokine, so deeply involved in his own ballets, had for once the opportunity to create a leading role, that of the Prince.

Despite the evidence of a great deal of hard work, the ballet eventually revealed itself as yet another cumbersome edifice supported on the weakest of foundations; there was no strength left in the plot once the delicate allegorical aspects, all about doing good and loving humanity at all costs, had been translated—none too clearly—into stage action, snuffing out the whimsical charm of Aksakov's writing. Unlike the original story, the ballet seemed overburdened and pretentious. Some of the critics thought it merely interminable. Legat had put his greatest efforts into the grand pas in the last act, and it was a gross misfortune that Nijinsky, who had been cast as Kchessinskaya's partner, should have fallen ill the night before the premiere. Poor Legat had to go on in his place, and it was hardly surprising that his dancing in this section gave a certain appearance of improvisation. Coming so soon after the enthusiastic reception accorded *Le Pavillon d'Armide*, the coldness toward the new work was a sharp reminder that the public had a mind of its own, and that it had been nurtured on the soundest of choreographic principles; but with all the expense that had been poured into it, the work could not be abandoned.

In addition to appearances as Annunciata in *The Little Red Flower* and as Madeleine in *Le Pavillon*, Pavlova was rehearsing for her long-awaited accession to the role of Aurora in *The Sleeping Beauty*. It was the part an eight-year-old had declared would be her own, yet for so many years she had been forced to content herself with minor roles in the work. She had seen Trefilova score a notable success in the leading role, and the previous April it had also been given to Sedova. Now it was Pavlova's turn, and her first and only performance of it during the season was to be on January 6, 1908. Alas, when the time came she did not arouse in her audience the kind of enthusiasm that always greeted her Giselles and Nikiyas. The reaction was polite and considered, but the feeling was that the role of Princess Aurora did not suit Pavlova's timbre of dancing in the way her other roles did. It was understood that her talent was great and her future assured, but it was also felt that *The Sleeping Beauty* would never be one of "her" ballets. Audiences had seen the haunting conviction she brought to the death throes of a swan, but a light-hearted princess resisted her penetrating intuition.

Significantly, Petipa had never suggested the role for her. The review in the *New Times* came straight to the point:

> For the first time, Mme Pavlova appeared yesterday as the Sleeping Beauty. The role of Aurora in this exquisite ballet is quite unsuited to Mme Pavlova, and it only remains for one to wonder what could have induced her to assume it. The artist nowhere has an opportunity to express her dramatic ability, and the genre of dancing of the Italian school is also not compatible with her talents. A famous bass does not attempt the part of a tenor, and Mme Pavlova achieved nothing in this role. A number of floral tributes and a degree of applause do not alter the matter: Mme Pavlova's debut was a failure.

What was perhaps worse, Karsavina was described as "deserving of all praise" in her role of the Lilac Fairy.

Kchessinskaya seemed to be in irrepressible form, emboldened perhaps by her exhilarating new partner, Nijinsky. She even took the young prodigy to Moscow, where they danced in *La Bayadère* on January 13. Pavlova had thought that she had put her own imprint on Nikiya, so that it was no longer indelibly associated with Kchessinskaya, but the general excitement that Nijinsky lent to any performance was sufficient to focus renewed attention on Kchessinskaya's appearances. Mathilde had never doubted her suitability as a princess, and she was back in *The Sleeping Beauty* on February 17. Guiding Aurora's destinies in this performance was a new Lilac Fairy—none other than Pavlova, in her more familiar guise as a supernatural being.*

Fokine, by the early days of 1908, was planning a new work based on Egyptian culture; archeological digging at Thebes was much in the news. The new ballet was to be called *Egyptian Nights*. Its premiere was scheduled for a charity performance on March 8, with a freshly revised *Chopiniana*—Fokine was dissatisfied with his initial version, considering that the whole thing should become soft and romantic in tone, without the ballroom elements, which he knew to be reeking of the "old order." (It is perhaps significant that Duncan was on view again in mid February; Fokine's response to her was always immediate and positive.) The only thing Fokine did not want to lose was the waltz that Pavlova had performed with Oboukhov, so he left this as a centerpiece and proceeded to make fresh pearls around it. He also proposed that Pavlova dance to some new music. He found a Chopin mazurka (Op. 33, no. 2) that contained gathered impulsions followed by releases, which he interpreted as jumps, and this seemed a good chance to show off Pavlova's aerial qualities. Fokine allotted another waltz (Op. 70, no. 1) to Tamara Karsavina; and with the young Nijinsky emerging as a performer of rare talent, Fokine eliminated all the other men from the ballet, leaving Nijinsky in a pivotal role which became that of a daydreaming poet haunted by muses. All the selections were now

---

* Nijinska's reference in her memoirs to her brother and Pavlova having danced the Blue Bird pas de deux for the first time places this event in February, but it could only have taken place on March 28, the remaining performance of *The Sleeping Beauty* for that season. The Yearbook did not specify who danced the secondary roles on this date, but Nijinsky's personal entry does state that he danced the Blue Bird three times that season. (As a ballerina, Pavlova's Yearbook entries tended to concentrate on leading roles.)

orchestrated by composer Maurice Keller, with the exception of the C-sharp minor waltz, which retained the Glazunov orchestration.* One of the singers from the Maryinsky chanced upon a rehearsal and noticed for the first time the conjunction of the Etude and the Waltz. He strode about the theatre declaiming on the artistic barbarity of the ballet dancers, for whom apparently nothing was sacred. Fokine had to suggest that he complain in the Conservatory across the street for the benefit of his own director, Glazunov.

The dancers who were taking part in Fokine's Egyptian ballet had some bewildering new ideas to cope with; like Gorsky in Moscow, Fokine was afire with innovative choreographic devices that were striking at the most ingrained beliefs about classical ballet. The music that Fokine was using had been written in 1900 by Arensky for Ivanov, who was preparing an entertainment to take place at Peterhof, the Tsar's summer residence, with the mise en scène making use of the lake and island that had been dug out near the palace. Ivanov died before completing the ballet, but costumes had already been made for it, and Fokine unearthed them in the wardrobe building where they were stored; all the girls' costumes were conventional short tutus, with only a hint of an Egyptian motif here and there. He went on searching through endless racks of opera and ballet costumes from all sorts of productions until he did come across the odd element that was more suited to his needs, and with the help of carefully chosen accessories, together with freshly designed wigs, and sandals to replace the ballet slippers, he gradually built up a new decorative scheme for his ballet. Fokine was not entirely satisfied until he had redesigned the dancers themselves, persuading them to wear all-over brown body paint and a heavily stylized face make-up.

At one point in the ballet, Pavlova, as Veronika, the principal female dancing role, had to wear a snake as well; Fokine had seen a snake dance illustrated in an Egyptian painting in the Hermitage Museum and felt that such an incident would add authenticity to his own work. The zoo supplied the newest recruit. Fokine's idea was that Veronika should perform a dance for Cleopatra in which the snake would prefigure the queen's own death. However, the link was tenuous, since the ballet had nothing to do with Cleopatra's demise; she was very much alive at the end of it, and it was Amoun, the young hunter (played by Fokine), who lay sprawled on the stage. Still, for Fokine the snake was an Egyptian accessory, just as it had been Indian for Petipa in La Bayadère. Pavlova watched quite calmly at the rehearsal when Fokine introduced her silent, sinuous partner. He demonstrated the steps of the dance he wanted Pavlova to execute, until the snake joined in and began moving around too, and Fokine nearly

fainted with the sensation of it. Pavlova had something of a reputation as an animal lover, and she did not argue when the choreographer insisted that she carry on rehearsing with the reptile, but she looked far from delighted, and it is a measure of her willingness to pursue Fokine's every aim that she persevered until the opening night. In the event, the snake became thoroughly blasé about its role, settling into a comfortable coil around Pavlova's arm on its first entrance and moving not so much as a scale during the performance. For the second night, one week later, it suffered the ignominy of being replaced by a piece of stuffed oilcloth and was returned to the zoo.

Gerdt had to manage a chariot of white horses for his entrance as Mark Antony, and there was a mounted bodyguard as well. Corps de ballet dancers and extras poured onto the stage as legionnaires, their prisoners, and accompanying rabble, and everyone walked in an exaggeratedly stylized manner that echoed the figures in Egyptian wall paintings. Each position was angular and presented in profile; it may have baffled those in the audience who did not have a nodding acquaintance with ancient Egyptian friezes, but for those who recognized the source of the imagery, the adventurousness of the choreography was thoroughly exciting, with the passions portrayed in a vivid and daring way. Pavlova and Fokine both had great personal successes in their roles, though Elizaveta Tihmé as Cleopatra gave the most anguished performance, due to toothache. Nijinsky and Preobrajenskaya were outstanding as two slaves dancing with a billowing veil, as was Karsavina in her Jewish Dance. The story line was the usual one of thwarted love, with Veronika left disconsolate with the apparently lifeless body of the one she loved. In fact, Pavlova gave the role tremendous pathos, so that toward the end the audience was deeply touched by the tragedy of the situation, and the horses and all the other distractions were entirely forgotten.

No one could exceed Anna Pavlova in determination; her wholehearted absorption in her career remained something of a phenomenon for the times. To Pavlova, dancing was an end in itself and not the means by which some haven of security was to be reached. Like other ballerinas, she acquired admirers; but Pavlova kept them in the background. She also acquired beautiful jewelry, yet she seldom actually wore any of it, taking a simple pleasure in its possession. She was a paradox in that she held conventional views about her position within the company and about the works she performed, yet her behavior on numerous occasions suggested that of a rank nonconformist.

* The Fokine ballets were part of a "private" evening in the eyes of the Maryinsky directorate; it merely lent costumes and music, and the ballets were in fact preceded by a one-act play. Though Fokine did adapt Chopiniana for a student presentation the following month, neither it nor Egyptian Nights entered the regular repertory until February 19, 1909. With a gap of nearly a year, no doubt further alterations took place. Nijinska in her memoirs says that the Chopin ballet and Eunice were first given at a charity performance on February 16, 1908, and that the March 8 presentation of Chopiniana (given with Egyptian Nights) was thus its second performance. In Eunice on February 16,

Pavlova took over Kchessinskaya's title role, while Karsavina stepped up to the part of Acté. According to Nijinska, Fokine canceled a planned divertissement section on the program of February 16, rather than get involved in any jockeying for position between Kchessinskaya and Pavlova, the former having ambitions to dance Kulichevskaya's Chopin Nocturne with Nijinsky. I cannot help feeling that this was the real reason for Fokine's changing the program: since he was planning to present the revised version of Chopiniana with himself partnering Pavlova in the Waltz, he would hardly want a rival Chopin number on the program; Kulichevskaya's Nocturne included a Chopin waltz.

ABOVE & OPPOSITE In costume for the Panaderos in *Raymonda*, with personal jewelry.

The directors who controlled her career were wary of her. Pavlova had a respect for authority where that authority sprang from solid achievement, but hierarchical offices of command did not impress her unduly. In one instance, when the management of the theatre replaced a costume of hers with a newer one of more sumptuous design, she reacted as if a favored pet had been destroyed and tore the new costume to pieces in front of the baffled director. In this instance she was fined, but she also won the right to wear the old costume again. Tears and tantrums came to her aid when she wanted something badly enough and could find no more reasoned way of getting it. Some interpreted her behavior as base ambition, a consolidation of her status, with all the attendant material benefits; but others detected something else: a fervor about the very act of dancing that was akin almost to a religious mania. She seemed impelled by forces she did not necessarily understand herself. Whatever the motive, the result made the public eager to see everything she did. The initial group of ardent followers, the *"Pavlovtzi,"* were no longer remarkable; their ardor had been taken up by most of the regular St. Petersburg audiences, and even those of Moscow.

Perhaps it was this very success that produced anxiety in the management about Pavlova's increasing interest in touring. When the motivation to tour sprang from a dancer herself rather than from the directors, official reaction was cool; after all, the Tsar's dancers were not to trail around like a band of gypsies. After an initial rebuff to her suggestion of another tour, this time beyond the bounds of the Motherland, it became clear that internal diplomacy would have to be employed. Pavlova's admirers got to work until the management finally relented, and the pilgrimage suddenly had official blessing. The tentative arrangements allowed for Pavlova and a group from the Maryinsky, including Adolph Bolm as artistic director, to travel as "The Imperial Ballet from the Maryinsky Theatre." This was a mark of confidence on the part of the management, which could so easily have withheld this official banner.

The northern arc of the Baltic was the path Pavlova chose for her first sortie abroad, with Helsinki as her starting point; Stockholm followed, then Copenhagen, before she went south into Germany, across the border to Prague, and then back into Germany for the tour's conclusion in Berlin. It was an untried circuit, and the Maryinsky management could not know if it would succeed; nevertheless, for this 1908 tour they apportioned to Pavlova's group twelve girls and eight boys. Presumably opera house corps de ballet dancers were recruited in each city, since the ballets being shown were far from modest: these included three acts of *Paquita,* two acts of *Coppélia,* all of *Giselle,* and the middle two acts of *Swan Lake* (perhaps Pavlova was smarting at Trefilova's success in this work), as well as two shorter Petipa ballets, *The Cavalry Halt* and *Les Millions d'Arlequin.* Several of Fokine's more recent works were also included in the repertoire—probably nervously—by the directors; but they suited Pavlova, and the productions were not cumbersome. On the

Scandinavian leg of the tour, there were four performances in Helsinki, six in Stockholm, and two in Copenhagen.

In the Finnish capital, Pavlova's reputation had preceded her, and the audience welcomed her enthusiastically. In Stockholm the monarch himself attended the opening night and, liking what he saw, attended each subsequent night as well. Seeing the royal box occupied each evening was the greatest reward for the dancers, but Pavlova and Bolm received a special accolade from the King: they were summoned to the palace for an investiture of the Swedish order Litteris et Artibus. The people of Sweden demonstrated in their own way, rewarding Pavlova with a vigil outside her hotel, until she was obliged to go out onto the balcony. The crowd, which had been silently respectful up to now, gave a great roar of approval. Pavlova was startled and deeply touched, and when the crowd began to sing national songs for her, she was more astonished than ever. In an effort to show her appreciation, she darted back into her room and returned with an armful of flowers that had been given to her on stage that evening. These she tossed to the people below, and the enthusiasm was redoubled. When the company came to leave Stockholm, they found the railway station crowded with people. Thinking that Stockholm boasted an exceptionally busy terminal, Pavlova and her entourage braced themselves for battle; to

ABOVE With Adolph Bolm in the *Chopiniana* waltz.
His costume may be the one borrowed from the
Legat production of *The Fairy Doll*.

BELOW Program for *The Cavalry Halt* in Helsinki.

ABOVE Program for *Giselle* in Stockholm.

BELOW Rare photograph from *The Cavalry Halt*.

their amazement, the crowd parted before them as they advanced. It all happened with such quiet decorum that it was some while before it dawned on the dancers that the majority of the crowd was there to witness their departure.

To face such a haven of dance tradition as Copenhagen must have been daunting, particularly as newspaper articles had prepared the Danes for something special, but the Russians had the sort of success to which they were becoming accustomed. Members of the audience noticed one elderly member of the royal family in the opera house for the first time in eighteen years, and it was explained to the dancers that this benediction constituted true fame for them.*

Prague and its May Festival was approached with some trepidation. There had been sensational stories of the fate meted out to a group of dancers from the Paris Opéra a few weeks prior to the Russians' arrival. The audience thought the standard of the French dancers so low that the theatre emptied itself before the first performance was half over. But by the time the Russian company's first performance was half over, the auditorium seemed even fuller than before. The newspapers contained glowing tributes the following morning. At the end of the engagement, the stagehands had been persuaded to contrive a petal drop, and as the dancers took their final bows, a shower of fragrant blossoms swirled down on them from behind the proscenium. The visitors were thoroughly exhilarated by this display of affection, and they left in high spirits for the station, where they decorated the locomotive of the night train with many of their bouquets and wreaths.

In Berlin the following day, a somber group of waiting managers and journalists were astonished when the Russians' train pulled into the station; it was like a festival excursion. The dancers tumbled out of the carriages in the highest of spirits, pelting the train staff with the remains of their bouquets, and presenting the Prussian capital with anything but a stoical Russian "front." Their merriment abated when they saw the stage of the Komische Oper, which cramped the sets and much of the choreography; but the dancers concealed the difficulties from the audience, which duly proclaimed another success. The *Berliner Tageblatt* in its preliminary announcement had managed to suggest that the principal performer would be "Soloist Maria Pawlowa"; but whomever they were expecting, the goodwill of the audience was never in doubt, as many people had come to the house armed with flowers. During the divertissements that fol-

Ruth St. Denis in a "Hindoo" dance, Berlin, 1908.

lowed *Giselle,* the offerings were thrown indiscriminately from all parts of the theatre. Many flowers were crushed underfoot, and the stage became very slippery, so that the well-wishers finally brought to a conclusion the very activity they were encouraging. On the second night the Berlin audiences also enjoyed *Paquita* and its bravura dancing—their response providing a sharp contrast to the coolly detached reactions of the critics. The Berliners got their money's worth; each ballet evening stretched through four hours, and because of their success, three extra evenings were scheduled. Pavlova included the waltz from *Chopiniana.* In the audience at the Kroll on May 29 were Antonietta dell'Era, the original Sugar Plum Fairy in *The Nutcracker* and long-time prima ballerina of the Berlin Court Opera, and Ruth St. Denis, who was performing her "Hindoo" dances at the Komische Oper.

The dancers were like athletes high on adrenaline; they felt no distance was now beyond them. Though some were content to return to their home arena, many were fired with a desire to press on. Paris had always been on everyone's mind; its critics were international arbiters of taste, and its audiences dispensed success or failure with capricious decisiveness. Bolm found himself besieged with questions, advice, and simple exhortations to continue on at any cost. But the cost was being borne principally by the Imperial Theatres, and Bolm owed allegiance to the administration that had oiled the wheels thus far. There were stiff penalties for going against set plans.

---

* The opening night in Copenhagen had been put into jeopardy when Pavlova discovered that her jewel case was empty. Following the habit of leading ballerinas, who adorned their costumes with their own jewelry, Pavlova had taken her diamonds and emeralds to the theatre; in fact, she had taken the case without realizing it was empty. In the hysterical scene that followed, the stage manager was informed that the performance could not take place. Bolm saved the day by promising to hasten back to the hotel, having changed the order of the program to give him more time. He felt sure that some thief inside the hotel had taken the valuables on the spur of the moment, and the likelihood was that they were still on the premises. He was proved right when, during the frantic search that ensued, a detective fished the gems out of a laundry bag. Bolm could not face a performance like that again, and he persuaded Pavlova to send the jewelry back to St. Petersburg by special courier.

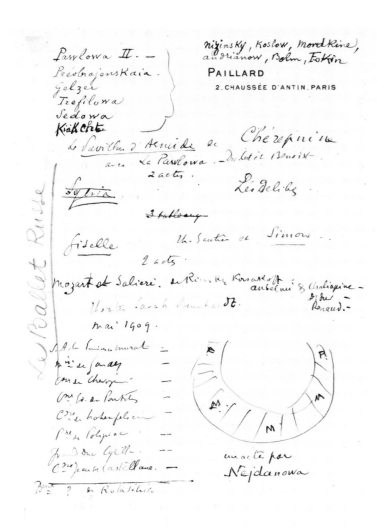

Diaghilev's jottings for his 1909 Paris season.

Diaghilev was in Paris at this time presenting Chaliapin in *Boris Godunov*. What the dancers did not know was that Bolm had been in almost continuous contact with Diaghilev, sending him news of their advance and their victories as they occurred. Not only was Diaghilev keeping in touch by post, but he also had a network of acquaintances who sent their own impressions from city to city, so that at the same time as Diaghilev was watching the mounting success of his season of Russian opera in Paris, he was receiving daily communiqués suggesting that Pavlova and her friends were advancing westward with their own uninterrupted success. If they came as far as Paris, Diaghilev's hoped-for combined opera and ballet season the following year would lose its projected impact; an eruption into Paris of Pavlova and her team performing their superbly schooled but tradition-bound repertoire would blunt the coup he was planning. His emissaries entreated Bolm to be patient, and Diaghilev bombarded him by mail with his plans and the part Bolm would play in them. What he was really seeking to protect was the potent appeal of Pavlova; he wanted to bring her from his sleeve at the right moment, like a conjurer. But it had to be his moment. Bolm decided not to test the patience of the Maryinsky directorship by asking for an extension of leave, and the fêted band returned east, receding mile by mile from the golden lure of Paris.

When, on June 2, 1908, Diaghilev sat down to supper at the Restaurant Paillard with the impresario Gabriel Astruc, and they tried to work out a roster of ballets and performers for their proposed Russian Season of opera and ballet in Paris the following year, there was nothing unusual about putting Pavlova's name at the top of their list of ballerinas. The glowing reports from her Baltic tour filtering back to Diaghilev could only have confirmed a fact that had always seemed obvious to him: any presentation of Russian ballet in the West must feature Pavlova as the principal jewel among the ballerinas. Besides, he admired her unreservedly as a performing artist, and he was often a guest when the ballerina gave intimate after-theatre supper parties in her apartment. In planning his 1909 season, Diaghilev must have felt more certain of gaining total cooperation from Pavlova than from almost anyone else.

The ballet for which Diaghilev had put forward Pavlova's name was *Le Pavillon d'Armide* and in writing down *Giselle* there can only have been one ballerina in mind. Equally, it was evident that Fokine's "new order" would feature prominently in any plans Diaghilev might have for presenting Russian ballet abroad. This was not a very extensive repertoire for a leading ballerina, but Diaghilev's ambition was to create an ensemble with the widest possible base of talent. He was treading a difficult path in such a jungle of back-office intrigue and jealously guarded stations of power. Not only was he attempting to placate a suspicious management, but he was also trying to make each principal dancer feel that his or her particular interests were of paramount importance—this, as well as juggle with the chauvinistic attitudes that prevailed in the two principal cities: St. Petersburg "knowing" that it ranked higher than Moscow, which likewise distrusted any product of rarified St. Petersburg thinking.

At the top of the list of male dancers Diaghilev placed the name of Nijinsky. Although the acquaintanceship was still slight, he already sensed that there was no one equal to him; Nijinsky was special, and the management as well as the other dancers tacitly acknowledged his importance. With the women it was not so easy. For one, there was the problem of Mathilde Kchessinskaya. She remained surprisingly unspoiled in view of the power she wielded; she was on good terms with the other dancers and was not given to unnecessary displays of temperament. But Fokine had not forgiven her capricious behavior toward him, and Diaghilev himself tended to bracket her with the "old order." In his initial discussions with Astruc, Diaghilev had not put forward her name for the roster of ballerinas, even though she was the most secure technician of them all and was absolutely professional. But they could not ignore the fact that the chance of an Imperial subsidy was inevitably linked to Kchessinskaya, and Diaghilev knew that such a subsidy was essential to his proposed enterprise; but for the staunch support of the Grand Duke Vladimir, the Tsar's uncle, it is unlikely that the performances of *Boris Godunov* at the Opéra would have taken place that spring. The success of this season had opened doors for Diaghilev; there was a powerful social circle in Paris that was ready to listen to any plans he might have, and hard cash supported their interest.

Even so, roubles were needed to attract francs, and an Imperial subsidy was the pledge against which all subsequent agreements lodged. Diaghilev knew that Kchessinskaya must be offered a part of the proposed season in Paris. At least she was already known to audiences there; that spring the ballerina had accepted an invitation from the Opéra. (Due to illness, the young Nijinsky had not been able to partner her as she had hoped; Nicolas Legat replaced him.) With apparent tact, Diaghilev offered Kchessinskaya the role of Madeleine in *Armide*, which he had originally planned for Pavlova.

By now Kchessinskaya had seen the success won by Fokine's ballet—and by Pavlova—and she considered the suggestion, meanwhile waiting for further roles to be submitted to her. Fokine, not having the worry of all this diplomatic juggling, could see no reason at all why Kchessinskaya should get the role, and he was adamant that she should not appear in Paris in *Chopiniana*—a suggestion that was being put forward in the Diaghilev headquarters. By the time Kchessinskaya herself made requests, Diaghilev probably demurred, with the argument that many other artists had to be considered and that much of the casting had already been agreed upon. Kchessinskaya felt—not unreasonably—that her position would be eroded by such a muted appearance in the season, and she declined to join the venture.

In 1908, though he was not recognized by the Maryinsky, Marius Petipa still cast a long shadow, but Pavlova was one of the few dancers with the sense to utilize his continuing presence in St. Petersburg; she went constantly to take advice from him. In addition, there had been two years of relentlessly firm tuition from Cecchetti, adjusting, admonishing, and urging analytical self-criticism. He had not regained a place within the School, but his availability to dancers at this time meant that his matchless understanding of the Italian school of dance was not lost to Russia. At the Maryinsky School, Nicolas Legat had become the principal teacher for the young men—though Nijinsky extricated himself from that class, in which Legat tried to re-create Johanssen's style very strictly, and took himself, with Pavlova's agreement, to Cecchetti's private sessions. At the end of his two-year stint, Cecchetti handed over his bound collection of music to Pavlova. Inside the cover he had inscribed a dedication and the date: August 1, 1908. He probably felt that for once his task was all but complete; from then on he gave open classes at his own studio, though he failed in his ambition to return to the Maryinsky fold.

The 1908–09 Maryinsky season was remarkable for the depth of talent evident among the dancers. At the opening performance, Preobrajenskaya in *La Source* was surrounded by Sedova, Karsavina, and Poliakova—the last replacing Lydia Kyaksht, who had gone to London for a season in music hall. (The Yearbook, in noting this departure, said that she had "left the stage of the Imperial Theatre for London," rather as if she had gone on the streets.) Making a debut on this opening night was Nijinsky's sister, Bronislava. Pavlova's first appearance of the season was as

Kitry in *Don Quixote*; Preobrajenskaya backed her up, in the two cameo roles, and both dancers had a great success. On September 21 they were both in *Raymonda*, and three days later Karsavina made her first appearance as a full-fledged ballerina in nothing less than *Swan Lake*. Four nights after this event, Pavlova got another chance to try to find the measure of Aurora in *The Sleeping Beauty*. Now it was noticed that "she contributed some interesting new interpretations in the miming parts of this role," according to the Yearbook. Trefilova had not been seen up to this point in the season because of a leg injury, but on October 5 her performance in *La Fille Mal Gardée* was wildly applauded, and the same enthusiasm was afforded Sedova in the lead in *Paquita* three nights later. The management obviously no longer felt any pressure to keep ballets as the exclusive domains of single ballerinas: on October 12 all the ladies were in *The Little Red Flower*; Pavlova had *Daughter of the Pharaoh* a week later; and then Karsavina was given the lead in *Le Corsaire*, and won the audience's firm approval. According to the *New Times*, "Her debut in this role was extremely successful, both for its tender and graceful rendering of the dances, and for the miming scenes, which were performed by her with great tact and liveliness of temperament." Trefilova's leg problem was recurring, and Preobrajenskaya had to replace her in *The Little Humpbacked Horse* on October 26. The night held other interest as well: in the words of the Yearbook, "The young dancer Nijinsky had an outstanding success with the astonishing power and lightness of his leaps, flights, entrechats, and assemblés."

The rest of Pavlova's roles for the 1908–09 season were in more traditional works. She made thirty-seven appearances in all, including three as Nikiya, her usual two as Giselle, two appearances each in *Les Saisons* (in the Bacchante role) and *The Little Red Flower*, three in *Paquita*, two in *Don Quixote*, two in *Daughter of the Pharaoh*, one in *The Sleeping Beauty*, and three as Diana in *Le Roi Candaule*. The first night of the revival of *Candaule* was allocated to the corps de ballet for its benefit night, by tradition the most glittering spectacle of the season, and one in which all the leading ballerinas were expected to take part. Kchessinskaya once again chose this occasion, December 14, to make her first appearance of the season; the only absentee was Trefilova, on the sick list again. Kchessinskaya, Preobrajenskaya, and Pavlova each had a great individual success that night, but the palm seemed to have gone to Karsavina, described by one critic as "a great classical dancer with a dazzling technique."

Kchessinskaya's rebuff to Diaghilev compounded the disaster of Grand Duke Vladimir's sudden death on February 4 (17 n.s.), 1909, for when she declined to lend her good offices to a wavering Imperial ministry, the promised subsidy for Diaghilev's new Paris season thus fell away. Diaghilev rushed off to lay the whole problem at Astruc's door. By the time the impresario had secured backing from his Jewish business friends, and Diaghilev

ABOVE Valentin Serov's *Chopiniana* sketch, used by Diaghilev for the poster announcing his 1909 Paris season.

BELOW In Alexandre Benois's costume, when the ballet was retitled *Les Sylphides*.

came to confirm arrangements with Pavlova, he found that she was already deeply involved in plans for her own tour through Germany, Austria, and Czechoslovakia. What was perhaps even worse, where he was experiencing so much trouble, she appeared to encounter no opposition at all. She again had the banner of the Imperial Ballet; she had Nicolas Legat as her partner; and, most importantly, she had well and truly raided the production storerooms. Her haul included her previous tour's full-length ballets as well as three acts of *Swan Lake*.

As business manager of Pavlova's previous tour, Edouard Fazer had established a position of trust with numerous foreign theatres and opera house managements, many of whom had experienced no previous dealings with artists from Russia, which was then considered to be a mysterious and unaccountable land—but for the new tour only Prague, Leipzig, and Berlin could guarantee a welcome; Dresden, Dusseldorf, Hamburg, and Vienna were untried. Vienna especially was a difficult testing ground; it had a heritage of its own as well as style and glamour, and to face it was an extremely brave undertaking.

But Diaghilev wanted Pavlova for his own brave venture, which would require her to be in Paris by the end of May and necessitate her canceling Vienna and curtailing Berlin. Under the circumstances, Pavlova made the right decision, opting to complete her scheduled tour and then go into Diaghilev's Paris season late. It was one thing to by-pass Berlin and its proven audiences, quite another to dodge the sophisticated and parochial Viennese theatre public—that would be a diplomatic blunder which could never be repaired. Both troupes, Pavlova's and Diaghilev's, faced critical and uncertain audiences; but in some ways Pavlova's was the more difficult task, since anyone arriving in Vienna trailing glory from Berlin was bound to start off with a distinct disadvantage, as rivalry between the two cities was almost absurd; and there was the added problem of a frigid political climate between Russia and Austria. Paris, on the other hand, had already shown itself to be open to conversion in matters of Russian art and artists. Diaghilev was left to settle casts without Pavlova for the first two weeks of his season. (The crucial factor in these moves was that Pavlova's group was traveling under the Tsar's banner, as the Imperial Russian Ballet. By comparison, what was going on in Paris was a semi-private venture, and Pavlova's first allegiance had to be to her own, official group.)

When Diaghilev and Astruc sat down in the restaurant in Paris and made their tentative programs, Diaghilev had written down "Giselle . . . 2 acts." It must have been an appealing thought to return the old Romantic ballet to the city of its origin with its greatest contemporary interpreter in the title role. But there would be no point in bringing the production simply to hold it back until the second part of the season, awaiting Pavlova's arrival; by then the whole venture would already have been won or lost, and a gloriously performed *Giselle* would make little difference. As it happened, the rights to any Imperial Theatres costumes and sets were withdrawn along with the subsidy; but even if Diaghilev had nurtured some initial hopes of taking the Maryinsky production of *Giselle* to Paris, they would have been dashed when he returned to Russia and discovered that Pavlova had prior claim on it for her own tour.

Still, there was a truly Romantic ballet for Paris: Fokine's Chopin ballet. For all his readiness to amaze once the curtain went up, Diaghilev knew that his advance publicity should lull Paris with a traditional vision. In Valentin Serov's studio, Diaghilev saw a large working sketch for a planned portrait of Pavlova in *Chopiniana*. The artist had elected to depict the ballerina in aerial movement, and for hours she had held difficult poses and made taxing jumps while he worked out the design. The sessions had become distinctly irksome to her, since they took place late at night after rehearsals and performances, but her professionalism and her respect for Serov kept her from rebelling, and he was able to make some exquisitely observed studies. The one Diaghilev chose was in charcoal and white chalk on a large stretcher of blue-stained linen; it had a simplicity of design, was clear and tender in profile, and caught the mood of Fokine's ballet, as well as showing Pavlova's characteristic absorption. Benois had designed the costume with little cap sleeves, but Serov showed off the set of Pavlova's head and neck by pulling the sleeves down off her shoulders. This drawing had already been purchased by Dr. Sergei Botkine, but he allowed Diaghilev to borrow it so that lithographers could reproduce it as a poster for the impending Russian Season of opera and ballet at the Théâtre du Châtelet. Ironically, by the time Pavlova set off for Germany, her image was already hovering over the streets of Paris.

ABOVE The original Bakst *Chopiniana* costume, 1908.

BELOW By 1910 it had acquired new wings and a higher cummerbund, and the skirt had been freed.

In Berlin, Pavlova received the by now customary acclaim, though one critic made extraordinarily ungallant remarks about her personal appearance, writing that although her name was printed in fat letters on the program, she was as thin as a skeleton, and her ugliness was off-putting. It was admitted that her actual dancing was scintillating, but because she lacked the *embonpoint* of cream-fed local girls, her skills could not really be enjoyed. Another critic found her to be a talented—if gaunt—Giselle and thought her colleagues to be equally scrawny.

After the performances, Pavlova would unwind by playing poker; she was something of a compulsive card player and liked the stakes to be worth the playing. Although far from brilliant (as usual, her emotions betrayed her), some of her fellows were worse; Legat had such a bad run at one point that Pavlova had to lend him a thousand roubles. Pavlova kept all her money and her jewelry in a small case during the tour, and miraculously it survived, though there was an alarum when she managed to leave the bag in a cab on the day she arrived in Berlin. Pavlova, aided by Legat and others, spent a night being driven around the city, vainly trying to recognize the original cabman. In the morning, exhausted and despondent, they made their way to the central police station to report the loss. The first person they saw when they entered the building was the cabman, sitting on a bench with the bag on his knees. (Years later, in an interview, Pavlova recalled the standoff between herself, with no large reward in her pocket, and the cabman, waiting for just that. "We were both

La Fille Mal Gardée:
ABOVE Berlin, 1909; (left) with Nicolas Legat.
BELOW Pavlova's Act One costume was soon modernized.

suspicous of one another, and I kept my eye on him, while he kept his eye on me. It was a sort of I-shan't-give-you-yours-till-you-give-me-mine, and in the end it came very near being an exhibition of let-go-and-grab—horribly undignified!")

About the only thing that Vienna seemed to share with Berlin was a delight in amply proportioned young ladies. As the critic for the *Illustriertes Wiener Extrablatt* put it, "Ladies of the ballet must be very, very pretty if one is to believe in them. With melancholy and gratitude I thought back to the unforgettable legs that march out when our opera ballet takes the field; to the blooming faces and pleasing figures that stir our belief."

The Russians had opened in Vienna with *Giselle*, followed by five divertissements, in one of which Pavlova and Ivan Kussov were one of five couples in the Panaderos from *Raymonda*. The same critic who had expressed unhappiness about Pavlova's build plainly detested *Giselle* and its music ("like the day before yesterday's soup, dispensed in driblets"), though he allowed that in it Pavlova had an opportunity to show "her magic talent, her grace and lightness, and the bravura of her toe dancing." The critic of the *Neues Wiener Tageblatt* agreed about the quality of Pavlova's dancing but was extremely bored by the ballet itself. (On the following evening he found *Swan Lake* less boring than *Giselle*, but more tasteless, and he considered it might just as easily have been composed by any ballet conductor as by Russia's leading composer.) The *Neue Freie Presse* also thought *Giselle* an unhappy choice, particularly in view of Adam's music, which was described as one-toned. But Pavlova's dancing saved the evening:

> Despite a certain resistance from the audience, the Petersburg guests created a considerable success, above all Miss Anna Pavlova. Her name has become famous so quickly that some skeptics were reluctant to agree with the general assessment, but her virtuoso technique, and an equilibrium that allows rapid shifts in her point of balance, her impressive mime, and her patent sincerity in her art, convinced, astonished, and finally aroused everyone. Her waltz in the first act, which she danced with the acrobatic Nicolas Legat; her shattering death scene in the finale; her gliding, floating, and rapid revolving on pointe in the ghost scene of the second act, appealed to the audience more and more, until the applause after the last pas de deux broke like a storm.

The writer went on to mention the divertissements that were given after *Giselle*, and then concluded, "Altogether an interesting evening for everyone who loves the art of classical dance, this odd, half-forgotten art that one scarcely remembers, apart from old, faded etchings, and that now Miss Anna Pavlova, ballerina of the Imperial Russian Ballet, brings alive again" —thus giving the lie to protestations about the excellence of the local ballet; certainly the audiences were in no doubt that they were seeing classical style and training far superior to their usual fare.

Among the divertissements presented on the second night following *Swan Lake* was Legat's *La Nuit*, to music of Rubinstein, which he and Pavlova danced to such effect that they were obliged to encore the entire number. Success of this sort was remarkable, given the fact that the medium was ballet and the

ABOVE Bakst's Act One *Giselle* costume, in Pavlova's early touring version. This was not a popular ballet in Germany in 1909.

BELOW *La Fille Mal Gardée* was better liked by the German audiences.

ABOVE With Legat in *Swan Lake*, photographed in Berlin, 1909.

BELOW In her Bakst *Swan Lake* costume. With her left hand, Pavlova supported herself by a post (later touched out) during the long exposure time.

execution Russian; but if newspaper readers in Vienna were aware that the Imperial Russian Ballet was performing in their city, this intelligence arose chiefly because the Hofoperntheater traditionally claimed first place in the review columns. Certainly anyone who skimmed through the reviews probably got the impression that the Russians had nothing to teach the Viennese. Pavlova tried to ignore this rubbish, and the enthusiastic reaction proved that audiences were either uncritical, predominantly female, or full of men who nursed a secret interest in slim ladies. In fact, the Russians were a huge box-office attraction. Even the most parochial of the critics were forced to concede that the audiences were responding to these Russian dancers with exceptional warmth. The critic of the *Illustriertes Wiener Extrablatt* went so far as to say that in the second-act adagio in *Swan Lake,* Pavlova carried the burden of the solo passage much better than did the violinist: "Miss Pavlova danced love and longing with a truly convincing bearing. Her dancing is without the usual pauses. Her body is in restless motion; the way in which she manages the transitions is distinctive of her mastery. A single flowing line accompanies the cantilena. With regard to Pavlova, it is possible to speak of an art of dissolving the inner being of the melody into movement." Such flashes of unguarded critical ardor kept disrupting the supercilious veneer of the reviews, but on the whole it seemed almost impossible that *Giselle* or *Swan Lake* could survive the critical mauling that was going on at this time. (See Appendix, p. 397.) The *Neue Freie Presse*, rather late in the day, decided to devote its lead article to the Tsar's ballet, and a long feature appeared on Saturday, May 29. (See Appendix, p. 398.) At last the average reader knew that something exceptional was happening in town. Such had been the clamor after *Swan Lake* that the opera directors felt impelled to offer the Russians one more performance. To do this they had to cancel the performance of *Elektra* scheduled for that Sunday. Pavlova acceded and offered *Paquita,* though she was cutting her schedule exceedingly close if she wished to have any sort of private rehearsal with the team in Paris.

By this time, Pavlova knew that Diaghilev's troupe had triumphed in Paris. She did not know, however, that their overnight success had attracted to the Théâtre du Châtelet a swarm of English agents searching for talent. London's extensive range of music halls was capable of absorbing an almost unlimited supply of new "acts," from Australian comedians to Russian dancers. The Danish ballerina Adeline Genée had already shown that pure ballet could hold its own in a mixed program. Her exquisitely crafted performances, full of demure wit and delicately mannered precision, had earned her a faithful and adoring public. She had the inestimable quality of true charm, and it won her a position that became, over the years, inviolable; but her loyalty was to the Empire Theatre, and the other managements fretted over their own lack of "toe dancers." When Genée decided to test her charms in America under the aegis of Florenz Ziegfeld, the Empire was without its petite star for the first time in over ten years, and there was an open field for any dance acts new to London. The Empire had the advantage of having a permanent ballet master—Genée's uncle, Alexandre—and it quickly established direct links with the Maryinsky directors, who allowed Lydia Kyaksht to go to London for a season during the summer of 1908. Kyaksht took with her Adolph Bolm (after Pavlova's tour), and she changed the transliteration of her name from Kyaksht to the more manageable Kyasht. Forty pounds a week for a month was a great lure for Miss Kyasht, and the public evidently thought her worth every penny of it. Encouraged by her reception, she requested permission from the Maryinsky directors for another London season in the summer of 1909. The Tsar signed her release, although this time she lost her Imperial Theatres stipend for a year. Once again Diaghilev had been penciling in a dancer for his Paris season just when she was aiming in another direction.

Across the Channel, Kyasht's friend and schoolmate Tamara Karsavina was becoming the object of particular attention as the result of her enormous success in Diaghilev's Russian Season. Among those inquiring at the stage door for her was Oswald Stoll, the managing director of the London Coliseum, whose seats outnumbered those of the Theatre Royal in Drury Lane, as well as of the Royal Opera House nearby. Stoll felt that the delightful Karsavina could help fill those seats—all twenty-nine hundred of them—with or without Nijinsky, who seemed at this point to be something of a forbidden fruit to the outside world. The key to Nijinsky was lodged with Diaghilev—near to his heart, it seemed—and though Stoll and others attempted to entice him, through Karsavina, they knew that they were really pursuing her alone. Although the ballerina received offers from as far afield as Australia, it was London that seems to have caught her interest—a combination, perhaps, of Stoll's mannerly charm, her friend Lydia's presence there, and her abiding love of Dickens, whose unfettered descriptive prose provided every educated Russian with a pungent image of England and its seething capital.

Even before Pavlova arrived in Paris, she must have seen the French newspapers and read of "Mlle Karsavina of the irresistible charm." She would certainly have spotted the copy of *Le Figaro* that mentioned her new young rival "whose subtle technique and marvelous sense of music are combined with expressive grace and poetic feeling and whose success in *L'Oiseau de Feu** stopped the show." Here was an unexpected challenge. Pavlova had seen the younger dancer encouraged by certain segments of the St. Petersburg audience, but she had not envisaged this popularity taking wing in Paris, which Pavlova had probably hoped would be another plum in her own basket. When Pavlova had left on her own tour that summer, she had known that Vera Karalli would precede her in Paris in *Le Pavillon d'Armide*, but Pavlova probably felt that the Moscow ballerina posed no great threat.

---

* Actually the Blue Bird pas de deux from *The Sleeping Beauty*, now part of the divertissement section known as *Le Festin*. Bakst's scarlet and yellow costume probably provoked the title.

ABOVE With Legat in *Swan Lake*, Berlin, 1909.

BELOW *Swan Lake*, Berlin, 1908 or 1909. The difficulty of achieving this flare photograph without support must have been great.

Studio portraits by Bert, Paris, 1909: (opposite) in costume for *Giselle*.
At this point Pavlova may still have been expecting to dance this ballet at the Opéra.

ABOVE Karsavina in the two versions of Benois's costume for the pas de trois in *Le Pavillon d'Armide:* (left) St. Petersburg, 1907, (right) Paris, 1909.

BELOW Studio portrait by Bert, in the costume Pavlova presumably wore in the pas de deux with Mordkin in *Le Festin.*

Pavlova could not know that Karalli would elope in Paris with the tenor Sobinov, precipitating Karsavina into the role and thus consolidating her reputation in a city that was already enamored of her as a result of her performance in the pas de trois in this same ballet and in *L'Oiseau de Feu.* Nijinsky and Karsavina were the toast of Parisian theatre-goers that spring.

Still, the press was predisposed toward Pavlova even before she arrived, and advance publicity items suggested that Diaghilev and Astruc continued to view her as the real figurehead of their enterprise; there had been preliminary "puff pieces" about Pavlova on May 28 and 29. Raoul Brévannes of *Le Figaro* was in the habit of attending closed rehearsals and then publishing "appreciations" of one or two of the principals on show. On May 27 he did half a column on Preobrajenskaya, who was due to appear at the Opéra, and his column on June 1 was devoted to Lipkovska (singing at the Châtelet) and Pavlova. It was in the middle of the front page and was a day before the *répétition générale* that would reveal Pavlova to a Paris audience for the first time.[*]

La Pavlova! This one is a glory. She is dark, tall, slender, her waist more supple than any other. There is a sacred fire burning within her. The energy and accuracy of her technique are a means and not an end; when she is inspired, her dancing becomes a masterpiece. Lightness is but one of her gifts; she also has *élévation* and *ballon,* further gifts in this field. But she has much more than these. She encompasses an extreme range of qualities, any one of which would proclaim her a star. . . .

At the end of his article, Brévannes picked up a nice touch that had appeared in an esoteric dance sheet:

But it is "The Balletomane" yet again which discloses the most apt and delicate compliment that has been paid to the celebrated artist: a balletomane from the upper gallery, from "Paradise," was leaving the Maryinsky one evening and delivered himself of this quatrain:

> *Everyone speaks of the ballet's decline*
> *Have they forgotten that Pavlova still dances?*
> *Only when she is away from the stage*
> *Does the ballet cease to exist.*

At the *répétition générale* for the third program change in Diaghilev's Russian Season of opera and ballet, every vantage point was occupied, and there was a feeling of barely suppressed excitement. After one act of Glinka's opera *Russlan and Ludmilla,* there was a break; then, as the orchestra completed Chopin's Prelude in A Major (Op. 28, no. 7) and began his Nocturne (Op. 32, no. 2), the curtain parted to reveal Fokine's wonderful grouping for *Les Sylphides* (as the revised *Chopiniana* was now titled). A sigh of sheer delight rose from the darkened

[*] Technically a rehearsal, the *répétition générale* was traditionally the evening on which the press attended, prior to the official opening night. Brévannes's article was published on June 1 (not June 5, as has been suggested), and his views must therefore have been based on sightings of Pavlova in St. Petersburg. Her extra performance in Vienna did not begin until 8 p.m. on Sunday, and the earliest train connection could have got her to Paris no earlier than the small hours of June 1.

auditorium. In a pearly blue light, the girls seemed to be hovering, motionless, in the midst of Benois's gothic glade. In their center stood a poetic-looking young man in a Byronic white shirt and black tunic. Two sylphs each claimed a shoulder on which to rest a blossom-wreathed head, and a third vision reclined gently at his feet. This rapt group formed a cameo of deep significance; it could be seen as the entablature of Diaghilev's Temple to the Dance. It was Fokine's child and they were Diaghilev's children: the loved, the wayward, and the loyal; for above the reclining figure of the blond-haired Alexandra Baldina stood Nijinsky, with Pavlova on his right and Karsavina on his left.

Pavlova, like everyone else, was exhilarated by the heady approval that enveloped them in Paris that spring. Fokine, watching her on stage as she marked out a role—she was dressed in a simple street outfit—thought she had never looked more elegant and spirited. Her arrival must have been a whirl. Even as she stepped off the train she was embroiled in new plans; a syndicate of the Paris press was striving to shape a gala to aid victims of the recent earthquake in the Midi region of France. Pavlova indicated her willingness to accept any plans made for this special evening, tentatively announced for June 26, at the Opéra. The Paris correspondent of *The Tatler* used the venture as an excuse to indulge in some fantastic gossip: "Isadora Duncan was asked to dance at the gala, but when she saw that La Pavlova was on the programme also, she utterly refused, on the grounds that Pavlova had copied her style of dancing and attitudes." The reporter had the grace to add that such an accusation was absurd.

For the remainder of the Paris season, Pavlova was scheduled only for the reworked version of *Egyptian Nights*, in which Veronika had been renamed Ta-Hor; the ballet itself had become *Cléopâtre*, and it followed *Les Sylphides* at the *générale*. "Interim," in *Le Gaulois*, had this to say:

> Mlle Rubinstein brings to the role of Cleopatra a sinuous elegance, and an understanding of the attitudes and quirky movements, that makes her remarkable. But Mlle Pavlova invests the role of Ta-Hor with something really unique. . . . She creates a miracle whereby we are able to understand word for word (which must need be spoken gesture by gesture) all that is going through the mind of the pathetic Ta-Hor, the priestess who would rival the queen.

Then, on June 8, *Le Figaro* announced: "La Pavlova enjoys such a triumph every time she dances at the Châtelet that policy has dictated that she be included in each one of its ballet programs. For this reason a supplementary showing of *Le Pavillon d'Armide* and *Le Festin* has been booked for Monday, June 14." So Pavlova took over her original role in *Le Pavillon d'Armide*. She was by now indelibly associated with the part, despite the fact that it was not one of her favorites, being too confined and episodic, and she viewed appearances in it as more of a duty than a pleasure. Nevertheless, the performances were always warmly applauded. When the ballet had first been presented in St. Petersburg, there were comments in the press that foreign audiences would never tolerate Benois's "garish" costumes, and these were indeed changed for Paris; but the results represented moderation

ABOVE As Ta-Hor in *Cléopâtre*, with Fokine as Amoun.

BELOW With Koslov as the Vicomte in *Le Pavillon d'Armide*. Benois made unhappy revisions to the ballerina's costume for the Paris season. (Compare with the original costume on p. 70.)

89

Stravinsky, Diaghilev, Bakst, and Nijinsky, Paris, 1909.

rather than any fresh thinking, and the ballerina's costume in particular lost some of its joyous opulence. Nijinsky, by contrast, took on ermine trims, and also a glittering choker to show off the beautiful column of his neck. In his role of a favored slave he attracted the audience's attention out of all proportion to his time on the stage, yet Robert Brussel's review in *Le Figaro* on June 9 managed to ignore him:

> We admired *Le Pavillon d'Armide* and *Le Festin*. Both ballets always receive their just and considerable success. Yesterday we acclaimed the prodigious technique, the supple and undulating grace of Mme Pavlova, the incomparable wit and charm of Mme Karsavina, the scintillating talent of the corps de ballet. In addition we also admired the invention, the taste, and finally the subtle art of Michel Fokine, who understands how to give life to his dances and groupings.

During this second week in June some extraordinary plans seem to have been brewing behind the scenes. On June 11 *Le Figaro* printed the following notice: "On June 19 Messrs Messager and Broussan present once more the great Russian artists. *Giselle*, in two scenes, by Adolphe Adam, will be danced by Mme Pavlova, *danseuse étoile*; M. Nijinsky, *premier danseur*; Mmes Karsavina and Fedorova, *premières danseuses*, and the entire corps de ballet."* It would seem, then, that the ambition of Diaghilev and Astruc to show Paris *Giselle* had not died so readily. Of course, they had no production of the ballet; either the Opéra would

have had to unearth some of its old scenery, or Pavlova's touring production could have been diverted (it was probably still in the packing cases after Vienna). But it was wildly ambitious thinking with only ten days to go, and in practical terms it must very soon have proved impossible; for one thing, the prince in *Giselle* was an untried role for Nijinsky. And at that moment, in the excitement of the adulation of Paris society, did he really want to partner Pavlova in her greatest role? Was that to be the climax of his Paris season? The only person who could be assured of personal success in the ballet was Pavlova.

For whatever reason, the plan foundered. Fate was about to deal bad cards to Nijinsky, but that had not happened by the time the decision about *Giselle* must have been reached. If Nijinsky's views about his own importance (not to mention those of Karsavina, who was rapidly acquiring a taste for being treated as a star) carried weight with Diaghilev, it would be understandable but no less annoying to Pavlova; she was, after all, an established and widely acclaimed ballerina who deserved at least one chance to show her real range. But suggestions that Pavlova was jealous of Nijinsky and the attention paid him are simply not borne out by factual evidence. More to the point, Nijinsky must have been amazed at the way Pavlova could arrive in town late and still establish dominance.

The extra gala evening by the Russians went ahead at the Opéra, but *Boris Godunov* was paired not with *Giselle*, but with *Les Sylphides* followed by the section of divertissements known as *Le Festin*. Nijinsky was suffering from a severe sore throat, which would prove to be typhoid fever; in *Les Sylphides* he had to be replaced by Theodore Koslov. For this last night at which the public could see and applaud the Russian Ballet as an entity, it must have been a problem deciding how to fit Pavlova into *Le Festin*. Karsavina would not have wished to relinquish *L'Oiseau de Feu* (and if she had, she would have required something else), and Fokine may not have wanted to be seen in a bravura role. An obvious solution would have been to have Nijinsky partner Karsavina *and* Pavlova. He may well have been practicing with Pavlova, for an article in *Le Figaro* on June 21 was suggesting, with innocent hope, that the earthquake gala at the end of the week would reveal "Mme Pavlova et Nijinsky dans un divertissement russe." But it was only wishful thinking, and the contretemps threw forward the one obvious alternative—Pavlova and Mordkin. Though it was almost five years since they had danced together, there was little problem in putting together a pas de deux from Gorsky's *Daughter of the Pharaoh*, and Pavlova went to the boulevard des Capucines to have more photographs taken by Bert. Karsavina ended up dancing with George Rosai.

At a party after the performance, it was announced that Pavlova, Karsavina, Nijinsky, Fokine, and Sergei Grigoriev (as régisseur) had been awarded the Palme Académique.

---

* Messager and Broussan were Paris Opéra directors. The term "once more" means over and above the scheduled season at the Châtelet, which was to end on June 18, while the absence of a fourth ballerina suggests that Karsavina and Fedorova were to dance Moyna and Zulme, leaving the role of Myrtha still to be cast. When she was interviewed in St. Petersburg later in the year, Pavlova said that she had been willing to dance *Giselle* with a minimum of scenery, but that Diaghilev had been "afraid." He may have used the scenery problem as an excuse to mask a revolt by Nijinsky and Karsavina; he could hardly have cast the ballet without them.

It is unlikely that Diaghilev risked raising Nijinsky's temperature by reading him the article in the following morning's *Le Figaro*. It spoke of the forthcoming gala in aid of the earthquake victims, and after discussing the proposed operatic excerpts, it went on to say: "The choreographic art will also be acclaimed in the person of its most luminous star, Mme Pavlova. We do not know whether she will be dancing with Nijinsky. It hardly matters. We do know that she will be all grace, lightness, and charm—a dream." This Press Syndicate gala did not involve Diaghilev, though several of his artists were asked to donate their services. In addition, Kchessinskaya was in town* and eager to join in this charity event—not unreasonably, since she had a villa in the south of France. Any potential battle over having Nijinsky as a partner was neatly eliminated by the typhoid bacillus, so Kchessinskaya summoned Nicolas Legat, who had already danced with her at the Opéra, after Pavlova's tour had ended. Karsavina was off to London, taking with her a group that included both Koslov brothers. However, Mikhail Mordkin was still in town—principally because he was head-over-heels in love with Pavlova, who appeared to return the sentiment. This swiftly blossoming romance solved the problem of a partner for Pavlova, but there remained the matter of the actual dances. As is often the case with charity galas of this nature, the exact content was not discussed in the press, and reviews spoke in the broadest generalizations. In the actual program, the main dance section was listed under an all-embracing heading, "Russian Dances," and though Alexandra Vassilieva and Mikhail Alexandrov were to dance a mazurka, there was nothing obviously "national" about the other two items: Kchessinskaya and Legat, and Pavlova and Mordkin, were merely listed for "pas de deux." The overall title for this section of the program seems to have created the impression that Pavlova and Mordkin did a character dance; yet their success was out of all proportion to that which could be achieved in stately, cumbersome robes and heeled shoes. Paris had seen all that before. An interview with Mordkin suggests that it was, rather, an exciting bacchanalian dance that he and Pavlova performed that evening; he said that he would never forget the success they had had that night at the Opéra, when "in the Bacchanale, Pavlova was aflame. . . ." One review mentioned Pavlova and Kchessinskaya, and spoke of "the poetry of the one and the prestigious virtuosity of the other." "*Poésie*" would be a strange word to pick for a character dance. Pavlova's *Bacchanale,* danced to the "Autumn" music from Glazunov's *The Seasons,* is, with her *Swan,* indelibly associated with the world's image of this ballerina, and its exact origins have always been clouded and confused. When it was first done in London it was credited to Mordkin—but only so long as he was in it. Dandré, in his book on Pavlova published shortly after her death, attributes the choreography to Fokine, and this seems reasonable; at this stage he

In her *Giselle* costume, photographed by Bert.

certainly owed Pavlova his support, since she had been his ally in his battles with the Maryinsky directorate.**

Fokine interpolated the Glazunov "Autumn" music from *The Seasons* into his reworking of *Egyptian Nights* for Diaghilev's 1909 Paris season, and he composed a dance for Vera Fokina and Anna Fedorova that was described in the press after the *répétition générale* as "sheer voluptuousness." In his memoirs, Fokine recalled the creation of this scene, in one short rehearsal, and noted its importance to his career. For the Finale, they all "ended by crashing down to the floor in violent ecstasy." This end to the bacchanale scene (not the end of the ballet itself) involved youths, fauns, and bacchantes, who must have rushed on stage after the two girls finished their cavortings. In the same ballet, Karsavina and Nijinsky ran on beneath a fluttering veil to the music of the Turkish Dance from *Russlan and Ludmilla*. In the *Bacchanale* as danced by Pavlova and Mordkin, the two ran on stage under a veil and, amid much rushing about, occasionally froze in sensual poses during an adagio section. Then, after a torrid chase, it ended with Pavlova falling to the ground in a state of ecstatic exhaustion.

Pavlova must have considered that she would have only a few minutes in which to make her effect on the stage of the Opéra, and that it would have to be in something sensational. At the same time, it would need to be confined to music for which orchestral parts were readily available. If Kchessinskaya was

* The Tsar's two senior ballerinas, whom Diaghilev had excluded from his plans, had contrived to get engagements as guest artists at the Paris Opéra at the same time that his troupe was appearing at the Châtelet: Kchessinskaya in *Coppélia* on June 5, and Preobrajenskaya in *Javotte* two nights later. Both were received warmly.

** That autumn, when Fokine wanted to put the Glazunov bacchanale into the Maryinsky production of *Egyptian Nights,* it seems that Pavlova was against it. Fokine, grumbling to a reporter, said, "Madame Pavlova has her own bacchanale; she should not worry if others have one also." If she had her own bacchanale, where had she danced it?

bringing in Legat, it would not be difficult to guess that they would do a classical pas de deux. Vassilieva and Alexandrov were strictly character dancers. What was left? It would be natural to think of the bacchanale scene from *Cléopâtre*, which had created such a sensation; and certainly Fokine, with his usual quickness, would be able to reshape something to the same music, using some of the elements from the existing dances.

On the night of the gala, some jockeying was going on backstage. Kchessinskaya was adamant about appearing last; in her memoirs she tells us that word came through that the costumes for Pavlova and Mordkin were not ready and that she and Legat were asked to go on first. Kchessinskaya refused, giving as her reason that such an alteration would be incorrect procedure; she was sufficiently ready herself to note that the costumes for the other pair seemed perfectly in order when they duly went out first. She does not mention the reception afforded the dancing of Pavlova and Mordkin, so one can only reconstruct what the audience must have seen that night. After a static singing duo, the orchestra suddenly launched into Glazunov's thumping piece, and on swept a glorious pair, she so petite and lissome, he well formed and virile, accentuating further her femininity and frailness. They let their billowing veil drop, threw rose garlands at one another, ducked and twisted with almost animal vigor, and even went into kissing clinches. Mordkin was wildly extroverted and untrammeled, and his sheer physicality brought out the vamp in Pavlova. Together they struck gold in this autumn bacchanal, which proved itself a display of finely tuned eroticism.

In the audience that evening was Otto Kahn, chairman of New York's Metropolitan Opera. Gatti-Casazza, the general manager, had been present at the opening of the Russian Season at the Châtelet by special invitation of Astruc, but he was deeply wary of Diaghilev and had remained strangely silent. Kahn, as chairman, did not have Gatti-Casazza's fears that Diaghilev might, given half a chance, supplant him in New York; he saw the effect that Pavlova and Mordkin had on the audience, and he acted promptly, extending to the pair an offer to dance at the Metropolitan. (There had been concern about the turgid state of opera patronage.) As it happened, Kahn found himself in competition with a representative of the English agent Daniel Mayer.

The American offer was exciting, and Pavlova had no wish to forfeit such an opportunity, but she was equally eager to appear in London. After her late start in the season she had been left listening to other dancers' plans, and watching a general exodus from the Gare du Nord at the end of the season. It must have seemed intolerable to Pavlova, in the light of her 1907 visit to London, that Kyasht, and now Karsavina, had beaten her there. Astruc observed Pavlova's restless curiosity toward London and tried to help. With Mayer's representative there evolved a crosshatching of plans: Pavlova would persuade Mordkin (who hardly needed persuading) to accompany her to London, where, for a guaranteed sum, Pavlova would dance privately for one of Astruc's rich contacts. Following this (and here Mayer had a trump

card), the Countess of Londesborough would be pleased to present Pavlova and her partner as the special entertainment during a soirée in her town house. Furthermore, the likelihood was that her guests of honor would be none other than King Edward and Queen Alexandra. Of course nothing more than this could be stated; it would have been the height of impropriety to use the Sovereign's name in any capacity relating to a business arrangement, just as etiquette forbade a king making overt invitations on behalf of his hostess. On the other hand, discreet inquiries could be made as to whether Their Majesties would like to see two of their nephew the Tsar's finest dancers. Nothing could have been better calculated to woo Pavlova from her perch, and with the compliant Mordkin she swooped across the Channel. There was just over three weeks to fill before the Londesborough party. What of the other engagement?

Conclusive evidence for the identity of the pioneering hostess arises only in the reports of a 1911 court case. On that evidence the friend of Astruc was Mrs. Brown Potter. The *Times* reporter was the only one who wrote down "Mrs. Potter Palmer." Confusion was perhaps inevitable. Both ladies were American, both had great wealth, and both set enormous store by their standing in London society. But there the similarity ended. Bertha Potter Palmer was a Chicago matron renowned for the way she had hounded vice from the World's Fair in 1893. If she was known as "the Mrs. Astor of the Middle West," then Cora Brown Potter was perhaps New Orleans's answer to Lillie Langtry. Having detached herself from Mr. Brown Potter—though not from his money—she pursued her career as an actress, cutting a swathe through many capitals. She even managed London's Savoy Theatre for a spell, and appeared with Beerbohm Tree in a play at Windsor Castle. It was Bertha from Chicago, with her seven-strand pearl necklace and her towering silver hair, who gave a party on July 12, at which the highlight was a display by Russian Imperial dancers—none other than Karsavina and her friends from the Coliseum. The imagination boggles at Cora scheming to top *that*, but it seems she may have done so.

Part of the appeal of Daniel Mayer's agency lay in Mayer's personal entrée to the good offices of Alfred Butt, who controlled the immensely popular Palace Theatre. Mayer's ambition was to get Pavlova and Mordkin top billing at the Palace for a season beginning the following spring, immediately following the close of the Imperial Theatres' season. For two years Butt had been presenting Maud Allan's spectacularly provocative Salome, but now he was lacking a good dancing act: Maud had been Butt's mistress, but she left him for the immensely rich Duke of Westminster, whose charms must have exceeded the phenomenal £500 weekly salary she was drawing from Alfred. Mayer and Butt argued about the worthiness of Pavlova and Mordkin as an alternative to Maud Allan, and since no contract was signed prior to Lady Londesborough's party on July 19, it seems likely that Butt was waiting to observe their true effect for himself; it is reasonable to suppose that he had angled an invitation to the soirée. As a background to all this, Edouard Fazer seems to have been trying to set up some plan for Pavlova to head another touring group, with London as the objective; we know that Pavlova addressed a letter around this time to "Cher Edouard," and in it she (or Dandré) mounted a convincing argument against trying to present a complete Russian ballet ensemble within the framework of English music hall.* By this stage she must have been aware that she could pick up as much money as a "star turn" as she could leading a troublesome company.

The Londesborough party was the real turning point. The countess had arranged for a low platform to be constructed at one end of the ballroom in St. Dunstan's Lodge; this was to act as a stage. Distinguished guests arriving at this corner of Regent's Park were dined lavishly, and then, after a suitable interval, they were conducted to the seating arranged in the body of the ballroom, where an orchestral group was ready to play. We can let Pavlova herself pick up the story, for she gave an interview to the *Daily Mail* the following day:

> "Well—I danced first with M. Mordkin to a valse and two mazurkas by Chopin. I wore an exact replica of the costume which in the 'Thirties Taglioni, the great Italian ballerina, wore in Paris and London. It has delicate pastel shades, which harmonise exquisitely with the tender and somewhat morbid music of the Polish composer. The second number was a dance of mine to 'La Nuit' of Rubinstein. In this I appeared in flowing greyish-blue garments, holding white lilies. A pale mauve light played on me.**
>
> "The King and Queen seemed eagerly to appreciate the charm of that dance, for they applauded with much enthusiasm. After dances to an adagio, and variations [the *Pharaoh* pas de deux from the first Opéra gala], M. Mordkin and I appeared in Russian dances. Naturally I wore one of our old Russian garbs—a sarafan of white and gold tissue and the classical *kokoshnik*. . . . These dances seemed to carry everyone away, especially that which is performed to Alabieff's famous 'Nightingale' tune."

Pavlova had had three weeks to sort out this costume, as well as the choreography. (There was no way she would have risked dancing an erotic bacchanale within a few feet of foreign royalty; she was representing *Russia*.)

The royal couple led enthusiastic applause after this last number, and as the dancers took their bows Lady Londesborough came forward and told Pavlova that the King and Queen would like to meet her. In her cumbersome costume, Pavlova hesitated on the edge of the platform, uncertain as to how to negotiate the step; the King noticed her predicament and with natural simplicity immediately stepped forward to help her down. At that moment England utterly charmed her. This was the informal style of royalty that she had grown to respect from childhood, and it gave her a sudden positive view for any future dealings in the city. Pavlova continued:

> "Just as Their Majesties were leaving, Cassano's band struck up 'Paraguay,' a South American tune to which I have danced hundreds of times. The Queen turned. 'I know this air so well,' she

Maud Allan

exclaimed, and I was asked to give this encore. Quickly I tied a red 'kerchief round my head, for local colour's sake—'Paraguay' being really a Spanish dance—and I did my best, I at once forgot my fatigue; and although I had been performing for over one hour I think I danced better than I ever did before."

By the following day, July 20, Mayer had contracts ready to present, and he took them to the Grosvenor Hotel in Victoria; when he arrived he found Victor Dandré was present and acting as interpreter, though his English was not perfect. Pavlova was eager to have Mordkin as her partner—she enjoyed his full-blooded Moscow approach—but she definitely saw herself as the motivating force in the new arrangement. Mordkin was just beginning to appreciate his own ability to please an audience (which was in contrast to Nijinsky's mysterious insinuation on the stage), though he knew that he could not achieve a success on his own. He agreed to be engaged for £80 a week, while Pavlova was to get five times as much; but from her £400 she was required to pay for any soloists or corps de ballet dancers she might wish to engage for the program. Mayer agreed to undertake to secure private engagements for the two dancers as a supplement to the basic income, and these special engagements would be very highly paid: 300 to 400 guineas was the suggested range. For all this work, Mayer was to receive 10 percent as agent and sole representative in England for the two dancers. The authority was for five years. Dandré explained the details of the contract to Mordkin, whose English was nonexistent.

---

* It is a supposition that the "Edouard" in question was Fazer. In 1956 the Paris Opéra Bibliothèque had the letter catalogued as being to Edward Kagan.
**Presumably this was a free adaptation of Legat's piece, originally a pas de deux.

Studio portrait by Bert, Paris, 1909.

As they had already realized, there was no chance of commencing engagements before the spring of 1910, since Mordkin had not secured a release from his duties in Moscow, and Pavlova had commitments at the Maryinsky: that autumn she would be accorded a benefit night to honor her ten years of service on the Imperial stage. She was twenty-eight years old; in seven years she would be faced with compulsory retirement, according to the rules of the Tsar's theatres.

With the outline of the contract with Butt established, Pavlova was free to return to St. Petersburg. She got no farther than Paris when she encountered Diaghilev, and immediately he was putting fresh plans before her. Unbeknown to Pavlova, Diaghilev and Astruc had been engaged in efforts to bring the Russian dancers back to Paris for a return engagement the following year. Astruc's letters had bombarded Diaghilev after the Paris season ended: who should dance what, when, and how much it might cost. Diaghilev was careful to conceal from Pavlova his desperate financial predicament, laying the blame for any imprecision on forces beyond his control. (Though it was an artistic success, the Paris season had ended in a deficit, and Astruc had instituted bankruptcy proceedings against Diaghilev.) Undeterred, Diaghilev wanted to take the ballet to London in 1910, and though he had yet to secure a suitable theatre, in the interim he could state—with complete assurance—that he had decided to sign a contract with the directors of the Paris Opéra for fifteen performances to be given the following spring. He asked Pavlova to be available from May 15 to June 15. She was eager to oblige, and if she gave any thought at all to the Palace contract, it must have been only that she would have to charm Butt into delaying her first public appearance in London.

Mordkin had gone back to Moscow, and no sooner had Pavlova and Dandré arrived in St. Petersburg than a series of telegrams fluttered after them from Diaghilev. Things were hotting up. Diaghilev told Pavlova that he had signed a contract with the Theatre Royal, Drury Lane, and that he would give a Russian Season in London from June 15 to August 1 under the patronage of the Grand Duchess Vladimir (Maria Pavlovna), whose London representative would be Lady de Grey (Marchioness of Ripon, after the death of her father-in-law in 1909). Next came the crunch: Diaghilev wanted Pavlova to renounce the Palace agreement altogether and dance for him throughout the Drury Lane season. Questioning none of this, Pavlova merely set about finding a way to accommodate these latest plans. The most immediate problem was that the Palace contracts had already arrived, duly signed by Butt; Mordkin's had been forwarded to him in Moscow. Pavlova replied to Diaghilev that she felt that she was unable to break the contract as such, but she agreed in principle to begin the season at Drury Lane before going over to the Palace. Dandré then penned a letter to Daniel Mayer, writing as from Pavlova (and indeed, she did sign and date the letter, on August 15). Having outlined the recent series of events, Dandré came up with a persuasive argument for her:

> I think that my debut in London in proper ballets with a troupe of one hundred artists from the Imperial Theatres would make an excellent advertisement not only for me but also for the Palace. In view of this I beg you to obtain from Mr. Butt the consent to begin my performances at the Palace the first of July, certainly in the case of Mr. Diaghilev coming with the Ballet to London. I beg of you please let me know of Mr. Butt's reply by telegram addressed to Mr. Dandré. . . .

Pavlova was not living at Dandré's address; she was probably about to go off to Ligovo with her mother for a holiday.

Although Pavlova at this stage wanted Diaghilev quite as much as he wanted her, confidence in him must have been severely shaken when she found out that his offers had been baseless. Diaghilev, in the event, forfeited his £500 deposit on Drury Lane (or rather, he forfeited his right to avoid ultimate settlement for the sum, as he had had no £500 when he took the option), and it was not long before word was all over St. Petersburg. Pavlova had been offered almost as big a sum for each week's work for Alfred Butt, and already she had got off on the wrong foot by trying to make him bend to Diaghilev's whims—an annoying situation, quite apart from her disappointment in knowing that her London debut would not, after all, take place in the favorable circumstances of a Diaghilev presentation.*

Pavlova opened the 1909–10 Maryinsky season dancing Aurora in *The Sleeping Beauty*. Perhaps as a result of the press reports from Paris, Karsavina's repertoire was extensive at the beginning of the season: all of *Swan Lake*, a debut as Raymonda, and then the lead in *Le Corsaire* at the end of the month. Pavlova had *Paquita* and *Don Quixote*:

> Mme Pavlova dances with ever-increasing perfection; her talent shines more brightly with every season. Yesterday's *Don Quixote* was an unmitigated triumph for this incomparable artist. One should overlook a few slight faults (an unnatural and ungainly port de bras in the arabesques), so full of inexpressible charm is the character she creates of a young and passionate Spanish girl, such is the nobility and perfection of her dancing in the last act, particularly the pas de deux with Legat, the variations from Ivanov's ballet *Bestalka*, and those to the music of Garnier.

The *New Times* thought that Pavlova and Karsavina were having to bear the entire repertoire on their shoulders because the other artists had not yet finished their vacations. On October 4 Preobrajenskaya returned (she had been dancing in Dresden, not prolonging her vacation). Now she danced the Tsar Maiden in *The Little Humpbacked Horse,* and then danced a string of big roles in quick succession, including *Swan Lake, La Fille Mal Gardée,* and *The Sleeping Beauty.* The enthusiasm over Preobrajenskaya's return rather overshadowed Pavlova's debut in the leading role of Nisia in *Le Roi Candaule* on October 11. Even with the added interest of having Sedova and Nijinsky dancing together, the ballet, sprawling through an entire evening, still made no impression on its audience—despite a mad scene for Nisia, when she is confronted by the ghost of her husband, the King of Lydia. By the time of its second scheduled appearance, in February, Pavlova was no longer in the country. She had concluded arrangements with Otto Kahn, and she and Mordkin had been given permission to leave the season early: the Tsar had been told flattering things about Pavlova's exploits abroad.

Pavlova's benefit for ten years of service to the Imperial Theatres took place on November 25, and she chose to perform *La Bayadère.* The *New Times* reported on the evening:

> Yesterday at the Maryinsky the whole theatre world of St. Petersburg celebrated the ten-year period of ballerina A. P. Pavlova's artistic activities. *La Bayadère*, Minkus's old ballet, was presented, and the public, always enthusiastic about the ballerina in this, her best role, was naturally particularly demonstrative.

---

*The collapse of Diaghilev's 1910 London season is generally attributed to the death of King Edward, but this excuse is spurious; theatre in London continued without a tremor. One can assume that finance was the deciding factor.

After the tableau of the Kingdom of the Shades, the scene was transformed into a flower garden. It seemed as if we were no longer in St. Petersburg but in the eternally benign Riviera. The public had subscribed to an enormous 27-carat solitaire, which adorned Pavlova's head like a star. She also received samples of the artistic work of L. S. Bakst, together with the text of a speech by Mr. Andreievsky, two elegant vases, flowers of every kind, a wreath with the inscription "To a Divine Talent," and even the skin of a huge brown bear.

Although Preobrajenskaya was still at the height of her popularity, she was told that her farewell benefit night was to take place on November 29—and this despite the fact that, like Kchessinskaya, she had the talent and the box-office appeal to withstand compulsory retirement. Legat revived *The Talisman* for her, with new scenery and costumes, and even a new orchestration by Drigo. As a result of this extensive face-lift, the ballet struck the audience as a genuine novelty. But for some reason, the expensive new production, billed for its second performance on December 20, was suddenly canceled, and Pavlova had to dance *La Bayadère* in its place.

Events of considerable significance were taking place in December 1909, and the reverberations would affect the whole course of ballet in this century. At the traditional corps de ballet benefit on December 13, Kchessinskaya made her customary first appearance of the season, dancing as the Sugar Plum Fairy in *The Nutcracker.* Trefilova was back after a long absence, and Pavlova naturally graced the occasion too; she first did the Spanish dance in *Nutcracker,* and then appeared in the divertissements that concluded the evening. Of these, the *New Times* reported: "Once again there flew onto the stage Madame Pavlova with Nijinsky, but the music and presentation of this number was of no interest. [This seems to have been Legat's arrangement of Asafiev's *Papillon.*] Pavlova, who also has not a few admirers, exchanged greetings with them, charmingly copying Madame Duncan, and the public responded to this joke with a storm of applause." It was evident that news of Duncan's outburst in Paris had got back to St. Petersburg.

Apart from demonstrating Pavlova's sense of humor, the event indicates that she was not jealous of Nijinsky, as some have believed. Diaghilev must have been eager to see how the two would work together—Nijinsky could have found a way out of it, if he had been prompted; in fact (as subsequent evidence will show), it was the trial run for big plans involving Pavlova and Nijinsky as a partnership. Pavlova appears to have been eminently satisfied with the experiment: within forty-eight hours she signed a contract with Diaghilev! This contract, dated December 15, obtained for Diaghilev her exclusive services for the period June 12 to July 25, 1910. Pavlova signed it as an Artist of the Imperial Theatres. She was to be paid 15,000 francs—not a fortune in view of Butt's offer, but not unreasonable. (In the spring of 1909 the payments for the Paris season had been 2,500 francs to Nijinsky, and 55,000 francs to Chaliapin, the undisputed "name.") Had the archives of London's Palace Theatre not been destroyed in the Second World War, we might have been able to trace the feelings of Alfred Butt at this juncture, but we must assume that, by degrees, he was being maneuvered into a postponement of Pavlova's debut at the Palace. He was probably grateful for any small mercies, knowing that the Coliseum would again be offering the charms of Karsavina. Her willingness to give London first call on her services during her free spells from the Maryinsky seems to have annoyed Diaghilev considerably, and in view of her subsequent importance to Diaghilev's enterprise, it is remarkable the extent to which she does not feature in the major plans of this time. Paris certainly had an affection for her, and Astruc saw her as one of the draws in any further season there; but as far as Diaghilev was concerned, the cornerstone of his edifice was to be the partnership of Pavlova and Nijinsky.

Events moved on apace. Diaghilev was juggling a variety of imponderables, not least a total absence of finance to underpin the offering of contracts, and Astruc in Paris was moving ahead independently. It was Diaghilev who had the problem of keeping Pavlova happy; in his initial discussions he had wanted her for a minimum of fifteen performances; the enticement was to be a new role, devised for her by her favored Fokine. The twenty-seven-year-old Igor Stravinsky, who had already been entrusted with the orchestration of some of the Chopin pieces that went into *Les Sylphides,* had been offered the commission for the new work after a false start with Liadov, who took weeks just to buy the ruled music paper. The theme for the ballet was an amalgam of old Russian folk tales held loosely on the framework of a legend concerning a mysterious Firebird possessed of supernatural powers. Everyone in Diaghilev's immediate circle assumed that Pavlova would be the Firebird; with the faintly exotic, withdrawn, fey side to her character, she seemed ideal.

Pavlova did listen to a piano transcription of the composition, but she could make nothing of it at all; to her ears it seemed very ugly and modern, and indeed, to someone not trained to envisage the color of a full orchestral score, the piano rendering must have sounded bizarre. The Paris dates were still hopelessly fluid, and the whole enterprise must have looked like quicksand viewed from the early days of 1910. Diaghilev's efforts at brick making seemed to lack clay as well as straw, though Pavlova must have realized that her own talents could provide the necessary binding ingredient. But for what? Underpinning performances by Nijinsky? Or the other "genius," Stravinsky, whose reputation had yet to be established? Within the ranks of the Maryinsky there were already signs of "cutting down" a ballerina who thought to display her independence by traveling abroad. The *Petersburg Gazette* thought there was something "artificial" about Pavlova's current performances. How quickly one could be tainted! Coupled with their snide hints in November that she was a legitimate ballerina of illegitimate background, this must have been enough to set her against the whole suffocating structure that came between her and her art.

When Pavlova left St. Petersburg in mid-January, she probably did not realize the extent to which she was still seen by Diaghilev as a concomitant of his own plans. Although Karsavina was being used at the Maryinsky as a replacement for Pavlova, the former's name did not figure in the forefront of the correspondence shuttling between Diaghilev and Astruc at this time; everything seems to point to the conclusion that they both still saw Pavlova as the obvious partner to Nijinsky. In fact, she is so paired in the draft of a letter sent from Robert Brussel, acting as Astruc's envoy, to Diaghilev, then in Paris, dated January 24, in which Brussel discusses a fundraising dinner at which Diaghilev planned for Pavlova and Nijinsky to be the attraction.*

It seems extraordinary that Diaghilev was talking of presenting Pavlova with Nijinsky the following month (the dinner was to be on February 27) when Astruc's office already knew that Pavlova would be in America. But we know that Diaghilev and Astruc were working independently on many matters. Diaghilev set great faith by his own powers of persuasion, but he must have taken the hint when Pavlova complained to St. Petersburg reporters that she had not been given a chance to show her full range in Paris. Despite Nijinsky's last-minute illness, she seems to have viewed the abrupt cancellation of *Giselle* as a conspiracy, and she was clearly not going to leave herself open to a repeat of the situation. She went ahead with her American plans. She had by then received her official leave of absence from the Maryinsky. For some reason, they saw this as a lengthy affair, and the Yearbook reviewing the 1910–11 season noted that "Karsavina's talent burgeoned, a fact greatly assisted by the fortuitous circumstance of Pavlova's taking a two-years' leave of absence to tour America—to the sorrow of her numerous admirers." (The Yearbook was commenting retrospectively. By the time they wrote their editorial they must have got wind of fresh plans.)

Karsavina seems to have been unaware that Pavlova's was the name still being touted as the obvious partner to Nijinsky—which was just as well, for she was soon to be seen by Diaghilev as a necessary replacement cog in his machinery. By February he knew he had to secure her services for his next venture, and all his charm and persuasion might have been met with some suspicion if she had known a little more of his real ambitions. Fokine was another cog. Ironically, *Egyptian Nights* was back in the Christmas repertory at the Maryinsky, with the original score and no outward sign that it had been to Paris in the guise of *Cléopâtre.* If the Maryinsky management felt threatened at this point, they were careful not to show it.

The steamship *Augusta Victoria* sailed from Southampton in early February 1910, with Pavlova and Mordkin among the first-class passengers. Mordkin found the whole experience to his liking, particularly as he was made much of by the captain and the trophy-hunting socialites. His partner did not occlude his limelight; she was seasick for much of the time and hardly left her

---

* Nijinska's memoirs tell us that Pavlova and Nijinsky had rehearsed *Giselle* frequently, but that the actual performances were always deferred, until it became clear that Nijinsky's debut in this ballet would be with "another dancer." According to Nijinska, Pavlova's explanation for the canceled partnership was: "Let the public that comes to see Pavlova see only Pavlova! Vassia has enough of his own public to fill the Theatre to overflowing." Nijinska was obviously unaware that Pavlova was accepting a contract from Diaghilev—hardly the best way to avoid appearing with Nijinsky.

cabin. It was a relief to her when the ship finally docked in New York and the creaking and vibration ceased.

The first press conference took place on February 12. It was carefully orchestrated. The room was packed with journalists and photographers, the latter with an army of sodium flare assistants adding to the crush. Pavlova arrived quietly and in a dignified manner, with no attempt at an "entrance," but Mordkin appeared to chafe in his role of escort, flapping a glove in his left hand and carrying his head excessively high. The journalists observed that he had not removed his headgear, and the graphic artist Aspell had time to make a careful note of the silk hat, as well as Pavlova's huge froth of black net bows enveloping her turban. The New York *Telegraph* was amazed by this millinery: "Some hat authorities claim it is two feet high, others two and one half. It has yards of black net that somebody started to wind about it and evidently began thinking of something else, winding meanwhile." After Mordkin's silk hat, Pavlova's pearl earrings seemed to be the most lustrous items in the room. The writers' general impressions centered on the physical appearance of the two dancers, and not on the rather stilted question-and-answer routine, conducted by a flustered interpreter who had difficulty making himself heard amid the commotion. Pavlova sat in a chair, with erect grace, while Mordkin elected to sit on a table, which gave him a vantage point from which he did not have to look up to his interrogators. Pavlova's petiteness, despite the towering millinery, was obvious. Some observers thought her thin to the point of emaciation, with fragile wrists and ankles markedly at variance with the normal ideas of robust dancers. Others were impressed: "If there are more girls like Pavlova, Russia ought to be made to send them over. Put your name to any old paper the Tsar demands, only get the girls." Pavlova had yet to dance. One exchange did get through the hubbub.

"What do you like most on earth?"
"Dancing."
"Are you in love?"
"I am not one little bit in love. I did not realize I had to be."
"That being the case, are you married?"
"Not at all. Are not Americans queer and interesting? You ask interesting questions a little different than those in other countries."

Other interviews were given the following day, at the hotel. (See Appendix, p. 400.)

At the Metropolitan Opera House Pavlova and Mordkin faced the problem of integrating the rather scratch opera corps de ballet into the production of *Coppélia*, and nothing was made any easier by the language difficulties; American-English, French, and Russian collided and overlapped with every new instruction and imprecation. The opening was set for Monday, February 28; two acts of *Coppélia* were to follow the opera *Werther*. Bookings had picked up conspicuously since the announcement of the Russians' impending first appearance. Mrs. Harry Payne Whitney was persuaded that it would be something of a social coup to have the two dancers perform at a soirée at her home prior to their debut, and Pavlova and Mordkin were persuaded that Mrs. Whitney

certainly equated with Lady Londesborough as far as American society was concerned. Pavlova and Mordkin did all that was expected of them in delighting the Whitney guests, with the result that word soon spread from those who felt it their duty to tell others what they had missed. By the time of the first night at the Metropolitan, expectations were running high.

The afternoon of Pavlova's entrée at the Metropolitan had its own excitements. She left the rehearsal to take tea with the Mandelkein family at the Wilhelmina on Seventh Avenue. She had asked the taxi driver to wait, but then changed her mind and sent young Miss Mandelkein downstairs with a ten-dollar gold piece to pay the driver. He said he could not change it, crossed the road to a cigar store to do so, then returned, giving Miss Mandelkein the balance from five dollars. The young girl, momentarily confused, was still astute enough to note the number of the cab before it was driven away.

Upstairs, Pavlova confirmed that she had indeed given the girl ten dollars. Armed with the taxi's number, she set off immediately, hailing another cab. For the next two hours Pavlova drove around Manhattan looking for a red taxi bearing the incriminating registration. When finally she returned to her base at the Navarre Hotel, who should be there but the object of her hunt. Pavlova enlisted the help of the doorman and had the driver detained. Miss Mandelkein was sent for, the police arrived, and the truth of the matter was gradually pieced together. The driver surrendered a further five dollars and faced a charge of fraud when the man from the cigar store testified that the driver had indeed changed a ten-dollar piece; the coin was still in a separate drawer of the till. Pavlova was quite happy. "It was not the money so much as the principle of the thing. My, but I've had a most strenuous afternoon!" And off she went for her much delayed glass of Russian tea.

That evening a glamorous audience sat through all four acts of Massenet's opera and then crowded back into the auditorium again after the fourth intermission. It was already past eleven o'clock, and less-than-eager critics noted with some astonishment that the society boxes were almost as full as they had been for the opera—a sufficiently surprising occurrence that it warranted recording. The first strains of Delibes's music came as something of a pleasurable novelty, and many ears were charmed as it progressed. Total silence greeted Pavlova's first appearance, so perfectly did she make her entrance a part of the group scene on stage, but when the delicate little figure had completed the first waltz, the audience burst into spontaneous applause and was thereafter entranced by all the elements of the dancing and the mime that bubbled from her. For the opera lovers there was a further bonus: Pavlova decorated the music with a thousand different accents, giving it a highly embellished visual line that spoke to them as a great coloratura might. For anyone who had seen Genée's appearances for Ziegfeld two years earlier, this new exposition of classical dancing was totally unexpected. The Danish ballerina had charmed her audience, and indeed she had also astonished: in one scene she dismounted from a horse (following a pack of live hounds across the stage!) and danced an extremely provocative number in her riding boots. Pavlova did not have quite the same challenge, but with equal resource she put her own complicated vocabulary of performance before an untutored audience, and she won that audience on her own terms.

Those who had noted that the house had remained packed for the beginning of the ballet were further amazed that there was very little drifting away; countless after-show supper parties must have been in disorder as a result. The critics peered at their watches as their normal deadlines came and went. But their editors would be told that in this instance, something special was taking place.

It was one o'clock when Pavlova and Mordkin took their last curtain call and the clamor of applause finally died down to a buzz of general exclamation. Met regulars could scarcely recall such a night of genuine fervor. Newspaper editors scribbled hasty headlines as they read through the ecstatic reports of an opera evening in which the opera earned barely a line of comment.

Coppélia, London, c.1910.

This costume is at variance with a description of the New York costume: "In the first act . . . Pavlova wears first a white ballet costume. The many flounces are covered coat-like with white satin edged in fur. The second is the handsomest ballet dress ever worn here. The skirt seems to be in many shades of pink, with the entire top in cerise velvet, heavily embroidered in gold."

By dawn the verdict was on the streets:

ANNA PAVLOVA A WONDERFUL DANCER

LITTLE RUSSIAN, LITHE, EXQUISITELY FORMED, CAPTURES METROPOLITAN AUDIENCE IN FIRST WALTZ

Her Technique of a Sort to Dazzle the Eye, and She Has Grace and Humor Mordkin Assists

Poor Mikhail! It was not easy to find a way of glamourizing the phrase in interpretation, and he had to wait for the following day's papers before he received his due. Bewildered editors let through chunks of prose with the merest resemblance to intelligible English. At best, these outpourings had to be taken as a form of prose poetry that sought to express the inexpressible:

What other dancers, on the technical side, do considerately, Miss Pavlowa accomplished vaporously: or rather like the motion of light itself. What, with men of the ballet, would be a feat, Mr. Mordkin makes an impulse. The mathematicians, the physicists, have their notions of bodiless things—of motion as absolute motion apart from the moving object. Of such is the motion of the Russian dancers: only it is motion made fluid loveliness, and quick with imaginative impulse. Other dancers dance with their technique. They dance by their technique with their spirits: and he in a bodily ambiance, when there is chance thought of it, that is like some young figure off the frieze of the Parthenon, and she with the thighs and legs of a Venus of Milo.

The second night was a benefit for the Metropolitan Opera's pension and endowment fund, and four acts of different operas filled out the evening. Otto Kahn needed something special for this gala evening, and he must surely have asked for something that he already knew was a safe bet—something he had seen at the Opéra gala in Paris, perhaps? In the event, it was the *Bacchanale* that closed the benefit night program. When Mordkin caught Pavlova near the footlights at the end, forced a kiss upon her as she bent back from him, half-yielding, and then almost threw her to the ground in a gesture of triumph, she lay in her usual sculpted pose for a second or two, languorous and seemingly drained of energy, and there was a moment's breathless stillness from the audience; then she let her head fall back to reveal the exulting smile, and the light of that smile, as always, released the audience's exhilaration. Cheers and whistles punctuated the crash of applause, which was triggered by Pavlova's mischievously quick scramble to her feet. The calls were innumerable, and the full house gave the box office a return of $15,000.

The only people with any problem were the critics, who continued to tear sheet after sheet from their typewriters in their efforts to limn their experiences. Totally untutored in the art they were observing, they had watched attentively and then described, as best they could, exactly what they had seen. In the end, they described the impression rather than the actuality, as in this review by Carl Van Vechten for the *New York Times* describing the classical pas de deux:

Probably the Act Two costume from *La Fille Mal Gardée*, c.1912
(though occasionally identified as from *Coppélia*).

Pavlova twirled on her toes. With her left toe pointed out behind her, maintaining her body poised to make a straight line with it, she leapt backward step by step on her right foot. She swooped into the air like a bird and floated down. She never dropped. At times she seemed to defy the laws of gravitation. The divertissement ended with Pavlova, supported by Mordkin, flying through the air, circling his body around and around. The curtain fell. The applause was deafening.

The Metropolitan Opera management also had the franchise for the New Theatre, which was used for alternative programs of opera and variety. In order to boost ticket sales there, Pavlova and Mordkin were booked for that house as well. Since there was no scenery or corps de ballet for anything other than *Coppélia,* some of the special dance programs had to rely entirely on the two stars performing various pas de deux and solos, with songs to bulk out the show.*

Van Vechten thought Pavlova's *Swan* to be "the most exquisite specimen of her art she has yet given to this public." The average viewer was still taking in the most elementary aspects of the dancers' art:

> The three costumes she wore had short, fluffy skirts. Her legs were incased in fleshings, and on her feet she had the pink coverings ballerinas have worn from time immemorial. Her first movements were mere regulation: quick steps forward and sideways; the sudden lift to tiptoes and rapid, gliding motions on extended feet. But gradually the extraordinary proficiency of this tall, slender woman evolved itself before the astonished eyes of the crowd and then there was no stemming the tide of applause.

(The fact that Pavlova appeared tall on the stage was due to her slight build; such dancers as had been seen, usually in the opera corps de ballet, were invariably short and solid. Pavlova's height was about 5 feet, 3 inches.) There followed a lengthy, sincere

---

* Pavlova danced *The Swan,* and she and Mordkin presented several pas de deux, including *Le Papillon,* the current title for the dance to Chopin's "Minute Waltz" that she had done with Fokine at Maria Petipa's benefit in 1907. This was now clearly acknowledged as being "arranged by Fokine." Nobody at all was credited with the choreography for *Simple Aveu,* a pas de deux to music of Thomé, or for a pas de deux to a waltz by Rubinstein; and since Mordkin was always eager to get printed acknowledgment for anything that remotely concerned him, it is unlikely that these were his; more likely they came from the Gorsky repertoire in Moscow. Mordkin's principal contributions to "arranging" were "Danses Orientales" and "Danses Classiques." The first gave Pavlova and

Mordkin a sequence that began with an adagio pas de deux to Giraud, followed by variations: Mordkin's to music of Arends and Pavlova's to Rubinstein. On March 6 this variation was credited to Fokine—otherwise one might be certain that the whole number was an Assyrian interlude from Gorsky's version of *Daughter of the Pharaoh.* The second was Bleichmann's "Adagio Classique," which switched to Tchaikovsky for a bow-and-arrow dance by Mordkin; then came Pavlova's variation, to music of Homer Bartlett, followed by a finale to Bleichmann. This pas de deux was to crop up time and again in all sorts of permutations. Mordkin's bow-and-arrow dance was so popular that he soon extracted it as a separate solo.

The Swan. In 1910, when this portrait was taken in New York, photographs still required
a long exposure time. In this instance, Pavlova was supported at the shoulders by a clothesline strung across
the studio and later removed in the retouching. Even so, some movement is still evident.

attempt to describe exactly what Pavlova did, much as a gymnast's floor program might be analyzed for its components.

Nevertheless, it was the opera that, by tradition, held command, and most of the patrons were seeing ballet in spite of themselves. When *Coppélia* was announced in tandem with *Madama Butterfly* at the New Theatre, the box office was sold out there for the very first time for an opera performance; yet it was still the opera that took first place and the ballet that tagged along at the end, so that the final curtain did not close on the dancers until 12:30 a.m. The conductor, tired and unfamiliar with Delibes, plowed his way through the score, and the opera corps de ballet took matters not very seriously; yet the heart of the work survived and indeed triumphed. Only a few members of the audience knew that the ballet *Coppélia* contained three acts and wondered why all of it could not be seen, even if it meant—heavens!—showing only a one-act opera.

March 18 was the Metropolitan Opera's premiere of Frederick Shepherd Converse's *The Pipe of Desire*, the first opera by an American to play the Met. *Cavalleria Rusticana* was also being given, and a ballet divertissement was billed as a coda for the evening. It was said that the Russian dancers and the entire corps de ballet would appear in something called *Hungary* (actually the Grand Pas Hongrois from *Raymonda*). The opera patrons, by now distinctly loyal to these little extras dashed off by the foreigners, stayed on, but they failed to see any connection between Hungary and Pavlova, who was drifting about the stage under a blue spotlight in a costume of swan's wings. They were enthralled by what they saw; but nobody had thought it necessary to announce that the program had been changed. Nor had the stage crew any idea of what was happening. When Pavlova disappeared again after a few minutes of drifting about, they kept the lights down and the curtain up. The conductor then got the green light to begin playing Bleichmann's "Adagio Classique," and Pavlova appeared again, in a different costume, with Mordkin, and—miraculously—abreast of the music. When the dancers took bows that very obviously signaled the conclusion of the piece, the great Met curtains swept down, and in the dimly lit auditorium the audience began streaming into the aisles. So *that* was *Hungary!* Backstage there was utter confusion as Pavlova and Mordkin frantically changed into their *Bacchanale* costumes while a distracted house manager tried to prevent the audience from leaving. He had the curtains run up again, and the tide of patrons was stemmed. The conductor launched into Glazunov's thumping piece, and Pavlova and Mordkin swept on beneath their fluttering gauze cloak. But they did not move fast enough; a minute later the curtains zoomed down again, in mid-score. Mordkin's browned arm was seen struggling to part them.

Pavlova was undeterred; it was pioneer work. At the end of the first week, on March 6, she gave another long and reasoned newspaper interview. (Mordkin was questioned as well, and could not resist taking a dig at the Metropolitan Opera patrons who had applauded in the middle of a dance, drowning out the music that the dancers were attempting to follow.) In her room at the Knickerbocker Hotel Pavlova relaxed after a matinee, picking at a box of candy and lulling herself slowly in a rocking chair. Her quick, staccato voice etched in for the reporter a detailed picture of her background. (See Appendix, p. 400.)

The New York press was mentioning with ill-concealed envy that Alfred Butt had Pavlova under contract for the forthcoming London season, but it seemed that George Edwardes in London was also to get a chance to present Pavlova, by arrangement with Butt, "later on." There was a surprise lurking in the wings of the New Theatre on the night of April 1: not a joke, but a subpoena.

"I was just through dancing and had bowed before the burst of appreciative applause," Pavlova explained through an interpreter, "when a man threw a paper in my face. I was surprised. I felt insulted. 'How is this?' I said to a friend, a gentleman who was standing near. He said it was a call to appear in court. Then I was greatly excited. Then I was more excited. I imagined that I was charged with an awful crime. It was explained to me that Gabriel Astruc, my agent, was suing a newspaper [or was it Diaghilev?], and I was wanted to testify. In Russia such a thing could not take place. A legal paper must be served upon one only when in one's own house. If you are not at home the server must come again. He must come many times—perhaps a hundred times."

Pavlova had a remarkable natural talent for providing reporters with copy, so that the activities of Astruc's lawyer were immediately lost amid fresh revelations: what Pavlova ate, what she weighed, what she did with her spare time (she had none), and what she thought about American girls: it seemed they were inclined to sit down and cross their legs rather too abruptly. She rattled on in French, and columns and columns of English translations were the result. "I find it most difficult to understand English, though not so hard to speak it." Nevertheless she was picking it up rapidly, and before long she was able to respond with some wonderful replies before the interpreter could open his mouth. When one whimsical reporter suggested that she must surely exist on a diet of rose petals, she said tartly, "I prefer German cooking." At all interviews she spoke extremely fast, and flustered reporters often had to wave a hand to get her to slow down. She was plainly annoyed that the early press releases had described her as *Madame* Pavlova. "*Jamais!*" she cried, with a stamp of her foot.

Observers had been astonished by the dancers' capacity for work and their willingness to perform under extreme pressure, though even Pavlova admitted that she had never before gone through an experience like that of the Monday evening before they left. They had been engaged to dance at a charity concert for the Russian Immigrants' Home. This performance, at the Waldorf-Astoria, was to begin at 9:00 p.m. They were also scheduled to dance that night with the Metropolitan Opera, at the Brooklyn Academy of Music after a performance of *Madama Butterfly.* Pavlova and Mordkin went on first at the concert; they danced six numbers and did not finish until 10:00. The Metropolitan's Charles Strakosch hovered nervously; he had a large touring car waiting outside the Waldorf. The dancers rushed

With Mordkin in the *Bacchanale*, New York, 1910.

out, still in costume, with only cloaks to protect them from the chill. Maids threw in hastily packed suitcases with more costumes; there were also armloads of sheet music and Mordkin's huge bow and arrows. The car sped off into a thick mist while the occupants disentangled themselves and then tried to see something of the city they had scarcely glimpsed so far; but they were not able to recognize much except the Brooklyn Bridge itself. The driver got them to the Academy safely in under half an hour, and Miss Farrar was still singing her last notes as Cio-Cio-San when the Russians hurried into the building. By the time the stage was reset, Pavlova had got out of her *Bacchanale* costume and back into her *Swan* costume and was ready. She and Mordkin later danced the Chopin C-sharp minor Waltz, as well as the "Papillon" Waltz, and the *Bacchanale*, and Mordkin also did his variation with the bow and arrow. It was a wonder he could still aim straight.

There were lightning visits to Boston and Baltimore. On March 30 *Coppélia* had to follow a performance of Flotow's *Martha* at the Boston Opera House, where they were nursing some indifferent local singing talent. By the time Pavlova and Mordkin came to leave New York, the rumor was circulating that they intended to marry. Pavlova let out a peal of laughter

when a reporter cornered her with the suggestion. Adroitly as ever, she fended the subject. "We are too busy to think of marriage." The reporter then tried Mordkin.

"Engaged?" stammered Mordkin, blushing like a schoolgirl. "Why I can't say—that is (looking at his beaming companion, who stood near) not at present. I mean—no. Of course not. You see we have our art to think of. Mlle. Pavlowa is a great artist. With her, dancing comes before all else. She must think first of that—all the time. Is it not so?" And Mordkin vanished, followed by the trim Pavlowa, who threw a mischievous glance over her shoulder.

The same day came the announcement that the dancers had been engaged for the fall season at the Metropolitan, and that they would remain in America for five months thereafter. Rival theatrical producers were astonished, having been led to believe that their only chance of securing the dancers would be during the Lent break at the Imperial Theatres. It was also public knowledge that the decision had been taken against the advice of Gatti-Casazza, who believed that the dancers' success was dangerous for the opera; but the General Manager had been overruled by the board of directors. For the New York season, the sum negotiated was said to be 40,000 francs (about $8,000) for thirty performances, but as this represented a mere single night's takings, it was probably way off the mark. At this stage there was no knowledge of the ramifications involved with the Tsar's representatives—sufficient that other New York houses thought that the Met had stolen a march on them. The Shuberts were trying to drum up interest in a production of *La Belle au Bois Dormant*. There might have been more immediate enthusiasm if they had eschewed the French title, but at this stage snobbish entertainment seemed to be the thing.

In all, Pavlova and Mordkin appeared for four different charities in the ballroom at the Waldorf, and they even delayed their sailing date in order to help the Widowed Mothers' Fund by appearing in the two-act operetta *The Millinery Shop* on April 5. They then went to a party at Mrs. George Gould's until the early hours of the morning, and were on the *Campania* when she sailed a few hours later. Even at the quay, Pavlova was still coping with the gentlemen of the press:

> "I have been asked why it is that I haven't muscular legs like other dancers, considering that my technique is as good as it is. The reason, I think, is that those other dancers are always seeking to astonish by feats of force, strength, and dexterity. They are not supple and they are not plastic. They do not recognize often the differences between different kinds of dances. A dancer should be able to change his manner with every costume, and that is what Mr. Mordkin and I try to do. We have enjoyed our success in America very much, and we shall be very glad to come back in the fall."

When Pavlova left America she was still under the impression that she would be dancing in Paris that summer. She was quite clear in her plans when she spoke with the reporters: she would dance in London for Alfred Butt, then at the Opéra, return to London, and then, in September, go to St. Petersburg for two ballets at the Maryinsky. But somehow, the Diaghilev plans were about to go awry again.

The Palace Theatre in its press releases had advanced the names of Pavlova and Mordkin as star performers of what it described as its "Saison Russe," and it was made clear that the dancers were making their first appearance in England—insofar as the general public was concerned. The program at the Palace contained a number of popular "turns," including an illusionist and a comedian from Australia, but on the evening of April 18 most of the audience was waiting with some impatience for the Russian dancers. Pavlova and Mordkin had six couples, all from Russia, supporting them on the bill. In the foyer of the theatre, patrons had made their way under the outstretched arm of a statuette of the ballerina; it was an agreeable work by Mrs. Bert Longworth of Chicago showing Pavlova in a Romantic tarlatan as the sort of fairy sylph the audience must have been expecting. At last the big moment came, and the general excitement was barely suppressed as the conductor raised his baton. There was a further moment's suspense when two dancers appeared in the middle of the stage. They were not Pavlova and Mordkin, but a

Miss Eduardova and a Mr. Monahoff, who launched into a brisk number that was described in the program as "Danse Charactéristique, petite Russien [*sic*]." After polite applause there was a moment's silence; the lights changed, and the orchestra began playing Bleichmann's "Adagio Classique." Pavlova and Mordkin were at last on stage, beginning their pas de deux. The style, precision, and extreme lightness of execution were quite new to the audience. The two dancers created a stunning impression from the very first, and by the time the coda was reached, Pavlova and Mordkin were a hit. They took ten curtain calls, which was most unusual for a music-hall turn.

In devising the program, Butt had been persuaded that the *Bacchanale* should end the ballet section; although the English took to it unreservedly, they were equally delighted by Legat's *Valse Caprice*, an "old familiar" from the Maryinsky repertoire, but surprisingly avant-garde in manner. Pavlova wore a gauzy dress suffused with violet and green, and its exceptional lightness enhanced the effect of freedom, not normally associated with exponents of strictly classical dancing. Because of the critical response to *Valse Caprice*, it was soon transferred to the closing spot. The dance was a showy, extroverted number that con-

Bacchanale portrait.

Palace Theatre, London.

affaire between Pavlova and Mordkin had waned, and Mordkin consoled himself with Bronislava Pajitzkaya, one of the ten soloists of the dance troupe.*

If we follow Dandré's evidence, he was with Pavlova once the English season started. Dandré appeared to have a surprising amount of freedom from his duties in the Duma; his arrival in London seemed to coincide more with the end of the ballet season in St. Petersburg than with any cessation of council duties. Pavlova loved the variety of parks throughout central London; for the first week she and Dandré stayed at the Hyde Park Hotel. From her room she could survey a vast leafy vista, with sheep grazing under the trees—something quite unknown to central St. Petersburg. Her passion for trees and all growing things was marked—a continuation of her Ligovo childhood—and when it became clear that the Palace season was a success that would run its full course, she hankered for something more relaxing as a base. The agents suggested that detached houses with gardens were available in the vicinity of Hampstead Heath, and in a few days they had located, in Golders Green, a small house with its own garden, and this Pavlova rented on a weekly basis for the remainder of the season. Nothing more was heard of Paris.**

tained several difficult feats of partnering relying on Mordkin's strength, which he displayed to very good advantage. There was no question where the eyes of the ladies in the audience were focused. Mordkin's athletic build and his open, "Moscow" manner of presentation were refreshingly different; if male dancers had been seen on the London stage at all, they had been supernumeraries whose role was to carry and support, with strict instructions not to advance into the ballerina's limelight. Mordkin swept all that away with his youthful charm and his knowledge that a male dancer had a right to the stage equal to that of his female partner.

Mordkin had quickly grown accustomed to the American enthusiasm for his manly charms, and he was a little dismayed to discover that followers in London were more evenly divided in their loyalties, and indeed a little bit more demure in singing his praises. However, high society, with its usual lack of inhibition, soon began to betray its interest in the off-stage Mordkin. He was much in demand for appearances at charity functions and dinners, and only his bruising encounters with the English language spoiled his success. There was no chance of an English society girl knowing any Russian, and most conversations limped along with a display of execrable French coming from both sides. The

London's "Russian Season" was the talk of the town; journalists assessed the audience reaction as "a frenzy of enthusiasm." After the opening night, even the overseas news services were told that Anna Pavlova and Mikhail Mordkin would certainly be the rage of the season. An editorial in *The Graphic* at the end of the month gave considered thoughts about the *Bacchanale* and the *Valse Caprice*:

These dances occupy a mid position between the old ballet dancing of La Scala and the descriptive posturing of which Miss Isadora Duncan is the chief. Mr. Mordkin, in the first place, is particularly unlike the conventional dancer, resembling the Greek god of sculpture more than the master of ballet. He is an extremely handsome, well-built man, with powerful limbs, which he uses with great suppleness. He dances in his bare legs, so that you can see the movement of every muscle. He is at his very best dancing to Tchaikowsky's famous variations, appearing as a hunter, with bow and arrow. His whole note is that of joyousness, and the sense of life with which he is instinct makes it a vivifying experience to watch him. This sense of joyousness keeps his *Bacchanale* dance far away from the spirit of corruption to which it might very readily degenerate. Mlle. Pavlova is at her best in the concluding item, the *Valse Caprice*, which is of such rare delicacy that it is almost impossible to find words to convey its charm. She is in complete contrast to Mr. Mordkin, especially in those particular items where he acts the part of the splendid athletic pursuer, while she for all the

* Many years later, Mordkin said that he had been madly in love with Pavlova, and she with him, but that it all ended very quickly. Most of Mordkin's ventures had an uncanny knack of going wrong.
** There is an inexplicable gap in documentation about this break between Pavlova and Diaghilev (and Astruc). Perhaps there was more to the subpoena at the New Theatre than Pavlova was allowing. From a practical point of view it would seem that Butt had stood firm on his prior contract; in the light of the success in America he would have

been foolish to have done otherwise. This would almost certainly mean that the longed-for partnership with Nijinsky was in jeopardy, as Nijinsky was a slow learner of roles. Mordkin, too, was a problem. After the sudden fame he could hardly be discarded again. One can imagine a fear of Paris factions looming in the mind of Astruc, if not in Diaghilev's. Pavlova may have been willing to partner Nijinsky *and* Mordkin; this would not suit Diaghilev at all. It would have to be Nijinsky or no one. The binding contract with Butt meant that Pavlova was really bound to Mordkin—as well as to Butt's theatre.

earth is like a fantastic fairy eluding his grasp. To see her in his arms throwing back her head in an attitude of would-be escape brings the house to that point of murmured admiration which is very rarely heard in England. The appearance of these very Russian artists suggests the query—Why does not the Empire or the Alhambra give us one of Tchaikowsky's ballets?

Pavlova's variation in the first pas de deux used a brief snatch of Delibes, and Liszt, Glazunov, Glinka, and Rubinstein were all given their moments. There was one extraordinary interlude in which Pavlova and Mordkin danced the Paraguay. This was mistakenly assumed to be of interest to a general audience, since Queen Alexandra had requested to see it the previous summer, but like most "sensations" it was already passé a year later and was quickly taken out of the program, though the audience was entirely well disposed toward anything the Russians were prepared to do, and the press cheerfully included the Paraguay among the triumphs. According to *The Star:*

> The Palace has set the fashion, and Pavlova's the only wear. Judging by her triumphant success last night, Russian dancing is going to have a bigger "boom" in London during the next few months than either here or in Paris last year. Mlle. Pavlova's dancing, compared with that of most of her compatriots (however highly trained though they might be), is a representation, say, of *Hamlet* at His Majesty's Theatre compared with a performance at a fit-up booth on a country race course.

The *Daily Mail*, referring to a little-publicized sortie by Preobrajenskaya into London the previous year, said of Pavlova and Mordkin that they would convince London of the supremacy of the Russian ballet "which London began to doubt last year when Mme. Preobrajenskaya disappointed her Covent Garden audience." The *Pall Mall Gazette* must have endeared itself to Pavlova by saying that it could not recall a dancer of her genre who had revealed so exquisite a grace of form:

> As a rule the limbs of the *première danseuse* are powerful rather than shapely, but those of Mlle. Pavlova are as beautiful as were those of Taglioni in her portraits by Challen [Chalon]. She appeared last night in a diversity of dances, and had equally delightful moments of movement and of repose in each. She can suggest the fire and the languor of passion in a quite wonderful way; she moves with the lightness of thistledown being blown across a heath; and so far as the usual familiar *tours de force* are concerned she can apparently accomplish them all with ease as well as grace. Her success last night was complete, and—a more important point—it was deserved.

And from the *Evening Standard:*

> La Pavlova is electric—a faun, a sprite, a bacchante—and a most feminine woman. Sometimes she is one, sometimes she is the other, and sometimes she is all at once. She pirouettes with the rapidity of a tee-to-tum at the first impulse; she is demure, arch, a she-devil and a spirit of goodness. She scowls, she laughs, she suggests chastity and passion. Her movements are sudden and they are languorous. Her poses are quick as lightning and as expressive and as seemingly spontaneous. And with all there is the trained perfection of the supreme artiste.

Mordkin publicity photos, c.1910.

Publicity photographs for the first season at the Palace Theatre. Pavlova's was a
Maryinsky costume, possibly from *Paquita*; Mordkin's was from the Moscow production of
Daughter of the Pharaoh, which was now being used in the *Bleichmann* pas de deux.

The enthusiasm of the audiences at the Palace was remarkable, and there were numerous floral tributes added to the clapping and shouting, which went on long after there was any hope of an encore. Far from demeaning themselves before a music-hall audience, Pavlova and her fellows were receiving adulation coupled with a genuine appreciation of their artistry. This warmth delighted Pavlova, and she responded with a number of interviews in which she seldom failed to return the compliment. She told a reporter for the *Daily News:* "Of all the places I have visited—including Vienna, Paris, and New York—London is the one that has impressed me the most favourably." The *Daily Chronicle's* reporter was completely bowled over by his quarry:

I have been to the Palace to "interview" Pavlova. Fancy interviewing Pavlova! Fancy asking her where she was born, by whom she was trained, what were the place and date of her first appearance, and so on! It was a wicked thing to do, and I felt that it would be a relief to me, after such an experience, to go to a great poet and ask him for a complete analysis of his best beloved work. That would have been a happy holiday to the conscience. . . .

Pavlova "breath'd a song into the air. It fell to earth, I know not where"—for the earth was spinning round. She had come from the stage after thrilling the Palace audience in the pas de deux *L'Automne Bacchanale;* and of the song she breathed into the air I care only to remember such words as help me to believe that her parents were the moonbeams, and that she made her debut in the fairy ring. If people want to know hateful hard facts about Pavlova, they can go to her agent and learn from him—perhaps from the very books in his office. . . .

But these are mere "interview" matters, and must be forgotten as mundane atoms painfully out of place in the fairy atmosphere of Pavlova. She is uninterviewable—unphotographable—undrawable. But she is not uncaricaturable; for are not all phrases of the pen and strokes of the pencil but caricatures that attempt to describe and picture Perfection? And what is Perfection but Pavlova?

A certain Marcelle Azra Hincks fired off a letter to *The Times* in which she described the Russian dancers as having solved the problem of the dance, adding, "For the given form of the ballet, whilst adhering strictly to the rigid rules of their art, they possess the emotional and expressive qualities which Noverre and Blasis, and the founders and systematisers of the ballet in the 18th century, deemed essential to the dance."

Francis Toye in *Vanity Fair* lamented the absence of a British national school of dancing:

. . . So-called ballets at the Empire and the Alhambra are nothing more than variations on a musical comedy theme. . . . And now, in the midst of this desolation, the Russian dancers have appeared and conquered immediately. Who shall wonder at it? Anybody can recognize good dancing. No knowledge of technique is necessary to appreciate beauty of line, lightness of movement, or gracefulness of pose. Furthermore, the Russians, particularly Pavlova, excel in emotional qualities. So that we may reasonably hope to have seen the last of the so-called "classical" prancings which so long—and so profitably—appealed to our national love of amateurishness.

Toye, who had a strong musical background, went on to comment on the excellence of the composers used by the dancers.

The *Bleichmann* pas de deux. Like the music and the choreography, the costumes underwent many changes over the years.

Austin Harrison wrote in the *Daily Mail:*

Can there be anything more truly beautiful in the world than the Bacchanalian dance [Pavlova] performs to the gorgeously inspired music of Glazounov? Here is a vision of love and forest revelry, of fauns and rhapsody, and wood nymphs wild and shrieking in some Pagan Saturnalia. The frenzy, the bravura, the magic of music and rhythm, and the fierce rush, the joy, the sheer mad beauty of grace and motion—this is a thing which reels into the senses. A splendid figure is the man, like a Greek athlete. The atmosphere of Glazounov's music is superb, transporting. We are no longer in our places in the theatre, but on the stage in the wild flight, the coy provocations, the retreats, the magnificent abandon of this sylvan nymph toying with her male pursuer. He is like an ancient statue come to life, fired with the passion of centuries. She is the symbol of life and femininity and beauty, which is the soul of life.

Art can go no further than this. It is the combination of the music with the perfection of dancing, interpreted as an art rather than a corybantic ingenuity, that makes this dance so true and beautiful a thing, the contrast of the superb virility of the male with the supreme grace of woman; or, again, see her marvellous dexterity of "elevation," the sureness with which she stops suddenly on tiptoe, with leg and arms extended as in flight, the plasticity of her body when she is dancing in the classic style with her cavalier and he raises her up in the air as if she were a child, and takes her by the waist and throws her here and there, now with her head cast back upon her heels, now in the air hanging like a bird; the beauty of this must be seen to be at all believed in. It is the intensity of the effect

ABOVE In *Rose* costume, with blooms
from the *Bacchanale*.

BELOW In new *Valse Caprice* costume,
London, c.1911.

which is so overwhelming. Every detail is right, the complementary colour scheme of the dresses, the accent of the picture, the man, the woman, and the rapture of movement—this is no artistry of the stage. It is the result of a school of dancing trained for decades as an art for art's sake, maintained regardless of expense, and inspired directly by critical enthusiasm.

Marcelle Azra Hincks, in a newspaper article, expanded on the importance of individuality in dancing, which she felt had hitherto been considered very little, either by dancers themselves or their public:

We never, in fact, think of criticising or analysing the personality of a dancer in the same way as a dramatic critic endeavours to seize and define those particular characteristics of which an actor's personality consists. With a few exceptions, such as dancers who have left the beaten track, and therefore call for especial consideration and criticism, as, for instance, Isadora Duncan or Ruth St. Denis, the only way in which dancers have been mentioned by the critics, or looked upon by audiences, has been entirely from the point of view of purely superficial and external qualities: the beauty of the figure, their grace of movement, the lightness, quickness and agility. . . .

I think that the time has come when we must approach the dance from a completely new standpoint and judge it by another standard; the same methods of criticism which are applied to the other arts should be applied to the dance. . . . Dancers, like actors, must first of all have certain artistic and temperamental gifts, and secondly, they must learn how to reveal and express these perfectly by means of art forms. Anna Pavlova has shown that it is possible to do this in the dance as in all the arts. She is above all an interpreter of emotions; she has an extraordinarily interesting personality, an artistic temperament of the finest order, and she expresses herself through the medium, and within the limits, of the most severe art-forms. . . .

Pavlova had a curious ability to keep these personal performing characteristics intact, while at the same time accepting the fact that being a dancer placed her squarely in the role of popular entertainer. She knew her art was something of a novelty—even a passing vogue—and she did not lose her sense of humor or expect a false measure of seriousness to be applied to everything she did. Unlike Mordkin, who took himself very seriously indeed,* Pavlova was content to let her work find its own level of acceptance: if it pleased, then that was reward enough; but if it led to a deeper understanding of musical impulse and human expressiveness, then so much the better.

Wealthy Americans in London for the season were among those who saw Pavlova primarily as a novelty. A certain Mrs. Vincent gave a cotillion in London at which the principal entertainment was an appearance by thirty-five especially talented ballroom dance couples. These were in action when the band leader suddenly stopped the music, and there was wheeled into the room a huge basket of flowers. In the silence that followed its

---

*He once took huge exception to a menu featuring "Frogs' Legs à la Pavlova." He thought it was a conspiracy by his partner. "Where are 'Frogs' Legs à la Mordkin'?" he demanded, banging the table in fury.

entry, the flowers fell apart and out jumped Anna Pavlova—or "Mme. Paverola," as the Duluth (Minnesota) *Herald* had it, adding for clarification, "the famous Russian dancer." There was no room in the basket for Mordkin, but he was there waiting for his partner to emerge from her floral bower. She had contrived a costume of loose draperies with appliquéd silk rose petals, and a headdress of more roses. They danced in the center of the ballroom; at one point Pavlova slipped on the parquet, but she recovered without injury, to the relief of the hostess, who exclaimed gleefully: "If she had injured her ankle I would have been obliged to pension her with thousands of pounds. How fortunate!" As it was, Mrs. Vincent was paying out $500 each time Pavlova and Mordkin took the floor between sections of the cotillion.

London in the spring of 1910 was a city of massive resource and vested power, the heart of an empire that spread around the globe; but in the wake of Edwardian opulence and complacency, there was emerging an understanding of the brittle peace that pertained between Austria and the Slavic states, and the reality of the English Channel being a watery bastion of supreme importance. The people of England were thus expected to finance a massive shipbuilding policy for the Royal Navy; duties on tobacco and spirits were up, and incomes over £5,000 were hit with a super-tax of sixpence in the pound. In an escape from the horrid reality of the Finance Bill, patrons crowded the theatres seeking distraction, and even the Prince of Wales took his wife to the Palace Theatre on Tuesday, May 3, having already seen the program there on April 23, when he had taken the young Prince Edward at the end of the first week's program, with Pavlova and Mordkin topping the bill. While the heir to the throne was at the theatre taking his mind off things, urgent messages were being sent to his mother, Queen Alexandra, who was on a yacht in the Mediterranean; the King's health was giving cause for alarm, though he was still attending to state business. The Queen's precipitous return started rumors flying two nights later. That same evening—Thursday, May 5—a new production was launched at the Empire: *Dance Idylls* (which *The Stage* reported as a "Series of Dance Ideals"), starring Lydia Kyasht and Adolph Bolm, the latter being given credit for their arrangement. An English girl, Phyllis Bedells, did the Little Red Riding Hood dance from *The Sleeping Beauty*.

On the afternoon of May 6, while anxious crowds gathered outside the gates of Buckingham Palace, the King lay unconscious and fighting for breath. He was dead before midnight struck, and because of the new miracle of wireless, British subjects at sea learned of their monarch's death before the majority of their countrymen, but within minutes of opening time the following morning, shop windows were filled with swags of black and purple crêpe, and the carriages rolling into the forecourt of Buckingham Palace were all similarly draped. Theatre audiences suddenly became a sea of black, and their response to entertainment was muted, but performances continued uninterrupted, just

Publicity photograph in the original *Valse Caprice* costume, soon abandoned for the version seen opposite.

as the streets outside bustled and surged in their usual overcrowded manner. There was a low-key fortnight, waiting for the King's funeral, but during this period several new dance programs opened on the London music-hall circuit, as managers were desperate to compete with the Empire and the Palace. Monday, May 16, was a public holiday, and the Hippodrome and the Coliseum launched rival attractions on the same night. Preobrajenskaya was risking part of *Swan Lake* with a London audience again, while Karsavina and Baldina renewed their successful association with the management of Oswald Stoll, giving a version, of sorts, of *Les Sylphides*. Critics considered it "rather long and pitched too much in the same key," but the rest of the performance was thought to be bright and varied and "decidedly improves on further acquaintance." Rather more interest was shown in a young lady from California who dived repeatedly into a tank of water. At the Alhambra the nubile French charmer Gaby Deslys was about to give way to the Moscow ballerina Ekaterina Geltzer, who was to be embroiled in a new ballet announced as dealing with the history of dress "from the costumes of earliest times down to the present day 'creations' of Paris and London."

On Whit-Monday the weather in London was cloudless, with the heat tempered by a pleasant breeze. Because of the traditional attitude of "The King is dead; long live the King," the crowds were torn between Madame Tussaud's exhibition, where there was a model of King Edward, and the Zoological Gardens, where some of the more delicate animals were withdrawn from the public areas, since forty thousand bun-bearing visitors threatened many cases of gastric suicide.

"Russia's Greatest Dancers" seemed to be everywhere; the Palace and the Hippodrome (where Preobrajenskaya and Georgi Kyaksht were in *Swan Lake*) both claimed this title for their stars, while the Coliseum settled for "The Famous Russian Dancers" in their advertising of Karsavina, Baldina, and Koslov. Karsavina was thought by the *Daily Mail* to be "the most exquisite fairy imaginable, a dream of pearl, and pink, and gold, light as a flower, smiling, elegant, and dainty," while Koslov was described as "incomparably the finest male dancer seen in London." Pavlova, noting this rash of competition for the Whit-Monday holiday, introduced a novelty—the Pas de Diane from *Le Roi Candaule* (though the audience was not told of its origin), and there was a new costume designed by Bakst. But the press felt that this item was not as remarkable as the *Valse Caprice*—"partly due, perhaps, to the depression in the national atmosphere which penetrates even the walls of a theatre." The *Bacchanale*, however, "proved even more wonderful at a second seeing than at the first."

On May 27, a week after King Edward's funeral, the Palace Theatre was able to include in its program a bioscope film of the funeral procession, made more remarkable by the introduction of Kinemacolor, a hand-tinting process. The matinees were in the nature of a memorial ceremony, heightened by a number of dead marches played by the orchestra. The funeral scenes and the Russian dancing were reckoned to be suitably complementary entertainments for the second half of the program, leaving the first half to such as Miss Margaret Cooper singing old established favorites like "My Moon" and "Hello! Tu-Tu," as well as her newer additions "Bunny" and "Catch Me, Catch Me, Clarence." The orchestra contrived to support both Pavlova and Miss Cooper with devoted attention, and even managed to underpin the bioscope scenes with a felicitous selection of music.

Karsavina must have infuriated Pavlova by introducing at the Coliseum a version of *Giselle*, known as *Gisella, or La Sylphide*, with the dances credited to Petipa. It was, for the most part, the second act of the ballet, complete with the Adam score. But by early June this work had to be suspended; Baldina and Koslov carried on with divertissements while Karsavina was on leave for Diaghilev's 1910 Paris season. The Coliseum audience may have been relieved to see the end of *Gisella; The Stage* had thought it "rather a tedious affair, mainly on account of the darkened stage. The fact that the dancing is reduced to a minimum while pantomime occupies the greater length of time also detracts somewhat from its value as a turn pure and simple of a musical entertainment, though artistically the ballet may be considered to be of a very high order." At the Palace, Pavlova's understanding

of the limited concentration that could be expected of a music-hall audience showed in her selection of relatively inconsequential items, in which she put maximum effort into a minimum time-span and usually managed to create a furor. Over at the Hippodrome, *Swan Lake*, though considered "charming," was having to compete with comedy bicyclists, a model airship, and a Chinese conjurer who appeared to produce an endless supply of livestock out of a cauldron of boiling water.

Although the variety of the programs suggested otherwise, the ballet dancers were making a decided impression on the theatre-going public. In mid July, *The Times* drama critic, A. B. Walkley, headed his long theatre article "If Pavlova Had Never Danced." The noted legal counsellor F. E. Smith had just made a speech in the Woman Suffrage debate in which he had said that if Sarah Siddons had never played, the sum total of human happiness, knowledge, and achievement would have been almost unaffected. Walkley took up the theme:

If Pavlova had never danced—though Mr. F. E. Smith's "sum of human happiness" might have been unaffected—the public stock of harmless pleasure during the past theatrical season would certainly have been diminished. Nothing like it has been seen before in the London of our time. There was, to be sure, the delightful Genée, with her gaiety and brilliance, and there was the seductive posturing of Isadora Duncan and Maud Allan. But Pavlova and the Russian dancers of the present moment (including not only those of Pavlova's own troupe, but the beautiful Lydia Kyasht of the Empire—a rival who runs, or rather dances, her very close—and others at the Coliseum and the Hippodrome) have given us Londoners something really new: an extraordinary technical accomplishment, an unfailing sense of rhythm, an unerring feeling for the elegant in fantasy, and what Hazlitt would have called "gusto," a passionate enjoyment. The dancing of Anna Pavlova is a thing of perfect beauty. This is no case of Mr. Pepys and his "best legs that ever I saw."

In the presence of art of this stamp, one's pleasure is purely aesthetic. Indeed the sex-element (though of course necessarily somewhere in the unconsciousness) counts for very little; for a man the dancing of Mr. Mordkin is *almost* as pleasure-giving as that of Mlle. Pavlova. The combination of the two, above all in their Bacchanalian dance, is an even choicer thing than their *pas seuls. . . .*

This is a very different thing from the ballet to which Londoners used once upon a time to be mercilessly subjected—rank after rank and file after file of honest bread-winners from Camberwell and Peckham Rye performing mechanical manoeuvres with the dogged perseverance of a company of Boy Scouts. When people tell you, as they sometimes will, that ballet dancing is a bore, you recognise the trail of the honest British bread-winners. Once they have seen the Russian dancers, they will hardly again be guilty of that *bêtise.*

Across the Atlantic, *Variety* reviewed the Palace bill of fare and decided that it would be impossible to describe Pavlova's dancing, sufficing with the information that "the Russian woman held her audience astounded during the forty minutes." *Variety's* assessment was that Mordkin was an important figure: "It is not putting it too strongly to say he all but shared the honors with the star. His dancing in itself is enough to make them sit up and take notice. The man is almost perfectly built, and if he doesn't start havoc among the matinee girls, the dope is all wrong." The *Telegraph,* with a short memory, took a poke at the London papers: "One wonders what would happen if such hysterics as are printed beneath were submitted to a New York editor":

> And then from the other side of the stage, like a rose leaf blown on the wind, Pavlova dances toward the triumphantly virile Mordkin. Dancing does not describe the lightness of her movements. She floats. The tips of her feet tremble on the stage like the quivering, shimmering wings of a butterfly. She seems to be a thing of air—a ghost of lightness—gliding across the garden with trembling feet. The pas de deux is danced, and every pose, every change of expression, speaks its story to the looker-on. They personify the music. She, light, laughing, and elusive, is the rippling stream wooed by the sun, the brown, strong Mordkin. It is a poem of motion.

Even before this season had ended, Pavlova had taken particular note of potential home-grown talent for classical dancing: "Sometimes I feel I want to adopt all the little girls in London and take them away to an island and teach every one of them how to conquer London! I am not what you call 'dog in the manger,' you see."

By early autumn, a great deal of material was being sent to the New York press in advance of the dancers' appearance there in mid-October. Most editors followed the convention that had been established by American writers in spelling the ballerina's name as "Pavlowa." This confusion was compounded in certain quarters, noticeably Cleveland, where potential patrons were informed that "wherever Pavlowa and Mordkin appear everyone talks about them, so you might as well learn early how to pronounce their names. Mme. Pavlowa is enunciated 'Pavlova' as though no 'w' entered the last syllable. The 'a' is spoken softly and the 'o' as in 'go.' M. Mordkin's surname is pronounced phonetically, but his given name has a thoroughly Russian individual twist—'Mick-ah-eel.' And there you have it—à la Russe." Nevertheless, Mikhail lost the battle early on, ending up with the Anglicized form. The Irish element seized on the prosaic "Michael" and suggested—tongue in cheek—that "Michael Mordkin" was nothing less than a cover-up for one Mike O'Mordkin, with no possible claim to the steppes. Mordkin rose to the bait. Harnessing French and English in unruly tandem, he fired off a cable:

INFORM EDITEURS VOUS AVEZ TORT. I AM A COSSACK. NAME IS MIKAIL, NOT MIKE. MAKE IT SO IN EVERY ANNOUNCEMENTS.

Mordkin was developing something of a love-hate relationship with the press. He loved the attention but was unhappy when tougher members of the journalistic brethren peeked behind the Imperial façade. One reporter, feigning deep interest, infiltrated the publicity office of Ben Atwell and discovered that Mordkin himself was keeping a sharp eye on all the releases, particularly relishing one quote, which he unabashedly asked to be repeated at every opportunity. Readers thus learned of "... 'the perfect

ABOVE Cover of the souvenir album for the first American tour, autumn 1910. Their pose approximates the entrance in the *Bacchanale*.

BELOW Cover of a brochure advertising the forthcoming appearance of Pavlova and Mordkin in Grand Rapids, Michigan, 1910.

Mordkin,' as Anna Pavlova's dancing partner frequently terms himself in ultra critical moods. . . ."

Otto Kahn's involvement in the first American presentation of Pavlova and Mordkin had been something of a social amusement and a business expedient, rather than a committed policy of presenting ballet to uncommitted audiences. In the first instance he had taken a qualified risk with a very limited season in key opera houses on the East Coast only. He was able to conclude contracts with the dancers at a time when they were already on leave from the Imperial Theatres; at worst they had merely to ask for an extension of their leave in order to embrace the New World—a very different matter from being involved in protracted negotiations with the Tsar's personal representatives. This aspect of presenting any of the St. Petersburg dancers was not taken up lightly by anyone with any knowledge of the complexities involved. It needed tough, attraction-hungry managers with stamina, nerve, and a great deal of hard cash.

As soon as advance publicity from the Metropolitan Opera management betrayed the fact that the Russian dancers were not envisaged as a permanent adjunct to the usual Metropolitan fare, a new presenter put himself forward. G. P. Centanini was a comparative youngster in the world of musical management, but a position as secretary of the Metropolitan Opera Company had given him an ideal base for learning about the complexities of the business, and he was ambitious and forceful; furthermore, he was quick to see that the excitement generated by the Russian pair was not a chance success but something that could revitalize any flagging opera season that lacked musical novelty. He saw too that the existing investments in standard opera productions could not be jettisoned. The productions really had to be squeezed dry if the books were to balance; classical music was competing for audiences in a cutthroat business. There was no subsidy from the state; private patronage usually expected a return on its investments; and if one was investing, many attractions looked a better bet than opera. There were numerous programs of vaudeville acts, circuses, and female revues; the accent was on superficial amusement. As an example, in Philadelphia the fine building of the Grand Opera House usually featured vaudeville and moving pictures, while at the same time, the six other principal theatres in town competed for attention with—to quote the summer bill of fare for 1910—circus acts, a revue called "Girls," burlesque, vaudeville, more circus, and more vaudeville.

Into this froth of lightweight distraction, opera (and dancing) dipped an occasional net for loyal patrons, but for any such season to be financially safe, a percentage of customers had to be wooed from other houses. Centanini was convinced that this was now possible—that it could in fact be guaranteed, given the Russian dancers as bait—and he joined forces with Max Rabinoff, who had been well to the fore in the fierce skirmishes taking place on the Chicago musical front, where a consortium was bidding for outright control of the opera house. Rabinoff and his team won there, and the Chicago Grand Opera Company was registered. Both Rabinoff and Centanini embraced culture wholeheartedly; Centanini's bride was the beautiful American songbird Jane Noria, while Rabinoff, not to be outdone, caused something of a flutter when he married his young musical protégée Maria La Salle, a coloratura soprano said to be "the most wonderful musical discovery of the decade." Rabinoff wore gold pince-nez and bore a disconcerting resemblance to Rudyard Kipling. He had also been a partner with Ben Atwell during the stormy battle for control of the opera concession in Chicago.

Centanini, Rabinoff, and Atwell all joined forces to woo Pavlova and Mordkin, and they knew that they were in for high stakes when Pavlova airily brushed aside an initial offer guaranteeing $12,000 for a six-week season. This rebuff merely strengthened their interest; they were convinced that there was money to be made, no matter what the outlay. One other aspect was almost of more importance: the chance of establishing a reputable bridgehead in musical management, with a subsequent pressure being exerted on other managements. But the Chicago team was forced to look beyond its own immediate horizon if the undertaking was to be anything more lasting than Otto Kahn's brief flirtation with foreign exotica. Touring was a concomitant of big financial outlay in the musical field, and the person with real experience of touring a musical company was Harry Snow, who had been chargé d'affaires for numerous road tours and concerts presented by Oscar Hammerstein. Snow joined the team, which was completed by a backer, Alexander J. Quilez, a member of the Guatemalan diplomatic corps, whose name never got as far as the brochure, even if his cash did.

This executive army doubtless felt itself ready for all comers, but it found itself in deep and uncharted waters once it got into serious dealings with the Russian government, which acted as a front for the vested interest of the Imperial family. There were long lists of conditions pertaining to any release of the Tsar's select entertainers, and the required financial guarantees were assessed in absolute ratio to the outlay at home. Centanini, Rabinoff et al. were expected to deposit over a quarter of a million dollars as a pledge against the fulfillment of all obligations. This was the big league with a vengeance, but somehow they met the obligation, even if the Guatemalan national economy stood at risk. The Philadelphia *Times* thought the deal newsworthy and commented suavely that "as an amusement manager, Czar Nicholas can teach the Paris and London impresarios, who usually supply the American market with novelties, a few business tricks."

With a dispensation from the Imperial Theatres of half a year's absence, the dancers signed the major contracts. (Rabinoff had inserted options for five years.) Centanini had then to devise a schedule that could, in principle, recoup the outlay. In addition to the pledge to the Russian government, the actual running costs looked to be enormous, since the schedule was breaking new ground in terms of the distance traveled and the number of artists involved. The enterprise needed the detailed planning of a large-scale military maneuver if it was to infiltrate the entire North American continent. The plan was for just that:

after the initial engagement in New York (a return to past triumphs, it was hoped), the company was to board a private train consisting of seven cars, and travel to and fro for ten weeks, taking in cities all over the United States and Canada.

The important thing was to secure maximum saturation with minimum exposure. The largest auditorium in each city was allocated one, or at most two, performances, so that patrons would fill every available seat. The train would then whisk the entire company and its massive amount of equipment on through the remainder of the night until the next destination was reached. Boston, Chicago, St. Louis, Cleveland, Cincinnati, Kansas City, Omaha, Denver, Seattle, Portland, Philadelphia, Pittsburgh, Washington, D.C., Baltimore, Salt Lake City . . . the list seemed without end. It embraced the Pacific coast, with San Francisco and Los Angeles, and then there was Canada as well. (Cleveland got a second bite of the apple on January 23, when an alert local manager spotted a rare gap in the schedule and claimed it.) New York was allocated the three weeks over the Christmas period, which was considered a particularly unpredictable time for any theatre bookings, and then the whole process of train shuttling would begin again, with eighty-one dates to be filled between January 9 and March 9, in cities ranging from Montreal to New Orleans. Even before January was out, the train would have covered more than 20,000 miles. And finally there was a further three weeks at the Metropolitan Opera House in New York. July 7, 1911, was the date set by the Russian government as a deadline for the whole enterprise; all personnel under contract to the Imperial Theatres had to be home by then or the bond would be forfeited in its entirety.

Rabinoff and Centanini had to some extent covered themselves against any really massive loss by spreading the risk. The individual managers in the various cities underwrote each engagement by guaranteeing a certain box-office figure, so that the promoters' main concern was that nothing should prevent them from maintaining the strict timetable. That, and the frightening imponderable: could Pavlova and Mordkin stay the course? The tour was as nothing without them. And there was one final pressure: Centanini and Rabinoff were committed to returning the whole ensemble to Alfred Butt in London for a ten-week season at the Palace Theatre beginning on April 17. Daniel Mayer, the London agent, was determined that the momentum gained in England should not be lost.

During the dancers' initial visit to America in the spring, when they had made fleeting appearances in Boston and Baltimore as well as the more widely publicized New York performances, audiences had had difficulties not only with the dancers' names but with the terminology of the art being purveyed; one newspaper article had referred throughout to the various "ballots." The word "ballet" was common enough coinage in metropolitan New York, but for the coast-to-coast tour Centanini's brochure required an explanation on its cover, coupled with the usual bombast. The company was said to be "introduc-

With Mordkin in poses from the *Bleichmann* pas de deux, taken for the first American tour. The poses as well as the costumes seem to be from *Daughter of the Pharaoh* or *Egyptian Nights*.

ing an art new to America, the interpretation of the ponderous messages of the great composers through the most primitive and yet potent of mediums—motion!" The New York *Review* ran an article on "ocular opera" being the latest thing for the stage, and under the subheading "New Classification" ran the explanation, "Term Had to Be Coined Because None Existed to Describe the Russian Dancers' Act." It went on:

> Critics, all-wise in most things, are perplexed over what classification to give the performances of Anna Pavlowa, Mikhail Mordkin and the Imperial Russian Ballet, which will tour America next season. . . . It is a moot question whether the attraction is operatic, a spectacle, or belongs in the concert field. . . . Indeed the management styles the performances of the famous Russian dancers "ocular opera" or "opera in action." This because the programs include operas, or plays, especially written for interpretation through the medium of this national Russian art.

It was noticeable that Mordkin, usually photographed in his bow-and-arrow costume, which left a goodly expanse of bare legs, was most often the figure dominating the pictorial side of all this advance publicity. Ben Atwell's press office was probably hauled over the coals by Pavlova in the matter of *Variety's* talk of Mordkin's sharing honors with the star, and things were not helped by a fulsome missive to the male dancer penned by Centanini:

> Of the many unique and novel features that cluster about the tour, one that has been nearly overlooked is the almost unprecedented fact in this country of the presentation of a male dancer as a terpsichorean marvel. Paris, London, New York and Boston have raved over the beauty of Anna Pavlova and her wonderful art as compared with other great dancers who have visited America. When it came to criticising Michael Mordkin they were at a loss for any basis for comparison, for he stands alone in a field distinctly his own. Mordkin has been likened to a Greek statue leaping into life, and called by some enthusiasts the incarnation of a Greek god. The apotheosis of masculine strength and force, with a head and face remarkable for classic outline, he possesses a deft grace of movement and an agility known only to the Russian school of dancing.

Pavlova's ambivalent attitude toward personal publicity (she had been distressed to see her name on a placard of a London omnibus) meant that Mordkin, with his enthusiastic approach to self-advertisement, was achieving the top berth in American news items. "Mordkin to Open New Chicago Opera House" trumpeted the New York *Telegraph* on June 20. "Mikail Mordkin" splashed the Chicago *Tribune* helpfully, under a picture of Mordkin in Roman garb, adding in small print the information that Anna Pavlova and Mikhail Mordkin had the honor of opening the newly decorated Auditorium Theatre, the home of the new Chicago opera.

After all the negotiations, the American team must have had a moment of collective doubt. What had they risked so much investment on? Centanini rushed off to Europe to reassure himself and his partners that Diaghilev's company contained nothing more interesting. It was not long before he had arranged for a supposedly private letter to a New York friend to be "leaked" to journalists. For their ultimate benefit, he wrote from Paris: "I have been over to London in order to see Pavlowa and Mordkin. They have achieved a success there beyond all belief—a success so great that Mr. Butt, manager of the Palace Theater, canceled Pavlowa's engagement at the Grand Opera at the sacrifice of a large sum in order to keep her as the star attraction of the London season." After this falsehood, Centanini artlessly rearranged a few more facts:

> The Russian Season at the Opera was no more than half a success on account of Pavlowa's absence. As a matter of fact, when it was known that Pavlowa would not dance at all in Paris, numerous subscribers canceled their subscriptions, and, notwithstanding the beauty of the costumes and scenery, ballets like *Sylphides* and others that achieved great triumphs last year owing to Pavlowa were this year not more than a demi-success, as they call it here in Paris. After seeing all the dancers that are starred here I am absolutely convinced that no other dancer can be considered for one moment in the same classification as Pavlowa.

How would Centanini square this view were he forced to replace an injured Pavlova with some other performer?

It was on the first day of July 1910 that the great Petipa died. His death closed an era and even ended a certain approach to ballet life. It severed a direct link with an astonishing heritage, and it cut the true filial link that Anna Pavlova felt with her St. Petersburg upbringing. She was adrift, and there was no longer a secure anchorage where the lighthouse beam was true and constant. If the King had died in London, certainly another kind of king had vanished from the world of ballet. Pavlova's thoughts turned more and more toward the New World, for she was now aware that with her success in London, her position there was safe for as long as she cared to exercise her prerogative. Thus it no longer satisfied her.

The death of Petipa emphasized one more brutal fact: Pavlova could now rely for suitable new choreography on Fokine—and who else? She listened to Mordkin's ambitions for producing new images in ballet, and they both realized that to avoid Diaghilev was to compete with him. Fokine's *Schéhérazade* had been a wild success in Paris at the beginning of June, and it had been talked about as a concept for months. Mordkin, knowing that their American tour would need an exotic spectacle, had his own ideas for an Oriental dance-drama; it was a rehash of everything he had already learned from Fokine's *Cléopâtre* and everything he thought *Schéhérazade* probably was. His own Arabian Nights confection was to be known as *The Legend of Azyiade*. (In its initial stages of preparation it was actually referred to as *The Arabian Nights*.) Being a Mordkin enterprise, it was not strictly a vehicle for Pavlova alone, but rather an interminable duet in which danseur and ballerina vied for attention. Mordkin had been left with selecting the music, and his conservative tastes matched those of Pavlova; he selected from melodic, if only faintly exotic, scores, drawing on Glazunov, Chaminade, and of

Pavlova happily demonstrating that she was not "gaunt." The presentation is a hybrid:
the headdress is from *Daughter of the Pharaoh*, the veil is from the *Bacchanale*, and the pose
suggests her first appearance in *The Legend of Azyiade*. New York, 1910.

With Mordkin in *The Legend of Azyiade*.

formed hips were far more accommodating of male fantasies than Rubinstein's attenuated form. When it became apparent that any further unveiling of Pavlova would be indiscreet, the lights dimmed for the next scene. Pavlova emerged in harem attire; it was really a female version of Nijinsky's slave costume in *Schéhérazade*. Her quaintly daring culottes were something of a show-stopper for customers who had not imagined that "ocular opera" could extend to blatant eroticism.

Being under opera management meant that there was a tremendous emphasis on the musical presentation. It was one thing to collect music, quite another to know that one could get that music played in an intelligent manner. Pavlova had been conscious of the dispiriting performances given by the rather disdainful orchestra members during her first visit to America. Their performances had sufficed, since the engagements had been few and the ballet itself such a novelty that its musical content was of secondary consideration; nevertheless, even then there had been murmurings of discontent from influential quarters. Boston had a critic who did not temper his views. During the spring visit with *Coppélia* he had been in no way antagonistic to the music of Delibes, noting that it was "often as fine, subtle, soft of texture, and lovely of design as lace, and the rhythms are the spangles by which it shines." But then came his assessment of the conductor's handling of this music:

> Mr. Podesti conducted the music like the stone-breaker of Strauss's song. And Delibes did not compose mazurkas with a mallet and a chisel or conceive the fall of the dancers' feet in a czardas as like to the descent of a steam hammer in a foundry, or even write the waltz of the automatons to overwhelm the clatter of tongues at a table d'hôte. Perhaps he saw, too, his music translated into motion and pantomime by the practiced and imaginative dancers of the [Paris] Opera as they were in the '70s by Rita Sangalli and in the '80s by Rosita Mauri, and not by the clumsy, hesitating, rhythmless, expressionless coryphées of the Metropolitan. To be half a beat behind or half a beat ahead—and Mr. Podesti's beats were blows—was their terpsichorean pastime. And *Coppélia* is all delicate fantasy, humor, light, shade, and always artistry.

"Poetry in motion" would not win any converts if reviews like that were to be the order of the day. It was clear that the forthcoming American itinerary demanded not only a traveling orchestra fully versed in the entire repertoire, but a musical director who could bridge the gap between the stage requirements and the demands of a relatively discerning audience, drawn for the most part from established opera patrons.

course Rimsky-Korsakov, as well as Rubinstein, Borodin, and Bourgault-Ducoudray. This last composer, much in favor at the time for soupy concert pieces, was also entrusted with the transcriptions for the new ballet. He handed them over to Mordkin on July 2—and died four days later.

The libretto of *Azyiade* was certainly drama; as Centanini would have said (and his brochure did), "Not a line is spoken, not a word sung. Only the graceful movement of the ballet and the rhythmic sway of the character dancers, supplemented by music especially written for the purpose, illuminate the theme, or plot." The poetry of motion! By some strange chance (understood all too well by those who worked in the rather incestuous world of the theatre), George Bernard Shaw had revealed his Cleopatra from the folds of a carpet, Fokine had unwrapped his Cleopatra from a mummifying swathe of twelve veils (shades of Pavlova in *Eunice*), and Mordkin, not to be outdone, unrolled his heroine from a fabulous rug, revealing a beautiful captive, "fair as the lilies that deck the banks of the Euphrates." Like Ida Rubinstein in Fokine's ballet, Pavlova was first revealed to view swaddled in veils, and Pavlova's supposed gauntness, which had earned strictures in Europe, was seen to be a calumny. Her strong, well-

In London, Pavlova and Mordkin were already rehearsing new ballets, in addition to those others they were planning to present in America, and they knew the futility of arriving without a musical director. Daniel Mayer spotted the obvious opportunity for one of his own clients and quickly put forward the name of Theodore Stier, an émigré Austrian at that time conducting in the Bechstein (now Wigmore) Hall. Pavlova made a surreptitious visit to one of his concerts and approved of what she heard, so Mayer quickly produced Stier at Golders Green for an interview. One of the conductor's assets was that he was bilingual—but this skill was not really called upon, as Pavlova had clearly decided already to offer him the engagement. After five minutes, Stier was on his way back across Hampstead Heath. Pavlova had been sitting for a portrait, so there was some excuse for the brevity of the interview; but she had relied on her sharp intuition, and as usual it did not betray her. Stier proved an admirable choice.

Mordkin had been given an added responsibility for the approaching tour—that of ballet master. It was his job also to recruit the soloists. He chose five couples from his own Moscow company, and although the advance publicity suggested that the entire tour was a traveling version of the Imperial Russian Ballet, any extra corps de ballet dancers were to be recruited in America from opera house companies. Mordkin's girlfriend Pajitzkaya was given billing as "first solo danseuse," and in any ballet in which the two stars were not performing, her name was to be in the program in a typeface the same size as that used for Pavlova and Mordkin. This rash move by Rabinoff could only lead to trouble.* There was already a strong bias toward the Mordkin side of the enterprise, with his name liberally sprinkled about the programs wherever there was the slightest opportunity—as co-star, ballet "composer," or revivifier of such as the long-suffering Giselle, for Pavlova had decided to take the chance that interpretive passion could keep opera audiences involved in Giselle's fate, and at the same time distract them from Adam's score. She could not know how the Arabian confection would be received. The rest was a collection of bits and pieces, including the two London favorites, Valse Caprice and the Bacchanale, as well as the Bleichmann pas de deux, the Grand Pas de Deux from the third act of The Sleeping Beauty, and The Swan, as well as the usual character dances for the company.

While the summer season at the Palace was in progress, Mordkin received an invitation to appear with Carlotta Zambelli at an entertainment given by Baron Maurice de Rothschild at his country chateau outside Paris. Butt could not agree to Mordkin's taking leave, though the French foreign minister was luckier when he asked for Pavlova and Mordkin to put in an appearance at a soirée he was giving in Paris. The combination of the French government *and* Pavlova was sufficient to make the English impresario relent. Both dancers returned with specially struck gold medals as a token of the minister's appreciation for this fleeting visit.

It was a prelude to a far more hectic and sustained period of travel. The dancers had proved in London that they could cope with nightly appearances as well as specially extended Wednesday matinees, a schedule that a cosseted Imperial dancer, used to the usual two or three performances a week, might well have thought crushing. Yet even this weekly stint was nothing as compared to the long haul looming across the Atlantic, where they would never have fewer than eight performances a week, and in some instances would have eleven.

Once more Pavlova's constitution battled with the Atlantic; once more American publicists heralded the impending arrival of the two dancers as an event of the greatest magnitude; and once more Mordkin looked forward to being received as a conquering hero. Apart from the little matter of the first review of the spring tour, which had credited him with "assisting" Pavlova, the rest of that visit had been a smooth conquest, nowhere more blazoned than in the New York *Telegraph*, which had provided balm for his soul: "While Madame Pavlova, whose fame preceded her appearance in New York by many months, quite fulfilled expectations, it was Mordkin who took us entirely by storm and created by far the greater sensation." Even then Pavlova must have reflected that she could easily have asked for Theodore Koslov, whom London had thought the finest of male dancers, yet one who had not encroached into Karsavina's limelight. By the autumn, *Valse Caprice* was being listed as a solo for Pavlova; she was already looking for more *pas seul*.

AU REVOIR!

A snapshot of Mlle. Anna Pavlova, the famous Russian dancer, whose triumphal season at the Palace concludes at the end of this month, after which she will probably return to America for a short season. On the right is Prince Tschagadaeff, who has done so much to popularise Russian music and dancing in London. On the left is M. Mordkin, who has appeared with Mlle. Pavlova during her engagement at the Palace

---

* The other girls were talented classical soloists: Hilda Bewicke (Bewickova), Stanislava Kuhn, Stephania Plaskowieczka, and Alina Schmolz. The men were Kyprian Barboe, Mikhail Moisseyev, Sergei Moroseff, Alexis Trojanovski, and Veronine West, one of two brothers—*which* brother the programs did not specify.

Act One of the Pavlova-Mordkin *Giselle*, New York, October 1910.

Stier had his problems from the moment of his arrival. At the first rehearsal at the Metropolitan Opera House he was barely into his stride when an official of the Musicians' Union stayed his arm. It seemed that unless Stier complied with the regulations, he could not conduct the orchestra, and he could not comply with the regulations until he was a full member of the union. And to be a member of the union, he had to be an American citizen. The official wrapped up his argument rather succinctly by suggesting to Stier that if he did not "come along" he was liable to find himself "in a jackpot." Events took an easier turn after this intimidating overture; someone placed a violin in Stier's hands, he drew a single chord from it, became a musician at a stroke,

and could thereafter pay his dues, conduct the orchestra, and take out what was known as the First Paper relating to the American Aliens Board.

The diplomatic go-between who might have smoothed over all these troublesome ripples was back in St. Petersburg. Victor Dandré had returned to his city council duties; he sat at the Senior Procurator's table of the main department of the ruling senate. Dandré certainly had a way with figures; Pavlova on her own was less able to juggle with the financial requirements of the disparate departments surrounding her own contributions to the art of dancing. Money went out and money came in, as often as not directly into her own traveling bag, along with the jewels and

118

Act Two of *Giselle*. Obviously a rehearsal pose, given the irregularities in footwear and headgear.

the diary of coming events, which represented her real worldly wealth. The Tsar was gaining a handsome recompense for the absence of two of his leading dancers. It was said that the stipend Pavlova had forfeited at the Maryinsky in order to pursue her art (and financial gain) abroad had been in the region of 21,000 roubles—the sum that would have been guaranteed her, as a ballerina, had she given the Maryinsky first call on her services for the remaining years of her statutory employment. The wealth that was now available to her was infinitely greater, but the long-term security was less.

Centanini and Rabinoff had contrived to schedule two performances for the opening date of October 15: a matinee at the

Met for the press, and a subscription night at the Brooklyn Academy of Music. The dancers began with their Louis Quinze version of *Giselle*, followed it with a couple of solos, emoted their way through *The Legend of Azyiade,* and ended up with the *Bacchanale*. It turned out not to have been such a good idea to give the press plenty of time to polish their phrases for the following morning's editions. The influential New York *Telegraph* had sent Algernon St. John-Brenon to view the proceedings, and he was in irrepressible form. Nobody was spared.

The Count G. P. Centanini and the Samovar Max Rabinoff (a Russian nobleman) have gone to extreme pains in presenting Mlle.

Pavlowa and Mikhail Mordkin to the general American public. A part of their presentation took place yesterday afternoon at the Metropolitan Opera House, and the noble stage so often devoted to the music drama was entirely devoted to legs, mostly archangelic. . . . The owners of Pavlowa and Mordkin were fully aware that these two had captured the imagination of opera goers during the past season, so they advanced Michael—low! vulgar! Mikhail we meant to write—and Mlle. Pavlowa under the extraordinary denomination of "ocular opera," which means opera with eyes, as if some there were particularly distinguished (like many singers) for its ears. . . .

Ourselves did not think it as much opera as it was legs. Mordkin's are particularly magnificent. In certain companies they would be starred. Tacitly, I believe they are starred in this. They received a round of applause all to themselves yesterday, when they came along, with Mordkin safely fixed on them holding a bow and arrow, the arrow being recklessly discharged at George Maxwell in the wings and hitting him directly above the fifth royalty. Mordkin's legs were painted brown, out of compliment to the Comptroller of the House, Mr. John Brown; for this and other reasons they were frequently encored. The enthusiasm of the elderly ladies in the audience was remarkable. . . . Aye, and we had much of Mr. Mordkin. He appeared as a romantic creature in the time of Louis Quinze, in love and finally in a tomb. He appeared as a Terrible Turk, with a polygamic of salutary non-suffragists tripping it lightly by the sunlit Bosphorus to the pleasing accompaniment of an officer of the harem with a meat ax, which he waved to and fro menacingly in order to keep the ladies the victims of polygamy—though women are not the only victims of polygamy—in good humor with themselves.

And what did one enjoy most? Was it the ballet *Giselle* with a mad scene and a tomb, invaluable properties in any opera, ocular or opiate? Was it *Azyiade or the Arabian Knight?* 'Twasn't. 'Twasn't nothing of the kind, no how. It was the Bacchanale, music by Glazounow, dancing by Mlle. Anna Pavlowa, poses and smiles by

Rehearsing *Giselle* with Mordkin at the Metropolitan Opera House, New York, October 1910. The final moments of Act One.

Mikhail Mordkin, ocular lyrics by Theodore Stier, silent jokes by Joe Herbert, Esq., wigs by Hepner, legs by Mikhail Mordkin. Herein Mlle. Pavlowa, simulating the gesture and bearing that we see on precious vases dug up in Athens or Birmingham, showed the full amount of gracefulness and dashfulness that resides in her. As a dancer she has a redoubtable technique, genuine poetry and sometimes dazzling execution. The gracefulness alluded to accounts for her positive genius in concealing—at least making us forget—the length and gauntness of her figure. Of the exquisite daintiness, the insuperable bewitchment of Genée she has—or shows—but little, but she has done much by virtue of the complete and exhaustive discipline she received in the training schools of Russia and by virtue of an innate talent to restore to its ancient pedestal the prone figure of the muse of dancing, the primal mimetic art to which we owe those supreme histrionic types, music and acting.

The range of feelings that can be expressed by dancing is but scant, and as we saw yesterday a pirouette in a moment of tempestuous emotion is as absurd as a vocalization in the midst of a dramatic agony. A few years ago too little was claimed for dancing and today too much. But there are always the legs. . . . The last glimpse of the chestnut legs was obtained at 5:30 o'clock.

The music-hall atmosphere of the Palace Theatre in London, with the pervading scent of oranges, the noisy shelling of nuts in the upper galleries, and the not inaudible calls of meat pie vendors, must have seemed blissful compared to the daunting prospect of getting ballet some form of serious consideration in America. If this was what a leading New York newspaper offered as a summary of the entertainment, what hope was there once the entourage headed west? To some extent Centanini and Mordkin had dug a pit for themselves with their absurdly inflated advance publicity, but Pavlova must have felt that she was battling with the Viennese all over again. Had they known what the papers were dishing out, it is doubtful that the dancers would have found the energy for the evening performance. But there was simply no time to rage or sulk. And if the truth had been reported with a little more objectivity, one would have learned that the audience had enjoyed itself.

But the program as a whole was heavy going, and fears that *Giselle* might be too much of an antique for American audiences looked well founded. Although the dancers had the very evident goodwill of their audiences, it was an uphill battle getting any kind of critical acceptance of the Romantic tragedy. A syndicated article reported the dancers' success, all the more astonishing in view of the hurdles:

The atmosphere of the theater was stifling. The orchestra was execrable. It recalled the worst of the gutter bands ever brought here by Strauss or Mascagni. It set the teeth of the audience on edge, and in the Russian mazurka almost brought the dancers to a standstill. Then the waits were interminable, and *Giselle*, Adam's old ballet, which began the program, is a weariness to the flesh. Yet, over all these obstacles, the art of the two dancers triumphed.

The article explained that Karsavina had been dancing the role of Giselle in Paris the previous summer, and that it had been

The ubiquitous bow-and-arrow dance:
(left) Mordkin, (center) Alexandre Volinine, (right) Anatole Oboukhov.
Mordkin actually released his arrows into the wings during performances;
Oboukhov, on the other hand, managed without any arrows at all.

"incarnated two years ago, in the plump person of Mme. Alda," and then went on to give the work a further drubbing:

> The piece dates from the days in which the ballet was recognized as a possible means of tragic expression. The heroine even lets down her hair and goes mad. Operatic insanity, with its invariable flute, is hardly plausible in these days, and even the frequent anguish expressed on Mme. Pavlowa's face could not relieve the tedium. . . . In the second act the dancer was exquisitely ethereal and moved through the air with melting beauty of pose. That there can be poetry in motion her every attitude reveals, and the old platitude takes on the commonplace literalness of a breakfast food advertisement when applied to the fay who hovered and twinkled over the stage of the Metropolitan Opera House yesterday afternoon. The music has a certain old-fashioned charm and there is a faded prettiness about the action of *Giselle*. Yet it pre-supposes that the ballet can be accepted as the vehicle of serious dramatic expression, and its conventions became ridiculous years ago when they were put to any such test. Possibly some of the ones who are constantly prating of the dry eloquence of pantomime may find delight in *Giselle,* but the ballet is just about as interesting to ordinary play goers now as looking over the files of *Godey's Lady's Book* for 1858 might prove.

The *Bleichmann Adagio* did not seem to win much favor, but Mordkin's *Bow and Arrow* variation, now a separate solo, broke through the audience's reserve, and the *Bacchanale* worked up a whirlwind of applause. There were also on the program some Russian dances to Tchaikovsky, some czardas to Liszt, and *The Legend of Azyiade*. This work in itself was fifty minutes long, so Pavlova and Mordkin danced rather more than a normal three-act work would have demanded. American audiences of the time would have fainted at the prospect of sitting through a four- or five-act work such as St. Petersburg audiences often enjoyed.

Their train whirled along relentlessly, and there was no time for the troupe to pause and reconsider, and little enough time to rest; but as they progressed, so they encountered more tolerance for their programs. By the time they reached St. Louis, in early November, not only was the Odeon Theatre packed, but every possible standing space had been taken as well. Centanini's plan was working: the one-night stands were ensuring a rush for seats. Significantly, *Giselle* had still not put in a reappearance, and the reporter for the *Globe* did not seem disappointed:

> To call what was offered on the stage dancing is to use a heavy, earth-clinging term. The evolutions of M. Mordkin seemed more like flying and the presentations of Mlle. Pavlowa more like the mid-air gyrations of a Bleriot monoplane. In the Bleichman pas de deux, performed by the principals with complete orchestral accom-

121

Two Famous Russian Dancers as They Look Off the Stage. Anna Pavlowa and Lydia Lopoukowa.

San Francisco, 1910.

paniment, the audience caught the elevating spirit of the performance to such unwonted extent that rapturous applause broke forth in the middle of this act, so impatient was the house to show its approval. Mlle. Pavlowa's solo dance *The Swan,* to the familiar Saint-Saëns music, was bird-like grace itself, accentuated by the finest human mimicry. Here truly it became apparent what the visitors gave forth in advance of their coming, namely, that they are introducing an art new to America. If this be Russian dancing it is difficult to see how the dancing of any other nation or people can stand in preference to it.

The climate changed in more than one sense by the time the tour reached the West Coast, where San Francisco had made it clear that it was not prepared to imitate blindly the distant adulation. As George Shoals pointed out in the San Francisco *Argus,* "The fame of the Russian artists had extended to San Francisco before their coming was announced, but it did not ensure their success here. Other famous artists have come to this city and found a strange indifference to their claims. But Pavlowa and Mordkin, and their managers, have no reason to question the interest of San Franciscans in an artistic novelty or the lavish appreciation shown when they are pleased." Shoals was summing up after a week in which the first signs were emerging of the crucial strain under which the dancers were performing—in Pavlova's case exacerbated by the attention given to Mordkin, his name often preceding hers at the head of the reviews. Just as Mordkin had suffered in New York in the spring, so now Pavlova could hardly have been pleased to observe in a review the subheading "Pavlowa Also Charms."

On the opening night at the Valencia Theatre in San Francisco there was a turmoil backstage, which resulted in Pavlova, after only one brief appearance early in the evening, storming out of the theatre. When it became apparent that she would not dance during the remainder of the evening, a considerable proportion of the audience asked for its money back at the box office. They received it. Ironically, the incident underlined the drawing power that she did actually wield. The manager of the theatre drew upon all his resources of diplomacy in order to repair the dollar damage, and he persuaded the company to return for an extra performance on the Sunday following their brief sojourn in Los Angeles.

Extraordinarily, they were not the only Russian dancers in San Francisco at that time. Over at the Orpheum ("the safest and most magnificent theater in America") Lydia Lopokhova, her brother Theodore, and Alexandre Volinine were paying a week's visit as part of a vaudeville program.* There was the usual trouble with names—"Lapokawa" and "Valinene" in the first review—but these "Imperial Russian Dancers—by special permission of the Czar of Russia" gave a program that, though very short, was popular. It gave the San Francisco *Chronicle* a chance to take a swipe at the Valencia's temperamental star. After rhapsodizing about the pretty, well-rounded, and flower-like Lydia and her consorts, it continued: "When these performers, who have technique at the tips of the fingers (and toes), can be seen in conjunction with a number of other interesting acts for six bits [the cheapest seat at the Orpheum that week was actually 10 cents], why pay more than three times that amount for the doubtful pleasure of watching the dances of a countrywoman of theirs who cannot dance?"

Pavlova was back in action for the full program on the second evening in San Francisco, and patrons and critics alike were in a forgiving mood. Shoals wrote in the *Argus:*

> Mlle. Pavlowa is much more than the *premier* [sic] *ballerina assoluta* familiar as the star of the ballet in grand opera. She has mastered the technique of her art as few have done before her, and those few the great ones of earlier days. She is young, slender, and symmetrical, and endowed with a beauty that gives a peculiar charm to her dramatic expression. For she is an actress of genuine power, as well as a dancer. The set smile of the ballet is not for her. Entreaty, coquetry, passion, fear, terror, even madness, and the simulated convulsion of approaching death, are all equally at her command. And the spirit of youth, the seemingly unstudied grace of nature, gaiety and freedom, pervade all her movements. Years of instruction, application and practice were necessary to acquire such finish. Her ability comes of knowledge and not of inspiration.

If Mr. Shoals had watched Pavlova longer, he might have noticed that certain day-to-day refinements in her performances were more the result of intuitive improvisation than a blind

---

* Lydia, a St. Petersburg product, was having her first taste of widespread travel that year, following Diaghilev's seasons in Berlin and Paris. Volinine, schooled in Moscow, had also done the Diaghilev tour; but at the age of twenty-eight he was a seasoned traveler, and had been as far as Australia with Genée. He also partnered the prima ballerina Geltzer, in Moscow and abroad. Little did he know what travels lay ahead of him still.

following of pattern—even if the set pattern was her own. But he was an alert observer, and he was the first to point out the similarity between the famous nineteenth-century Romantic painting "The Storm" by Pierre Cot, widely reproduced in its day, and the entrance with the veil in the *Bacchanale*. Mordkin won his customary paean of praise:

> He is physically fit to be a sculptor's model, and thought and emotion as well as manly beauty mark his face. There are feminine graces of the ballet which are set apart, but in lightness, swiftness, harmony of posing, he is no shade less of accomplishment than his co-star. Invaluable as he is as an aide and partner in the dances with Pavlowa, strengthening and perfecting every phrase of interpretation, he is quite as attractive a figure when dancing alone. The productions of the company are also of his arrangement.

This understanding, fostered by the programs, banished Fokine and Petipa, to say nothing of Perrot, though Mordkin may have made such changes as would have made the great choreographers delighted to let their works pass into anonymity.

After the unfortunate start, Pavlova was clearly on her mettle. With a schedule so hectic, she may not at first have realized that the other Russians were already in town, but it must have been brought home to her that San Francisco was not a city to dismiss; the earthquake of four years before was a momentary interruption in a long history of excellence on its stages, and Shoals had been right to point out that the city had proved a graveyard for many overinflated reputations. San Francisco was the first to wonder why *Giselle* opened the program, when it seemed to be the tour de force of the evening.

In the divertissements, Pavlova made a program change, substituting *The Fire Bird* for *La Nuit*, and "in a costume of tattered orange and vermilion, proceeded to emulate a flame with results that were at once artistic and realistic." As the critic pointed out, she had not done the Blue Bird pas de deux (for such it was) since leaving the Maryinsky. The "tattered" costume was one so similar to that worn by Karsavina in the Diaghilev repertory that it was only a matter of days before there was a small outcry from Paris, with the dressmaker being accused of copying the original Bakst costume. This accusation she denied with spirit. It was, she said, from a Paquereau sketch on a postcard handed to her by Ivan Clustine, ballet master at the Opéra. Nobody seemed to remember that a photograph of the Bakst costume had been in the program for the first Opéra gala in June 1909; the plagiarism could have been subconscious. (It had been accompanied in the program by a picture of Nijinsky, in his turban and tunic costume. The caption read "Mlle Nijinska.")

Notwithstanding the Orpheum's cheap seats, patrons in the Valencia on November 22 got remarkable value for their money. Apart from *Giselle*, and the *Fire Bird* pas de deux, they had *The Swan* and *Bow and Arrow*, and two more: "A Chopin valse was charged with quaint coquetry and rare humor. Her last offering, which might have been called 'variations on the hue of orange,' was danced to a harp obligato." The Chopin piece may well have been the Minute Waltz. For the other, one might suppose that Mordkin had remembered Gorsky's most recent (1908) version of *Raymonda*, in which there was a dance called "En Orange"; it cropped up later, with a solo violin playing an air by Giraud, in a transcription that was probably by Glazunov.

Before ending his review, Ralph Renaud delivered some sharp observations in the San Francisco *Chronicle*:

> I would like to say a word concerning a curious misconception which has spread in regard to these dancers. Many came expecting to find certain qualities which there is no pretense made of offering. These performers are primarily dancers and not interpreters. They dance to the accompaniment of music, and do not, for the most part, attempt to suggest its esoteric raptures in their bodily motions, which remain largely an extension of themselves. First of all their art is the artificial and formally beautiful one of the ballet, though they present variations, to be sure, and elaborate developments. Their groundwork, however, is that of the trained toe-dancer and all their efforts are built on that. It is fundamentally different from what Maud Allan, Isadora Duncan and their disciples are trying to do. They seek to give the music a visual form. Yet there is no reason why each school should not be judged on its merits and every reason why neither should be judged by the standard of the other. Those prejudiced in favor of Allan and Duncan will call Mordkin and Pavlowa superficial. Those swayed toward the Russians will call the classic [i.e., "Greek"] dancers vague. This is all very foolish. It means both motes and beams in the point of view.

In December at the Alvin Theatre in Pittsburgh, Bronislava Pajitzkaya received enthusiastic requests for encores in a Russian dance; and it was only later that the *Dispatch* saved the day, saying of Pavlova that she "combines the exquisite daintiness of Genée, the classic grace of Isadora Duncan, . . . and the languid orientalism of Ruth St. Denis, with much besides that is all hers alone."

Back in Chicago, where they played together with short opera performances, the dancers were treated as old friends rather than foreign invaders. In a general theatre review, Felix Borowsky thought that "if the quite extraordinary success of Miss Pavlowa

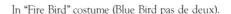

In "Fire Bird" costume (Blue Bird pas de deux).

and her partner is any indication that the fickle public is about to take the ballet to its heart once more, it is possible that the association of the dance with operatic music will not be due to an occasional condescension on the part of impresarios, but that the ballet will hop about the stage with a consciousness of its inalienable rights." From his description of the program, one gets the impression that Pavlova was making very free adaptations of dances that had started life as duets, in order that her solos should outnumber those of Mordkin. She was said to have been seen in "an adagio by Drigo, a 'piece' of the music of which consisted of an exceedingly commonplace tune played by the harp; the *Fire Bird* of Tchaikowsky, a Valse of Chopin, and Saint-Saëns's *Le Cygne*," while Mordkin appeared in his *Bow and Arrow* dance and in "some offerings with Mlle. Pavlowa."

Amazingly, there was no serious interruption to the travelers' physical progression, which was like some medieval caravan bearing strange treasures across an uncharted land; and the two rarest jewels were neither lost nor stolen, nor did they stray. Without any serious physical incapacity, Pavlova, Mordkin, and their hard-working troupe settled into a regime which, because there were really no days for rest, kept them at a fine pitch; but it was doubtful if, from week to week, they were fully aware which city lay beyond each theatre and each hotel—that is, when the luxury of more than a night in one place freed the dancers from their train accommodations.

By December 14 they were back in New York to test the traditional apathy toward theatrical entertainments associated with the Christmas period. The opening night seemed to confirm all their fears, since the Metropolitan was far from full; but the audience was loyal and welcoming, and greeted everything with prolonged applause. "Anna Pavlowa and Mikail Mordkin Again Captivate by Their Seductive Art" ran one headline. Once they had bowed in, the dancers shared the programs with opera: *Orfeo ed Euridice* was being given again, in Italian, after many years' absence. The composer's namesake, Alma Gluck, was singing, and Toscanini led the orchestra with his usual electrifying command. At a quarter past eleven he yielded the podium to Stier, and the ballet began. Again the society boxes remained full of interested patrons, who found Pajitzkaya's solo Russian Dance a distinct hit.

Two days before Christmas the troupe made a quick sortie to Boston. The *Evening Transcript* reported on the event: "For forty minutes Miss Pavlova with Mr. Mordkine and ten of the little company that they have now brought with them to America danced at the Opera House last night. An audience of exceptional numbers that might easily have been bored by the lifeless and careless performance of *Pagliacci* that preceded the dancers watched them with rapt interest and applauded them as only in recent memory Mme. Melba has been applauded." Behind the curtains, Centanini still left nothing to chance, and an exhausted Pavlova was always instructed as to which box should receive her first curtsey.

For the first time in her life, Pavlova found herself in a foreign country at Christmas time, already dislocated by the fact that it was being celebrated according to the Gregorian calendar, thirteen days ahead of Russia's Julian calendar. For the dancers it was work as usual. The tour was heading north into Canada; obdurate members of the American Musicians' Union had to acquire an ability to play the British national anthem—and in a recognizable manner. It was a polyglot little empire of its own that traveled on the train; and at the performances, an Austrian conducted Americans for Russians, all in the name of art and dollars.

A rare bit of drama occurred in Hamilton, Ontario, on the night of January 18, 1911, when a steel clamp from the handle of a sword wielded by Mordkin during the fight scene in *Azyiade* flew into the audience and embedded itself in the skull of an assistant manager of a local dry-goods company. This luckless young man had been seated in the eighth row of the orchestra, and the missile lodged itself above his right eye. Several women seated nearby fainted; the victim clapped his hands to his head, staggered out into the lobby (with some assistance), and there collapsed, unconscious. When he reached the hospital it was discovered that there had been no serious penetration of the brain, but pressure had already caused paralysis and other grave symptoms, necessitating an immediate operation. All that the dismayed dancers could learn the following day was that the condition of the ballet-struck Hamiltonian was considered "hopeful." A police investigation of the accident was promptly made, but no person was held, and after depositing a $5,000 bond, the company was allowed to depart.

Two days later they were back on American soil, in Detroit. This city liked *Giselle*, and in this ballet Pavlova was considered to be a supreme artist: "She has poetry in her soul, for she gives expression to poetic images. She is an actress, for she depicts human emotions. She has a sense of color, of rhythm, of perspective and of proportion. Her medium is the unspoken story, and through that medium she is enabled by the matchless perfection of her art to attain heights of poetic beauty hitherto undreamed of in all the wide domain of Terpsichore." In New

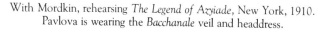

With Mordkin, rehearsing *The Legend of Azyiade,* New York, 1910.
Pavlova is wearing the *Bacchanale* veil and headdress.

Haven at the close of the program, hundreds of Yale students waited outside the theatre to form an escort of honor that followed the stars' automobiles all the way back to the private train, with much singing and cheering along the route. The following day, professors in several departments used this enthusiasm as an excuse to assign papers and give lectures relating to dance as a medium of art, and Cole Porter, then a student, would later effortlessly rhyme "Mordkin" with "lordkin." At the vast Boston Opera House, which was crowded to capacity, hundreds of people were turned away, and seats were even sold behind the wings on the stage. With such appallingly disconcerting practices, it is little wonder there were occasional flare-ups and bouts of tears in the relative privacy of the dressing rooms.

Pavlova had been away from Russia for a year, but she was certainly not forgotten in her homeland. The Tsar sent her a large gold medal bearing his portrait and an inscription expressing his pleasure at the way in which she was carrying Russian artistry abroad. At the Maryinsky, Gerdt had just celebrated his benefit night for fifty years' service, with a revision by Legat of Petipa's *Bluebeard*, in which Kchessinskaya danced with the beneficiary. The St. Petersburg audience had just seen Fokine's *Carnaval* for the first time; a few nights later Kchessinskaya celebrated her twenty-year jubilee, and she was thought to have lost nothing of her brilliance and virtuosity. Although Legat retained the title of Ballet Master, the same position had been bestowed on Fokine the previous autumn, the management perhaps hoping that his creative urge would spread itself a little more freely on their stage rather than on those of foreign cities.

Away in Toledo, Ohio, Fokine's erstwhile dancing partner was performing a medley of items in which choreographic exactitude sometimes gave way to experimentation, depending on mood, the orchestra's finesse, and the degree of encouragement from the audience. Toledo seemed to assess the dancing by the brilliance of the modern transport outside the theatre's doors: "Were the Russian dancers popular? If 27 hired carriages, 42 private horse vehicles of the single and double-barreled variety, 72 electrics and 31 other autos, from an $8,000 touring car to the humble and nimble Hupmobile, are any criterion, then they were." The reporter was so busy tabulating the vehicles that there was no time left to comment on the event that had attracted them. He concluded that there was on display "something like $250,000 worth of the means of locomotion of the privileged classes."

By March, as the marathon drew to its end, the thirty-five members of the orchestra were entering into the spirit of things. As each performance ended they were one stage nearer the final effort, and at the end of the *Bacchanale*, which invariably closed each program, the musicians were often seen to be cheering as delightedly as the audience. Centanini's military planning was standing the test. Apart from one Pullman car breaking down (with the result that the musicians, demanding their rights, invaded Pavlova's own car in order to continue their all-night poker game in the "first quality" accommodations to which they were entitled), the schedule was adhered to, and even the peripheral travel arrangements seemed to go without a hitch. In places like Canton, Ohio, there were special cars running on the suburban lines, and patrons were drawn from as far afield as Akron, Massillon, Alliance, Salem, Wooster, and Ullrichsville; Sherrodsville even ran its own train. Pavlova and Mordkin together danced a Chopin waltz on this occasion, and she was thought to be "looking truly like a dream child, a creature of fancy, ready to flutter out of sight at any moment." In the hope of finding the reality behind the dream, the writer of these lines worked his way backstage. After the applause had ended, the reality of the situation was noted carefully:

> The little woman placed herself in the hands of her two maids and her secretary and doffed the tights and slippers and frilly fluffed short skirts and a few minutes later was threading her way among the busy stage-hands, an unobtrusive little figure, sharp-eyed, sharp-featured and somewhat angular, apparently of no more consequence than her maid in the hurly burly about her. . . . Mikhail Mordkin strode away to his dressing room and re-appeared in clothes that made him look much the same as the men about him but with considerably less hair on his head than when he was dancing. Girls, he wears a wig.

The manager of the theatre in Canton had no difficulty in meeting the pre-performance guarantee to Centanini, as nearly thirty-five hundred people had paid to see the Russians. The orchestra could have noted that its work was considered "good, yet left something to be desired in the way of tone quality and airiness and freshness of style."

The tour was now on the final loop heading back toward New York City. In Rochester the reception was ecstatic, and *Giselle* was winning a more than tolerant audience: "To see these people is an education in rhythm, in unobvious poetry, in a sort of silent music like that dreamed of by young Keats." By March 8 they had reached Hartford, where they were to perform at the Parsons Theatre. There stagehands were on strike and refused to allow the railway cars to be unloaded; the performance was given with some "house" scenery put in place by members of the management, who were unable to contrive a presentable stage before 8:40 p.m. A local newspaper the next morning was tactful: "The scene was supposed to be Oriental and the costumes and dancing were entirely so." (This was for *The Legend of Azyiade*.)

Pavlova arrived back in New York to face problems somewhat removed from the stage. At exactly that time in St. Petersburg the first signs of a scandal were brewing, and it appeared to involve her, obliquely. On February 27, 1911 (March 12 n.s.), in the St. Petersburg magazine *Footlights and Life,* a column headed "Items of Theatrical Life" contained the following statement: "Soon there will be an enquiry made by Senator Neidgard about the famous ballerina Pavlova in connection with the revision of the Town Council. The artist because of this is especially returning from America." This startling, if obscure, information must have been obtained some days prior to the publication date, for on that same day the *New Times* reported that the Bureau of Information had announced that Inspector

General D. B. Neidgard had indeed initiated an investigation—into one Romanov, a lawyer and Chairman of the Executive Committee concerned with the construction of the Okhtensky Bridge, a town planning project. All the paper could do was to outline Romanov's duties, pointing out that one of the functions of the committee of which he was chairman was to safeguard the interests of the city in connection with the building of the bridge. It was revealed that Romanov had asked the managing director of the contracting firm, Rudzki & Co., to lend him 15,000 roubles in bills of exchange. The matter was referred to the board of the company, who agreed. This favor granted by Rudzki & Co. was connected—so it was assumed—with a subsequent decision by the Executive Committee to grant the contracting company 80,000 roubles as disbursements for the drawing up of plans for the bridge. Now, the senatorial investigative body was demanding explanations from Romanov, and finding them unsatisfactory. Thus the matter was submitted to the prosecutor, and Romanov was relieved of his duties.

The day after the article in the *New Times* appeared, it was revealed that Judicial Interrogator Yurevich had been cross-examining the Chairman of the Commission of Inspectors to the St. Petersburg City Council. Victor Dandré, "in his capacity of accused," was cross-examined from morning until 7:00 in the evening. At the end of this time, the only significant fact to emerge was the move by the Judicial Interrogator to suppress any measures by Dandré "to evade interrogation or restraint by the court. V. E. Dandré left the Interrogation Room under escort for the House of Preliminary Confinement." In a word, he was arrested. It must be noted that due to *Footlights and Life* having blown the gaffe hours—if not days—before anyone else, Dandré would have had time to fire off warning words to America. Once the story broke officially, the more gossipy St. Petersburg newspapers were plainly making bricks with very little straw: Dandré was supposed to have made remarks such as "Wouldn't it be nice to be able to travel away somewhere?" It appeared that he was writing numerous letters, and it was said that a number of these were addressed to America.

In New York, Pavlova was settling the tour accounts with Rabinoff. Dandré seems to have been in communication with Pavlova during this fortnight; certainly it is to the New York offices that he would have written, since communications with the tour were chaotic. Pavlova asked Rabinoff to transmit the greater proportion of her earnings directly to Russia; it was nearly $18,000, the equivalent of the 35,000-rouble bail. Just as Pavlova was about to embark, the first hint of her problem appeared in the press; on April 6 the Atlanta *Journal* reported: "In some mysterious way some favorite at the palace—oh, a lady, of course, and a jealous one—got word to America that Anna, who has been dancing over here, had received a big share of the small fortune which a certain M. Dandré is accused of having looted from the Russian treasury." After suggesting that Pavlova had lurked in her dressing room at the Metropolitan for three days, refusing to dance because of the gossip, the *Journal* brought in the name of Dmitri Smirnoff as someone who had agreed to

Being met in London on arrival for her second season at the Palace Theatre, 1911.

make representations in St. Petersburg on behalf of the maligned dancer. Pavlova was credited with saying, "It was some jealous old cat who started the story."

Pavlova probably never saw the worst of it; she was back in England on April 10. Alighting from the *Mauretania* boat train, she professed to be delighted to be back, saying that she felt as if she were home. In among her personal luggage was a wooden crate containing a 30-inch baby alligator from Florida, named "Goosh," the latest "pet." (He got as far as St. Petersburg, where he perished from the cold and was turned into a handbag for his erstwhile mistress.) Alfred Butt's representative announced that Pavlova's dressing room at the Palace Theatre had been specially done up for the season and that this year she was securing the services of a Russian cook. With these tidbits, the press was momentarily satisfied, and Pavlova was able to depart for Golders Green, where another small suburban house had been rented for the duration of the season at the Palace.

Both Pavlova and Mordkin had renegotiated their contracts with Butt in August 1910, when the impresario had given notice that he would avail himself of a clause that enabled him to re-engage the artists on the same terms and conditions as before. At that stage Daniel Mayer had applied, on Mordkin's behalf, for better terms; Mordkin wanted £200 a week. Butt demurred, at which point Pavlova suggested replacing Mordkin with Alexei Koslov, who was performing in New York with a group of Russian dancers under contract to Morris Gest. While Mordkin and Butt wrangled over pay, overtures were made to Koslov, who actually cabled his acceptance, only to discover that he could not be released from his contract. His subsequent *volte-face* left Pavlova hopelessly out of countenance with Mordkin, who pressed home the advantage. Butt then agreed to a fee of £100 a week plus £25 extra for matinees, and also that he, Butt, would take the risk of private engagements, or lack thereof, and pay Mordkin £50 a week in consideration of such engagements. Mordkin asked for a concerted public relations campaign as well. Pavlova negotiated an increase for 1911 that, in favorable circumstances, could bring her income up to £1,200 a week, though she still had the responsibility of paying supporting artists.

As soon as the dancers' new season had begun at the Palace Theatre, it became clear that Mordkin was kicking against Mayer's extraction of 10 percent on all the engagements. Since these engagements were showing every sign of proliferating, Mayer was anxious to establish the validity of the initial contract,

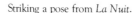

Striking a pose from *La Nuit*.

and he was forced to test his claims in a court of law to recover the relatively paltry sum of £106. The action in the Division of the King's Bench was scheduled for Monday, June 26, the day planned for the Coronation Gala at Covent Garden, King George V's coronation having been set for the preceding Thursday. Pavlova had no dispute with Mayer, whom she found thoroughly satisfactory as an agent, though it must have been disagreeable to her when he taxed her with the problem he was having with Mordkin, as he undoubtedly did, since she was the only other original signatory to the agreement.

Pavlova and Mordkin were welcomed by the Palace audiences with the clamor accorded particular favorites, and patrons could hardly believe their ears when, on the Friday evening of their first week, Pavlova was heard to administer a hearty slap to her partner at the conclusion of the *Bacchanale*. Nobody actually saw what happened, as the curtains were coming down at the time, but people in the front rows clearly heard a slap on stage, and it was unlikely to have been a tiff between stagehands. The truth of the matter was confirmed when the dancers took solo calls and did not appear together. They were number 13 on the program the following evening, and when that portentous number went into the frame, Mordkin appeared alone, bounding upon the stage, smiling, as *The Tatler* put it, "as if he were suddenly going to bite." The troupe then appeared, and then Pavlova, alone, in *La Nuit*. Pavlova made it a thing of beauty. With her flowing dress of pale blue and the large bouquet of marguerite daisies, her entrance was the more effective for being gentle and unobtrusive. She danced like a young girl surrendering herself to the mood of a summer's evening, as if taking hints borne on the night air. These seemed gradually to provoke a more passionate response, so that finally the flowers were discarded in a rapture of pure dance.

After this, there was some dancing by the little company of soloists, and then Pavlova did further dances alone, including a Chopin waltz that *The Tatler* thought "lost a great deal by being performed as a solo and not as a duet." Then there was *La Rose Qui Meurt* and *The Swan*, and finally *Papillons*. This was London's first sight of a shimmering little solo that electrified its audience. It too was based on pas de bourrée; but in contrast to *The Swan*, this piece was given a tremulous attack. It was all quivering speed and lightness, suddenly in view and—it seemed—just as quickly gone again.* As soon as she fluttered off, the curtain descended. Mordkin came out and bowed, then gesticulated toward the wings and shook his head. He appeared to be shouting something, but no one could hear him on account of the applause. He was wearing his costume for the *Bacchanale*, but no more was seen of his partner, so after a degree of further confusion the program continued with the bioscope films. Scenes

---

* Though the *Papillons* music was credited on the program to Drigo, Winifred Edwards remembers it as being Kitry's variation from the famous *Don Quixote* pas de deux—which means the credit should go to Minkus. Pavlova seems to have experimented with different music on different occasions. In later years, such was her nervousness before dancing the piece that she could never remember the music, and needed the first two or three bars to be hummed to her in the wings.

In costume for the Chopin *Variations* (also known as *Love's Message*).

of the Football Cup tie were greeted with hisses and shrill whistling, interspersed with cries of "Mordkin!" and "*Bacchanale!*" It was a full twenty minutes before the clamor subsided. Alfred Butt was forced to explain later to reporters that the quarrel, which he tacitly admitted, was entirely a personal one, and that the dancers had no differences with the management of the theatre. "I hope to be able to bring about a reconciliation shortly," he said, "but if this is impossible it will be necessary to find other partners for Pavlova and Mordkin in their double dances." And in double-quick time, he might have added.

Butt must have begun consulting his short list of replacements that weekend. By Monday night the dance portion of the Palace program was looking decidedly thin, with Pavlova and Mordkin doing only two spots each, and no *Bacchanale;* but the ebullient *Tatler* correspondent was enjoying the whole affair, saying that the dancing of Pavlova and Mordkin now held the added attraction of a bloodless war:

> Everybody is talking of the quarrel which prevents these two artists dancing together in those pieces which were the sensational joy of the last London season. Because, too, everybody has a theory as to its cause. . . . It is all quite funny and absurd and somewhat impertinent, but booing is wonderfully catching, and one never knows if one will not get a pretty scene of reconciliation for one's money. So

we continue to kick up a great shindy until we get turned out and spread the news of the matinee's disaster and failure through the whole of England. "I call it perfectly tragic," bemoaned "the creature" [society slang, in this case the writer's lady companion, who featured regularly in his column]. "I call it a perfect *coup de génie* of an advertisement," I retorted. And we booked our seats for the next performance.

Of course, he was right. It was marvelous publicity for the Palace, and it vied in the newspapers with matters such as Moroccan uprisings, the Veto Bill's passage through the House of Lords, and even the absurd event of an undertaker driving his hearse past the Albert Memorial in the mistaken belief that it led into a cemetery. Evening newspapers containing accounts of the latest bites and scratches sold like hot cakes. The *Tatler* writer got his wish for a reconciliation scene almost before his copy had gone to the printers. On Thursday night, April 27, it had been whispered that such an event might take place, and there was a general sense of disappointment when the Russian dancers' program came to an end without the expected pas de deux from the two stars. Then, according to the cool eye of *The Times,*

when the troupe came to take their final call, Pavlova led forward one of the ladies of the ballet, while Mordkin was at the other end

129

of the line of dancers. There were loud calls of *"Bacchanale"* from the audience, and after an interval Pavlova and Mordkin appeared on the stage together. Amid a scene of much enthusiasm Pavlova stepped forward and said, "To please you, I will dance the *Bacchanale.*" The two then gave their celebrated dance, and at its close they were warmly cheered and repeatedly recalled.

There was a change in the cast list right at the beginning of the season: Pajitzkaya was banished. She had become Mrs. Mordkin in America, and her husband was soon to suggest to the press that Pavlova had become insanely jealous of her popularity with audiences and had demanded that she be left out of the London season. Pajitzkaya was replaced by one Miss Pružena. The rest battled on: a little band of ten supporters all told, headed by two very newsworthy stars. Though rough partnering in the *Bacchanale* may have triggered the notorious slap, feelings must have been running very high for such a slip in professional conduct. There had been no comparable drama since the opening night in San Francisco five months earlier.

A leading article in *The Times* on May 2 eulogized the *Bacchanale* and its interpreters, and then went on to describe their pas de deux to a Chopin waltz:

> You will not easily forget the two in that Chopin valse. Mlle. Pavlova wears the ballet costume, and M. Mordkin is in something that might as well be Early Victorian as anything else. But the dance is a crystallization of the mannered grace and sentiment of the eighteenth century—a Greuze or a Fragonard in terms of dance—a thing wonderfully finished, delicate, of far-sought design, and with a faint, subtle, sensuous appeal.

Programs of the time gave very scant information; Pavlova's swan was designated strictly in accordance with Saint-Saëns's title, *Le Cygne,* and audiences were not always certain of the fact that the swan was supposed to be dying. The rose number also caused problems. It began public life on May 1 as a dying rose, but later became a fading one. When it was first performed, *The Tatler* thought it ranked with *The Swan* as the most exquisite thing in Pavlova's repertoire, but the Palace audiences were unlikely to have sorted out the French and they were always a little nonplussed when the vision suddenly collapsed. Even *The Tatler* became confused a year later and grumbled that there was no warning that death was imminent. (Presumably the writer had never observed a fine tea rose shatter in an instant.) The *Rose* was notable for the way in which Pavlova abandoned all technical virtuosity and relied instead on her ability to summon up a mood. At the Palace there was an all-purpose backdrop for the dance items, and since this represented a bower of cupids and roses, the issue may sometimes have been somewhat confused. *La Nuit* was thought to have a rather mystical atmosphere because a forget-me-not-blue light drowned the detail of the décor and brought a hush on the audience. Even the footlights were faded away during this number, which was unusual for a music hall, where the audience always liked to see things clearly. As a result, there was a tendency for a standard bank of stage lights to

La Rose Mourante: a new title and a new costume, 1913.

be in operation at all times, and there was a limit to lighting plans that technicians cared to accommodate with the theatre's straining dynamos.

Because of the exceptional success of Pavlova and Mordkin, the Palace ran special all-dance matinees during their "Saison Russe," and in these performances extra numbers were given, though the program notes were no more forthcoming in their information. Experience seems to have shown that if an audience liked something, then it did not want any explanation, and if it did not like it, then the offending item was quickly removed from the program. "Arrangers" were sometimes given credit: Petipa (always listed as "Petitpa"), Fokine, and, of course, Mordkin. Since this last did not claim any credit for *Variation Grecque,* to Giraud, nor *Variations,* to Tchaikovsky, one can only guess that they might have started life under Gorsky's hands, as his choreography was often created on Mordkin. Pavlova was probably rather shy of admitting to "arrangements," perhaps fearing that a certain male chauvinism might rear its head; but at that time she seems genuinely to have had no real confidence in choreographic innovation, and certainly not overt experimentation. (That past autumn in Indianapolis she had said, "I would love to interpret the dancing flight of a golden maple leaf such as I saw falling today. But I came to your country too late. My formative days are over.")

On May 18, Lydia Kyasht opened at the Empire in a version of *Sylvia.* It was described in the program as "rearranged in one scene by C. Wilhelm" (the Empire's resident designer) and had never before been attempted, in any guise, in London. *The Stage* regretted the curtailing of the original but gave the usual warm greeting to Kyasht. A week later there was an extra charity matinee at the Palace. According to *The Stage,* "in one way at least, the matinee in aid of the Prince Francis of Teck Memorial Fund made history, as every artist announced to appear duly performed." The *Bacchanale* was on the program, as well as songs, juggling, and "a unique bubble-blowing exhibition."

As a result of his wife Pajitzkaya's banishment from the troupe, Mordkin was intent on stirring up trouble. During the third week of May he gossiped to the *Evening News:* "In my opinion the London public should show the very greatest indulgence to Mlle Pavlova. While she was in America she received news that a friend to whom she was deeply attached has been arrested in St. Petersburg on a political charge. He is still in prison, and it is not known when he will be brought up for trial, or what fate awaits him." Mordkin, this time, had sealed his fate as far as Pavlova was concerned.

Summer was settling in, hot and dry, and London seemed noisier and dustier than ever, with crowds of foreign visitors starting to arrive for the Coronation excitements. It was not long before fresh scenes of discord occurred in the Palace auditorium. On Monday, June 12, the program of Russian dancing was concluded in a little over a quarter of an hour. Mordkin contributed the one solo dance that was now allocated him (there had been a considerable erosion of his territory), and Pavlova danced only briefly, omitting three items from her program. When the curtain fell it was generally assumed that it would rise again for the *Bacchanale,* and there were shouts of protest when an attendant changed the numbers and an attempt was made to proceed with the bioscope pictures. The audience erupted into such a storm of hooting and shouting that the film had to be stopped. The house manager announced from the stage that Miss Pavlova had been seized with illness after her first dance, and in the circumstances the audience's indulgence was asked for. There continued to be loud demands that at least Mordkin might contribute another solo. The management's representative had to go back on stage and explain that Mr. Mordkin had performed the one dance allotted to him. It would be more than understandable if Mordkin was resting on his dignity behind the scenes, since he felt that only Pavlova was to blame for his dwindling program; however, these feelings were of no importance to the audience beyond the curtain, and there were frequent signs of dissent throughout the remainder of the evening.

While Monday's upsets were taking place at the Palace, Genée was over at the Coliseum, back in town under new management—Stoll. Lydia Kyasht had filled the space left by Genée at Alfred Moul's Empire, so Adeline had now to entice her fervent and long-standing admirers elsewhere; indeed, she had claimed an Englishman as husband on her return from America. Genée was performing a pretty little fantasy called *A Dream of Roses and Butterflies.* The first number displayed the dancer in a crinoline, showing once more, according to a rapturous *Times,* "what a fascinating garment a crinoline can be for (we are sure we shall not be misunderstood) a demure minx. Then she is transformed into a yellow-and-black butterfly; and her lover M. Sherer Be-kefi—a very graceful and capable dancer—is transformed into a grey and tawny butterfly and, together or separately, they dance about among eight young ladies transformed into very full-blown roses."

Pavlova's sudden illness, whether physical or psychosomatic, presented Butt with an enormous problem: Coronation crowds packing the city, rival dancing stars in the other theatres, and a volatile audience that could quickly transfer its allegiance elsewhere. (Theatre-going was then a spur-of-the-moment activity, with very few advance bookings, and an enormous number of seats were available for London patrons on any given day.) Kchessinskaya was then at her Grand Duke's villa in Cannes, and Butt telegraphed his problems that Monday night. Whatever else she might have been, Kchessinskaya was also a trouper in the best sense of the word, and she was on the train within hours. Besides, London at that moment was the magnet for everyone because of the impending Coronation, and visions of royal favor may have opened up before her eyes.

Some Grand Ducal diplomacy had ensured that by the time she reached London, a suite was available for her at the Savoy, bookings notwithstanding. Mathilde was in her element; within hours she had organized a reception at the hotel for all the ladies of society who had met her in St. Petersburg, though she did not speak English and her French—rather surprisingly—was said to be "little." Nevertheless, she made clear her desire to make a reputation in London, where she was unknown; but she also made it clear that on such a hastily contrived visit she could stay only two weeks. Mordkin was absolutely delighted at the prospect of adding the number-one Imperial star to his list of partners. But word of Kchessinskaya's arrival must have shot up the hill to Hampstead with the speed of a comet, and following on newspaper reports of Genée's triumphant return, its tonic effect was astounding. La Pavlova was well; she would dance.

Poor Alfred Butt must have been wishing he had another profession; for while Kchessinskaya, all unwittingly, was explaining her presence to the society ladies (including one from the *Daily Sketch*), the occupant of the Hampstead eyrie was already swooping back to her territory at the Palace, having conveyed certain information to *The Times* theatre correspondent on Tuesday night. This particular evening a theatrical Coronation Ball was being held at the Savoy, with supper tables separately organized and managed by different theatres and artists. The *Daily Sketch* thought that a popular table would be "that run by Michael Mordkin, the Russian dancer from the Palace Theatre. He is to preside at a Russian table, which will invite with all the delicacies of the St. Petersburg supper. Mordkin is forbidden to dance outside his contract, but it is easy to imagine that he might be induced to forget, and break out into a really characteristic northern dance."

One can only assume that Butt was in something of a funk, and that at the Savoy *The Times* was not examined too closely, as a glance at that august journal's Wednesday theatre column would have revealed that "Mlle. Pavlova, having recovered from her indisposition, will appear at the usual matinee at the Palace Theatre today and tomorrow, when she will introduce two new dances, the *Blue Danube* and the Variations from *Coppélia.* She will also dance the *Bacchanale* with M. Mordkin." It was not the business of *The Times* to hover around the Strand checking the

Savoy register; equally, the *Daily Sketch* did not check the theatre columns of *The Times,* so it went ahead and set up word of "Mordkin's New Partner" for the Thursday morning edition. The orchestra at the Palace, rehearsing many new numbers, presumably had no time to read any of the papers.

Thus, by mid-afternoon on Wednesday, the rising curtain of the Palace did not reveal Butt's latest import, who was gathering herself together for a dignified retreat back to the Riviera. One week later, on Wednesday, June 21, *The Tatler's* latest issue appeared, adorned with a portrait photograph of Kchessinskaya, who had given it to them the previous Wednesday. The whole thing seems to have been too much for Mordkin, and the handbills for the Palace for that day showed his name absent from the line-up. To make up for this, Pavlova had to do nine numbers: *La Rose Qui Meurt, Danse Hongroise* (to Brahms), the *Blue Danube,* the Valse and Variations to Chopin (still with the arrangements credited to Fokine), *La Nuit,* the *Coppélia* variations, *The Swan,* and finally *Papillons.* This was just the matinee; the iron butterfly had an evening performance after that, while over at the opera house, the Diaghilev company was giving its first London performance.

The following day was the Coronation itself—and business as usual for Mlles Genée, Pavlova, Kyasht, and, at the Hippodrome, "Mme Viriasova Sobinoff," who was described as "a favourite at the Court of the Czar" and who sang and danced in boyar costume to the accompaniment of an orchestra of balalaikas. The King of England had only to go through a single ritual performance at Westminster Abbey, but the aforementioned ladies were expected to do both matinee and evening performances on the great day. Because the Alhambra management had decided against a matinee, at least one ballerina had a chance of observing the royal procession: Ekaterina Geltzer, who had opened on May 29 in *The Dance Dream.* "Catrina," as she was billed, was dancing in a specially commissioned Gorsky confection that allowed her numerous changes of costume: she appeared as "The Ideal," "A Cloud," "An Amazon," "A Tzigane," and "A Boyarishnic." Her partner was Vassili Tikhomirov, at thirty-five years old already as noted for his teaching as for his dancing. Tikhomirov was a combination of St. Petersburg and Moscow training; he had had two years in the *classes de perfection* of Gerdt and Johanssen at the Maryinsky before he was eighteen. Among his students were his near-contemporaries Mordkin, Volinine, and Alexei Koslov. The sixth scene of Gorsky's ballet contained a war dance in which the leading pair were joined by two more of Tikhomirov's gifted pupils, Zhukov and Laurent Novikov. Pavlova contrived to slip over to the Alhambra between her own performances to see her erstwhile Moscow rival. She seems to have thought Novikov underused and of some potential. He certainly had huge legs. More interesting than the legs was the music for the war dance: none other than Glazunov's "Autumn" bacchanal. Was nothing sacred?

Coronation Day was followed by a Royal Progress in which other parts of the city got a chance to glimpse a great cavalcade of royalty, visiting heads of state, and Princes of the Empire. Newspaper space was at a premium, but *The Times* found room for a lengthy review by George Calderon of Diaghilev's first program at Covent Garden. Calderon was a specialist in Russian affairs and had a sure grasp of the background to Russian ballet and its artistic intentions. In the midst of his article was this observation:

> How much of the work of a ballet-master suffers from being given piece-meal may be seen by comparing the effect of the detached "turns" of Pavlova and her company at the Palace Theatre before an irrelevant, purely "decorative" back-cloth, with the effect of *Carnaval* in its entirety at Covent Garden. *Carnaval* is an exquisitely delicate artistic whole . . . and not a detail of it could be spared.

Certainly the opera house was across a "class" divide, drawing an audience, in the main, trained to absorb lengthy musical presentations in which the varying components were all given due consideration, while Pavlova was giving a series of brief, intense vignettes in which she went for maximum effect in minimum time. Not only was this an accurate assessment of what was wanted for music-hall audiences, but it suited her febrile approach to performing. In her *Papillons* solo she could never have sustained the quivering, electric energy for more than a minute or two; it imprinted its image and then was gone. Always, the audience clamored for more. Pavlova knew she was appealing to a wide sector of the public, and it was her desire to do so; but Calderon's article could only have made her wonder whether she had traded more for less.

The weather was breaking: Monday was the first day of the lawn tennis championship at Wimbledon, and the committee had prudently spent £340 on a "huge sea-green mackintosh" that could be erected in tent-like fashion over the center court. At the Royal Opera House the newly installed electroliers revealed an army of workers striving to complete the decorations for the Coronation Gala that night, with one hundred thousand artificial roses being wired to panels of trellis all over the auditorium. And in the King's Bench Division of the High Court, *Mayer* v. *Mordkin* had been called before Mr. Justice Bankes.

Daniel Mayer, in the witness box, was being cross-examined by the counsel for the defense, Mr. George Elliott.

"Do you know that through Mr. Astruc of Paris Mr. Mordkin entered into a contract with the Palace in 1909?"

"Not to my knowledge," replied Mayer, adding that he had no desire to take advantage of Mordkin in any way. He did not think that an agreement to appoint him sole agent for five years was an engagement for such a time as amounted to taking advantage of an artist. Then he added: "They [Pavlova and Mordkin] had the help of a Russian gentleman, a Monsieur Dandré, throughout, and the contract was read over and explained thoroughly."

Elliott, well briefed by Mordkin, seized the chance.

"He, unfortunately, is detained in Russia just now."

Mayer realized his mistake.

"I don't think it necessary to go into that."

"Oh! I am not making any imputation," murmured Elliott suavely. "We know their little ways in Russia."

Mayer concluded his evidence by saying that it was entirely a fabrication to suggest that he had approached Mordkin in the street and tried to get him to sign the commission note there, in a great hurry, and implying that it related only to private engagements. Mayer also volunteered the fact that Mordkin complained that he was not sufficiently advertised in comparison with Pavlova, and that there was "a little trouble at the theatre for some time." While the negotiations were taking place over the matter of revised salaries, it appeared that Mordkin used to make long calculations in francs on the mirror of his dressing room at the Palace.

Pavlova was then called to the stand. She was dressed in dove-colored silk with a beehive-shaped hat covered in pale green lace. She chose to speak in Russian and used an interpreter—always a useful ploy if a tricky question should arise.

Pavlova was examined by Mr. Shearman, the counsel acting for the plaintiff, and she said that she was prima ballerina in the Imperial Ballet at St. Petersburg. She had several times been in London before 1909 but had never performed before that year in England. In 1909 she had, however, danced at the house of Mrs. Brown Potter, and later at Lady Londesborough's before the King and Queen. Mordkin danced there too, volunteered Pavlova, adding that Mayer had made all the arrangements, that she was well pleased with him, and that she still employed him as agent. In answer to further questions from Mr. Shearman concerning the interview at the Grosvenor Hotel, Pavlova said that the defendant could understand French and that they had also discussed the contracts together. She herself was quite satisfied with the agreement for five years.

Mr. Elliott took over, for the defendant. "In July 1909, I think you were very friendly with Mr. Mordkin?"

Pavlova, smiling sweetly, and with ample gestures accompanying the Russian monosyllable, said "Yes."

"I am afraid you are not quite such good friends now?"

Here, Pavlova smiled even more sweetly, indeed was observed to be almost laughing as she replied "No." At this, there was a lot of laughter from the public benches.

Mr. Elliott continued: "Is Mr. Mordkin's knowledge of French very imperfect?"

The interpreter, replying for Pavlova: "He does not know it well." At this juncture, a discussion in the Mordkin camp resulted in Elliott suggesting that Pavlova's reply in Russian could be interpreted as "He knows it badly." This was too much for Pavlova, who interrupted both counsels to point out that although she used the word "badly," she meant that Mordkin did not know the language very well.

The judge: "She has corrected *both* interpreters!"

The remarkable witness was then allowed to step down. (She made her way out of the courtroom before Mordkin was very far advanced in his evidence.)

Papillons

The general content of Pavlova's evidence had put a broadside into Mordkin's leaky craft well below the water line, and Alfred Butt, who followed Pavlova to the stand, did not seem a particularly helpful character reference for one of his star performers.

Mr. Elliott, with his briefing suddenly a little less secure, asked him: "Am I to understand that he [Mordkin] had not performed at the Palace until 1909?"

Butt put the record straight: "Not until 1910 I think; I engaged him in 1909. He performed in 1910, and before that he had not performed in London."

The judge intervened: "What language did Mordkin use to you?"

"Broken French," replied Butt, "until this year when he came with his secretary. I could generally make him understand."

"You would not suggest he is a past master in the language?" asked the judge.

"I think he is like a good many more artists. They understand what they want to and not what they don't," replied Butt. There was a ripple of laughter in the courtroom.

Elliott then tried to retrieve Mordkin's situation by cross-examining Butt about the antagonism between Pavlova and Mordkin, and the witness was forced to agree that the dancers were not quite such good friends as they had been in 1909, but he added by way of gratuitous explanation that Mordkin had become "rather swollen-headed."

For the defense, Elliott said that if Mayer's account was to be accepted, then the defendant could not dispute the claim, but if, on the other hand, his client's story received credence, it must lead to the conclusion that the commission note was signed under circumstances that would disentitle the plaintiff from reaping advantage from it. Elliott, seeking to plug the leaking ship, commented that it was noticeable that there had been no conversation between the defendant and Mme. Pavlova about his refusal to pay. The judge himself supplied the answer: they were not on friendly terms; that had been established.

Mordkin took the stand next and told the court that he had been engaged as a dancer in the Russian Opera at Moscow before coming to London.

"You are on very friendly terms with Mme. Pavlova?"

Mordkin replied—in startlingly good English—"Formerly. Not now." Then he exploded: "At this moment, absolutely NO!" He then went on to explain that he had left all arrangements in Pavlova's hands when they were in Paris because he did not understand the language. With respect to the alleged contract, he had understood from Mayer that the arrangement related merely to special soirées and had nothing whatever to do with the Palace Theatre, and he reiterated that Mayer had one day approached him in a great hurry outside the Palace and persuaded him to sign a document under the belief that it related to private performances. Mordkin was at pains to deny the events at the Grosvenor Hotel, even though his signature was on a document dated July 20, 1909.

There was a lengthy summing up, at the end of which His Lordship gave judgment for the plaintiff, Mayer, for the amount claimed, with costs. It was all over, and the reporters scurried off to file their stories.

Most of the newspapers carried lengthy reports the following morning. *The Times,* with cruel exactitude, was the only one to mention Victor Dandré by name; of course it would be the English paper read first in St. Petersburg. If there was any damage, it was done. The *Daily Express,* which probably did not find its way into any diplomatic bag, was the least forthcoming about the suit, giving it only four and a half inches but playing up the juicier bits. It also gave coverage to the Covent Garden gala:

> The performance concluded with a Russian ballet, and the superb dancers who have just come to Covent Garden supplied the supremely artistic item on the Gala programme. It was noticeable that German music was unrepresented. So was English music. The applause was gentle and restrained, as it always is on these occasions, but the arrangements were perfect, and the whole performance went smoothly, the curtain finally falling soon after eleven.

The paper then devoted most of a column to a description of everything that was happening backstage.

By the end of June, Butt's threats about canceling contracts seemed to have instilled some reason into his two performers, and Pavlova donned a forgiving air after her agent's victory, though it had Pyrrhic overtones for herself. She and Mordkin were dancing the *Bacchanale* together, but the general atmosphere was far from rhapsodic. By July 8 Mordkin had dictated a letter and sent it off to the office of the *Evening News,* which printed the headline "Pavlova Souvenir" and then—infuriatingly for Mordkin—in slightly smaller print: "Minus Mordkin." They described the problem as an echo of the "Quarrel in Fairyland" at the Palace. Mordkin's letter (obviously the product of some English-speaking confidant, most probably his solicitor) read as follows:

> "As the management of the Palace Theatre has announced a Pavlova-Mordkin souvenir in its advertisements, and as it contains no mention of me or my photographs, I have received a large number of letters asking me the reason for the omission of my pictures.
>
> "As I am unable to reply to these letters individually, may I trespass on the courtesy of your columns to be allowed to state that I know nothing of the reasons which caused the suppression of my photographs after I had been asked for them and had supplied a large number in various costumes and poses.
>
> "The publication of this statement will, I hope, dispel any idea the public may have entertained that I am in any way concerned with this matter.
>
> "My efforts to please have been received with an enthusiastic appreciation far beyond anything I had dared hope, and it would, therefore, be out of the question to suppose for one moment that I would do anything that would place me in an objectionable light in the eyes of the public, for which I entertain so profound an esteem."

There was every justification for Mordkin's complaint. The anonymous introduction to the souvenir booklet had needed to fall back on the use of such words as "her consort" when trying to describe who else was in the *Bacchanale* pas de deux. Nowhere in

The *Bacchanale*, Berlin, c.1912.

the lengthy reviews quoted in connection with the 1910 season was Mordkin's name to be seen, but one or two clues had been missed, so that a sharp reader could discover mention of Pavlova's "no less amazing partner" and her "male pursuer." Francis Toye's 1910 quote that it was "a pity Pavlova does not dance a little more alone" seems to have been taken to heart a year later. During July 1911, the *Bacchanale* was the only thing that brought the warring artists into contact with each other. Still, it was enough to keep the house happy, and there were always crowds lining up for each performance.

London was truly seething with entertainments. Geltzer had been recalled to Russia, and her place in *The Dance Dream* at the Alhambra was filled by Alexandra Balashova, a first soloist from Moscow. *The Times* thought that Novikov and Zhukov were kept subservient to Tikhomirov's "leaps and twirls," though the two soloists displayed "panther-like grace and ardour." A report sent to the New York *Evening Sun* said that Russian

dancers were like a plague in London, where more and more buildings were needed to house every sort of entertainment. On Kingsway, Oscar Hammerstein was overseeing the final decorations for his new London Opera House. This huge edifice even allowed for three hundred costumiers to work on site. Faced with such competition, Oswald Stoll took over the Old Mogul in Drury Lane and razed the site for a vast new music hall, the Middlesex, an uncompromising structure of red brick, limestone, and polished granite. It had many novel features, including two cantilevered tiers with steel cores which allowed for uninterrupted views from every seat, of which there were three thousand. Another novelty was that any seat in the house could be booked in advance for a threepenny surcharge; this was designed to do away with the disappointment of a "house full" sign suddenly confronting a long-suffering line.

"Improvements" were a symbol of confidence and prosperity, a defiance of increasing taxation and the preoccupation with instability in Europe. The *Daily Mail* ran its huge "Ideal Homes Exhibition" at Olympia in July, and readers were able to see a page of pictures of Pavlova in one of her eye-catching hats getting involved with numerous products, among them Robinson's Patent Barley, a proprietary mush for infants; on July 26 Pavlova was photographed holding a squalling baby firmly while a powerful nurse shoveled in the gruel. "Mme. Pavlova was delighted to witness the satisfaction with which the child took this nourishment and greatly enjoyed the novel experience," read the account. She also handled a box of caramels, and readers were told that at Mr. Batger's exhibit, "the virtues of the firm's celebrated Jersey caramels were explained to Mme. Pavlova so convincingly that she acquired a supply." (In fact, she had a marked weakness for sweets.) Pavlova's views about promotion were undergoing something of a change; she seems to have had an ardent desire to earn extra money at this particular time and even maintained an alert and vivacious mien when confronted with Day and Martin's Boot Polish, and Molassine Biscuits for dogs.

Much of July and August was stiflingly hot and cloudless. The mood was not improved by general industrial unrest throughout the country, with dock workers on strike, troops called in, extra police drafted in Manchester and Liverpool, and the Liberal government running ragged in its attempts to conclude truces with the various elements. Perhaps to escape these problems, people flocked to the theatre. The drawing power of the Russian dance acts remained potent, and no self-respecting music hall in the West End could afford to be without them. Genée, by now an institution in London, was the only other safe ticket in town as far as toe-dancing was concerned.

The bickering over the notorious slap reached as far as America. The Detroit *News-Tribune,* on August 5, ran quotes from the two antagonists:

"Four months I have suffered in silence. Although I am tempted to speak out after this incident," said Miss Pavlova. "For ten years I have been dancing, but I have never before had anything like the difficulty of the present engagement. It has spoiled my work."

"The truth ought to be known," declared Mordkin after the accident. "It was impossible for Pavlova to lose her balance, as I held her by the wrists. She slipped to the floor after trying to trip me."

In New York, Rabinoff was agitating for a return season to begin in the autumn, as before. The options on the original contracts still had the full five years to run, and Mordkin was quite ready to make himself available for another coast-to-coast conquest. For Pavlova it was not so easy. She had to evaluate a number of possibilities and imponderables: there was the chance of a four-month English provincial tour with a quick sortie to Dublin, beginning in November; she was concerned to find out more about the legal case involving Dandré (not least because the major part of her American earnings had been tied up in this matter); she did not want to continue dancing with Mordkin on account of the personal antagonism that had arisen between them; and there was one further matter that could not be ignored—the Tsar had made it known that he would like to see her

dance again, and that could only be at the Maryinsky. There was also talk of the Diaghilev company returning to London for an autumn season. Would its leading performers establish too much of a bridgehead in the English capital? It was four months since the gossip item in St. Petersburg had implied that Pavlova was returning from America at the instigation of Senator Neidgard, and it would be another six weeks before she would actually set off for her homeland, since she had tentatively agreed to extend her summer season at the Palace until the beginning of September. Mordkin, on the other hand, was unwilling to give Butt any extension. He was deep in plans with Rabinoff and must already have come to some sort of agreement with Geltzer, prior to her departure, since her name soon cropped up in the preliminary announcements for the new American tour—as did Kchessinskaya's. There was probably considerable pressure directed toward Pavlova from Rabinoff's office in an endeavor to persuade her to accommodate the plans being made in New York, but in her moment of extreme indecision two things were to her advantage: if she chose to use the Tsar's invitation as an excuse to return to Russia, Rabinoff could hardly take exception, since he was dependent on the Tsar's goodwill if he was to show Mordkin with any other dancers from the Imperial Theatres; and as long as Pavlova was not making any move in the direction of any other American impresario, she could not be said to be breaking her contract with Rabinoff.

By the first week in August, Mordkin was coming to the end of his contract with Butt. Pavlova and Mordkin danced together for the last time on Saturday, August 5, 1911. The stage was lined with baskets and bouquets of flowers, and among them Pavlova caught sight of a simple glass vase with a handful of roses in it. She must have guessed it was from the upper echelons of the house, for she picked it up and glanced to the "heavens" before bestowing a kiss upon it. It was really a love affair between Pavlova and the audience; Mordkin had to watch mutely while she picked up bunches of roses and lilies from the stage and threw them out over the ecstatic audience.

Then the big letters came down from the grid on the Palace Theatre's façade, and by Monday the sign was reading "Pavlova & Co." At the same time, Mordkin was unburdening himself to an American correspondent:

Mme. Pavlowa is jealous of my success, not of mine alone, but of the success of all the members of the company, no matter how small a part they may take. She does not want the audience to applaud anyone but her. The great trouble began, so far as the public was concerned, when she refused to let me take my curtain bow at the conclusion of each performance. When she went out to take her bow she held the ends of both curtains tightly in her hands so that I could not pass.

I went to my dressing room in disgust and when she was quite sure that I had gone she would turn around in view of the audience and say: "Where is Mordkin?" That was to give the audience the impression that I did not want to come out. Mme. Pavlowa is a clever woman.

Just because Pavlowa did not wish it the management for some time refused to allow my flowers to be handed to me from the

MME. PAVLOVA TRAINING CHILDREN FOR HER NEW RUSSIAN BALLET

Rehearsing *Snowflakes,* August 1911.

orchestra. They had to be sent by the stage door, and my dressing room is full of flowers that were sent to me in this way. At this time, Pavlowa was receiving flowers across the footlights at every performance.

The management of the theater decided to get out a Pavlowa-Mordkin souvenir in the form of a booklet. Mr. Butt asked me for my photographs, and I gave them to him. At the last moment Mme. Pavlowa said: "No, it must not be a Pavlowa-Mordkin souvenir: it must be a Pavlowa souvenir." All my photographs were cut out, all the newspaper criticisms of me were left out and one would hardly know from the souvenir that I was appearing at the theater at all.

Originally, at these special Wednesday matinees, Pavlowa and I had an equal number of solo dances. All that was changed by the management and eventually I was cut down to two numbers, while my partner had seven or eight. Madame was also allowed to give postcard souvenirs of herself in the theater, while I was compelled to give them at the stage door. After every performance a couple of hundred men and women wait for me there and I am compelled to sign postcards in the street. Is that fair treatment for a star?

Then Mordkin suddenly announced his plans for an American season. While he displayed trunks full of costumes that he had not been able to use during the Palace season because of his restricted solo spots, he declared:

I hope to surprise the United States this time. I am to visit more than 100 cities in six months under the management of the Metropolitan Opera Company. I will also visit Mexico, at the invitation of the government, and Cuba. I will have with me my wife and Mme. Geltzer, who has made such a great and instantaneous success during the last few weeks at the Alhambra Theatre here.

Such plans must have been in the process of discussion for weeks, but it seemed that London might still be big enough to contain both Pavlova and Mordkin in the future, for Mordkin concluded his diatribe with news of his long-term plans:

In the spring I am returning to London to start a school for dancing. I am teaching about a dozen young women, some of whom pay £10 an hour and some of whom I teach free, because they are poor and cannot pay.

It is not quite clear what sort of talents earned a free pass from Mordkin; society ladies would have paid even more than £10 an hour for any sort of instruction from the star, but he must have been very busy recruiting potential dancers for the American tour. The Duluth *Herald* announced on August 3 that Mordkin and Pavlova would dance together again in America. Under a photograph of Mordkin wearing an American Indian head-dress—and, apart from the ubiquitous bow and arrow, not much else—the paper informed its readers:

Mikhail Mordkin is coming back to America to dance. When he went away last spring he was doubtful if he would return because he and his associate, Pavlowa, were in the midst of a bitter quarrel growing out of jealousy. But for purely commercial reasons this quarrel has been settled and Mordkin announces that he is once more on good terms with his associate and is preparing to come back after some more of those dear American dollars.

In London, Pavlova had other ideas, and after roubles it was dear English pounds that held her interest: she seems to have decided that if she was to base herself anywhere other than in Russia, then England was the country in which she felt most at ease. But there was still the Palace season to complete. During the July of background skirmishing she had been active in every spare moment from her usual schedule planning a little ballet based loosely on Ivanov's snowflakes scene from *The Nutcracker.* She wanted to use children, much as at the Maryinsky, and to

With Laurent Novikov in *Valse Caprice*, New York, c.1912.

this end Pavlova scouted around among the London dancing classes, where hordes of little girls were trying to develop a sense of rhythm that might later distinguish them on the ballroom floor.

On August 7 the children were ready for their big adventure to the strains of Tchaikovsky. Pavlova had watched Kchessinskaya and Preobrajenskaya dance the Sugar Plum Fairy on numerous occasions in St. Petersburg, and she had a choreographic framework to use for a solo. All of this had involved the Palace orchestra in a lot of extra rehearsal work, and at the end of the first performance Pavlova handed across the footlights a huge laurel wreath. She needed some assistance, since it was bigger than she was. The wreath was bound in the Russian national colors, and across its six-foot span was a message reading "To the charming maestro Herman Finck, gratefully, Anna Pavlova, 'Snowflake' August 7, 1911." *Snowflakes* was warmly applauded, and it had kept the audience's attention. The use of children was a shrewd move for a music-hall audience; only a small furry animal could have been more popular.

The Era gave the work its serious consideration:

There is no thought of the cold white shroud about the production, with its tripping diminutive fairies, who emulate the lightness of the glistening flakes and dance with joyousness in a glowing winter-scape of blue and white. There are concerted numbers, and they dance in trios, and more than one little maiden shows excellent promise. There is a small soloist too, who has already wonderful technique, with a career before her. Pavlova, alternately dashing and languorous, trips in her own inimitable fashion, and the little ballet, which is refreshingly simple in character, is just long enough.

After *Snowflakes,* Pavlova had unveiled her replacement for Mordkin: Novikov had managed to learn the *Bleichmann* number. He put his own variation in, to Glazunov. The compilation was now an entrée to Bleichmann, an adagio to Thomé, solo variations (Pavlova's to Drigo), and finally a coda, again to Bleichmann. Pavlova's decision to extend the season caused some alterations in the company: Plaskowieczka, Schmolz, and Kuhn took leave, as did three men. A second Veronine West had arrived (they were now called "Veroni-West"), and there was an English girl, "Mdlle Courtenay"—she too had another member of the family waiting in the wings, but for the moment she was only the second British girl (after Bewicke) to join Pavlova's troupe. There was curiosity about Novikov, following in the turbulent wake of Mordkin: "The newcomer has made a very favourable impression and is a remarkable executant," concluded *The Era.* Pavlova must have heaved more than one sigh of relief at the end of the evening's performance. She had smoothed over the departure of Mordkin with her choice of Novikov, and, perhaps even more important, she had discovered a way of peopling the stage with supernumeraries who did not need to be imported from Russia. Laurent Novikov was quiet and unambitious, and he seemed more than content with his new role as supporting partner to the famous Anna Pavlova. He was not a quick learner, but he practiced assiduously, and before the end of the season

Pavlova had taught him the *Valse Caprice*. On Saturday, September 2, they danced together in this work when Pavlova completed her second season at the Palace. Yvette Guilbert arrived to take over the star spot, and Pavlova was free to face the problems in St. Petersburg.

While Pavlova headed back to the commitments and uncertainties, Mordkin was gathering together numerous associates from Moscow and St. Petersburg in order to fulfill Rabinoff's requirements for a Russian dance troupe, which had the Tsar's approval to the extent that they were allowed to say that they were from the Imperial Russian Ballet.* When the liner *President Lincoln* docked in New York on September 19, it was carrying Mordkin, Karalli, and Julie Sedova (who was being described as "prima ballerina assoluta"), as well as thirty-eight other dancers. It was made clear that eleven more members of the company had missed the ship and would follow, most particularly Geltzer, who was described as "the most authoritative dancer of Russia." Rabinoff announced that the tour would "encircle the globe" and would cover a period of three years.

Even before Mordkin arrived there had been a great deal of speculation about an appearance by Pavlova; by mid-August certain society ladies were quite convinced that "the Russian Apollo and his airy consort" would be putting in appearances at such as Sherwood Lodge, the home of Mr. and Mrs. Pembroke of Newport. It was thought that just prior to the horse show which was to begin on Labor Day, Mordkin would give Mrs. Jones and her friends some dancing lessons, and they were optimistic enough to suppose that the *Bacchanale* itself might be adapted for their own enjoyment on the ballroom floor.

Mordkin kept up the bluff until the bitter end. During his interview at the Navarre Hotel on the day after his arrival in New York, he was busy with his old friends the reporters, whom he had learned to respect. "Yes, Pavlova will come here to dance again this season," he insisted. "The trouble between Pavlova and me was not near so violent as you had it," he explained. "Just now Pavlova must stay abroad for a while to finish up her part in some legal affairs. But she is under contract with M. Rabinoff until 1915 and therefore will be ready to dance when wanted here."

Whether Mordkin wished to imply that Pavlova was not actually wanted at this stage is open to conjecture, but such an attitude would have served to camouflage her absence. By now Pajitzkaya was being described as his wife of six years' standing. "The best character dancer in Russia, and the prettiest," he said as he introduced her. "Mme. Geltzer is of the older school." A reporter could not resist asking exactly *how* old. "No, no, not in years; I mean the school, not Madame. She has been to Moscow as the great Kchessinskaya is to St. Petersburg, but Mme. Geltzer is Russia's authoritative dancer." Mordkin endeavored to keep up

a light-hearted front, but behind the scenes he was confessing to feeling unwell.

Four days earlier, in St. Petersburg, Karsavina had opened the Maryinsky season in a performance of *Swan Lake*. Pavlova's first appearance after her long absence was to be in her favored role of Nikiya on October 1 (September 18 o.s.). She had also agreed to do two performances of *Giselle* as well as two further performances of *La Bayadère*. There was a decided shortage of ballerinas who could carry these big works: Preobrajenskaya was out with a long and serious illness, and Kchessinskaya could not be persuaded to get herself back into trim before December.

Diaghilev was back in St. Petersburg and eager to involve Pavlova in his plans. He had the opportunity of an immediate return season in London playing at Covent Garden in the autumn, in tandem with German opera, but he needed a roster of high-level ballerinas to sustain the season, and his favored Karsavina could only take two full weeks from the middle of her heavy commitment at the Maryinsky. Kchessinskaya was back in the running; memories of her obduracy over the first Paris season seemed to have been put aside, and she, no doubt still smarting over her abortive sortie to London that summer, was in an accommodating mood—even ready to talk to the Imperial Theatres management on the subject of a production of *Swan Lake* that she might earmark for London. There were two weeks left to fill between Karsavina's departure from London and Kchessinskaya's arrival, even though Karsavina was able to share the last two weeks of the eight-week season, which was to continue with Kchessinskaya.

Pavlova was the obvious choice. She was fully occupied with rehearsals and performances at the Maryinsky during the first three weeks of October, but she concluded tentative plans with Diaghilev by the end of the first week, and when he arrived in London on October 10 he was able to announce the arrangements. It certainly made sense for Pavlova to agree to dance *Giselle* for Diaghilev in London, since she was at that moment rehearsing the same ballet in St. Petersburg, but in the decision there must also have been the understanding of an old debt about to be repaid. As to the rest of the London stint, Pavlova was to dance in *Les Sylphides* and to take on her old role of Armide, and also Ta-Hor in *Cléopâtre*. There was a tentative suggestion that she might dance the Blue Bird pas de deux with Nijinsky, as Diaghilev was seeking a short "filler" to bolster his program of one-act ballets. (By now this pas de deux, which had already done service in Paris as *L'Oiseau de Feu*, was having to be renamed *L'Oiseau d'Or*, because the true Firebird had at last been launched.)

For an interviewer from the *Stock Exchange Register*, Pavlova had a few words about talent outside of Russia: "I heard the renowned Caruso. He sang divinely, but does not know the beginning of what acting means. He just stands in any chance pose and spreads out his enormous hands." Although Dandré was out on bail, Diaghilev may have sensed that this complication could

---

*Six of the company were actually straight from Miss Phipps's Academy in London. They had been photographed in Brixton in a group pose; the print was joined with a reverse image of the same photo to double the numbers, and anyone looking closely must have thought that the company had a heavy preponderance of identical twins.

intrude on his London plans, for at the same time as he was releasing his news to the English press he cabled Astruc in Paris to see whether Carlotta Zambelli might be free on the dates penciled in for Pavlova.*

Things were not going smoothly for Mordkin either. On October 4 it became known that his absence over several days from rehearsals of his company had been due to more than fatigue. It was said that he was seriously ill, but while Ben Atwell, his manager, was busy trying to cloak the nature of his illness, other reporters had discovered that the dancer had already undergone surgery. Atwell was finally cornered and had to make a statement to the press:

> It is true that M. Mordkin was operated on last Monday, but he has at no time been in any danger and is in such a condition that he was singing and joking yesterday.
>
> M. Mordkin arrived in this country feeling decidedly indisposed after a rough voyage. He ventured upon rehearsals without paying any attention to a growth under the skin of his body, which was apparently the source of his trouble.
>
> Despite the fact that it continued to increase in size he rehearsed the organization until last Monday, when, in compliance with the insistent request of his management, he submitted to a medical examination. The group of physicians who conducted the examination recommended an immediate operation if he was to attempt to appear throughout the season mapped out for him, which is to open next Monday night at Hartford, Connecticut. The operation was then performed and was highly successful. Naturally his whereabouts has not been made public in order to avoid the flood of inquiries and calls which would not tend to hasten his recovery.
>
> Before the operation, M. Mordkin named Alexander Volinine as his successor to complete the training of the ballet and imparted to him all his ideas concerning the details.

The mention of Volinine presented a fresh problem. Morris Gest, who had shown a troupe of Russian dancers in New York in 1910, realized suddenly that he still had options on the dancers who had appeared during that little-publicized visit; not only was Volinine one of their number, but Lydia Lopokhova as well, now with Mordkin's troupe. The two dancers found themselves restrained by a temporary injunction even from rehearsing with the new company. They had to spend a morning in court before they were freed to rejoin their colleagues.**

Legal matters in St. Petersburg were a little more indeterminate. What place did Victor Dandré occupy at this point in Pavlova's life? Was he a former lover and protector who now found himself in trouble and worthy of her sympathy; or was his situation the direct result of her own extravagances, as a ballerina "living in style" within the materialistic society of St. Petersburg? Had she accepted financial aid from him wittingly, or unwittingly? Did she hold herself responsible for his predicament, or did she discover, on being reunited with him, that he was a person she could not do without, whatever his misdeeds? Did his proven ability at organization suddenly loom as an ideal replacement for Mordkin? Temperamentally they were an oddly assorted pair, he so placid and traditional in outlook, she so mercurial, swinging between volatile gaiety and a certain withdrawn melancholy, when even those closest to her were unable to divine her thoughts.

During the years of Pavlova's rise to eminence in St. Petersburg, Dandré for much of the time had acted as a sort of knightly protector in the background; he appeared to take no particular delight in parading her publicly. He was in that sense exactly the escort and admirer that Pavlova needed. It was evident that she had a fond regard for him, though it was equally clear that she was not romantically in love with him, a fact that must have caused him anguish, since he still worshipped her. Pavlova had a clear sense of her own importance, insofar as she had been brought up in a world taught to respect position and authority; equally, she often resented such power when it was wielded by others. Although she was something of an orphan in the world at large and had sought a father figure, she did have a family at this time, and about them she needed to worry: her mother's earning capacity was precarious at the best of times, and although it is not absolutely clear whether her grandmother was still alive, there may well have been that added complication, since the senior member of the family had been referred to only a year earlier as being one of the reasons why Pavlova had a desire to return to Russia.†

If Dandré had been the prime mover in furthering Pavlova's ends and ideals, then he was the one who had given her the wherewithal to fly from the cage and discover her new freedom. Dandré was worthy of her support. If he left Russia surreptitiously and joined her in London, the bail would be forfeited; he would become, in effect, an exile. If the alternative looked so bleak that Pavlova decided she had to support him in such a

---

* Serge Lifar has suggested that Diaghilev, who had an uncle on the Magistrate's Bench in St. Petersburg, was asked by Pavlova to intercede on Dandré's behalf but that Diaghilev refused. One can see that Diaghilev had no desire to become involved in any nefarious goings-on in the city while he was still dependent on artists and material from that source; equally, he would realize that such a failure might turn Pavlova against him, and that she might even be forced to cancel her return to London.

** Gest's claim seems to have been shaky. By the autumn of 1910 the dancers were said to be under the management of Charles Frohman and C. B. Dillingham. The Orpheum circuit advised patrons that they had been seen at the Globe Theatre in New York, as well as in Paris and Berlin.

† In Indiana during the long tour, Pavlova had been interviewed by a cub reporter. He was eager, she was amused by his extreme youth, and the evening's performance was

over. Although Atwell was monitoring the interview, and it was only fairly innocuous stuff that found its way into the Indianapolis Sun the next day, the censored material emerged in a manuscript drafted, years later, from the reporter's original notes. After referring to her mother and grandmother as a reason for her to return to Russia, Pavlova added: "But I have seen freedom in the outside world. I shall not spend so much time there [in Russia] as before. How would you feel toward a country where it is possible for a Grand Duke to come backstage and order the maître de ballet to line up the ballet corps for his inspection? Then, as he strolls down the line, he points with his cane. 'There. That one! Put her in my carriage. I will take that one for tonight.'" Pavlova made it quite clear that she had equivocal feelings toward her homeland and its class system wherein she had had to struggle to be accepted and promoted, though the anecdote was illustrative more of the 1840s than of her own era.

FASHION, 1908–1914

Pavlova's unfailing sense of style in her personal dress, and her rare ability to display clothes for the camera in what was, for the time, a very modern and relaxed manner, is self-evident throughout her pictures. In the sphere of fashion, as in dancing, she was a "natural." She had some very fine pieces of jewelry (see the diamond necklace, above) but she seldom wore them, preferring relative simplicity. She let the clothes make the statement without distraction, and designers obviously loved her for that. Pavlova always seemed to be six months or so *ahead* of fashion, and was never its slave. Her hats were often a source of wonder, even in the age of the hat; the Secessionist painter Schuster-Woldan exhibited a portrait of her wearing the millinery with the vast taffeta bow (p. 145), and it filled much of the canvas. She was often given to wearing Liberty clothes from London (p. 144), but her wardrobe also took in rather exclusive designer labels, such as Fortuny (p. 147), as long as they stayed on the right side of extravagance. She could make the plainest dress look custom-made.

146

move, then escape was the principal objective during this period. But it would have been folly for him to travel with her, since she was bound to attract a certain amount of attention. It seems likely that she slipped out of St. Petersburg without any undue fuss after she had fulfilled her obligations to the Tsar; her performances would at least have placed her in good favor in that quarter. Dandré must have been left to choose the right moment for his leap into Europe.

When Pavlova arrived back in London in October, she checked into a hotel and immediately began rehearsals at Covent Garden. The country's general unrest was evident within the city, and much of the public transport system was affected by strike action. Pavlova was missing at the beginning of her first scheduled rehearsal, and after a long wait the worried management sent out envoys to scour the surrounding streets, imagining that she might have been unable to find the opera house within the vast clutter of the surrounding market. She was eventually spotted standing in the midst of a crowd of porters, where she was listening with rapt attention to an orator expounding the cause of the working man.

Her first real chance to assess the general appearance of the Diaghilev company and its current repertoire came on October 24, and she was noticed in the audience, which had much increased since the opening of the season. The program consisted of *Carnaval*, *Les Sylphides*, *Le Spectre de la Rose*, and *Schéhérazade*. With the exception of *Sylphides*, probably everything was new to Pavlova;* in all of the works she saw Karsavina with Nijinsky. Pavlova must have remembered the review that had compared her "turns" at the Palace unfavorably with Fokine's beautifully crafted *Carnaval*, and it seems that she asked Diaghilev to let her try one or two performances if the ballet could be scheduled during the ensuing fortnight. Then she made a surprising decision about *Cléopâtre*: she wanted to abandon her role of Ta-Hor and take on the relatively minor role of the favored female slave. Could this have been because it would give her another chance to dance with Nijinsky? Diaghilev and Fokine agreed to her request; they had no option and probably viewed the experiment with some interest; there was always the possibility that she might return to the fold.

On October 26, *The Lady* published—rather belatedly—its views on the opening of the latest Russian Ballet season; being to a great extent about *Giselle*, it would have been of particular interest to Pavlova:

> It remains to be seen whether the autumn opera-goers, who are quite a distinct class from the summer ones, are going to take to classic ballet with the same fervour. I think it was a mistake to try *Giselle* on the opening night. Frankly, *Giselle*, whether in summer

---

* During the Diaghilev company's summer season in London, Pavlova had had no break in her own schedule; she could only snatch glimpses of a rival program and then rush back to the Palace. Nor did the Diaghilev company give any matinees in its first London season.

or autumn, will not do. I do not object to its being Early Victorian. *Les Sylphides* is also Early Victorian, and yet from the dance point of view it is almost too advanced for the majority of us. The trouble with *Giselle* is not the Victorian story of a peasant hero who is a noble prince in disguise, and of a love-sick heroine, who goes mad in a genteel way; nor yet its rather watered Gautier element of the supernatural; the use of traps and other old-fashioned appliances; the white tarlatan skirts and Taglioni wreaths. All these might be charming and, indeed, were charming in the second act of *Giselle*. But what we cannot stand at this time of day is the score of *Giselle*. Those 1840 sentimental strains, meaning absolutely nothing, are wearisome to a degree. The little jerky "tunes" are unendurable. No! *Giselle* will not do! And this in spite of the superb work done in the ballet by Nijinsky, who not only gives us some wonderful double pirouettes, but acts quite beautifully. There is really a touch of Hamlet in his romantic impersonation of Loys [the Prince].

Pavlova must have realized that she would be trying to persuade a very reluctant audience to enjoy her precious ballet. There was also the risk that the English would treat Cecchetti's performance in the travesti role of Giselle's mother as a rollicking "dame" act.

The *Sunday Times* on October 29 was the first to assess whether or not Pavlova had turned the tide then running against the Romantic saga:

> By her mimetic art and subtle suggestion Mme. Pavlova raised the whole representation from a conventional plane to the region of real drama. Every gesture was full of meaning and every movement a poem. It was her acting even more than her dancing that held one captive, for she represented so faithfully all the complex emotions that must have troubled the soul of Giselle. In *Cléopâtre*, with its vivid mental colouring, its mystery of life, and its mystery of death, its lurid story, and pathetic close, Pavlova again was superb as the slave, so well did she illustrate the part by her finely wrought acting, suggestive dancing, and eloquent movements, which called forth enthusiasm from all parts of the large audience and brought the distinguished artist repeatedly before the curtain. Nijinsky, too, won honours for his share in the performances. His lissome and agile dancing as Loys in *Giselle* and his acrobatic feats as the slave in *Cléopâtre* were alike remarkable.

It had been the first performance of *Cléopâtre* that season, and the rest of the cast was thought to have acquitted itself well: Sophie Fedorova as Ta-Hor, Serafina Astafieva as Cleopatra, and Adolph Bolm as Amoun. The *Morning Post* that Monday made note of Pavlova's "new powers" as an actress, and her dancing was thought to be "something more fairy-like and more exquisitely graceful than has been seen before on these particular boards, and at once produced its wonted effect of charming the whole house. Her numbers with M. Nijinsky were a delightful exposition of the art of dancing in its purest aspect." The *Daily News* thought it all an "unqualified success," despite the weakness of *Giselle*. The *Bacchanale*'s veil floated high again, this time in its original place in the ballet: "Pavlova and Nijinsky are less important figures in this sumptuous *Cléopâtre*, but their cringing admiration of their mistress was full of subtle by-play, and the veil dance as fascinating as anything in the production. Perhaps,

ABOVE *Amarilla.*

BELOW *Greek Dance.*

though, the most vivid impression one takes away from *Cléopâtre* is the wonderful Bacchanale." The *Evening News* spoke of Pavlova's "supreme dancing in an atrocious ballet" (*Giselle*), while the *Evening Standard* focused on her reputation:

Were anything to make the Russian Ballet performances more popular than they have been all along it would be the engagement of Mme. Pavlova. Apart from the eminence and achievements of any other visitors in the same line to these shores, she has by her previous engagements in London made her name to the man in the street synonymous with Russian dancing, in the same way that Maud Allan's stands in his mind for classical [i.e., "Greek"] dancing and Caruso's for operatic singing. . . .

George Calderon in *The Times* wrote another of his long and well-researched reviews, which showed his knowledge of the whole genre of this ballet and of Pavlova's strengths within it. If *Giselle* itself got a negative reaction, it did so at the end of a most reasoned thesis:

The main thing about Pavlova is that, when she dances, the whole of her dances. With others our attention, and their own, is drawn at any given moment to this part or that; the rest is accessory. With Pavlova there are no accessory parts. She dances with her feet, her fingers, her neck (how much expression there is in the various inclinings of the head), her smile, her eyes, her dress. There is nothing left over, not even a personality watching its own evolutions. She is all dance and all drama at the same time. After the wildest caper she and Nijinsky are instantly poised in perfect balance, ready to stand stock still or start off again in any direction. Her gestures seem swifter than those of others, though they are fitted to the same music, partly because they are bolder and therefore cover more space, partly because they are perfectly timed, and partly because they are full of subtly-imagined variety. The drama of her successive emotions is perfectly clear; her changes of sentiment are instantly echoed by little thrills and murmurs, even in the inexpressive audience that fills Covent Garden. That roguery of hers is so deliciously feminine in its combination of full-grown intelligence with the mien of childhood. How delightful she is in *Giselle* with her old mother, Cecchetti! It seems impossible that two such expansive people can live in such a very little cottage.

But Giselle, though a big role, does injustice to Pavlova's genius. The part exhibits many moods and conditions—love, coyness, fear, anger, despair, madness, death, resurrection; but it is all about nothing; there is no sequence or motive. In fact *Giselle* is a good subject spoilt. The Wilis ought to be either vampirish and terrible or else plaintive and pathetic. But these are neither one thing nor the other, and pretend to be both. Who could really be alarmed by these nice young ladies in their white ballet-skirts? We all felt that the forester was a poor, fuddled coward to be so frightened. Heine, who gave Gautier the story, was not concerned with the vampirish side, but only with the pathos of the fate of girls who had never "had their proper whack" of dancing, and tried so feebly and unsubstantially to make it up of a moonlight night. No wonder they danced him to death if a young man came wandering by.

On November 1, Pavlova appeared in a truncated version of *Le Pavillon d'Armide*, as well as in *Les Sylphides* and another performance of *Cléopâtre*. L. H. Hayward in *The Times* was the first to suggest that Armide was actually given anything more in the way of partnering than the occasional support by her slave. Had Pavlova persuaded Fokine to do a little "adapting" for her?

Even the wonderful dancing of Mme. Pavlova as Armide in the magic garden cannot reconcile us to the dullness of the story in which she takes part, nor to the ugliness of the crude mixtures of pink, blue and green in which the characters are dressed. Armide herself, dancing in blue and white a pas de deux with her favourite slave in cream and yellow (once more a favourite slave, and once more M. Nijinsky to play him), provides the five minutes' relief (and exquisite relief it is) from dullness, but even here the tunes of M. Tcherepnin, though clearly the work of one who lives in an atmosphere of dance music, are not inspiring, and constantly suggest that they have tumbled out of someone else's score.

The *Morning Post* suggested that Pavlova had nothing to fear from dancing among her peers—or from the artistic efforts of Alexandre Benois:

The factor that was wanting in the performances of the Russian Ballet is supplied by Mlle. Pavlova. Last night she appeared in numbers that are for the most part familiar to patrons of the entertainment, but which, with the elegance of style, the grace, and total absence of the acrobatic she brought to bear, were made to appear as glossy new. . . . The effortless nature of her dancing, its delicacy, and its astonishing finish gave a fresh zest, and enabled the more sensitive to become oblivious for once to the clashing of the gaudy coloured dresses, and to be blind to the hideousness of the scenery.

The *Evening Standard's* reference to Pavlova's name being known to "the man in the street" was a tribute to something more than her extraordinary dancing skills, or even her physical retort to Mordkin. It had to do with her acceptance of the role that advertising played in an unsubsidized theatre world. Having discerned that it was an essential concomitant of her being able to dance as her own mistress rather than as the pawn of some all-powerful management, she fell in readily with the publicity requests of her promoters—but always in the most stylish and expensive manner. Gordon Selfridge, the merchandising magnate, had a penchant for "star ladies" and courted their association; he was much given to parading the charms of such as the Dolly Sisters. For Pavlova he mounted an unusually subtle bit of advertising, taking a whole page in the *Daily Mail* and laying it out as an eye-catching journalistic feature. It was perhaps inconsequential stuff: an alert lady writer (already known to Pavlova) being sent to accompany the dancer on a shopping spree in the House of Selfridge and reporting on the fun. But in another way it is a surprisingly clear-eyed and even rare document, for it portrays Pavlova over a span of several hours—as much as and probably more than anyone other than one of her dancing colleagues would ever see of Pavlova the woman. It is the inconsequential but real woman—the one who had such a fragmentary existence beyond the far edges of stages and rehearsal halls. (See Appendix, p. 404.)

At the other end of the journalistic spectrum, the social column in *The Lady* was pinpointing the smartness of the occasion that had taken place the previous week:

The first appearance of Pavlova at the Royal Opera House in the Russian ballet on Saturday attracted a very large company. The Grand Duke Alexander came with his gentleman-in-waiting and Major Fowler Burton to Mrs. Leopold Albu's box on the grand tier, and the Duchess of Manchester, in electric chiffon, with a pearl rope, and diamond pins catching her coiled hair, was with the Duke of Manchester in the front row of the stalls, where, too, was Lady Ripon, in sparkling grey, and a brush aigrette in her hair.

The Marchioness of Ripon's daughter, Lady Juliet Duff, was wearing *diamanté* lace on the corsage of a clinging pink gown, and a "sparkling headband" (which *The Lady* did not venture to suggest was diamonds) was fastened with an aigrette in front. All the aigrettes and the gold net turbans—spawned by *Schéhérazade* and by Poiret—must have made the view from the stalls even more of a hit-or-miss affair than usual, even though the seats had been raised since the summer. Lady Ottoline Morrell wore a black gown with great gathered Venetian sleeves and a square décolletage outlined with antique lace, obviously a marvelous contrast to all the pinks, greys, and mauves around her.

The Lady's "Musical Notes" section had some observations about the spectacle taking place on the stage:

Familiar as London audiences are with Madame Pavlova as a "turn" at the Palace, they have probably never yet seen her at her best, unless the centrepiece of a mosaic pavement is seen at its best when torn out of its proper surroundings. It is hardly necessary to praise Pavlova at this time of day, but it is interesting to find that there has been a great divergence of critical opinion over her dancing. When she was in Paris in 1909, one critic wrote that she had a very good style, but no great talent, and that her dancing was "sèche." Another said, "All the essentials of the dance, nobility of gesture, beauty of line, lightness, elevation, have united in her to produce the perfect dancer. She does not dance; she flies."

The Lady then went on to discuss an article that had appeared in *The Mask*—"the only journal in existence where the art of the theatre is written of by people who really know their subject." (The article and the production in general were the solo effort of Edward Gordon Craig.)

[*The Mask*] makes an attack on the Russian dancers, and on Bakst and Benois, the two painters who do most of the pictorial work of their ballets. In this article it is asserted that the Russian ballet masters learned all their modern improvements from Miss Isadora Duncan when she visited St. Petersburg in 1904, and that before that date they "had not understood the value of the curve." Nijinsky and Pavlova are declared to be the most perfect of the Russian dancers, because they have been "the most successful in acquiring the grace taught them by the American." . . . This is rather severe, and is it quite true? If the Russians stole ideas from Miss Duncan, they have used them in a way entirely their own, and only a small proportion of their dances are on the Duncan lines. . . .

It is not the work of the ballet in the "natural" school that I most admire. I admire the Russians because they have eliminated what is ugly and meaningless and mechanical in the classic school; have shown us that there is something essentially artificial in dancing on the toes, just as there is something essentially artificial in expressing thought in rhyme. The dancer's art is indeed in more senses than one akin to the poet's. Poetry is not a "natural" expression of the mind, any more than dancing is a "natural" expression of the body. We don't attack poetry and wish all expression could be in prose because there are bad poets. We ought to preserve the same attitude towards dancing, the "poetry of motion."

Motion in the streets was noticeably less, on account of a public transport strike, but the newly proliferating taxicabs were finding rich pickings from those patrons who could afford their services. For Pavlova's third appearance at Covent Garden, on November 3,* people got there by whatever means they could commandeer, though it meant that *Le Pavillon d'Armide* started to a thin house and was constantly interrupted by the arrival of more and more frustrated patrons. They were still arriving during *Les Sylphides,* which followed. There was panic backstage when Ludmilla Schollar fainted just as she was about to go on, but the situation was saved by Maria Piltz (just arrived from Warsaw), who volunteered to go on in Schollar's place, though she had never danced the roles before. The audience remained blissfully ignorant of the problem. The main excitement was generated by the latest novelty of the season's repertoire: on the same night, Pavlova and Nijinsky danced the Blue Bird pas de deux, which was masquerading as *L'Oiseau d'Or.* The *Evening Standard* thought it "a delightful little trifle [that] afforded an excellent medium for the display of Mme. Pavlova's unrivalled talents":

> Mme. Pavlova's every gesture and action was instinct with significance. Decked with resplendent feathers, she invested her movements with a rare sense of suggestion. Of no other dancer can it be said that her performances are the ideal combination of music, dancing, and acting. M. Nijinsky, too, was in one of his most agile moods, though the more one sees of the methods of the Russian ballet the more one is persuaded that the scope of the man dancer is more limited than that of the woman.

One can begin to see that the Pavlova-Nijinsky partnership was doomed to be fleeting, if only because Pavlova could have diverted too much of the attention that Diaghilev intended should center on Nijinsky.

H. C. Collis in *The Times* considered this pas de deux as "little more than a display of . . . virtuosity" but was still fascinated:

> Here the pointed toe step, which Mme. Pavlova does with an entrancing grace which no one else can quite attain, is used in a new way, with little clawing movements as though only a small thread held her to the ground and she were trying to free herself and sail away into mid-air. As in her famous *Papillon* dance, so in *L'Oiseau d'Or* her art is more suggestive than imitative. She does not copy a bird, but she seems for the moment to partake of its nature.

This seems to suggest that Pavlova had firmly discarded the Maryinsky echoes of Petipa's Princess Florine and was going wholeheartedly for the golden bird image of the title—if not of the costume, which was surprisingly heavy, with no finch-like simplicity but a panoply of adornment like some overburdened Chinese pheasant. Her agitated footwork probably made all the scarlet and yellow feathers quiver in an exciting way. The Polovtsian Dances from *Prince Igor* completed the program for that night.

On Monday, November 6, Pavlova returned to *Giselle* and then essayed Columbine in *Carnaval* for the first time. Rather extraordinarily, the program was not thought to warrant a further visit from the press, even though Collis's review in *The Times* three days earlier had concluded with the thought that the management at Covent Garden might give more consideration to that part of the audience which would have wished to see "three or even two whole ballets, rather than four maimed ones." So there was nothing printed to tell how Pavlova must have trilled on her delicate pointes as the coquettish Columbine to Nijinsky's impish Harlequin in what would have been an astonishing contrast to her poor, love-torn Giselle. The following evening, November 7, the King and Queen were in the audience. Pavlova and Nijinsky again danced *Carnaval,* as well as *Le Pavillon d'Armide* and *Les Sylphides.* That night King George made his customary diary entry, and on this occasion he confided that "Madame Pavlova and Mr. Nijinsky certainly dance beautifully."

Pavlova danced again with Nijinsky at the Wednesday matinee in *Cléopâtre, Les Sylphides,* and *L'Oiseau d'Or,* and *The Lady* recognized in the afternoon's performance an artistic partnership that seemed to possess elements of magic:

> Those who had not seen Pavlova before in her proper setting will surely admit that her dancing at Covent Garden was infinitely more beautiful and noble than it was at the Palace Theatre. I have always asserted that the secret of her pre-eminence, apart from a singularly poetic personality, is her miraculous sense of time. She dances so exquisitely on the beat that she seems to play the music. This perfect time is also one of the chief charms of Nijinsky's dancing, and Pavlova in her dances with him seems more joyous, more spirited, more free than she ever was in her pas de deux with Mordkin at the Palace, for this dancer, with all his merits, has not anything like the rhythmic excellence of Nijinsky. The Chopin waltz in *Les Sylphides* demonstrated exactly why these two dancers, Nijinsky and Pavlova, have achieved such a unique position in the ballet world. They are poets and musicians as well as dancers. . . .
>
> The dancing of Pavlova and Nijinsky in [*L'Oiseau d'Or*] was superb. They seemed to be creatures come from a world as different from the de Musset-like world of *Les Sylphides* as is a wood in a fairy tale from a panelled room. They are gentle and wild at the same time, this Prince and his Bird. They have been nourished on magic philtres and have learned the lore of feathered things. Those who saw *L'Oiseau d'Or* at Covent Garden last Wednesday should keep the vision in their memory zealously, joyously, for they are not likely to see anything so beautiful again in a lifetime.

Finally, Richard Capell of the *Daily Mail* summed up Pavlova's season with the Diaghilev troupe:

---

* In Washington on the previous night, Mordkin, returning to the stage after his operation, was responsible for a bit of ballet history: he was giving America its first sight of the full, four-act version of *Swan Lake.* It was twenty-eight days before Diaghilev's two-act production was seen for the first time, in London. The ballet got a much better reception in America than it did in England, where Kchessinskaya was starring.

Mme. Anna Pavlova, who has been dancing at Covent Garden for a fortnight, bade farewell there to her admirers on Saturday. She appeared as Armida, as the chief nymph in the Chopinesque *Les Sylphides*—surely, as interpreted by this peerless corps de ballet, the most enchanting exhibition of purely classic dancing ever seen—and as the Golden Bird in the extract from Tchaikovsky's *Sleeping Beauty* ballet. And she has perhaps never before danced so beautifully. Closer acquaintance with the Covent Garden stage, the orchestra, and her fellow dancers evidently had greatly increased her confidence, and things like the dance following the Scene of the Scarf in *Armida* and the C sharp minor waltz in *The Sylphides* were done with a self-abandonment, a "fine, careless rapture," that were entrancing. After *The Sylphides* . . . there was a storm of applause, flowers for Mme. Pavlova, and laurels for M. Michael Fokin, the inspired ballet-master of the troupe, to whom Mme. Pavlova, in an amusing scene, paid homage, handing over to him, in gesture, all the audience's applause.

Sometime after midnight on Saturday, November 11, 1911, Pavlova left Covent Garden—left it to Nijinsky and Diaghilev, to Kchessinskaya and her Grand Duke, and to the last of the diamond-bright crowds. She was headed elsewhere; the English provincial tour with a small group of soloists had been organized, and it was due to start that Monday, in a coal-mining center called Newcastle. To Pavlova, the good folk of Newcastle appeared ripe for conversion.

While Pavlova was dancing in Newcastle, Mordkin was being quizzed by Count de Beaufort for the Chicago *Examiner*.

"Tell me, Monsieur Mordkin, what is the real, mind you the *real*, not the press agent reason, that Mlle. Pavlowa is not with you this year?"

"Ah, mon ami, I will tell you with pleasure; no, no, I did not mean that; with regret I mean, because I am very sorry. The reason is this: Pavlowa is engaged to a Russian nobleman. Last year he got in some kind of trouble in St. Petersburg and Pavlowa put up a certain amount of money as a guarantee. When the case came up she left London, where at the time she was playing with me, and the moment she arrived on Russian territory she was put under surveillance of the police department and has been ever since. It is forbidden of her to leave Russia. This and this *only* is the reason that Pavlowa is no longer with me, but as soon as her affairs are settled she will come back."

At this moment Enrico Caruso interrupted the fairy tale to tell Mordkin that he was the Caruso of dancers!

Whether it was an audience at the Lyceum in Edinburgh, or at the Prince of Wales' in Birmingham, or at the Royal in Manchester, it was an audience with one objective: to see the most famous Russian dancer in the world. And see her they did, night after night, all over Britain. Provincial audiences were not concerned with the expertise of the raggle-taggle group that accompanied Pavlova, nor were they particularly concerned with the efforts of the self-effacing Novikov; they wanted Pavlova, and Pavlova wanted them, and this affair between the star

This 1912 photograph of Pavlova as Columbine was reproduced from a color original on the brochure for her British provincial tour.

Les Coquetteries de Columbine:
(above) with Novikov and Zaylich, 1912; (below) with Novikov,
in new costumes for the 1913-14 American tour.

and her subjects was carried out nightly, with passion and enjoyment on both sides.

The audiences loved the little delicacies of emotion, the small swoonings, the charming embroideries of physical grace, the fragility, the fleeting quality, and, too, the accessibility of the music and the uses to which it was put. The potpourri programs, with their interludes of piano playing and singing to fill out the evening, were carefully tailored to make a minimum amount of material go the maximum distance. There were only four girls in support; the youngest was a fourteen-year-old English girl, Winifred Linder, parading as Linda Lindovska. They could not carry the stage for long on their own, and the very nature of Pavlova's snippets meant that it was a taxing program for her, since her energy was always required to be at a peak; there was no chance for the pacing of a sustained role. She had a voracious appetite for performing—or, more particularly, for the adrenaline charge that came from her instantaneous success with each new audience—and without it she was something of a lost being, restless and unfulfilled. But withal, she had the discipline of her early training, and she knew that weakness on her part would quickly erode the faith of any organization that was backing her. She had learned the lesson of Mordkin, noticing how quickly he could antagonize managements; she, by contrast, usually managed to escape any long-term acrimony, and her occasional outbursts were always credited to a nervous artistic temperament being put under momentary stress. She had a way of giving full measure which always obliterated any memories of irrational behavior.

The tour went well, though in neither Dublin nor Belfast did her visit start auspiciously. In Dublin a scenery flat collapsed on top of Pavlova, but she clambered out and continued as if it were an everyday occurrence. In Belfast the opening night provided fourteen people in the audience; the dancers had clashed with a political speech being delivered by Winston Churchill. (For once Pavlova encountered someone who could top her.) But the fourteen people got their money's worth and cheered her heartily for it, and the rest of the performances were packed.

When the group returned to London at the beginning of March 1912, with just over a month to get ready for a new season at the Palace Theatre, Pavlova was confronted with the reality of Dandré—having slipped out of Russia and forfeited his bail—now being an exile, to all intents and purposes dependent on her.* Her attachment to Dandré was by this stage based purely on loyalty. Even in the early years of their association in St. Petersburg they had never lived together openly. Now her

---

* Dandré's "problem" was later the subject of gossip within Pavlova's company. It was generally understood that she had bailed him out; the gossip related not to the civil engineering project but to the misuse of a Grand Duchess's milk fund. Later, references were made to a long-standing court case, known as the Gurko-Ester-Lidval-Dandré case, which spluttered along for years before being snuffed out by the Revolution. There was a suggestion that municipal funds had been "borrowed" for temporary investment elsewhere in order that the profit could be creamed off. The stock was more sluggish than expected, and the discrepancies emerged before the original financing could be returned.

small house in Golders Green suddenly became a claustrophobic base, and Pavlova looked for something larger. By chance, nearby there was an agent's sign signifying that a large house behind an ivy-clad wall in Hampstead's North End Road was to let or for sale. Pavlova saw the property in company with Dandré and Daniel Mayer and his son Rudolph, and she fell for the house immediately; once inside, an unexpected view opened up from the main rooms, which looked out over a descending garden covering well over an acre, and this was flanked by a large municipal park, so that the vista of trees gave an appearance almost of open countryside. And it had a verandah, which must have clinched things. The house had not been lived in for some years, and the garden was very neglected but was alive with birds using it as a sanctuary. When Pavlova saw the pond at the far end of the property, she exclaimed, "There I will have swans! I take the house." She agreed to rent the property, known as Ivy House, for an extended term from the Golders Hill and General Estates Company.*

The house was ideal for Pavlova: it was in the vicinity of the relatively unspoiled surroundings of Hampstead Heath, it had light and outlook, and it had lots of space, most particularly a huge central hall, very airy and lit by a sort of clerestory. Upper rooms opened onto a balcony which overlooked this central space. It meant that Pavlova could duplicate her St. Petersburg living arrangement, with her own rehearsal hall. And the hall also meant that her company could sometimes go to her; and the children's classes, which she was so eager to promote, could be held there as well.

At Ivy House:
(below) displaying her *Russian Dance*
costume in the central hall, 1912.

Pavlova was due to open her new season at the Palace on April 15. When her motorcar arrived at the theatre for the first performance, newsboys in the street were shouting of a calamity that fixed the attention of every person within earshot: the great *Titanic* had met with a disaster on her maiden voyage. It was inconceivable—the greatest ship afloat, claimed to be unsinkable, and yet the placards for the *Evening News* read "Great Loss of Life." Information was confused and conflicting; at this stage it was not known that the vessel had actually sunk, merely that she was stricken after colliding with an iceberg and that the lives of more than twenty-three hundred people were at risk. Somewhere in icy waters the great floating hotel, with its Aubusson carpets and Jacobean carvings, had already gone through its death throes. Pavlova, preparing for the show, had ample time to think of her own sea voyages to America, of her hatred of sea travel, with everyone assuring her that it was the safest thing in the world to step on board a great ocean-going liner and be transported in utter comfort. All the luxury in the world had not availed those poor souls on the *Titanic*.

---

* The agents seem to have suggested to Pavlova that at some point in its history, the house had been tenanted by the painter J. M. W. Turner. There was absolutely no justification for this, though there may have been some honest confusion with a house called Wyldes further up the road, which had been frequented by numerous well-known painters in the nineteenth century.

With Novikov as the gypsy brother in *Amarilla*.

The opening program consisted of eleven numbers, including two directly attributable to Gorsky. These had been rehearsed by Alexander Shirayev, who had last traveled with Pavlova on her 1909 European tour and had now joined the company in something of a leading position as second partner and general régisseur. The Palace audience's first sight of Pavlova was in *La Nuit*. She also appeared in *Les Coquetteries de Colombine*, which was actually a pas de trois to Drigo interpolated by the Legats into *The Fairy Doll*; as the program put it, Pavlova was "assisted" in this flirtatious number by Novikov and Shirayev. Pavlova and Novikov danced Legat's *Valse Caprice* in the second half and ended with the still wildly popular *Bacchanale*. When Pavlova made her entrance in *La Nuit*, there were displays of tremendous enthusiasm in the audience, and the dancer seemed physically to bloom with this outpouring of regard; the evening became the accustomed triumph, and as the audience streamed out the most frequently heard comments were "Isn't she divine?" and "More splendid than ever!"

The Times, for once, was not overscrupulous; everything in the Palace garden was lovely: "M. Novikoff, if we are not mistaken, will create an even bigger *furore* than his predecessors. He is not only a picture of a youthful male, handsome from crown to sole, but a dancer of all the accomplishment we expect." As for the *Bacchanale*, it had become a crazy scamper, but *The Times* seemed to adore it: "We have never seen it so madly danced. If the rout in Titian's *Bacchus and Ariadne* came to life, they could not outdo this revel of wine and sunshine and love." *The Times* continued with the thought that Pavlova's hour-long program was all too short. (This benevolent review suggests that it came from other than Calderon, who had in the past made such pertinent remarks about the artistic content of Pavlova's presentations.)

The musical critic of *The Lady* had time during the first week to analyze the program's actual content with a far cooler eye than most of the critics writing for the dailies:

> . . . I began to wonder what was wrong with me that, on the whole, this Pavlova reappearance had made me very sad, and that I could not with sincerity have joined in the eulogy of this "Saison Russe" à l'anglaise. For there is hardly a trace left of the discipline, of the delicacy, of the admirable restraint which distinguish the Russian ballet at its best. I am not going to say that the movement in favour of greater natural grace is not precisely that which has raised Pavlova and Nijinsky above the heads of their comrades, and has leavened the formal steps of "classic" dancing with a breath of new life. So long as this movement was translated by the Russians in their own way, it was all for good. But since Pavlova emancipated herself from the discipline of the Imperial Ballet and became the idol of the British public, is it not true that she has begun to translate natural dancing into American? Over the performance at the Palace the other night I could not help noticing the trail of American influence. Everything was exaggerated. Vivacity degenerated into mere tricks; passion became a coarse "letting go." Instead of that exquisite impersonal purity of the emotion of the dance, we had personal feeling—we had Pavlova getting on terms with her audience as their favourite, not as a dancer.

The scenery for *Amarilla* was an extensive departure from the usual Palace stagings.

It is useless to deny that there is very little art about the present Pavlova show. The scenery and the dresses are certainly not good in design and colour, and as the new spirits who guide the Russian Imperial Ballet [*sic*] have done so much in this direction that is uncommon and beautiful, there is really no excuse for this relapse. The male dancer who supports Pavlova is really a caricature of Mordkin, and the *Glazounov Bacchanale,* which used to be so beautiful when that dancer and Pavlova danced it together, is now a wild romp. . . . Shall we make an appeal to Pavlova not to sell her dancer's birthright for a mess of pottage in the form of numberless baskets of flowers and bouquets?

Yoshio Markino, a Japanese observer, saw Pavlova as a kindred spirit to figures in his own cultural background:

While I was watching her dances, two symmetrical pictures came into my mind. When she dances calmfully [*sic*] all her draperies come into that graceful curved line which Utamaro invented in his pictures, and when she dances with abandon all her draperies become those wavy lines which Hokusai invented in his late works. Utamaro and Hokusai both invented those lines entirely from their imaginations, and how strange to see them actually visible in Pavlova's dancing!

Strange, perhaps; and yet one was a stylized observation of natural movement, the other natural movement resulting from stylization. The critic André Levinson had also noticed that certain elements of Pavlova's dance had a Japanese-like "color."

A month into the Palace season, Pavlova introduced into her program the Grand Pas from *Paquita;* in this she showed audiences the true splendor of an Imperial ballerina, in manner and in dress. Her many-layered black skirt was embroidered with gold spangles, and she wore a diamond necklace and a big fan of osprey feathers in her hair. Then, as contrast to all this classicism, Pavlova decided to test her music-hall audiences by staging a half-hour ballet on a dramatic theme.* *Amarilla* was set to an arrangement of pieces by Glazunov, Drigo, and Dargomizhsky, and had a standard plot involving a countess at the time of Louis XVI, her noble young fiancé, and the gypsy girl of the title whom he had loved and left. It was said to be taken from the libretto of a gypsy folk song. Like Nikiya in *La Bayadère,* the heroine is compelled to dance before the man she loves, while he watches in the company of a high-born fiancée. Amarilla had a pas de deux with her gypsy brother in which she supported herself by the tambourine he was holding; then she would go into an arabesque on pointe and hold it, unsupported, while Novikov withdrew into the wings. The quivering pose seemed to last an

---

* The choreography was later credited to Ivan Clustine, and also to Pyotr Zaylich. Clustine was at this point pursuing a career in Paris after having left the Imperial Ballet in Moscow in 1903, when Gorsky had taken his place as ballet master, while Zaylich had yet to join the company, but other contenders would be Shirayev or even Novikov; however, Pavlova had been in contact with Clustine and there were plenty of occasions when he could have been in London.

On the lawn at Ivy House.

ABOVE & BELOW June 12 dress rehearsal for the garden party.

eternity, before a flourish ended it as Novikov stepped back into view. Elsewhere she drifted backward in a "faint," employing a ripple of fine pas de bourrées that fascinated audiences.

The Times, for one, was uncertain of the value of this poignant little drama of blighted love as an entertainment, thinking it rather too episodic to have dramatic unity and with an over-abundance of pantomime, but for the *Daily Graphic*, Pavlova made it all worthwhile: "Her last pose, when the shadows of a purple twilight are creeping over the rose-hung terrace and green lawns of the garden, when she is abandoned to the tears of solitude and humiliation—would that it could be perfectly rea-lised by some deft and sympathetic sculptor. . . . But even then you would not be so profoundly moved as when the spirit of Pavlova breathes tears and little heart gasps into the flickering movements of a dance."

The audience was fully appeased by Pavlova's appearances in the second half of the program, in which she danced her *Swan*, her *Butterfly*, and, invariably, the *Bacchanale*. The diminutive Matveyeva (Shirayev's wife) usually won a storm of applause for her dance to music of Liadov, in which she portrayed a French baby doll—on pointe throughout. After Pavlova's last dance there was always a clamor for an encore, with flowers thrown to her from all parts of the house. Although encores were never given, Pavlova made such a play of her curtain calls, with endless little effects and gestures, caressing the flowers and bestowing her magnetic glance in turn on all sections of the auditorium, that the patrons were usually teased into thinking that they might succeed in their objective if they continued their enthusiasm for long enough. The calls always differed in style according to the dance. After *The Swan* she might run forward to center-stage with arms outstretched, totter a short distance on full pointe, and then collapse into a marvelous drooping pose by the footlights; for a return call she would run on from one of the downstage wings. A third call and she would emerge from quite another spot. By this time the audience would be in a fever, wondering where she would appear next. At the end, they had been given, in effect, another ten-minute entertainment, which sent them into the streets in a happy mood. Many people did not choose to stay for the bioscope pictures.

In June, Pavlova had an entertainment of her own to consider: she decided to give her new address a traditional housewarm-ing. Though she had no desire to curry any sort of favor on the social front, she did like things to be done properly if done at all, and she took advice on the composition of her guest list, which began very high up the social scale. Mrs. Asquith, the Prime Minister's wife, was somehow missed from the initial list, but the omission was noticed before an irretrievable social faux pas had been committed. Pavlova picked a Thursday in mid June, the week before Ascot Gold Cup day. It was also the day after the Diaghilev company's opening at Covent Garden; but even in the guise of hostess, Pavlova still managed to be the number-one entertainment.

Ivy House garden party, June 13, 1912:
LEFT & BELOW Performing *En Orange* with Novikov.

The Bystander, June 19, 1912

PAVLOVA'S HOUSE-WARMING: GREAT D...

At the Pavlova Garden Party

MRS. ASQUITH

MADAME PAVLOVA

THE DUCHESS OF RUTLAND AND COUNT BENCKENDORFF

159

The weather was on her side, with a cloudless sky and only a light breeze, so that despite the provision of a tent, the tea tables could be arranged around the perimeter of the upper lawn. By mid-afternoon some four hundred guests were on the grounds of Ivy House, having made their way through the central hall, which had been hung with garlands of smilax and gilded baskets filled with pink flowers. There were flowers everywhere, set off by the white-painted woodwork of the rooms in the house; and even in the garden itself the tables were all decorated with bowls of sweet peas.

Circulating among her guests, the hostess wore a clever echo of the sweet pea colors: a diaphanous frock of palest mauve with its sash in powder blue and a bodice band in cerise. A "Charlotte Corday" hat, also mauve, with a big bow and a cluster of flowers to one side completed the effect. The Palace Theatre orchestra had been persuaded to play, and there were all sorts of surprise entertainments, including a tiny boy playing violin solos, a conjurer, and seven young dance students cavorting as nymphs. Pavlova also thought to bring in the young English dancer Phyllis Bedells, who performed at the Empire. The setting was really very sylvan, despite the ladies in vast millinery creations and the gentlemen in frock coats and toppers or an occasional blazer and boater.

As the lowering sun slanted through the poplars lining the garden boundary, Pavlova provided the best possible climax to the afternoon's entertainments: dressed as some archaic shepherdess in flame-colored crêpe de Chine, with golden sandals and a bandeau of roses entwined in her dark hair, she emerged sud-

Adeline Genée as Camargo.

denly from a shrubbery and danced on the grass with Novikov supporting her. He wore a sleeveless pinafore with a pair of shaggy goatskins girdled fore and aft, while his great legs terminated in Attic boots. The pas de deux was new to England: Gorsky's arrangement, known as *En Orange*, with the principal Giraud air now played by a violinist. Pavlova had rehearsed it on the grass the day before, but with an audience she seemed encouraged to adapt, and she contrived to fling herself to the ground at one point with a gesture that had a certain bacchanalian abandon to it. This entertainment had an added audience craning over the fence of the North End Road boundary to the property. After she had finished dancing, Pavlova went to thank the perspiring leader of the orchestra and handed him a glass, announcing with a smile that it was "Orangeade." Finck missed the point of her joke but replied with one of his own: "Orangeade? What I need is first aid!"

Considered opinion in society columns was that the garden party was one of the most delightful ever held in London; prompted by the Louis Seize costumes of the *Amarilla* court dances, the *Pall Mall Gazette* thought that it brought back Versailles in the days of its *fêtes galantes*. The new hostess was showered with invitations after this spectacular entrée, but she would never submit herself to the usual society circuit and was so adamant about this that Mrs. Asquith was finally driven to describe her as "an impossible woman."

Even in 1912, royal favor was still viewed as a magic pass to some inner realm of grace. King George maintained his regard for the Palace Theatre and its entertainments, and he consented to a Royal Command Performance for the Music-Hall Benevolent Fund, to be staged on Monday, July 1. Many thought that the event would signify a new degree of respectability for music-hall entertainment. As the *Daily Telegraph* said, "Millions of British subjects patronise the music-halls, and a thrill of satisfaction was felt by them all when their favourite, if one-time derided, form of amusement was thus declared 'fit for a King.' The social elevation to which the music-hall has attained has been both exalted and real, but never formally acknowledged." The King, perhaps unwittingly, gave the lie to the sentiments of prestige by appearing on the night in simple evening dress with his only decoration a white carnation; but the royal couple seemed determined to enjoy themselves and were noticeably of good humor throughout the performance.

The Executive Committee, which included managers like Oswald Stoll as well as Butt himself, had been determined to outdo Covent Garden in the magnificence of the decorations. The royal party was framed by a great arch of palms, with Dorothy Perkins roses and blue wisteria intertwined in front, and the interior of the box was lined with Louis XVI paneling. There was a new backdrop in imitation of a Beauvais tapestry, with the central painting representing Fontaine's picture of the gardens at Versailles, and the rest of the auditorium was a phenomenal bower of roses—reportedly 3 million, both real and artificial.

Garden party performances in London:
LEFT Drigo's *Polka Pizzicato*. In this group Gorshkova (center) is the only true Russian;
the others are English recruits: Zalmanova, Lindovska, Fredova, and Butsova.
RIGHT Pavlova in her *Bleichmann* costume, in a pas de deux with Novikov.

At the end of a long evening (Pavlova and her "assistants" were Number 22 of twenty-five different acts), the King announced that he was charmed with the program, though he admitted that at first sight he felt it was going to be too long. Such a great favorite as Little Tich had been included (fortunately for Nijinsky, in the audience, who always wanted to see the diminutive comedian more than anyone else), but there were some notable absentees: the *Daily News* lamented the absence of Marie Lloyd, Eugene Stratton, Albert Chevalier, and Ada Reeve. "A variety gala without these artists cannot be called complete. There were several turns which might have been omitted, and room should have been found for Adeline Genée and Lydia Kyasht, which could easily have been done by limiting Pavlova's dances." Still, the *Telegraph* commented on the feeling of expectancy that took possession of the house when Pavlova's number went into the frame, and they thought she danced "as she has rarely danced before." Genée was having a triumph of her own over at the Coliseum in her version of *Camargo*. There was really a tremendous choice of entertainment for London theatre-goers, ranging from Irving Berlin singing ragtime at the Hippodrome to Chaliapin singing *Ivan le Terrible* at Drury Lane.

Despite the pressure of work at the Palace, Pavlova still found time to fulfill some of the extra engagements that had been promised by Mayer: she and Novikov, together with a group of her dancers, performed at a garden party given by Viscountess Michelham at Strawberry Hill, where Pavlova managed also to get onto the program eight little girls she had auditioned for tuition at Ivy House. Later in July, Diaghilev's dilettante business associate Baron de Gunsbourg pulled off a remarkable coup when he persuaded Pavlova, Karsavina, and Kyasht to appear together as the entertainment for a supper party given by him at the Carlton Hotel.[*]

At the Palace, Pavlova continued to experiment with the introduction of one-act ballets, hoping no doubt to educate the music-hall audiences; there was still a gulf between them and the crowds over at Covent Garden, where *Thamar* and *The Firebird* were causing great excitement. She decided to present a version of *La Fille Mal Gardée* in which Shirayev followed fairly strictly the Dauberval structure (revived by Ivanov at the Maryinsky), with its score by Hertel. Although the program stated that only the first scene of the ballet was being given (this possibly to allay nervousness in the audience), it was actually the entire work in slightly condensed form. The program also claimed that it was being shown for the first time in England, but Dauberval himself had revived it at the Pantheon Theatre in London in 1791, when it was more accurately described as "an entire new ballet," and it appeared at frequent intervals in the King's Theatre during the following twenty-five years. Nevertheless, Pavlova's production was most certainly a novelty for modern London, and it afforded a chance to see her delicious sense of comedy in the role of Eliza (as the heroine was now named). Shirayev played Marcelline, the mother; Novikov was Colin; and the simpleton, here called Nikass, was played by Monahoff.

---

[*] Ballerinas were not in the least bit timid about gracing these entertainments. Pavlova also revived her flower basket party trick, and burst forth at the Ritz one night. The pay for these jollities was high.

ABOVE Bursting out of a basket of flowers at
a society party, in her *Rose* costume.

BELOW This illustration, originally in full color, was presumably
reconstructed from the photograph of Pavlova in *La Fille Mal Gardée*
on p. 82. In the artist's version, Pavlova appears to be wearing
her 1908 *Chopiniana* costume.

THE QUEEN OF DANCE AT THE SAVOY HOTEL, LONDON. MADAME PAVLOVA'S "PAS DE SEUL" AT A FANCY DRESS BALL.

In some ways the work was almost ideal fare for a music hall, and the audiences loved the cleverness of the ribbon pas de deux, the clog dance done by four girls, and the corps de ballet dancing with bouquets of wildflowers. Pavlova's ability to play the soubrette was something of a revelation, but equally amusing was Shirayev in the travesti role of the mother, which accorded well with the tradition of English music-hall "dames." Colin's four friends (one of whom was played by the young soloist Stanislas Idzikowsky) carried sheaves of real corn, and although the company was unevenly divided, with a preponderance of female dancers, the boys usually managed to support two girls each when they were not toting corn.

The audience seemed genuinely enchanted by *Fille*, but after the performance on its first night, Shirayev summoned the dancers on stage and proceeded to enumerate a string of complaints. He was quite prepared to commandeer the stage for another run-through, but the stagehands had other ideas, and so everyone adjourned to Hampstead to continue the post mortem at Ivy House, where a replay continued until the early hours of the morning. Pavlova actively encouraged this martinet approach, and she was as concerned as anyone that standards should not deteriorate simply because the dancing was no longer taking place in the hallowed setting of the Maryinsky. Most of her company members were taking this extra work during their summer vacations from the Imperial Theatres, and there was always a temptation to treat the London season as something of an amusing adventure; but Pavlova was very conscious of the increasingly wide range of dancing available to London audiences, and she was well aware of the criticism of falling standards that had already been leveled at her from some quarters. Nevertheless, *La Fille Mal Gardée* was given for one week only, due to the prevailing idea that music halls had to keep changing their programs in order to keep the interest of their patrons, many of whom owed a certain allegiance to a hall rather than to its program, and perhaps also to Francis Toye's end-of-week review, which dismissed *Fille* as a pantomimic aberration with derivative music. Audiences on the whole were sympathetic to whatever Pavlova offered, and although her supporting company was still billed as "Russian Artists from the Imperial Theatres," Pavlova could at last see the clear possibilities of a career as an independent star, *à la* Taglioni. But she still needed sympathetic vehicles for her talent. Audiences wanted novelties, and she needed to sustain her own interest. Fokine was still the safest source for material that would display her qualities to the best advantage, and to this end she had re-established contact with him back in June when she had heard of his break with Diaghilev. Fokine tried to interest Pavlova in a production based on a suite from *Le Coq d'Or*, which encapsulated the Rimsky-Korsakov opera in dance form and offered a perfect role for Pavlova in the person of the Queen of Shemakhan, the Daughter of the Air. Unfortunately, at this juncture the weight of Victor Dandré's counsel became evident in matters artistic, and it was suggested to Fokine that the satirical element involving the character of Tsar Dodon might be interpreted in Europe as an antiroyalist jibe. Fokine's

La Fille Mal Gardée, Act One

Novikov in costume for the Pirate's Dance.

Shirayev in costume for the Sailor's Hornpipe.

suggested innovations, which showed that he was attempting to swim with the modernist tide, alarmed Dandré, who was quick to instill doubts in Pavlova's mind, so that the brilliant concept of *Le Coq d'Or* was put aside. Instead they settled for two less contentious works: *Les Préludes,* to Liszt, and a work using Alexander Spendiarov's tone poem *The Three Palms.*

Both ballets were to have a similar underlying thread of poetical mysticism—almost fatalism; Liszt's Symphonic Poem No. 3 was to be used for a choreographic essay interpreting Lamartine's *Poetic Meditations,* in which Pavlova would play the role of the Spirit of Love; in contrast, in *The Three Palms* she was to play a Persian princess in the tale of the visit of an Oriental Prince and his knights to the mountain height where dwelt the seven daughters of the chief of the djinns, who had immured them there to keep them safe from the eyes of mortals. During the Ghost King's absence, Prince Hassam and six knights reached the retreat. All of the daughters gave themselves to the knights, with the exception of the youngest. The wrath of the Ghost King caused them to be cast into a fiery pit, except for the seventh daughter, though she was secretly mourning the loss of Prince Hassam as well as her sisters, and the weight of such melancholy brought about her death too.

Having appeased Dandré by rejecting *Le Coq d'Or,* Pavlova rather artfully conspired with Fokine and allowed him a free hand in the Spendiarov ballet (which was first given with the

alternative title *The Seven Daughters of the Ghost King),* so that he was able to envisage a well-integrated work in which the components of Spendiarov's music and Boris Anisfeld's designs would be every bit as important to the overall effect as the choreography and the dancers who interpreted it. Fokine admired Pavlova's marked ability to assume Oriental languor, and he planned for the ending a striking little theatrical effect, with the Princess subsiding to the ground in concert with a dwindling jet of water from a fountain.

During all this planning, the programs at the Palace continued, and there were as well the social engagements enlivened by Pavlova's appearances as an entertainer or as guest of honor for charities. In addition, the young girl students had to be prepared. They worked assiduously at Ivy House, and by the end of July they were ready to make a public appearance at the theatre. Pavlova and Shirayev worked out various dances for them; apart from the *Blue Danube* waltz with Grace Desbrisay, a slightly older girl, there was a Chopin *Idyll* for Maisie McDonald and the diminutive June Tripp, a *Danse Calabraise* to Pugni for Beatrice Beauchamp, Aileen Bowerman, and May Smith, and a pas de trois to Czibulka in which Beatrice Griffiths and Muriel Popper[*] were supported by the clever young Stanislas Idzikowsky.

[*] Muriel Mary Stuart Popper, to give her full name. Miss Stuart recalls only Kostia Kobelev in the pas de trois. Kobelev took over the part the following year, with Beatrice Beauchamp (Collenette) replacing Beatrice Griffiths.

With her pupils, 1913: (standing, left to right) Mabel Warren,
Grace Curnock, Aileen Bowerman, Beatrice Beauchamp,
Muriel Popper; (seated) Beatrice Griffiths, June Tripp.

With her pupils, 1912. The Steinberg (1909) portrait had
recently been shipped from St. Petersburg to Ivy House.

But most exciting for them was a divertissement in which they appeared with their teacher. It was called *La Naissance du Papillon*, and in it Pavlova was a butterfly. (There was an obsession with depicting butterflies in dancing; they figured endlessly at the Maryinsky and elsewhere.) She was surrounded by seven "flowers": clover, poppy, bluebell, daisy, lily of the valley, buttercup, and cornflower. The tunes were a selection from Delibes, and the dances were worked out according to each girl's capability; there was no attempt to marry movement to any particular floral image.

For the special matinee in which they were appearing, on August 1, the little girls were sent to the fitting room in their tarlatans prior to the performance, and there Pavlova dipped into various boxes of artificial flowers, quickly deciding which girl would be suitable for which bloom. These were then stitched onto the dresses, and circlets were made for the girls' hair. It was a considerable strain for the children, despite their eagerness, since they had to cope with their earlier dances in the program before their appearance with Pavlova. There was so little time between numbers that improvised dressing rooms had to be arranged at the sides of the stage, painfully far from the "facilities." After having danced a Chopin waltz, a pas de trois, and *La Nuit*, Pavlova darted out of her dressing room, already changed but still breathless, in order to watch the girls' early dances. Then she had to perform a solo Chopin variation, take calls, hurriedly shed her costume for the butterfly one, find time to arrange little

June's wreath of cornflowers, and be ready to emerge at the right moment from the swathes of her silk gauze chrysalis. She still had to do the *Valse Caprice* and the *Bacchanale* in the second half of the program. Anyone not sated with this outpouring of energy could have stayed on after the dancing and seen strong men exerting themselves at the Royal Henley Regatta—on film.

The appearance of Pavlova's young pupils held out the promise of native English talent in dance. But according to one writer, "It would need experienced judgment such as the layman cannot command to tell whether this is genuine and precocious promise of a high order, or only that dramatic imitative faculty which some English children possess in marked degree, only to develop later into the most level, sober, not to say stodgy, specimens of their awkward tribe." He laid much of the blame for the current state of English dancing on the quality of the music that generally accompanied it:

> And finally and fundamentally there is the music. Our dancing has been negligible largely because our music in general has been contemptible. Much of the accomplished dancing which has visited us has been to the accompaniment of a music which simply is too trivial to sustain a great art. Even now, of course, we have not by any means learnt to listen to dancing, to understand that the ear, as well as eye, must be perfectly focussed. So that one may sum up the limitations of a possible development of a native modernist English school of dancing as lack of temperament—lack of sufficient general standard of musical culture.

So another season of summer dancing in London came to an end, and Pavlova was replaced at the Palace by the popular Australian entertainer Annette Kellermann (billed as "The Perfect Woman"), who was performing with a company in *Undine,* "An Idyll of Forest and Stream"—it was actually a swimming act.

The forthcoming provincial tour had firm bookings that filled three full months, including two weeks across the border in Edinburgh and Glasgow. There was a month's respite before it all started—barely time to plan all the new ballets and engage fresh artists. Tikhomirov's name appeared among the male soloists with no star billing or solos, and there were two more local girls to join Lindovska and Hilda Bewicke, already established members. Winifred Edwards became Fredova, and Rita Zalmani (actually of Spanish-Polish-Jewish stock) became Zalmanova, to accord with the smokescreen that all the dancers were members of the Imperial Russian Ballet—all, that is, except the Anglo-Indian girl who performed under the stage name of Roshanara and who had a section of the program all to herself. She had learned her four dances—*Indian God, Warrior, Harvest,* and *Snake*—during travels throughout India with her father, a minor government official in that country. The girl packed in an extremely varied career over a brief span; she had danced with Loie Fuller, performed in *Kismet,* and even done a short stint in Diaghilev's company, following Karsavina in the role of Zobeide in *Schéhérazade.* Among the men who joined in the autumn was Piotr Zaylich, a Polish dancer who was soon to reveal a talent for

English provincial tour, winter 1912–13:
at the railway station in Liverpool.

OVERLEAF In the gardens at Ivy House.

choreography. He took on the role of ballet master for the troupe, replacing Shirayev, who had returned to Russia.

For musical interludes (included to lend variety and to give a small company some much-needed breathing space) there was Helen Fairbank singing Mascagni, Wagner, Purcell, and Sir Frederick Cowen; solo cello spots for Paulo Gruppe; and Walford Hyden at the piano whenever needed. Pavlova herself was to be the centerpiece of the *Coquetteries de Colombine* pas de trois, and, with Novikov, to lead extracts from *Coppélia*. There was really something for everyone: the war-horses were not forgotten (*The Swan* and the *Bacchanale* were in), and Novikov was dusting off the bow and arrow. In the spring, Pavlova had chided her audiences gently in an interview. "Alas! It seems that the public will not let me do anything new; they demand the old things." But she managed to slip new things into the programs along with the old.

Pavlova was resigned to the fact that she was already stuck irreversibly with the swan image, and after her comment about swans on the pond at the end of her garden, Mayer arranged for someone to present her with a pair. The cob was thoroughly bad tempered and before long had pinned an unsuspecting workman to the ground. When not on the attack, the cob was unapproachable; but Pavlova persisted in trying to win him over. A few days before the tour began, both swans managed to take off, clearing the trees (though not a neighbor's chimney pot, which was sent flying) en route to an adjacent borough. They were soon enough down again, landing in Edgware, and after a series of chases were taken into custody. Newspaper publicity about Pavlova's missing swans quickly resulted in the culprits being returned to North End Road, where they suffered the indignity of having their wings clipped; further adventures would have to be on foot. Pavlova made it up to them by leaving instructions that the pond was to be improved, and then she gathered herself for flight. The provincial tour of England was about to begin, with the first stop Eastbourne.

The week Pavlova spent in Birmingham brought her before the attention of the Birmingham *Post*'s musical correspondent (there were, of course, no dance critics then), and since this gentleman was the redoubtable Ernest Newman, his views assume perhaps more interest than those of anyone else in England at this time. For once, someone set out to analyze the precise manner of Pavlova's use of music:

The secret of Pavlova's predominance seems to be that the whole personality dances, and nature has evidently taken the utmost pains to make Pavlova's personality multiplex and perfect for the special ends for which it has been designed. We can easily see the truth of this by imagining even the most beautiful face among the other dancers substituted for hers. Her dancing might remain externally the same, yet something of the charm and suggestive mystery of it would be gone. For Pavlova's face, like the rest of her, is an enigma that she probably does not comprehend herself. Who can say whether that fascinating but baffling expression comes from extreme simplicity or extreme subtlety of soul? One can think of

nothing quite so eloquent, yet so elusive and indefinable, since the smile of Mona Lisa. The charming lights and contours of Pavlova's eyes and mouth are always one with her limbs and her hands. She is the complete dancer, in fact, a dancing soul where the others are only dancing bodies.

How fully this is so was evident from the curious aspect the music took on relative to the dancing when she was there, and when she gave place to the others. With the best of those one always felt that it was the music that has been written first and that was now being translated into bodily movement; and good as it all was, the derived version [was like] the best translation from another tongue. With Pavlova one had the extraordinary sensation that the dancing was the original medium of expression, and the music— even such music as a waltz of Chopin—the translation. Her consummate art, indeed, seems to rob music of the quality that we thought was its greatest glory—the lovely bodiless play of tones and rhythms and colours that have no counterpart in grosser nature.

When the others dance, it is they who seem to be rendering the immaterial into the material; when Pavlova dances, she refines the movement and gesture so far down to their pure essence that it is the music that seems in comparison slow and heavy with the burden of mere crude matter in it. The thing would be unbelievable had not one seen it. . . .

It is in the C-sharp minor waltz of Chopin [from *Les Sylphides*], however, that Pavlova most effectually makes the music, tenuous as it is, seem a merely coarsened reflection of herself. Here one was amazed at the fidelity with which every nuance in the rhythm, the colour, or even the tonal intensity of the music had its counterpart in the dancing. At one point, where the music fell from a piano to a pianissimo, Pavlova actually, by some incredible and unanalysable magic, gave the illusion of toning down her own normal silence of motion to an even greater degree, as it were of noiselessness. There seems nothing, in fact, that her art cannot express. She correlates the music and the movements so perfectly that the two seem only the obverse and reverse of the same thing. We do well to see her again and again, for this generation is not likely to provide us with her equal.

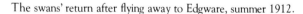

The swans' return after flying away to Edgware, summer 1912.

170

Newman's appraisal must have been a tremendously encouraging item for Pavlova to encounter in the middle of an English provincial tour, and it would have underlined her inherent faith in the sensibilities of audiences away from international cities: if Birmingham could supply a critic of such insight, then there was no reason why other cities should not contain equally perspicacious observers. It was, too, a commendation of Stier's handling of the orchestra that Newman could concentrate so utterly on the nuances of the music without being distracted by shortcomings in that department.

The tour proceeded quite calmly, until one of Novikov's not-infrequent malaises necessitated an appearance by a corps de ballet dancer, Edward Kurylo, who had to partner Pavlova at short notice. Kurylo was Polish, with a rough-and-ready manner, but he had had experience partnering Kyasht during a season at the Empire. Lydia was no sylph, and Kurylo was amazed to find how much easier his present task seemed. He discovered Pavlova to be perfectly placed for supported pirouettes and remarkably light in lifts; he thought that she projected herself mentally into the air and never waited for the partner to provide all the impetus.

A greater dislocation in the company occurred in Bristol, when the charming Hilda Bewicke met with one of Pavlova's occasional bouts of irrational anger and as a result left the company precipitously. Bewicke was a real loss; she was a useful dancer, and among her other assets was a remarkable flair for languages. Not only was she the first British dancer with Pavlova, but she was the first to be allowed to cast off the silly contortion of her stage name and revert to her true surname. (Pavlova may have considered that the "ck" looked Polish in some way.) This Anglo-Scottish girl was equally at home in Russian, Polish, and French (with a fair grasp of several others) and had done a lot of extra work helping Pavlova and Dandré with their business correspondence. In doing this extra work, the girl unwittingly established a daily pattern that did not include Pavlova at certain hours. When the latter finally became overworked and irritable, the office regime became the target for comment. Bewicke might have realized that the storm was really directed at Dandré, but of course she retreated in floods of tears. She was greatly liked by company members and she adored Pavlova. The breach was a distressing episode.

To replace Bewicke, Pavlova summoned a student she had seen at Stedman's Academy in London. This particular girl had been one of two pupils used by Diaghilev to fill the back row of the corps de ballet at Covent Garden the year before. One had been Ivy Sawyer, the other Hilda Boot, and it was the latter who received Pavlova's summons. The girl came from Nottingham, where her father was the proprietor of a sweet shop; her name was now quickly changed to Butsova. She had an unhappy introduction to the company, having to face the icy regard of

Hilda Boot (Butsova), 1912.

Shirayev, who disapproved of the upheaval. The new Hilda (it was malign chance that she was replacing a much-liked Hilda) found that hardly anyone spoke English—apart from the Austrian Stier, who advised her against infiltrating the small morning class that Madame Shirayev sometimes conducted. Pavlova, following the precept that angry dogs are less trouble when not approached, avoided a confrontation by telling Hilda to work with her.

Unhappily, the departure of Bewicke had left Pavlova in a rare turmoil, and it was the replacement Hilda who bore the brunt. The new recruit was "stupid"—it was the one English word she used, emphasized in the midst of a stream of Russian and French, all of it disdainful in tone. The girl would never dance; she should go home; her mother had wasted her money. Hilda, deep in misery, trailed back to the dressing rooms, there to wait, as she imagined, until someone handed her a train ticket. Indubitably, such an encounter with a black Russian mood would have been treated with a degree of equanimity by an established member of the company, but for a novice there was no way of knowing that Pavlova was merely working the upset out of her system. It was Pavlova's maid, Maria, who came in with the news that the storm clouds had lifted slightly. (Maria was a senior Swiss lady with a no-nonsense approach to life. She would take just so much, and

A snapshot of Pavlova taken by Butsova, c.1914.

no more, and Pavlova was slightly in awe of her.) Hilda was taken back to the hotel to hear her fate. There Pavlova settled the girl on her knee and told her soothingly that it was all for Hilda's own good. This impenetrable logic soon gave way to a lot of excited chatter about the fact that Fokine was going to make two new ballets for the company. Boris Anisfeld's designs were laid on a table, and Hilda sat mutely as Pavlova pointed out various details while serving tea. Although the girl was still inconsolable, and so thoroughly English that she could not bring herself to reveal her feelings on the matter, her longing to be a part of the company must have transmitted itself to Pavlova, and Hilda began to realize that she was being taken into the team after all. Thereafter, she found herself working every day with Pavlova, and in such deep water that she had no choice but to swim. She made no pretense at sophistication, but her attributes stood her in good stead; she had shapely legs and feet and a natural facility, and before long she had a small part in *Coppélia*.

The English tour ended in Cardiff on December 14, and the plan was to make a series of train connections through to Harwich, and thus on to Berlin. In the midst of the packing, young Rudolph Mayer appeared as envoy for his father and set about amending all of the contracts that were not valid for the German tour. Another new English acquisition had been little Madge Abercrombie, who joined late because of a foot injury. Pavlova decided that she was a useful long-term prospect after all. The news was no comfort to the prospect, who stood weeping while Mayer determinedly ignored the sight and pressed on with the revision to her contract. The vertiginous horizon opening up before someone as young as Madge (who was parading under the name of Crombova) was really a little frightening. Company members were left to fend for themselves once a contract had been signed, and the never-ending quest for lodgings took on fresh horror once a tour strayed into foreign lands. But though on these occasions the younger girls began to hate the very thought of ballet, they knew they were no match for Pavlova if she decided to charm them into submission.

A full complement set off from Cardiff, and thirty hours later the English girls had their first view of Berlin's new Kroll Opera House. The Diaghilev company was still playing out the last few performances of its four-week season, and Hilda Bewicke was now of its number. There was a phenomenal concentration of dancing talent in Berlin during these few days, and it became a testing ground of marked significance—the polarization of company styles.

The common denominator was Fokine, who had so recently been the mainstay of the Diaghilev repertoire. The rift had occurred when Diaghilev had betrayed the fact that he thought Fokine's inventiveness was exhausted. So here was Fokine about to be used by Pavlova, who—in Diaghilev's eyes, at least—represented everything in ballet that was reactionary. Fokine was out to prove Diaghilev wrong, and this spirit intrigued and excited Pavlova, though Dandré was still agitating for moderation. It was inevitable that battle lines were drawn up, with artistic rivalry taking on the color of direct confrontation, and these overtones lay like a minefield under the renewed association between Pavlova and her earliest dancing associate. Fokine was undismayed; the challenge exhilarated him, despite the fact that at this stage he also wielded real power at the Maryinsky, which absorbed much of his energies. Nicolas Legat was already a spent force, and unwell, and Fokine was the great hope for the Maryinsky's immediate future.

When Fokine left for Berlin with a group of dancers to augment Pavlova's team, Gorsky was busy with a revival of *The Little Humpbacked Horse*, which was part of the strongly traditional fare that the Maryinsky paraded during the Christmas season. Fokine's thoughts were still fixed firmly on the exotic, and he decided that Pavlova's programs should include a divertissement in which his wife would be the principal adornment. It followed in his Eastern vein, which Paris had seen in his *Dieu Bleu* the previous May, and St. Petersburg in *Islami* in September, when musical copyright problems caused a reshuffling of *Schéhérazade* to a different score, by Balakirev. The newest number was called *Induski*, or *Indischer Tanz* in Germany. At this time there was only a vague understanding in Russian ballet of real Indian dancing, and Fokine had the trouser-clad girls shaking their beads in a frenzied dance that seemed rather warlike, with echoes of his *Polovtsian Dances* from *Prince Igor*.

On Christmas Eve there were little parties in the hotel rooms. Shirayev and his wife gave the English girls Russian tea with strawberry jam, and he played the balalaika for them; Madge and Hilda received from Pavlova individual hampers of traditional English fare packed by a London store. It was the sort of inimitable gesture by which Pavlova was able to erase the memory of black Russian moods and outbursts.

Although Fokine worked at his usual white heat, it proved impossible for any of his ballets to enter the repertoire before the New Year, so Pavlova's first few programs had to rely on trusted favorites. They began the season with *Coppélia* on Christmas Day—thanks to a special dispensation by the Generalintendant of the opera house. It was evident that Pavlova still exercised her hold over the Berliners, but there was an inevitable sense of the lightweight, and the critics in particular wanted to see Pavlova, "who is distinguished by an outstanding personality, taking on more important roles of greater psychological depth." Fokine worked on at frantic speed against a threnody of disapproval from many members of the company. Negro slaves were de rigueur in Eastern ballets, and Madame Shirayev had been very put out to discover that she had been allocated to this group in *The Seven Daughters of the Ghost King*; it meant a lot of extremely unpleasant sepia grease paint. She thought to overcome the make-up problem by devious means, and at the New Year's Day premiere, with the composer conducting, she appeared with her head wrapped up in a black muslin scarf, onto which she had applied a large red mouth. Fokine exploded with fury. There were other impromptu decorations in red, caused by razor-sharp strips of cut tin, which had been incorporated into some of the

costumes; but Dandré, imperturbable in moments of real crisis, materialized in the wings with a bottle of "New Skin" and calmly restored the damage as it occurred. The added vehicle for Fokina meant that many of the corps had to learn three new works at the same time, and when they were not being harried by Fokine they were trailing back and forth, far into the night, through the opera buildings to the workshops, where Boris Anisfeld sweated over the realization of his designs. Dandré stood around making "helpful" criticisms.

For *The Seven Daughters of the Ghost King* the designer provided the djinn's family with costumes that had enormous angel wings sprouting from the shoulders, while the scenery was markedly Persian in mood; but coming to a theatre that had recently housed the full-blooded palette of Bakst, the colors appeared curiously muted by comparison. This latest ballet did get its fountain, as well as a fiery pit (whose tongues of flame were streamers of silk activated by a fan under the stage), though by the time one lot of scenery had been finished, there was barely time to complete the next, and the floor cloth for *Les Préludes*—bright green covered in white daisies—transferred much of its vividness to the dancers. The scenery for this work consisted of a painted landscape piling into jagged architectural forms; but this violent linear quality had no echo in the costumes, which were softly draped in the manner of Botticelli nymphs. The girls wore greenish-colored wigs, and under the draperies they wore body stockings tinted to match the costumes. There was a striving for novelty in every department: filters on the limelights sifted various color primaries—first violets and greens for the spirits of Darkness and Death, and then reds and yellows for the emergence of Joy and Light. These "spirits" had to dance without shoes; they had instead elastic anklets, also tinted, which went over the tights.

The reaction to Pavlova's season was strangely mixed. The well-known ballets were as popular as ever, and many people thought that Fokine's ballets for Pavlova had interesting elements. Distinguished visitors such as Richard Strauss and the conductor Arthur Nikisch took the trouble to go backstage and express their delight. Strauss in particular was eager to hear and see everything, as Diaghilev was courting him for a ballet score. (He had emerged from a performance of *Petrushka* on December 4 saying dryly, "It is always interesting to hear one's successor.") But the general public did not really share his enthusiasm for Pavlova's Fokine ballets, and *The Seven Daughters* in particular, seemed to be box-office poison. Berlin audiences disliked seeing their adored Pavlova disfigured with futurist make-up and with no chance to display the glory of her pointe work. Shirayev was openly delighted that this attempt by Pavlova to follow Diaghilev's precepts had not succeeded, and when Dandré sent a cable to London with a frantic request for the scenery and costumes of *La Fille Mal Gardée*, Shirayev saw it as a triumph. He abhorred Fokine's emancipated movements of the torso and arms, and frequently averred, "Dancing is dancing, and it is the feet that have to do it!" With such an ally, Victor Dandré felt more secure in his arguments against experimentation, but Pavlova dismissed

With Novikov in *Les Préludes*.

the poor reaction as a momentary setback. She desperately wanted the ballets to succeed and would not hear of their being abandoned. Pavlova's quandary revealed itself clearly: whether to be artistically progressive with Fokine and court financial headaches, or to let Dandré play safe with such as *Fille*, which the Berliners had approved in 1909.

At the end of the four-week Berlin season, Dandré and the company made their way back to London, while Pavlova continued in the opposite direction to renew her bonds with the St. Petersburg audiences. She had less than a fortnight to prepare for a string of performances in *Don Quixote*, on February 2, 5, and 9 (o.s.), quickly followed by four performances of *Daughter of the Pharaoh*, and then a final appearance in the favorite role of Nikiya in *La Bayadère*. Svetlov felt impelled to comment after her opening night that Pavlova had acquired some mannerisms, and that "the lack of big stages, so essential to her, shows in her dancing." (Pavlova might have pointed out to him that some of the stages she had been dancing on in the previous three years had been the biggest in her experience.) Still, the audiences received her rapturously, and Pavlova was immensely popular in all that she did. The Tsar made a point of receiving her on the two occasions when he attended her performances. He seemed rather eager to ensure that she should return in a year's time, yet when Pavlova pointed out to him that she had already made tentative arrangements to tour America again, he diplomatically accommodated her plans and said, "Well, come and dance for me in September before you go to America."

Mindful of the Dandré complication, Pavlova trod a delicate path in St. Petersburg, charming everyone from the Tsar on downward. While she was performing, a visiting Tibetan diplomatic deputation was sent to the Maryinsky, and its members enjoyed the experience so much that they made a point of seeing Pavlova in her two other ballets. She later described these visitations as "the only political success I had during my absence from London." She was seen several times at the British Embassy and even managed to go to Moscow and present a program that included her London music-hall bits, all of which were novelties for the Muscovites. Fokine, also back in St. Petersburg, wasted no time in utilizing *Les Préludes* for the Maryinsky; Pavlova could hardly have left the railway station before Karsavina was taking her role in the ballet on April 13.

Pavlova presented the same work as the second part of her program on the opening night of her new season at the Palace Theatre a week later. In the first part she had danced an adagio arranged by Legat to Glazunov (which seems to have been an adaptation from *Raymonda*) as well as the *Valse Caprice*, both of them with Novikov. They were also joined by Piotr Zaylich for *Danse Espagnolle* (*sic*); the program printed a dash where the composer should have been listed. A review described this dance as giving Pavlova a chance to display swift changes of emotion, with vivacity and vitality, as she played the "tantalising devil" to her two admirers.

The presentation of *Les Préludes* on a music-hall program was really a brave step, and it demonstrated just how far Pavlova could carry an audience with her. The shorter numbers, which fitted the accepted format better, had their customary triumph: the *Westminster Gazette* noted "masculine cheers (undisguised, and from the stalls too) and split gloves commonplace and unnoticed," though it felt obliged to comment that the Liszt work, "well arranged for the most part as it was, hardly seemed to become the ethereal grace of Pavlova." *The Times* found the dancing in this ballet pleasing but considered the settings and costumes "a strange mixture of the wholly charming and the quaintly grotesque." None of the papers dismissed the work; the theatre correspondents considered it carefully, and there was an awareness that it represented an attempt by Pavlova to do more than rely on her own stellar appeal. The *Daily Mail* gave a generally rapturous review, but it too ended on a qualified note:

Mr. Anisfeld's scenery and dresses (the scenery bizarre, the dresses all airy webs) are engaging, and show Mme Pavlova to have concerned herself with matters in which, now and then in the past, she did not quite do her radiant self justice. The pastorale movement of Liszt's work gives her opportunities for measures of ravishing grace. The music's military finale has presented the ballet-master with a problem he has not quite convincingly solved.

The *Daily Telegraph* gave *Les Préludes* a rave; the *Daily Chronicle* recorded without bias that the close of the work "brought a great outburst of applause." Perhaps it was the *Evening Standard* that sealed the fate of this ballet:

The scene ends with the lovers caressing fondly within the very shadow of death. Like the scenery, the audience could read such meaning as they pleased into the ballet, and one went away with the feeling that it would have been nicer if Pavlova had danced more, and in the simpler surroundings where her great genius would have shone even more brightly.

Pavlova kept the ballet going for a week and then allowed it to be put away. She was not abandoning the work as such, but she had to face the fact that the Palace audience was in great measure a recirculating one, and *Les Préludes* was not the sort of thing they could be persuaded to sit through very often. The premise of music-hall life was that frequent visits provided either favorite numbers or new ones; there was no place for a favorite performer in a not-so-favorite role. Pavlova accepted this outlook calmly; she knew exactly the tone of her setting and the extent to which she could change its emphasis. In general, she had an astonishingly secure bridgehead, with a company in which the genuine Russian and Polish members had been augmented by English talent that was in no way conspicuous—neither outstandingly better nor noticeably worse than the others. Rita Leggerio, a well-known child actress, and of Italian parentage, became Leggierova; Helen Sykes became Saxova; and Sheila Courtney, back from a rough spell with the Mordkin troupe, went on at the Palace as Kortnova. There were never fewer than sixteen girls and eight men. The company now had a feeling of permanence about it.

Pavlova tried to carry this mood through to Ivy House, though it was still the property of the Golders Hill and General Estates Company. (Pavlova did not begin paying rates as a registered occupier until April 1, 1913.) Financing continued to be a headache, to the extent that it was advantageous to let the house from time to time at the height of the season. She had furnished it well, with many of her possessions from St. Petersburg, including the full-length, life-size portrait by Steinberg that had dominated her Anglisky Prospekt studio. It was now fixed to the wall of the practice hall, with handrails neatly butting up to it.

To the seven little girls who trained with "Madame" in this studio, she was an exalted being. When Pavlova was in residence at Ivy House, they had a strict schedule: she worked them from 10:30 until midday, and they did their best to please her, but there were times when frustration got the upper hand. Pavlova was in the habit of drinking hot milk after her own solitary morning class, and she would sit sipping this while the girls began. One morning one of the children teetered into the studio on pointe. Pavlova surmised in an instant that an ambitious parent had been taking her child for extra tuition elsewhere, in an attempt to circumvent the apparent slowness of the child's progression to that stage of facility which distinguished a real "toe-dancer." With a flash of anger, Pavlova hurled her glass to the floor, producing an inevitable scene of tears and fright from the children. These occasional flourishes were spasmodic, but not so rare that the students were not on the lookout. They learned to divine Pavlova's mood by the color of the practice tunic she wore: pale tints meant calm, but one particular black dress always heralded a storm of some sort, and on those days it seemed impossible to do anything right, try though they might. Victor Dandré would sometimes come into the studio with a glass of milk or a choice fruit—not for Pavlova, but for whichever he considered the most upset of the pupils. Sometimes he would take them by the hand and walk them out into the garden to look at the flowers or the swans down on the pond.

In reality, the children adored Pavlova and suffered only when they felt they could not please her. Often she would be in an expansive mood, and then she would gather the children about her and give them some simple homily, perhaps about life, or about art springing first and foremost from awareness: "Soon you will be going home on the train. Observe carefully, and try to understand the people you see. You must not sit there with dead faces like so many English maids. Why is that person sad? Perhaps she has to work very hard. Who is that elderly man? What do you get from watching him?" In the matter of dancing itself, Pavlova wanted the children to "reach out" toward some person in the audience: "Something must impel you to move. It must be *for* someone. It must not be mechanical. The movement must come from a feeling within you; it must be inevitable. It has to be more than port de bras one, two, three, four. We are not performing tricks! Those we can see at the circus."

Much of this wisdom about the theatre of dance was over the heads of Pavlova's young pupils, but they did remember the

ANNA IN ALABASTER

exact nature of the talks, so all was not wasted. Little girls like Muriel Popper were overwhelmed by Pavlova's sincerity and conviction on these occasions. They all knew she was someone special, and hard words or broken glass never altered their basic attitude of adoration. Pavlova was perfectly aware of the precepts of Stanislavsky's teachings, and much of that basic approach sat easily on her own methods, even though these sprang from inner convictions of which she was the medium rather than the conscious creator. Despite the heady analyses of dancing, the children were taken along slowly in the physical domain. While Pavlova was waiting until she thought them strong enough to attempt some pointe work, she compensated for this slow progression (slow to eager children, that is) with careful lessons in other departments of performing: how to put on a hair piece correctly, how to sit on stage in a graceful yet natural manner. Pavlova never tired of preparing the children for the hurdles that she had encountered as a student. She had a rare ability to present profound problems in a simple manner, and never expected results from blind obedience to command.

Even with her pupils and her endless schedule at the Palace, Pavlova cheerfully took on extra jobs. She chaired the annual dinner of the London Stage Society on May 18 and even made a brief speech. She opened the Ionic Picture Theatre (a sign of the times) in Finchley Road; she helped at the bazaar held at Grosvenor House in aid of the Colonial Intelligence League (leaving the dancing on this occasion to Maud Allan and others);

she even made an ascent in a Maurice Farman biplane, which took her up for a circuit above Hendon one Sunday. It was a summer when other women were determinedly making the news in their search for emancipation. The premier horse race, the Derby, was run on June 4 that year. At Tattenham Corner (a strategic bend on Epsom Racecourse), Emily Davison, a schoolteacher, darted out under the rails just as the field came thundering past. She had suffragette colors sewn inside her coat, and the horse she brought down belonged to the King. Her terrible injuries resulted in her death soon after.

Society's greatest interest and concern seemed to lie with the huge ball taking place at the Albert Hall the following day. This was a late-night costume pageant called "Fête at Versailles"; it was in aid of the Soldiers and Sailors Help Society. The central device was the re-creation of a reception such as might have been given for Louis XIV at the Palace of Versailles. Hundreds of "names" took part in rehearsed processions that formed part of the general tableau, which had Pavlova, supported by Novikov and a group of her dancers, as the central attraction. The star was rather dismayed by the huge expanse of floor on which she was expected to perform, and she was also perplexed as to whether she should face the mock King of France (actually the Grand Duke of Mecklenburg-Strelitz) or genuine royalty in the form of Queen Mary, who was going to grace the Royal Box. Pavlova solved the problem neatly, performing a Mozart minuet for "Louis" and then turning to present the rest of the program to the Queen of England. Pavlova wore pink ostrich feathers in her high powdered wig, and pink silk looped in panniers over a lace under-

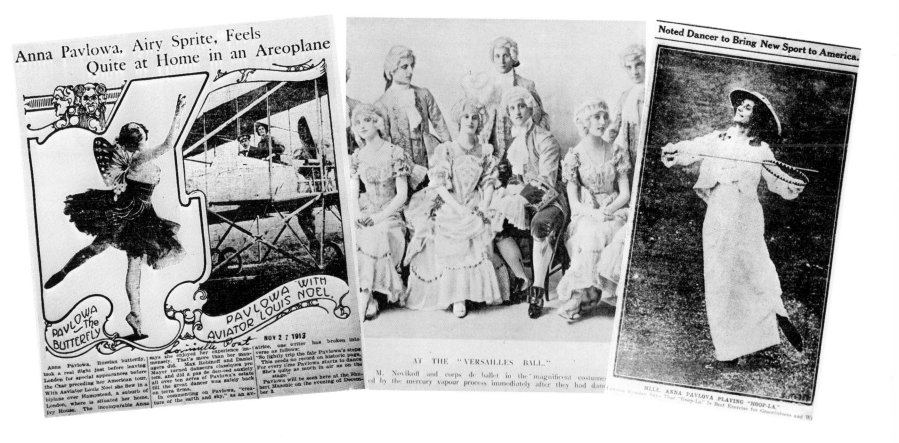

dress, which was swagged with tiny flowers and pink roses. And she glittered with gems—it was one of the rare occasions when she bothered to get her beautiful jewelry out of the bank.

Pavlova was not lured to the ten-day Suffragette Summer Festival going on at the Empress Rooms in Kensington. (She once said: "Were I given a choice, I would choose the ballet rather than the ballot.") Her nod in the direction of female emancipation took the form of a vocal distaste for corsets. "If you want to dance, either the modern dances or the classic, you simply cannot wear the old-fashioned corset," she declared firmly. Many interviewers had observed for themselves that her spare body seemed free of any form of harness, off stage as well as on. She was adept at keeping the press happy. Despite her intensely private nature, she saw clearly everybody's role in the interlocking dependency of the entertainment world, and she never took an unapproachable stance. She could give the press a quote on almost anything: "But the lovely English horses! Where are they all going to? I see none now in London streets and parks as I did when I first came to London on a private visit eight years ago . . . oh, where are they now? They were so much more lovely than the automobile." Fan mail came from as far away as Australia. One girl's letter explained, "Every big English magazine we get sent out to us, and nearly every one contains a picture of the World's greatest dancer." No self-respecting music hall could afford to dismiss the new craving for classical dancing, and one flustered West End variety agent was quoted as saying: "The rush on Russian dancers is most annoying. At this rate France will never be able to turn them out quickly enough."

In the second week of June, the audiences at the Palace were given a new ballet: Piotr Zaylich had produced a bland, elegantly mannered construction to Berlioz's orchestration of Weber's "Invitation to the Dance." Fokine had used it eighteen months earlier for *Le Spectre de la Rose*, with the happiest of results. Zaylich too stayed safely in the Biedermeier period, except that his setting became a rather grand domestic ballroom, with the program following very strictly that laid down by the composer. The stage was filled with crinolined young ladies and their dancing partners, with the focus centered on one particular young girl (Pavlova) and the youth she impresses (Novikov). There were several pleasing touches for Pavlova: the moment when she fended off two gallants competing for her, and a solo waltz in which the demure debutante gradually abandoned herself to the happiness of the occasion. Here Pavlova displayed an exultant gaiety that was ravishing. There was poignancy at the end when the couple had to part, and the little romance was terminated almost before it had begun. The ballet was utterly undemanding of an audience, and yet its saccharine simplicity worked.

Pavlova was again eager to present to the public the progress made by her pupils, and this time they were allocated a special matinee at the Palace, on August 7. At this same performance Pavlova danced a little novelty, *Etoile du Soir*, to a piece of music from a ballet score by Maude Valérie White that incorporated Russian folk melodies. The children had various bits and pieces, including the *Blue Danube* waltz and a dance from *Coppélia*. During the program they ran on stage with a gift for Pavlova, which produced a gasp of surprise. Mr. Otto Popper on behalf of

the parents had organized the purchase of a silver-plate casket of classical design that had inscribed upon it: "To Madame Anna Pavlova, from her loving and devoted pupils, London, August 1913." On the opposite side of the casket were engraved the names of the seven students. The happiest touch of all was discovered only later, when Pavlova opened a drawer in the casket and discovered seven silver hearts, each inscribed with one of the girls' first names.

Pavlova made sure the girls were photographed for the press so that the attendant publicity would provoke further interest in classical dancing. She posed them for the benefit of the cameramen, either on the lawns or in the hall of the house, with the background of the cool white walls and the numerous pictures: the prints of Taglioni, the drawings by Bakst, and Steinberg's life-sized image of Pavlova as a laurel-crowned muse carrying a lyre on a flower-studded path by a stream.

So popular was the program with the children, simple as their dance numbers were, that they earned themselves a repeat appearance just before Pavlova finished her summer engagement at the Palace. Toward the end of this same season there was a replay of the famous slap; this time the corrective was administered to Laurent Novikov. He was well-meaning but not always adept as a partner. On one occasion he drew blood when he stepped in too close and caught Pavlova's heel during a supported turn; on this latest occasion he had strayed too close during the beginning of the *Raymonda* adagio, and Pavlova, in turning, had struck him on the shoulder. Without ceremony, Novikov immediately strode off into the wings, leaving Pavlova no alternative but to do likewise—which she did in the opposite direction. The orchestra played the piece out to an empty stage, while the audience waited avidly for developments. As with the previous "discord in Fairyland," the net result was no *Bacchanale*. The *Evening News* reported that "M. Novikoff did not appear again, but Mme. Pavlova was seen in the *Pavilion* [*Papillon*], and in another solo dance. Earlier in the evening she and M. Novikoff had danced the *Prelude* in perfect accord."

Despite the newspaper's assurance that "the peace has not been marred, and . . . the two great dancers will unite in harmonious art this evening," the next performance took place without Novikov, who was saying he was ill. Pavlova attempted to straighten out the press versions of the event:

> "What happened was this. While I was dancing, Monsieur Novikoff, who was dancing on the stage with me, came close to me, and to prevent myself having to stop the dance I was compelled to push him away. It was quite by accident that I pushed Monsieur Novikoff with my two arms to avoid knocking into him, as I fully believe that it was quite by accident that he swayed so near to me as almost to throw me over! Anyhow Monsieur Novikoff seemed offended and left the stage. He did not dance again with me that evening. And this is all."

If Pavlova thought that such tiffs were all very normal, the English considered them extremely Russian; some even suspected that it was part of the entertainment. Such little dramas certainly attracted full-scale publicity, and the final night of Pavlova's season found the Palace crowded to the roof. It was impossible to find a seat by eight o'clock, and by nine there was no standing room either. When Pavlova came on at ten o'clock (with Zaylich; Novikov was still sulking), there was a rapturous reception, and after every dance she was rewarded with numerous bouquets handed up over the footlights. At the end there were still further flowers accompanying the applause, which went on for more than a quarter of an hour. It was an astonishing display of regard from a music-hall audience, but it was an audience that had come to think of Pavlova as its own. They went on cheering until the dancer was persuaded to give them a few words of farewell. The reporters gave the color of her accent faithfully: "Sank you ver' moch. I am ver' 'appy. Adieu." Finally the audience began to leave, and then there could be heard a great burst of cheering from behind the curtain as the other dancers, the stagehands, and the technicians all joined in honoring their famous colleague. She had gifts for all of them, and it was after midnight before she could get away from the theatre; but at the stage door a huge crowd still waited, trying to get a glimpse of her. When she came out to her motorcar, there was a fresh burst of cheering.

When Pavlova ended her 1913 summer season in London, she seems to have been contemplating a tour not only of America but of Australia as well. The previous December, Daniel Mayer had inserted the name of that country into an agreement outlining tours for either 1913–14 or 1914–15. Mayer's draft had originally mentioned both seasons, but Pavlova amended the agreement so that she was committed to one or the other, but not both. Either way, Australia seems to have been difficult to organize, and the usual six-week delays with mail cannot have helped; but the intention was there. Behind-the-scenes activity also included a rapprochement between Pavlova and Novikov, who apparently realized that his partner was the raison d'être for his continued employment. On August 22 the *Daily Sketch* had four lines tucked away on an inner page: "Whatever the rights and wrongs of that slap on the stage of the Palace, Mme. Pavlova and M. Novikoff have become friends again. They were reconciled before they left London."

Pavlova was thought to be looking tired, yet there was no let-up: there were to be engagements in Dresden, Munich, Nuremberg, and Baden-Baden en route to Russia. She dismissed the inquiries about her health, saying that she felt excellent but that she thought the change would do her good. In all of the schedule for the next period of work there was room for only one week's real break, for she was due back in London the following month to prepare for the trip to America. She had already offered Cecchetti a job on the tour; the attraction for him was a free trip to California, where one of his sons was living. When the new American tour was confirmed, the news caused despair among Pavlova's young pupils, but she softened the blow by persuading the parents of three of the children to have their training continued under Ivan Clustine in Paris.

Pavlova punches Novikoff,
The Palace audience to astound;
Her partner promptly marches off,
Knocked out in but a single round!

ABOVE *John Bull* views a contretemps.

BELOW H. M. Bateman's view of Pavlova and Novikov for *The Sketch*, May 1913. Pavlova seems like some denizen of Bloomsbury, complete with rubber boots.

At the County Fair in Aid of Our Dumb Friends League (above)
and a theatrical garden party in Chelsea (below), June 1913.

BELOW Being fêted in Baden-Baden, 1913.

Pavlova was in St. Petersburg for the briefest of private visits, and she did not accommodate the Tsar in his request of the previous winter; the Maryinsky leads were divided among Preobrajenskaya, Karsavina, and Egorova. The word had just come through of Vaslav Nijinsky's marriage while on tour in Buenos Aires, which caused amused gossip in St. Petersburg and London and meant that Fokine would surely be back in favor as a choreographer for Diaghilev. His company had only one rival abroad—Pavlova and her ensemble—and talent such as Fokine's was still a trump card. Pavlova knew that she had already lost the choreographer after the lukewarm response to his works in Berlin, but she may have wished that he would concentrate his energies on the Maryinsky stage rather than rejoining Diaghilev. Clustine, at the Paris Opéra, represented to Pavlova the one real alternative to Fokine; if he lacked Fokine's deep-seated individuality, he certainly matched him in facility. In a span of three weeks Clustine put together a remarkable amount of new choreography for Pavlova and her company.

By 1913 Pavlova could no longer ignore the huge popularity of social dancing, and she allowed the New York *Evening Sun* to use her for a long-running series on "The New Social Dances." The Tango alone occupied an entire week, with steps like the "Sensational Whirl" and the "Forward Glide" demonstrated by Pavlova and Novikov, the latter in white tie and tails. All of these poses were photographed in London and the results dispatched across the Atlantic. It was good advance publicity, though the sight of Pavlova and Novikov playing at being Irene and Vernon Castle may have blurred the concept of ballet dancing in the American public's mind; it had been only three years since ballet had had to be explained as "ocular opera," and here was Pavlova selling social dances.

In view of the length of the American tour, which in some aspects provoked dread, Pavlova decided to give two "farewell" performances for her London fans. In some ways it was an attempt to obliterate the music-hall image: she wanted to leave London with a memory of her as a great ballerina, performing suitable works in a suitable setting. (The London performances would also serve as elaborate dress rehearsals to prove that everything was in working order before the Atlantic crossing.) Since there was no way that this sort of program could be given at the Palace, it was agreed that performances should take place at Hammerstein's London Opera House, at matinees on October 6 and 7. It was a measure of her extraordinary popularity that the huge auditorium was sold out almost as soon as Pavlova's two extra programs were announced.

Pavlova contrived to present on one day no fewer than three ballets that were new to London. On October 6 she gave a version of Ivanov's *The Magic Flute,* recalled—with the aid of Cecchetti—from Maryinsky days. This was followed by a Clustine version of *Chopiniana* called *Une Soirée de Chopin,* with a variety of orchestrations of polonaises, nocturnes, preludes, valses, mazurkas, and indeed the C-sharp-minor waltz with the

The New Social Dances:
By Mlle. Anna Pavlowa

The One-Step: Introduction and Lesson No. 1

Mlle. Anna Pavlowa

Fig. A. Position for Start of One-step. The Lady Stands Easily, Right Arm Extended. Left Arm and Hand Resting Gently on the Right Arm of Partner. The Man Holds His Body as Shown, Being Careful Not to Hold the Lady Too Close

Fig. B. First Figure in the One-step. Both Dancers Move to the Right, the Man Stepping Back With the Idea of Completing a Full Revolution. On the Fourth Count There Should Be a Slight Dip from the Knees No Action ... Line Up

The Tango: Lesson 1
The Sensational Whirl and the Forward Glide

"Tangoing is One of the Best Health De-velopers I Know," Declares Pavlowa.

Fig. A. Conclusion of the Sensational Whirl.

Fig. B. A Passing Step in the Forward Glide.

The Tango: Lesson 7
The Half-Arch and the Double Turn

Figure A---The Half-Arch, One of the Easiest of the Tango Poses

Figure B---The Double Turn, a Complete Cir-cle With Hands Held High

The Good Tango Dancer Is the One Who Constantly Tries New Figures

Confidence in Oneself and Much Practice Required for Expert Tangoing

Illustrated Interview with Mme. Pavlova

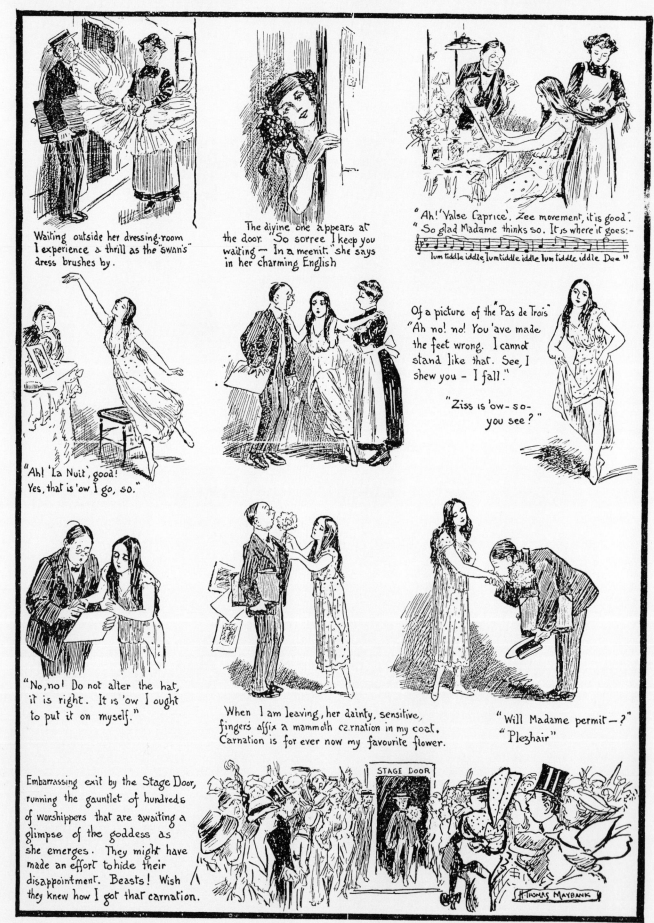

Our artist having had a commission to do some water-colour pictures of Pavlova the Incomparable, is graciously permitted an interview for the purpose of correcting technical points, etc., with results as truthfully depicted above

original Fokine choreography, all placed in a setting that owed most to Watteau. With this confection, Pavlova knew that the breast of the most savage audience would be calmed. Finally, Zaylich put together *Oriental Fantasy*, employing for the most part music of Serov and Moussorgsky, with other bits from Rimsky-Korsakov scissored to fit the libretto. Bakst was asked to provide designs for this ballet, all about a young knight returned from the wars bearing a talisman to guard him against misfortune, but which did not prevent him from losing his way and falling foul of an enchantress who tried—unsuccessfully—to lure him to destruction. Although this ballet had various references to *Schéhérazade* and particularly to *Thamar*, it had as well many distinct novelties, not least of which was a Dance of the Serpents done to a solo piano, which had to be placed below the stage, producing an effect that was strange and disconcerting. This interlude took some of the strain off Theodore Stier, who was having to make his London debut as Pavlova's orchestral leader with a somewhat scratch orchestra. (Finck always led the Palace orchestra.) But nothing worried this audience; it loved everything and cheered itself hoarse. *The Times* was impressed by *Oriental Fantasy* and, while acknowledging the evident debt to Fokine, still thought the ballet was distinctly original, "a little work of art which it is a great pleasure to record." The *Daily News and Leader*, on the other hand, was offended:

> There was too much practical allurement shown by this Eastern Enchantress in her desire to possess the young knight's talisman. One need not be a prude to object to the public embraces which are considered necessary in Russian ballets when dealing with Eastern subjects. The *Oriental Fantasy* is a rather weak example of the decadence which, admire them as one may, runs through these Russian ballets of action.*

The company was looking immeasurably stronger, and Pavlova's confidence was reflected in the fact that one English girl escaped having to be Sheltonova: Shelton stood out bravely in the program. There were promising young men, too, among them Serge Oukrainsky, Andreas Pavley, Marcel Bergé, and Ernest Marini. For the second "farewell" matinee, on October 7, Pavlova intended that London should keep an image of her as a great dramatic ballerina. She presented *Giselle,* and this time there were no half measures about the public's response to the intensity of Pavlova's depicted madness and the pathos of her wraith in the second act, though *The Times* grumbled about "the

apparelling of Giselle and the other wilis in meaningless draperies instead of the orthodox white ballet skirt." (These were William Walter's costumes from the 1910–11 American tour, when the ballet had first displayed his Directoire period designs, with long clinging dresses in the second act, rather than Romantic tarlatans.)

After *Giselle* there were eight divertissements, several of them novelties. Pavlova, with Bergé and Oukrainsky, danced a pas de trois arranged by Clustine to Godard's Berceuse from the opera *Jocelyn*; Pavlova was a sylvan nymph cavorting with a shepherd and a satyr. The *Daily Telegraph* reviewer spoke of this and *Le Papillon* (it was now singular) as repeats of "triumphs familiar to everybody." The girls circling around in red and green to the tune of Meyer-Helmund's *Danse du Printemps* were also familiar; it was a Zaylich work from the summer season. But *Moments Musicaux* was probably being seen for the first time. Pavlova had arranged this "Greek" dance for Plaskowieczka, supported by Butsova and Crombova; it was a pastorale with Attic draperies, sandals, and shepherd pipes. New too was Clustine's *The Bird and the Serpent*, for Bergé, who was very slim and supple, and Oukrainsky, who danced on pointe as the bird. *Bow and Arrow*, and *Rhapsodie Hongroise* were also seen, and then Pavlova and Novikov signed off with the perennial *Bacchanale*, which evoked the inevitable tumult of cheering and a fresh avalanche of floral tributes.

Coming from a normally blasé London audience, this fervor was a remarkable demonstration of goodwill and affection, and Pavlova was quite overcome by its obvious sincerity. Normally secure in addressing a few words of English to her Palace audiences, at the London Opera House she had to enlist the help of Stier, who expressed thanks to the people who were still jamming every corner of the theatre. Even the orchestra was applauding. The curtain descended once more, and when it rose again Pavlova was surrounded by all the principal dancers of the company. A magnesium flash lit up the group as the tableau was recorded. In her dressing room, Pavlova asked the *Evening News* reporter to give the public a message: "Express my profound gratitude for all the kindnesses I have received during my visits to London. Already I long for the time when I shall be with my dear English public again."

The following morning, Pavlova discovered in her mail a letter from a Mr. A. R. Harvey, responding to a communication from her solicitors. They had intervened in a quarrel that had

---

*The American response to Zaylich's Oriental ballet later in the year was to be positive, perhaps because it was America's first chance to see the full panoply of a Bakst-designed production. His name was everywhere at this time, and Pavlova opened a Bakst exhibition in New York on November 2. She had lent four drawings relating to the new ballet, which was now billed as *Orientale*. The costumes were described as "strange fragments of every shape and shade, but all bold, flat colors, crude, barbaric," and the settings were "great splashes of gray and purple and yellow." They included the obligatory hanging lanterns and also a suggestion of great roof beams striking a diagonal above the ochrous walls, where a lapiz sky glinted through the fretted windows of the Enchantress's palace. But what really seemed to excite audiences was the smell of incense that gradually permeated beyond the proscenium.

Pavlova's characterization was totally unexpected. In a dance with Novikov "she did

not caress; she commanded": "Power was in the miming and savagery in the dance. Then came the climax, when her hand was almost upon her prey, and fierce anticipation played out the graphic glance and dancing body. Then the moment of fierce bewilderment when the warrior baffles her. Finally the slow sinking, with the very voice and line of the music, into the waiting—indomitable and devouring. Miming of such imagination and intensity, so stark and so elemental, is new to our stage and new as a revelation of a power in Pavlova that hitherto she has hidden." For much of the ballet Pavlova reclined on a throne-like divan, but when she uncoiled herself and joined in a dance with her female slaves, she was "a whirling flash of animation, crimson and gold radiating from her," in a costume "of such cobweb texture that the Seven Veils of Salome are Arctic furs in comparison." Pavlova does not seem to have posed for the camera in this ballet. Malvina Hoffman's drawings show that the costume was indeed scant.

"FARE THEE WELL, FOR I MUST LEAVE THEE"

Madame Pavlova is next week giving her farewell performances before leaving on a tour of the world, which will in all probability keep her away from London for the next two years. These performances will take place at the London Opera House on October 6 and 7, and the programme, besides including four new ballets that will be performed in London for the first time, will also contain "Papillons," "Valse Caprice," and "Le Cygne" the famous dance which Mme. Pavlova has made so popular. She leaves for New York on October 8

Pavlova Bids Au Revoir to London.

Pavlova's farewell matinee at the London Opera House yesterday was the occasion of great enthusiasm, and the picture illustrates the scene at the close of the performance. The incomparable dancer, who will be away for two years, is seen in the circle.—(*Daily Mirror* and Foulsham and Banfield.)

arisen when Pavlova altered the terms to which she had previously agreed in relation to letting Ivy House to Mr. Harvey. The disruption of his own plans had apparently led to an outburst in which he had described Pavlova's behavior as "immoral," perhaps not realizing that Pavlova would treat the remark as the grossest imputation. The letter started off benignly enough:

> I can assure you that no English lawyer or judge could possibly read any such meaning into the words I used, as I was speaking not of your personal relations with others, but of your immoral conduct in regard to a contract which you had made and were forcibly breaking, thereby putting me to great inconvenience and considerable expense. It was your unjust act I was referring to, and not in any way reflecting upon your moral character.

Hereafter, Harvey launched into a vein of bizarre fantasy that promptly reduced to nil the credibility of his complaint:

> You are fully aware that you have instructed your chauffeur over and over again to exceed the speed limit, which is illegal in Eng-

land, and which I would call immoral, and that you have been fined for breaking the law. You have even ordered him—and this will come out in court—to drive over the side path and to drive over people who were in your way. I must point out that if this is brought out in court—and proved—as it will be—your receipts will drop more than fifty per cent in this country, and you will be hissed on the other side when you appear.

Pavlova left the diatribe for her solicitors to handle and departed from Waterloo Station at eight o'clock that evening. A musical band of Hampstead boy scouts was among the throng bidding her farewell. Pavlova received roses, pinned a few to her coat, and held her Pekinese up to the carriage window to share in the moment.

When the White Star Line's *Kaiser Wilhelm II* docked in New York on the evening of October 14, it was at the end of a six-day struggle through appalling weather. Pavlova went straight to her favorite hotel, the Knickerbocker, leaving the luggage to be cleared by a courier. She had gone through the customs area wearing a modest hat, and perhaps for that reason no mention was made to her of aigrettes. A new American law forbade the importation of the plumage so esteemed by fashionable milliners, and customs officials were under orders to confiscate any articles carrying the tail feathers of the threatened egret. The following morning, dock officials began opening all 194 trunks labeled "Pavlova Co." and assiduously noted that the contents were principally "3,000 gowns," which they apparently attributed solely to Pavlova's personal extravagance. Among the costumes were five headdresses incorporating the forbidden feathers. These were seized.

Pavlova was irate when the law was explained to her. "It is too silly for anything. If the birds were hurt the harm is already done, and they will suffer no more injury through my bringing the aigrettes here than they will if the officers destroy them." The customs officials were unmoved but allowed a stay of execution so that Pavlova could appeal to Washington for permission to bring the feathers into the country in bond. The aigrettes languished in custody while Pavlova played New York before starting another of her nightmare transcontinental parades.

Pavlova's 1913–14 tour was tiring enough in terms of dancing, but behind the scenes there were management disputes that carried their disruptive effects right to the stage itself. Rabinoff and Atwell were involved in a long-running private feud over matters of profit and loss and past internal agreements; Atwell felt he was being cut out, and Rabinoff felt the partnership was extinct. In November, Atwell moved. His lawyer, Simon Pollock, began issuing writs of attachment against the weekly takings, and, in lieu of these, against the scenery and costumes. Each claim necessitated a local court order and a sum of money to be deposited against the claim. In Cleveland it was $14,000 and in Washington, $6,000. The judge in Boston took a lighter view and made the order for $3,000. In all these instances Pavlova was expected to file bonds as security. In less than a month she had deposited

$23,000, in her view "as security for somebody else's debts." Dandré did not improve the situation when, in exasperation, he manhandled a law clerk off the stage. The clerk immediately procured papers to ensure a $250 deposit from Dandré against a suit for assault. Given the task of serving this latest batch of papers was Jacob Bier, a deputy sheriff. He could not have picked a worse day. At the Metropolitan in New York, a matinee to benefit a music school was already forty minutes late in starting, due to the nonarrival of a costume van. (Nobody was quite sure whether or not Atwell's representatives had hijacked it.) A restive audience, paying premium prices, finally gave *The Cavalry Halt* a lukewarm welcome. At this point it was realized that a public tea, for which patrons had paid extra in the hope of having more of Madame Pavlova, was due to begin at 5 p.m. Stier stood by his podium and announced to the audience that the "Oriental" ballet had been canceled. At that moment there was a huge fracas taking place backstage, and Stier, half aware of the drama, felt unable to tell the audience *why* there was a cut in the program, because he could already envisage an announcement curtailing the tea as well. He quickly disappeared from view, leaving the hissing audience to its fate.

Backstage, Jacob Bier—with great tact—had elected to wait until the first intermission before serving the papers. Dandré trumpeted with rage. Bier then disappeared to seek the aid of a policeman. Thus emboldened, he returned and thrust the papers at Dandré, who was standing in the wings trying to get the show moving again. Dandré snatched the papers and threw them down, and then began to run across the stage. Bier scooped up the papers and darted after Dandré, detaining him in mid-stage by his coattails. Dandré's weight (and his tailor's excellence) was more than a match for this impediment, and Bier found himself being dragged into the opposite wings. At this point the policeman contributed the weight of the law, and a period of respite followed. The curtain remained down, shutting off an increasingly disgruntled sea of patrons. Alfred Selisberg, the Metropolitan's lawyer, arrived on stage to sort out the muddle. Then the lawyer Nathan Goldberger arrived, having been summoned by Pavlova, and arranged to guarantee Dandré's appearance in court the following morning. The audience was given one more ballet, and the threatened tea was served—without Pavlova's presence. The audience for all this hidden entertainment had raised $10,000 for the music school. Goldberger, on behalf of Pavlova, took the sting out of the situation by issuing a counterclaim on Pavlova's behalf with a suit for harassment, asking for a stay of execution against Atwell and Pollock, which would compel litigation in the Federal District Court. At this point the contenders all stood back and began to settle their differences privately.

Before leaving London, Pavlova had put her signature to an agreement whereby she undertook to endorse the benefits of Pond's Vanishing Cream, which advertisement ("The Great Pavlova is warm in her praises . . . *'I find it is very good for softening and whitening my skin'*") began appearing in December,

WITH HER TRIPLEX-GLASSED CAR: MME. PAVLOVA, THE FAMOUS RUSSIAN DANCER.

MME. PAVLOVA'S DEPARTURE.

Mme. Pavlova waving farewell to her own troop of boy scouts, who gave her a hearty send-off to America at Waterloo Station yesterday. In one of the circles the popular dancer is seen with her mascot.—(*Daily Mirror* photographs.)

with exhortations to apply for a free sample. "Wintry winds, frost, and fogs have little or no effect upon the face that is protected by a morning-and-evening application of Pond's Vanishing Cream."

By the time Pavlova's tour had reached the West Coast of America in the late autumn, it had encountered one climatic phenomenon against which Pond's Vanishing Cream was no proof: floods. For a while they were marooned at Santa Barbara, when a night trip turned into a long-drawn-out ordeal. The train had to be halted while a bridge was patched up, and the waters swirled level with the floor of the carriages. Pavlova made light of the situation in an effort to keep the European contingent from panic, and she spent a lot of time walking up and down the carriages talking cheerfully, until eventually the train was able to cross the bridge, which then started to collapse again as the last of the coaches cleared it.

Pavlova barely concealed the fact that she was far from well at this point. She was very weak and suffering from acute tonsillitis,

Photograph used by Pond's Vanishing Cream
in its 1913 advertising campaign.

but she insisted on completing all the performances. It was a thin house for the matinee in Los Angeles, but those who were present enjoyed themselves, little realizing that every time the effervescent figure of Pavlova disappeared into the wings, it was only to collapse onto a couch (one had been placed on either side for the purpose). She took her curtain calls in a daze. There were no flowers, but Pavlova came into the wings rhapsodizing in a stream of French about the beauty of the bouquet she had been given. Her arms were weaving about. It took some time for her confederates to realize that she was not being ironic but was actually hallucinating. An attendant doctor muttered ineffectual threats. "If her temperature rises one more point, I forbid her to do the evening performance." He drove her to the hospital for treatment, but she was back in time for the evening curtain. And she went on. At the end the audience clamored for more, but Stier slammed his baton onto the music stand and walked out. He thought the situation impossible and would not be a party to its being prolonged for one more minute. Naturally, nothing and no one could prevent Pavlova from getting back on board the train that night, insisting that the company should return to San Francisco for a special Sunday concert performance.

The trip back was as horrendous as before; the train was so late that the concert was half over before the dancers arrived, and they could give only the final divertissements. Then they were off again, across the Bay to Oakland. The floods farther south were bad enough for Fresno and Bakersfield to be struck off the itinerary, which left the little band heading east toward

Salt Lake City. The dancers peered out of the carriages at blizzard conditions as the train inched toward Cheyenne, through numerous high-mountain snowsheds protecting the passes.

With every day the winter was biting harder and harder; Denver, Spokane—the dancers were hardly conscious of where they were, only that they were surrounded by endless snow and appalling cold, with the train conductors warning them against frostbite. One girl broke her leg; it was bandaged tightly and she was put back on the train. What else was there to do—leave her in Dodge City? Christmas, the hallowed festival for Pavlova, was spent in Montreal. All the water mains either were frozen or had already burst, and drinking water had to be delivered by sledge.

The tour worked its way back through the central United States until winter's grasp weakened—but not before it had weakened, in its turn, everyone who had sought to travel in the teeth of its hateful energy during all those months. The strain had got to everyone. In the Odeon Theatre in St. Louis on March 16, just after the start of *Valse Caprice,* in which Pavlova was dancing on demi-pointe, in sandals, the audience was startled to see her falter and fall back with a look of anguish, unable to put one foot to the ground. Novikov supported her while the curtains were rung down and she was carried, fainting, to her dressing room. A local doctor could not discover what was wrong and advised Pavlova to have her foot x-rayed at the hospital; but the results provided no conclusive evidence of any fracture, despite the fact that some members of the audience claimed to have heard a snapping sound. The real cause of the accident lay in the fact that Pavlova's normal practice routine had been disrupted by the conditions of incessant travel, to the point where muscular tone became impaired through general debilitation. So the damage was done, and there was no chance of keeping engagements in the following days. Without Pavlova, there was no show, and many prospective patrons were disappointed by a string of cancellations.

Pavlova traveled straight to Chicago, where the tour was due, but doctors there could not agree: one surgeon diagnosed a broken bone at the back of the instep, while a professor from the University of Chicago concluded that the problem was merely a sprain. The foot was bound in an adhesive bandage, and Pavlova could do nothing but wait until the strength gradually returned. During the first few performances she gave after recovering from the injury, tears of pain would sometimes catch the lights as she danced. Word of the mishap had reached London within days, and there was a lively exchange of messages in the press, with Pavlova thanking the editor of the *Daily Telegraph* for the sympathy tendered on behalf of the readers.

OPPOSITE Snapshots from the 1913-14 American tour:
1. Christmas 1913   2. Dandré exercising the dog   3. With Theodore Stier
4. Resting   5. Montreal   6. Spokane   7. Niagara   8. Cecchetti (flanked
by Novikov and Zaylich) stocking up at a wayside halt   9. To New York
10. Returning home   11. Novikov and his wife   12. With her girls

Invitation to the Dance, 1913. Pavlova (with a new costume) is at far right with Zaylich and Novikov.

The company was in better shape by the spring of 1914, when it was due to return to New York; they were not at the Met this time, but at Hammerstein's Manhattan Opera House on West Thirty-fourth Street. Pavlova decided to test New York with the comedy of *La Fille Mal Gardée*, particularly as she was able to present Cecchetti in the travesti role of the Widow Marcelline. It was the sort of thing he could do to devastating effect, and it made its own distinct contribution to the whole-hearted acceptance of the work when it was seen on April 15. Novikov's Colin was thought to be rather ponderous, but Pavlova's deft and delicate comedy won the house. Even so, the ballet appeared only briefly, and usually at matinees. Compared with the repertoire of her first overseas trips, the available works from which they could now draw had become extensive, and whenever a new member was taken into the company from Russia there was a chance to reconstitute fresh items from the parent company. There was no copyright for choreography, and because of the tradition whereby new dances were often inter-polated into some established work, a constant reshaping of ballets was not considered in any way disrespectful or unethical.

Determined that they should not be wasted, Pavlova continued performing the new Fokine ballets in America; but it was rather depressing to discover just how many people in the audience shared Dandré's outlook about them. She persevered, leavening the programs with more accessible works, including Zaylich's Oriental concoction and his *Invitation to the Dance*, which was becoming one of the mainstays of the repertoire, as was the *Gavotte*, which Pavlova danced with Marcel Bergé. This *Gavotte*, arranged by Clustine to Paul Lincke's "Glowworm" music from the operetta *Lysistrata*, had curious overtones of the number that Pavlova had danced with Fokine in the charity concert in St. Petersburg back in 1902. Certainly the costumes were in the same manner—Pavlova's was of gold satin, with écru lace edging and black velvet ribbons; she wore gold sandals and gold laurel leaves on her bonnet. Pavlova presented herself with incredible élan in this piece: her bearing was immensely proud and yet provocative at the same time. The slit dress flashed a lacy underslip and the deep poke bonnet was employed coquettishly, in the same way as a fan would be used, now hiding the face, now revealing it. The eyes flashed from the rim of shadow when the chin was tilted high; at other times only the piquant mouth betrayed the dancer's amusement. The wonderful ankles and insteps caught the eye more than ever with their cross-strapping from the heeled sandals, and the right hand swirled the train of the dress like a matador's cloak. Over the trite palm-court music Pavlova spread an infectious sense of exhilaration. For sheer elegance it was without rival. Among the one-act works there was Ivanov's *The Magic Flute*. Petipa was represented by the ballroom scene from *Paquita* and *The Cavalry Halt*. Whereas *Paquita* presented the hummable music of Minkus with pure dance, *The Cavalry Halt* suffered from a surfeit of swashbuckling mime and a mediocre score by Armsheimer. A typical program might consist of *Paquita* followed by *Les Préludes,* with divertissements in the third part, or *The Cavalry Halt* might be followed by *Une Soirée de Danse* (as Clustine's Chopin ballet was now called), again with the usual divertissements. These drew on music by Rimsky-Korsakov, Johann Strauss, Drigo, Paderewski, Lincke, Chopin, and Glinka—to take an average line-up. On other occasions it might be Moniuszko, Godard, Schubert, Grossman, and Grieg. It was always an eclectic selection.

ABOVE With Zaylich and Novikov in *Invitation to the Dance*, 1913.
BELOW With Marcel Bergé in the *Gavotte*, 1914.

Because the idea of visiting Australia was still being discussed in October 1913, it was assumed then that Pavlova would not be seen in London for a long spell. Press releases were conflicting: one paper said "two years or thereabouts"; another spoke of a "five years' world tour." Although Butt would have been only too happy to sponsor another of Pavlova's immensely popular seasons, no engagement was planned for London for 1914. Pavlova's wish to appease her Tsar was another factor; she was, after all, a Russian citizen and still had family in that country. When the Australian trip finally seemed impossible, Butt already had other commitments, and Pavlova turned her thoughts to Russia. Her schedule meant that she could not arrive before the Maryinsky season ended, so she had to agree to give several summer recitals in the newly rebuilt People's Palace in St. Petersburg and in the Hermitage Theatre in Moscow. In addition there was to be an appearance in the Pavlovsk Residence, a palace situated about 15 miles southwest of St. Petersburg, in which there was a large hall for concerts.

After agreeing to these commitments for late May, Pavlova was able to plan for engagements in Germany and Austria on her way to Russia. But Novikov had the winds of Russia in his nostrils and elected to return there without further delay, wishing to try to re-establish himself within the Imperial Theatre in Moscow, despite his resignation at the time he first joined Pavlova. She took this latest decision in her stride and immediately engaged Tikhomirov on a short-term basis; it was essential for her to have a skilled partner with her in Germany, even if her further plans were fluid. Apart from the Prince's role in *Giselle,* he was

THIS PAGE & OPPOSITE With Novikov in
The Magic Flute at the Manhattan Opera House,
New York, 1914.

expected to learn the *Bacchanale, Une Soirée de Danse, Les Préludes, Invitation to the Dance,* and *The Magic Flute.* Shirayev also agreed to join the tour in Germany.

While still in America, Pavlova must have had her ear to the ground for Diaghilev's plans, if only so as not to find herself in direct competition with him. By February she would have known that he had lined up a German tour, including Hanover and Berlin, where she had hopes of appearing herself. She also knew by then that Nijinsky, having earned his dismissal by getting married, was going to take her old spot at the Palace for a season beginning on March 2. In fact, the following account had appeared in *Musical America* in December:

> The [Diaghilev] company spent the summer season down in Buenos Aires and other South American cities, and it was not until the beginning of this month that Nijinsky arrived in Vienna after the return voyage. Immediately after his arrival he received a telegram from Djagilew notifying him that his services would be no longer required. Thereupon the dancer promptly informed Richard Strauss, who had been composing a ballet, *Potiphar's Wife,* for the Djagilew company, and with Nijinsky especially in view for the principal male rôle. The result is that Nijinsky himself will arrange to produce the ballet in London.

Presumably, Strauss knew on which side his contract was buttered; Fokine was soon adapting the work for Leonid Massine, Diaghilev's new protégé.

Nijinsky spoke to the press in London on February 24 about his Palace season. The program was one of "safe" ballets, and he was careful not to make the mistake of repeating such earlier remarks as "Grace and charm make me seasick!" Instead he mentioned that Boris Anisfeld had been chosen to do the scenery for his production of *Les Sylphides.* "It has an atmosphere all its own," confided the dancer. The same could be said for the Palace Theatre itself, a setting alien to most of Nijinsky's fans:

> Devotees of Nijinsky flocked to the Palace with high expectations; but many of them left it with a curious sense of disappointment, for though the chief items, *Les Sylphides* and *Le Spectre de la Rose,* were the same as we have so often seen and loved at Covent Garden,* there was a subtle sense of anti-climax about their reappearance in Cambridge Circus. What was it? One could detect no difference, no decline in the dancing, but it did not seem to fit in with the background. . . . Of course, those who have not seen Covent Garden— and perhaps the bulk of the Palace audience has not—notice nothing, so that when the curtain fell on the *Spectre,* M. Nijinsky and his sister, who becomes the *première,* were received with immense enthusiasm.

Pavlova could not resist sending Nijinsky a telegram of "congratulations," but he was unable to see any humor in the situation. He was being paid £1,000 a week for his troupe—and for changing his old views about music halls. His conversion had probably come about in the summer of 1912, when he had seen the Palace under the glittering overlay of the Royal Command

---

* Sic. This *Sylphides* had a different selection of Chopin pieces newly orchestrated by Ravel, plus Anisfeld's décor, while *Le Spectre* was danced in front of black curtains.

Performance and graced by the Sovereign of the land; after that, he could hardly have gone on saying it was not quite respectable. Even so, its normal daily guise was a little more down-to-earth; furthermore, its performers were expected to talk to the press representatives in the dressing rooms, not at carefully controlled press calls. One interviewer had a perfectly rational conversation with Nijinsky (presumably via an interpreter) until the moment when the reporter took his leave. At this point the dancer took from a cardboard box a tiny ivory crucifix and said, "Take it with you everywhere. I cannot save you if you do not."

Things soon started to go wrong. *Variety* reported on March 18 that Nijinsky "failed to appear on Monday evening, without having given the management notice":

The Tuesday papers reported his illness, and the management announced he would go on later in the week. Any number believe

Nijinsky will not appear at the Palace unless under desperate persuasion. He is considered "through" there, and is also termed "London's greatest flop." Nijinsky is a classical dancer. He opened the Palace last week as a vaudeville turn for his first appearance here, and was well praised by the press, favorable opinion that did not seem to be shared by the audiences.

There was soon more detail about the drama:

It is stated that the illness of Nijinsky, the famous Russian dancer, is much more serious than is generally realized. There was quite a sensation at the Palace Theatre on Monday [March 16] when Mr. Butt appeared on the stage and announced that Nijinsky was too ill to appear. He is said to be suffering from a nervous breakdown, induced by overwork in the planning and rehearsing of new dances.

Three days later, the contracts of Nijinsky and his company were canceled. Butt had learned a lot about dancers since the

tantrums between Pavlova and Mordkin in 1911: now he had a clause that allowed only three missed performances before he was free to pull the plug. *The Era* commented coolly: "There are really very few Pavlovas, and as a male dancer has not got quite the same personality and charm, the chance of a success out of the general environment is very small." By the time Pavlova returned to England that spring, the convalescent Nijinsky was preparing to take his heavily pregnant wife to Austria, and Mordkin was preparing to bring Alexandra Balashova from Moscow for a summer season at the Empire.

Passing through London on her way to Bremen, Pavlova was able to divulge to the press that she was to appear at the Century Opera House in New York in October for a ten-week season. This was to be under the management of Andreas Dippel, who had commissioned (so it was announced) "a ballet opera, *The Rose Queen,* written expressly for Madame Pavlova and the Century Theatre by Leoncavallo" (*La Reginetta delle Rose,* actually already produced in Rome in 1912). Australia was still being mentioned as a possibility at this point, but for the moment Pavlova was heading back to her roots.

T his return was taking place at a time when the news from Russia was exceptionally disquieting for anyone who chose to look beneath the superficial calm of Court Circulars and widely publicized royal hobnobbing. Over one million Russian workers were on strike in the spring of 1914, and two-thirds of them had not been at their jobs since the previous autumn. This was in the background; more openly, a cross-hatching of state visits in the early days of the hot 1914 summer revealed the chess match being played across Central Europe: Kaiser Wilhelm to Archduke Ferdinand, King George V to the President of France, the President to the Tsar of Russia. With the innocent impartiality of a single-minded artist, Pavlova accepted invitations from the two royal houses most acutely involved in these power-bloc deliberations; setting forth from her English residence, she would dance for the Tsar as well as the Kaiser.

In Germany, the Royal Command Performance took place on May 9 in Brunswick, where the Duchess had organized a gala for the occasion of her baby son's christening. The Duchess of Brunswick was the Kaiser's only daughter, and matters took a slightly confusing turn when her father decided that he would be godfather to his own grandson. The Hohenzollerns and the Brunswicks had not been on friendly terms, and during this time protocol was rigidly observed at the functions in Brunswick, which were attended by representatives of all the German courts. Before the ballet performance, an official assembled the company and warned that there would be no applause at any point during the evening. This would not have come as a particular surprise to Pavlova, who had experienced similar protocol at semiprivate royal performances in St. Petersburg, but it may have been disconcerting for some of the others. Stier found himself once more coping with Teutonic exactitude, being told to begin the overture at the exact moment the Emperor sat down. This was important;

ABOVE & OPPOSITE Two previously unpublished photographs by Arnold Genthe, whose fashionable (if murky) pictures were much in demand. *La Nuit* was often danced in flowing drapes such as these.

The Swan, Berlin, c.1913.

Herr Emil Pauer had once been wiping his glasses at the crucial instant, and the slight delay in the music's commencing had cost him his job.

For Kaiser Wilhelm, Pavlova danced first in *The Magic Flute* and then in *Invitation to the Dance*; the silence after each work was chilling. It was only in the divertissements, when Pavlova subsided to the ground at the end of *The Swan*, that the stillness was suddenly broken by a throaty voice exclaiming "Wunderbar! Wunderbar! Brava!" It was the Emperor, and the audience realized that it was a signal that they might dispense with protocol. The house roared its own approval. At the end, Pavlova was asked by the sternly disapproving Master of Ceremonies to make her way to the Royal Box to speak with the occupants. When Stier arrived in Pavlova's dressing room to congratulate her, he was astonished to find her silent and in a distracted state. It was some while before she could be persuaded to unburden herself: it transpired that in kissing the Kaiserin's glove, Pavlova had left behind a vivid smear of crimson grease paint. Even if it was not seen by Pavlova as an omen—a sinister hint of some impending bloodshed—it was at the least an example of careless social etiquette, and a week later the English press was describing the

incident in some detail. The Kaiser had apparently noticed Pavlova's distress and had said in a kindly manner that the mark on the Kaiserin's glove was of no account. "I was never so frightened in my life," said Pavlova, to a reporter from the *Daily Express*. "In Russia such an offence would have had very serious consequences." (The *Evening Sun* actually reported that Pavlova had told the Kaiser that his disapproval of the tango had had the satisfactory result of getting the dance banned in America!)

Stier had looked forward to the Vienna engagement, as his aged parents were going to be able to attend a performance at which their son was musical director. Alas, they were out of luck for the opening night; no tickets had been made available, and Stier had to be content with a box for the second night. On the morning after the opening performance, Stier Senior was taken ill; he was dead before evening. His son hurried from the deathbed to conduct *The Magic Flute*. In such devotion to his task, Stier was revealing that he had acquired all the hallmarks of his employer's relentless professionalism.

Pavlova's arrival in Prague had been planned to coincide with the seventh annual May Celebrations. She was playing at the New German Theatre, the scene of past triumphs; but by the

cheeks—intimations of a thoroughly spiritual nature welling straight from the heart. This, then, is the true Pavlova.

Yesterday we waited two whole hours to have more of her than just a charming promise, waited for her to give of herself totally; and it came when, with shattering pathos, she portrayed a dying swan. This yearning, this soaring into the heights, this fluttering wing-beat of the hands, this battering against an implacable fate—expressed only by the vibrating arms and the bending neck—this was Duse without words.

Prague succumbed all over again. When Pavlova left for Breslau, her art continued to be discussed. One newspaper reproduced an essay on Pavlova that had been published in Berlin by Fischer as part of a series on the ballet. Emil Ludwig's thoughtful essays probed beneath the surface of a performer's presentation, while at the same time he could create a vivid little pen picture.

While these feet bred to the high school of Italian ballet play their part with the assurance of well-trained adjutants, her whole being seems to quiver beneath the two sensations of surprise and sudden inspiration. In a mazurka she looks down at those little feet with a charming coquetry, and her expression clearly asks: "Are you crazy? Do you want to get away from me? What are you doing, then, down there?"

Though Ludwig considered that never did a female body have so large a component of the spiritual as did Pavlova's, he also picked up a most subtle distinction:

If the impression made by an ordinary dancer is one of spirituality, then for the most part it is also one of tedium. But because Pavlova achieves a spiritual effect which has, however, an erotic basis, she both excites and elevates. This degree of neutrality can at times drive the spectator mad. She resembles in this respect certain portraits of the Milanese and Roman renaissance, behind whose cool expressions there lurks a world of danger. This is a part of her mystery.

After performing in Budapest, Pavlova went next to the Theater des Westens in the Berlin suburb of Charlottenburg. Patrons used to seeing her at the Kroll still flocked to Pavlova's opening program on June 3; it consisted of *The Magic Flute, Invitation to the Dance,* and the obligatory divertissements, in this instance *Pizzicato* (Delibes), *The Swan,* the *Gavotte,* and a Chopin *Nocturne,* "in which she was partnered by the somewhat phlegmatic Tikhomirov." Bergé partnered Pavlova in the *Gavotte,* which ended the evening to a storm of applause. One fastidious Berlin critic concluded that "Lincke's 'Glowworm' is itself drowned out, extinguished, by the musicality of those limbs; and that which to most minds would appear as purest kitsch, she succeeds with her very first step in transforming from the ridiculous into the sublime." The critic continued:

If an appreciation of this art were dependent on this night's performance alone, then at least we would have the assurance that that which is often seen can be seen again and again—not with the same, but with an even greater enjoyment. Anna Pavlova is always the same. Every item of her performance is like the creation of a sculptor, thought out, felt, modeled, perfected down to the last detail.

time she arrived on this occasion the critics had already noted the Berlin papers' praise for the Brunswick gala, "enough to turn any normal stomach, and make one lose any taste for her." Pavlova went on stage knowing that the critics were gunning for her.

So yesterday one was prepared for disappointment and ready to oppose so much excessive enthusiasm. But that was not the way it turned out. Naturally, one had not yet forgotten Nijinsky and the nerve-tingling sensation made by the Russian Ballet with all its splendor, and for which Bakst designed his orgies. Nijinsky was the Kainz of the ballet, but Pavlova is its Duse. It is nearly five years since her conquest of Prague, and one had recovered from the discovery that the good old School of Ballet had its merits after all; one was no longer overcome because a dancer could control her muscles and had learned to throw a leg straight up into the air and revolve on the tips of her toes. Yet one must with all due veneration acknowledge that these techniques are once again worthy of respect, since Pavlova has developed them to the highest peak of perfection. One can only marvel at the feather-light jumps, the inflections of those marvelous wrists, the faultless pirouettes and fouettés. But always there is something more, something which is not technique, but which could not exist without it: such a movement of the noble head, such a tremulous lifting of the delicate arms, such sensitivity in the fugitive expressions brushing the wan

With Dandré in Germany, 1914, immediately before crossing into Russia for the last time.

Here, not a finger is allowed to improvise. This art is irreducible, like the letters in a great book, in which fresh beauties appear every time we read it.

Though *Giselle* was labeled an "essentially kitschy-creepy ballet," it won wholehearted approval; Pavlova's skill was "impossible to analyze." As for her appearance in the Chopin ballet: "Out of the earthbound, kaleidoscopic scene of dancing forms there emerges, again and again, the little white cloud which is Pavlova, 'weightlessly floating' as if stepping down onto a ground of elastic, a dream of moonlit loveliness." There were *The Magic Flute, La Fille Mal Gardée, Les Préludes,* and "an Egyptian dance with music by Arensky," which suggests something from *Egyptian Nights.* There were *Valse Caprice,* Clustine's Godard Pas de Trois, and the *Butterfly;* and "Delche's pas de deux, which she danced with Tikhomirov, had to be repeated several times." (This may have been intended as Deldevez, which would suggest something from *Paquita.*) Least popular was *Oriental Fantasy:* "No, this is not for you, Madame Pavlova, and the public were also well aware of it. The applause was loud but cold. How different it sounded after Weber's *Invitation to the Dance.*"

At the conclusion of the final evening, on June 8, the fire curtain was eventually lowered in an attempt to persuade the patrons to leave, "but still, from beyond the iron curtain, they called for her again and again with roars of applause, the one and only, whose captivating grace in Lincke's *Gavotte* had taken the audience by storm."

When Pavlova finally returned to her homeland, one of the first things she had to do was to apply for a Russian national's passport; this was issued to her on June 12 in St. Petersburg. The following day, a Saturday, Pavlova presented a ballet concert in the Narodny Dom (the People's Palace, rebuilt after a fire at the beginning of 1912). People there certainly were: thousands flocked to see the famous ballerina, and when the critic Plescheyev arrived, his cabman asked him, "Is it Chaliapin, then?" Everyone was prepared to overlook the fact that their heroine was a migrating creature who would soon take off again: "All is forgiven her for the sake of her amazing talent. She entranced the audience of the huge, crowded hall and was tirelessly applauded by both fans of the ballet and those seeing her for the first time." Plescheyev wrote what was to be his last article on Pavlova in Russia, for the *New Times:*

Her whole figure gives an impression of a slim, waxlike fragility, with its pale and lovely lines. When she appears on stage it is as if she were taking shape from out of a mist. Her first movements transform Pavlova into a creature of the spirit who is yet in total command of the vast auditorium. There is a fusion of her talent and the spectators, which subjugates and totally enthralls them. Such is her power. Pavlova speaks to us all; everyone feels for her. One may not understand the ballet, its techniques or intricacies, but for all of us the art of Pavlova is as clear and as uncomplicated as the light of God. The artist's femininity is expressed in the marvelous poetry of her dancing, in the animation of her expressions and the piercing regard of her eyes. Mood succeeds mood: the naive and charmingly coquettish minuet [Paderewski] is replaced by the wistful melancholy of her dying Swan; a dreamlike sequence [Chopin], by a wild and stirring mood of passion [Godard Pas de Trois].

I find it impossible—and indeed it is pointless for anyone—to pause, even momentarily, and consider the subtleties of Pavlova's technique, of her professional choreographic skills, hoping to arrive thereby at an exact appreciation of her talent. The creativity of this artist is *sui generis*, and at this present time has reached such a peak of perfection that it must be regarded as something entirely unique. It would be a different matter if Pavlova were to appear in a ballet where everything is presented for the sake of the eye, and nothing for the heart. Where the heart, the soul, and psychology are called for, Pavlova is inimitable.

It was a small group of soloists that Pavlova took into Russia. (Dandré was, of necessity, absent at this juncture.) Bergé and Oukrainsky went to St. Petersburg, though Pavlova began rehearsing with the promising young graduate Anatole Oboukhov once she arrived. Plaskowieczka was the principal female soloist, supported by the two English girls Butsova and Crombova. Pavlova was rather proud of her protégées' progress; in Russia they did the *Moment Musical* pas de trois with Plaskowieczka, and also a Pastorale from *Tales from the Vienna Woods*, arranged by Zaylich. Madge and Hilda were provided with an escort wherever they went, and although this seemed on the surface no more than a social necessity for the care of two young English lasses, it could not have escaped Pavlova's notice, once she arrived in St. Petersburg, that there was an air of unease distinctly reminiscent of the troubles of 1905, although now, as then, a veneer of calm prevailed.

In Moscow the little company was in the habit of dining at an open-air restaurant in the theatre's surrounding pleasure grounds, laid out around an ornamental lake. These luncheons were happy, drawn-out affairs dictated by Pavlova, who loved to linger over such meals. One burning hot day she left the shade of the table and wandered off down a slope to the lake, where the others watched her from a distance, content not to have to move. After a while they noticed her crouching by the water's edge, quite still. Madge and Hilda were longing to get back to the cool of the hotel, and went to see if they could encourage Pavlova to leave. They found her watching several huge bronze dragonflies working in and out among the water plants. "Look at them! Aren't they marvelous? I am going to make a dance out of them. You see? Watch!" She continued to stare intently at the glittering insects, while her hands quivered and weaved, as if they had an independent life of their own and no connection with her otherwise still body. Madge and Hilda began to wilt. "Wait—just a little longer. I will come in a minute." But another

twenty minutes went by before Pavlova could be persuaded to leave.

They went back to St. Petersburg in mid-week for what was supposed to be their last appearance of the season, at the Pavlovsk Residence on Saturday, June 20, where the late-afternoon performance—a benefit in aid of orphans and children of servicemen—was to be concluded by a display of fireworks on the grounds. Pavlova had already done one performance there, and this second one was so crowded that extra stools and benches were moved in wherever there was space. There were loud demands from the back of the hall for the ladies to remove their millinery. Pavlova included the *Butterfly* in her program—she had done it in Moscow, where two encores had been demanded, but it was a novelty for St. Petersburg and provoked a tremendous clamor. The audience was reluctant to let their star go; they deluged the stage with flowers, and Pavlova threw a lot of them back into the audience, where there was great competition to catch them. When, finally, the audience left the building, most were content to find carriages and make their way home; the promised fireworks seemed to be considered an anticlimax, certainly not worth the risk of having to walk miles and miles.

At this juncture Pavlova was already aware that Moscow wanted her back for yet another performance, and, as well, it had been made known to her that the Tsar hoped she would grace the Maryinsky in the autumn. A decision had been promised by that Sunday, June 21, the day that Preobrajenskaya was celebrating her jubilee for twenty-five years' service to the Maryinsky with a performance in the People's Palace—a sign that rules about retirement were not binding, if the talent remained great enough to make such rules absurd. Already Preobrajenskaya was billed to appear in Cairo during October, with Egyptian society being offered *The Trials of Damis* and *Swan Lake*—a safe export of Petipa in staunchest European vein. There had never been much real hope that Pavlova would fit in any performance at the Maryinsky in September; St. Petersburg knew that she was already booked for appearances in England and Germany and that America was beckoning again. Even if she were to make only one or two appearances at the Maryinsky, her European schedule would suffer; it was said publicly that Pavlova's own company was costing her 700 roubles a day and that any idle time spent by her dancers during a contracted season was a direct drain on the ballerina's own resources. There was talk of three command performances at the Peterhof, but over the long term, refusing the Tsar's management had fewer repercussions than would have been the case at any other time, since the curtain was about to go up on far greater dramas than the Maryinsky could provide.

On June 28, 1914, in the capital of Bosnia, a chauffeur managed to forget the explicit instructions he had been given a few minutes earlier and led a procession with the Austrian Archduke Franz Ferdinand's car into the prearranged, and therefore dangerous, route away from the city hall. They had already escaped an attempt on the Archduke's life on the way to

Pavlova and Clustine demonstrating their new
social dances in the *Ladies' Home Journal*, 1915.

the city hall. Now their luck ran out. The spark of Sarajevo ignited the volatile forces of European power politics, and King George made another entry in his diary: "Terrible shock for the dear old Emperor."

It was a shock for a great many people, not least of them Pavlova, who had so recently appeared in Vienna and who had a deep respect for royalty. The people most affected by the violent event were real in every sense to Pavlova: she knew the tenor of their voices, the color of their moustaches, the manner of their bearing. Hands that had held hers now held the fates of millions. Those hands could pick up a pen and unleash forces that could sweep aside the work of generations.

Pavlova's sense of self-preservation at this point does not appear to have been marked by any unseemly haste. Her two English protégées, true to their backgrounds, displayed an insular awareness that extended no further than the intolerable difficulties of coping with strange foods and a different language. They were bored and homesick, and nothing made an impression—except the attendant at the New Hermitage art gallery; a tremendous tussle took place with young Hilda, who did not want to relinquish her umbrella. In the end she sat glum but victorious in the vestibule, while Madge trailed around the paintings and sculpture. Pavlova dodged such attempts to instill culture into the girls, deputing Kostia Kobelev to the Olympian task. But when the time came for them to be sent back to England, there was no escort, and the girls were expected to make their own way. Pavlova was extremely agitated about this. The girls were due at the railway station late on the night of a performance; they

were packed and ready before Pavlova herself had finished performing and they had to make their farewells in the wings of the theatre. Their mentor produced a crucifix from somewhere and held it over the girls' heads while she spoke a great many prayers for their safety. There were tears in her eyes, and she laid great stress on the "hope" that they might soon be together again.

On July 20 President Poincaré arrived in St. Petersburg to the usual brilliance of its court scene, with a dazzling display of military (and social) might paraded in his honor. It was not immediately apparent to the French contingent that one and a half million striking workers were also parading throughout the country, and that in some parts of St. Petersburg mobs were erecting barricades in streets already deep in broken glass. The new French ambassador was fascinated most by the military review at Krasnoye Selo; there "the light toilettes of the women their white hats and parasols, made the stands look like azalea beds."

Although there was an impervious calm among the middle and upper classes, there were some signs of preoccupation: Pavlova's Peterhof performances were "postponed," and as a result she left the even more imperturbably provincial atmosphere of Moscow and made her way directly to Nijni Novgorod for a few days' rest. At the same time Austria made its impossible ultimatum to Serbia—which unexpectedly groveled; Kaiser Wilhelm thought that all grounds for war had disappeared, and almost as

his thought took wing, Austro-Hungarian shells started whistling across the Danube into the middle of Belgrade. Russian troops were mobilizing along the Austrian frontier, the cousin emperors "Nicky" and "Willy" bombarded each other with telegrams, and while the hours ticked on, July took with it the last days of peace between Germany and Russia.

When Germany declared itself in a state of war with Russia on August 2, 1914, Pavlova and Karsavina were both traveling in Germany—but in opposite directions. Karsavina has left a vivid account of her cruel disappointment in being stopped at the German frontier and made to get back on the train when the very crossing was in sight. Pavlova, by contrast, never reminisced about the problems she had experienced; only some contemporary newspaper articles gave the odd clue, and these emerged many weeks later. At the time, Daniel Mayer was sending telegrams to all of Pavlova's dancers: "Madame Pavlova's whereabouts unknown. Hold yourself in readiness for rehearsals." In fact, Pavlova had left Russia three days before the suspension of the St. Petersburg–Berlin express, and she arrived in Berlin before the Kaiser's mobilization order was issued. She was traveling on her new Russian passport, but she seems to have applied for visas to complete her journey to London. Of course Dandré had no passport, due to his self-promoted exile, and he had been marking time in Germany. After Pavlova's highly popular season at the Theater des Westens, the Germans had suggested that she should cancel a planned English tour and repeat the German tour instead, during August and September. This seems to have been agreed upon, for productions and costumes were held back, with

a tentative plan that the subsequent American trip would start from Bremerhaven rather than Southampton.

With the realization that war was imminent, Dandré may already have crossed into Belgium. Pavlova arrived at the Belgian frontier a few hours too late; the Kaiser had ordered a general mobilization. As a result, Pavlova, a Russian national, was arrested. Reports of the length of this detention range from eighteen hours to "several days." Dandré in his account casts a fog over the whole period, and the word "we" is conspicuously absent: "The declaration of war found her in Berlin. She managed to get to England via Belgium." Pavlova's onetime pianist, years later, wrote: "But for the merest of accidents she might have been destined to remain interned throughout the whole of the War period. She managed to get through, but all her luggage and personal effects were detained in Germany."

She managed—but how? It is inconceivable that Pavlova did not think to seek the help of the Duchess of Brunswick; she was the obvious link to ultimate authority, although suspicious and intractable levels of command probably delayed the communication for many hours. But Pavlova was finally released and allowed to pass across the frontier—by now meaningless—into Belgium. Here there were more difficulties: her train was stopped dozens of times, by successive military and civilian authorities. It seems that in Brussels Pavlova appealed to friends in the nobility and received Royal consent to pass unmolested. Winifred Edwards (Fredova) was later told by Dandré: "We had very little money, and near Brussels I offered the coachman a golden sovereign. When he refused it, I knew that England was at war."

The annual Moratorium, when all the European banks closed at the beginning of August, must have caused untold extra confusion. They got through to France, where Pavlova's passport was honored, and probably traveled via Paris in the hope of getting some help from friends; certainly Pavlova appears to have gathered up Ivan Clustine at this point. He was lamenting the imminent closing of the Opéra and was desperate for a job. Pavlova hastened on, with "Uncle Ivan" in tow. (He was Uncle Ivan to most of the dancers, but he was the real uncle of Mikhail Mordkin.) According to contemporary reports, Pavlova left France via Calais, on a packet boat loaded to the rails with fleeing tourists.

England's ultimatum to Germany over Belgian neutrality expired at midnight on August 4, and the two great powers were thus at war. The world might have achieved its greatest display of collective madness at that moment, but crowds were cheering outside Buckingham Palace. Part of the euphoria and bravado came from the belief that the conflict could not continue beyond the end of the year; everyone seemed to refer to Christmas as though it would be a time for double rejoicing, but Pavlova, who loved and guarded that festival with a childlike intensity, could only speculate as to where she might be at that time.

THIS PAGE & OPPOSITE At Ivy House, summer 1914.
As well as swans and pigeons, the photographic session included
"Polly" and the Pekinese "Bijou" and "Purchok."

Ivy House was cool and welcoming after the tension and the travel weariness. It was high summer, and an untroubled drowsiness lay about that hill, cushioned from the sprawl of central London. Pigeons strutted along the gables, and from the upper windows it was possible to look out across the tree tops to a green haze of countryside, distanced and tranquil. In the late afternoons, the surface of the pond threw back a fractured reflection of the sky as the swans fussed at skeins of cut grass.

Ivy House had become home to all the people who made up Pavlova's "family": Victorushka, Lily, Big Shura, Manya (whose sighing, as she sewed, could be heard along corridors, and whose occasional shrieks could be heard well down Golders Hill), and Kuzma, eternally shifting the wardrobe cases in the basement. It was home for the swans and for the pigeons, who increased their families with such regularity; and now it was a refuge for "Uncle Ivan" too. But it was not home for Pavlova; it was still the property of the Golders Hill and General Estates Company. And there was a shock lurking in those soulless offices: the price of Ivy House—to Madame Pavlova, the famous, highly paid Madame Pavlova of the Palace Theatre—was £10,000. For the locality and the times it was an outrageous price, but Pavlova was over a barrel and the agents knew it. If she wanted it she had but to sign the deeds—and find the money.

The brutal fact about Pavlova's "wealth" was that she and Dandré had arrived back in London with a single cheque to the value of £100—and this drawn on a German bank. It was common gossip locally that the occupants of Ivy House were in straitened circumstances, and neighboring residents "passed the hat" to tide them over. Pavlova's jewelry was the only sound currency left, and even that glittering collection could not provide forever. America represented the obvious answer. There had been requests from film companies; Andreas Dippel had a scheme to present her under license from Max Rabinoff; and Rabinoff himself was trying to secure regional support for another of those terrifying expeditions across America.

One of the questions facing Pavlova at this time was whether the appeal of classical dancing would remain as potent to audiences, now that ragtime was the rage. Pavlova found the new music ugly, but she could not ignore the trend; already some of her experiences in parts of America had shown that audiences could be apathetic about the idea of paying for an evening of classical ballet. She could convert them once they came in the door; it was getting them to the door that was the worry. Pavlova's astute manner of playing to the press helped, and she was careful never to lose patience with these demands on her time. The photographs of the social dances the year before had been a pointer. Pavlova now took the idea a stage further. She would take on the manner but present alternatives: dances that preserved the old European tradition. It was reactionary, her striving for new gavottes and quadrilles, and yet it was understandable—a clinging to the styles and values that were disappearing before the headlong advance of the tango.

Pavlova and Clustine worked relentlessly, choosing music (even commissioning new melodies) and planning the move-

ments, and they were soon sufficiently advanced that a photographer was employed to take a series of pictures showing the comprehensive stages of several of these dances. *The Pavlowana,* in 2/4 time, was thought to have a suggestion of the maxixe, and there was also the *Czarina Waltz* and the *New Gavotte Pavlowa.* Clustine squired Pavlova in all the photographs, and for some sequences she wore a hair piece with bangs. With it she also wore a rather whimsical headband; this she forgot in some of the sessions, so that in the final assembly it came and went, rather disconcertingly, as the sequence progressed.

When Malvina Hoffman and her mother arrived in London in August 1914, they made a point of visiting Pavlova. Although the American sculptress had been depicting the ballerina over the course of the previous four years, they had never actually met until the previous April at the New York home of Mrs. Otto Kahn, when Hoffman began slaking her thirst for firsthand observations: "I watch her, as a panther might crouch in a thicket and watch a bird." The first impression had been vivid: "The fragile, pallid little sprite comes into the room—dressed in black—with fiery flashing eyes—quick, unexpected movements—nervous, breathless French conversation. Simple, *real,* inspired from within, a child of nature—a great artist—this is at once evident." Hoffman put it all down in her diary, including her quite unguarded ambition that she would make Pavlova "proud to be my muse before it is all over between us."

The object of this intensity seems to have sensed it immediately and kept it at bay for the remainder of the season in New York. Hoffman was given a pass to allow her backstage so that she might sketch, and Pavlova was complimentary about the drawings; she remained friendly, but guarded. Hoffman drank it all in, like every artist who discovers the exotic confusion of

backstage life for the first time. But Pavlova was then still a foreign creature to Hoffman, seen from a distance. It was enough for her to observe the ballerina's little rituals in the wings each night: the extraordinary feet dipping and stabbing in the rosin box; the nervous return to the chair, where the maid had set out a little collection of necessities: a mirror, a glass of water, cologne, scissors, needle and thread, a bowl of powder with a puff, which the dancer frequently used to dust her shoulders. Then, as the music began, the quick sign of the cross, the entry into the enveloping warmth of the spotlight, and the applause crashing like surf. This was the view seen and remembered by many privileged people; it was like a close-up impression of the most memorable creature at the zoo.

Pavlova at Ivy House was the rarer thing; behind the bars, with the public gates closed, the creature dropped its guard. And of course the plumage was tucked away: Hoffman registered shock when she noticed how much grey there was in Pavlova's hair. After the escape from the threat of internment, she was still looking drawn and tired, but she received her guests warmly and took an obvious delight in showing them the beautiful house and garden. At lunch Pavlova, Dandré, Marjorie Ford (Pavlova's secretary), and Hoffman planned Greek ballets and drank to "the victorious Allies." Later, driving in Pavlova's car to see Mrs. Otto Kahn, who was staying at St. Dunstan's Lodge, Hoffman had a few minutes to claim Pavlova's attention without interruption. "We recognize that two human creatures adrift in such a whirlpool of bloody chaos can be of service and comfort to one another," the sculptress wrote in her diary. "She becomes enthusiastic about posing and helping me in every way to interpret her art." Back at Ivy House, Pavlova whirled about the room presenting little cameos of the *Bacchanale,* and when she sprawled on the floor poring over tracings of Greek friezes, her very naturalness was in itself enthralling. Not for the first time Pavlova had bewitched an admirer, and from that day Hoffman's very considerable energies found a more direct focus.

Rehearsing *The Awakening of Flora* with Volinine
at the Palace Theatre, London, 1914, for the
Red Cross. Pavlova also returned briefly to France
for the same organization.

After the first six weeks of the war, the carnage was beginning to register on the national consciousness in England, and the undisturbed calm of daily life appeared more contrived than natural. In September Pavlova made brief appearances in the English provinces, and also showed up at the Shaftesbury Theatre for a matinee in aid of the Allied Forces' Base Hospital in Grosvenor Street, where in the midst of numbers by well-known stage artists, she contributed *The Swan*. Pavlova had concluded her plans for America: she would tour under the aegis of Dippel and his Century Opera Company, by arrangement with Rabinoff. Before leaving she decided to give one final matinee at the Palace, as a benefit for the British and Russian Red Cross. A card was printed with a facsimile of her own stylish handwriting:

My heart bleeds for the British soldiers and those of my country and their Allies, who are laying down their lives in a common cause. I can do nothing—I can offer nothing but my Art. It is a poor thing when such brave deeds are being done, yet, if you will help me I will do my utmost, give the best that is in me to ease the terrible sufferings of our brave brothers.

On October 12 she presented the English premiere of *The Awakening of Flora*, with scenery and costumes by "the well-known English artist A. Rothenstein." Queen Alexandra was in a box in the circle; significantly, the audience seemed composed almost entirely of women. Pavlova was also unveiling a new partner at this performance: she had contracted Genée's erstwhile associate Alexandre Volinine, whose previous contract had expired. He had not been back to his homeland since 1910. The

war, and Pavlova, contrived to deter him further. As well as *Flora,* in the first half of the program there were orchestral selections under the baton of the Palace conductor, Herman Finck; Boris Bornoff and Maggie Teyte both sang; and there were ten dance divertissements. Though Clustine was not given any credit on the program as the creator of the *Gavotte* (which a London audience was seeing for the first time), he was credited with having "arranged" *Flora*. Fourteen years separated Pavlova from the day when she had pleased "Papa" Petipa with this first milestone in her career. This time Flora earned more than praise: she earned £730 for the first casualties of the Great War. And Pavlova had danced in London in 1914, after all.

Within hours of the last curtain call at the Palace, the Pavlova company was on the boat train. The purchase of Ivy House had still not been finalized, and Pavlova had to leave an agent with power of attorney on her behalf. He did not achieve this goal until November 17, when, presumably, advances were available from Rabinoff and any sale of jewelry had been effected. (Pavlova had begun corresponding with Otto Kahn in August, asking that securities which he held on her behalf be used as collateral for cash advances to Rabinoff.) When the papers for Ivy House were finally signed, the new owner had just left Rochester, New York. The previous evening's program had included *The Awakening of Flora,* and in the newspaper review the following morning it was said that this ballet showed "a maiden in her dream-land." In a sense the maiden had acquired her own "dream-land" that day; and yet, as a true home it was now as far away as home had ever been.

Did the immediate future seem less clouded to Pavlova than to others at this time? If she saw herself as some sort of harbinger of poetic light, a simple missionary dispensing brief moments of beauty and happiness to depressed spirits, then it was no more than the role others cast her for: Anna Pavlova was viewed as someone bestowing her gift in a mood of genuine communion, and in most places there was still a clamor to see and partake of it. It was not unknown for working-class mothers to hold up small children at the stage door and beg Pavlova to touch them; and although this extravagance sometimes worried and confused her, Pavlova understood the simplicity behind the reasoning. The blazing truth in her expressions of human emotional forces—and animal forces—came in part from her own immutable belief in the rightness of her work, and its general impact made it not too fanciful to suppose that she was perhaps the agency for some other greater truth.

More simply, she was a great crowd-puller, a superstar, in an age that was only just discovering that certain theatrical talents could transcend all ethnic frontiers, provided they had stamina and a comprehensible medium of expression. Pavlova's fortune was in the fact that her medium was universal; she also had the desire to prove that it was so. At a more mundane level, it was the thing she did best, and she wanted to continue earning a living from it. She had simple tastes, but on the other hand she had acquired an expensive manner of protecting that simplicity; she had discovered more and more that her art brought with it commitments, and that these involved a continuing financial drain, quite apart from the massive problem of Ivy House. She was increasing her company—it was no longer a hired-and-fired gypsy band but a supportive "family" providing the framework for her own flowering. Despite the differences in temperament and the inevitable stresses that arose, Victor Dandré had proved his worth to her in countless different ways: calm, forgiving, impressive in matters of organization, a behind-the-scenes diplomat, a buffer between Pavlova and the pressures that focused increasingly on her. But that very efficiency had promulgated the treadmill progression—she had wanted to dance, and suddenly the reins of command had been transferred to a driver who steered a course for just that purpose. She had found an ally in her obsessive cause.

Once the "train" began to move, Pavlova became the self-regenerative fuel for it. Nobody stood the pace consistently, except herself; she was a comet carrying with her a tail of lesser brilliance that constantly expended itself. She now used people, rather like firewood, for her own pyre. No one was indispensable; if they did not measure up to her specific needs—and exactly when she needed them—she put them aside. Her confederates were expected to sacrifice themselves. If she drove herself impossibly hard, then that was the yardstick for all. Novikov's departure had been a sign of the exhaustion felt by everyone, although for him other factors may have intruded: he suffered from a slight heart condition which at times became the basis of hypochondriac displays that did not win all the sympathy that he felt was his due. But he had enjoyed his position as senior danseur with its attendant privileges, including his wife allowed to travel with the company free of charge. The stresses were far greater for lesser members of the company, and on the whole they displayed astonishing resilience.

America in the autumn of 1914 was experiencing an economic boom, and this confidence was reflected in the overtures made to Pavlova once she arrived there: one was a guarantee of $75,000 in cash plus a quarter interest for a film that would show the ballerina in one complete ballet and two divertissements. Yet Pavlova turned down the offer, saying that she did not have the time. In truth she did not, though the pressure was of her own devising. Vaudeville managers noticed this capacity for sustained effort, and they tried to lure her onto their own circuits. The rewards would have been phenomenal by prevailing standards, but Pavlova would not cross the thin dividing line between music hall and true American vaudeville. Refusing a lure of $210,000 for twenty weeks' work, she said: "I am not a circus performer and will never appear on stage with trained animals."

Pavlova faced the familiar and seemingly endless skein of halts that lay ahead, tracing a cat's cradle all over the map of North America. Just to look at it was to recoil with fatigue. They had

MME. PAVLOWA HERE AFTER ARREST AS SPY.

n.f. World Oct 23. 1914

Dancer Held as Enemy Few Days After Receiving Decoration From the Kaiser.

Mme. Anna Pavlowa, who will dance at the Metropolitan Opera House, beginning Nov. 3, arrived yesterday on the White Star liner Adriatic. She said that just before the war began she was dancing in Berlin and was applauded by the Kaiser, who gave her the Order of Merit. But when war was declared this did not save her from arrest as a spy. She was detained several days, all her baggage was searched and she was freed only on condition that she leave the country at once. In London she reassembled her scattered company.

Mme. Rita Fornia said she served as a Red Cross nurse in the French field hospitals and was at Senlis when the Germans occupied the town. "They were so confident of reaching Paris that they issued notes for supplies marked 'Payable at the German pro-

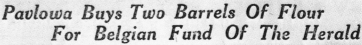

Pavlowa Buys Two Barrels Of Flour For Belgian Fund Of The Herald

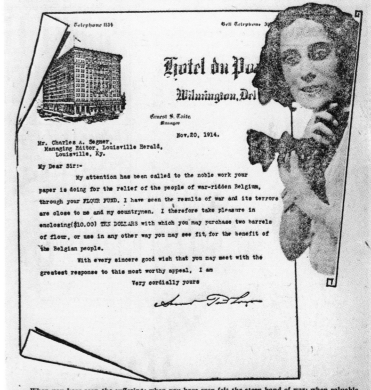

When you have seen the suffering; when you have even felt the stern hand of war; when valuable property has been taken from you and you have been forced to make your weary way, on foot or aboard a bumpy cart, out of a war-torn country, then you realize the plight of the poor, unfortunate people who are stripped of all they own and are left destitute and dependent upon charity.

Perhaps that experience, combined with a sympathetic nature, had something to do with the contribution received yesterday from Anna Pavlowa by The Louisville Herald Belgian Flour Fund. This dainty little interpreter of classic dances sent a letter to The Herald from Wilmington, Del., enclosing a ten-dollar gold certificate for the purchase of two barrels of flour for the Belgians. She expressed the wish that the movement may meet with hearty response.

Mlle. Pavlowa was in Berlin at the outbreak of hostilities, and it was some time before she was permitted to leave. With great difficulty she made her way, by circuitous route, to London, where she arrived with no baggage and mourning the loss of all her stage properties. These latter were valued at thousands of dollars, and it was impossible at once to replace them. Undaunted, Mlle. Pavlowa appeared a number of times in London, and later made a trip into France, where she danced for charity and to aid the Red Cross. Her heart was deeply touched by the pathetic sights she witnessed while making her way out of the war zone, and she has contributed liberally to the relief of the sufferers.

1914

Nov. 2	Bridgeport	Park Theatre
Nov. 3	New York	Metropolitan
Nov. 4	Brooklyn	Academy of Music
Nov. 5	Worcester	Worcester Theatre
Nov. 6–7	Boston	Boston Opera House
Nov. 8–9	Providence	Providence Opera House
Nov. 10	Springfield	Court Square Theatre
Nov. 11	Albany	Harmonics Bleecker Hall
Nov. 12	Syracuse	Wietings Theatre
Nov. 13	Hamilton	Hamilton Opera House
Nov. 14	Toronto	Macy Hall
Nov. 15	Buffalo	Teck Theatre
Nov. 16	Rochester	Lyceum
Nov. 17	Ithaca	Bailey Hall
Nov. 18	Elmira	Lyceum
Nov. 19	Scranton	
	Wilkes Barre	
Nov. 20	Wilmington	Playhouse
Nov. 21–22	Atlantic City	Apollo Theatre
Nov. 23	Philadelphia	Opera House
Nov. 24	New York	Metropolitan Opera House
Nov. 25	Richmond	Academy
Nov. 26–27	Washington	New National
Nov. 28	Baltimore	Lyric Theatre
Nov. 29	(travel)	
Nov. 30	Akron	Music Hall
Dec. 1	Wheeling	Court Theatre
Dec. 2	Parkersburg	Auditorium
Dec. 3	Charleston	Berlew Theatre
Dec. 4	Huntingdon	Huntingdon Theatre
Dec. 5–6	Cincinnati	Music Hall
Dec. 7	Dayton	Victoria Hall
Dec. 8	Columbus	Hartman Theatre
Dec. 9	Lexington	Ben Ali Theatre
Dec. 10	Louisville	Macauley's Theatre
Dec. 11	Nashville	Ryman's Theatre
Dec. 12	Evansville	Well's Bijou Theatre
Dec. 13	(travel)	
Dec. 14	St. Louis	Odeon Theatre
Dec. 15	Kansas City	Convention Hall
Dec. 16	Omaha	Auditorium
Dec. 17	Des Moines	Coliseum
Dec. 18	Chicago	Auditorium

Chopin Waltz with Volinine.

Dec. 19	Milwaukee	Pabst Theatre
Dec. 20–21	Chicago	Auditorium Theatre
Dec. 22	Cleveland	Central Armory
Dec. 23–27	Chicago	Auditorium Theatre
Dec. 28	Davenport	Burtis Opera House
Dec. 29	Peoria	Majestic Theatre
Dec. 30	Springfield	Chatterton's Theatre
Dec. 31	Chicago	Studebaker Theatre

1915

Jan. 1	Battle Creek	Armory
	Kalamazoo	Post Theatre
Jan. 2	Muncie	Grand Wysor
Jan. 3–4	Indianapolis	Schubert Murat Theatre
Jan. 5	Lansing	Gladman's Theatre
Jan. 6	Grand Rapids	Power's Theatre
Jan. 7	Saginaw	Auditorium
Jan. 8	Ann Arbor	Whitney's Theatre
Jan. 9	Toledo	Valentine Theatre
Jan. 10–11	Detroit	Broadway Theatre
Jan. 12	Fort Wayne	Majestic Theatre
Jan. 13	Columbus	Southern Theatre
Jan. 14	Springfield	Fairbanks Theatre
Jan. 15	Canton	Opera House
Jan. 16	Erie	Majestic Theatre
Jan. 17–18	Youngstown	Grand Theatre
Jan. 19	Pittsburgh	Schenley Theatre
Jan. 20	Lynchburg	Academy of Music
Jan. 21	(travel)	
Jan. 22	Washington	New Lyric National
	Baltimore	
Jan. 23	Philadelphia	Metropolitan Opera House
Jan. 24	(travel)	
Jan. 25	Brooklyn	Academy of Music
Jan. 26–31	New York	Century Opera House
Feb. 1	New Haven	

Feb. 2–28	New York	Century Opera House
Mar. 1–6	Boston	Boston Theatre
Mar. 7	(in New York)	
Mar. 8	Savannah	
Mar. 9	Jacksonville	Duval Theatre
Mar. 10	St. Petersburg	Casino Theatre
	Tampa	Casino
Mar. 11	(travel)	
Mar. 12–22	Havana	Payret Theatre
Mar. 23	Cienfuegos	
Mar. 24–25	Havana	Payret Theatre
Mar. 26	Matanzas	
Mar. 27–28	Havana	Payret Theatre
Mar. 29	Key West	San Carlos Theatre
Mar. 30	Miami	Grand Theatre
Mar. 31	St. Augustine	Jefferson Theatre
Apr. 1	Jacksonville	Duval Theatre
Apr. 2–3	Pensacola	Grand Theatre
Apr. 4–7	New Orleans	Tulane Theatre
Apr. 8	Mobile	
Apr. 9	Montgomery	Grand Opera
Apr. 10	Birmingham	Jefferson Theatre
Apr. 11–12	Atlanta	Atlanta Theatre
Apr. 13	Chattanooga	Bijou Theatre
Apr. 14	Knoxville	Staub Theatre
Apr. 15	Nashville	Music Hall
Apr. 16	Louisville	Macauley's Theatre
Apr. 17	Cincinnati	Music Hall
Apr. 18–19	Pittsburgh	Shenley Theatre
Apr. 20–21	Buffalo	Teck Theatre
Apr. 22	Detroit	Lyceum
	Toledo	Valentine Theatre
Apr. 23	Terre Haute	(no performance)
Apr. 24	Indianapolis	Shubert Marat Theatre
Apr. 25	Chicago	Auditorium Theatre
Apr. 26	Milwaukee	Pabst Theatre
Apr. 27	St. Louis	Odeon Theatre
Apr. 28	St. Joseph	Lyceum Theatre
Apr. 29	Topeka	
Apr. 30	Wichita	Forum Theatre

Dance of the Hours with Volinine

Raymonda

ANNA PAVLOVA COMPANY 1914–1915 NORTH AMERICAN TOUR AND BOSTON GRAND OPERA TOUR

Elysian Fields

May 1	Denver	Auditorium
May 2–3	Colorado Springs	Opera House
May 4	Albuquerque	Crystal Theatre
May 5	El Paso	Texas Grand Theatre
May 6	(travel)	
May 7–9	San Diego	Spreckles Theatre
May 10–16	Los Angeles	Mason Opera House
May 17	Fresno	
May 18–19	Sacramento	
May 20	Stockton	
May 21	San Jose	Yosemite Theatre
May 22	Oakland	Auditorium
May 23–June 5	San Francisco	Cort Theatre
June 6	(travel)	
June 7–8	Portland	Baker Theatre
June 9	Aberdeen	
June 10	Tacoma	Tacoma Theatre
June 11–12	Seattle	Moore's Theatre
June 13–14	Victoria	Victoria Theatre
June 15	Vancouver	Avenue Theatre
June 16	Billingham	
June 17	North Yakima	Yakima Theatre
June 18	Walla Walla	
June 19	Spokane	
June 20–21	Butte	
June 22	Billing	
June 23	Bismarck	
June 24	Grand Forks	
June 25–26	Winnipeg	
June 27–28	Fargo	
June 29	Duluth	Lyceum Theatre
June 30	St. Paul	Metropolitan
July 1	Minneapolis	Metropolitan
July 2–Aug.1	Chicago	Midway Gardens

(Company vacation; Pavlova continues filming in Chicago
and then goes to West Coast for more filming.)

(Boston Grand Opera Company Tour begins)

Oct. 4–9	Chicago	Auditorium Theatre
Oct. 10–13	St. Louis	Odeon Theatre
Oct. 14–16	Louisville	Schubert Theatre
Oct. 17–20	Detroit	Lyceum Theatre
Oct. 21–23	Toronto	Opera House
Oct. 24	(travel)	
Oct. 25–Nov. 6	New York	Manhattan Opera House
Nov. 7–13	Philadelphia	Opera House
Nov. 14	(arrive Boston)	
Nov. 15–Dec. 15	Boston	Boston Opera House
Dec. 16	(travel)	
Dec. 17–21	Washington, D.C.	Belasco Theatre
Dec. 22–26	Atlantic City	Keith's Theatre
Dec. 27–28	Baltimore	Lyric Theatre
Dec. 29–30	Wilmington	Playhouse
Dec. 31–Jan. 1	Philadelphia	Opera House

1916

Jan. 2	(travel)	
Jan. 6–12	New York	44th Street Theatre
Jan. 9, 16		Hippodrome
Jan. 17	Syracuse	Wieting Opera House
Jan. 18–19	Toronto	Royal Alexandra Theatre
Jan. 20–22	Buffalo	Teck Theatre
Jan. 23–26	Cleveland	Hippodrome
Jan. 27	Grand Rapids	Power's Theatre
Jan. 28	Detroit	Lyceum
Jan. 29	Toledo	Valentine Theatre
Jan. 30–Feb. 2	Cincinnati	Music Hall
Feb. 3–5	Pittsburgh	Schenley Theatre
Feb. 6–7	Dayton	
Feb. 8–9	Indianapolis	Murat Theatre

Scène Dansante

Feb. 10	Evansville	Well's Bijou Theatre
Feb. 11–12	Nashville	Vendome
Feb. 13–15	Birmingham	Bijou Theatre
Feb. 16–17	Memphis	Lyric Theatre
Feb. 18–19	Atlanta	Atlanta Theatre
Feb. 20–27	New Orleans	French Playhouse
Feb. 28–29	Houston	Majestic Theatre
Mar. 1–2	Dallas	Coliseum
Mar. 3	(travel)	
Mar. 4	El Paso	Texas Grand Theatre
Mar. 5	(travel)	
Mar. 6–11	Los Angeles	Mason Opera House
Mar. 12	(travel)	
Mar. 13–19	San Francisco	Cort Theatre
Mar. 20–21	Oakland	Auditorium
Mar. 22–23	(travel)	
Mar. 24–25	Portland	Hylig's Theatre
Mar. 26–28	Seattle	Moore's Theatre
Mar. 29	Tacoma	Tacoma Theatre

Walpurgisnacht

Mar. 30	Spokane	Auditorium
Mar. 31	Walla Walla	Keylor Grand Theatre
Apr. 1	Boise	Pinney's Theatre
Apr. 2–4	Salt Lake City	Opera House
Apr. 5–8	Denver	Auditorium
Apr. 9–12	Kansas City	Convention Hall
Apr. 13–14	Omaha	Auditorium
Apr. 15	Sioux City	
Apr. 24–26	St. Paul	Auditorium
Apr. 27–30	Chicago	Blackstone Theatre
May 1–2	Milwaukee	Pabst Theatre
May 3	Grand Rapids	Power's Theatre
May 4	(travel)	
May 5	Saginaw	Auditorium
May 6	Columbus	Southern Theatre
May 7	New York	Hippodrome

As Helen of Troy in the Walpurgisnacht scene
from *Faust*, 1915: (opposite) with Volinine.

With the vast numbers of the entire ballet as revealed to the present writer at Drury Lane Theater in London in June, such brilliant and thrilling scenes, setting all the nerves in the body a-tingle, were comparatively easy of accomplishment. It is to the credit of Clustine and Pavlowa herself that she is able with her thirty dancers to approximate the lightning power of striking clean to the heart of our feelings and sweeping us into a world of emotion and enthusiasm of which we have never dreamed ourselves capable. It was that one moment at the close of *Walpurgis Night* which sets off the Russian ballet against all other forms of present-day art as a vital part of our emotional life, a stimulus that comes all too seldom into our lives to thrill us into new worlds of sense and sound and sight.

Pavlova persisted with *Oriental Fantasy,* even though some audiences were disconcerted by the preponderance of mime over dance. Like the critics in London and the audiences in Berlin, some people in America could not accept the work as suitable for Pavlova's attention. But with the vivid description in Henry Taylor Parker's review, we get a further glimpse of the reason it was so unusual in Pavlova's repertoire. This ballet showed her as "the enchantress prone on her couch, watching, hungering, devouring herself while she waited to devour others. Baleful imagination seemed to shape each outline of her body, each glance that played across her face. There she lay, remote, solitary in her dreams and desires. . . . And when this enchantress danced, it was with the sensuality that bites rather than caresses."

Clustine was now acting as ballet master in place of the hapless Zaylich, who had been interned in Germany at the outbreak of war. His replacement was a powdered and painted dandy, not very good in terms of class discipline or even exact schooling; but his adroitness at stringing together serviceable choreography satisfied Pavlova's greatest need. He had a retentive memory, which gave him the raw material for a stream of pastiches from more considerable works. For this 1914–15 tour everything was ripe for plunder, from the vast storehouse of Petipa treasures to the best of the Legat brothers' work, *The Fairy Doll.* In a divertissement called *Valse des Visions,* six dancers performed in filmy, floating draperies under colored lights. It was really a hybrid extract from the Vision scene of *The Sleeping Beauty,* with a hint of Loie Fuller to add spice. The only surprising musical choice was Boccherini, for a pas de deux called *Scène Dansante,* which Pavlova first danced with Oukrainsky. Volinine had his own solo, *Pierrot,* to Dvořák's "Humoresque." The reactions to the ballroom dances in contemporary style were mixed; some critics saw them as a sop to a mistaken conception of American public taste, and though three of the dances were published in the January, February, and March issues of *Ladies' Home Journal**

been in thirty-six different places by the time they left Des Moines on the night of December 17, and they were due in Chicago for a short Christmas season, with excursions to Milwaukee and Cleveland sandwiched into that time. Mercifully, the Chicago engagement was almost in the nature of a vacation, since the ballet was performing in conjunction with the Century Opera Company at the Auditorium Theatre, and in five acts of *Faust* their principal duty was to provide the Walpurgis Night scene in Act Four. Patrons were content as long as they had Pavlova on stage at some point in the evening: "Mlle. Pavlowa finally revealed herself, not as Helen of Troy, but as herself, and everyone, I think, forgot the opera."

The Indianapolis *News* critic had been to London the previous summer and had seen the Diaghilev company at Drury Lane. Like a great many people, to him Russian ballet meant the Ballets Russes, and vice versa, so that in reviewing Pavlova and her company he saw them as a touring extension of the other group:

---

* Pavlova's elegant poses in the *Gavotte* series were in marked contrast to a rather skittish series posed by Irene and Vernon Castle. Their "Castle Gavotte" appeared in the November 1914 *Ladies' Home Journal* and drew such ire from matronly readers that the editor canceled the series. The Pavlova lessons began two issues later, with the pictures that had been taken in London in the summer of 1914. In the text that accompanied the ill-fated Castle series, Vernon Castle had said, "It was Mademoiselle Pavlova who has shown how beautiful the Gavotte really is." He was probably referring to a spring performance of the Lincke *Gavotte* rather than the 1913 newspaper series.

—copiously illustrated with the series of photographs that had been taken of Pavlova and Clustine in London—the divertissement itself was retired early in January 1915.

One of the replacements proved to be the fruit of Pavlova's summer musing by the lake in Moscow: after hearing Fritz Kreisler play his "Schön Rosmarin" at a concert, Pavlova created for herself a solo, *Dragonfly*. For this she designed a clever costume of bronze-green chiffon. The outer skirt was an arrangement of irregular, wire-rimmed panels which floated free. In movement, the drapery seemed to be in a state of constant agitation, and the floating panels enhanced the many swirling turns in the dance. The costume also had four long, wire-framed wings, and Pavlova was able to curve her arms over the lower pair and draw them forward with vibrating movements. At other times there would be stabbing little bourrées, and the hands would suddenly flick over, palms uppermost, then flick back again. It was not straightforward mimicry, but the tempo of the flicking hands seemed to catch exactly a dragonfly's random shifts in direction. Much of the dance picked up the lilting, almost waltzing melody, with lots of turns, but here again it seemed apposite, because the movement had a sunny quality. The verisimilitude of her portrayal of a dragonfly lay in the mood she created as much as anything. Vital to it was the way Pavlova seemed almost to hypnotize herself so that no move appeared prefigured by any mental preparation: it gave the movements an unpredictability that was electrifying. The audiences invariably tried to persuade Pavlova to repeat the *Dragonfly*, but she never risked overexposure of these little "tone poems," which relied on an intense output of mental and physical energies.

Pavlova's most important test in America came in February. The initial plan had been for the company to share a season with Andreas Dippel's Opera Comique Company at the Century Opera House in New York (on Central Park West, between West Sixty-second and Sixty-third streets, and considered daringly "uptown"), but this had been placed in jeopardy. Dippel, like many others in the musical world at this time, thought that the war in Europe would cut off the supply of first-rate artists who might normally have graced the New York winter season, thus leaving the field wide open for home-bred talent that had not previously emerged in the front ranks. The expected shortage did not occur, and the competition between the various managements was as hot as ever. Dippel went in search of enthusiasm for his line-up from audiences in Salt Lake City, but he met with disaster and had to ask that his planned New York appearances be canceled.

Undaunted, Pavlova decided to carry the enterprise herself, with the run reduced to four weeks. She knew the risk she was taking, but she was confident that the season could be sustained. This was one of the rare times when Pavlova relied on a "safe" and relatively captive audience, for economic reasons, rather than pressing on in her normal adventurous manner, leaving the worry of box office returns to others. But she minimized the risk.

Dragonfly

With Volinine in *Raymonda*. (Photographed in Mexico City, 1919.)

There were to be fourteen ballets new to the city, and the social dances were coming back on certain days in a different guise, as *thés dansants* held on the stage. On Tuesday and Thursday afternoons a "selected list of patrons" showed who was to be permitted to dance, and tea would be served by a well-known restaurateur. Mondays were kept free, partly in order not to clash with subscription nights at the Metropolitan Opera; and the orchestra, which had been augmented to opera proportions and was now called the Russian Symphony, filled the Sunday evening slots with programs of Russian music.

The season was launched on February 2 with Clustine's staging of Petipa's *Raymonda,* giving New York its first sight of the ballet, and giving Pavlova her first chance to dance the title role. Clustine had condensed the work somewhat, and the scenario struck people as being extremely vague. Pavlova herself was assured of an affectionate welcome; she had an army of staunch admirers, and there was the novelty of the program. The following day, the reviews were mixed. "The Russian danseuse last night produced within herself a new vitality, a youth and a grace more spontaneous and overpowering than she has shown in years, a perfection of poise and a resourceful versatility nothing short of amazing," wrote the *Evening Mail's* critic. The *New York Times* was more begrudging:

Except for a certain effectiveness of costuming which goes with the period of thirteenth-century France, there is little of note in the

new ballet that differs from most of the others in which Pavlova has been seen. The scenario has little power to hold by itself, and there are dull and characterless stretches in the music, which was not particularly well played last night. Nevertheless opportunities for the display of the principal dancer's talents and those of certain members of her company are not lacking, and this was what the audience was most interested in. There was as much tumultuous enthusiasm as usually accompanies a Pavlowa performance.

Two new divertissements closed the program. The *Evening Mail* commented that in the *Dragonfly* Pavlova "becomes for the moment an actual winged creature," and it also described a "startlingly frank *Hebrew Dance*" in which "the voluptuous joy of life quivers through every gesture." (This pas de deux, danced with Volinine, used music of Saint-Saëns, and though it was tried as a finale, it did not survive in the repertoire at this time.)

On the afternoon of Pavlova's premiere, Isadora Duncan and her pupils had given a matinee of a program that she described as "Dionysion"; by enlisting the support of her brother Augustin with readings and Madame Namara-Toye with songs, Duncan had managed to fill the Metropolitan Opera House for the third time that week. Pavlova insisted on several of her soloists going to the Met to see Duncan, and especially to observe the manner in which she used her arms. At the end of the matinee most of the audience filed out rather hurriedly, but the visiting dancers, and some loyal Duncan admirers, crowded to the front of the

In the new *Fairy Doll* costume, Chicago, c.1915.

theatre, continuing to applaud. Duncan said to them: "Now I am among friends; I shall dance for *you*," and she did some further items for the few people who were left.

The February 1915 issue of *Vanity Fair* carried an article "by Anna Pavlova" that outlined a Russian ballet girl's education. The last sentence read: "As it is the custom to retire Russian ballet dancers at the age of thirty-five, it is evident that they must use their best energies to make hay while the sun shines." Pavlova had just entered her thirty-fifth year. Her name day was celebrated on February 16 with a little ceremony on the stage of the Century, in view of the audience. After a performance of *The Fairy Doll* the curtain was taken up again to reveal the entire company gathered on the stage. Attendants carried in tables laden with flowers and other gifts, and Max Hirsch, the company manager, explained to the audience that the custom of the Russian opera houses in presenting gifts in public on such occasions would be followed. There were short speeches: from Clustine on behalf of the ballet, from Stier on behalf of the orchestra, and from Plaskowieczka on behalf of the dancers. Pavlova thanked each of them with a kiss. *The Seven Daughters of the Ghost King* was given its New York premiere that night, but the general impression was that the happenings on stage bore faint resemblance to the scenario. Sylvester Rawling wrote in the New York *World*: "Was it the accidental breaking of one of her wings or the slowness of her sisters to fall into the abyss of fire that caused Mlle Pavlowa to proclaim so volubly her dissatisfaction? It was a bit of a shock to hear an irate voice in the pantomime." (This winged costume seems to have escaped any photographic record.)

The uncertainty in Europe and the contrasting mood of confidence in America meant that all sorts of grand theatrical plans were discussed during this period in New York. Rabinoff had received news of the Cuban National Opera's new theatre in Havana: a magnificent building erected at a cost of $4 million, subscribed to by thirty thousand stockholders. He rushed off to see for himself. By February 12 he was cabling that Pavlova and her company would be the first professional performers to appear on the new stage. His other plans were equally grand. Aiming at the Panama-Pacific International Exposition in San Francisco and San Diego, he thought to take Pavlova to the West Coast via the Panama Canal, with performing stops at Caracas, Cartagena (Colombia), Colón, and Panama City. No sooner had Rabinoff announced this plan to the press than fresh alternatives showed themselves: a joint venture of ballet and opera seemed a possibility. The impresario knew where there was an opera company for the picking—he had simply to harness it to a financially successful ballet company. He must have won Victor Dandré's confidence over this scheme, because Pavlova was persuaded that she should put money into the enterprise, which was to utilize the assets of the sagging Boston Opera Company; she was expected

The Woman with Million-Dollar Feet

FAVORITE RECIPES OF THE GREAT RUSSIAN DANCER

PAVLOWA'S RECIPES DO NOT INCLUDE BUTTERMAKING — BUT HERE SHE IS AS A BUTTERFLY

Hartford Courant Sept. 29, 1913

WHEN Pavlowa made her first foreign tour, and played in Stockholm, King Oscar came every night to see her, and crowds followed her from the theater to her hotel. One night she asked her maid why the people outside were so stirred. The girl answered: "Madame, for an hour you make them forget the sorrow of life."

MADAME PAVLOWA began studying at the Imperial Ballet School when she was ten years old. A ballet school is more like a convent than anything else—up at eight sharp in the morning, dress under the eyes of a matron, hustle downstairs to prayers, and then dancing lessons till noon. After lunch a walk, lessons till four, and then dinner, followed by fencing, and a little music. No, there's no nonsense about life in a ballet school.

SHE doesn't often idle about her English life like this, for when she isn't working she sleeps. Pavlowa sleeps at least five hours a day, and always seven hours at night when possible. She hasn't time for a husband and "I can not immerse myself in the cares of housekeeping," she said, "I dare not desire a life full of peaceful happiness by the domestic hearth."

A BALLET dancer hasn't much more chance for that back-to-nature business than a bank president. He runs down to the cottage at Newport and pokes around with a spade now and then, just to be human for a change, and the ballet dancer can have a cage of birds brought up to her dressing-room, and pretend she is out in the wild-and-woolly for the moment.

When Mlle. Anna Pavlowa, queen of the dance, arrives in this city there will be other Russians with her besides her big company of Imperial dancers. Her numerous personal retinue includes two Muscovite cooks. Although the London Daily Mail calls her "London's principal and peerless idol" and although she is as much in demand in France and Germany as here in America, Pavlowa still keeps by her the manners and customs of the land of the Little Father. Russian cookery is particularly dear to her heart, and—well, let it go at heart.

Here are the recipes for the things Pavlowa's cooks are most often called upon to prepare:

Consomme Pavlowa.

To be served hot or jellied, sometimes erroneously called Borsch. To the ingredients used for ordinary consomme for six persons add four medium sized beets chopped quite fine, also one or two tablespoonfuls of fresh grated horseradish. Strain the consomme into another saucepan. Have ready one turnip, scraped very fine and seasoned with half a teaspoonful of sugar, and the same quantity of salt. Put the turnip pulp into a saucepan and pour in a pint of the consomme. Boil till quite soft, or about thirty-five minutes. Then mix with the other consomme.

Borsch.

Real borsch is a great deal more elaborate, although it is sometimes called simply "beet soup." It is the national dish of Poland, and all Russians love borsch too. To make enough for six people put two pounds of soup meat in a pot, earthenware preferable. Add four quarts of water and sprinkle in an even tablespoonful of salt. As soon as the pot boils skim off the fat. In the meantime lightly roast a small duck for about twenty-five minutes. Put the duck in the soup pot, together

with a quarter of a pound of lean bacon, uncooked; two carrots, two onions, a small bunch of parsley, chopped fine; two bunches of celery, two beetroots, peeled; some thyme, bay leaf, two cloves and a teaspoonful of allspice. Put the lid on the pot and let it simmer for an hour and a half, skimming off the fat every now and then. Put in a smoked sausage then and let the simmering go on for another half hour. Then lift the vegetables and meat from the pot. Cut the beets into tiny slices and also slice a small portion of the beef and a bit of the bacon. Slice all the sausage. Put all this in the soup tureen and strain in your soup. The duck and the remainder of the bacon are, of course, to be saved for a subsequent meal.

Salade Russe.

There are a number of salads to which restaurateurs give the name of Russian. But real Russian salad is either a forcement dish or else it is made of lobster and shrimp, with anchovies. The best Russian salad is made like this:

Chop into small cubes the meat of a small, cold, boiled lobster, the meat of a dozen cold cooked shrimp, a dozen anchovies in oil, a cold boiled beet, carrot and potato. Put in a salad bowl and add a bit of cold cooked string beans, cut in pieces; add some cold

add a quart of granulated sugar. Boil for five minutes, then cool. Add the juice of the lemons and oranges and a dash of sherry and some rum, as desired. Serve in glasses with shaved ice.

Valank Tsorbassi.

Here is a delicious dish, most popular in the south of Russia, particularly Odessa:

With two pounds of fresh whitefish, including bones and heads, put a sliced onion, two branches of celery sliced, a sliced carrot, a branch of chervil and two branches of parsley, a sprig of thyme, a bean of crushed garlic, three cloves and a bay leaf. Pour in three quarts of water and half a gill of white wine. Boil fifty minutes, seasoning with salt and paprika. Strain the broth through a cheesecloth into a saucepan containing three ounces of raw rice and boil on a slow fire for forty minutes. Add about eight cooked shrimp shelled and cut small. Boil for another five minutes and serve.

Russian Jelly.

And here is a Russian dessert: With one ounce of clear gelatin mix half a pound of sugar. Add the juice of one lemon and a pint and a half of water. Put on the fire till thoroughly melted, mixing constantly with a wooden spoon. Strain through a cloth and put

Taglioni and Elssler Were as Famous In Their Day as Pavlowa Is Now

ELSSLER.   PAVLOWA IN OLD TIME BALLET GARB.   TAGLIONI.

Pavlowa Sways Big Audience

Motion Her Way of Expression

Anna Pavlowa, Russian Dancer, With Her Pet Dog

Los Angeles Examiner Jan 29, 1914

Russian Ballerina Declares She Almost Has Lost Her Voice From Pantomiming

Admit You're Over 30! Why Not? For Younger You Haven't Any Poise

N.Y. Evening Mail APR 15 1914

Pavlowa tells her real age —29—and is a little ashamed it is not more —She aspires to love, wisdom and poise as true success.

So the lady with the wrinkle under her chin will please forget her troubles and think how graceful her mind is—perhaps.

By ZOE BECKLEY.

PAVLOWA AND HER BIRTHDAY GIFTS.

WHAT age is woman's best? A century ago the answer to this ancient but indestructible query would have been "seventeen."

AROUND THE CLOCK WITH PAVLOWA; HEALTH RULES OF THE BUSY DANCER

N. Y. Herald

Russian Artist's Only Complaint Is That There's Not Time to Do All She Has to Do.

Feb 7 1915

IF she could have her own way about it, Pavlowa would make over the universe and make each working day forty-eight hours long.

The famous Russian dancer has just begun an engagement at the Century Opera House. When a HERALD reporter saw her the other afternoon in the green room, which adjoins her dressing room, ...

dozen orders, speaking rapid fire Russian and French; had dashed to the elevator and rushed across the stage, entered her dressing room, followed by most of the managerial staff, a HERALD cartoonist and the reporter.

She threw her fur coat across a chair, grabbed a huge flower pot of blossoming tulips, put them in the centre of the green room table, placed her own and some other chairs around it, and, presto! the scene had been set for her interview.

"My creed," said Pavlowa, her face wreathed in the fascinating smile that is so familiar to her audiences, "is that there is happiness alone in work. When I work make you realize that twenty-four hours is a stingy arrangement of time."

So the HERALD presents in this connection the Pavlowa time table. Read it. It puts the tired business man to shame to learn how much more than he this frail little Russian woman accomplishes—not only accomplishes, but wails for more time in which to work.

"Of course," sighed the famous ballerina, "I only have the pleasure of doing this much when I am in a city for an uninterrupted day or more, for when we are travelling the journey takes up so much time, and my manager, Mr. Rabinoff, seems to have a habit of choosing cities that are far ... other. He takes a map, ... nts to a speck far away ... and says, 'We are go- ...

work. So I have just finished embroidering a huge carpet for my church in Russia. My girls all helped me with it, and we all worked with big, long needles until we had finished the carpet; but then, oh, la! la! la! It was so dirty from train riding and from so much handling that I had to have it all cleaned before I could send it to my beloved church in Russia.

"Now that job is done I spend a lot of time with my ballet master, Ivan Clustine, and while travelling we map out new ballet effects. We use a board like a checker board, which represents the stage, and then we scheme out groupings and positions, letting two fingers of each hand travel across the board like a ballet dancer's legs. After that is done we make diagrams of the ballet and then ... Then I have to help in designi...

PAVLOWA DANCES AROUND THE CLOCK

9:00 A. M.—Rises; exercises before open window.
9:10 A. M.—Bath, tepid.
9:30 A. M.—Breakfast, fruit, tea, toast.
10:00 A. M.—At theatre; practice one hour.
11:00 A. M.—At theatre; rehearse one hour.
12:00 noon.—Luncheon; conference with costumer or other employes.
1:00 P. M.—Interviews; fresh air.
2:00 P. M.—Music study, one hour.
3:00 P. M.—Instruction to six private pupils of corps de ballet.
4:00 P. M.—Dictation to secretary, &c.
5:00 P. M.—Siesta; relaxation and sleep one hour.
6:00 P. M.—Tea; discussion with staff.
6:30 P. M.—At theatre; inspecting costumes, altering shoes, &c.
7:15 P. M.—At theatre; in practice clothes, "warming up," forty-five minutes.
8:00 P. M.—At theatre; dress for performance.
8:15 P. M.—At theatre; evening performance.
11:00 P. M.—At theatre; performance over; rubbed down by masseuse.
11:15 P. M.—At theatre; relaxation in dressing room, fifteen minutes.
11:30 P. M.—At theatre; dress for street.
11:45 P. M.—Conference with artistic staff, discussion and criticism of performance, orders for routine of coming day.
12:15 A. M.—Light supper with managerial staff, with discussion of business.
1:00 A. M.—Retire.

Pavlowa Opens Local Season

PAVLOWA, PARTIAL TO NO PARTICULAR PET, HAS A REGULAR MENAGERIE.

But Famous Dancer, Who Has No Fads, Says That a Pet's Place Is In the Home, and a Country Home at That---Not Even a Pekinese Spaniel Travels With Pavlowa---At Home She Has Swans, Pigeons, Parrots, a Gazelle and Dogs, Both Real and Toy---And Now She Wants a Coyote.

KEEPING pets is a serious business with Pavlowa. No, the incomparable Anna has not turned fancier to eke out her income. The highest paid artist on the stage hardly needs any pin money. It is to study their graceful movements that Pavlowa has a pond with swans and an aviary of pigeons at her English summer home, Ivy House, near London, and also a gazelle frolicking about the lawns. Her polyglot

GOOSH the LAMENTED 'GATOR HAS BEEN GATHERED TO HIS FATHERS

THE DANCER SAYS THAT SHE FINDS INSPIRATION IN THE GRACEFUL EFFORTLESS MOVEMENTS of her SWANS

PAVLOWA and HER POLYGLOT PARROT.

© by UNDERWOOD & UNDERWOOD.

parrots, masters of five tongues; her prize winning Pekinese spaniels and her blue ribbon bulldogs are just pets for their own sake.

Pavlowa has two country places, one outside London, the other near St. Petersburg. While she is appearing in either city for a season the menagerie is with her. But when she travels as on her 1913-14 American tour, which includes besides this city almost every other city of importance on the continent, the swans and the pigeons, the dogs, the parrots and the gazelle stay in London. She leaves them there because the English climate is so much milder than the Russian.

Rights of Dogs.

"Even a tiny toy dog has a right to have a lawn to play upon," says the Russian danseuse. "My two Pekinese would be miserable living in trains and hotels, and I should be miserable because they were miserable. And naturally my two big bulldogs wouldn't enjoy the American tour a bit.

"Speaking of pets in general and of dogs in particular, they should not be kept in cities. It's not healthful for their owners who live in crowded quarters, and it breaks a dog's heart to have no big, free, open spaces in which to run and play."

The ballerina says that when she can have them about she finds in her swans and gazelle and pigeons inspiration for her art. "You see," says the great ballerina, "the life of a dancer is work, work, work, and then more work. Somebody asked me the other day if it wasn't satisfying to have attained the zenith of my art. Just as if I could keep my art without constant daily practice! Since I have to dance from two to eight hours out of every twenty-four, even during the few short days when I am not making professional appearances, I diversify these exercises.

"I love best to practice on my own lawn. With the trees and the sunshine and the flowers and my pets I imagine myself in some old glade of Thessaly. Of course only folk, dramatic and character dances can be done on a lawn. The ballerina's steps I must practice indoors on a smooth floor.

Swans Her Favorites.

"Of my pets the swans are, of course, my favorites, because I so love the dance 'The Dying Swan.' I can stand for an hour watching my white beauties float, proud and stately, in and out and round and round. They are very fond of me, principally because, the gluttons, I feed them cakes and crackers. Sometimes when I am blue—and sometimes I am—the swans will cheer me up. When, as will happen now and then, I take my work too seriously and grow introspective and sad I rush to my swan pond. I watch the swans; then I call Fifi, the gazelle, and then I don't take myself so seriously. Why? Because I realize that nature is greater than art. My swans and my gazelle are, oh, so graceful without an effort at all, and I must work so hard. I cry to myself, 'Oh, to be a swan or a gazelle!' But soon I say, 'No!' For, though the swan and the gazelle are, without giving thought to it, so wonderfully graceful, they have not the intellectual ecstasy and the joy that comes from hard work and things accomplished. Nature is greater than art, but the mind is greater than all things else."

Parrots Speak "American."

Pavlowa's two parrots speak five languages—English, Russian, French and German, also American. Before her regular season at the Palace necessitated her living in London in the summer time the ballerina kept the two birds at her Russian country place. There they learned Russian and, of course, French, which is the "polite" language of all educated Muscovites. Their German vocabulary they picked up in Berlin and Vienna

LIKE HER TOY DOGS, PEKINESE, HER REAL DOGS, ENGLISH BULLS, ARE PRIZE WINNERS.

© by UNDERWOOD & UNDERWOOD

PAVLOWA'S PEKINESE SPANIELS are of ROYAL LINEAGE and BLUE RIBBON TAKERS

THE HARDEST WORKING PERSON IN CHICAGO

Yes, This Is She. If You Don't Believe, Read the Story by the Hattons on Page 8.

with an eloquent wave of her hands in the direction of the small army of "movie" directors and actors. She dived into her dressing-room for a few moments and then came for her luncheon in the knee-length peasant dress required for the next scene.

Her Italian appearance suddenly gave us a clew to the real Pavlowa. She has been widely described as the spirit of the new Russia, the artist spirit of the new Russia, the artist emerging in that great northland now finding a spiritual voice.

Pavlowa is not Russian in that sense at all. She is emphatically southern. Without making any intentional effort she is infinitely more Greek than Isadora Duncan. She has all the Attic qualities, energy, mental and spiritual vivacity, a pagan joy in physical perfection and a wonderful "creative" ability. She is one of the few twen-

Chicago Herald JUL 13 1915

them in her widely-copied gavotte.

by Anna PAVLOWA

The Fascinating Russian Artiste, Foremost Living Exponent of the Classical, Here Applies Her Technique to the Modern Dances, and Gives Personal Illustration of the Principles of Grace and Dignity, Especially for American Amateurs.

Anna Pavlowa.

HALF the dancers of America do not know what the other half are doing, with results glaringly apparent at the social functions of the day. At present even the most formal balls are apt to resolve themselves into a series of isolated lessons in which one partner tries to initiate the other into the mysteries of his or her latest acquisition in steps.

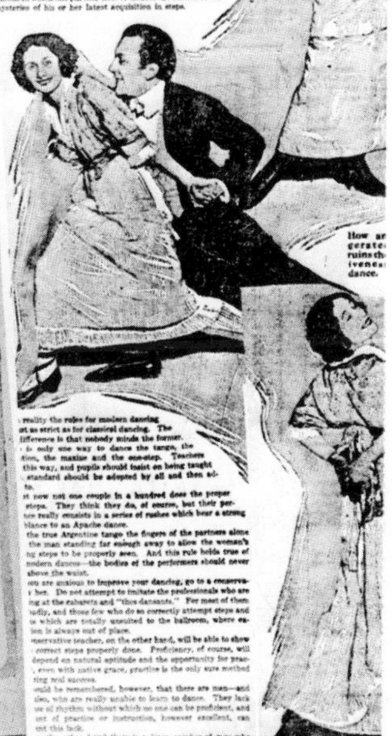

On the *Olivette* to Cuba, March 1915: (top right) with Volinine;
(above) Dandré, Stefa Plaskowieczka, Pavlova, Ernest Marini.

"Ever since I was old enough to know what the stage meant I have been possessed of a desire to play the role of Fenella. It has always been my one anticipation that I might some day be seen in a sort of dramatization of Auber's great opera, for I realized that it offered great opportunities for pantomimic work.

When I visited Universal City some time ago I was greatly interested in the wonderful facilities offered there for great productions, and so when I was asked by Mr. Laemmle if I would do a picture for him, the first thought that came to my mind was *Masaniello*. I was not over-anxious to go into pictures, and I recall that I stipulated if I did consent to make a screen début it would have to be as the dumb girl of Portici. I was not easily converted to picture work. . . .

Just what arrangements I made financially I do not think is of interest to the public. When the documents had been signed and the date agreed upon as to when my work should begin, I began to feel somewhat nervous and apprehensive as to how I would look in pictures. So I bought a camera and spent some of my idle time out in the country, where I had some of the members of my company take various photographs of me in different poses. Some of these were quite satisfactory; some were quite otherwise."

The budget for the film was a mammoth one—a quarter of a million dollars, not including the star's fee, which Pavlova wanted paid in advance. All this meant that the producer, Phillips Smalley, was competing with any epic that D. W. Griffith might produce. Most surprising was the fact that the director was to be a woman, Lois Weber; she was married to Smalley and was responsible for the screenplay, which was soon enough wrenching the opera's libretto into novel shape. Pavlova made sure that the opera itself was penciled in for the repertoire of the new touring company.

Universal mapped out its production plans to accommodate Pavlova, who made it clear that her first duty was toward continuing her live appearances without any significant break in schedule. The fact that Universal tolerated this viewpoint was a sign of just how much faith they placed in the drawing power of their new star. Film performers at this time were not considered demigods, and the salaries of even the most well known were moderate; yet for Pavlova there was a flat fee negotiated at a sum of $50,000. This was a mighty salary by film standards, and even at the Palace Theatre in London Pavlova would have had to work for the best part of a year to earn it. Furthermore, Pavlova's insistence that she should continue touring meant that the production company had to split its activities between the West Coast and Chicago. (A revised schedule for American touring by the Pavlova Company had now been finalized, with the Panama Canal jaunt dropped in favor of transcontinental appearances, ending with a season in Chicago.) This presented obvious headaches, solved only by Universal's having the bright idea of leasing Sans Souci Park from the Chicago municipal authorities. The park was adjacent to the open-air Midway Gardens Auditorium, where the dancers were due to perform for the month of July, before their usual August holiday. The full company was to be employed for court dances in a scene set in a palace, and the plan was for a huge outdoor studio to be erected in the park, so that

to make a huge initial investment of $75,000, and furthermore she was not to draw a salary. Presumably the creditors of the opera company needed a guarantee before they would authorize the release of any of the assets, such as scenery and lighting equipment. Certainly Pavlova was not averse to escaping from the music-hall image and recovering the surroundings of a high-minded artistic ensemble, and she desperately wanted a genuinely supportive company to share the load, but she was discovering for herself the reason for Diaghilev's never-ending financial escapades. It was all too clear that good art cost good money, and there was no guarantee that there would be enough good patrons to make up the deficit. It took a huge number of people to add up to one Tsar.

Pavlova agreed to the deal, but she was able to supply the money only by also agreeing, finally, to one of the many film offers. This one was from the newly inaugurated Universal Film Manufacturing Company. Pavlova explained everything to *Motion Picture* magazine:

Pavlova and the others could shuttle between the film work and the stage with minimum disruption to either schedule.

While Rabinoff tried to assemble the components for the new opera and ballet company, Pavlova was on hand for consultation. She and Clustine were confident that they could revive several Russian productions that melded opera with dance, and since novelty was the name of the game, all sorts of suggestions received an airing, including the use of a new operatic score by the English composer Josef Holbrooke, whom Rabinoff was endeavoring to promote in America. Ambroise Thomas's *Hamlet* was also mooted, with the point being made that many sections of the score had always been cut because they had been specifically written for balletic interludes, just as the ballroom scene in Gounod's *Romeo and Juliet* was invariably lost for lack of skilled executants. Rachmaninoff's *Aleko*, with its libretto after Pushkin, was another contender.

I n the midst of all this adventurous planning, Pavlova took off for a farther frontier, to fulfill the invitation from Havana. The company gave several performances in Georgia and Florida before leaving from Tampa on the morning of March 11. A small steamship, the *Olivette*, carried the dancers out into the Bay of Mexico. The change was utterly exhilarating; there was a clear blue sky, a light breeze, and a balmy warmth that dictated a change into summer clothing.

When the dancers drove past the huge white stone building of Havana's opera house, they thought it looked like a splendid building. In fact, the decorators were still struggling with the interior fittings, and the ballet had to appear at the Payret Theatre. But for Havana, it was still a huge social success; there had been no ballerina there in living memory. After the first night an article about Pavlova appeared in *La Noche de la Habana*: "All motions and evolutions of her body proceed in accordance with an order, a system whose principal element is line—by the application of which she is able to express anything, from the most primitive forms of feeling to the most complex action." Laura de Zayas-Bazan, writing in *La Prensa*, was in a breathless mood: "Words cannot express the artistic emotion which overcame me during the marvelous spectacle afforded by that peerless artist, Anna Pavlova. I should never have thought that the rhythms of motion and plastic perfection could affect me so deeply." By the time she came to interview Pavlova, she was more affected than ever. "Those who meet Pavlova for the first time seem to lose all power of speech," she wrote. "They feel they are in the presence of a superior being. A serious intellectual force emanates from her person."

The serious and superior being was actually enjoying herself in Cuba and was quite prepared to countenance a trip to the other side of the island to perform at Cienfuegos. The weather changed to steady rain, the old theatre was dank and musty, the inn was primitive, and the audience on the night of March 23 would hardly have made two football teams. Added to this, Pavlova found herself without a partner. Volinine had had a tiff

with his girlfriend and then gone out to ease his sorrows by sampling the beverages of Cuba. He was soon oblivious to the passage of time and missed entirely the joys of Cienfuegos, where Clustine gallantly struggled to get into the white tights and turquoise doublet of Volinine's Prince Charming costume from *The Fairy Doll*. Savage work with a pair of scissors and a great deal of temporary stitching accommodated the bulges just long enough; at one point it seemed touch-and-go as to whether the tights would descend before the curtain. It was all something of an adventure, including the "facilities." Plaintive cries from the girls finally achieved the surrender of a treasured roll of toilet paper, bowled under the door by a swarthy masculine hand. Pavlova remained cheerful and announced a visit to Matanzas, which news was greeted with suppressed groans, but they went there too, before a final performance back in Havana.

Then it was embarkation, but this time they went only half the distance back. Key West, that tiny dot of land at the end of the Florida Keys, boasted a theatre by the name of San Carlos, and after March 29 it could also boast of an appearance by the Russian dancers. It was on to the Grand Theatre in Miami the next night, and then the American trek began: St. Augustine, Jacksonville, Pensacola, New Orleans, Mobile, Montgomery . . . one-night stands stretching into the limitless distance.

Danse Espagnol, c.1915.

California Poppy

Leaving El Paso in the first week of May 1915, there was a day's train journey, and then the Pacific was sighted as the company pulled into San Diego. Three nights at the Spreckles Theatre seemed like luxury. The same hotel bed two nights running, washing allowed to dry, and the chance to memorize a street name without referring to a bit of paper. The same pitfalls in the stage surface already marked and remembered. Costumes hanging to air, freshly ironed and not clammy from the previous night's perspiration. But there was dreadful news on the day they arrived: the Cunard liner *Lusitania* had been sunk by a German U-boat off Ireland, and twelve hundred passengers had been drowned, many of them Americans. The company danced relentlessly each night—a week in Los Angeles, a night in Fresno, two nights in Sacramento, successive evenings in San Jose and Oakland, and then on to San Francisco for a fortnight at the Cort Theatre.

Before leaving San Francisco, Pavlova gave her West Coast admirers one glimpse of a new solo; it was her gesture to them. To the swan, the bacchante, the butterfly, and the dragonfly, she added the *California Poppy*—her latest embodiment. The ubiquitous *Eschscholtzia californica* was in rampant display, and the bloom's habit of closing as each evening approached lent it an individuality that had placed it immediately in Pavlova's private pantheon of favorite flowers. Accompanied by Tchaikovsky's *Melodie in E-flat*, she was discovered on stage as a deep crimson flower bud that gradually turned back the segmented "petals" of its dress to reveal the blazing golden reverse. Her little dance soon became a twirling, joyous paean to the speeding hours of

daylight that marked the life span of the poppy; at the end she drew the petals up again, one by one, until they concealed the vivid eyes and the pale, powdered features under the golden wig. Thus extinguished, the creature folded herself to the stage and was finally still, as the closing darkness shrouded her from sight. The audience was greatly touched by this poetic sentiment; it was, after all, a novelty that sprang from their immediate environment, not some hand-me-down from the dim and distant shelves of European legend.

The Midway Gardens in Chicago was as strange in its way as any setting graced by the dancers. The sprawling brick enclosure had been designed by Frank Lloyd Wright like some Assyrian courtyard, surrounded by balconied walks on two levels. For the ballet, the rudimentary open-air concert platform had to be deepened with a temporary construction that projected far beyond the false proscenium. This was an equally makeshift affair, supporting swags of material concealing the overhead scaffolding, from which the scenery flats were unwound. There were stands of calcium lights in the wings, and beyond, more by way of decoration, tall poles studded with dozens of light bulbs looked like spires of glowing hollyhocks when darkness fell. The orchestral enclosure butted into the first two rows of seats; there were then six more rows before steps admitted patrons to raised terraces studded with half an acre of tea tables, each fully decked with a damask cloth and accessories. The whole complex was able to admit up to five thousand customers at a time.

Besides tea and cakes, the fare included *The Magic Flute, The Awakening of Flora, The Fairy Doll, Amarilla, Coppélia, Invitation to the Dance, Walpurgis Night, Chopiniana*, and a shortened version of *Raymonda*, which consisted of the substance of Act One, under the title of *Raymonda's Dream*. There were divertissements by the score, including *California Poppy*, which got its second public performance during this season and soon became one of the established favorites. The people of Chicago flocked to see all this, but they were constantly beset by bad weather, and on many evenings the performances had to come to a premature conclusion when rain settled in steadily. There was rain on twenty-three of the thirty-one evenings. Sometimes Pavlova would battle on, facing a forest of umbrellas. The music librarian would hold a large umbrella over Stier, hoping to keep the conductor's score dry, and bedraggled musicians struggled to turn damp sheets of music that had stuck together, while above them dancers found that sodden draperies plastered themselves in all the wrong places. Other dancers huddled unhappily in the wings awaiting their cue, while the calcium lights hissed and steamed ominously and the flats shuddered and slapped like the mainsails of a rudderless ship.

The inclement weather was playing havoc with the filming schedules in Sans Souci Park, and burglars played havoc with the receipts of the first three days' performances. They blew up the safe and got away with $20,000, three-quarters of which belonged to Pavlova. There was no time to grieve, however; if the mornings dawned clear, there was pressure to get under way as soon as possible. Afternoons for Pavlova were invariably interrupted by matinees in the brick courtyard. Those locals who had time on their hands hung about the perimeters of the park in droves, curious about the comings and goings. On the day when the Smalleys invited Mary Pickford to meet Pavlova at the "studios," the rain settled in early. Undefeated crowds still crouched under umbrellas, scanning the faces of each arrival in the hope of seeing not Pickford, who was there incognito, but the mystery film star at the center of so much activity. One elegant limousine created a stampede, but it was merely a cameraman accompanying equipment swathed in coats to protect it from the damp. In the midst of the downpour Pavlova arrived on foot wearing canvas shoes, a dripping hat jammed over her ears and with no umbrella. The waif-like figure found no difficulty in slipping through the crowd. Inside, she announced cheerfully, "I like the rain—it is healthy. I walked all the way. It is good to feel the cold sweet air on the face." And she propped her little shoes in front of the fire to dry.

In all she worked for five weeks on the filming in Chicago. According to official time sheets, she managed to fit in from three to five hours a day, with five working days a week. (This meant that Pavlova's hourly take was working out at about $500.) Despite the disruptions, she was uncomplaining, punctual—and exact. If a time was set for her to be at the park for work, she was there, ready and waiting, to the minute. She left on the minute

MLLE. PAVLOWA'S OPINION OF CHICAGO WEATHER CONDITIONS CAN BEST BE EXPRESSED IN RUSSIAN.

ABOVE *Invitation to the Dance*, Midway Gardens, Chicago, summer 1915. The umbrellas appear to be a protection against the sun on this occasion.

BELOW During the filming of *The Dumb Girl of Portici*, with cameraman Dallen Clawson. Pavlova is dressed for *Danse Espagnol*, presumably for a matinee at the Midway Gardens.

One of Eugene Hutchinson's many superb portraits of Pavlova in *The Dumb Girl of Portici*.

too. She had her own timekeeper, who maintained a detailed record of her work periods. It was his duty to find out from Universal when she was wanted, and to establish, in advance, what time she would be permitted to leave. This was quite contrary to normal practice—working hours tended to be open-ended—but Pavlova purchased a stopwatch (which she called her "Portici watch"), and her work was entirely governed by it.

Although the initial rushes dismayed her, Pavlova quickly learned about the techniques needed in working close to a camera. Her fellow performers were happy to give her tips, and before long her acting was quite as compelling as that of any experienced movie actor in the production. The part of the dumb girl Fenella was a purely dramatic role, but Lois Weber was conscious of the great risk she was taking in denying audiences a view of Pavlova the dancer, so she devised three interludes, in the manner of "visions," with Pavlova drifting around on pointe. One scene contained a bit of trickery with a male dancer clad totally in black velvet acting as an invisible partner, which enabled Pavlova to make an airy ascent that denied gravity. Elsewhere in the film she was given some gypsy dances with a tambourine, filmed later on location in California.

The action of *The Dumb Girl of Portici* was placed in the seventeenth century, during the uprising of the people against the Viceroy of Naples. The fisherman Masaniello was their leader in a revolt against persecution and the increasing taxation that went to support a profligate court. The Viceroy's son, Alphonso, was in the habit of moving about among the common people incognito, and it was thus that he wooed lightheartedly Masaniello's sister, the beautiful but congenitally dumb Fenella, who fell in love with this dashing admirer. Alphonso was actually engaged to Elvira, a Spanish princess, so the deceit inevitably led to anguish and confrontations, in the best *Giselle*-like traditions of blighted love. The great crowd scenes centered on the revolutionary populace, armed only with clubs, confronting the pikemen and armored horsemen of the Viceroy in hand-to-hand battles, and then overrunning the palace in an orgy of destruction. Side plots were rampant. Some of the film's scenario made breathless reading:

The Duke [i.e., the Viceroy] hears of his son's amour and by a subterfuge snares Fenella. In jail the Duke has her flogged because she will not answer his questions. [She cannot, of course.] When the guards get drunk on the wedding day of Alphonso, she escapes from the cell. Bewildered by her surroundings Fenella, in rags, her back torn from the strokes of the lash, runs headlong into the wedding party. The princess senses the relationship between the dumb girl and her husband. The princess sets her free but the Duke throws her into jail again. She is freed when the mob breaking into the castle opens the prison doors. Alphonso and the princess flee and the dumb girl saves their lives. Masaniello is poisoned by a neighbor who hoped to marry Fenella, and [Masaniello] goes mad. Alphonso returns to his father's power, overturns the rule of the people, which has become debased since Masaniello's madness, and he is saved from death by Masaniello's sword, as Fenella jumps between them and receives the weapon. Masaniello then falls on his own sword.

It was at this point that the white-robed spirit of Fenella was seen dancing its way up through the clouds to some Elysian Fields of perpetual happiness.*

Despite the stopwatch and her enormous salary, finance was still a recurring worry for Pavlova as the plans for the opera and ballet tour were consolidated. She actually accepted a "donation" of $5,000 from an ardent fan, wealthy attorney Charles Dickinson Stickney, who assured her that she need not repay him if her touring enterprise was not a success. Stickney was a fifty-eight-year-old bachelor who occupied a box near the stage every night that Pavlova danced in New York. At one period it was assessed that the flowers sent by him to the Century had cost over $500, so it was not surprising when he told the dancer, "I'm rich enough to put some money in your art!" Despite the openness of the loan, Pavlova signed a promissory note.

In the first week of September, while Pavlova was back on the West Coast completing the filming of beach scenes for the movie, Rabinoff was able to make his preliminary public announcements in New York. It was revealed that he had acquired the properties (and many of the artists) of the Boston Opera Company after it had fallen on hard times, and at this point it

---

* Having seen the entire and uncut version of this epic, I can testify that it is a genuinely remarkable opus for the times, with large-scale effects that would be the envy of many contemporary film makers. Pavlova displays a vivid personality, and her dramatic effects are really no more overblown than those of her fellow professionals; it was a time when styles of film (melodrama, lyric romance, etc.) dictated the style of acting employed, and audiences knew which to expect. Some of the scenes in the film, such as the flogging and Fenella's incarceration in a cell swarming with very real rats, are quite disturbing. It is an exceptionally long film for the era.

Rehearsing *The Dumb Girl of Portici* on location in California, 1915.

was hoped that Pavlova's New York appearances would take place in Hammerstein's Lexington Opera House. It would be the first time that the big East Side building would house the type of entertainment for which it had been built. In fact, there were so many curious legal ramifications surrounding the theatre's attempting to compete with the Metropolitan that troubles were soon clouding that particular issue. So many important names had been gathered by Rabinoff that he felt some justification in calling the new company "The Pre-eminent Grand Opera Company." In the brochure this title was bracketed with the ballet's banner, which had become "The Pavlowa Imperial Russian Ballet"—no less. All this bombast was pretty quickly toned down once Pavlova arrived back from Los Angeles, and by the end of the month it was established that the billing would read "Boston Grand Opera Company in conjunction with Mlle. Anna Pavlowa and her Ballet Russe." Among the singers already signed were Maria Gay, Amelita Galli-Curci, and Maggie Teyte, as well as Marie Kouznetzova from the Imperial Opera in Petrograd. The orchestra of sixty musicians and the chorus of seventy were taken over directly from the Boston Opera Company.

All of this represented a huge undertaking even for a fixed base, but the whole organization was designed to tour, and on a weekly basis. Pavlova's coast-to-coast tours with the ballet had taken the art to areas where it had been scarcely envisaged, and it was pioneer work with a vengeance. But the Boston Grand

Opera Company tour was promising something very different: it was taking the format of Diaghilev's famed 1909 Paris season and saying, in effect, "Anything you've read about Paris, we are going to show you from St. Louis to Spokane." And they meant it. Diaghilev, for all his renowned energy, would never have contemplated a fraction of this present undertaking. The rash optimism of Rabinoff and the sheer bravery of Pavlova were astounding. Although Rabinoff was the titular managing director, it is clear that the force for the company's existence was Pavlova herself. It was her name and prestige that were singularly responsible for getting the bookings, and she, quite as much as Rabinoff or Dandré, had the experience of combined opera and ballet as it was presented at the Imperial Theatres in Russia, so that she contributed in large measure to the choice of programs. She was desperately concerned about standards and knew that opera in particular needed to be raised to a higher level than was usual in most areas. She was not playing at being Diaghilev; she was from the start providing an infinitely greater mixed repertoire than he had attempted in the 1909 Paris season. She chose to present several operas that were rarely heard, and revitalized an old standby like *Carmen* by including dances intended by the composer but subsequently abandoned. Outside New York, cities did not have a good record in the patronage of opera, and even Boston and Philadelphia, for all their pretensions in this field, had a frightening capacity for apathy.

The proud venture was launched on October 4 in the Auditorium Theatre in Chicago. There were no concessions to public ideas about the strict frontiers between opera and ballet: *La Muette de Portici* was performed, with the silent heroine played by the famous dancer. What could be more disconcerting?

Giovanni Zenatello was a Neapolitan fisherman, putting aside for the moment something of the elegance of the operatic tenor and playing into the part with the fire of his race. His voice had the dominating force that was not merely volume of tone for display, but seemed to sound a call to vengeance. Miss Felice Lyne made her Chicago debut as the Spanish Princess and showed both a pleasing personality and flexible voice, although not apparently quite at her ease in the opening aria. But it was rather the spirit of the whole performance that held the attention than the individual parts. Of course, lacking an extraordinary artist for the dumb girl it would fall apart, but Mme. Pavlowa gave the atmosphere for all that it was the thing itself and not individual display that was to count, and they all caught her spirit. . . .

The performance revealed one of our national weaknesses in that many people found it difficult to adjust themselves to the pantomime. They could tell it was brilliantly done, but it is a form of art to which they were not accustomed and they were not quite sure of their own feelings. . . . Could one who has earned a place so incontestable in one art also excel in another? The voice of authority had not spoken, and they hardly dared trust their own judgment. It may well be that this *Muette* will not find a permanent place in our modern repertory, but it was a thing well worth seeing and hearing again, and the performance by the combined forces of the Boston opera company and the Pavlowa ballet was one of distinction.

That reasoned assessment (with some more besides) was the first notice won by the new company, and it was on this optimistic note that they assembled the following day. Yet as if to underline the issue of who played the key part in the entire enterprise, despite her happy ability to integrate her performance into the operatic ensemble, there was the Boston *Monitor* headline: "Mimic Art of Mme. Pavlowa Wins Applause."

The company arrived in New York on October 24. The problems at the Lexington Opera House had proved insurmountable, and they were forced to go under the management of Comstock and Gest at the Manhattan Opera House for a two-week season. This was the program for the first week:

Monday	*La Muette de Portici*
Tuesday	*L'Amore dei Tre Re* followed by the Elysian Fields scene from Gluck's *Orfeo ed Euridice*
Wednesday	*The Fairy Doll* followed by *Snowflakes* at the matinee; *Carmen* in the evening
Thursday	*Madama Butterfly* followed by *Snowflakes*
Friday	*Otello*
Saturday	*Madama Butterfly* and *Snowflakes* at the matinee; *La Muette de Portici* in the evening

Nobody could complain that there was not something for every possible taste. Strikingly, Cio-Cio-San was played by the Japa-

Portraits by Eugene Hutchinson, Chicago, 1915: (above) in costume for *Danse Espagnol*.

The Boston Grand Opera Company production of *La Muette de Portici*, 1915: (right) with Pado Ananian.

nese soprano Tamaki Miura, with a novel and effective impersonation. A general assessment after the first week commented that "the reviewers, after the manner and the obligation of their kind, have found shortcomings in the performances, as after only three weeks of preliminary work there were bound to be. They have also found many things to commend." In an interview in the *New York Times,* Pavlova spoke of her hopes of introducing large-scale Russian works to foreign audiences:

I have wanted to conduct an opera company for many years, but never until now were the circumstances right. What interests me in having an opera company to work with instead of only a ballet is that much broader opportunities are offered. In the Russian school there are many pieces that combine mime and ballet work with operas and dramas. If our venture proves a success I have ambitious plans for broadening the scope, and making known some of those pieces, the existence of which is hardly even suspected here.

In a long article in its issue of November 13, *Harper's Weekly* brought up this very issue. After pointing out that the program in its current form was varied and already contained much that was new to the American public, it continued:

All this is, of course, extremely worthwhile and laudable. At the same time, however, one cannot but feel that a great opportunity is being let slip by. Just now the world is agog in search of everything Russian. Since the first season of Russian ballet, music-lovers have been fired with a desire to know more of the artistic expression of a country which had produced such marvelous dancers. That interest has continued to grow; lately the war has stimulated it. Now Pavlowa has been here, not simply with her corps de ballet, but as impresario of the Boston Opera Co. A great hope sprung up at the news of her undertaking. We felt sure that she would not content

herself with florid Italian operas and that she must draw upon the Russian store for the best expression of her art—operas where music is adjusted to the necessities of expression rather than to a display of technique, and where rhythmical expressiveness is emphasized by the ballet instead of acrobatics. She knows the wealth of sound and color at her disposal, but we must wait a little longer it seems. Yet it is just now that we turn almost instinctively to Russia for the satisfaction of our music hunger.

No allowances were made for Pavlova's involvement being little more than one month at that stage. In fact, on November 1 the *New York Times* had carried an article that gave fresh news on this subject:

Mlle. Anna Pavlowa, who has announced her intention of introducing Russian operas and choreographic works here with the Boston Opera Company, may obtain the cooperation of the Russian Imperial Opera Company, according to a statement sent out yesterday from the Manhattan Opera House, where the Boston organization is appearing. The statement is from Prince Peter Lieven, who is in this country representing the Russian government in financial matters connected with the war and war supplies. . . . While it is not represented that Prince Lieven is directly connected with Russian operatic institutions, the statement says that "his influence both at the Russian court and in all circles of society is unquestionable."

That was true, but the Tsar had a war on his hands. He had as well a disintegrating government, brought about by the corrosive influence of a maniacal monk and an interfering Empress, who pleaded—usually with success—that the Tsar accept the advice of "the Man of God." And wherever Rasputin's prime interest lay, it was not with the arts. Lieven was a roving satellite from an impotent bureaucratic machine.

Already there was a nervous assessment of the likely future pattern of attendances, since the houses were never really full, and the weekly outgoings were enormous; but takings, day by day, did at least show a steady—if not dramatic—increase. Philadelphia supported them tolerably for a week, and then it was time for Boston and the arrival of the phoenix with its resplendent new feathers.

Boston was the real testing ground, with four weeks in a city that had already shown its inability to sustain an operatic ensemble on anything other than restricted showings. As feared, its opera-goers now looked at the remarkably rich fare freshly provided, and picked at this or that, fussily. Some of the music critics were eager to chastise Auber no matter how well the general production underpinned the score of *La Muette de Portici,* while the audience had to adjust to accepting Pavlova as a purely mimic artist. Some were disturbed by this new Fenella. The Boston *Globe* thought that

> her suffering, her shame, her aspirations, her triumph in love over hate, and her noble sacrifice had vividity and often eloquence [but] its characteristic appeal was marred at times by exaggeration. There was incongruous and disturbing restlessness. In the first act she embodied hysteria rather than suggested it; [however] the scene of self-abnegation in her brother's hut was done with transforming beauty.

This was the intensity of characterization that chilled some people when it took form as Giselle. But of the same performance, the Boston *Monitor* had no difficulty responding to this vivid Fenella:

> Not once throughout the entire evening did she lose the feeling of that Neopolitan maiden that flashed through the scene like a burn-

ing flame. The fire of that passion that burns under the southern sun was in her every move and gesture, each glance of her eye, and in the spirit that animated her. She sketched the whole outline of the story with a force no one could miss and that gained even greater power from the silence of her tongue amid all the thunder of the stage.

This critic was well aware of Auber's weaknesses to the modern ear, but he was all for the revival as an experiment worth the undertaking.

During the second act of *Carmen* on November 16, Lindovska began a letter to her mother:

> It was not a very good house last night. I think it is better tonight. The newspapers write very well about everything, it all depends upon the houses how long we stop here, and I have heard the whole company may smash. What is to happen after Boston nobody knows. Some think Pavlova may go into vaudeville.... I have just heard from someone who has been in the public—they say the house is empty. It really is serious.

A few days later she took up the letter where she had left off:

> We had a lesson this morning and a rehearsal for Chopin. Two more new girls have come. They are not even good dancers. We are furious about it. Business is so bad they can't possibly give us a raise—in fact later on salaries might have to be cut down—and yet they can afford new girls and their *mothers.* Maybe they are paying to come. Tonight we should be playing *La Muta di Portici,* but the tenor is very ill so the programme has to be changed.

Toward the end of her letter, Winifred added the news that, for once, there would be no special Christmas celebration within the group. This seems to suggest that Pavlova's finances were so

severely depleted she felt unable to indulge in her usual extravagant round of presents for the company.

The distinguished music critic Henry Taylor Parker wrote an article summing up the first half of the Boston season in the Boston *Evening Transcript*. Headlined "Pavlova and Her Opera," it emerged as a lucid appraisal of the situation that could stand as the full-term report on an artistic gamble of heroic proportions:

Perseverance is not the least of Miss Pavlova's virtues. Having embarked upon an undertaking and having accomplished it to the utmost of her ability and means, she does not whimper and complain, if for a time the public remains indifferent. Ambition, faith and will sustain her while she waits for it to discover the pleasures she has set before it and, as her experience has gone, especially in this town of Boston, it usually finds them out. For a fortnight, her forces at the Opera House have been giving the best performances of opera that a touring company has accomplished here in recent years. . . . In fine, the whole quality of the performances has risen well above the level that the defunct Boston Opera Company used to maintain. True, the public was none too eager for it; but until the end of last week it seemed even less well-disposed toward its successor.

Meanwhile Miss Pavlova and all her associates patiently endured undeserved neglect. Nobody lectured the town as though the hearing of opera and the watching of ballets was an "obligation" or anything but a pleasure like other entertainment in the theatre. Nobody prated in the old silly fashion about the "educational" or the "social" or the "communal" value of opera. Nobody made large and vague promises for the future or embarked on the vexed question whether it were better for Boston to make another attempt to maintain an opera of its own or rest content with the visits of the Metropolitan or of touring companies. Instead, with a wisdom, will and faith that was the fine crown of unrewarded efforts, all concerned did their utmost to make the performances as pleasurable as possible, hopeful that sooner or later the tide of public indifference would turn. Seemingly, it has. There was a considerable audience for *La Bohème* and *Chopiniana* on Friday; there was a yet more numerous one for *Madama Butterfly* on Saturday afternoon; it was by no means small for the dances of Saturday evening. From the beginning the public of the cheaper places has been quick to discover that the most pleasurable opera Boston has known in five or six years awaited them; now the public of the dearer places seems to be awakening as well. A little more and Miss Pavlova's faith and—what is more important—her practice will enter upon the reward that they deserve.

Of all these trials and tribulations, of all this strain of hoping and waiting, there has not been a hint in Miss Pavlova's own dancing and miming. She has been as busy as ever by day with the rehearsal of a ballet that from various causes has been much changed in personnel; by night she has danced with a beauty, a fire, a mingled play of technical skill, quickening imagination and poetizing glamor that she has never before in Boston attained so completely or sustained so evenly. If she bears now some of the burdens of management, she has not to dance evening after evening through two or three unbroken hours of the ballet; and, she has gained accordingly in alertness of unfatigued body and in quickness of

On tour in America. A rare moment of repose.

unspent spirit. In the mimed scene from Gluck's *Orpheus*, she and her dancers wrought poetic illusion of remote and spiritualized figures in tranquil play in their Elysium; in the Spanish dances of *Carmen*, she struck pictorial and rhythmic fire until the stage blazed with it; in *Snowflakes* she summoned the formal beauty of the old "classic" ballet and glamorized it with her visualizing and suggesting imagination; in the Egyptian dances from *Aida*, she and her train carved upon the air the reliefs of the monuments in line and color; in *Coppélia* she was matchless among the dancers of our time in the illusion of the playfulness, the archness, the quick-coming moods, the gay humors and the passing chagrins of Swanilda and the beauty of line, the finesse of detail, the rhythmic elan, the variety of aspect and suggestion that she imparted to her dances.

In the moonlit glade and to the music of Chopin, last Friday, Miss Pavlova was like a being all compact of white light and white fire, cleaving the air with its own beauty or hanging for an instant radiant upon it. In *Amarilla* on Saturday, she danced as one enkindled with a flame-like ardor of motion and ardor of spirit, as though each instant brought new impulse. It was like to rhapsody, yet it was unerring. At the same time her mimed suggestion of the gypsy girl's hopes and fears and longings before the lover that will now have none of her touched equally the eye and the heart. All that her miming had lacked in *The Dumb Girl* of implicit and human suggestion was now incarnate in it. All the fire of Amarilla burned through her dancing; all the wistfulness and the piteousness of the girl shone clear in her miming. Then, as it were in a moment, Miss Pavlova was the shimmering, the playful, the fairy-tale figure of her ballet of the toy-shop, all innocent grace, all gay sparkle, writing her bravura of the dance upon the eye as lightly as the singer writes her ornaments of song upon the ear. Once more, in the "divertissements" she mimed the dying swan, idealizing every drooping motion into the white loveliness of her picturing; or rose, an Undine from the waters, fascinating and enchaining mortal youth in the bonds of a strange beauty of pale motion and still suggestion.* Once more, as in the ballet of the Elysian Fields, Miss Pavlova wrote with her body the poetry of her spirit. To an indifferent public and with the cares of an opera company upon her, never in all her visits to Boston has she danced with such perfection of accomplishment, with such fire or spirit, with such fulness of imagination and with such poetry of illusion as are now hers. To see her now is to see her at the very acme of her powers.

The dances interpolated into *Carmen* became so popular with audiences that a suite, called *Spanish Dances*, was put together by Clustine and thereafter given after operas that did not allow for any dance in their scenarios, such as *Rigoletto* and *La Bohème*. It made a long evening, with four intermissions, but it appealed to the public, and that was justification enough. It was noticed that Pavlova varied her "Spanish" style between the opera dances and the new divertissement: "This Carmen is schooled in the coquetry of Andalusia. And she could wind up the day with a dance on the table—no reckless, scatterwit table dance, but a poetic one, and with Spanish dignity kept, just the same as on the floor." The *Spanish Dances* were actually presented against the

Spanish Dances, 1915.

---

*This was *Undine*, in effect a solo for Pavlova, enlarged in January 1916 to a company work, under the title *Undines* (also known as *The Ondines*).

Rondo, 1916.

second-act set of *Carmen,* but the lighting was radically altered for a night scene, with the balconied court of the tavern awash with shadowy pools of light, and an indigo sky glimpsed between the arches, which were hung with glowing orange lamps. The whole thing was likened to a Sargent painting. The music was a series of fragments from Massenet *(Le Cid),* Moskowski *(Boabdil),* and Glazunov. (Pavlova led the Panaderos from *Raymonda* at one point.) Elsewhere, the dancers were allowed to be vocal, with cries of "Olé!" punctuating their handclapping.

Pavlova added to the company's repertoire constantly: in *Aida* she restored the ballet to the second act; she put the rarely heard Humperdinck *Hansel and Gretel* back on the stage; and she added to the ballet divertissements. One such confection was called *Danse des Roses,* described as "perhaps the most successful from the popular pictorial standpoint. . . . Roses fell and fell from the ceiling onto the poised figures of the girls in their pale scarfs, in their rose-colored dresses, and on the charming head of the woman who has plotted so much beauty, devised so many dreams and re-created an ancient art."

But as December came in, murky and chill, the rumors that the company was in danger of imminent financial collapse assumed painful substance. The New York Calcium Light Company had already felt impelled to sue Pavlova and Rabinoff for the recovery of a thousand dollars due on the rental of apparatus. Their argument was that receipts that might normally have gone to the ballet side of the organization (the all-ballet matinees were usually full) got siphoned straight into the parent company, so that the Pavlova Ballet seemed to be without assets. Dandré and Rabinoff must have known what they were up to—and Pavlova was probably still making up the initial $75,000 investment—but $1,500 had to be paid into court at this juncture, pending a hearing of the case.

Pavlova faced the situation in Boston bravely and with dignity. She did not plead for support but made a reasoned statement to the press about her hopes and aspirations:

The greatest artistic efforts of myself and of our company will be concentrated in the final four performances of the Boston Grand Opera Company and the Russian Ballet, next Monday, Tuesday and Wednesday. It is my confident hope that the house will be crowded on these last days of our stay in Boston. . . . We have tried to arrange for the final series as comprehensive a repertoire as possible, one that would give the artists their best opportunity before their "home folks," as you Americans say. I want to take this opportunity to thank the people of Boston and to say that I am gratified at the appreciation that they have shown us, at the praise we have received at their hands, and at the many opinions expressed that ours has been the best operatic effort ever made in Boston. This praise and this appreciation has served as a great encouragement to me and my associates, and I cannot help but see in them the harbingers of better days to come. Whatever may be the ultimate result, it shall ever be a source of great pride to me that it is generally acknowledged that we have maintained the highest artistic ideals, and I am happy in the belief that our sacrifices have not been entirely in vain.

On December 21 Pavlova made an appearance at Mrs. Astor's home during an evening organized to raise money for Serbian refugees, and she and Volinine danced in a Sunday evening concert at the Hippodrome five nights later, while the company was in Atlantic City. They played Baltimore for two nights, and Wilmington for two nights, before arriving in Philadelphia for the New Year. This brought with it a sinister knell: Rabinoff was forced to declare the company technically bankrupt. Pavlova was deeply committed to the concept of the whole venture, quite apart from feeling a loyalty to the individual singers, who had given their best to make the performances noteworthy, and she was determined that the group should not be disbanded summarily. She made the decision to finance the salaries and the day-to-day running expenses herself. It was a frightening risk, and she was pinning her faith on the fact that the itinerary was taking them back to New York, where her personal prestige was perhaps held highest; but the wires had been humming, and every preplanned move encountered freshly erected obstacles. There was a make-or-break fortnight in which to get the whole cumbersome caravan on the move again, and a handful of ballet performances at the Forty-fourth Street Theatre during the first days of 1916 were barely enough to keep the creditors at bay.

In order to provoke some interest, a new one-act ballet was presented: *L'Ecole en Crinoline,* to various bits of music by Chaminade. Pavlova played Emilie, Kobelev Pierrot, and Zalevski a curate. One of the girls was the schoolmistress and the remainder filled in as pupils. The ballet's scenario was devised by a Mrs. Christian Hemmick; in Baltimore on December 28 Clustine had been credited with the "arranging," but now he was listed as "Choreographic Director." If Pavlova was trying to give a budding female choreographer the encouragement of seeing her work mounted on stage, the gesture does not appear to have spawned a blazing talent, and the work was soon put aside.

Pavlova made two more appearances in Sunday concerts; at the final one, on January 16, she gave *The Swan* and then *Rondo,* a new solo with a lot of flirtatious use of an eye-glass, to a Kreisler adaptation of a Beethoven theme. Pavlova and Volinine also danced the *Gavotte,* and another novelty, Sousa's waltz "Land of the Golden Fleece." Sousa, who was conducting, managed to disregard a planned cut, so that the dancers were almost on their knees by the end, having had to perform repeats and improvisations while the conductor beamed happily at their efforts to accommodate a seemingly endless stream of his own music. (Afterward he explained that he had not forgotten the cut, but that the dancing was so beautiful he could not bear to shorten it!)

Pavlova and Volinine left New York before they were confronted with some of the new advertisements that were helping to pay for the company's progress—endorsements for such as Cutex Liquid Polish: "'My hands, too, must dance . . .' says charming Anna Pavlova." Diaghilev was in town—his company opened at the Century the night following the Hippodrome concert—and one wonders what he must have thought of an Impe-

Anna Pavlowa paints as well as dances. When she has a fence or a balustrade to paint on her summer place at Los Angeles she is happy.

Pavlova was a never-ending source of news for American reporters.

rial ballerina so wedded to base commerce. But at that stage he could desperately have done with such a dancer; his ballerina was the solid Maclezova. Pavlova had looked in on the rivals at their dress rehearsal.

Fortified with renewed confidence, a great many paper guarantees, and the willing support of the other artists, the massive company set off once more. The new schedule seldom allowed for more than two or three performances in any given place; Cleveland was an exception with four, while Grand Rapids, Detroit, and Toledo only got one evening each, which meant that the progress was as frenetic as that previously experienced by the ballet company—only now there were tons more scenery, more musicians, more staff, more everything. The chorus alone was twice the number of the original corps de ballet. Pavlova's return to places like Nashville could not have been in greater contrast to her previous appearances. Now they were being shown in that city's principal theatre, the Vendome, but Pavlova's abiding memory of her first visit was of a performance that took place in a mission hall, with a decorous audience sitting in pews. She had changed in the organ loft and then descended, imperturbably, to dance the *Bacchanale*.

The progression was relentless, and while thousands of miles were logged by train, thousands of figures mounted up in the ledger books. But, precariously, these figures balanced, and the

accountants did not feel impelled to snap the books shut and lock the chequebooks away, so that when rumors began circulating from Otto Kahn's office at the Metropolitan Opera in New York to the effect that Diaghilev would be predisposed to Pavlova's leading his forthcoming season there, Rabinoff was quick to react. He was down, but not entirely out, and was not admitting that Pavlova's contract had expired and that she was committed to the tour rather than to her director. She kept going, with a judicious leavening of ballet often given at the conclusion of an opera. In Cincinnati on February 1 there had been a new "Egyptian" ballet by Clustine, to music of Luigini; and even if it owed as much to Ruth St. Denis's cavortings as to Fokine, it had novelty value for most people. And the new ballet, *The Ondines*, quickly established itself in the repertory at this time.

The success of the *Dumb Girl* film had become a matter of importance to Pavlova. She had initially agreed to the project as a temporary expedient; but she was hoping to gain some screen reputation—not because she wanted to be a movie star, but because her marketable value in that area would act as a form of collateral for her other endeavors. She also held a half-interest in the profits of the film. It had been seen in San Francisco at the end of January 1916, but it did not go into general release until the beginning of April. In New York it opened at the Globe Theatre; unusually, it also opened in several other states simultaneously. The New York premiere coincided with the opening of the Diaghilev season at the Metropolitan. They were without Nijinsky, since the ship bringing him and his family to America, after his release from internment, was not due to dock until the following day. Pavlova was actually performing in Salt Lake City on that night, but she managed to scoop the theatre page headlines in New York:

PAVLOWA AGAIN IS "INCOMPARABLE"
ON THE SCREEN
Achieves Wonderful Triumph in Picture
"The Dumb Girl of Portici"
SPLENDID FILM DRAMA
Auber's Opera "Masaniello"
Furnishes a Story of Unusual Power

To the many who have seen her as a dancer in the flesh and to the many more who have not because of the prohibitive prices, Anna Pavlowa, the inimitable, proved a revelation because of her wonderful power as an actress.... Pavlowa, in her first attempt, has revealed so marvelous a histrionic ability as to call from many in the brilliant first-night audience the opinion that she would make the greatest Carmen of them all. If the great film plays of recent years can be superlatived [*sic*], the consensus of opinion would place *Cabiria* at the head as a spectacle, *The Birth of a Nation* for emotional thrill, *Carmen* for individual force, and *The Dumb Girl of Portici* for artistry. But in all fairness to Mme. Pavlowa's production, it must be said that, although it stands pre-eminently as the artistic picture of the year, if not of all other years, it combines in high degree the other three qualities. The picture is as big as it is beautiful, and gives the new film-star an opportunity for the display of every emotion, every one of which is done in a most original way.

It must have been an unusual occurrence for an acclaimed new movie star to be absent from her own premiere. But Pavlova had five more weeks to go before the long haul of the tour was due to end, and though she had every excuse for calling a halt, she was determined to see it through to the end. Meanwhile, *The Dumb Girl* soon picked up the tag of an "all women's" production, about which feminists were said to be especially enthusiastic; many women's clubs were buying blocks of seats and attending en masse. Despite widespread enthusiasm for Pavlova, and for the production in general, occasional adverse reaction was inevitable because the dancer's name carried the production; yet she did not provide a continuous display of the skill for which she was best known. There were, too, some references to the fact that Pavlova did not possess a conventionally pretty "screen" face.

Rabinoff's five-year option on Pavlova's services had expired (along with his bank account), and this meant that, by the spring of 1916, Pavlova was free to accept any new offers. For a short time she toyed with the idea of embarking from San Francisco on a Pacific tour, with ballet only. It was plain that the opera venture was at an end—an honorable end, of that there was no question—but the financial sacrifice had been massive,

and it would take a lengthy period of further unremitting work for the inroads to be repaired. There was talk of Hawaii, of Australia, even of the Orient: "I believe the Orient will give me many ideas for new dances, especially the Hindoo and Japanese," she had said in an interview on the West Coast. Pavlova also spoke of Ivy House, though she could hardly get farther from home.

"It is a great big place with, oh, so many windows for letting in the sunshine. It is not to live for show there, no, no. It is to live for life, you understand?

"A garden? Oh yes, a very big one, with all sorts of flowers. I dig the flowers, and work with them, make them bloom all summer, and get myself dirty like a pig, yes?" She laughed and clapped her hands at this idea. "I own birds, too, and they sing for me, and I like best the wild birds. And never am I home in summertime but I think of many plans for dances and costumes. One dance I do is from watching the hovering of a butterfly, another a hummingbird. And their colors suggest gowns.

"I have many friends lost in the war, yes; and often when I must dance I am sad. Tonight I have a letter from a dear friend in London; her husband is just killed in the war. He, too, was my friend. But one must think of the people out in front, so that you not make them sad too, is it not so?"

She did not mention that Ivy House was being used as a hospital for wounded officers. Like Isadora Duncan, Maud Allan was a "dear friend" of Pavlova's: "Miss Allan has a room in my London house that's her own whenever she cares to use it."

Pavlova had recently lost her Pekinese, Purchok ("Powder Puff"), and the replacement was a Boston terrier bought in Los Angeles and named Poppy. The new recruit quickly had to get used to the traveling, just as Purchok had done. During the week she was at the Mason Opera House in Los Angeles, Pavlova attended a rodeo and was very impressed by the activity, particularly the skill of the riders. Though her voice was usually withheld from the public, it was noted that here its staccato sweetness filled the air as she cried "Bravo!" at the events that excited her most. A small boy sold her peanuts, and when he was told who his famous client was, he returned and asked to have one of the peanuts back to remember her by. He got it, and a kiss as well. Pavlova loved children, but there was obviously no place in her life for any of her own; indeed, she sometimes hinted that there was a physical reason that precluded the possibility. For years she carried in her handbag a newspaper clipping of a woman posing with her thirteen children. "You see," Pavlova would exclaim, unfolding the faded relic time and again, "she has so many children, and I have none." Instead, the characters she created on stage became a sort of family, just as the loyal team of her household was. They were the familiars who seldom altered, even though their surroundings were an endlessly blurring kaleidoscope of hotels and theatres and railway carriages.

Work was the anodyne, the insidious drug that could not be denied, and now it hovered perpetually, just beyond the field of vision, as a coachman to a horse in harness. When asked if it was not all terribly hard work, she replied, "Oh yes; one could not do

Scenes from the film *The Dumb Girl of Portici*.

On the steps of the Hollywood Hotel, June 1916: (bottom) Vajinsky, Stuart, Plaskowieczka, Volinine; (middle) Saxova, an actor, Pavlova, a local friend, Stier, a local friend; (top) Dandré.

it if one did not love it. I love my art, and always want to use it." Like all dancers, Pavlova had submitted her body to physical stress for so long that the acceptance of all those little pains and agonies had become a mental ritual. All dancers are masochistic to a greater or lesser degree, but in Pavlova's case there was also a compulsion to give pleasure and joy to others until, it seemed, she was being torn apart. The more the audience called her back to the footlights, the more she played up to its demands, devising fresh ways to assuage the clamor until it had spent itself, satisfied. She did not appear to derive excessive gratification from the outpouring of the audience; it was merely the confirmation that a need existed.

When, sometimes, Pavlova gave the appearance of resenting the warmth of applause afforded others, it was not from so basic an emotion as jealousy. It was a combination of things. It was a demonstration that her own contribution had perhaps not been sufficiently far-reaching; it was proof that she was not entirely irreplaceable and thus an undermining of her belief in the essential nature of her "mission"; and it was sometimes a clear-eyed assessment of a fellow performer: she could be aroused to fury by an undiscerning audience, considering it a betrayal of standards.

The impresario Charles Dillingham had secured the services of Pavlova when he and Florenz Ziegfeld had taken over the running of the Century in New York from the struggling Dippel. There was some degree of secrecy surrounding her capture, and although it was never actually stated that she would appear at the Century, she was committed to that management very shortly after the Boston Grand Opera Company gave its final performance on May 7, in Dillingham's Hippodrome. On that particular evening there had been another gala concert, with John Philip Sousa conducting. He did his own arrangement of Rubinstein's "Valse Caprice" for the occasion. At the end of the evening, Pavlova went before the curtain and made what was thought to be an exceptionally charming speech of farewell.

For a while it was still not clear whether she would appear next at Dillingham's Century Theatre or at the vast Hippodrome; but one thing was certain: she would undertake a South American tour in the spring of 1917 (at this point it was thought the tour would begin in April), and it would be for the impresario Adolfo Bracale. Then came the big news: Pavlova would be the star attraction at the Hippodrome in a vast new vaudeville show, which Dillingham was planning for an early opening in late summer. The ballerina had decided to present herself in that touchstone from childhood, *The Sleeping Beauty*. It would have to be a condensed version, but it would bring Tchaikovsky to the masses, as well as more than a hint of Petipa's genius, and it would have the panoply of the most famous stage designer in the world, Léon Bakst. Pavlova was to receive a fee of $8,500 a week, from which she would pay her own company salaries in the usual way. It was a handsome recompense.

At the beginning of June, Pavlova was back on the West Coast. When she arrived at the Beverly Hills Hotel, it was thought that her presence must be in connection with the film industry, though she professed she was taking a vacation. A release stated that she did not intend any picture work that summer—"at least she has contracted for none so far." The columnists thought she would take a house either in Hollywood or at the beach, which was a safe assumption; but as was usual with Pavlova, restlessness soon set in, and she was off again before the end of the month, having persuaded Volinine and a small group of girls to join her in some concert appearances around southern California, including three performances at the Majestic Theatre in Los Angeles and one at the Potter Theatre in San Diego. It was a mixed bill, with divertissements and musical interludes provided by two ladies, a pianist and a violinist. Pavlova never danced fewer than six items in an evening: four duets with Volinine and two solos. On June 25 she caused some excitement in San Diego when she appeared as guest of honor at a reception given at the headquarters of the Women's Board of the Panama-Pacific International Exposition. In the Art Palace of the great fair in San Francisco there could be seen a number of Malvina Hoffman's bronzes based on Pavlova, with various partners.

Pavlova's name was often in the headlines. Toward the end of July there was space devoted to her thoughts on musicality in dancing. She created something of a stir by announcing that dancers did not need a sense of time, and that in fact it was often a handicap. She then qualified this by pointing out that rhythmic instinct was something different:

> Time is a simple matter. It consists merely in keeping track of the beat, which in most music is fairly obvious. But a sense of rhythm, that is something different. Without a highly developed sense of rhythm no one can dance really well. A too accurate sense of time, on the other hand, often interferes with good dancing.... Technique is a necessity, of course, but an artist must always guard against becoming too dependent on it. Even within the limits of technique, it is possible to make every performance of a dance, to a certain degree, spontaneous and self-expressive.

In an earlier interview, she had propounded an ambition startling for the time:

> It has been my dream to perfect the dancing of myself and of my company to the extent that music should become only an accentuation instead of the dominating factor. I have no doubt that this is possible, for whenever I think of new dances, these dances suggest tonalities to me. I am not a composer, so I could not express in black dots the music that is running through my brain, but I can hear it, and so could the audience, provided the plastic art of the dancers could be brought to perfection.... When we speak of

Anna Pavlowa and Her Ballet Master, M. Christine, on the Lawn of Her Hollywood Bungalow.
Motion Picture World Oct. 30, 1915

SHOULDER ARMS! The inimitable Charlie and the incomparable Anna smile for the camera man in the California sunshine outside the former's Hollywood studios, during Mme. Pavlova's recent visit to Los Angeles. Sans the Chaplin mustache and derby, the screen comedian is an even less familiar figure to the public eye than is the famous dancer all dolled up in her best tailor-made.

ABOVE Bakst's program cover for *The Sleeping Beauty* at the
New York Hippodrome, showing Pavlova "in flight."

BELOW The original photograph was of a pose from the Elysian Fields
ballet in *Orfeo*. It was turned on its side, and the resulting image
became the logo for the Hippodrome's "Big Show."

music creating certain pictures in the minds of the hearers we state an incontrovertible fact, and it is logical to suppose that dancing should call forth a melody in the brain of those who witness it, provided, in both cases, that the respective art has reached a high mark.

No doubt should I or somebody else decide upon presenting a ballet without the musical accompaniment the idea would be greeted with derision. But it would be an interesting experiment, making every man and woman his or her own composer, and if the dancers possessed the necessary talent it would be well worth while. I am planning to try the experiment of a ballet without music some day. Of course it would have to be before an invited audience, for the innovation would be too radical to attract the masses; besides I do not believe anybody would be willing to pay for a performance of that kind.

Pavlova and her company began rehearsals for *The Sleeping Beauty* at the Seventy-first Regiment Armory in New York. Clustine had carved up the big ballet into four principal scenes that together added up to fifty minutes: the Christening was followed by the traditional Birthday scene, which allowed the audience its first glimpse of Pavlova; then came the Vision scene, which was followed by a panorama for the Prince's journey; next was the Awakening; and finally, there was the Wedding, in which Pavlova wore heeled slippers and was given a less taxing pas de deux in the manner of a stately court dance, similar to her *Gavotte*. Another innovation was the introduction of operatic recitatives to explain the story line at some points.

Bakst was sending his designs piecemeal from Europe via his London agent as he completed them, until finally only the design for one of Pavlova's costumes was missing. The days passed, and Dillingham actually detailed one of his staff to voyage to London to track it down. But while the quest was in progress, the Adams Express Company gave notice that a small package from London awaited identification; it had Dillingham's name on it, but no address. Inside was the missing art work. Pavlova's principal costume had a wide, panniered skirt, and she had to wear a towering golden wig decked with ostrich feathers and ropes of pearls.

The new Hippodrome spectacle was mounted by R. H. Burnside, and for want of a better title it had come to be known during its formative days as "The Big Show." Dillingham rather warmed to that description and decided to keep it. Everything was big in truth: the billboards, the quotes ("Bigger and Better Than Ever"), the Hippodrome itself. Even Pavlova became big. The publicists took a photograph of the dancer on demi-pointe and wearing the loose costume from the Elysian Fields ballet from *Orfeo*. They then silhouetted the figure, with all its ballooning draperies, and laid it horizontally against a background of fluffy white clouds. Thus converted and enlarged, Pavlova appeared to be zooming through the air like some female version of Batman. She was horrified when she first saw the result, but the publicity experts were pleased with the effect, and the image was reproduced in all The Big Show's classified advertising. It became synonymous with the Hippodrome, where, as they were

Rehearsing *The Sleeping Beauty*, August 1916:

LEFT (top) Backstage discussion with (left to right) rehearsal pianist Alexander Smallens, Stier, Volinine, Pavlova, and Clustine; (bottom) Volinine, Pavlova, Clustine, and an unidentified woman, possibly a singer

BELOW Volinine and Pavlova working out.

ABOVE Bakst's costumes for the Maids of Honor in *The Sleeping Beauty*:
(left) Linda Lindovska; (right) Muriel Stuart.

BELOW Pavlova with some of her leading girls in *The Sleeping Beauty*:
Stuart, Plaskowieczka, Kuhn, Smoller, Butsova, and Leggeriova.

quick to point out, everything was big but the prices. The name "Pavlowa" was often printed the same size as the title of the show. She was further billed as "the Incomparable," and under her name some bright fellow came up with one further exotic line: "Dwarfs the Grandeur of the Durbar."

There were several previews at the end of August, and the critics were able to have their say after the opening on August 31. This was the New York *Tribune's* assessment:

It is noteworthy that, for the first time, beauty has invaded the mammoth playhouse. There has been much that was novel and striking in various effects produced at the big theater in previous years, but it has remained for Bakst to bring the beautiful. Strangely enough, not the scenery, but the costumes, are the triumphant feature of the work which the Russian artist has contributed to the Pavlowa ballet. . . .

The Sleeping Beauty in four tableaus is interesting and at times enchanting, but it is not a thing of joy in its entirety. The ballet is not Russian and it is not American. It lacks coherence. Pavlowa, however, delighted the audience. This great dancer has not all the fire which she once possessed, but her art flames as brightly as ever. Classical dancing of the finest sort was shown by her. It is a pleasure to watch Pavlowa dance, since you can applaud her without being told when. Then too, we have always admired her art because she is the only toe dancer in the world who has not fat legs. The best part of the entertainment is Russian, for Russia contributed the ballet, the costumes and scenery of Bakst and the music of Tschaikowsky. . . .

America is creditably represented by "The Mammoth Minstrels," "400—Count 'em—400," says the program. We did, and it added up to 418, so there is no deception. . . . The performance begins with a street parade and Powers's elephants, which do a ball game. This year they are imitating the Giants, and the elephant with the bat hits nothing. The second number is a strange thing called "The Revenge of the Lions." It consists of a more or less meaningless motion picture [it was an animal hunt in Africa] and then a scene where a man with an iron bar and a whip annoys a lot of unoffending lions shamelessly. Just what revenge the lions get was not made apparent, but whatever it is they deserve it. "Somewhere in Spiritland" follows the lions. This will be an effective number later on, but last night, through a mishap, it was marred by falling bits of scenery, one of which nearly carried away a girl who was dancing on a piano in mid-air. Maybe it will be a lesson to her not to dance on a piano again. Later, as a startling finale to the ballet, a number of chorus girls were raised high on wires. But with the memory of the earlier aviatrix well in mind, none looked particularly happy. George Hermann pleased in a dancing specialty, and so did Toto in one of his stunts. Frank Fogerty followed, and learned to his chagrin that the Hippodrome was much too big for a Ford joke. However, the pair who came after decided to forgive and forget. "We'll Stand by Our Country" was the burden of their song, and two effective tableaus followed of West Pointers and naval cadets. The entertainment is indeed a big show, and, like the Matterhorn, William H. Taft, the Atlantic Ocean and all big things, it has its bad and its good spots.

The *Tribune's* reporter was Heywood Broun (he had suffered at the hands of a ballerina, having been jilted by Lopokhova), and

The Sleeping Beauty: (below) with Volinine.

ABOVE & OPPOSITE *The Sleeping Beauty,* in Bakst's costume for Aurora's wedding.

238

he went to file his story before midnight, thus missing a huge ice ballet, "The Merry Doll," which preceded a ten-minute solo spot by a skater named Charlotte, "The Pavlowa of the Ice." (*Musical America,* with a certain one-upmanship, saw fit to describe Charlotte as "a Karsavina on skates.") As one reporter said succinctly: "The Big Show should diet."

A great many supernumeraries were required to stand around in *The Sleeping Beauty* in order to fill the stage, and as the days progressed it became clear that this human padding was doing nothing for Petipa's original concept. Twice a day they filed on and off, gum-chewing automatons who felt like shift workers and who betrayed the thought. "Apparently no one can mold a Hippodrome chorus into the semblance of a ballet worthy of Mme. Pavlowa," wrote one critic. "With all its shortcomings, however, the second act of the show will attract thousands daily. Mme. Pavlowa herself is sufficient for that." Although it was thought that she was "a jewel in a garish setting," she was undoubtedly the star, and five thousand people at each performance caught a glimpse of the quality that had earned her such a position. The New York *Herald* was quite clear as to where the honors lay; the headline ran: "Pavlowa and Bakst Heighten New Pageant at Hippodrome."

There were many stars, and the greatest of these was Pavlowa, Anna the Great, probably the most famous of woman dancers, certainly the greatest that American theatregoers have seen. She is the new acquisition at the Hippodrome, and she promises to be the most notable single star the house has ever had. She appeared against a background of scenery by her countryman Leon Bakst, master of color, who also designed the costumes. *The Sleeping Beauty,* a ballet in four tableaux, from Charles Perrault's story with Tschkarkowsky's [sic] music, served to present Pavlowa and her company, including the high-bounding A. Volinine. The little star danced as she alone can. She danced alone and with the corps. Never did she dance better. The entire second act was given over to her. She was worth it. The ballet told a pretty story with the engagement of the prince and princess at the end. Of course she was the princess and Volinine was the prince. The Bakst decorations evoked "Ohs" and "Ahs" and various and divers "Wonderfuls" all over the house. Just before the curtain the flying ballet comes down to the footlights and then flies almost to the top of the proscenium where it forms a semicircle in mid air and awaits the curtain, which ascends [sic] and hides it from view.

The organization of the entire show, quite apart from the ballet section, which in itself was complex, was similar to that of an army in the field. The hundreds of performers and stage staff would begin to check in at the stage door on Forty-third Street around one o'clock for the matinee. Curiously, the advertisements for the Hippodrome seldom bothered to say when the matinees started, but it was the sort of show that unwound like a frieze, and it was not absolutely vital where one began. There were soon changes in the running order, so that the circus procession with the elephants took place downstage, while behind the drop curtain carpenters and property men were given more time to construct the representation of the Capitol in Washing-

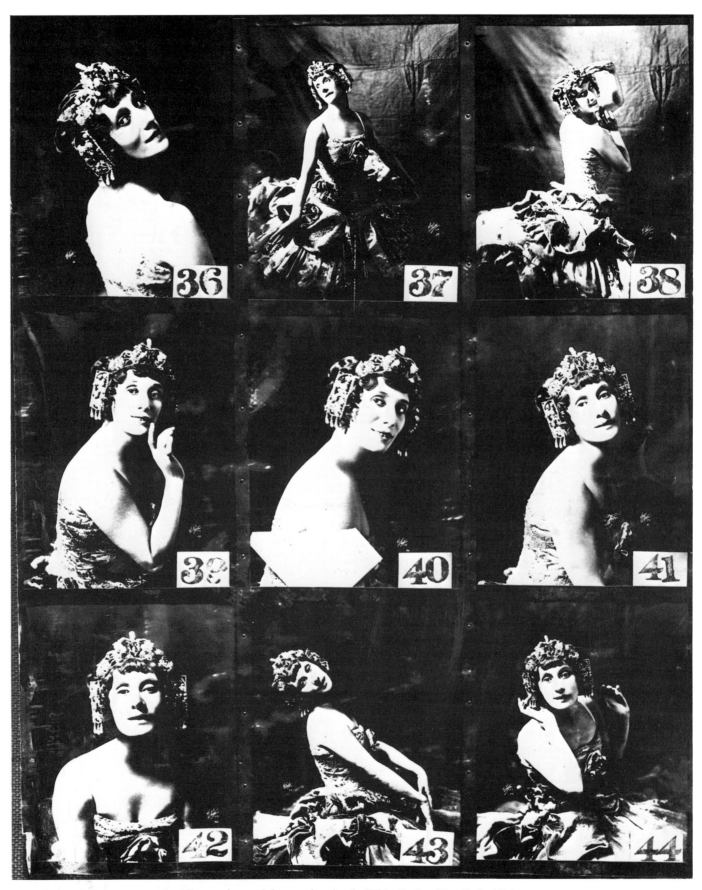

Contact sheets of photographs taken by White Studios, New York, 1916:
(above) Pavlova in Bakst's all-gold costume for Act One; (opposite) scenes from The Big Show, including
the dancer twirling on the piano in midair, and Charlotte, "The Pavlowa of the Ice."

ton, with the steps built up from a series of collapsible platforms and wagon stages. When the curtain finally went up, the steps were dressed with serried ranks of West Point cadets in white dress uniform. (They were actually professional chorus men—and women—drafted from all over Broadway.) The chorus master had to carry a pocket card-index system detailing the human units for each of the tableaux, and since there were four hundred singers, the inevitable one or two absences always had to be concealed by a reshuffle at the last minute.

There was a strong patriotic fervor to the opening part of the show, and this seemed to rouse the audience; it was becoming increasingly clear that it was only a matter of time before America became physically involved in the war in Europe. The choir sang "We'll Stand by Our Country"; then, during a black-out, and while a spotlit group downstage sang about how America was going to frighten off U-boats like so many sardines, the carpenters and stagehands assembled the prow of a dread-nought. The Capitol steps were trundled away and replaced by a gun turret, the dome flew up into the flies and passed a mast and a crow's nest coming down, and as soon as this was locked into position, "officers" climbed up to man powerful searchlights. And then counter-searchlights raked the battleship for the benefit of the startled audience, which discovered a fresh swarm of song-sters, "middies" this time, all determined to "Stand by Our Country." The girl on the piano then showed other aspects of American bravery. Heywood Broun's review had failed to ex-plain that while the girl twirled on the piano's lid, a pianist was also up there playing the spotlit white instrument as it swung back and forth at a giddy height. He had his legs locked around the piano stool, which was bracketed to the piano, while the girl had suspension wires looped under her armpits and a revolving housing on the piano's lid, into which she could fit a toe. It was to compete with all this daredevilry that the ballet fairies in *The Sleeping Beauty* had to take to the air.

And so The Big Show settled in. Dillingham was far too skilled a campaigner to have got the mixture entirely wrong; there was indeed something for everyone, and no one was ever deterred from a banquet because there was too much of every-thing, so that for anyone who found ballet resistible, there were always the elephants and the long-suffering lions. Twelve times a week you could take your pick. Pavlova had exchanged one sort of waking nightmare for another; in many ways she now had even less spare time than on tour. At least on the train journeys there had been enforced moments of ease, when there was nothing one could do but sit and talk, or read, or play cards. Pavlova herself had started to embroider a 65-foot-long gros point runner for the aisle of her old school chapel at the Maryinsky, and the huge roll was lugged around America as part of Pavlova's "private" luggage—along with the dog and the fold-ing card table and the tea urn. The mechanically repetitive labor of the carpet looping was soothing, and it absorbed her nervous energy. Pavlova was incapable of remaining still and totally re-laxed, and she could never concentrate on reading for very long. In strange towns, invariably she had been the first to set off on a brisk walk to see what was what. "Come along, Kobelev!" He was a similarly energetic walker, and so off she would go with her dutiful consort of the morning, while the others were still sorting out their luggage. That had been a pattern, a sort of ritual, for months and months, all over America. But now, in New York, the variety of it had gone. There was still the carpet, and more and more of the girls in the company grew to hate the sight of it, as they were commandeered to help in its completion, though they were now scattered in different lodging houses, and Pavlova saw less of them in her off-duty hours. She and Dandré had left the Majestic Hotel as soon as the show settled in and taken an apartment in the Red House on Eightieth Street.

The OPERA NEWS

PUBLISHED BY JOHN WANAMAKER NEW YORK
PHILADELPHIA   PARIS   LONDON

Volume VIII   New York, Tuesday, October 10, 1916   Number 1

The Pavlowa Ballet, a wonderful scene designed by   Leon Bakst to music of Tschaikowsky at the Hippodrome

THE HIPPODROME'S NEW AND WONDERFUL SPECTACLE

PAVLOWA, Volinine and the Russian Ballet (not to be confused with the Ballet Russe), occupies the entire second act of the very entertaining show at the Hippodrome.

The entertainment is divided into three acts, each entirely independent of the other and each containing a great many novelties. So much is offered that the audience is nearly bewildered.

The first act has animal numbers and spectacular scenes introducing one "Some-

ANNA PAVLOWA
In the "Sleeping Beauty" at the Hippodrome

where in Minstrel Land." Hundreds of performers appear in row after row. End men, banjoists, trombonists, etc., filling the entire stage.

THE Pavlowa ballet is beautifully done, it being entitled "The Sleeping Beauty," and is given in three scenes.

The Ice Ballet is still a great novelty and is more interesting than even last year. Charlotte is alone with her exquisite grace and is the chief feature of this ballet.

Mr. Dillingham deserves the gratitude of all for the splendid manner in which the production has been staged.

This cover of *The Opera News* showing the Garland Dance in *The Sleeping Beauty* indicates the size of the Hippodrome stage and the sheer number of performers needed to fill it.

Pavlova did have one time-consuming preoccupation at this time: the desire to start ballet schools for the young. On tour, she had often managed to preside over meetings in far away towns or look in on classes, where she would explain fundamentals patiently or sometimes scold if she found bad rudimentary training methods. In New York, Charles Dillingham allowed her the use of the ballet room at the Hippodrome, and it was there that she decided to institute classes, under the direction of Clustine. Applications (with parental consent) were solicited. Pavlova saw no reason why America should not spawn natural dancers:

> The longer I remain in America, the more convinced I am that there lie distinct possibilities in an entirely American ballet. It merely requires an awakening on the part of the musicians before this reality is accomplished. I have often dreamed of an American ballet, because I can see infinite possibilities in the action and vitality of the native dancers. . . . I can see it all—the grandeur of the West, the romance of the South, the pastoral beauty of the East and all. The complications are apparent, but one could weave into the ballet dances of a fantastic as well as a realistic nature. For a ballet to be really striking, the accompaniment must be striking. Feeble music is fatal and no matter how cleverly the dancers perform and the stage manager directs, there is no effect without a

vivid musical accompaniment. I have heard some of the American folksongs. They are charming and mystical, and they would make an excellent foundation for a great artistic ballet. But these melodies would have to be orchestrated by a complete musician, and one who understood the traditions. . . .

> Just at present I am as much interested in my productions new to America, and in helping young Americans to learn to dance correctly. It is quite thrilling to have pupils and watch them follow instructions. I don't think an artist can ever do greater service to her generation than to teach the younger folk whatever she has learned by experience and labor.

(*Variety* later had some fun by way of a misquote, so that "native dancers" became "native dances": "Perhaps Pavlowa eats what we should call a heavy supper. Nothing but lobster or Welsh rarebit could account for such a fantastic dream, with our native dances, including the Jitney Bus, the Corkscrew Glide, and Walking the Dog, as reflections of the 'American soul.'")

Pavlova's Free Ballet School (as it was titled) was deluged with applications from young hopefuls, and at a meeting on September 24, Pavlova, Clustine, Stier, and Burnside tried to work out how the applicants would be processed. There were over twelve hundred of them; eight hundred were residents of the greater New York area, and the balance were from throughout the country. There was even one from Winnipeg. Although they all seemed worthy of at least a trial, with their professing a serious desire to become ballet dancers, it was determined with reluctance that while the system was being organized, only residents of New York should be handled. The numbers were still impossible, so it was decided that the first class would be limited to fifty members, and that after these students had shown some aptitude and ability and were assigned to advanced practice, then a second class would begin. So that there should not seem to be any partiality in the selection, it was announced that the pupils would be taken in the order of receipt of their applications—though this could scarcely have been a practical possibility.

That autumn there were domestic aggravations behind the scenes. Dandré was at a thoroughly loose end, since there was no place for him in the Dillingham organization, and there were an increasing number of quarrels between him and Pavlova. At one point he walked out. Financial problems were often the root of the stress, much of them carried over from the collapse of the Boston Grand Opera Company. Annoyingly, one aspect of this problem had got into the newspapers. Charles Stickney, the attorney who had given Pavlova the $5,000 contribution, had died in March, and that summer his executors had found the promissory note signed by Pavlova. They filed a suit to collect on what they saw as a straightforward loan, so that Pavlova had to file an answer in return. The *New York Times* ran the details: that the money had been a voluntary gesture, given with the understanding that if the venture showed a profit in December of the same year, the money would be returned, but that if there was a loss, then it was not to be repaid. Pavlova declared that the venture had lost "at least $25,000" and that "before his death, Mr. Stickney promised to return the note, but failed to do so."

This same issue of the *Times* carried an advertisement for Diaghilev's Ballets Russes, which was due to open at the Manhattan Opera House on the following Monday, October 16. The opening night had been postponed for a week because Nijinsky had sprained his ankle on October 3, and it was with extreme optimism that his name still headed the list in an advertisement on October 10. Pavlova sent Nijinsky a basket of flowers, and later she telephoned his wife, Romola, to ask if it was true that he had broken a bone. (Rumors had been most colorful.) Romola— at this stage quite paranoid on her husband's behalf—thought that Pavlova sounded rather disappointed when she heard that the injury was less serious.*

It was certainly galling for Pavlova to find that her business affairs were again being aired in the papers at the exact time the Diaghilev troupe was in town. Although Diaghilev himself lived constantly with the burden of financial stresses, he did somehow manage to keep the details within his own circle. Pavlova had to suffer public gossip, which suggested that she had taken on her present engagement only because her tour had cost her all she had saved. On top of everything, the audiences were apathetic toward *The Sleeping Beauty,* and after five weeks Pavlova began to make alterations. She introduced more divertissements, paring away from the long-suffering work all of its ensemble numbers, with the result that the time occupied by the ballet continued to shrink. But nobody seemed to mind; the point was that Pavlova *appeared.* She retained all her personal magnetism, even though she did make her dancing a little more "flashy" for the Hippodrome audience.

All her habits were watched and catalogued from a respectful distance at the Hippodrome. Usually the wings were packed with people, but when Pavlova came off the stage, a space always opened before her. There was never any of the usual jostling. A backstage observer reported one such exit:

> This time it is Mlle. Pavlowa and not the elephants. There is no particular reason why everyone should stand aside, for the great danseuse is less temperamental than the average chorus girl, and makes no foolish demands of her professional inferiors. But such is the brilliance of her art that she seems to shed an aura which mere mortals would not think of profaning by entering. So she makes her entrances and exits through a lane of hushed admirers, as a Queen of pre-Revolutionary France must have moved among her retinue.

This queen of ballet never had an idle moment. The selection for the ballet school finally took place on October 26, when seventy-five hopefuls assembled at the Hippodrome in order to be assessed by Pavlova. Although it had been requested that no one under the age of sixteen was to appear, it was perhaps

ABOVE Nijinsky, after arriving in New York on board the *Espagne*, April 5, 1916.

BELOW Diaghilev arriving in New York on board the *Lafayette*, January 11, 1916.

---

*Romola's acid interpretation seems unlikely under the circumstances. Pavlova had no cause to exult in an injury to another dancer. A few performances by Nijinsky at the Manhattan Opera House would not present a threat to bookings for the Hippodrome's Big Show, which was directed toward a vaudeville-oriented audience and which packed competitively priced seats over a long season.

Pavlova with Clustine and some of the pupils selected
for her Free Ballet School at the Hippodrome.

inevitable that a number of tots infiltrated their way into the throng. They were weeded out, with much audible distress, until at the last moment Pavlova took pity on them and said that a younger group could assemble again the following week. The rest were put through their paces, and by the end of the day Pavlova had narrowed the field to ten pupils. (She had also disappeared for a while to fill her slot in the matinee.)

The strain on the little ones, when it came their turn, was intense, and there must have been tremendous parental pressure in the background. One small girl was quite overcome by the occasion, and despite everyone's coaxing sat down on the floor and sobbed uncontrollably. Pavlova went over and picked her up, took her back to her chair, and settled her on her lap. Presently the girl got down and performed everything just as she had been taught, her eyes fixed steadfastly on the ballerina's face throughout.

The first class was held at the Hippodrome on November 2, and by this time the original ten girls had been augmented to

eighteen, all between the ages of fifteen and twenty-two. Clustine took the older students on Mondays and Fridays, and Pavlova took the youngsters on Saturday mornings. The classes progressed, though the pressure of external activities—not to mention the advanced ages of some of the students—meant that it was really more of a sop toward the image of American children being inducted into classical ballet than a serious belief that the experiment would bring on a whole generation of adequate performers overnight.*

Pavlova tried to explain her long-term aims and where she thought indigenous American talent would spring from: "California, with its flowers and sunshine and hills, should make great dancing, but not so your skyscrapers." When she said that before

---

* A prophetic article appeared in the *Evening Sun* on November 7, with a headline declaring: "Some Day Russia May Do Homage to a Visiting American Ballet—But not immediately, thinks Pavlowa, who is aiding the establishment of a Free Ballet School in New York."

American girls could become good dancers they would have to learn good manners, she accompanied the comment with a delicious bit of dumb show that was instantly recognizable as a chorus girl being insubordinate in the presence of a senior chorus master. Pavlova had never quite come to terms with the natural arrogance of youth that she encountered in America, nor with the casual attitudes that prevailed in many matters: "We of Russia are a people who have lived a stern life, and that makes great dancing. We dance as a reaction to the stress of our daily lives. . . . But make no mistake; one does not become a great dancer without work, and that is what you must learn over here."

The reporter to whom Pavlova was laying down these strictures was won over by her personal charm:

When Mme. Pavlowa first began to speak, she had impressed her listener as being rather plain looking. She was chic, in a little blue serge frock that hung loosely from her shoulders, accentuating the suppleness of her body, and a smart little fur-trimmed toque; but except for great lustrous eyes, her beauty at least was not arresting. But when she spoke, with ceaseless, incisive gestures that seemed to begin, hang pendant, and end in one fraction of a second, each movement of the head, arms and body as graceful and clean-cut as the myriad motions that melt into one another to form her dancing, her countenance illumined by the reflective brilliance of her eyes, and a smile that flickered but never died—then indeed she was truly beautiful.

To another, Pavlova tried to explain her theory of teaching, drawing on her own experience as a student at the Imperial Ballet School:

I do not lay down rules for my pupils. When I dance before them it is not that they may copy me. I do not want them to begin their dancing careers by being "like Pavlowa" by doing some of Pavlowa's dances. My dances interpret my ideas. But how do I know that my pupils' ideas are the same? I want them to try to succeed by dancing their own ideas in their own way. I can advise them how to do this—that is quite another matter.

I remember when I too was only a student at dancing. I was in a class one day with four fellow pupils. There was a mirror in the hall, and looking into it, I suddenly noticed that one of the other girls— she is a famous dancer now—was copying my every movement, the motions of my hands and arms and feet, and even my smile. Even when, purposely, I did the wrong thing, *still* she copied me! I was so angry, I never went to that classroom again. It seemed such an affront to art. I was learning to dance my own thoughts, my hopes and my fancies. She was dancing—just a copy of Pavlowa.

Coming from someone else, this might have sounded like self-aggrandizement. But Pavlova's self-respect and her burning belief in the rightness of individuality emerged spontaneously. She did not check her own pride in her performances or water it down with artificial humility. She exhorted others to show their emotions as she showed hers. She could laugh one minute and be sad the next, flush red with anger and cry with vexation; her moods sped past unchecked.

Two days after Pavlova had given her first class, Charles Dillingham's press office sent out a release suggesting that Pavlova was busy preparing an autobiography for release among her friends. How anyone could have thought she had the time for all this cannot be imagined; however, the office had extracted from her a page of quotes, sufficient to fill half a column in the newspapers (which was probably the object of the exercise after all): "Russians Are Gay, Not Gloomy, Says Mme. Pavlowa—Great dancer declares her countryfolk have been misunderstood."

The Sleeping Beauty—or what was left of it—finally disappeared on November 27, and from then on Pavlova and her company performed a program of divertissements in front of plain velvet curtains. The selections were supposedly chosen "by popular demand." Apart from Lewandowski's *Obertass* (a type of very fast mazurka), Delibes's *Pizzicato* (from *Sylvia*), Bizet's *Farandole* (from *L'Arlésienne*), Massenet's Fandango (from *Le Cid*), and some Russian polkas, Pavlova introduced for herself the Olé from *Carmen*. It had not been among her *Carmen* dances on the opera tour but was a memory of the one often danced at the Maryinsky, in Pavlova's time most often by Preobrajenskaya, when Pavlova herself would dance the Fandango, with two male partners. *The Swan* was given a rest at the Hippodrome, but

An audition for stunned adjudicators.

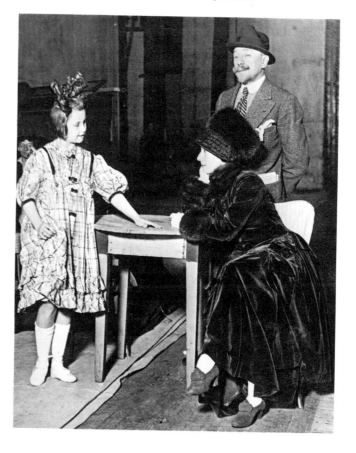

245

Pavlowa, All Nations Are Thine

PAVLOWA, all nations are thine,
    No country thy country alone.
Terpsichore who shall confine?
    Has genius a land or a zone?
    You have danced at the foot of a throne;
Republics have worshipped your shrine—
Pavlowa, all nations are thine,
    No country thy country alone.

Pavlowa, O dancer divine,
    Thou art not one woman alone.
For thou art all women—the wine
    That all of life's lovers have known.
    The love in thy eyes that has shone
Another has looked into mine—
Pavlowa, O dancer divine,
    Thou art not one woman alone.

Now Dance for Me the Bacchanale

NOW dance for me the Bacchanale,
    Pavlowa, Bacchus' airy sprite,
And we shall tread the fields of folly
    Through purple gardens of delight.
However mad your merry measure,
    However amorous your sighs,
Wherever lies the path of pleasure
    There I shall follow with my eyes.

She Poises Like a Panting Bird

SHE poises like a panting bird
    Suspended on the edge of things,
A messenger that waits the word
    To voyage upward on her wings
        Where sister swallows flutter by.
The air above is music-stirred,
    The world about is singing mirth,
    Until we wonder if the earth
    Or sky supernal gave her birth—
        This creature of both earth and sky.

Pavlova usually did her *Dragonfly*, and with Volinine her *Gavotte*. The *Gavotte* seemed to be far and away the most popular item on the program. All told, the ballet section lasted only eighteen minutes, and Pavlova made a brief, well-balanced contribution of three dances which she performed twice a day. In that respect it was a great deal easier than the old days at the Palace. They even made an experiment, distributing among the audience slips of paper listing various solos, with an announcement that since Pavlova's programs would be changed at regular intervals, patrons might like to indicate which dances they would like to see again. It was around this time that Nijinsky showed up at the Hippodrome to see what Pavlova was up to. He probably admired the way she could maintain the integrity of her performances within the context of the overall vaudeville atmosphere. Since his 1914 experience at the Palace, he had discovered that this was no mean feat.

America seemed to be fascinated with things Russian. At the annual Christmas Week Bazaar at the Seventy-first Regiment Armory, the theme for 1916 was Russia, and the proceeds were to go for the relief of the sick and wounded of that country. In the armory's concourse one could have tea in the Russian Tea Garden, listen to a balalaika orchestra, and enter numerous competitions, some of which were judged by Pavlova. She also danced in the hall each day during the hours when she was not needed on stage at the Hippodrome. Edward Kurylo, who had been in her company in 1912, was in New York with a small group of dancers of his own (he was now Edouard de Kurylo), and his group and Pavlova's alternated each day at the bazaar, afternoons and evenings. Pavlova and her partner were thus doing three performances a day during this week.

It was at the bazaar that they tried out a new divertissement with a seasonal flavor, which they called simply *Christmas*. Pavlova played a carefree beauty arriving at a Christmas party with an escort and then flirting with four attentive swains who plied her with gifts. She entered in a glamorous rose taffeta cloak with a swansdown trim, which also decorated a bonnet, and when all this was discarded it revealed a hooped dress of filmy white *point d'esprit* with little garlands of forget-me-nots and pink roses. The ballet was a bit like *Invitation to the Dance* in atmosphere, though high-spirited instead of poignant. The music was the "December" waltz from Tchaikovsky's *The Seasons*.

Pavlova also found the time to paint a self-portrait in a Russian peasant costume, and she had this reproduced in color as a calendar so that she could sign each one and have them sold at the Hippodrome and in the foyers of various hotels as a further means of raising funds for Russian war victims. Her readiness to help others did not always find its true reward. When the Hippodrome management gave a Sunday evening performance in aid of the Home for Hebrew Infants on December 10, the backstage area was suddenly swarming with police, who claimed that "cer-

From a booklet of poems and photographs published
by Douglas Malloch in 1913.

Working on a self-portrait.

Almost every waking hour of December brought fresh demands on Pavlova's time. Some were from old friends and associates who wanted her to grace their own Christmas parties. (Otto Kahn was able to give an entertainment almost beyond imagining: Caruso sang, Pavlova danced, and Bernhardt declaimed.) When the Hippodrome held a benefit performance for the *Evening Mail*'s Save-a-Home Fund (for the assistance of "worthy poor families in danger of being dispossessed of their homes during the holiday period") on Christmas Eve—again, a Sunday—Pavlova confined herself to the role of mistress of ceremonies, it being apparent that it was dancing (and the display of legs) that antagonized the civic authorities. On the other hand, ice skating was considered a thoroughly healthy activity to pursue on a Sunday, and it escaped censure. The following day, Pavlova gave the Hippodrome patrons a Christmas treat by repeating the new dance she had introduced at the Armory bazaar. Burnside had four beautiful Christmas trees put on stage for her, which cheered up the customary plain drapes.

Pavlova was in a bubbling mood; she must have felt a tremendous relief at the thought that her Hippodrome marathon was nearing its end. She had stayed the course in her usual miraculous fashion and could depart with honor as well as dollars. Pavlova's was going to be a difficult name to replace. Her in-flight image had zoomed across the Hippodrome's banner in all the newspaper advertisements at the height of the Christmas season, competing with Sarah Bernhardt at the Empire, Yvette Guilbert at the Maxine Elliott Theatre, and Douglas Fairbanks (also billed as "the Incomparable") over at the Eighty-first Street Theatre in a romp called *The Matrimaniac*. Culture buffs could enjoy Caruso singing Samson at the Metropolitan Opera House, and for those who were tone deaf, Annette Kellermann was swimming at the Lyric. Skating was also tremendously popular, and apart from the pre-eminent Ulrich Salchow, most of the other performers at the rinks seemed to be Russian. However, when Dillingham gave an "Ice Tea" at the Hippodrome rink, Pavlova merely watched the other guests cutting graceful figures. "I would give anything if I could only learn this skating," she said. "It is very graceful—but it is not for me."

Dillingham finally secured the water nymph to replace his ballet star, and one of the city's large engineering companies began constructing a long steel tank with plate glass panels in readiness for "the living Venus," Miss Kellermann. Someone worked out that if there had been any mistake in earlier calculations of stress, or if a defect should develop, no one at orchestra level would escape with dry feet. Bakst had never provided such risks.

tain of the performers" were violating the Sunday blue laws in an open and provocative manner. Anna Pavlova and Toto the Clown were considered to be the principal offenders, and they were arrested. At the end of a thoroughly absurd evening, the case was adjourned.

A week later Pavlova was being discussed in court again on the matter of the Stickney loan. Dandré was back and gave evidence to the effect that he had "overheard" a conversation between Pavlova and the late Mr. Stickney at the Century in which Stickney had offered to put money into the ballet and opera venture. Dandré averred that Stickney definitely did not expect to get his money back unless business was good, and he went on to testify that the company finished its tour $75,000 in arrears. Dandré had not been present (or had failed to take due regard of the fact) when Pavlova, in her initial answer at the earlier hearing, had stated that the loss had been $25,000. Dandré was simply giving the figure that Pavlova had invested—and indubitably lost. The court accepted this statement without asking for any clarification, and the jury subsequently decided that the money need not be repaid. Dandré gave his evidence as Pavlova's "manager."

On New Year's Eve, Pavlova and Dandré gave a party for the ballet company in the apartment on Eightieth Street, and there Pavlova announced that plans had been finalized for her tour of Latin America, with a start two months earlier than had originally been envisaged. There was much talk of the magnificence of the showcase opera house in Buenos Aires, the superb Teatro Colón, where ballet was already known as a result of the Diaghilev company's 1913 visit; so a certain standard would be expected. Although the company had been rehearsing a repertoire of ballets during their spare moments at the Hippodrome, it was made clear by Pavlova that everybody would have to work harder. They were representing Russian ballet, and Russian ballet had to be seen at its best. There were cheers, and vodka, and Pavlova handed out an expensive present to each member of the company.* She still thought of Christmas by the old calendar—her calendar—but the distinction was blurring, and she was beginning to meet the New World halfway.

In staying on to complete the long season at the Hippodrome, and in making the plans for Latin America, Pavlova had put aside a tentative agreement with Alfred Butt that she would return for a winter season in London. Still, she was continually pressed by him, and she agreed in the first week of the new year that she would return for the 1917–18 season; her passage was actually booked for October 1. She dreaded the very idea of crossing the Atlantic (the U-boat menace was then at its height), though several of her company had sailed the previous May, immediately after the opera-ballet tour had finished in New York. They had boarded the alarmingly small *Noordam* and crossed safely to Falmouth, but by that time Britain had already lost over three hundred ocean-going ships, and there was serious talk that these losses were reducing the country to starvation. From the American side of the Atlantic it was difficult to take in such facts, with everything absurdly plentiful; even so, many of the dancers longed to return to their homelands, and Pavlova herself indulged in a lot of talk about reopening Ivy House.

On January 18 the summonses against Pavlova and Toto were dismissed when the magistrate refused the police application for warrants against the two performers. Two nights later was Pavlova's farewell performance at the Hippodrome. She had played to more than a million patrons during her engagement (the seating capacity was over five thousand), which was an amazing milestone, even if classical ballet itself had not been all-conquering.

The New York *World* analyzed the apathy of the huge crowds toward Pavlova's medium with the witticism that "she was dancing over the heads of her audience." It continued:

When it was announced last August that Pavlowa was to be the superlative feature of this year's show, the master-stroke in the Hippodrome career seemed to have been accomplished. But from the outset, the expected appreciation of her wonderful art failed to manifest itself. . . . It is not that Pavlowa did not give her Hippodrome audience the best of her art. At the Metropolitan Opera House the same dancing would have created a furore. The apathy of the great crowds which found so much to delight them in other features of "The Big Show" must have been a great disappointment

---

* Pavlova's generosity could be extraordinary. At the end of November Lindovska, who was completing five years' service with Pavlova, was presented with a jewel box inscribed in gold and containing a silver horseshoe brooch studded with diamonds. Pavlova then took the astonished girl to a surprise party she had arranged for the entire company.

Christmas: (above) in the rose taffeta costume, photographed by Baron de Meyer; (below) with Volinine and other cavaliers, Berlin, 1926.

New York, 1916.

to her, but she was philosophical enough to recognize that she was dancing in the wrong place. She persevered until her contract was fulfilled and did not once complain. The real eccentricity of Pavlowa's genius is her self-discipline.

For her last performance at the Hippodrome, Pavlova danced *Spring Waltz* (to Strauss), the Delibes *Pizzicato*, and the ever-popular *Gavotte*. None of that was over anybody's head. In taking her final bow, Pavlova graciously led out onto the stage Annette Kellermann, her successor to the "star spot." There were numerous floral tributes handed up the aisles, and Harriet Patchin, one of Pavlova's students, presented her teacher with a bronze statuette representing "The Divinity of the Dance," by Malvina Hoffman.

A *Bacchanale* pose for Malvina Hoffman.

T he sculptress had used Pavlova's extended stay in New York as a chance to add to an enormous number of studies for an ambitiously planned frieze of the *Bacchanale* in bas-relief. There were to be twenty-five panels all told, and by the end of 1916 Hoffman was well advanced on her project of molding Pavlova for posterity. The dancer had always accommodated the artist whenever time permitted, and she would hold difficult poses uncomplainingly. Some of the free-standing figures were very successful, and apart from the group at the Panama-Pacific Exposition, others had taken a first prize in the Paris Grand Salon of 1914. In the *Bacchanale* frieze the male partner was an amalgam of four years' sketching: of Mordkin, Novikov, Volinine and Pavley, the last of whom had been photographed with Pavlova in poses from the *Bacchanale*. The first three panels depicted the famous entrance of this dance: the dancers are running side by side under the billowing gauze veil, and they hold stiffened garlands of roses as well. As soon as the two separated, the male dancer always threw his garland to Pavlova across the width of the stage. Hoffman's designs for the frieze were done in a style that was an uneasy mixture of Greek classical and Japanese rococo; but her small wax model of a pose from the *Gavotte* was perhaps the most successful of many artists' depictions of Pavlova. The ballerina allowed the sculptress to have it produced in a limited edition, and the replicas of the 15-inch figure were sold for $600 each, with the orders handled through Rabinoff's office.

Though Pavlova attracted a number of artists, it was a curious mischance that the majority of renderings remained at an undistinguished level. In Russia there had been paintings and drawings, and Soudbinine had modeled her at the express wish of the Tsar, but though he had produced strong head studies, his full-length figurines left her conventionally doll-like. The Italian artist Emanuele de Rosales made several figures, but he found it difficult to resist fussy detail in the costuming—a fault he recognized himself, for he was provoked to another attempt, this time showing the dancer nude (ostensibly in Zaylich's *Printemps*) and this statuette was displayed in the Goubil Gallery in New York in 1916, when the critics described it as the sculptor's best work.

The Austrian sculptress Baronne Vranyczamy also depicted Pavlova nude, in 1914, in the final pose from *The Swan*; only the headdress and two great wings made any allusion to the stage view. Pavlova's own attempts at figurines, in wax and in clay (which were afterward cast), showed a talent hardly less than that of the people who were working from her.

Painters too found trouble in her strange beauty, though numerous pictures testify to their determination. Sir John Lavery did three pictures in London and exhibited them in 1912, when the Tate Gallery promptly bought one for its permanent collection; it showed the ballerina in her swan costume languishing beside the pond at Ivy House. But Pavlova seemed to follow a creed that did not distinguish between artists; they were all a band of fellow travelers. Although Lady Lavery had had to act as a stand-in for the dancer in numerous sittings, Pavlova posed for a relatively unknown young English artist, Archibald Barnes, who was at that time confined to a couch through injury. Her willingness to pose for him while he was incapacitated was said by the artist to have given him hope and inspiration. A leg up, too—the Royal Academy accepted his picture for exhibition in 1914. Still, it was a tragedy that Valentin Serov had died in 1911 without completing the work for which he was ideally suited. Only the beautiful preliminary drawings were left to show that he had detected in his subject the remoteness and astringency, as well as the allure.

The Pavlova Company was due to leave for Cuba on February 2, 1917, but before they could head off on their new adventure Pavlova's name was twice more in the headlines. It was finance again. On January 29 the Appellate Division of the State Supreme Court sat to assess the previous judgment relating to Charles Dickinson Stickney's "gift." The executors were still trying to get their hands on the $5,000 and had claimed a further sum in interest. Dandré had to give evidence again, and he repeated that he had overheard Stickney's "no strings" offer. "It was only upon the insistence of Madame Pavlova that Mr. Stickney gave her a paper, which was introduced in evidence as the note, payable at the Fifth Avenue Bank, December 21, 1915," he stated. Dandré went on to explain that when the note became due, Pavlova complained to Mr. Stickney that she was "annoyed" about the bank's sending her the notice; that Mr. Stickney had "apologized," saying that she would not be bothered again; and that he would give an order to the bank canceling the note. At this point in the evidence the losses of the tour were gone into in more detail, and it was now asserted that there had been a deficit of more than $140,000. The figure was creeping up steadily. Furthermore, the court heard that Pavlova had not been paid for her services and was technically owed $26,400. Justice Newberger may have been aware that Stickney's estate had been estimated at more than a million; in the event, he ruled for Pavlova, affirming the previous judgment.

Then, on the eve of the departure for Cuba, another headline caught everyone's eye: "Danced Away $50,000 Is Charged in Court—Pavlowa's tour, financed by Rabinoff, used up her inheritance, impresario's ex-wife says." It seemed that Max Rabinoff's attorney brother, Samuel, was being sued by his former wife, now Mrs. Evelyn Hart, for neglecting to support their two children. He had been ordered to pay $150 a month in a decree awarded in 1915, and he had also been instructed to return a $50,000 inheritance belonging to his wife. "The $50,000 I inherited went to finance a tour of the United States by Anna Pavlowa," said Mrs. Hart. "My former husband, with his brother Max Rabinoff, who is Pavlowa's manager, spent the money." Mrs. Hart was a little behind the news in the Rabinoff family.

The Wall Street skyline slowly receded as their ship headed down river. In the hold were crates of new costumes and scenery, for which Pavlova had just paid. What else could she do? Havana was very smart, and there was that huge white granite opera house, which would be packed with discerning patrons. Only the best would satisfy them.

Cuba, as it transpired, was on the verge of a revolution. High-ranking members of the social structure in Havana made something of an effort for Pavlova's opening night at the Teatro Nacional, but from then on the attendance trailed off alarmingly, with rumors and counter-rumors rampant throughout the city. The streets were almost empty, and it must have been strangely reminiscent of St. Petersburg in the autumn of 1905. Before the first week was concluded, it was evident that Pavlova's enterprise was once more passing through dangerous financial straits. Dandré assumed a statesman-like mien, and putting aside his usual avuncular attitude toward the company he came sternly to the point: business was a fiasco, and Pavlova was simply not in a position to risk another disastrous season. The dancers were either to accept his temporary solution, which was a 25 percent reduction of salary, to three dollars a day, or accept the fact that the tour would have to be abandoned.

The meeting in the hotel room developed into an uproar. The younger and newer members, who had nothing to lose and everything to gain by traveling with Pavlova, were quite prepared to go along on bread and water if need be, but the senior members—the Poles and Russians, who were seasoned and cynical campaigners—were in no mood to make any sacrifices for art. For a while it looked as if the vote would go against Dandré (the Poles usually spent three dollars a day on drink alone), but someone reasoned that nothing could be worse than Cuba, and so Dandré won the day. Pavlova stayed out of the brouhaha, awaiting the verdict. The theatre management tried to help in its own way: on February 23 they gave the company a benefit night, at which *Cavalleria Rusticana* was followed by part of *Faust* and then the ballet divertissements.

The original intention had been to return to America from Cuba and then to sail to Rio de Janeiro; but all that was changed. Adolfo Bracale cobbled together a fresh itinerary, and after two performances at Matanzas, in the north, they sailed due south for Costa Rica and Panama on March 1. Their transport was another of the small, dirty steamers that the company was rapidly coming to detest. The S.S. *Tenadores* was no better and perhaps no worse than the others: vibrating, sooty, airless carriers in which human cargo was treated as an afterthought. Stier was still in America, tangled in the red tape of visa applications and faced with the knowledge that if America entered the war, he would become an internee. The rehearsal pianist, Alexander Smallens, took over the orchestra. (A month earlier he had taken a job with the new Inter-State Opera Company, but it folded after ten days.) On the Boston Grand Opera Company tour he had often deputized for the opera conductor Schmid. Stier had always been a dependable and a kindly soul, and the company missed him, but Pavlova was very happy with Smallens because of his expansive attitude toward music; he could maintain a legato quality while still accommodating Pavlova's capricious moods of interpretation. He could also be utterly firm, when he felt that a composer's intent was being threatened, so that at certain points Pavlova lost the battle; Smallens simply refused to conduct. By birth he was Russian, and at these times it was a case of one Russian dealing with another, and peace was invariably established without lasting rancor.

It was while she was in Costa Rica that Pavlova heard of Kerensky's coup d'état in Russia. The Tsar removed! It was amazing news. There had been no word of Pavlova's mother for many months. Most of the company had family to worry about, and the realization brought them closer together, so that even the sight of the S.S. *Quilpué* did not provoke instant insurrection.

at Marianao

Pavlowa loves children!

Pavlowa enjoys bananas!

Pavlowa goes ashopping

She was a South American cattle boat heading for Ecuador. The sixty-five members of the Pavlova Company were expected to fit in as best they could; only one deck separated the bovine passengers from the rest, and the mournful complaints from the hold, as well as the accompanying odor, seemed to permeate the entire vessel. There was the brief novelty of the locks in the Panama Canal, but it was extremely hot and humid, and the ship was extremely slow, so that it was not long before most of the company members left the stifling cabins in which they were crammed, to make the best use they could of the small open forward deck. At night, in the Pacific moonlight, Pavlova wandered around from group to group offering words of cheer, until the dreadful bellowing from the open hold drove her back to the refuge of her cabin. Even when they had arrived in the Gulf of Guayaquil there was still a two-day journey up to the mouth of the Los Ríos River to Guayaquil itself, and the moment when the anchor chain rattled out and the ship slowed to a halt in the soupy brown water.

Guayaquil was a trading port that made no effort to disguise its basic poverty. The squalor started at the waterfront. The cattle stench was exchanged for the almost equally nauseating smell of raw cocoa, an insidious sweetness drifting everywhere from huge mounds of beans awaiting shipment. Pavlova, head bravely erect, set off for the hotel with Dandré in the only available

victoria; the rest of the band picked up their belongings and began walking in the same direction, surrounded by bemused natives. What was the Russian Ballet doing there? It was another of Bracale's bright ideas. It seemed he had thought to fill in time with engagements until the smart season got under way in Peru, so after Panama, where else but Guayaquil?

The shabby old Teatro Almedo was actually packed for the opening on May 2. Hordes of ragged spectators peered down from the galleries, as incredulously wide-eyed as they had been in the streets, while hidden behind lattice screens in the upper circle English cocoa merchants and a few rich Ecuadorians sat back in style. (The higher social orders desired to see Pavlova, but at the same time did not wish to mix with the lower orders, for fear of the contagious diseases that were rife at the time. The screens concealed the presence of the "upper rank" from those below and avoided the odium of overt segregation.) Below them the locals watched the strange foreign rituals with wonder and increasing delight. The dancing was a hit. During the intermissions the performers were ushered up to the higher boxes to be offered drinks, as was the custom, and the characters from the toy shop of *The Fairy Doll* were all mixed up with the real clients at one point, so that the "Englishman" tried to understand what a real Englishman was saying, while his wife handed *piñas frias* to a "chimney sweep." That night, some of the dancers met another

The Vision scene from *The Sleeping Beauty*, Lima, 1917.

Englishman. He tried to explain the charms of Guayaquil. "Six months of it would make a living corpse of anyone," he observed as he picked up his opium pipe. Swamp fever was prevalent, and everyone was considered at risk.

It took only two weeks for the cosmopolitan dancers to feel they had come to the end of the earth, and even Pavlova's morale cracked. She was in a tearful, overwrought state toward the end of the engagement, and she began to voice a morbid conviction that the boat would not arrive to take them away, and that they would be stranded. Her fears were unfounded, and another sluggish steamer, the *Chile,* appeared as a deliverance. They were headed south, to Callao, and each mile between them and Guayaquil raised their spirits. In Lima there was the excitement of Election Day when they arrived, and little reflection of the uncertainties associated with the terrible war in Europe, except for interned German ships at anchor in the harbor. The Pavlova Company had a month-long engagement at the Teatro Municipal, and from the start the Peruvians were wildly appreciative of the dancers' work. It was the first time that Bracale's preliminary publicity had had a chance to take effect, so that there was a certain expectation in the city, and rich patrons strove to outdo each other in displays of appreciation. There were huge floral tributes, and during the season each soloist in the company was given a benefit night at which he or she was spotlit, while gifts were handed up to the stage and white pigeons were released into the auditorium.

The affection shown her company in Lima seems to have inspired in Pavlova a recovery of her martinet approach. On a heavily overcast Good Friday morning she walked into the theatre from the main entrance and discovered a rehearsal in progress on the stage. Clustine was overseeing a run-through of *The Seven Daughters of the Ghost King.* Pavlova watched from the orchestra for a few moments. It was one of the two Fokine ballets she had fought for so tenaciously; it was almost a symbol of Russian ballet proving that it could embrace the twentieth century, that it could deploy fable and fantasy through the medium of a classical vocabulary honed by the great talents of the nineteenth century, and still remain valid. But this particular ballet had always had weaknesses, and Pavlova knew it required every ounce of effort and conviction to conceal them. Clustine was no great respecter of Fokine's work, and his attitude showed. The situation was not helped by the increasingly polyglot nature of the present company. Among the non-Russians was André Oliveroff, whose real name was Oliver Grimes. He later recalled the scene on that Good Friday morning.

The first intimation of Pavlova's presence had been the swift clicking of her street shoes advancing down the bare stone aisle. Then:

"Ivan Nicolaiovitch! Ivan Nicolaiovitch! What are you doing there! This is terrible work. Everything looks *rotten!*"

At the sound of the shrill voice, Clustine swung around to face Pavlova. "Anna Pavlovna! In the name of heaven what are you talking about? You don't like the way things are going? But why? What is wrong?"

Pavlova stamped her foot in vexation. "Old fool! The devil alone knows what you think you are doing! It can't go on like that!"

Clustine responded by telling Pavlova that she was impossible, that nobody could please her. Shouting "Konshuli!" ("I'm finished!"), he climbed down over the footlights and stormed to the back of the theatre, but since he was in Lima and not Paris, his threat was empty. Pavlova picked up his discarded stick and took over the rehearsal herself. Her anger soon centered on a pretty Russian girl who normally used generous physical charms to disguise the weakness of her footwork.

"Tatiana!" screamed Pavlova. "Why you not go on the pointe? Pianist, go back sixteen measures!"

The girl soon lapsed onto demi-pointe again. Instantly Pavlova's stick banged the floor, stopping the music and the dancing in mid-beat. "Tatiana! Why you not go on the pointe? You have expression like cook! You are artist or not?"

Tatiana tried to explain that her feet hurt, but Pavlova was unmoved. "Sore toes or not, you must do it! It must be done!" Pavlova's voice was taking on a sardonic tone that cut like a razor. "You want to be in Madame Pavlova's company. Then you must be artist!" The next words were all emphasized with a steady beating of the stick on the stage. "Otherwise you can take your passport and go home. Now—go through it again, by yourself. You other girls stand aside. Begin. On the pointe!"

The girl tried a few more steps and then suddenly rushed from the stage, sobbing uncontrollably. Without a word, Pavlova got up from the chair she had been seated on and flung it in the direction of the vanished dancer. Then she turned and called to Clustine, knowing he would still be in the theatre. He shambled out of the gloom, looking apologetic.

"Anna Pavlovna, why you do like that? Why you do, Anna Pavlovna? I was doing the best I could. But look at them! They are a bunch of fools!"

Pavlova handed him the stick and, without a word, stalked off to her dressing room. She was soon back, wearing her practice tunic, and while Clustine resumed the rehearsal, his employer watched from the shadowy edge of the stage as she went through her morning exercises, grasping the edge of a scenery flat for support. Her free hand constantly made the sign of the cross as she muttered to herself. Sometimes the dancers overheard her:

"This will never do. It can't go on like this."

"Oozshassno!"

"Terrible, terrible, terrible!"

It is a moot point whether Pavlova was thinking entirely in terms of artistic standards. Her situation was scarcely to be envied by the most vainglorious exhibitionist. She was the head of a volatile, bickering "family" that had the added complication of emotional cross-currents and sexual jealousies that would have been spared any normal family. Her own relationship with Victor Dandré was suffocated by layers of shared experience over more than a decade. He understood her and was content to serve her,

absorbing her frustrated explosions like a huge punching bag that always swung back to the same epicenter. She envied the relatively casual freedom of her corps de ballet, and she watched the artistic progress of her soloists with mixed feelings. They could encroach upon her territory with the confidence bred of a lack of responsibility, while she was forced to provide the platform from which they sprang; then she had to vault higher. The irony was that if she failed to do so, it was they who were lost. Tatiana, with her recalcitrant feet, embodied perfectly the sort of company members who most upset Pavlova's equilibrium. She was aware of the girl's off-stage life: in Lima she had been seen frequently with a rich local admirer, and it was becoming plainly apparent that her love of dancing was equaled by a fondness for the comforts such an admirer could provide. It was not the relationship that worried Pavlova—far from it; it was the fact that it was not kept subservient to the girl's art. This was the crux. To Pavlova's way of thinking this was the true betrayal, the more insidious because the attractions that caused it were all too potent. She lashed out at Tatiana in the knowledge that she, Pavlova, had failed in the advocacy of her own particular art.

But there were other pressures in Lima that compounded the strain, including the fact that America had now entered the Great War. Whatever hope this presaged for the long term, with vital support for the exhausted Allies in Europe, its immediate effect was a frightening new degree of uncertainty. There were shifting German sympathies in certain South American states, and for a band of European nationals traveling in that continent, each frontier would henceforth provide an alarming new challenge. The journeying itself was going to be more hazardous, since shipping lanes—in the Atlantic, at least—were increasingly part of the arena of war, and American tonnage was no longer neutral. Pavlova was, effectively, in one further stage of exile.

Arriving in Callao, en route to Lima, May 1917. Pavlova is flanked by Volinine and Dandré.

Invitation to the Dance, Lima, 1917.

Yet she was famous and adored, presidents did her honor, and all her associates were in awe of her—and rightly so. Her art gave her a rare power, but it also isolated her. She was condemned to be forever pushing onward, and always she had to be in the vanguard; the company was nothing without her. She was its head, its heart, its pulse, and its armor; her will power was its collective energy. That removed, the whole enterprise would blow away in the night like dead leaves. Without her the dancers would become gypsies begging for alms, whereas with her they could press on, plying their trade with honor and gaining recompense in the process. In a turbulent and uncertain world, that was something of a privilege. Only Pavlova herself could not leave it at that; for her there was a more burning commitment. She was not a fugitive from Russia, she was a missionary; and that being so, it was not difficult to view the whole world as being peopled by the unconverted.

The savagery and chaos that festered across Europe during 1917 had scarcely an echo in South America during the time that Anna Pavlova's company was in isolation there. At worst there were inconveniences of divided national sympathies, when certain passports (or lack thereof) caused some dancers to be stranded at frontiers, watching others waved through with the briefest of formalities. On the rare occasions when diplomacy could not solve a problem, Pavlova was forced to leave the victims behind—with a handsome allowance and assurances that the main group would ultimately return.* Theirs was going to prove a restricted circuit, even though the distances between stops were hundreds of miles.

In all of Latin America the strands of society were still archaically distinct, and theatrical performers created suspicion by their very calling. In Lima at a soirée where she was guest of honor, Pavlova was astonished to find herself surrounded entirely by men; it was not quite proper for women to attend such an occasion, and indeed the leading newspaper editors sometimes accused Dandré of traveling with a very dubious female contingent under his command, since photographs clearly showed these girls brazenly walking about with uncovered necks and bare arms. Even at tea dances there were equivocal attitudes toward the principal pastime. At one of them Pavlova noticed a young man displaying great elegance on the floor, and she was emboldened to suggest that perhaps he might be interested in joining her company for a season. The young man in question was of an

ABOVE Program cover, Lima, 1917.

BELOW Page from a Brazilian program.

* A typical example of these travel problems arose in Brazil, which had entered the war on the side of the Allies. A male dancer, a Czech, faced internment, despite the fact that he had left his native country fifteen years earlier and had in the interim married an American girl, who had a job with the company. After his arrest his wife decided to go back to her parents in New York, where they were looking after the couple's child. To her horror she was told that she could not re-enter the United States, since by marrying a Czech she had become, through international ramifications, an Austrian subject. Her protestations that she had never been to her husband's country, that she was American stock, had married in the United States, and had given birth to her child in that country all fell on deaf ears. Pavlova found financing to cover all these upsetting contingencies.

The *"Pavlowitas"* arriving in Lima.

English family named Ashton; Pavlova's suggestion utterly shocked him—though he had a young brother named Frederick who would have leaped at such a chance.

Despite the suspicions directed toward Pavlova's milieu, the dancer herself was hugely famous, and wherever she went all levels of society wanted to see her; even the "Pavlowitas"—the company girls—were recognized and followed in the streets—and not just because of their suggestive necklines. At the end of their first Lima season they were still giving ballets like *Coppélia,* but Clustine put into the program *Las Ondinas,* which was simply stated as being "from the Catalani opera *Loreley.*" In this small ensemble ballet Pavlova's heartless water nymph trapped her mortal lover in tendril-like arms that reminded onlookers of seaweed streamers. Lima loved everything, and on the last night the city bade them farewell with marked extravagance. The president was in his box, and society was decked in its finest apparel. The exotic Marchesa Casati was present, adrift from her normal European settings, and to compete with the Peruvian ladies on Pavlova's closing night, she wore cloth of gold, with a helmet of the same material, all surmounted by black ostrich feathers. At the end of the evening admirers of the ballet released dozens of caged birds into the air. While they clattered upward toward the vast marble dome, other sections of the audience showered the stage with flowers. Pavlova, making her incomparably graceful bows, urged her company to join her from the wings, and at this point the entire audience stood and there were innumerable fluttering handkerchiefs and cries of "Adiós!" It was a signal honor and a moving experience for the weary band of performers, and when they left the theatre by the front foyer (at the request of the management), they found a huge crowd there to cheer them. So as not to keep the public waiting unnecessarily, Pavlova had dressed hastily and covered her stage make-up with a veil, but it did not conceal the tears on her cheeks as she made her way through the vociferous throng of well-wishers.

The visit to Lima had turned into a triumph, a reward for all the stress and uncertainty. Could they expect as much elsewhere? Their plan was to sail down the coast to Valparaiso. When they left the port of Callao there were reminders of the outside world: a steamer painted in weirdly uneven geometric patterns, which had to be explained to them as camouflage, and the ships that held German internees, still anchored in the same positions they had occupied weeks earlier, with only the rust advanced.

Pavlova maintained a cheerful front and made jokes, but her associates knew it would be replaced, sooner or later, by one of her recurring fits of depression. Then she would sit staring, oblivious to her immediate surroundings; at such times she would bite a knuckle or suck distractedly on a piece of her amber necklace; and even when others were nearby, there were occasions when some internal anguish would cause tears to stream down her face unchecked. Because these moods were so baffling, nobody was certain as to how to offer comfort, and as a result nobody made a move; everyone pretended nothing was amiss, and Dandré was always conspicuously "busy." Pavlova would sit alone, staring out to sea through the chipped railings of some steamer, or through the window of a train, as miles and miles of landscape slid by, unseen. On at least one occasion the depression hit her in a theatre, and she failed to make an entrance for a divertissement; she sat in her dressing room sobbing, while the orchestra played to an empty stage. But in the environment of a theatre she was usually able to pull herself together and recover her equilibrium.

Apart from her instinctive responses as a natural performer, she had, too, the ever-present knowledge that the company's existence depended entirely on her. No matter how well the others performed, the public's box-office response was to Pavlova alone. She did gain a sense of comfort and security from the presence of such as Hilda Butsova, utterly dependable in any situation. Hilda had a placid temperament and a technical surety to her dancing that was enviable; she also seemed ordered in her personal behavior, whereas others stirred the worrying, mothering side of Pavlova's nature. Pavlova sometimes panicked when her injunctions about remaining open to the emotions of love were followed too wholeheartedly by one or two of the girls. In South America she thought that any friendship must surely end in tears; there was no likelihood that truly suitable husbands were thick on the ground. Nor would it have been convenient had they been. Pavlova fought to keep the girls in step and on a high-wire of behavior between dullness and dash.

As a countermeasure to being fêted by foreigners there was Pavlova's determination that the company should perform well at all times. She wanted its concentration on its work, and flashes of brief but violent temper lit up the general progress like summer lightning. Whether or not she consciously employed it, the uncertainty of her mood was a wonderful antidote to company lethargy and carelessness. Reprimanding someone for a mistake, she would cut short any vague or rambling explanation with a peremptory "Don't speak to me. *Answer* me!" There was surely a reason for everything; to have no reason was to be idiotic. Pavlova would take endless pains with anyone whom she considered was doing his best, even if that best was below standard; but less than full effort earned her scorn, and sheer stupidity made her lose her temper immediately. She was trying to inculcate the discipline of her own upbringing, but surrounded as she was by Latin American languor, there were times when the task was an uphill one.

The company, self-supporting in all that it did, was a remarkable enterprise, not least in the fact that Pavlova was able to pay her dancers a weekly salary more than matching European rates. In its mixture of nationalities, the company was as unlikely a team as could have been assembled. Some of the English girls continued to masquerade under phony Russian labels: besides Butsova and Lindovska, and Verina and Saxova, there was now Brunova (Enid Bryce Brown); but Stuart was flanked in the programs by Courtney, Cromer, Sheffield, and Shelton, and they all seemed equally exotic to Latin ears. On the male side, Oliver Grimes was irreversibly stuck with Oliveroff, but more recent recruits were not made to cloak their names if they were such as Parker or the brothers Horlick. There were numerous Americans in among the genuine Russians and Poles, including a Nebraska-born Angelino, Hubert Stowitts, who had just emerged from the cover of his first stage name, "Monsieur Hubert." As a graduate in commerce at Berkeley, he gained the public's attention when he appeared as Hermes in a "Greek" dance at a campus sports carnival in March 1915. By May he was dancing to Borodin in the students' "Senior Extravaganza"—apparently an apt title. Pavlova was at San Francisco's Cort Theatre shortly afterward, and young Stowitts tracked her down to her dressing room, where, in a further bit of extravagance, he kissed her hand. He had not practiced this bit of European gallantry, but it won Pavlova, who agreed to give the young man an audition the following day. He was aware of his own eye-catching physique, and his exotic costumes did little to conceal it; he managed to get in several changes during the one audition.

Stowitts was really a gifted natural athlete, not a proper dancer, but he was adept at falling into striking poses, and Pavlova thought he might have possibilities as a performer. She advised him to secure a vaudeville booking to increase his stage confidence. This he did, after graduation that year. By September, Pavlova was faced with some defections in the ranks, and she lost Serge Oukrainsky and Andreas Pavley, who had decided to go to Chicago and found their own school of dance. Oukrainsky had a hysterical sense of his own importance, and Pavlova may have been relieved to see him go; Pavley, on the other hand, was mild and cheerful, and had probably never deserved the description "that dumb Dutch boy" by which the company identified him in their private conversations. (He was the son of a Dutch father and a Russian mother.) Pavlova offered Stowitts a contract, which was accepted eagerly. He joined her at the conclusion of the *Dumb Girl* filming on the Coast, and they traveled together to Chicago, stopping to visit the Grand Canyon on the way.

Soloists of the Pavlova Company, Venezuela, 1917, in costume for *Printemps*. Muriel Stuart is in the foreground.

Stowitts was no retiring personality, but he was a young man eager to be in a dance company, and that, in America, was rare enough. Pavlova encouraged Stowitts in his drawing, and even gave him a chance to redesign some costumes. He soon displayed an active interest in all aspects of production and was clearly impatient to be given a chance to design a ballet. Clustine's view of the young American was acidic, since the boy was even showing signs of wanting to add his own "color" to established choreography—a latent talent to be discouraged at all costs. In fact, Stowitts lacked a proper classical training, and his sense of theatre outweighed his balletic vocabulary. Volinine also took a jaundiced view of Pavlova's apparent willingness to let raw theatricality usurp traditional values.

There were the usual jealousies and intrigues inherent in any such group, and the company's comparative isolation threw into sharp relief all differences of opinion, and also any *petites amours*, which might have passed unnoticed in other settings. Pavlova was so much the lifeblood of the company, so famous, so all-seeing, and so enviable in her personal style that she increasingly came to be treated as some exalted headmistress. The dancers developed the trick of calling her "X" in their private conversations, in case they should be overheard and reported. It accorded

with her Olympian position among them. Because they knew so little of her inner thoughts and scarcely understood the driving single-mindedness that was her raison d'être, they credited her with all their own feelings, unadorned with the complexities of her particular nature.

Since she and Dandré maintained a domestic front, it was assumed that the relationship followed a normal and averagely satisfying pattern; there was no real understanding that the interdependence of the two harbored a basic lack of compatibility that was almost suffocating. Dandré had not shared Pavlova's bed for years, and he saw no great reason why he should deny himself the occasional flirtatious overture toward one or another of the girls; because of his position of authority, their circumspect behavior often encouraged these passes unwittingly. But few of them found him romantically attractive, and it was a tribute to his own basic good nature that he would take their rebuffs without offense. The company understood nothing of the sacrifices Pavlova had made for Dandré at the time of his troubles in St. Petersburg, and the view was that the couple were together because Pavlova desired it.

Her own lighthearted and spasmodic flirtations with men in the company were short-lived and entirely superficial—usually with boys who were safely homosexual. They sensed her desperate need for distraction, but some of the girls in the company took the signs at face value and assumed that Madame had become romantically attached. This straightforward assessment accommodated their own down-to-earth and rather narrow view of life, and the idea helped to make Pavlova seem more human. She suffered from having no confidante, and indeed it would have been dangerous to have had one; instead she chose favorites and lavished upon them all sorts of extra considerations. Stefa Plaskowieczka was the most long-standing of the girls she admired; during the London seasons she usually stayed at Ivy House. The Polish girl had genuine dance talent, an agreeably sympathetic nature, and blond good looks of the sort Edwardians had enshrined. She took lovers with an openness that fascinated Pavlova, who often advocated unrestricted emotions but who was the first to become censorious if such emotions led to an "untidy" life. On stage she wanted full-bloodedness; off stage she wanted discretion, seemly manners, and quiet dress—which was not to be confused with dowdiness. One girl's hat so irritated her when it appeared without change week after week that she finally had money issued to the girl with explicit instructions to spend it all on some new piece of millinery. Pavlova felt that the general appearance of the company reflected directly on herself.

To an exhausted young dancer, a hat must have seemed of little significance. Their travel was arduous and their creature comforts minimal. After endless barren and inhospitable terrain, the cities always appeared as a violent contrast, most particularly to dancers who invariably found themselves performing in the municipal theatres or opera houses. These were usually baroque edifices of stupefying grandeur, palaces that pointed up the two sides of the dancers' lives: their glamorous presentation and the reality of dismal boardinghouses and second-class hotels.

A page from Alexander Smallens's scrapbook showing a 1917 Rosario program with Smallens's handwritten notations on repertory.

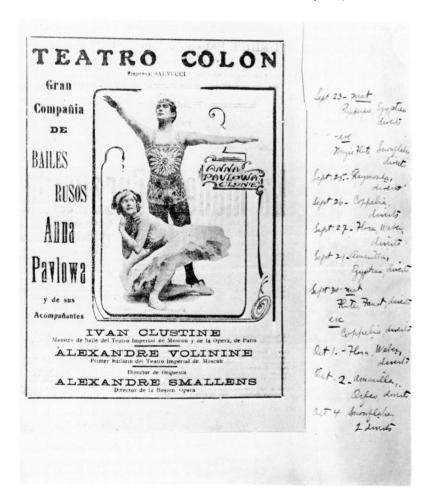

When she was in Chile at the end of July 1917, Pavlova reintroduced *Giselle* into the repertoire, and in both Valparaiso and Santiago the ballet was received with reverence. Everyone wanted to see the great Pavlova since the word had come down from Peru, and the theatres were packed with excited patrons who seemed genuinely to adore everything they saw. The choice of divertissements at this period seemed limitless. Two of them were to music of Grieg: *Anitra's Dance*, a solo first performed in 1912 and now being danced by Brunova, and a piece known as *Gnomos* in South America, performed by Pavlova and eight girls. Another novelty was a Japanese dance using music of Arthur Sullivan, which was performed by Dorothy Smoller, a beautiful girl who was not long with the company and who died of consumption at an early age. Pavlova's Russian national dance came in varying guises: from week to week the music varied between Kalinnikov and Tchaikovsky. Sometimes there would be two male partners, Jacoblieff and Popeloff, for instance, or the Horlick brothers; later it would revert to a single male partner for Pavlova, though still drawing on either of the composers. Meyer-Helmund's *Printemps* was still used; *Syrian Dance*, to music of Saint-Saëns,* had Pavlova with four boys (usually Stowitts, Veseloff, Parker, and Barté); and Neimanov played the Satyr to Pavlova and Volinine in the Godard *Pas de Trois*. Muriel Stuart was given her own ballet at this time: *The Enchanted Lake*. As Queen of the Nymphs, she waylaid a knight (usually Michael Nicholoff) to selections from Schubert. As the scenario was so vague, the ballet was given the alternative title *Schubertiana*. The permutations within a relatively small company were extensive. Volinine had his bow and arrow, and his *Pierrot*, all to himself; they were the concessions that singled him out as the male star of the troupe.

Pavlova's distinct personal quality always made the most overwhelming impression, even though she herself felt that the younger girls' charms weighed against her own chances with the audiences. She could never rid herself of the knowledge that the company's existence depended entirely upon her own pre-eminence; the impresarios and theatre managers hammered the theme continuously, and not without cause, since there was no preconditioned public for ballet as such, only for acclaimed exponents. There were times when she felt threatened. She was now thirty-six, an age that she had been brought up to believe marked the end of a ballerina's career, and though her deepest confidence (and the examples of Kchessinskaya and Preobrajenskaya) told her this was silly, she knew that the path could never get any easier. She had exchanged the security of a pampered Imperial ballerina for the total uncertainty of a wandering player, and if she never once doubted the exchange was worth it, then she was superhuman. Most onlookers considered her to be exactly so. She drove others hard, but only so long as she drove

Stefa Plaskowieczka

herself harder; she criticized others and was merciless with herself. She was incapable of understanding that the price might be too high. In her case, necessity did not allow any alternative.

From Chile there was the trip through the Andes into Argentina, where they had been booked for a season at the Teatro Coliseo in Buenos Aires. Their official debut in the city took place in the magnificent Colón opera house on August 11; they were in the Colón the following night as well. Maestro Paolantonio conducted the second and fifth acts of *Faust*, then yielded the podium to Smallens for the ballet. Pavlova and Volinine led the revels of *Walpurgisnacht* before the usual divertissements. The season in Buenos Aires started on a high note, and there was no falling off once they went over to the Coliseo; indeed, many of the regular opera patrons were deserting the Colón in favor of the other house. Pavlova's company left Buenos Aires for Montevideo, just as the Diaghilev company arrived from there. Pavlova's plan was to go from Montevideo to a series of "up country" appearances in Argentina, but she got no farther than Rosario, where she was halted by Argentina's first national rail strike (even chauffeurs and tram drivers joined in). The tour had to be abandoned, and the company made its way back to Buenos Aires by boat, arriving in time to see the rival company at the Colón, where it was performing in conjuction with the resident opera. Pavlova's company gave several hastily scheduled performances at the Coliseo in the time that was left before their planned return to Montevideo.

---

*In 1913 the composer had traveled to Ivy House to play for Pavlova; he was full of praise for the strength and beauty she brought to her interpretation of *The Swan*, and he hoped that she might find inspiration in more of his work. But nothing seemed to have caught her fancy then. When her pianist, Walford Hyden, asked her what she thought of the music, she replied rather elliptically that the great man emitted a glowing light!

With Stowitts in *Syrian Dance,* Paris, c.1920.

For Pavlova's entrée into South America Clustine had reintroduced his Egyptian ballet (it went on in Guayaquil), masquerading in the programs under the respectability of Verdi (always printed in large letters) "and other composers." While this placated stern opera-house patrons who might have sniffed at Luigini, it was in fact he who supplied the bulk of the musical fare in this ballet. His "Ballet Egyptien" suite, with its light, tuneful echoes of Delibes and Glazunov, was less of a hodgepodge than the medley contrived by Diaghilev for *Cléopâtre* in Paris in 1909. Clustine tried to capture some of the exoticism of *Cléopâtre,* with moments of pseudo-antique angularity in the choreography, and the décor (scenery by Samoiloff and costumes by Bain) owed a great deal to Bakst. There was thus a chance for Pavlova to re-create her Ta-Hor image from the earlier ballet, with its unusual make-up. Luigini's adagio sections were swooningly pretty, and they suited Pavlova to perfection. When the ballet was shown in Buenos Aires, members of the Diaghilev troupe could form their own opinions as to the merits of Clustine's Egypt, but they had no chance of outflanking it with the Egypt of Fokine and Bakst, since the *Cléopâtre* scenery had just been destroyed when one of the railway cars transporting their effects caught fire in a tunnel between Rio and São Paulo.

Buenos Aires was given further performances of a one-act ballet culled from Massenet's *Thaïs.* It had first been seen at the end of June; in it Pavlova had a double role, as a courtesan and as the vision of Thaïs. She had a big success in the work, but the choreographic material was desperately thin for the rest of the cast. They all had more of an even chance in *The Fairy Doll,* by now the stock-in-trade, yet Pavlova could hold attention by not moving at all. When the curtains of the doll's box were drawn aside halfway through the first scene, audiences would catch their breath at the sight of the ballerina in her wig of pinkish spun-glass curls topped by a net of pearls and her tutu encrusted with silver tinsel. Then there was the suspense of waiting for her to move; but of course she did not, as long as the "humans" were in the toy shop. Although the scenario demanded that she remain immobile at this point, Pavlova always breathed slowly and extra deeply so that the sequins on her bodice would sparkle and catch the light.

It was at this very time that Diaghilev and Massine, in Spain, were thinking that the theme of the toy shop would consort well with a series of Rossini compositions. Diaghilev had not traveled to South America, supposedly because of restrictions by the Russian "governmental committee," but more probably because of his phobia about crossing water; however, this was always a selective fear, and the suspicion and antagonism of Romola Nijinsky, who was traveling with her husband on the South American tour, must have tipped the scales against the crossing, perhaps even more than the thought of sea warfare. Massine's great predecessor was already causing unease among his colleagues; there were signs that some form of mental instability was beginning to darken his life. Pavlova was aware of this, and in Buenos Aires, though she found it a melancholy prospect, she became convinced that Nijinsky's dancing days were almost over.

Grigoriev, who was running the company for Diaghilev, went so far as to offer a contract to Oliveroff, while Nijinsky's principal partner, Lydia Lopokhova, turned up in Pavlova's dressing room one night on the verge of tears, voicing a willingness to transfer to the Pavlova Company.

But Pavlova had no need of being accused of poaching on another company's preserve while it was under stress. After dancing at a benefit for the poor on October 18, Pavlova departed for Montevideo. She left with Oliveroff and without Lopokhova. By chance, Nijinsky preceded them there. He had stayed behind in South America to perform at a gala in Montevideo in aid of the Red Cross, sharing the bill with the pianist Arthur Rubinstein on October 26; it was Nijinsky's last appearance in public as a dancer. Pavlova arrived back in Montevideo on October 20, and shortly afterward the manager of the Colón did likewise; he proposed to Pavlova that she return to Buenos Aires and run a season in conjunction with the opera at the Colón, just as the Diaghilev company had done. Pavlova refused, partly on the principle that a well-disposed audience should always be left wanting more, and partly because Adolfo Bracale had already mapped out more touring, northward. This was a desirable direction, even if it led into the arena of sea warfare. The Diaghilev company had risked sailing back to Spain, but shipping was at a premium, and the losses in the Atlantic were mounting due to the attempted blockade of Britain by German U-boats, a hazard Pavlova could not bear to face. In any event, there were such uncertainties about the state of theatre throughout Europe that Pavlova finally abandoned her idea of getting back to England for another of Alfred Butt's seasons.

Avoiding the more acute hazards of the Atlantic, Pavlova left Uruguay and sailed along the coast of Brazil toward Rio. The blur of travel merged into the blur of more continual performing: several weeks in Rio, then São Paulo, Bahia (now Salvador), Pernambuco, Belém, Trinidad, and Caracas. (A plaque in the Manaus Opera House suggests that Pavlova penetrated that far up river.) At Pernambuco two 1915 ballets were reintroduced into the program: *Visions,* to music of Berlioz, and a one-act reconstruction from *Paquita,* including the Grand Pas Classique. Pernambuco stuck in the memory because of the endless on-stage speeches in Portuguese; Trinidad was remembered because it was there that Volinine landed from a jump and went right through the stage, mercifully with no more serious damage than a severe scraping. The Trinidad performance was unscheduled; the ship was merely loading fruit. But Pavlova, impulsively, wanted to show the locals some dancing, and a show was cobbled together in an old cinema, with music played on a decaying upright. Other conditions were taking their toll. Stefa Plaskowieczka had need of a nursing home and took off on a long journey alone, back to New York. Pavlova gave one performance in Puerto Cabello, Venezuela, on December 9, and then came to a temporary halt in Puerto Rico when the ticket sales proved disastrous. They had done a week's performing in San Juan and a week more circling the island. Pavlova danced in Ponce, Guayama, Mayagüez, and

South America, 1917: Dancing the *Sleeping Beauty* pas de deux with Volinine at the Italian Consulate in Rio.

ABOVE Shopping for fruit in Trinidad.
BELOW In fancy dress, off the coast of southern Brazil.

263

Puerto Rico, Christmas 1917, with Poppy.

Arecibo before giving up. It seemed an opportune moment to stop and take stock, and certainly they were all in desperate need of a vacation. "Coming to Puerto Rico was a losing venture for me, from a financial point of view," Pavlova told a representative of the Puerto Rico *Progress*, "but there has been ample compensation for that in the restful pleasure of my stay here. . . . I did not make money here, but I rested, and an artist needs rest."

Pavlova had encountered a young American woman, Elizabeth Herrington, living in what seemed an ideal situation on the banks of the Condado River. There was a sandy foreshore running for miles where the river entered the sea, and the whole area was blessedly unspoiled. Miss Herrington knew of a similar house that was available for rental. Pavlova quickly established her miniature household: Dandré, the maid, and the Boston terrier; the rest of the company sought lodgings in the vicinity. There they idled for two whole months, all but cut off from the world and its upheavals. For exercise they swam constantly and walked for miles. Mail from New York filtered through infrequently; there was none at all from Russia. Pavlova had not heard any news of her mother for over a year—was she alive or dead?

Although Pavlova had every intention of keeping her touring company together, she had to face the fact that in America as well as Europe the state of unsubsidized theatre was uncertain. There were, in addition, the complications of passport regulations in a country that was actively at war. This ruled out that country for the company as a whole, so the main prospect was a return circuit in South America. Pavlova was disenchanted with Bracale, and turned an ear to overtures from another impresario, Renato Salvati, who envisaged a tour more or less reversing the sequence of the 1917 trip.

Even with her continuing fitness, Pavlova needed one or two experienced ballerinas to back her up. Plaskowieczka's future was uncertain at this stage, but Pavlova had been able to contact the Russian ballerina Vlasta Maslova, who had been dancing in America in glorified vaudeville programs. She was married to an officer in the Russian Army, but she knew that her fellow artists in Russia were beginning to suffer dreadful privations and that the army itself was divided and in disarray, and the offer from Pavlova presented a perfect respite from making a decision about returning to Europe. She traveled to Puerto Rico in February 1918, and by chance, Plaskowieczka was on the same boat. Stefa's beauty had taken some punishment in the months that preceded her return to the company, and she had put on weight. Pavlova's attitude was one of ruthless detachment: if Stefa was no longer suited to some of her former roles, then those would have to be distributed elsewhere. Stefa was deputed to teach two of her

264

favorite roles to Vlasta Maslova, and the task demoralized her.*

Pavlova had a deep-seated element of insecurity in her make-up, and she was constantly assessing the attributes of others, particularly women who combined talent with beauty. She was wistful when one such as Stefa was in her prime, and though her own true age was artfully concealed from everyone in the company, the truth of the matter contributed to her bouts of self-doubt. The outward appearance of such a state was usually assigned by others to pure jealousy, but such a straightforward diagnosis took no account of the uniquely difficult position occupied by Pavlova, at the head of a company whose wages were the direct result of her own skills, fortitude, and will power. In the case of Dandré, Pavlova knew that his managerial skills served their cause admirably, but she had too an uneasy awareness that his desperately conventional sensibilities about art always laid an overrestrictive hand on her own willingness to be adventurous. Diaghilev's aggressive search for novelty was a factor that Pavlova had always noted carefully, and in some ways tried to emulate. Dandré distrusted these trends utterly.

So Vlasta Maslova arrived, taking billing second only to the great Anna. The company, as it was reassembled, proved even bigger than before. Among the young recruits was Ruth Page, who had taken classes with the company in Chicago. She was only just sixteen and had to travel with her mother as chaperone. Ruth, a young lady of decided opinion, was soon writing down her views: Maslova was "not bad, but no personality—rather insignificant and vaudevillish, but does *wonderful* turns," while Hilda Butsova had apparently "improved a lot." The nucleus of an orchestra led by Smallens was strengthened in an effort to avoid the moments of chaos with local recruits, which could lead to the conductor's having to whistle scraps of melody to support the dancers. There were twenty principal ballets and enough costumes for seventy-five individual divertissements. All this paraphernalia, quite apart from the sixty-five individuals who needed it, made transportation, in wartime, almost impossibly difficult. Many of the usual steamship lines were discontinued, and most of the tramp steamers were hopelessly inadequate. It was now Dandré's turn to set off on a lone trip: he had to travel back to New York to make personal representations among the various national shipping bureaus. Eventually he was able to arrange for a ship to hold accommodations vacant while it diverted its route to Puerto Rico. The "Gran Compañía de Bailes

Clásicos Anna Pavlowa" finally set sail at the end of February 1918 in search of new gold, and it was still aboard the S.S. *Curvello* when Lenin signed the Brest-Litovsk peace, a stroke that made many of the dancers stateless persons overnight. Now there was no going back.

In Puerto Rico:
(above) with Maslova and Saxova.

* Oliveroff saw all this as a sinister plan on Pavlova's part, that she was exacting a strange form of revenge for Stefa's having "plied her conquests a little too close to Madame's heart. . . . " It is true that because of her own circumscribed life, Pavlova expected Victor Dandré to be equally monklike, but that was not his way, and she knew it—just as she knew that his deepest loyalty and devotion were laid unswervingly at her own feet. It was a hopelessly complex situation from which neither could free the other. Pavlova's apparent cruelty in this situation was subsequently presented by Oliveroff as an inexplicable dark side of Pavlova's character. Whatever was going through Pavlova's mind, her primary concern was the running of a tight ship, and there could be no room on the foredeck for a struggling, buxom ballerina. Had Pavlova allowed the girl to continue as before, that also could have been viewed as cruel. Plaskowieczka had been a fine performer, but her dedication was always less than total, because of her "life on the side." This would have exasperated Pavlova, who understood the nature of genuine sacrifice all too well.

On board the S.S. *Curvello* off the coast
of Brazil, 1918: (below) Pavlova in mid flight,
headed for one of her celebrated bellyflops;
(right) Pavlova is in the pool.

R uth Page's mother, Marion, kept a journal relating to the tour that she and her daughter had joined. In it she wrote: "Pavlova adores swimming and probably would have stayed in all day if M. Dandré, her husband, had permitted. He takes care of her just as one would a child. Such devotion as he lavishes upon her is seldom seen. He was so funny when he would try to get her to come out of the swimming pool (he never went in); he would stand on the upper deck and call "Annushka! Annushka! It is time to come out!" and she would laugh and make a face. Sometimes that would keep up for half an hour, and then she would come out protesting like a naughty child."

The company's first calls were to Pará, Pernambuco, and Bahia. After the last engagement many of the girls went on board ship with squirrel monkeys as pets. Pavlova, not to be outdone, had four of them in a cage, but they died of a surfeit of marmalade. One girl returned to her quarters to discover that her monkey had jumped into an electric fan and distributed itself all over

the cabin. Fragile creatures, few survived the trip, particularly as the weather grew steadily cooler as they progressed south. In Rio, on May 11, Maslova was allowed to do one performance of *Giselle*, but she does not seem to have been a success. Then an Italian naval ship took them on to Buenos Aires. There was war discipline on board, with dimmed lights in the evenings, which did not make the trip to the dining room any easier. (It could only be reached by way of the ship's storerooms, which seemed to be totally crammed with crates of bananas.) There was agreeable comment one evening about the fact that the strawberry jam actually had whole fruit in it; in the gloom several dancers had second and third helpings. Daylight later revealed the "solids" to be cockroaches. To ease the monotony (and soothe the digestion), Colin Quirk, the company's Irish pianist, often played the rehearsal piano in the hours of darkness during the five-day trip.

In Buenos Aires, Pavlova had to make her customary entrée at the opera house before moving over to the Coliseo. The season was to run from June 19 to July 10. *Rigoletto* occupied most of the evening at the Colón; only three divertissements were given: *The Swan*, *Moment Musical*, and the *Gavotte*. At the Coliseo, Dandré had to have portable heaters installed in the dressing rooms; but there was little that could be done about the chill draftiness of the stage. Still, the Argentineans' brief glimpse of Pavlova at the Colón had whetted appetites, and the Coliseo always had a full and appreciative audience. On June 22 the company gave a one-act version of Gounod's *Romeo and Juliet* for the first time. This ballet (sometimes billed as *Juliet's Dream*) was a vehicle for Maslova and Volinine. Pavlova was not tempted by the role of Juliet; she seemed not to have much sympathy with down-to-earth characters unless they were of the cheerful variety, such as in *La Fille Mal Gardée*, *The Magic Flute*, or *Christmas*. (Fokine once said that for all Pavlova's deserved fame as a spiritual inter-preter, her greatest achievements lay in lighthearted dances, for "Pavlova does not merely show us Pavlova in a gay mood, she expresses gaiety itself.")

For closing night on July 10, the Argentine "four hundred"—the city's social élite—was out in force. *Les Préludes* was followed by the ballet from *Thaïs*; then, after the second intermission, came a premiere: *Danza de las Flores*, to Delibes, with Pavlova as Mariposa (Butterfly), Volinine as El Sol (The Sun), and eleven girls as various flowers. It is more likely to have been a reshaping of Pavlova's Palace Theatre *Birth of the Butterfly* from 1913 than anything from the terrible Coppini version of *La Source* at the Maryinsky. There then followed *Anitra's Dance*, *Moment Musi-cal*, the *Gavotte*, and *Obertass*, and then another premiere: Clus-tine's *El Ultimo Canto*, to music of Augusto Maurage, danced by Pavlova and Volinine, with Stuart and Zalevsky. And in case all this was not considered sufficient for a grand evening, after the third intermission Pavlova led the company in dances from *Car-men*. If Buenos Aires had seemed dull and chill, the hospitality of its inhabitants had been so lavish that when it came time to leave, two or three of the girls announced their intention of remaining there. As there was no way that Pavlova could impel them to stay with the company, she shrugged off their desertion. Plaskowieczka was the principal loss. She had recovered some of her zest for life, and since Rio she had been followed by a wealthy German with Brazilian business interests, and with the ballet ceasing to hold any joy for her, she turned wholeheartedly to this latest admirer.

Two days after leaving Buenos Aires, and with only a brief halt at Mendoza, the Pavlova Company arrived at the transfer junction at the base of the Andes. At six o'clock in the morning they climbed aboard the narrow-gauge train that was to haul them through the pass at an altitude of fourteen thousand feet. The train often had to wait while snow was cleared, and during these delays, many of the dancers climbed down and ran along the track in an endeavor to loosen their muscles and get warm. Their arrival at Los Andes, at the Chilean end of the pass, was five hours behind schedule; they transferred back to a bigger train and did not reach Santiago until three o'clock the following morning.

ABOVE The cover of a program from the Coliseo, showing Pavlova in *Syrian Dance*.

BELOW Another page from Smallens's scrapbook, Buenos Aires, 1918.

Les Preludes in Buenos Aires:
(above) corps de ballet grouping;
(below) Pavlova.

The season there was unusually difficult because almost everyone was suffering from colds; but there were good audiences, and the theatre was luxurious. Impresario Salvati, making the most of his acquisitions, ventured to move the company into the southern parts of Chile with a string of visits down the coast, following a season in Valparaiso. In each city Pavlova gave one performance as a benefit for the Red Cross. *El Ultimo Canto* was given in Concepción on September 3 and was being billed as a premiere; it was now labeled "a musical elegy" in one act and two scenes, and with an intermission before and after, it seems to have been of some substance.

The company then moved on to Iquiqui; in port were the British cruisers *Avoca* and *Lancaster*—and also bubonic plague, according to worried European traders. The naval officers entertained the dancers on board *Lancaster,* and they all made plans to meet up again in Lima. Pavlova had to fit in Antofagasta first. The Pacific swells at this part of the coast were considerable, and since there was no deep-water harbor, it was necessary to transfer to a launch for the trip ashore. The company lined up on deck apprehensively, waiting for a signal to descend the companion ladder. Dandré had gone back to the cabins to arrange that personal hand baggage be lowered separately. Pavlova started down the ladder first; there was no one to help her, and only one sailor on the deck of the launch. Mrs. Page described the incident in her journal:

> She got down to the foot and was just ready to step into the launch when the big boat gave a sudden lurch and the water came way up on the stairs. Only her strength and presence of mind kept her from being washed off. Several of our men rushed down, and when the launch rose to the level of the stairs, she jumped on it. We were simply scared to death about her, but she was so calm. She said it was nothing—only wet feet and a scratched knee.

Mrs. Page had noted this calm more than once: "I thought her extraordinarily even-tempered, with remarkable self-control. Now and then at rehearsals she would get a bit sharp, but it certainly was justified. No one could be a better traveler. She never found fault or complained, and whatever had to be, she accepted it with a philosophical calm which was to be envied." She also admired the ballerina's stamina: "Pavlova works far harder than any member of her company. She seems to have endless endurance and vitality and never tires. She would come to the theatre at 10:30 every day, practice an hour or more herself, then help different ones or direct a rehearsal; come back to rehearsal in the afternoon, and then would practice again before the performance, dance two difficult ballets and two divertissements, and after all that did not show the slightest sign of fatigue."

In Lima, Pavlova gave a special performance for the crews of the two British cruisers. Many of the young men were on their first tour of duty. When some of the dancers were entertained onboard, a number of crew members were confined to their hammocks with influenza. It was the prelude to a disaster. Ten days after their ships sailed from Lima there was an outbreak of the virulent strain of influenza on board *Lancaster*; within days, two hundred and fifty of the men had died, including the young chief medical officer. The news was particularly distressing for the dancers, who had so recently made friends with many of the men who were now dead. By this time the company was suffering from some form of the same epidemic, but they had yet to hear of its catastrophic course in North America. In Lima, Pavlova succumbed the last but was affected the worst. After struggling on for several days, she was finally forced to her bed, and the performances on the last two days of the season had to be given without her. Her illness was common gossip, and the other dancers felt sure that the Lima audiences would desert them, but they were wrong; the houses remained full. It seemed the public had acquired a taste for ballet itself.

At the end of October the company was able to sail north for Panama. There was a week for recuperation, before the daily grind began again in Panama City. Because American marines at Ancon, in the Canal Zone, were forbidden to enter the city, a committee of young officers made a deputation to Pavlova with an offer that they would build a stage on one of their piers if the company would consent to dance for them. Pavlova agreed, particularly as part of the proceeds were to go to the Red Cross. The prices were kept low, and thousands of people got in to see the performances. Pier 18 was a cheerful sight, with a stage across the full width, fronted by a proscenium of palm branches and flags. More onlookers peered down from the decks of ships into the "wings," and there was a riot of cheering after the *Gavotte*.

News of the Armistice in Europe had not come through at this stage, and the program for November 14 was still running anti-German advertisements paid for by sympathetic subscribers: "To drive out the HUNS" was the frank message on one page. The success of the shows on Pier 18 brought forth more requests, so Pavlova took her company across the isthmus to appear in Colón in a huge hangar temporarily converted into a theatre by aviators who managed to hang the scenery from a dizzying 120 feet. Then it was back across to Ancon again. The first hint of an armistice seems to have been regarded as a false alarm after a brief bout of celebration, but soon enough there was confirmation, and joy erupted. Mrs. Page recorded: "Never shall we forget the procession of negroes, dancing and cake-walking, laughing, crying, embracing, and singing, while a big, out-of-tune calliope brought up the rear playing circus tunes. . . . As processions seemed to be in vogue, we joined some of our soldier friends in an army truck and paraded all around, singing and blowing horns, waving flags." There were parties everywhere.

Dandré soon scotched the rumors that peace meant an end to all the touring. He had previously given Bracale an option for a season in Havana, and had also agreed that the company would appear in Mexico. A trip to Jamaica was canceled only because of an influenza scare and a premium on shipping, which was also making the longer leg to Cuba problematical. They finally managed to get taken on board a French cargo boat carrying saltpeter. "There were only four

ABOVE Enid Brunova in *Anitra's Dance*.

BELOW Pavlova in costume for the *Godard Pas de Trois*, Buenos Aires, 1918.

On board the cattle steamer off the coast of Chile, 1918.

ABOVE Through the Andes.
BELOW At the party on board H.M.S. *Lancaster*.

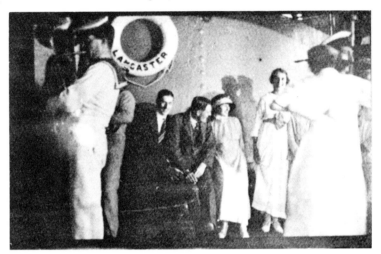

With Dandré.

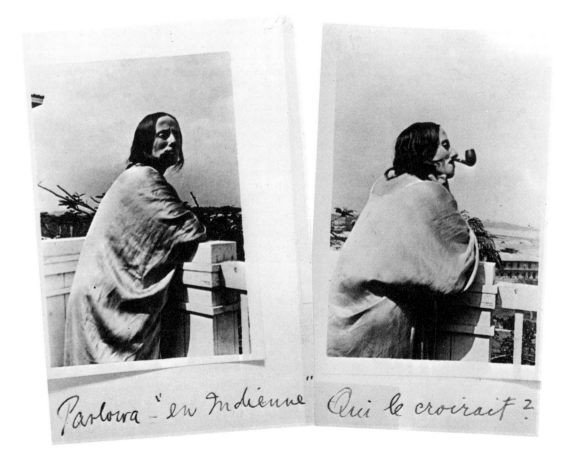

Parlowa - "en Indienne"   Qui le croirait?

On the balcony of the Tivoli Hotel, Panama,
clowning with Smallens's pipe.

Performing *Amarilla* in the bullring, Mexico City, 1919.

cabins and these were given the women for dressing rooms," Mrs. Page recorded, "and nearly everybody slept on army cots on deck. The voyage lasted seven days, but the weather was perfect and the food quite good, so we did not mind it much. As we had the whole boat to ourselves it was much nicer than the local Brazilian boats. Madame used to give a delightful tea-party every afternoon, which was the event of the day."

They docked at Santiago, Cuba, on December 8 only to find the town in the grip of a general strike; there was no transport to take them on to Havana. They were stuck in Santiago for two weeks, before some American soldiers got them onto a strike-breakers' train driven by a scratch crew, who seemed to have only the most rudimentary knowledge of the driving of a steam engine. The food ran out after the first day, since that was the normal span of the trip, but they had actually gone barely a third of the distance. The remainder took two more days, and the only food came from American soldiers camped at a site near one of the stations. Havana was not much of an improvement. Bracale had not booked any accommodations for the company; he was probably astonished to find they had arrived at all. On the first night, Pavlova made room for a number of girls on the floor of the sitting room in her hotel suite, where they tossed and turned all night while a drunk sang inexhaustibly in the street below. The company was to perform in conjunction with Bracale's opera. It was an uncomfortable and unmemorable season, enliv-

ened only by a Christmas celebration at which a toast was thankfully offered to the new peace.

A newspaper correspondent filing a story for the *New York Times* gave readers the first news of Pavlova in over a year. By this time she had reached the end of her patience with Bracale. She spoke of Guayaquil, at the beginning of their odyssey, twenty months ago: "Probably, as many others, I had not heard anything about this town, and only when we arrived there I understood how unclever, not to say more, it had been on the part of our impresario to let us come to this place." And still she was willing to face Mexico, despite tales of horrific banditry. The company sailed for Veracruz on the S. S. *Esperanza* in the middle of January 1919. To get them safely into Mexico City, the president insisted that troops guard their train; the "troops" appeared to be a rabble of peasants, but at least they were well armed. They disported themselves on the roofs of the carriages for the duration of the journey. The girls were appalled to see the corpses of bandits hanging from poles beside the railway track.

The season in Mexico began very well for Pavlova; she was received as a great star of the theatre, the company was fêted, and the president did her honor. At a matinee on February 2, Pablo Casals played *The Swan*. To keep his presence a surprise to Pavlova, the famous cellist was spirited into the wings after the lights had gone down for the third part of the program. Pavlova was amazed to hear the cello coming from the side of the stage and even more amazed at the beautiful tone; she bourréed closer and closer, trying to see into the darkness of the wings and discover the identity of the player. Casals saw the transfixing eyes searching for his and was so mesmerized that he had to shut his own tightly in order to be able to go on playing.

Unfortunately, the novelty of regular ballet performances in Mexico City soon wore off, and it proved regrettable that Pavlova was persuaded to outstay her initial welcome. Accounts of the company's "triumph" in Mexico have glossed over the fact that the visit went sour soon after the grand opening, which had been graced by the top echelons of society. They did not choose to book seats for the full season, and there was a disheartening slump in sales. Dandré and the impresario sought to repair the damage by extending the season in all sorts of makeshift ways, including performances in a bullring. It was a desperate endeavor, and a dying fall to what had been an amazing saga of artistic toil. By now the company was being run very ragged, and dancing at altitude added to the stress. Nor was there any comfort from the *Musical Courier*, which turned a cold-blooded eye on the events under a headline that read "Pavlova Dances—So Do Her Prices":

Mexican Dances, 1919:
(below) with Saxova and Verina.

With Mikhail Pianowski.

> The ballet was generally liked though it is admitted that the present company of this admirable Russian dancer is very incomplete and quite inferior to what it was when Nijinsky was the first male dancer in the troupe.* Pavlova has been much criticized for her disregard for public interests. When the season was announced at the Arbeu Theatre, the company which brought her from Havana advertised a series of fifteen ballets at eight pesos (four dollars) parquet per ballet or ten pesos single numbers. As the commencement of this season was practically a failure, due to the high prices, after a week single seats were lowered to six pesos without any consideration for those who had paid at eight pesos for the series. To add to this Pavlova, when she went over with her company to the Principal Theatre, lowered the price to five pesos a seat. In the "El Toro" Bull Ring (a splendid site for open air performances, with a capacity of 20,000 spectators), where she has given four or five Sunday performances, three pesos was charged, and finally she consented to work at the Cine Granat for 1.50 pesos a seat, commencing the 20th. Perhaps she will cheapen her work more still, as it is not nearly so popular. She announced her farewell for March 31, but as she has done this four or five times before, we do not know if it is true.

It was all very sad, the scramble for pesos to make the books balance; and yet the crowds who did turn up in the bullring enjoyed themselves immensely. Pavlova won their sympathies with *Mexican Dances*, a divertissement for three couples, led by herself and Mikhail Pianowski, the assistant ballet master. In it she translated a national dance step usually done on the heel into pointe work, which she did around the brim of a huge sombrero placed on the floor of the stage. At the first sight of this there was a riot of appreciative shouting, and many men hurled their own hats onto the stage, hoping that Pavlova would dance on them too. The ballet's costumes were renditions of traditional Mexican wear, and the draped backcloth had motifs copied from a peasant

---

*The writer was not the first to be under the misapprehension that there was only one company of Russian dancers touring around.

273

Léon Barté in the divertissement from
Schéhérazade, Mexico City, 1919.

shawl. Pavlova, Saxova, and Verina carried baskets of flowers on their heads. These were put aside before Pavlova did her solo on the hat's brim. The finale was a whirling dance with all three couples on stage. Pavlova wore long braids with bows at the end, and she began with a scene in mime, entering as a young girl scuffing along in a bored and sulky mood, which was dispelled when she encountered a handsome young man. It was all set to the music of Castro Padilla, which also appealed to the crowd; but it was dancing, not bullfighting, and the relatively poor receipts pointed up the difference.

When the Mexico City season came to a standstill at the end of March, there were some big questions to be answered: would the postwar world support the entire company, or would it be only Pavlova herself who could ensure the bookings? The experience in Mexico City had been chastening. Pavlova had tried every trick she knew; toward the end she had brought back Fokine's *Prince Igor* dances and a truncated version of *Schéhérazade* as divertissements, as well as a Sousa work from the New York Hippodrome. But that was clinging to old formulas. Her mind at this point was running to new ventures, but the direction and focus had yet to be fixed.

After the wearying slog of the Latin American journeying, North America might have seemed enticing, but the reality was less rosy. Even if various passport difficulties could be sorted out, there was the bitter experience of previous American tours to contemplate: endless one-night stands from coast to coast. Not only were these tours exhausting, but they were complicated to organize and required months of preplanning. No one could wait that long. Pavlova was utterly committed to the concept of her company, but its hunting grounds were altering; already the depressing realities of postwar life in Europe were being made known to them. (In Tiflis, Mordkin and his wife had been discovered virtually starving to death.) Most of the company members were not so blasé as to think that jobs like theirs were freely available; they stuck to Pavlova—though Maslova and Smallens each accepted a contract for the next opera season in Mexico City. The rest were willing to face South America again—for that was the only viable route.

The company re-formed in readiness for South America in the knowledge that their audiences there were captive, and that the theatres in Rio and Buenos Aires were on a par with anything that North America or Europe could offer. Dancers with passport problems struck out directly for Rio as best they could; others traveled with Pavlova to New York, where Theodore Stier was reclaimed as Pavlova's musical director (his internment had been canceled by the war's end). Volinine, remarkably, found no enticement in New York and stayed with the troupe.

They embarked on the S. S. *Vestris* on April 12, 1919, their route Barbados, Bahia, Rio, Santos, Montevideo, and finally Buenos Aires. There was a two-month breathing space in which to think about new ballets. In 1912 Clustine had choreographed *La Péri* for Natalia Trouhanova, at the instigation of the composer, Paul Dukas, who was then her lover. Bakst had created a décor showing gold mountains, crimson valleys, and trees bearing silver fruit, as a setting for the story of the Fallen Angel who guards the Lotus of Immortality. Clustine decided to reshape the ballet for Pavlova, and Hubert Stowitts was given the chance to create fresh designs. He was also going to get the chance to partner Pavlova by playing the part of Iskender, the Shah striving to gain possession of the lotus.*

It was intended that Pavlova's company would perform in conjunction with the opera in Buenos Aires for the duration of the season, but due to infrequent shipping from Italy, many of the intended singers trailed in hopelessly late, and the first full

* It has been suggested that *La Péri* was first performed in Buenos Aires in August 1917, but the scrapbook-journal of Alexander Smallens, who scrupulously logged every program for the 1917–18 period, does not mention this ballet. It would be an astonishing oversight for him. His energy in keeping the records finally deserted him in 1918—understandable, but to be regretted. Inside the cover of his journal he kept a handwritten list of the ballets and operas which he conducted during the Pavlova tours. One grouping, which seems to apply to the first half of 1918, contains *Romeo, Thaïs, Schubertiana,* and *Prince Igor,* and indeed all of these were seen in Rio and Buenos Aires in 1918. In a change of pen there are two final entries: "*Boudour* [sic]—Borowski; *L'Après-midi d'un faune*—Debussy." "*Boudour*" we can pin down as *Boudoir,* a ballet-pantomime composed in 1918 by the Anglo-American Felix Borowski. It is possible that Pavlova presented the premiere of this somewhere in Chile. But who was cavorting as a faun? Stowitts? A veil descends.

With Volinine and Vorontsoff
in the *Godard Pas de Trois*,
Mexico City, 1919.

ABOVE & OPPOSITE With Hubert Stowitts
in *La Péri*, Buenos Aires, 1919.

evening of opera could not take place until June 16, having been transferred from the Colón to the Coliseo, which had been lavishly redecorated. Massenet's *Thaïs* was chosen, and Pavlova and her company danced in the production—though presumably it was not her repertory ballet from the same opera score. Opera-goers frequently had the bonus of a Pavlova appearance; Antonio Gomes's *O Guaraní* was one of the operas she graced during this Coliseo season. In it she was an Indian woman of mysterious nature who haunted the rain forest. Stowitts played the hunter, drawing his bow on the creature, who kept vanishing and then reappearing, like some elusive tropical bird.

On July 23 a gala evening was given. Giulio Falconi conducted three acts of Rabaud's *Mârouf*, and then came *La Péri*, with Gino Marinuzzi conducting. It seems to have been an evening of rather blatant eroticism by the ballet company. They contributed a harem ballet to *Mârouf*, and then there were Pavlova and Stowitts climbing around one another in astonishing ways. Although Pavlova said later that the work that was needed to master the complex rhythms of *La Péri* made her soon wish she had never begun it, it seems she found the inner line of Dukas's music faultlessly. Clustine was annoyed to notice Stowitts adding his own embellishments to the choreography, just as the dancer had done in *Syrian Dance* when it was first performed in 1917; but Pavlova was merely amused by his cheek and viewed the new touches as improvements. The scenery was painted by Ferrarotti, from designs by Stowitts, who did much of the assembling of the costumes himself.* Still later in the evening, the March and Polovtsian Dances from *Prince Igor* were given. Although it seems to have escaped the notice of Diaghilev, the *Prince Igor* dances were often given by the Pavlova Company in 1918 and 1919. But for the fact that the programs nearly always credited Fokine, it might have been thought that these dances were a revision of Clustine's 1898 Moscow version.

During the sea voyage from New York, prior to the Buenos Aires season, Pavlova had begun to voice an interest in compiling a suite of Chopin pieces for a theme she had in mind as a full-company work. She had numerous Chopin pieces played over and over, selecting and discarding, until she had assembled a sequence to her satisfaction; it relied principally on the nocturnes. She was deeply engrossed with the exact form of the work and was later reported to have said that the ballet was in memory of a young student lover from her St. Petersburg days who had been drowned while trying to flee from the Bolsheviks. One cannot at this time make a guess as to his identity, or judge how youthful and how fleeting a romance it was; one can only speculate that some of her unhappiness, and her erratic response to the moral code of others, sprang from a brooding sense of loss—of what had been, and what might have been.

*Eyewitness accounts of these costumes vary. One reporter said Pavlova's costume was silver and turquoise, another, green and gold. Most probably it was the former, but changed color when the yellow floodlight was aimed at the lotus which Pavlova carried. It "blazed like the sun," according to one reviewer.

Autumn Leaves

Pavlova's ballet, which became *Autumn Leaves,* was simple, almost whimsical in outline. In a public park, a single surviving chrysanthemum bloom is buffeted by cruel blasts of wind tearing her from the flower bed. She is carried to and fro with eddies of falling leaves, until a poet, noticing the blossom's plight, attempts to restore her. He has no sooner done this, tenderly, than his attention is distracted by the arrival of his true love; he departs with the young lady, leaving the chrysanthemum to the mercy of the wind, which flings her to the ground, where she is left to die.

By all accounts, Pavlova's sensitivity to the theme and the music was exquisitely expressed. She took infinite pains with the fluid and apparently spontaneous patterns formed by the "leaves," and even after a successful premiere* she would not allow the curtain to go up on this ballet until she had personally rehearsed—and, if need be, adjusted—the running movements for the corps de ballet. She would take into account the exact area of each different stage thereafter, and with these last-minute rehearsals, the curtain for this ballet seldom went up on time. She demanded of the girls an utterly untrammeled freedom of physical movement, without any hint of artificiality. Once, when an

obdurate and unyielding girl consistently failed to follow the demonstrations of what was required, Pavlova at the last minute changed the program rather than let the ballet go on imperfectly. With a sense of defeat she said to the girl, "Someday, somewhere, *someone* will make you cry!" Hubert Stowitts, who won the part of the Autumn Wind, later described the original lighting effects:

> The stage was darkened while I was carrying and tossing her through the air, and there was a swirl of chilly pink, and icy blue, and frosty lights which eddied around us and obliterated the background entirely, and heightened the effect of a cruel wind maltreating a helpless flower. It was much more uncanny than the scene adopted four years later, without light effects.

Pavlova's extraordinary South American saga terminated in Bahia (Salvador) on November 4, 1919, when R.M.S. *Orbita* cast off, en route to Southampton, via Lisbon. Dandré could not resist the enticement of a new audience for Pavlova and had arranged that the company would disembark in Portugal; Pavlova's feelings on the matter can only be surmised. She was traveling as "Mrs. Anne Pavloff" and was not on view for much

---

* The earliest program I have found that mentions this ballet places it in Rio in September 1919.

Autumn Leaves

of the trip. She dutifully appeared in Lisbon, and then found herself headed for Madrid; there the King and Queen of Spain were often in the audience. *The Times* of London was there too:

> The opera season, which began so brilliantly with the appearance of Mlle. Pavlova's dancers, is now in full swing. Mlle. Pavlova arrived from Lisbon, where she had an enthusiastic reception. In Madrid, Russian dances had been presented during the war by Diaghilev's ballet, who had left an excellent impression as interpreters of the sense of the music to which they danced. Mlle. Pavlova was given out as being chiefly concerned with dancing rather than interpretation. When she appeared it was agreed that she combined both powers.

The Pavlova Company arrived in Paris at the beginning of December for a two-month season at the Théâtre des Champs-Elysées. The avenue Montaigne was thronged with excited patrons who used the occasion as an opportunity to present a *reprise de rigueur* in evening dress. Pavlova's appearance after an absence of eight years gave Parisians their first real excuse to revive a prewar severity of custom that was dear to their hearts. It was during this season that an emissary of the King of Spain asked Pavlova if she would make a return visit to Madrid; but to the monarch's disappointment, engagements had already been committed for Belgium and Holland.

During the Paris season (there was a sortie to Monte Carlo as well) Pavlova produced a novelty in the form of a little mime and dance story by Pierre Chantel. *Les Trois Pantins de Bois* had music by Michel Maurice-Lévy, who also conducted, and costumes by fashion illustrator Georges Lepape. The story line, in the form of a poem, was spoken from the stage. This rather disconcerted the audience, as did the fact that Pavlova's role was, in the main, all mime. She had the part of a poor girl, gravely ill, being cheered by the antics of three jumping jacks dancing to amuse her; when she complains piteously of the cold, they sacrifice themselves in the embers of the fire in order to give her a few moments of warmth. Critic Louis Laloy wrote:

> [Pavlova] displays the most exquisite feeling, and achieves, by dint of a virtuosity that can only be described as prodigious, effects of a most touching simplicity. See her, broken by illness, clasp to her heart the three Puppets that the Cruel Man, the heartless creditor, is preparing to take away! How delicate she is in her weakness when she collapses by the fireless hearth! And at the end, how incorporeal a joy ravishes and transfigures her when she revives, by virtue of the kindly little puppets' sacrifice, for a few instants—only too short for us—during which we see the Queen of Dancing dance at last!

The company moved on to Belgium, where performances were given in Liège for one week. During this run, word came

ABOVE *Les Trois Pantins de Bois*, Paris, early 1920.

At Ivy House, March 1920.

Underwood & Underwood

MME. ANNA PAVLOVA

Just returned from a dancing tour, is seen resting safe from Russian troubles on the porch of her English country home at Golders Green

through that the theatre in Antwerp, where they were due, had been destroyed by a fire, and with the cancellation of this engagement, Pavlova elected to use the time to take a short vacation in the south of France, rather than arrive at Ivy House before the planned date. The company's scenery and effects were loaded at Antwerp, where they proved more than one steamer could handle; a second had to be chartered to carry the excess. The luggage alone comprised 282 pieces.

The London theatre scene was something of an unknown quantity after all this time. Tastes had changed markedly during the Great War and its immediate aftermath. Music-hall programs were giving way to revues and musicals: *Chu-Chin-Chow* was well into its fourth year. Oswald Stoll had turned the Alhambra over to the films of D. W. Griffith, and even the huge London Opera House had become the Stoll Picture Theatre. Alfred Butt had a revue called *The Whirligig* at the Palace, but, together with Arthur Collins, he was also managing the Theatre Royal in Drury Lane, and it was there that Pavlova's return was billed—ten years after the disappointments with Diaghilev. His famous leading lady, Karsavina, was at the Coliseum ending a run in J. M. Barrie's one-act play *The Truth About the Russian Dancers*—"Showing How They Love, How They Marry, How They Are Made, with How They Die and Live Happy Ever Afterwards." The starring role in this mouthful was essentially one of mime and dance; Karsavina had taken it on when Lopokhova abandoned the production during an early stage of rehearsals.

In her wanderings abroad, Pavlova had referred with nostalgia to Ivy House on countless occasions. She had gone out the door on October 9, 1914; now, on March 29, 1920, she was back. It should not have come as a surprise that, after five and a half years, the swans ignored Pavlova's call. But the fact upset her, and she mentioned it in an interview. A few days later a letter arrived from a swan fancier who offered hints on the birds and their handling. Pavlova asked him to call, liked him, and, when she saw how quickly he gained the swans' confidence, agreed to his visiting Ivy House daily. She and Dandré referred to him as the "swan professor," and the cob soon became very tame as a result of the training. The pair even produced cygnets, and these too were trained to come when called; the lure was freshly cut grass. Pavlova had difficulty in distinguishing the pen from the cob and cheerfully called both adults Jack. Eventually the cob became so tame that he would come out onto the lawn and allow Pavlova to fondle him. Notwithstanding the initial professional training, there was still something strange in the degree of familiarity achieved by Pavlova, who could roughhouse with the bird in a manner more suitable for a friendly dog. The powerful creature was totally acquiescent in these games, and photographers were able to catch some wonderful poses.

Pavlova's long absence abroad had done nothing to dim her news value in England, and in view of the coming Drury Lane engagement she agreed to meet with various reporters asking for interviews and photographs. The strain of the previous five years was noticeable in her face; the piquant expression was unchanged, but there was a certain tautness, and the flesh had sunk under the eyes.

There were some clouds of dispute dimming the brightness of her return to her adopted homeland. Nationalism was evident everywhere, and some of the journalists caught the mood:

> One of the minor compensations of a great war is the opportunity it gives us of welcoming back the self-banished idols of peace. At the first breath of powder they flee from our midst—whether they be persons or institutions. When the trouble is over and we begin to tread the road back to peace, our journey is freshened by the sight of their return. In this way Madame Anna Pavlova with the Russian Ballet party has just come back to London after an absence of nearly six years.

Noting Theodore Stier's presence in the company, the National Orchestral Association issued an ultimatum: Pavlova would have to find a British substitute for Stier or face a musicians' strike at the opening of her Drury Lane season on April 12. Stier, who had been rehearsing for three weeks before the trouble showed itself, was at a loss: "My correct description is that I am an ally of Great Britain. I am alien only in the sense that any other non-British ally is one." With only a few days to go, it was apparent that no other conductor, British or otherwise, would handle the repertoire with any confidence, for, as Stier pointed out, "it is not a question of my being a good conductor; it simply means that my long experience in these same ballets enables me to watch the dancers' feet, and not the music. This can't be learned in twelve days." Pavlova fenced as best she could, pointing out that Stier had been conducting in England for the last twenty years. Her mathematics may have been awry, but her sentiments were sound. "England for the English" was, she thought, an admirable ideal, but not yet a practicable one. "I have in my company Americans, French, English, Russians—everybody. I could not do without any of them." Stier declared that he bore no malice toward anyone. "I know London too well to do so. I do not at all despair of a way out from this impasse, for I know the English love of fair play. Most of the orchestra are my very good friends. This season will only last some eight weeks, and I had arranged to leave London directly it was over." With the "fair play" taunt it was not long before there were signs of a change of heart, particularly as no other conductor was eager to be judged by severe musical critics such as Ernest Newman.

Pavlova tried to draw the sting out of the subject by waxing enthusiastic about the possibilities for the advancement of English dancers:

> "English girls, who have become increasingly interested in dancing, are most sincere, devoted, and conscientious in what they take up. There is a natural reserve, but you must throw your feeling into your art, and become expressive when the occasion demands it; to be happy you must *be* happy, and in crying you must *cry*. English girls have the feminine grace and charm, and the physical lines; many are very beautiful."

Snowflakes, c.1920.

When the Drury Lane engagement began, it was Stier who stepped onto the podium—to be greeted with an almost exaggerated round of applause. "Fair play" had won. Pavlova herself was received with rapture from a house, as one reporter put it, "chock full of distinguished and undistinguished people." The purist *Times* critic noted that the enthusiasm was of a kind that "cheerfully and ruthlessly breaks up a ballet by breaking into it, stopping the music, keeping the dancer curtseying and kissing her hand, when what we all really want is for the music to go on playing and the dancer to go on dancing to it." This same critic thought that *Snowflakes* was a dull and heavy thing to have fastened onto Tchaikovsky's *Nutcracker* music, but he conceded that it did give Pavlova a chance to do her "stunts," showing that she had lost none of her virtuosity, just as a returning violinist might play some impossible piece to prove that his fingers had not grown stiff. In *Amarilla* this virtuosity was seen to be but a means toward great dramatic expression, and by the time Pavlova came to dance *The Swan*, audience and critics were as one: "If we had imagined that a thing perfectly beautiful some years ago could not be perfectly beautiful still, we were mistaken." *The Times* reached its conclusion: "Well! Mme. Pavlova is still Pavlova, the incomparable. There are other great dancers. There is only one Pavlova."

Four nights later Pavlova introduced Vera Karalli to Drury Lane, in *Thaïs*. The *Times* critic seized on the weakness of the ballet's structure between the principal duets and observed that

With her swans, 1912–30: (right) with Chaliapin.

The Swan

the repertoire; London had only glimpsed it at the charity matinee in October 1914. The *Times* critic concluded that "a ballet should be a feast for the ears as well. This thin and trivial music by Drigo does not play its part. It is very poor stuff, and one grudges to see Mme. Pavlova wasting her art on it, but it is wonderful what opportunity she is able to find in it." Alas, *The Magic Flute* did not fare well either in this sternly realistic postwar London. "Heavy and dull" thought *The Times,* placing most of the blame on Drigo. "The clever work of Miss Butsova and M. Alexandre Volinine were, one felt, quite thrown away." But then came *Autumn Leaves,* and though its theme was slight, the whole was thought "quite charming, with the dancers' art and the beautiful and inspiring selection of music from Chopin. Movement on the stage and inspiration in the orchestra—then the audience is held. It was not surprising that the house was delighted last night. *Autumn Leaves* is a valuable addition to the repertory." Nobody saw fit to mention that the ballerina herself had created the work.

Orpheus and *La Péri* were both discussed at length, without a reference to Clustine. *Orpheus* (the "Elysian Fields" ballet, done without the vocal parts) was criticized for lacking drama and allowing only occasional glimpses of Pavlova. *The Times,* even so, was slightly fussed when she did appear: "Pavlova fills the stage as much when it is crowded as when it is empty, and the details suffer." With *La Péri* it was felt that Pavlova had taken a significant step toward Diaghilev's concept of presentation: "In a way, then, *La Péri* might be said to reveal a fresh aspect of [Pavlova's] genius," thought the *Daily Telegraph's* critic. *The Times* observed: "In this work Pavlova and M. Stowitts held the stage alone, and the effect was admirable. The setting has just those elements of fantastic landscape that make for plastic illusion, the costumes were strikingly apt, and of the dancing one need only say that Pavlova was herself and M. Stowitts was an excellent partner. Their performance enchanted the house." The *Daily Telegraph* gave the clue to Pavlova's final exit, which appears to have used a flying harness. "And in the end the king falls dead, while the triumphant peri, still clutching the emblem, is wafted on high up the side of a purple mountain till she is lost to view."

It was clear from the box-office receipts that London did still adore Pavlova in anything she cared to do, and in any setting; when the season was extended and transferred to the Prince's Theatre because of continuing demand, the crowds flocked there, too. Pavlova took the hints of critics who felt that more adventure might be displayed in the choice of new works. She accepted that modernity and change were to be the bases of the postwar era, and she was as anxious as anyone else not to miss the tide; but she had also to take counsel over economic considerations, as outlay always came directly from her own resources and not from wealthy patrons. In 1920 she went as far as letting Darius Milhaud travel over from Paris in order to play her a ballet score. She thought it was interesting and would have pursued the idea, but Dandré quickly put a stop to the project; he thought the score was far too modern for the average "Pavlova

Karalli, for all her reputation, only got a chance of being great "when the music leads, and that is what Massenet's music never does. It, like many of the pretty French ballets of its time, merely provides opportunities for graceful steps and postures; it never calls for the dancer's collaboration in the expression of more." *Chopiniana,* led by Pavlova and Volinine, went happily, and the *Dragonfly* fascinated everyone. By April 20 the *Times* critic was reeling from the number of program changes with which he had to deal. In the Vision scene of *The Sleeping Beauty* he thought Pavlova "perfect; her miming and dancing are on the same high level, and one's only regret must be that it could not last twice as long." Volinine won shouts of approval during *Walpurgis Night,* in which Karalli, playing Helen, reinforced the initial good impression she had made.

A week later Pavlova put *The Awakening of Flora* back into

Action photographs of *The Awakening of Flora*, London.

audience," an entity that, rightly or wrongly, he felt he knew precisely. Much of their thinking about repertoire was governed by the degree of tolerance they could expect in average North American towns; this receptivity governed the company's existence. It was no use carrying the sensibility of a sophisticated London music critic into these territories, as anything remotely avant-garde would empty the halls quicker than a fire. Pavlova gave in to these arguments, as she usually did in policy battles in which financial caution was urged.

The season in London ended on a triumphant note, with unprecedented applause prolonging the final evening. The partnership with Volinine seems to have been singularly free of discord, and despite his occasional complaints about the relentless schedules, he was game for another tour of the United States and Canada.* In some ways England was creeping back to its prewar style, and on July 7 Pavlova and Volinine danced at the Blue Ball, a big charity event held in the Royal Albert Hall to raise money for Russian refugees in Great Britain, and indeed British refugees from Russia: nationals who had fled from long-standing posts in Russia's foreign commerce. The company appeared in a minuet to music of Marinuzzi, the composer who had conducted for the company the previous year in Buenos Aires, where they had first danced this minuet in Louis XIV style. In addition, Pavlova danced a solo, *La Nuit*, which had not been seen in London for years. Vera Karalli and Lydia Kyasht also took part in the program.

W ith such a company to support it was inevitable that the lure of dollar-rich American pastures would not be ignored for long. Pavlova and her team arrived back in New York on the White Star liner *Adriatic* on October 15, 1920. There were company problems to contend with almost before they docked. Among the forty dancers was Joyce Coles, a fifteen-year-old recruit who had the alarming experience of being hustled off the ship by immigration officials enforcing the law that denied entry to any child under sixteen not accompanied by a relative or guardian. She disappeared in the throng en route to Ellis Island. Max Hirsch, the company manager, set off in pursuit of his abducted dancer. Once at the detention isle, he offered to furnish a bond that Joyce would not become a public charge, but the authorities insisted that the girl be held until the Secretary of Labor in Washington furnished authority for her release.

The opening night of Pavlova's American tour, which was being directed by Fortune Gallo, was a benefit for the Navy Club at the Manhattan Opera House on October 18. The auditorium was awash with flags and signals, and high-ranking navy men, including the admiral commanding the Atlantic fleet. It was a prestigious evening, and Gallo was able to report that 750 automobiles marked the return of society to the Manhattan Opera

House. They saw *Amarilla, La Péri, The Swan, Mexican Folk Dances,* and *Syrian Dance.* Local audiences had become used to Dukas's *Sorcerer's Apprentice* in the concert halls of New York, and they took *La Péri* in their stride. Critics thought Pavlova's attitudes in the role recalled "a Debussyan faun" and that her "poetic symbolism of action made you forget the dancer is a gymnast." Pavlova's Péri must have made a lot of people sit forward in surprise, not least of them Carl Van Vechten, who had thought to encapsulate Pavlova's image before her appearance that autumn:

> It may seem a little unprecise to describe a personality so vivid as that of Anna Pavlova as old-fashioned. Yet she is old-fashioned, in the delightful sense of that epithet; not old-fashioned like things of the day before yesterday: the slang of 1910, the bicycle, or "ballroom dancing"; but like the lambrequins, wax flowers, shell baskets, glazed chintzes, and mezzotints of our grandmothers, which the Baron de Meyer has so pleasantly revived. She is the last of the great school of classic dancers, a fragrant reminiscence of the early nineteenth century, born of the same tradition as Taglioni and Fanny Elssler and Carlotta Grisi, and as great as these, perhaps greater.

And here she was in silver and turquoise trousers and a conical hat, reclining seductively in the arms of a half-naked partner! Pavlova was not old-fashioned; she was utterly adaptable to fashions of any sort, using them to her own purpose.

B y any standards known to dance, the personal repertory of Anna Pavlova was huge, and even when the choreographic content of a piece was limited and repetitious, she was able to invest those same steps with infinite varieties of weight and color. She was like a master calligrapher, always alive to the possibility of new subtleties in rendering. And somehow, the instrument of this expression escaped the normal ration of wear and tear. On November 20, at the Massey Hall in Toronto, she did slip and fall heavily as she was making a jump toward Volinine, but she recovered immediately and there appeared to be no ill effects. The schedule continued unabated.

Christmas Day found Pavlova in Milwaukee—yet another Christmas celebrated far from home. In Minneapolis there were complaints that the company's fare was perhaps less than should have been expected in a leading opera house: a highly critical review was supported by a grumpy letter to the editor in the local newspaper. These complaints were from sophisticated music patrons who resented an orchestra with only twenty players, especially as it seems to have been known that Chicago had earned more respect, with thirty-five musicians in the pit. Underpopulation was also evident on the stage: the Minneapolis critics thought there were too few dancers to dress the stage adequately, and the pauses between ballets were "tedious." There was no quarter given over the exigencies of touring ballet on a nightly basis, or the physical stamina expected of the chief executant; each town was waiting for something world famous and judged it accordingly. Pavlova tried to give good measure. At the White

*Pavlova had a chance to talk with her erstwhile partner Laurent Novikov in May, when he turned up at the Coliseum for a special gala performance in aid of the London Fever Hospital. His partner for this performance was Phyllis Bedells, the young English dancer who had been Little Red Riding Hood at the garden parties before the war.

Christmas, c.1920.

Theatre in Fresno on January 31, a serious fire in the business section of town cut off the power supply, leaving audience and stage alike in darkness. Someone thought to bring in carbide lamps from parked automobiles, and with these linked to a portable generator and aimed center stage, Pavlova was able to dance two divertissements before the generator's fuel ran out.

Because of the size of the company's repertoire, some ballets would surface for a while and then be put away. *Christmas* was an obvious seasonal favorite, as was *Fairy Tales*—actually the third act of *The Sleeping Beauty,* with all the original variations of Petipa.* Pavlova's Russian dance at this period seemed to rely principally on Kalinnikov for its music, and on one partner, Stepanov—though there was a natural competition among the men for the right to say they "danced with Madame." Pavlova did

give the occasional chance to a junior, rather like a headmistress awarding a gold star.

Giselle made its appearance from time to time. Pavlova was still tremendously involved with the role, and the emotional energy she poured into it was often such as to produce marked symptoms of nervous tension, which did not always abate when the curtain came down. The girls dreaded having to hold Pavlova's hands during curtain calls; she would clutch them with such intensity that their hands were often bruised or even bleeding where Pavlova's nails had caught them. In Act One whoever played Giselle's mother was usually at some risk in the death scene; Pavlova would tear and clutch at her in an uncontrolled manner. Since this is the antithesis of really secure stagecraft, Pavlova must have put herself through some particular private agony on these occasions. The girls in the curtain calls sometimes noticed that her hands were icy cold. (Laura Knight once told this writer of her sketching *Giselle* from the wings at Covent

---

* Not to be confused with *A Russian Fairy Tale* (also known as *An Old Russian Folk Lore*), produced later.

Giselle: (below) with Volinine, New York, 1920.

Garden and her abiding memory being the sight of little wisps and strands of Pavlova's own hair lying on the stage when the working lights came up during the first intermission.) There was obviously good reason why *Giselle* was in the repertoire so seldom. The dancers dreaded its announcement. Pavlova was always particularly remote beforehand—rarely did anyone dare speak to her on a *Giselle* day, and even Dandré got nervous.

Dandré's tasks were never-ending. Since the days of the Boston Grand Opera Company he had acquired more and more of the duties that might normally have been shared among several executives. The Pavlova Company now traveled as an entourage requiring at least four hundred separate pieces of luggage, including forty packing cases for scenery and well over one hundred trunks for costumes. On train journeys the luggage had to be transferred from each station yard into vans, which then conveyed everything to the theatre. This often took so long that performers would be frantically searching the baskets with flashlights even as they were being unloaded. Divertissements always had to close an evening, because scenery for any principal ballet had to be packed and on the way back to the train by the time the performance had ended. For two seasons Pavlova and Dandré tried a system whereby they traveled in a motorcar with a trailer, but this method had to be abandoned, since it became apparent that they were always having to leave immediately after a performance and then drive through the night, whereas the company had time for a meal and an hour or two's relaxation before getting back on the train.

Dandré always orchestrated the press interviews, which were a requirement at every stop, and although Pavlova dutifully went through the motions time and again, that too was an added strain for her. The unswerving routine demanded that she be affable to an assembly of local dignitaries waiting upon her arrival in each town, and there were always shoals of social invitations to be fended off. Inevitably, there was also the matter of local dance tuition; it was usually uppermost in her mind, and though she often had to spend precious hours watching poorly trained executants perform for her "delight," she could never dismiss this aspect of her own proselytizing. And in the evening, the moment the curtain came down for the last time, the whole process began again—the same dignitaries now presenting their wives and business associates, as well as all the minor municipal officials and the senior staff attached to each theatre. Then the usual spate of importuning mothers would invade the backstage area and the dressing rooms, usually with their young hopefuls in tow. Pavlova always listened patiently and tried to give reasoned advice. Deputations from local groups, such as missions and charities, as well as youth societies, invariably tried to honor the dancer with specially prepared displays of their own, and it was difficult for Pavlova to avoid any of these without hurting feelings. All of these activities encroached upon the only time she might normally have had to rest or eat without interruption. The last dancers leaving the theatre on the way to a meal invariably passed Pavlova coping stoically with a line of people, who would keep her forty minutes or so beyond the time when she should

With Camp Fire Girls at the Manhattan Opera House, March 1921.

normally have left. Even if the stage staff turned them out of the building, Pavlova would merely move to a side street; there, clutching her coat about her, she would continue to listen and explain. She accepted this extra role each evening, but its demands were almost intolerable.

And yet it did not show in the performances. The New York *Herald*, reviewing a Manhattan Opera House gala that Pavlova gave for the Camp Fire Girls, noted:

> The new numbers on her program included a series of Mexican folk dances, the "Danza Mexicana," "Jarabe Tapatia," and "Diana Mexicana," which she performed with tempestuous abandon. Well past the middle of an evening of numbers exhausting to the ordinary artist, she could still show that sudden dash of fire which is one of the chief charms of her dancing. It is one of the triumphs of her personality that she can fit it in tempo and feeling not merely to the varied rhythms but also to the racial character and the inner meaning of a choreographic offering, and she did this supremely last night in "Amarilla" . . . and in her own poetic conception, "Autumn Leaves."

The 1920–21 tour had been carried out at a time when theatrical business for road shows was considered to be at its lowest ebb for many years, and yet the receipts for this most recent venture were the highest ever: $770,000, with a weekly aggregate of around $35,000. Pavlova had completed five major tours of America in a decade. Gallo, at the outset of this latest tour, had guaranteed the Pavlova Company a fixed weekly amount, with a percentage of all profits above that. The average weekly cost of maintaining the company worked out to $18,000—more in the biggest cities, where extras were taken on,

and less elsewhere. (In New York there were 128 people on the company payroll, whereas for touring it dwindled to 70 or so.) In Chicago they gave two performances in one day at the Medinah Temple and recovered their week's running costs; coming back through the same city they topped that figure with a single performance at the Auditorium Theatre. Gallo's personal share at the end of the tour was more than $75,000, while Pavlova pocketed nearly $200,000 for her unceasing labors. Before she sailed from New York, Gallo made an attempt to pin Pavlova down for a quick return in the autumn, but she left the decision in abeyance. For once she declared firmly that a reasonable vacation was a priority, and she penciled in six weeks for the tranquility of Lake Maggiore. All the dancers were exhausted; at the final performance at the Manhattan Opera House, on March 19, 1921, Volinine had strained a tendon, and while Madame de Markhoff played her polka "La Pavlowa" on the piano, Pavlova had had to improvise the new number as a solo.

Though the newspapers were revealing the big profits made by impresario Gallo, behind the scenes the situation was more complicated. Because of the financial climate of the time, Gallo had expressed extreme nervousness about the venture at the outset, and after the first few weeks he had allowed his young associate, Sol Hurok, to buy in. Gallo felt that the South and the Midwest would be unprofitable areas for ballet, but Hurok made the effort to travel along for the first part of the tour to observe things for himself, and he rapidly gained a clear idea of Pavlova's invincible drawing power in out-of-the-way communities. Inspired with confidence, he countered Gallo's misgivings with cheerful effrontery. Gallo may have thought Hurok a young fool headed for a fall; Pavlova recognized him for what he was: an ambitious young businessman trying to build up an agency of his own. She understood him, and, more to the point, she found him to be amusing company. For Hurok, Pavlova was the most fascinating woman he had ever encountered. She was Russian, which counted for a great deal, and he warmed to the Jewishness in her.

With Sol Hurok.

THIS PAGE & OPPOSITE On holiday in Salsomaggiore:
(above) with Alexander Jacovlev.

Above all this, she had style, which was something he hungered for. Though Pavlova was forty and might have been thought to be at the end of her career as a nonstop touring performer, Hurok had other plans. He sensed that she could—and would—go on, and he wanted to be the person who represented her.

At the end of March 1921, Pavlova sailed from New York on board the liner *Finland,* secure in the knowledge that the tour had provided a respite from financial concerns. She was bound for southern Switzerland and a much-needed rest. There she would learn to relax again, under spa treatment, and while away the hours with her painting and modeling, which allowed her to be creative at a less forcing pace. But it was not a time totally free of cares, for she had a number of reasons for continuing to dance at full pressure; not least was her ambition to earn enough money to set up a home for young Russian girls stranded in Paris as refugees. She had already tried to help students and graduates from the Academy in Petrograd, when she heard of the pitiful straits it was in. In an article put out under her name in the *Ladies' Home Journal,* she had explained how much her old school and all its associations meant to her:

> Certain Americans returning from Russia brought me word of the condition of the school, and that its children were starving. The knowledge was like a knife in my heart. I set about for some way to help. And it seemed so paltry little for me to do, to arrange a benefit performance for them which enabled me to send, through Mr. Hoover, two hundred and fifty parcels to each of the schools, the equivalent, I believe, of about five thousand dollars. To dance for them! It was such an easy thing. It seemed to me that I should be over there helping them, looking after them, caring for them myself. It was a foolish wish, of course. Naturally the money I could earn for them, dancing, meant a great deal more than my solitary personal services would. But still I felt that I should be giving them some very personal service, if only cooking broth for them. That was the kind of vital hold my school had on me. She was like a human thing, another mother to me; and it is disgraceful to withhold personal service and care and only to send money when one's mother is in sore distress.

In Paris, Pavlova revealed in a interview the difficulty of keeping the cares of postwar life in Europe from intruding into performances. (See Appendix, p. 407.) She did a week at the huge Trocadero, and the wife of the French president agreed to be patroness of a series of performances from which three-quarters of the profits were to go to the establishment of the charitable fund, the Fondation Anna Pavlova; the remaining quarter was to be put aside to aid orphans of French servicemen.

Four special performances were given, most successfully, at the Trocadero; a fifth was arranged for June 21 in the Parc des Bagatelles in the Bois de Boulogne—an open-air performance planned for mid-evening, with the surroundings lit by lanterns. Seating was laid out for several thousand people. Sadly, it rained heavily during the day, and although the weather cleared toward evening, when there was a beautiful sunset, many of the in-

With Novikov in *The Fauns,* New York, 1921.

tended public did not risk sitting outside in their evening clothes, and there were fewer than one thousand present. They experienced an evening of great beauty, including a performance of *Chopiniana* danced when the moon was up, but the receipts were not sufficient to cover the expenses. The organizers had insured the performance for a large sum, but the firm refused to pay up, on the pretext that there had been no rain during the actual entertainment. The exotic dancers Clothilde and Alexander Sakharoff also performed that evening, and Pavlova herself did a strange little novelty by Clustine. The number, which later became known as *The Fauns,* was arranged to a flute and horn duet by Ilia Satz, who had been music director of the Moscow Art Theatre, and it showed an obvious intention to accord with the rather "modern" score and the sylvan setting: Pavlova was a wood nymph pursued by a group of fauns. She had one entrance in which she was carried high by Stowitts and Bergé running across the stage—it made them very nervous to have to be so cavalier with everyone's idol.

Pavlova gave all of the charity money to the French fund and set about supporting a scheme of her own for the Russian orphans. She took the lease on a house at St. Cloud and had it adapted for the management of fifteen girls. The equipping of such a property, quite apart from the staff needed to run it, represented a continual outlay. Pavlova's thoughts turned naturally to America, where she was such a national favorite. Dandré had the idea of sending a letter to all the people listed in the tax records as being in the highest income group—in other words, millionaires. As there were 7,860 such people, the postage alone was not inconsiderable, but Dandré had worked it out that only a 5 percent return would solve their problems. He had not taken account of the fact that such people were being flooded with requests from war-devastated Europe. Hardly anyone responded

to Pavlova's orphans; the most generous benefactor proved to be Edsel Ford, who undertook to pay yearly for the support of one girl. The Camp Fire Girls, which had made Pavlova an honorary member the previous year, managed to raise one thousand dollars by collecting a few cents each from many thousands of girls.

On June 20, Pavlova had taken part in a gala program presented at the Opéra (it was repeated on June 22 and 24). She elected to perform *La Péri*—exotically avant-garde—perhaps because Fokine and Fokina were also on the bill, dancing his *Daphnis and Chloë.* Pavlova and Stowitts went on after two acts of Rameau's *Castor et Pollux* and before *Daphnis and Chloë.* Dukas had taken an interest in the rehearsals of his music, and most people thought that Pavlova's number definitely stole the show. For his part, Stowitts basked in the limelight; apart from partnering Pavlova at the Opéra, it was heady stuff to have his costume designs praised in Paris.

In the summer of 1921 all the traditional London theatres for dance seemed to be either closed or already booked. Diaghilev was in the midst of a season at the Prince's Theatre, with its unsuitable stage, while both Karsavina and Maud Allan were part of the mixed bill at the Coliseum. Now that the Palace had succumbed to moving pictures, and Alfred Butt's other franchise, Drury Lane, was temporarily closed, Pavlova took her chances under the management of Edmund Russen at the Queen's Hall. This was really a small concert hall, hopelessly ill-suited to dance. Pavlova opened there on June 27. Ernest Newman, who was now music critic for *The Sunday Times,* found that the seating left a lot to be desired: "I could see all the dancers from the chin up, and every now and then I caught a glimpse of one of them down to the feet; but under the circumstances, the most I can say is that whenever I did see Mme. Pavlova she was the incarnation of grace and lightness." The people in the balcony seats felt they were so close they could reach down and touch the dancers. There was no room for scenery, so everything had to be performed in front of drapes.

When one of her character dancers dropped out of the London season, Pavlova asked Natalia Trouhanova if she would fill in. Trouhanova was used to getting star billing when she gave concerts in Paris, but the only "extra" she demanded from Pavlova was that she receive billing in the program as "Princess" Trouhanova. In that guise she performed *Anitra's Dance* and led the company in the Lewandowski *Obertass.* Volinine was slightly injured, and though he was able to partner Pavlova in *Snowflakes* and in the Sibelius *Valse Triste,* for more energetic partnering Pavlova called on the services of Hubert Stowitts. He could not resist making capital out of this situation and precipitated a row, which resulted in Volinine's announcing that he was going back to Paris after the planned English provincial tour and would not be available for the next American tour, a commitment which seemed more and more likely at this stage.

Trouhanova stayed at Ivy House during the Queen's Hall season, and since she was given the bedroom adjoining Pavlova's,

With Stowitts in *La Péri*,
Paris, 1921.

With Novikov in *The Fairy Doll*, winter 1921–22.

they had long nocturnal conversations that allowed her to catch some glimpses of Pavlova's disordered and frustrated emotions:

"Oh, you won't understand what my life is like! I am a doomed creature. I was created to love and be loved, but I love no one, and no one loves me . . . "

"They adore you!"

"Yes, yes! They all do! I adore everyone and everyone adores me. But it isn't love! Take Dandré—you know how he adores me, but you have no idea how I adore him! I only pray to God to let me die before he does. I cannot live after he is gone. You say that I treat him badly? I simply adore him, and he adores me. Therefore, I have the right to abuse him. And believe me, his happiness is in this."

She told Trouhanova how Dandré had deflected her offer to marry him in the early days in St. Petersburg and that she was indebted to him for his support then.

"Afterwards, in America—there, you know, there is prejudice against living together in a hotel as man and wife without being married. Well, I decided . . . We were married in church, in secret.* No one was supposed to know it except the police, the hotels, and the witnesses. Do you understand? I told him: If you ever dare to say that we are married—everything is over between us. I will throw myself under a train. You understand: now I am 'Pavlova.' Now I care nothing for your 'Madame Dandré.' Now you must do everything in the world for me. He said nothing. He knew that he was to blame. Now it is only I, I! . . . And he will just have to accept it. Let everyone think that he is simply 'my escort.' He is mine after all, only mine, and I adore him . . . But I am unhappy, unhappy, unhappy . . . "

Trouhanova thought that Pavlova treated Dandré terribly, behaving like a capricious and sick child. Pavlova would drive him to tears and desperation by picking on him and then become hysterical herself, banging on the locked door of his study and begging him to let her in. After the inevitable reconciliation there would suddenly be another scene, with Pavlova shouting that she was insulted, that she would never forgive him, and that she was "ill of grief." Within hours there would be more frenzy of a different nature. "Who dares to make tea for him in my house?" Or, "Who dares to clean his shoes? Only I do that. That is my business. Out!" Trouhanova found herself relieved to get away from Ivy House—so hospitable, but with such unusual masters.

July was a vacation month for the company, but Pavlova was endlessly busy with preparations for a six-week English provincial tour beginning the following month, as well as with auditions, costume fittings, plans for America in the autumn, and the need to find a replacement for Alexandre Volinine. This last problem was temporarily solved on the provincial tour when Novikov came from Paris, where he had been rehearsing with Karsavina. Pavlova was careful to thank Karsavina for "the loan,"

---

* After Pavlova's death, Dandré claimed that they had married in 1914, but he lost Pavlova's English estate when he was unable to produce any evidence that he was her husband. On a visa application of October 1921, Pavlova was listed as "single."

Portrait, possibly in *Printemps*.

With Novikov in *Dionysus*, 1921.

Series of poses from a "Greek" dance.

ABOVE With Algeranoff in *The Fauns*.

OPPOSITE With Novikov in *Amarilla*.

With Pianowski in *A Polish Wedding.*

but at the same time she must have dropped hints to Novikov about future touring, for it was not long before he gave Karsavina his notice. She was incensed, viewing the desertion as a dirty deed perpetrated solely by Pavlova. Karsavina's view of Pavlova was continually soured by the realization that the latter could usually "top" her in any situation; the fact that she usually did it with a sweet smile added to the annoyance. Although Diaghilev was deeply immersed in his great plans to present *The Sleeping Princess* in London, he seems still to have been trying to secure the services of Pavlova for his long-term enterprise. On July 13 Walter Nouvel, in Paris, sent to Diaghilev, in Monte Carlo, the following cable:

> Bakst has impression Pavlova will agree dance Paris season but she is obstinate to appear only in Schéhérazade a condition to insert adagio music Rimsky of her choice. Telegraph if Bakst right to insist. Nouvel

Pavlova's "obstinacy" seems to have closed the last door between her and Diaghilev; she may even have intended it to do just that.

The schedule for the English tour was particularly grueling. One young recruit was Algernon Harcourt Essex, a pantomime dancer, who was given the name Algeranoff and told to report to Sheffield. Pianowski, the acting ballet master, enlightened Algeranoff about "flying matinees": they were to leave immediately after the afternoon performance, rush through to Newcastle-on-Tyne by train, give a late-afternoon performance, and then speed on to Harrogate for the evening. The company was a crazy jumble, the preponderance of the women now English and most of the men Poles, including several of the best male dancers from

the Wielki Theatre in Warsaw. The character dancer Karajaieff was pure Russian, but an Australian boy was disguised rather lamentably as Arthuroff. Volinine was being temperamental and at the slightest excuse would disappear for days at a time. He deserted breezy Yorkshire because someone left a scenery door open when he was practicing on the stage, and he was not seen again until Blackpool. In Liverpool, as the dancers were warming up on the stage before *Snowflakes* began, Pavlova was in one of her "up" moods and suddenly began jigging about in her glistening tutu, giving an instantly recognizable imitation of Charlie Chaplin, swinging an imaginary cane and tipping a nonexistent bowler. She vanished into the wings before the curtain swept up, leaving the company still giggling. Pavlova could be seen grinning at their efforts to compose themselves.

New dancers kept turning up at odd intervals throughout the tour, and in Edinburgh Clustine arrived to start rehearsing the American repertoire. When they got back to London there were still more additions: as well as Novikov there was Victorina Krigher, another exile from the Bolsheviks; Sigi Novak, previously with the Diaghilev company; and two more Poles, Zabrovski and Cieplinski. The latter had brought with him the Krupinski music for a ballet that had been done in Warsaw called *A Polish Wedding,* and Pianowski immediately started to put it together again. Pavlova had barely a week to work with Novikov on all the ballets that had come into the repertoire since 1914. She had decided that Stowitts was not as indispensable to her as he himself seemed to think he was, and she did not offer him a new contract. The company sailed from Liverpool on the *Empress of France* during the second week of October, and while Pavlova was safely at sea Stowitts found a sympathetic American

298

correspondent to whom he aired his grievances. It seemed he had spent his vacation traveling through Central Europe "counting the days until he should sail back for more triumphs in the United States":

He arrived with all his baggage in Paris on August 26. Straightaway, he recounts, he went to the Plaza-Athénée Hotel, where he was to meet Pavlowa, only to find that Pavlowa was in London. But her husband, M. Dandré, was at the Plaza and told Stowitts, so Stowitts says, that it would not do him the slightest good to see Pavlowa because the dancer was through with him and was going to sail with another dancing partner. Stowitts says that having only an oral contract, he saw he was really through. The youthful Californian, so far away from home, recalled wistfully that the last dance he danced with Pavlowa was the *Bacchanale,* at Queen's Hall, which he said was the last dance Pavlowa performed with Mordkin before breaking off with him. Stowitts blames his trouble on exactly the same circumstances he says caused Mordkin's difficulties. "Look," he said, lifting a big scrap-book from beneath his arms and showing numberless published pictures and articles about him. "Pavlowa can't stand that. I was too good. I had too much success. She only wants second-raters with her and so she fired me. Well, I shall never starve. I have so many offers I am puzzled to decide which one to take. Perhaps I shall dance at the Opera with Ida Rubinstein, and Pavlowa can have all the spotlight over there."

While the disgruntled Stowitts lugged his scrapbook around Paris, Pavlova and her "second-raters" arrived safely in Canada to give two performances in Quebec (where they introduced a new version of Pavlova's Russian dance) and four in Montreal. Hurok's new style of commercial presentation was apparent immediately: the first program had Pavlova endorsing a wine on the back page; worse, the synopsis for *Amarilla,* that pathetic story of blighted love, had underneath it a large advertisement lauding a quack cure for venereal disease. It was a far cry from the day when Pavlova had burst into tears because her name was on the side of an omnibus.

Pavlova's summer vacation had, like all her vacations, included an enormous list of preparations for future touring; in addition, she had made contact with Nicolas Tcherepnin, the composer of *Le Pavillon d'Armide,* who had just exiled himself and his family to Paris. Anxious to help, she accepted a score from him, which Clustine immediately studied for a new ballet, *Dionysus.* Pavlova wanted things to be novel for America—new works with new music, and, above all, new styles of presentation. For this aspect she turned to the brilliant young scenic innovator Nicolas de Lipsky, who had been experimenting with filters and light-sensitive pigments, winning for himself an esoteric following among people who had seen his initial experiments. His scientific approach produced effects that were often startling as well as beautiful. With the safety afforded by Pavlova's patronage he was able, for the first time, to exploit fully his understanding of color in relation to light. The first scene's depiction of a mountain gorge was extravagant rather than realistic, with

basalt rocks fluted like organ pipes; but the rendering was in the manner of traditional scene painting. Everything was bathed in a sunset glow. Pavlova entered as a High Priestess surrounded by attendants in loose Grecian robes. They performed oblations before a statue of the god Dionysus and then withdrew, leaving the High Priestess alone. She then cast off her outer veil and began to dance for the image of the god. Here Pavlova introduced a strongly erotic element, making it clear that she was worshipping the image yet at the same time physically hungering for the god himself. There was a mounting abandonment to raw feeling until some exhaustion, or release, caused her to droop in supplication before the god's image. Then there was a flash, and the image came to life (the statue swiveled around to reveal Novikov). With the transformation of Dionysus, the entire scene changed instantaneously. The gorge vanished as a night-blue pallor lit the stage, revealing pendulous willows and the sheen of moonlight on a wide lake. (In reality, both scenes were painted on the same backdrop; only the lights separated the components.) The god danced with the High Priestess "as shepherd might dance with Attic maid," in the words of one reviewer, and bacchanalian revelers joined the scene briefly. After their departure, the Priestess eventually sank to the ground, exhausted—this time by the god himself. As he vanished, the scenery reverted to the rocky gorge, with the Priestess asleep. The attendants returned for their mistress, and as she awoke, her mime conveyed the nature of an exultant dream.

When the ballet was first seen in New York, on November 4, at the Manhattan Opera House, audiences gasped during the transformation scenes, and they cheered at its end. *Musical America* thought that *Dionysus* heralded "a new era for the stage of fancy and fairy vision":

The producers of revue, and those who preside over the stage spectacular for the spectacle's sake, will quickly appraise the value of the innovation and adapt it to their needs. . . . As hand-maiden to the arts beautiful, the de Lipsky lights can shed their translating radiance beyond the ballet.

Interesting light effects were also created for *The Fauns,* with a glowing red sunset that gradually changed color, but the ballet was found to be too "modern" and "episodic" and was taken out of the repertoire after only two performances. *A Polish Wedding* was popular, but Pavlova found the footwork in heeled boots to be too straining, and after dancing two performances of it she handed the role over to Hilda Butsova. The English dancer also had to take over the role of Swanilda at short notice from Victorina Krigher, who had sought equal billing with Novikov on the posters and in the programs, as well as several other improvements in her status. Being terrified of elevators, she climbed the sixteen floors to Hurok's office on various occasions, but her efforts were in vain; none of her demands were met, and her contract was canceled. Also new to New York were *Norse Idyll* and *Fairy Tales;* but despite Hurok's ambition to present fresh programs, it was noticeable that the old favorites were the real favorites.

Although Pavlova was allergic to cats (she liked them but said they gave her sneezing fits) . . .

... she had no such problem with dogs.
Bull-nosed breeds were her favorites.

Printemps

There were many minor accidents during the season, and one serious one: Kuzma Savelieff, Pavlova's trusty wardrobe master, fell through a trap door that had been left open on the stage and was taken to the hospital with two broken ribs. There was terrible disorder during his absence. To add to the problems, Pavlova was coughing almost continually, though she continued to dance uncomplainingly. In the Mexican dances her appearance of youth and vivacity bewitched young Algeranoff when he watched one night from the front of the house:

> Pavlova's perfect control and the impeccable finish of her dancing only seemed to throw into relief the horrible chaos and anarchy among the rest of us. How often did I oversleep and rush to the theatre in a panic only to find that there was no sign of a rehearsal starting, and even when it was over several of the Poles had never appeared at all. . . . If only there had been a disciplinarian in charge of us, we could have given Pavlova the support she deserved at every performance.

Through eighty towns and cities it was the same. Hurok sometimes economized by not hiring sleeper cars for the train, but it made traveling even more wearing. For Pavlova herself they always reserved the center seats of a coach, where the vibration was less, but there were few other concessions. Though the settings changed, the procedure was relentlessly similar, day after day, until the dancers had very little idea of where they really were. At one town two dancers and one of Pavlova's dressers were missing for a performance. It transpired that when the train had been changed at a junction fifty miles back, the three had automatically rushed out of the station with their usual desire to be first into the hotel—a technique that avoided a half-hour delay once the check-in desk became crowded. The three had booked rooms, rested, then gone downstairs to ask the way to the theatre. "There is no theatre of that name in the town," they were told. Dancing for Pavlova? "But Pavlova is at Oshkosh. This is Sheboygan!"

By Christmas they were in St. Paul. Pavlova did her best to make the festive occasion a family event; there was the usual party with its Christmas tree, on which Pavlova had hung a present for each member of the company. The family aspect of the company called forth from Pavlova an attentive but headmistressy approach, as when she would look into the girls' dressing rooms while they were on stage to see if their make-up and personal effects were laid out in an orderly manner, or stroll up and down the railway cars, observing how the girls occupied their spare time. She liked them to read "improving" books and journals, or to sew. Hollywood magazines were greatly disapproved of; the girls tended to read them surreptitiously, behind the shield of some approved product, such as the *Ladies' Home Journal*. Pavlova herself was an inveterate card player, but she was less happy seeing the younger girls play. Some braved her disapproval, usually with unhappy results. At one temporary halt on a track she asked a card-playing girl the name of a tree that loomed outside the window. "I don't know, Madame," replied the girl with a certain insouciance. "It is fir," instructed Pavlova, before moving on. She came back through the car a little later, while the train was still held up. "What is that tree?" she asked the girl again. "I don't know, Madame," came the reply, as breezily unconcerned as before. "It is the same tree—you *idiot!*" exploded Pavlova. She could never understand why people did not have a continual desire to learn new things while traveling. She was forever sending them off to art galleries and then quizzing them on what they had seen, and when sleepy young dancers sometimes ducked out of these cultural missions, Pavlova was hurt and saddened. She would often arrive at some local gallery before it was open in the morning, and, having got in, she would be full of excitement at what she discovered.

She could juggle aestheticism with the frivolous aspects of her job: the serious artist could still be presented to the general public in a popular manner. At the end of March 1922 an article syndicated from Chicago appeared with a bold headline that read: "Anna Pavlova Rises to Defend Maligned Golosh from Critics":

Mme. Anna Pavlowa, the famous Russian classic dancer, refuses to believe that the American girl is becoming ungainly. All the artistic Pavlowa has is a man's word for it, and that's not enough. Andreas Pavley, called the greatest living male dancer, who is now in Chicago, says it's so. He says goloshes are giving our girls big feet and destroying the rhythm of their once charming walk. Bare knees, he avers, are making them stiff-legged, ungraceful and rheumatic. . . .

"What an indictment!" laughed the dark-eyed Pavlova, interviewed in her luxurious apartments here today. "It just can't be. Your girls are simply wonderful. They wear anything well, even goloshes. And they—I mean the girls!—are naturally graceful. I don't think it's what you wear that counts so much for grace or awkwardness—it's what you dance. Now why not the golosh? I've never worn goloshes, but I have worn Russian boots—seemingly without harm." Pavlova's slim ankles and dainty feet (insured for $100,000 against accident), which peeped out from beneath a silken Russian tea gown, attested to that fact. "It's what girls dance that counts," reiterated Pavlova. "Now, I would be concerned for your American girls if I thought they would stick to this—what you call it? This—oh, yes, this jazz dancing. That really would make them ungainly. What a dance!" "Madame," ventured the visitor, "have you ever tried it?" Pavlova paused. Finally, after passing the grapes, she said "Yes, once. Just once." "Why," she resumed quickly, "why must your graceful American girl dance it? It is so horrid, so vile, so inartistic. How much better would be proper ballroom dancing. Dancing should bring out the motion of the soul, character, the best in one. In Russia, the teaching of dancing is regarded as important as that of reading and writing. It should be so in America. You have not, if I may say it, the right kind of dancing teachers. Who are they? If your girls were taught clean, artistic dancing when they were very young, they would never accept jazz. But why worry over jazz? It is only a fad. It will go. When I was here before it was the bunny hug. It will be something different next time. Is it not so?"

Pavlova had the last laugh eight months later, when stores started selling something known as the "Pavlowa Boot." These new boots were rubberized, and it was expected that they would go a long way toward supplanting the galosh. In the realm of publicity, Pavley and his friend should have known better than to jostle for attention while Pavlova was in the vicinity.

With Novikov: (above) in the *Dance of the Hours* from *La Gioconda*; (below) in *Snowflakes*.

The Ondines: (above) Pavlova, in group at right, with
attendant water sprites, and (below) with Novikov.

Pavlova's fame was as great as that of any movie star, and in Hollywood all the big names flocked to see her. The younger dancers were agog at the famous faces out beyond the footlights: Chaplin, Pickford, Fairbanks, Valentino, Lillian Gish—they came night after night. With their beautiful homes to return to, these stars had no way of understanding what sort of life was led by the exotic foreign creature to whom they were paying homage. They had the contrast of deep comfort after any difficult working conditions. There was no such contrast for Pavlova. In Montgomery, Alabama, after a nine-hour train ride, a violent storm battered the iron roof of the hall and flashes of lightning came through the uncurtained windows; eventually a pool of rainwater formed in the middle of the stage—but none of the dancers thought it very exceptional. Even at the Metropolitan Opera House in New York someone turned on the central heating in mid-performance, so that Pavlova danced *The Swan* to a cacophony of hissing and gurgling that made nonsense of Saint-Saëns's melody.

Matters were not helped by the absence of discipline in the ranks. Clustine lacked authority as a ballet master, but Pianowski was in many ways an even greater liability, because he tried to undermine Pavlova's authority. If she interrupted a class during one of her strict moods, it was not unknown for him to stick his tongue out at her when she had her back to him. Dandré would have a periodic calling to order: "Ve do not expect you all to be great artists but ve expect you all to be artists. You vas all standing on ze stage and talking of things vich you should have been discussing in your own chambers, and taking no interest in your vork at all." The company would try to present contrite faces. Then Dandré might single out some girl by name. "Vy it vas zat you vas not looking vere you vas dancing, so zat you kicked ze scenery, and ve vas hearing you from ze public saying 'Hell on ze dam zing!'?" But Dandré could still be sympathetic to their problems, and in the privacy of his office he was avuncular, diplomatic, and lenient.

By the time Pavlova came back to New York in mid-April of 1922, she knew that her ambition to travel in the Orient would be realized later that year. Hurok saw all sorts of extravagant possibilities on a global scale, and he wasted no time in putting it about that—at least as far as New York was concerned—the appearances were in the nature of a farewell. Pavlova herself thought that this was a premature suggestion, but she had given up all attempts to keep control of the commercial brouhaha that eddied around her progressions. It was a changing world and she knew it. Her job was to dance, and as long as she was on stage, in command of her audience, the message came through clear and undistorted; the trimmings she left to others. She was a popular institution who had to accept the extremes of that role with equanimity: being attacked by Kansas City moralists who felt that her scanty stage clothes were an affront, or being given a beautiful silver vase from the manager and technical staff of the theatre in Memphis; she dealt with each event in

With Novikov in *The Ondines*.

the same manner. She was charming and restrained, never overreacting. It was a public skill, entirely at odds with her personal nature.

In New York, at the Metropolitan Opera House, the Memphis gesture was repeated. The gift was described as a loving cup—a two-handled vase, somewhat smaller than the Memphis one, but overflowing with sentiments. At the end of the second intermission, after *Giselle*, the stage was suddenly crowded with representatives of the artistic world in America, including foreign artists who had found refuge in the New World, such as Alexei Koslov. Pavlova soon realized that the publicity about her "farewell" was being taken seriously. When she stepped forward to accept her gift from Ruth St. Denis, who was the spokeswoman for the group, Pavlova saw the words "Au Revoir" engraved on the cup, and "To the incomparable Anna Pavlova, from her friends, admirers and fellow artists in America. Metropolitan Opera House, Tuesday, April 25th, 1922." As St. Denis handed the cup over, she suddenly knelt down and kissed Pavlova's foot. It made a tremendous impression on the audience, but Pavlova was acutely embarrassed and quickly pulled the American dancer up to receive a friendly embrace. St. Denis made a little speech. "Only a dancer could understand how great were the achievements, to whom America owes much, for the inspiration of beauty she has given."

Backstage in *Fairy Doll* costume.

Pavlova's company for the Far Eastern tour was reduced to twenty-five dancers and four musicians. Novikov thought that his heart would not stand the hot climate, so Pavlova lured Volinine away from Paris again. Clustine, on the other hand, returned there, to nurse his own hypochondria and a conviction that Pavlova would be either murdered or eaten by tigers. Oliveroff rejoined after an absence of four years, and Karajaieff, who had stayed behind in New York to take up a teaching appointment, was replaced in all the energetic Russian character roles by the young Algeranoff.

Tokyo in September was extraordinarily hot and humid, yet rehearsals had to begin at 9:30 in the morning if the newer members of the company were to learn such ballets as *The Enchanted Lake (Schubertiana)* and *The Awakening of Flora*—both of which were now being put back into the repertoire—before having to clear the stage for the Kabuki dramas, which began immediately after lunch. This sharing of the Imperial Theatre meant that in the afternoons Pavlova had to retreat to the rehearsal room, with its shoji screens and tatami.

There were few concessions to Western culture in Tokyo; the audiences did not applaud but merely whispered among themselves and lit up cigarettes after each ballet, and only the newspapers revealed that the little company of foreign dancers was considered a success. Theodore Stier struggled with the auxiliary musicians, who were playing Western music for the first time. Of the ballets, Clustine's enlarged version of *Russian Dance* was very popular. It included a corps of eight girls, all wearing Soudeikine's boldly figured costumes and moving against a crazy *izba*, complete with a rainbow, a duck pond, and cut-out pieces of scenery standing in the foreground depicting more peasants. The Japanese were nonplussed by this scenery, but they liked what went on in front of it.

Some of the dancers were equally nonplussed by the Japanese Nō drama, but Pavlova sat through the interminable event in rapt attention. Algeranoff, eager to follow Pavlova's exhortation that they should all learn as much of the rudiments of Japanese dancing as they could, found a parallel to her own constant direction to "*be* your part, don't just *do* it" in the Mirror Room just off stage, where a Nō performer would always take a final look at himself in his costumed guise before going on. The belief was that a good actor could absorb the character of the personage he represented by studying his outward form.

The hospitality in Japan was traditionally lavish, and at one entertainment the evening ended with a comic dance in which the dancer wore two masks, fore and aft, with the reverse being that of a woman. It was startling and theatrical, and at its conclusion Pavlova turned to Algeranoff and said, "This dance for you, Algy." She entered wholeheartedly into everything Japanese: she learned the tea ceremony, visited geisha houses, and organized lessons from a revered teacher, Matsumoto Koshiro VII. This was his inherited stage name; his wife—who also taught—remained Madame Fujima. There was also an assistant instructor, Miss Fumi. They taught Algeranoff and others who were interested, while Pavlova took lessons from the renowned

Leaving Vancouver, 1922:
(above) impromptu shipboard entertainment;
(below) sailing to the Orient.

Russian Dance: (opposite & below) with Simon Karajaieff;
(above) with Algeranoff and corps de ballet in Clustine's enlarged version.
(The true scenery can be glimpsed in this photograph; the others were
taken in front of backdrops from *The Fauns* and *Mexican Dances*.)

Kikugoro VI. For days Pavlova worked conscientiously to master the basic movements of Japanese dance, until Dandré noticed the strain she was putting on her tendons with the constant and unaccustomed turned-in positions, and persuaded her to cease the exercises. Pavlova loved Japan ("You know, there is nothing in this country one wants to throw away"), and she cheerfully put up with the rigors of country inns, with having to sleep on the floor with neck blocks instead of pillows, with the lack of privacy, with communal bathing, and with the terrifying variety of bats and insects that invaded the screened rooms. They visited all the principal towns and did a string of one-night stands in less well-known places. It was only in Yokohama and Tokyo that they could, in 1922, depend on there being any foreigners at all in the audiences; otherwise it was a case of upward of three thousand people entirely unaware of the rudiments of classical ballet, yet all sitting engrossed, and not merely politely stationary, until the very end. Opinions filtered out much later; Pavlova's Amarilla was thought to be a very disagreeable Western heroine, with no saving graces.

This alertness and interest from the local populations were singularly lacking in China, though the press releases put a brave front on matters. The enchantment of the East evaporated with the crossing of the Yellow Sea, which was extremely rough in the wake of a typhoon. Shanghai was cold, and Pavlova's whole stay

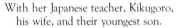
With her Japanese teacher, Kikugoro,
his wife, and their youngest son.

was clouded by an incident in the British sector, when a Sikh policeman brought to an end a rickshaw boy's minor squabble about fares by knocking him to the ground senseless with blows from a truncheon. The incident so distressed Pavlova that she refused to leave her hotel thereafter except to go to the theatre. The audiences were drawn mostly from the various foreign sectors, so that there was no real interaction with the native populace. Pavlova was further unsettled by the Russian émigrés she met, including one who was managing the hotel where she was staying. The shifting Russian population in Shanghai confirmed what she had heard of the conditions in Russia.*

When the moment came to leave Shanghai, Pavlova nearly lost her dancing partner. The tender taking them out to the ship bound for Manila drew up its gangplank, and Volinine was not on board. He had been wining and dining with the Russian Consul, but for once his absence was brief; he was spotted rushing along the quay, bags in hand, and he managed to make a grand jeté onto the prow of the boat just as it was reversing out into the tide. Pavlova was aghast, but Volinine was in a genial mood and told her, "You *know* I could never withstand a champagne lunch!"

In Manila the heat was dreadful, and it was there that Pavlova showed the first real signs of rationing her appearances—an attitude that could justifiably have emerged years earlier. There were two performances a day, with early evening matinees, and at these she made no appearance at all. Somehow this intention was always public knowledge immediately, and the net result was a pathetically small audience—a disheartening sight for a company slaving away in thick, heavy costumes. This indifference to the company itself underlined all too emphatically the impresarios' perpetual fears that with no Pavlova, there would be no show.

Manila did have its compensations: a bright social life that left many of the girls fending off admirers. Young Lona Bartlett seemed to be the belle of any evening, though the Poles in the company were horrified that the "quiet" English girls would actually dare to go out without chaperones. Pavlova was, as usual, busy with visits to local institutions. Her moods were as disconcertingly variable as everyone had come to expect. She came back from a long session at a dancing school in a buoyant frame of mind. "It was very sweet," she said. "All work very hard, you ask arabesque, they all do attitude! But very sweet." In the hotel supper room she experimented with some jazz dancing—the very thing she fulminated against in interviews. Diffident at first, she would dance only with Stier (who had been encouraged to practice by Muriel Stuart, a keen ballroom dancer), but eventually Pavlova risked dancing with others, though she was never enthusiastic.

Stier was Pavlova's escort when an argument about Poland broke out between Pavlova and Pianowski as they were walking

*In Tokyo, she had flown down the steps of the Imperial Hotel to greet Elizabeth Herrington (of Puerto Rico), just back from a trip to Russia. "You have been to Russia! My Russia! Tell me—I must know, I must bear it!" But the news was as somber as she had probably guessed.

in Manila one morning. The heat of the argument increased until Pavlova suddenly burst into a passion of tears, went scarlet with indignation, and walked swiftly away from their intended destination, leaving Pianowski dancing with rage on the sidewalk. The argument must have had a bitter core, because the ballet master, in a final paroxysm, snapped his favorite Malacca cane across his knee and hurled the pieces down the street. (With Stier's help, Pavlova later replaced the cane with an exact duplicate.) There were no pangs about leaving Manila, and in the voyage across the South China Sea, northward again to Hong Kong, the improving weather lifted everyone's spirits. There was a flat calm reflecting an amazing pink sky, and the harmonies of Debussy could be heard as the pianist Shura Chelmnitsky caught the mood. The *President Wilson* was a ship that hardly justified such a name, but when they docked, the Hong Kong press crowded around the famous passenger. On December 5 the *South China Morning Post* reviewed the company's appearance at Hong Kong's Theatre Royal, and the remarks were extraordinarily prescient:

> For Pavlova, in her art, is a peerless Queen, destined for immortal fame. Long after she ceases to glorify the theatre, people will recall the wonderful emotions she evoked, and when the last of those who saw her in the flesh has crossed the border, her name will be synonymous with a tradition of spiritual beauty which has seldom been attained and never surpassed.

At the same time, the American papers were carrying news of Isadora Duncan, who had just arrived in Boston after her latest trip to Russia; "Duncan Goes Red" ran one headline. It seemed she had waved a red scarf at her audience and sung out, "This is red and so are you. Don't let them tame you!" Pavlova, for the first time, was outraged by a Duncan action. There had already been signs that the Bolsheviks regarded Pavlova as a lackey of the West, yet she could not have been selling a Russian image more dutifully, and their dismissive attitude was hard to bear, particularly now, when she was so tantalizingly close to the country in which she had not set foot for eight years. She wanted to display the true glory of her Russian training, yet conditions so often worked against her. When the company arrived in Singapore, where they were expecting to perform at the Victoria Theatre, they found that Hurok's subagent, a Mr. Strok, had failed to confirm the itinerary, and the hall had already been booked by the local amateur dramatic society. Dandré, not unreasonably, suggested that they might perhaps postpone their Gilbert and Sullivan, in view of the famous ballerina's arrival in the Straits. This request took no account of the pride of a society that had been founded over one hundred years before. Why should they surrender to a foreign *artiste?* Pavlova thus had to make do with the cramped old German Club, twenty minutes by rickshaw beyond the center of the city. There, on a slippery little stage with a violent rake, she danced for the Governor of Singapore, who had to wait around until after ten o'clock because the club's manager had failed to organize not only curtains for the stage but lights as well. The company struggled to sort out other

problems backstage, including make-up that melted grotesquely as soon as it was put on perspiring faces. Domyslavski could not apply his fat false cheeks for the role of the Judge in *The Magic Flute* and, abandoning also the heavy stomach padding, finally came on stage looking so emaciated that the whole company did a double take. Most things were hastily improvised in Singapore, including the programs. In one change the only person who had not been warned was Pavlova; when she found out at the last moment, she took to her dressing room and refused to come out, so that the intermission stretched beyond half an hour and a restive audience had to be told that something had gone wrong with the lighting. That was entirely plausible. Pavlova was finally persuaded to go on in the wrong ballet, *Moment Musical,* because that was all the orchestra had rehearsed.

The heat, coupled with petty daily irritants, caused Pavlova to give way to hysteria much of the time. Her depressions also struck with regularity, and in 1922 she failed to celebrate Christmas in her usual manner. The company was on a cramped little steamer, the *Edavana,* traveling to Penang and Rangoon; it was the sort of situation that would normally have appealed to Pavlova's ingenuity, but nothing was organized. Certainly Christmas Eve had not been cheerful, with apprehension about the condition of Lona Bartlett, who had ignored Pavlova's strict instructions that no one was to sit on deck without some form of

Bombay, 1923.

311

Near Cairo, 1923.

headgear. As a result she had gone down with sunstroke, and seriously. She was a happy, popular girl who had accepted the marriage proposal of the manager of the American Express in Manila (a contract to be honored at the end of the tour); now she was showing symptoms of general delirium and could not be left alone. When they reached Rangoon she was taken to the hospital, ultimately to return to England under medical supervision. Oliveroff also had a spell in the hospital.

Still, these worries had to be cast aside as the company danced away the last few hours of 1922 for the benefit of an audience in the Excelsior, "Rangoon's Premier Place of Amusement," where the visitors were billed as "The Sensation of All the Civilized World." Pavlova's spirits appeared to lift, and she arranged for a little artificial fir tree to make a belated appearance at a New Year's party. She had the electric fans turned off for a few minutes so that she could light the tiny candles; there was a cake in the form of a book opened to a new chapter—1923—and there was also a Christmas pudding and champagne. And two more girls went to the hospital: one had a local fever, the other appendicitis.

In Burma, Pavlova made sure of seeing the Pwes—the traditional dance-dramas. She found them exotic but also undisciplined; there was too much casual Western influence, even to the extent that one dancer broke into the ditty "My Love Is Like a Little Bird" as a tribute to Pavlova's presence. The guest of honor kept a straight face, but she found the muddle of cultures dispiriting. Always she was looking for a national school with an untainted tradition producing a deep-seated and self-evident style. When she did encounter any such purity of method, she was able to draw from it inspiration; that was why she had been so engrossed with the Japanese Nō theatre and the Kabuki.

She had been looking forward to India with mounting excitement, hoping for some sort of revelation from a land of such ancient traditions. Throughout her life as a dancer she had been surrounded by varying suggestions of Indian dance: Petipa's Maryinsky repertory was studded with them; Fokine had added his versions; Ruth St. Denis had become famous by presenting a sort of "cigarette-card" impression of it; and Roshanara had approximated the real thing. But Pavlova was in for a shock: the reality—in 1923—proved a disaster.

In Calcutta the company was being presented in a rather handsome Western-style auditorium known as the Empire, which was managed by Bandman's Eastern Circuit Ltd. The British administrators who occupied the first few rows of seats did know ballet from Christmas shows, if nothing else; but the Parsees, Hindus, and Moslems could at best have had a vague notion that Pavlova's skills were some part of English variety, occasionally depicted in the *Illustrated London News*. Nevertheless, the entertainment given by Pavlova at the Empire proved tremendously popular throughout the audience, which saw ballets such as *Coppélia, Autumn Leaves,* and *The Ondines*. These unlikely subjects fascinated the locals, and they in turn made every effort to entertain Pavlova.

The whole company was invited to a matinee of nautch dancing at the Madan Theatre. The performance started after a police whistle gave the signal. The first hint of unease arose from the visitors almost immediately, when they heard the strains of a harmonium coming from the little orchestra. A large, shapeless woman then shuffled forward in an aimless manner; there was no refinement or clarity of movement, and the principal interest lay in the fact that every time her veil fell off (a frequent occurrence) she shuffled back upstage to use a large brass spittoon. The foreign guests watched all of this, stunned. In a group of secondary dancers, one was thought to be an improvement on her fellows—by contrast, she had graceful hand and head movements—but the rest were awful; and though a dance that followed for a man, a woman, and a dwarf displayed a marked rhythmic pulse, it also showed great vulgarity. The second half of the show reached unparalleled depths. Thirty or forty girls (many of them actually boys) came on, wearing pink flannelette dresses with black stockings and white tennis shoes peeping out. They all had long, lank hair crowned with hats like upturned chamber pots made of the same material as the dresses, and they formed vaguely defined groups in order to shake tiny bells in some sort of accord with the music. The pinnacle of the performance came with the emergence of a leader, who wandered up and down at the front of the stage waving a handkerchief while singing "It's a Long Way to Tipperary" with a voice like a parrot. Pavlova was struck dumb and made a polite but hurried exit.

This debacle was not a case of Westerners being unable to grasp the nuance of a foreign culture; the sad fact was that national dancing in India had reached an abysmal nadir through neglect and lack of administrative direction. The ruling British powers had not fostered the arts, and the native population was far too apathetic to make any spirited attempts to retrieve its own culture. The best of any natural talents were automatically assigned to various princely households and were thus never seen by the general public at all. There was no one to explain the difference between *natya* (nautch dance-drama), *nrtta* (stylized pure dance), and *nryta* (a sort of "beauty for beauty's sake"); these refinements were locked away in palaces, libraries, and the heads of aging gurus. Pavlova masked her acute disappointment by turning her attention to the seething natural life of India, to the Ganges, to the monuments, both Mogul and British. She was critical of the latter. "If they must make it English," she sighed, "why not beautiful English, like Chester?"

Eventually the company headed across the subcontinent, toward Delhi. Volinine missed the departure completely this time, together with Stier, when a taxi driver misunderstood their instructions and headed east into open country. There was one other absentee who was more sorely missed at this juncture: Kuzma, who controlled all the company bedding as well as the costumes. These problems were par for the course; in fact, they all met up in Delhi just in time for the first performance, which was attended by the Viceroy. This took place in a cinema called the Excelsior, which had been given a coat of paint for the occasion. Pavlova was finding the real India fascinating and was constantly urging everyone to go on sightseeing tours whenever the opportunity arose. The Taj Mahal had its customary effect, and she made sure they saw it a second time, by moonlight, as all the guidebooks recommended.

The visit to Bombay, which came next, ultimately assumed tremendous importance for Pavlova; it was there that she hap-

Alexandria, 1923.

Outside Shepheard's Hotel, Cairo, 1923.

Governor. On seeing a disgruntled jockey belaboring his horse after it had lost a race, she rushed across the unsaddling enclosure and accosted the culprit with a stream of rapid-fire French. The jockey could not understand a word of this, but the import was clear enough, and by the time a flushed Pavlova had rejoined her group, the jockey could be seen solicitously stroking his mount as he led it away. Just before leaving Bombay, Pavlova witnessed a second juvenile wedding; this time she asked to be allowed to give a few rupees as a wedding present. The groom was eleven and the bride nine.

The customs of India so intrigued Pavlova that her questions were sometimes embarrassingly direct. When she saw a young man cremating the body of his father in Calcutta, she thought the ritual beautiful, though her companions shrank from the sight. She said then that she would wish to be consumed by fire when she died. Nobody could deflect her from the topic. "I shall die before any of you. I could never grow old and die slowly."

In Cairo the company was performing at the decaying old Kursaal Theatre. The stage was full of holes, and the dressing rooms were cubicles. While Pavlova complained to the manager, several of the Poles eased their gloom with the local liquor, so that the chaos backstage took on operatic dimensions. There was also the usual struggle to meld a recruited orchestra into some sort of recognizable ensemble; as always it was the music that suffered most on these tours, since the dancers were already familiar with the repertoire and had only to find the best way of circumventing the physical pitfalls. Rather boldly, Pavlova allowed the *Egyptian Ballet* back into the repertoire for the occasion; but whatever its absurdities, the audience took the move as a compliment, and the theatre resounded with applause. The Queen of Egypt attended the opening.

Despite the political upheavals that were adding tensions to Cairo's life, the company followed the usual tourist rites, lurching across the sands by camel to see the monuments, and even going back to Giza for a second look, by moonlight, after one of the shows. Pavlova posed dutifully for the huge plate cameras of the Anglo-Swiss agents who materialized at every tourist spot, and she even climbed up onto the shoulder of the Sphinx for one picture. The surroundings were shattered and desolate, a far cry from the splendors once summoned up by Maryinsky scenery painters. As usual, the local rigors were taking their toll in the company, with fevers, influenza, and even mumps thinning the ranks.

The Mohammed Ali Theatre in Alexandria was a relief after the Kursaal. The city's principal house of respectable entertainment was ornately elegant; gilt glimmered in the curved auditorium, and when the dust had been banged out of it, the plush was still rosy. Audiences arrived smartly dressed, and huge floral tributes were carried onto the stage. In the streets, posters were announcing the impending visit of Maud Allan, who was already in Cairo dancing to scant audiences; Pavlova, unwittingly, had for the time being "drained the waterhole" for dance in Egypt.

pened to witness two Hindu wedding ceremonies, and from there that she visited the caves of Ajanta, 150 miles away, on one of the side trips she often organized for the company, and usually paid for herself. The deep chambers of the cave, with their extraordinarily rich carvings hewn out of the living rock, held an atmosphere so potent as to be almost sinister. The celebrated frescoes, which had recently been restored by the Italian experts Orsini and Cecconi, had a cumulative effect that was almost overwhelming. At last Pavlova had found an unsullied image of India. Back in Bombay, she was driving in a carriage with Stier when they spotted a marriage procession. They stopped to get a better look, and someone in the crowd recognized Pavlova and asked her if she would care to witness the actual ceremony. It turned out to be a double event: two brothers were marrying two sisters, and none of them was more than a child. Pavlova took in all the details with avidity: the showers of rice over the couples, the washing of the brides' feet with milk, the little fingers of the couples being tied together with string.

Pavlova was also subjected to more banal social conventions while in India, including attending a horse race as the guest of the

314

United States

AROUND THE WORLD

India

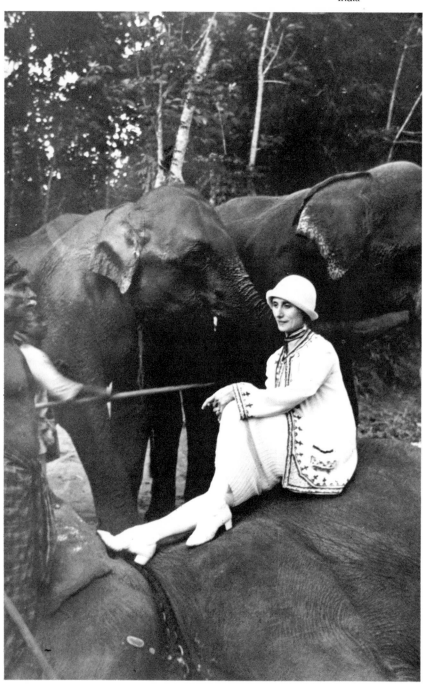

Ceylon

Egypt

ABOVE (clockwise from top left) England, Italy, Venezuela, South Africa.

OPPOSITE (top to bottom) Australia, Holland, Canada.

Japan

Pavlova sailed across the Mediterranean to Monte Carlo and a brief vacation—to hotels with fresh linen, to couture houses displaying the current season's hemline, to shoe shops (the eternal bugbear), and to the Casino. There, the baize seemed as exciting as any décor by Bakst. Pavlova used gambling as an anodyne, and once a year, in Monte Carlo, she abandoned herself to it; she dismissed the company, Dandré, and everything else from her mind and fell into the rhythm of play as easily as she took on the tongue of that setting. The other players were true strangers, mysterious, not her normal "family," striving merely to keep boredom at bay each night. And so she would unwind. Then, Pavlova was ready to rediscover England, to rush about her garden exclaiming at the new growth, even more vivid than Monte Carlo's baize.

The home for Russian girls in St. Cloud was a success from every point of view, and Pavlova devoted much thought and energy to it. Yet her actual visits there were fleeting: she could only sustain it as long as she was away from it, working. The financial aspect was always precarious, but invariably Pavlova would manage to give a gala performance in Paris during the summer months, and the proceeds would ensure the girls' security for a further year.

In considering finance, Pavlova frequently discussed the possibility of another film, as the improvements in cinematographic technique now provided the hope that dance might be recorded with some accuracy. She visited the Pathé studios in Paris during the filming of *Le Chiffonnier de Paris* to watch Mardi Gras festival scenes being shot in a fake boulevard. Observers thought she was looking very tired, but her interest was as keen as ever, and when she commented that the extras looked to be having such fun that she wished she could join them, the director said, "Why not?" Pavlova took on the guise of an apache dancer lingering under a street lamp in the next sequence being filmed. This little bit of fun delighted her, and since it was only a middle-distance shot, the director was able to leave the footage in the film.

By the end of July 1923 Pavlova knew that she had before her a schedule of work that would take her to the threshold of 1926. She had given in to Hurok's pleas for another North American tour, and already he was talking publicly about a tour to Australia; at this stage he was saying that she would be there in 1925. It was a lure, the last "unknown" continent, but letters still took six weeks to get there—along with passengers. Volinine for once seems to have quailed at the idea; he set up plans to open a school of dance in Paris, leaving Pavlova to face another London season and the enormity of what lay beyond. And she had still to find a way of utilizing the kaleidoscopic impressions of her journeys in the Orient.

Pavlova's first thoughts about extracting a ballet from her tour in the Orient had begun to form almost from the moment she left India in February 1923. At the time, she was on the S.S. *Kaisar i Hind* headed for Cairo, and planning to put her pseudo-Egyptian ballet back into the repertory. But the Ajanta Caves

ABOVE Playing croquet (American rules) with Chaliapin and Novikov, Ivy House, 1923.

BELOW With her old friend Adolph Bolm, Ivy House, 1923.

In costumes collected in Japan (above) and India (below).

had left a strong impression, and she began discussing ideas for a work using them as a theme. She wanted to stage a spectacle in which the teeming images on the caves' walls came to life in some way. (This followed the basic premise of *Le Pavillon d'Armide*, with its sleeping traveler disturbed by dreams of the figures in the tapestry adorning his room, while Benois's libretto was not entirely divorced from the opening scene of *Daughter of the Pharaoh*, in which the Englishman shelters in the tomb of the Egyptian princess and dreams that she comes to life.) Pavlova's first visit to India had of necessity missed out a greater part of the subcontinent, yet she had, by chance, traced a route exactly through the areas associated with the Guptas, who had given India a cultural renaissance between 320 and 467 A.D. Pavlova had absorbed the powerful impression of the frescoes and carvings and also seen examples of Mogul School miniaturist art.

Although the enthusiasm for all this was immediate, it was impossible to document what she had seen until she was back in London. The Victoria and Albert Museum had volumes relating to the frescoes at Ajanta, and many original examples of Mogul art showing scenes from the Krishna cycle—the stories so packed with pastoral symbolism and erotic undertones. Pavlova had read Tagore in Russian translations, but the English translations of ancient Indian poetry, such as the Narottama Das of the sixteenth century, contained remarkable imagery:

> Wild lightning in the lap of darkness;
> Radha ever more richly plays,
> while sidelong in the slippery path
> a way is felt;
> vermilion, musk, and sandal-mark all turn to mud
> in torrents of sweet rain.

Pavlova had brought back from India trunks packed with saris and bolts of fabrics, as well as the accessories of ornamentation, many of them almost identical to the minutely depicted details of costuming in the museum miniatures.

The Ajanta theme, with its particular antecedents, was to remain a typically Westernized bit of Orientalism, in the great tradition of the Fokine-Bakst collaborations, and it fell to Clustine to effect all this. Of course he had not seen Ajanta—that had been on the tour when he had expected Pavlova to be eaten by tigers—so it was hardly surprising that his construction missed the gentle lyricism inherent in the frescoes themselves, where the figures were so supple and so strangely simple, with none of the excessive gestures and exaggerations associated with later periods in Indian art. For the other collaborators, Pavlova was persuaded by Nicolas Tcherepnin that his son could handle a full ballet composition. Pavlova agreed, though Alexander was still only twenty-four. The idea about the frescoes coming to life remained the central theme, and the excuse for a "touch of orgy" lay in the story of Prince Gautama, who turned with disgust from the carnal world in order to seek a higher life.* Orest Allegri was

---

* Young Tcherepnin was to say later that the choice of story lay entirely with him, and that the Gautama episode was his device; but he also said that he did not compose the score until August, and a lot of preliminary work had been done by then.

Krishna and Radha: (above) with Uday Shankar; (below) with Algeranoff.

executing the designs, copying the pictures and cartographic sketches from collections in London, and he made great play of the elephant frieze from Cave Ten, but he too missed the harmony and tranquillity that pervaded many of the other caves, where flower-strewn backgrounds, with looping creepers and banana trees, blended in with the figures in a way that prefigured Botticelli's happiest compositions.

All of that was Pavlova playing safe, as indeed she was bound to do; but having made that concession, she was eager to experiment: there was the memory of the child wedding, and there were the miniatures, with their ever-smiling, sloe-eyed immortals. If these themes were to be followed with true sensitivity, then a real suggestion of Indian music posed the principal problem: scales of twenty-two notes, relationship between *tala* and *raga*—could any Western composer produce male and female tunes in anything but a Tchaikovskian manner? Dandré noticed that an Indian composer, Commalata Bannerjee, was giving a London recital of native music during the summer season. Algeranoff, who had shown the most marked interest in all things Oriental during the tour of the Far East, was dispatched to listen. On the basis of his favorable report, Bannerjee was immediately

invited to Ivy House to play a selection of her music. Pavlova was entranced, and there and then asked the composer to create a score suitable for a ballet suite. They chose two themes: the Hindu wedding, and the story of Krishna and Radha.

At this point Bannerjee made a vital contribution by telling Pavlova about a young Indian artist currently studying at the Royal College of Art, who might be of help. His name was Uday Shankar, and although he had never danced in public, he had studied Indian dancing from his father, and a questing mind had led him to some of the few remaining valid sources for true Indian style. Within days of going to Ivy House, Shankar was at work. Because he understood the pulse of Bannerjee's score he was able to start as soon as he heard it played for the first time. All this happy conjunction was not to continue in the tranquility of Ivy House and its peaceful vista; Pavlova was off on the inevitable English provincial tour leading to a two-week season at Covent Garden in September, and Shankar was expected to work during this tour. Although Pavlova had re-engaged Novikov, as a replacement for Volinine, she was sufficiently impressed by the graceful young Shankar to suggest that he dance with her in one of the ballets. He agreed, and throughout the second half

With Novikov in *Ajanta's Frescoes*, 1923:
(left) in rehearsal and (below) in performance.

With Novikov at Ivy House, 1923, in poses apparently from *Ballet Egyptien*, which had re-entered the repertory some months earlier. (Pavlova's foot and the mat have escaped the retoucher's brush in the center picture.) It is clear from these photographs and the ones of *Ajanta's Frescoes* that Clustine had only one approach to Orientalism.

of the tour worked continuously on the new pieces. Though Indian dancing employed no scenery, Western audiences had become so used to Bakst's Orientalism, which set stages awash with color and design, that it was decided to follow this lead. As in *Ajanta's Frescoes* (as the Clustine-Tcherepnin ballet was called), copies were made from some of the works in the museums, in this case the miniatures.

Shankar tried to suggest traditional groupings for the wedding scene, and in the love idyll of Krishna and Radha he gave the god a flute to signal that he was appearing in the guise of a cowherd. Only the steely blue skin would betray the fact that he was really the Eternal Lover. Whereas Fokine's 1912 ballet *Le Dieu Bleu* had carried hints of the Siamese court dancers who had visited St. Petersburg at the turn of the century, Shankar's *Krishna and Radha* was reaching back directly to the true Manipuri style of India, with the soft undulations speaking of Nature and all growing things. The corps de ballet girls, as *goppies*, were given beautiful flower formations, and at the center, Pavlova's Radha was tender and submissive before the sinuous virility of the young Indian artist's portrayal of Krishna.

Pavlova's return to Covent Garden in early September was her first appearance in the opera house since Diaghilev had presented her there in the autumn of 1911. This 1923 season was a test on more than one count. She was using the theatre in the dead part of the season, and she was having to appease an audience that was, on the whole, musically sophisticated. There was no certainty that her prewar "army," which had survived to

follow her to Drury Lane and elsewhere, would cross the great divide and become opera-house patrons in higher-priced seats. There was also the problem of the new repertory. A separate ballet derived from the experiences in Japan had not materialized; instead, three genuine Japanese dances were put together as the first section of an overall grouping that also included *Hindu Wedding* and *Krishna and Radha*, all of which were given the general title *Oriental Impressions*.

The reconstruction of the Japanese numbers relied heavily on the notebooks of the keen young Algeranoff, who had studied intently at the Fujima School. Thus aided, Pavlova was able to reproduce a suite of movements for fan-carrying Geishas from *Dojoji*, one of the classic Kabuki presentations; a solo called *Kappore*, which was a much-revered ancient comic dance about a coolie who fears that stormy weather will delay the arrival of oranges from the south; and *Takesu Bayashi*, another traditional number, which had dancers beating toy drums. The orchestral arrangements for these three pieces were done by Henry Geehl, who also wrote an overture, using traditional Japanese themes. Allegri's backcloth was in the manner of an eighteenth-century Japanese print. Matsumoto Koshiro, and his wife and assistant, who were responsible for the initial teaching of these classical Japanese numbers, were credited in programs with the "arrangements"; this led to endless confusion among critics, who thought the reference was to the music. Though Shankar had "arranged" *Hindu Wedding* and *Krishna and Radha*, this was seldom acknowledged in the programs.

Pavlova need not have feared for her popularity at the Opera House; on the night of September 10 the building was packed,

Pavlova took every opportunity to add Russian character dances in traditional costume to the repertory.
In the portrait above she displays the costume for *Russian Dance,* which she performed with Mordkin in London in 1911,
during the second season at the Palace. Opposite, she is seen (top) in the costume for the 1914 *Petite Danse Russe,* which
continued in the repertory in America for several years, and (bottom) as the Princess in the postwar *Russian Folk Lore.*

with (in the words of the *Daily Mail* critic) "the sort of audience that every artist would wish to win, an audience that only an artist with some spark of unhuman genius succeeds in winning. They were conquered beforehand, remembering what this slim, strange creature's art was already, years ago." It was as if Pavlova's other postwar appearances had never happened. Now that she was back at Covent Garden, she could be taken into account artistically:

> Those who remember Pavlova's last appearance at Covent Garden—in the heyday of the Diaghileff ballet—would not agree that last night the wondrous dancer had all the accessory graces worthy of her (for instance, the music of the evening started off by being poor and cheap). But Pavlova herself is the wonder she ever was. And when towards the end she repeated her two most famous poems-in-movement of the old days—the Saint-Saëns *Swan* and the *Autumn Bacchanale* of Glazunov—the most jealous eye could not see any falling away. There those exquisite achievements were, as surely as though we had gone back to a picture gallery to see again a masterpiece.

So Pavlova herself seemed unscathed. What of the rest of the repertory? *The Fairy Doll*, despite some fresh designs by Soudeikine, replacing the travel-weary sets by Doboujinsky, was dismissed as being a poor variant of Massine's *La Boutique Fantasque*; there was no awareness that Pavlova's ballet had predated Massine's by several years. On the other hand, the orgy element of *Ajanta's Frescoes* was thought to be a proper theme for a Russian ballet. The *Daily Mail* noted certain similarities with parts of *Schéhérazade* and *Le Dieu Bleu*, but thought that the new ballet was "worked out with brilliance . . . with a colour of its own. . . ." It noted too "the curious music—music that seemed to be seeking back for a prehistoric, naked primitiveness, rugged, obsessive, and artfully artless. . . . " The young composer's father was conducting; it was Nicolas Tcherepnin's twenty-fifth anniversary as a conductor. (Before the divertissements, Stier made him a presentation on stage on behalf of the orchestra. The members had primed Tcherepnin to be sure to kiss Stier, knowing how the Austrian would shudder. They were not disappointed.) *The Times* was very fair in recording that *Ajanta's Frescoes* was enthusiastically received, but then added, "If there is any criticism to be made it is that in the dances, and more especially in Madame Pavlova's own dancing, too many of the clichés of the conventional ballet make their appearance. The music of Alexander Tcherepnin has plenty of rhythmic character and might perhaps have been more closely studied in devising the steps. . . . "

The terrible extent of the Japanese earthquake in August 1923 had shocked the world, and the dancers realized that many of their new friends might have died. There was no way of knowing if the teachers whose names were on the program were still alive. Every day the lists were printed, with the estimate rising to above 90,000. Pavlova made the premiere of *Oriental Impressions* on September 13 a charity evening for the Lord Mayor's earthquake fund. The program sellers wore kimonos, and as a break between the Nipponese and Indian elements of the evening, there was a

Advertisements from the early 1920s involving Pavlova's
endorsements for various products . . .

small ceremony on stage in which the Japanese Ambassador made a speech of thanks and presented Pavlova with a bouquet. Although Pavlova had been persuaded against persisting with true Japanese dance steps for herself, for this special evening she did a dance to Grieg's "Butterfly," in which she flitted about briefly in a Geisha hair-do and a gauzy version of a kimono.* (Pavlova had arranged for an expert in Oriental make-up to attend to the company backstage.)

Hubert Griffith found *Oriental Impressions* "an entirely delightful surprise," though he could not vouch for its authenticity: "How far they recapture the spirit of Japan or India I cannot say, but in their simplicity, their colour, and their movement they are delicious." The *Japanese Butterfly* he found "definitely as un-Japanese as it can be. Mme. Pavlova's type is no more Japanese than is the Sistine Madonna; her light kimono was like the flowing gown of a Gainsborough duchess, she herself like something out of the French eighteenth century. But her dance was one of the gayest, quickest, and most beautiful things I have ever seen." For Griffith the real question was, "Is Pavlova herself now dancing with the same magic that made her name something apart from the name of any other dancer who had come to London in our generation?"

She has again danced the *Swan* and the *Bacchanale* and it can be seen that she is utterly unchanged. As before, one may judge Pavlova in different ways. One may—if one thinks one knows

enough—agree with the experts that her technique is perfection. Or one may take the layman's point of view: that she, alone of all dancers, seems to make technique not to exist; that when other dancers, walking on tiptoe, seem to be exhibiting the highest skill, Pavlova, doing the same thing, seems merely to have discovered a lighter and more effortless and more beautiful mode of ordinary progression—as, to Rostand, Alexandrines were merely a simpler way of saying the same thing than in prose.

The first section of the evening had been *Dionysus*. De Lipsky's lighting plans were not appreciated by the *Times* critic:

Mme. Pavlova is no priestess, but, what is better, [she is] Mme. Pavlova, a being possessed of wonderful gifts of movement, which she uses for our delight. But then why cumber it with this paraphernalia of red lights and green lights and revolving statues? The whole did not hang together, nor did the orchestral playing under the composer's baton. There is some excellent material in his score, but one wondered whether it had been rehearsed.

It may well have been a difficulty in setting up the complicated lighting filters—and a recalcitrant local crew—that prevented de Lipsky's lighting effects from making their true impact. The critics also seemed uneasy about committing themselves on *Oriental Impressions,* and at least one suggested that the break for the stage presentation disrupted the mood. It was certainly asking a lot of an audience to swing from intimations of a great human tragedy and the sight of Pavlova accepting flowers to the wavering percussive accents and drones of Bannerjee's music and Shankar's choreographic subtleties.

Pavlova's attempts to honor other cultures got a fuller, if be-

---

* In Gorsky's version of *Daughter of the Pharaoh,* a set of variations in Act Three included "Egyptian Butterflies," to music of Grieg.

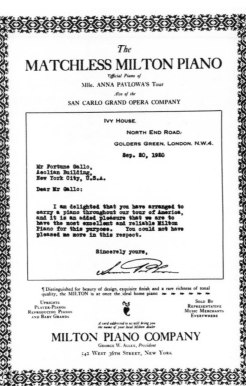

... including three different makes of piano.

lated, recognition in the Bombay *Chronicle,* which printed the views of an English art critic:

> Mme. Pavlova has understood the anguish of the artists in the Ajanta who for centuries have remained suppressed, who cry aloud but are not heard. She has dared to interpret the message in their heart. And her magic art, if it is the most difficult, is also the best medium of expression. It is probably the only medium that can approximate the Ajanta conceptions. That daring marks her out as an *artiste* of rare temperament. That rare temperament is the rarest of gifts. If it is the sensitive instrument that inspires, it is also the responsive soul competent to interpret aesthetic contacts and experiences. . . . It is true that the magic of the line of the Ajanta paintings is perhaps, even for this gifted *artiste,* the most difficult theme for translation. But the odds against her are not the consideration that would frighten Mme. Pavlova into renunciation of her rights and duties as an artist. It is an appeal that has already found a response. It is a challenge she is only too happy to accept.

In 1923 it was commonly believed that ballet had done all it could do and that what remained represented merely the dying embers of a few great exponents, pre-eminently Pavlova. *The Times* ran a thoughtful article whose author admitted that the Covent Garden season had been "beyond all question" a success; but he also included a recent quote from Lydia Lopokhova: "The great vogue of the Russian Ballet is over. I am now going to try to make myself an actress." (She had of course ducked out of the task in Barrie's play two years earlier.) The article pursued Lopokhova's startling statement. "Remembering her own tumultu-

ous reception whenever she now appears, and that Pavlova fills Covent Garden, can one square the statement into fact? It is at least not entirely fantastic. The applause is in each case for the dancer, not for the ballet." The article then noted London's faithfulness to certain performers:

> Critical it may not be—or at least not always, but those who have once found its favour are never in the space of long years allowed to forget it. It happens in [Pavlova's] case that it could equally well be either a manifestation of faithfulness or of judgement. Pavlova is dancing exactly as well as she has ever done. Those who saw her in former years will admit that there was no further magic to be brought to the art of dancing. Those who see her now will admit that no thrill of the former magic has abated. Her technique is still so perfect as to make all technique seem easy—but technique was never her greatest asset. Her physical beauty is unchanged—a suggestion of strength and maturity only adding to and not taking away from the wonder of its lithe grace—but it was never only her physical beauty that mattered. She has still the quality that is indefinable, that makes her different from other dancers—from Lopokova, who is a *comédienne* turned dancer; from Karsavina, who is a tragic actress turned dancer. Pavlova is still a dancer, and only a dancer, and brings to it, as she always did, the unknown eternal quality that will not go into words. The Opera House has good reason to be full.

Sol Hurok's presentation of Pavlova in the autumn of 1923 followed the pattern of her previous frenetic trips around America. The itinerary he mapped out was based on the lowest common denominator: proven audience response per city per week. His star was in her forty-third year, but she had the uncanny ability to keep this fact at bay. She recognized clearly the economic considerations that governed the touring of ballet in the postwar world, although she was not oblivious to the pressure, and at times she commented on it.

For Hurok the Pavlova Company was his safest bet for the long term. He had Chaliapin and Mischa Elman, and he dabbled with visits from the Folies-Bergère and even Ida Rubinstein, but there was nothing to compare with the solid garnering of receipts, week after steadfast week, by Pavlova as she tracked around the United States, performing at any place that could provide a platform for dancing and seating for an audience. Although Hurok could offer counsel, nobody knew American audiences better than Pavlova and Dandré, and it was they who made the basic decisions, juggling artistic considerations against economic practicalities. For every box-office uncertainty such as *Krishna and Radha* there had to be a *Fairy Doll* or its equivalent.

Novikov, on his reappearance with the company in England, had shown a desire to be seen as something more than a *porteur*, and to a score by Nicolas Tcherepnin he choreographed *An Old Russian Folk Lore*, based on a traditional folk tale, which emerged as a balletic hybrid of *Le Coq d'Or* and *The Firebird*. The thinking was not unsound, as they had neither of those masterpieces in the repertoire. Unfortunately, they did not have another Fokine either. When Novikov's ballet turned up in New York, critics were mildly dismissive of the choreography and they thought Bilibine's scenery conventional, but they went for the jugular over the score. *Musical America* called it "terrible; a mixture of modernism and feeble tunes, but modernism without method."[*] *Chopiniana* (still with its Pazetti scenery from 1913) had opened the program at the Manhattan Opera House, and the usual divertissements closed it. Curiously, *The Blue Danube* was described as having "brought the company onto the stage to form a living background for a new and wonderful bacchanale by Pavlova and Novikoff." Previously, there had been criticisms that this ballet was performed *à la grecque*, instead of in Empire dresses. On the second evening in New York *Oriental Impressions* was given. "The quaint posturings, mincing steps and automatic gestures of the figures . . . were interesting," according to one critic, but the music was "simple in design and tenuous to Western ears." *Krishna and Radha* fared better; in it Pavlova was thought to "impress the audience anew with her grace and versatility in the swaying and gliding of the scene."

There was a recurring fascination with the mechanics of Pavlova's craft. Journalists watched rehearsals and marveled that dancers could seem so prosaic in practice dress. Even *Musical America* indulged in some trivia:

It may interest you to hear that Pavlowa says that she uses a dozen pairs of shoes a week. She gets these shoes from a shoemaker in Milan, who every fortnight sends her two dozen wherever she may be. Sometimes she discards a pair after dancing in them for only half an hour—perhaps they stretch and get too wide. During a performance it may happen that she changes her shoes three times. What a shoe bill she must have. Happy shoemaker!

Pavlova herself was willing to chatter about any subject the reporters introduced. On fat men in America: "I'd say they should not eat so much candy and sweets and should drink more liquor. I would like to see every man in America have his daily glass of beer. Beer is good for men. Every good man should have his beer." Having had her fun at the expense of the Prohibition laws, she waited for another subject. Jazz dancing? "It will die out. It is too much like wrestling and boxing."

The 1923-24 American tour ran for seven months—an almost inconceivable progression in view of the constant daily traveling it entailed. Few places could sustain a six-day halt; for the most part it was arrive, unpack, show, pack, travel—all in a twenty-four-hour span. Although it was their own livelihood, many of the company members could not understand why Pavlova bothered to pursue such unremitting schedules. The truth seems to have been that her body and mind were so programmed to this routine that the thought of abandoning it opened up black chasms of the unknown that terrified her more than the remorselessness of further touring. She had unnatural amounts of nervous energy to burn up, and only the stage could produce the adrenaline charge that seemed to fire her metabolism to its peak. She lived on the stage; everything beyond it was merely a mirror land. Off-stage she was restless and uneasy, or listless, or overly passionate about minor matters; detached about wounded feelings in others; kind and gentle; sharp and persistent. All these conflicting qualities rose to the surface, glimmered dully or glittered brightly, and then submerged themselves again in an inexorable succession. For someone with such a manic disposition, a less binding life could have opened up a latitude in which these moods might have become ungovernable. Above all this, she was a dancer: disciplined from an early age, channeled into a corridor of life that had little to do with the lives of nondancers, precocious in the art of self-display, yet at the same time poorly trained in social deportment—adult children trapped inside school, self-absorbed, surrounded by mirrors, gazed at, protected, guided, relieved of day-to-day decisions. Childlike intensities and enthusiasms were a natural part of this atmosphere. (In England during a tour, Pavlova one morning took one of the pianist's gloves when he was not looking, tied a label of their next address to a finger of the glove, and dropped it in a mailbox. The prank kept her bubbling all day.) There had to be distractions, no matter how trivial, from the endless repetition, from the tinseled Fairy Doll waving her wand night after night. With all this mediocrity, she kept intact some inner core of her being which was never tarnished by physical or mental erosion. Because of

---

[*] By the following April, when the tour had wended its way back to Washington, *An Old Russian Folk Lore* was still thought boring—"Except for Pavlowa! She was entrancing as this will-o'-the-wisp enchanted birdling. All the caprice of her illusive technique was given. It was a marvel of virtuosity. . . . Then, too, Pavlowa is always a dramatic artist. When she is changed into the princess, in her Russian robes and huge headdress, she becomes humorous, coy and delectable." No one seemed to take as unusual the soprano voice in one section of the score; it was never mentioned.

Reading Tagore, on vacation in northern Italy, c.1924.

With her mother on the lawn at Ivy House, July 1924.

her belief in the message of dance, she would sacrifice everything else in order for that message to be seen. If first-rate collaborators meant that the end product would be seen and approved only by a relatively small and very esoteric audience, then she would abandon the refined artistic content. She did not believe that *Fairy Doll* was the ultimate in balletic expression, but she did believe that it and its kind were a password to a further audience. These ballets were accessible, undemanding, and agreeable to the majority, and within this framework Pavlova could, and did, work miracles. Hers was not lofty idealism, but missionary vigor.

The American tour finally ended in early May 1924, after a two-week New York engagement. Business had been good for the most part, and only a few outposts showed any empty seats. A journalist in Wilkes-Barre, Pennsylvania, tried to explain the local management's loss by equating ballet with Shakespeare: "One must become 'iddicated' to these things in order to derive the full benefit of their beauty and art, and outside of the large cities where the constant parade of all manner of productions makes every man and woman a student of art, this is well nigh impossible." The reporter must have been one of the "educated" ones, for he filed a rave review.

Sometime that spring, Pavlova received news that her mother was alive and well and had reached Odessa safely, and it was decided that she would travel to England that summer. (One wonders at this timid soul, who spoke only Russian, making the long journey to a foreign land alone. Surely Pavlova, or an envoy, must have traveled to the Mediterranean to collect her.) There was a sense of excitement at Ivy House, and an Orthodox priest blessed all the rooms in preparation for the visit. A few snapshots bear testimony to those gentle days in high summer,

with mother and daughter feeding pigeons on the lawn or wandering around the garden walks. Anna leans protectively toward the composed figure of her mother, but both women look years older than their age. Her mother must have found the Hampstead retreat rather overwhelming, and her daughter a stranger. She would have looked at the appurtenances of a successful and worldly life and seen her daughter at the center of it—forcing the gaiety, tired, aging, and endlessly interrupted by the outside world calling on her time. Almost beyond belief, Pavlova had agreed to another American tour for Hurok, beginning in the autumn. The pattern was repeating itself: English provincial appearances, a season at Covent Garden (four weeks this time), and then the Atlantic; on the other side, six months of touring lay in wait. It was a frightening treadmill. Her mother saw her dance, in Bournemouth, in the peak of summer; then she returned to Russia, to the country and the way of life she understood best.

The usual syndicated interviews began appearing in the American press as a result of Hurok's advance publicity. The September 1924 issue of the *Ladies' Home Journal* ran a feature under Pavlova's own byline. It rehashed the years of dedication, the hierarchy at the Maryinsky in the days of the Tsar, the travels, the successes, the differences in the American approach to life versus the Russian. There was also a paragraph on the careful choosing of a marriage partner in Russia: " . . . and we married for keeps. The years that I have been Victor Dandré's wife will attest to that."

Novikov had been at work throughout the summer reconstructing a version of Gorsky's *Don Quixote,* and Clustine had begun shaping another bit of Egyptian nonsense to a Nicolas Tcherepnin score. *The Romance of a Mummy* was in a long line of descent from Petipa's *Daughter of the Pharaoh,* through Fokine's *Egyptian Nights* and *Cléopâtre,* to Clustine's own Egyptian ballet. The line was becoming enfeebled—and so was Clustine; he fell ill, and Novikov had to complete the ballet the following year. Meanwhile, Pavlova was making inquiries about Fokine's whereabouts; she wanted him to overhaul *Les Préludes,* and she may well have thought to charm a new work out of him as well.

The revival of *Don Quixote* made sense: it was new to the West, it had spectacle and color, and it provided plenty of action for the company as well as two contrasting showcase roles for Pavlova herself, which framed her to advantage in a style she could carry with personality as much as with physical bravado. As usual, reporters crowded the rehearsals at Covent Garden. Among them was Trevor Allen, unabashed in his sense of wonder when in proximity to a figure of such international fame:

> And then, out of the gloom comes—Pavlova: half shy, half tangible, exquisitely diminutive against this vast, dark cavern of undraped stage. She has on a frail ballet frock of apple green, Grecian in line. She greets you with an impulsive pressure of the hands which at once dispels all aloofness. What a baffling, perplexing thing is Pavlova, vis-à-vis! Night-dark eyes, night-dark hair over a face so tending to thinness as to be half transparent, as though a light—the light of the dancer's soul, if you will—transfigures mere cell and tissue. When she speaks, it is musically, ecstatically, with a captivating abandon. She hardly shares your three-dimensional world. All the time you have the impression that she is merely a strange visitant hovering on its verge, and that even in the middle of a sentence, you may suddenly lose her.
>
> Immediately she joins the ballet you have indeed lost her utterly. She becomes a possessed thing. Her whole consciousness turns, in a trice, inward. In contour, rhythm, gesture, she is tracing out a language, an esoteric script, of which you know only the surface meaning. Suddenly she stops, and interpolates a swift exclamation in Russian. In that moment you can almost hear her drop tangibly to earth.

With her mother and her maid, May Chapman, at Ivy House.

Pavlova had cause for a lot of exclamations that week. Her personal costumes for the ballet were being embroidered in Paris, but a customs strike prevented their entry into England. In the end Manya, Pavlova's dresser, had only a few hours to tack together makeshift substitutions for the first night. N. G. Royde-Smith assessed the evening in *The Queen* magazine:

> Madame Pavlova, received by an enthusiastic and crowded house, opened her four weeks' season at Covent Garden on September 8th with *Don Quixote,* an operatic ballet, arranged by Laurent Novikoff to music by a nineteenth-century composer called Minkus. It was not a happy idea to put Don Quixote into dancing, and it was not a happy idea to get Minkus to set him to music even for the middle of the nineteenth century, and its revival is an even less happy notion, though the opening scene in a great and gloomy Spanish library, with Don Quixote as mad as mad and Sancho Panza as fat as fat, is very well staged by Korovine and Allegri, and quite adequately mimed by M. Damoslavski and M. Markovski. But after that everything goes a little wrong. Two of the Don's adventures were presented, one in a Barcelona public market-place, the other in an Enchanted Forest opening into Dulcinea's garden. The marketplace was full and busy: the corps de ballet, described rather disconcertingly on the programme as "a grovelling crowd," danced as
>
> Spanishly as possible, but their efforts were almost obliterated by the vivid insistence of the scenery, which, with its heavy outline and its violent colour, did everything a background should not do to the picture it is to enhance. The forest was better, being dimmer, and the dances in Dulcinea's garden were really charming, though it was a shock to discover that Dulcinea was not the cloaked and dignified figure in the centre of the group which formed the first part of Don Quixote's vision, but a prima ballerina of the most glittering conventionality who danced as only Pavlova can dance and made up for everything else, so that we forgot the tale in adoring the enchantress who had so completely mangled it for us.
>
> We had been annoyed with the commonplace and obvious setting, bored with the long dull dances and the tireless perversion of a great story; and then Pavlova came along with the hardworking M. Novikoff to lift and swing her into her most perfect poses, and all was well. And she did it on the first night without the aid of the wonderful dresses she is now wearing, because the Customs would not let them through. So her dresser improvised raiment for her, and her personal triumph was the more complete.

Most of the daily papers were less severe in their criticisms, and all agreed that Pavlova carried the evening; but the company must have braced itself for Ernest Newman's critique in *The*

Don Quixote, 1924: Pavlova as Kitri, Novikov as Basilio, Domyslawski as the Don.
BELOW (right) The dream sequence, with Pavlova as Dulcinea and Novikov as the Knight.

Sunday Times. Newman had consolidated a reputation as a highly opinionated, ruthless avenger of musical excellence, and he occupied a pivotal position in criticism in the way that George Bernard Shaw did. Newman launched his article on September 14 with a provocative paragraph that ran directly counter to his fellows' views: he was of the opinion that as an actress Pavlova was not convincing, citing her work in *Amarilla* to support this. Nevertheless, he wrote, "In herself she is a wonder; as a dancer she is still, in her own line, without a superior. She is a soloist and, like all artists of her type, difficult to fit into the scheme of a big work." On the matter of *Don Quixote* and Ludwig Minkus, however, Newman was unremitting:

> To build up a big ballet into a complete work of art, again, one needs something more than supreme perfection as a solo dancer; and it is this something more that Mme. Pavlova seems to lack. Her taste in music appears to be, to put it very mildly, somewhat accommodating. We had come to believe that we should never be asked to listen to more commonplace music than that of Glazounov and Drigo to *Amarilla*, or that of Bayer to *The Fairy Doll.* But we had congratulated ourselves too soon. On Monday night Mme. Pavlova introduced us to *Don Quixote*, the music of which is by one Ludwig Minkus, a long-forgotten mediocrity of the mid-nineteenth century, who was ballet composer at the Petersburg Imperial Theatre in the 'seventies. In a long experience of bad music I have never come across anything so utterly banal, so inane, so thoroughly incompetent in every respect, as that of Minkus to *Don Quixote.* The stuff is an insult to the intelligence of any musical hearer; I had to summon up all my respect for Mme. Pavlova to persuade myself to sit it out.
>
> The ballet is not much more satisfactory than the music. It has one or two charming dances for Mme. Pavlova, and an excellent one for M. Novikoff; but for the rest it is mostly the kind of thing one would expect to see in any music hall or at any pantomime. It has the minimum of connection with Don Quixote, which perhaps is as well; for the wretched Minkus is obviously incapable of writing five bars of music that could be supposed by the most generous-minded listener to be characteristic of Don Quixote or Sancho Panza. M. Korovine's scenery and costumes are so good that they deserve a better fate than to be associated with such a work.

Surprisingly, the appearances of a horse and a donkey in *Don Quixote* did not draw particular mention from reviewers, though a make-up artist had drawn rib shadows on the plump white charger to such effect that one old lady complained to the Royal Society for the Prevention of Cruelty to Animals, which sent an inspector to Covent Garden to investigate the horse's well-being. The blue lights of the night scene invariably made this animal nervous, with the inevitable results, and the dancers derived some innocent amusement from Dandré's voice in the wings calling for the stage manager: "Mack! Mack!" With Dandré's accent, this came out as "Muck! Muck!"

Alexandre Volinine rejoined the company during this London season. Pavlova had persuaded him to leave Paris for a while and share the burden of the American tour with her and Novikov. Not without a little foresight she said, "If either of you gets troublesome, I will always have the other to rely on."

THE ANNA PAVLOVA FOUNDATION

SPECIAL MATINEE

Thursday, October 2nd, at 2.30 p.m.

Madame Pavlova is devoting the whole of her proceeds to the Refugee Home.

PRICES AS USUAL

During the year 1921, when in Paris, the worst hardships I witnessed were those endured by the little Russian children, some without homes, many actually starving—little refugees of my own land mutely pleading for help in a strange country. Something had to be done at once, so at St. Cloud, near Paris, I rented for some of them a suitable home, where they now live in happiness and are well cared for. That little band is ever increasing; already it has assumed proportions beyond my private purse to entirely support.

I am most anxious to continue this work—**will you please help me?**

1924

To Madame ANNA PAVLOVA,
Ivy House,
North End Road, Hampstead.

I enclose £ : : as a Donation to the ANNA PAVLOVA FOUNDATION.

Signature

Address

ANNA PAVLOWA'S HOME
FOR RUSSIAN CHILDREN
7, BIS RUE DU CHEMIN DE FER
SAINT CLOUD, PARIS

Cheques should be made payable to Anna Pavlowa and sent to the above address.

TO MY COMPANY:

I wish to express to all of you my deepest gratitude for the excellent services which you have rendered me during my long season.

I also thank you from all my heart for the kind attention you have shown me by giving me your full support in my Charity Performance for my "Home for Russian Children".

With my sincere appreciation,

Yours very sincerely,

The Pavlova girls looking toward familiar horizons, 1924.

For once Pavlova was content that her tour should be billed as a "farewell." She was faced with 238 booked performances in 77 different places; the pitcher was returning to the well dangerously often. And she was troubled, for the first time in her life, with a nagging ailment—a knee problem. In the past, physical damage had been nonrecurring: the foot in St. Louis, an injured finger, an infected toe—they had been fleeting inconveniences. But now her left knee was a constant factor—surmounted without outward sign, but nevertheless impinging on her general concentration in a way she had not known previously. Pavlova had been luckier than most dancers, but then no other dancer had carried the constant performing schedule that she had. This unremitting work had a positive side in that she was constantly tuned to a fine performing pitch, which was to her physical advantage; but it also aggravated the slightest impairment.

New York audiences found *Don Quixote* agreeable, and no one was as brutal as Newman had been over the score. "The

music, by a mysterious stranger named Minkus, was rhythmic and tuneful," reported *Musical America*. Hurok had announced the three-week season, starting on October 17, as the "Farewell New York Season," though he knew perfectly well that when the time came, he would happily try to convince Pavlova that she should return again to the city of her triumphs. The "star system" was already big business on the American musical scene. Karsavina had followed Pavlova into New York; but whereas the former's name was virtually unknown in America outside musical circles, Pavlova's was a household word. Karsavina gave a matinee at Carnegie Hall on November 1; she had no company, only a partner, the talented Petrograd dancer Pierre Vladimiroff. Hurok had just concluded an agreement whereby he controlled all bookings at the Manhattan Opera House, and his offering Karsavina and Vladimiroff a single appearance there, after Pavlova had left, was his assessment of the star system as it then pertained.

The reviews for Karsavina's Carnegie Hall debut tended to enforce his view. *Musical America* thought that "the program, consisting of solo numbers and dances with her partner, Pierre Vladimiroff, presented many difficulties, especially to an artist who, like Mme. Karsavina, is renowned as much for her pantomimic work as for her skill as a ballet dancer; but these obstacles were quite successfully overcome. More rehearsals with the orchestra, too, would apparently have resulted in a smoother performance; but the volume of applause proved that Mme. Karsavina's art was not unappreciated." It was scarcely an idolatrous reception for a "renowned" dancer. When she joined up with Adolph Bolm's small company, Ballet Intime, for some concert appearances in Boston and elsewhere during November, her contribution to the evening was described as "gracious dancing." With her pretty command of English, she did her best to accommodate the American press, flattering them on the "wonderful material for dancing in this country, especially among the girls between the ages of 14 and 16."

On November 30 the *Sunday Eagle* magazine ran a full-page interview with Pavlova under the headline "Anna Pavlowa Wishes to Preserve Her Art on the Films," in which it was stated that the ballerina "has already screened [i.e., filmed] all of her divertissements." (See Appendix, p. 408.) It is unlikely that Pavlova had all of her solos recorded, and no one knows how many of the films she actually did make have been lost. But she had certainly taken part in film experiments prior to the 1915 *Dumb Girl* venture: in 1913 during her season in Berlin she let herself be filmed dancing *La Nuit* in a studio; this was to help a group of journalists who wanted a special attraction for a Widows and Orphans Fund gala, which was to take place after Pavlova had left the city. She did not like the result but agreed that it could have one showing. The thought that she might preserve her art on film was welcomed by Pavlova; the limitations of the medium never discouraged her from further attempts, and by the autumn of 1924 she had completed other experiments toward this end. She danced at least four solos for Dr. Lee de Forest, whose invention of the vacuum tube had transformed the development of radio at the time, and whose refinements to filming technique included a method of synchronizing sound and running the camera at a faster speed. The footage that exists today is garnered principally from the commemorative film *The Immortal Swan*, which was put together by Victor Dandré after Pavlova's death. (See Appendix, p. 411.)

As Pavlova had hoped, Fokine did rehearse *Les Préludes* in New York, and it was performed there; but there was no new work. As much as anything, the crushing schedules were precluding the development of new ballets. As Pavlova began progressing through the country after the initial New York engagement, it was noticeable that much of the press coverage was perfunctory, and the excitement that normally surrounded any

ABOVE Frame enlargements from the film of *The Swan* taken at the Fairbanks studio in Hollywood in 1925.

OPPOSITE At the Fairbanks studio: (top) in *The Fairy Doll*; (middle) in *Columbine* costume, with Mary Pickford; (bottom) in *Greek Dance*.

arrival by Pavlova was often missing. There were various factors at work: apart from Pavlova herself no longer being an unfamiliar entity, her East Coast appearances came in the wake of scattered performances by a company led by Adolph Bolm, with Karsavina as guest artist, as well as the Pavley-Oukrainsky company, which was hopping around the country both before and after Pavlova, like an annoying terrier snapping at an ex-mistress's heels. Hurok's press agent, Rufus Dewey, was nonplussed by the unaccustomed lack of interest, and during a meeting one morning he hit on the bright idea of finding Pavlova a husband. The journalists were apprised of this little "discovery" and were instructed to turn up at the Copley-Plaza hotel in Boston to coincide with Pavlova's arrival there. She followed the rules of the game adroitly, as reported the following day to readers of the Boston *Post:*

> Pavlowa arrived in Boston with a husband yesterday, but where she acquired him the famous toe dancer refused to say. "He just belongs to me," she answered demurely when newspaper men and women spotted the tall, fair-haired man who was trying to make himself inconspicuous at the far end of Madame's reception room at the Copley-Plaza. "His name, oh, no!" and the slender little woman raised her hands in gesture more convincing than her "oh, no," and the fair-haired man at the far end of the room smiled back in acquiescence.
>
> For a moment, it looked like a great mystery. Everybody fumbled for a question until a unanimous "Why?" won the day. Pavlowa called over the fair-haried man to help her give her reasons why she didn't want the world to know his name. "For the artist there is no husband. Yes, he is my husband, but that's just for me. No one else." She began speaking slowly, as if trying to make a great attempt to be understood. Every now and then she called upon her husband to supply a word, but never did he add more than the word. He simply smiled, and Madame seemed pleased. Like the famous dancer, he is a foreigner, possibly French. "When were you married? Where? Everybody is interested in the husband of the world's most famous toe dancer." But to all these complimentary queries Madame turned a deaf ear, and would do no more than admit that he was her husband and he's been around a long, long time.

> Not until the enquiring press sought the hotel register was it learned that the husband of Madame was M. V. Dandré. Throughout the long interview in which she discussed art, American girls, and all those things that the distinguished are called upon to tell the public, she constantly made veiled remarks about the beauty of companionship. She whetted the curiosity, and it was apparent she knew it. Her smile was always engaging, and it seemed that she was enjoying the humor of the occasion. Whenever she spoke, she looked around to be sure she was taking everyone into her confidence. It should be said that though Madame has never been hailed as a great beauty, she has about her that rare "something" called magnetism, that is so compelling that after a while one sees beauty in her that was not apparent on meeting her. Recently, it was reported in the papers of the country that she is 50. [She was at this time forty-three.] If she is, she certainly conceals it miraculously. She is not afraid of the camera, and she uses no make-up, with the exception of carmine for her lips. No rouge on her cheeks. And in the glaring noonday sun, one had to look hard to find even the faintest wrinkles.

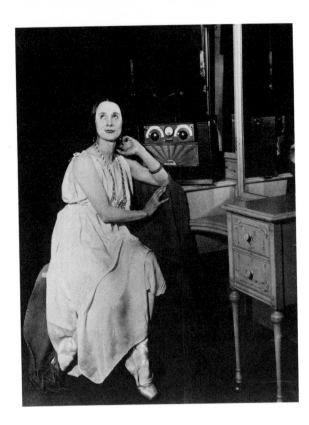

Backstage photographs, typical and not so typical.
The artificiality of the "radio pose" should not conceal the fact
that the medium represented a vital source of musical material
for consideration, even if in Pavlova's case the broadcasting
times did coincide with her own working hours.

She is, of course, the acme of grace, but more, she is distinctly feminine both in dress and in manner. She created the impression throughout the entire chat that the tall, fair-haired man close by was her protector, and once she gave voice to this feeling.

Pavlova's adroitness was certainly exceptional. She had told the world that Dandré was her protector; it was for the world to judge the accuracy of the definition.

Victor Dandré's protection of Anna Pavlova included the booking agreement for Chicago, which stipulated two performances on Christmas Day. She was undeterred; during the intermissions, dancers were summoned to her dressing room in relays, and each was presented with a carefully wrapped present. When Algeranoff opened his, he found a gold watch. In the world beyond the ballet, some people might have waited twenty-five years for such a gift from their employer; Algeranoff had been with Pavlova's company for three years.

But there were still the occasional tart admonitions, administered like a whip across the backs of honest but prosaic toilers. One girl, at work in the corner of a room one morning practicing "graceful" arm movements, had her satisfaction shattered by Pavlova, who had been observing the girl out of the corner of her eye. She stopped her own work after a while and said: "You know, in England there are first-class hotels, and second-class hotels, and there is something called the boardinghouse." She paused, then added, "You have the boardinghouse arms." When another girl was not giving her "all," Pavlova put her face close to the girl's and said, "You are a cow," then qualified this by adding, "But a nice, contented cow." It says much for Pavlova's authority that the recipients would later tell these anecdotes against themselves.

The final performance of Pavlova's farewell tour of America took place in El Paso, Texas, on March 25, 1925; but as far as touring went, it was merely one more notch: Mexico was next on the list. Though the visit was exciting for younger members of the company, for those who had been there before it was evident that five years had wrought few changes: there were still armed guards on the carriage roofs, hungry beggars and starving dogs at the railway stops, and barrenness from horizon to horizon. The contrast came with the capital city, swarming with extra visitors for Holy Week. There was a scramble for rooms; Pavlova made a point of staying at a hotel run by a Frenchman who had once befriended a stranded Russian opera company solely because he loved music.

There were several days with only a minimum of rehearsal before the season was to begin at the Teatro Esperanza Iris. Many of the company, including Pavlova, paid a visit to the Teatro Lirico, where a motley Mexican revue was playing. After an intermission, as the audience was waiting for the lights to go down, the manager walked in front of the curtain and announced that Pavlova was in the theatre. With one accord the entire audience stood and began looking around. When she was spotted in one of the boxes, they began cheering. Pavlova took it

ABOVE Rehearsal pose. Despite the extra cavaliers, the port de bras in this
press photograph show a stylistic affinity to Pavlova's own ballet *Autumn Leaves*.

BELOW *Autumn Leaves*, c.1926: (left) with Novikov.

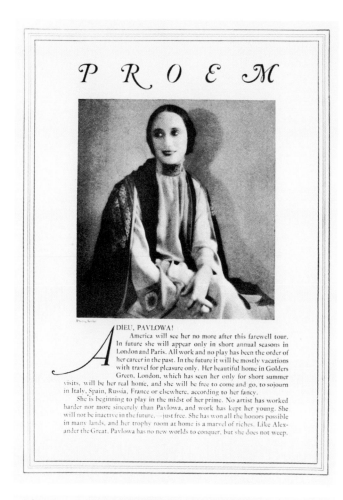

PROEM

ADIEU, PAVLOWA!

America will see her no more after this farewell tour. In future she will appear only in short annual seasons in London and Paris. All work and no play has been the order of her career in the past. In the future it will be mostly vacations with travel for pleasure only. Her beautiful home in Golders Green, London, which has seen her only for short summer visits, will be her real home, and she will be free to come and go, to sojourn in Italy, Spain, Russia, France or elsewhere, according to her fancy.

She is beginning to play in the midst of her prime. No artist has worked harder nor more sincerely than Pavlowa, and work has kept her young. She will not be inactive in the future,—just free. She has won all the honors possible in many lands, and her trophy room at home is a marvel of riches. Like Alexander the Great, Pavlowa has no new worlds to conquer, but she does not weep.

"Ralph, this is Poetry."
"Margaret, this is Religion."

THESE classic observations passed between two of the great literary minds of the last century, Ralph Waldo Emerson and Margaret Fuller Ossoli, as they sat entranced by the performance of Fanny Ellsler, one of the great predecessors of Anna Pavlowa.

Throughout the Orient, where the dance is the handmaiden of religion, and in the Occident, where her art is held the essence of poetry, Pavlowa reigns supreme. Last year, for the first time, she visited Japan, China, Manila, the Malay States, the Straits Settlements, India and Egypt. The plaudits she had won in the western world for many years were equalled in the enthusiasm with which she was received in the Far and Near East. In these strange climes she added many choreographic jewels to her repertoire, in which she was given hearty assistance by native artists, musicians, dancers and historians.

---

bravely and graciously, though she disliked that sort of attention. She took off her tight-fitting little evening hat with a cavalier's gesture and nodded with modest dignity to various corners of the auditorium. Near the end of the program there was another commotion as a line of Mexican beauties came on stage carrying baskets of souvenirs to be thrown to the audience. All of them aimed the straw dolls and beribboned flowers toward Pavlova's box; anything that fell short and was picked up by some other member of the audience immediately provoked a rash of hissing, so that the abashed recipient had to make strenuous efforts to get the souvenir back to its original target.

Pavlova's own performances in Mexico were received just as happily, but it was hard going. As before, the altitude played tricks. In the wings one evening Volinine was asked if it affected him. "No," he replied, "I not notice anything different." Moments later he slid down the side of a scenery flat, feet foremost, and was out of action for the rest of the evening. Pavlova improvised and summoned spur-of-the-moment replacements from the wings. The Mexicans were crazy about Pavlova's Radha; there were endless curtain calls. And, of course, she had to show them her *Mexican Dances,* and her sombrero dance created a riot.

Subtle shifts were taking place in the company at this time, and indeed in the outside world that governed it. Butsova, on whom Pavlova relied a great deal, succumbed to the charms of Hurok's young tour manager, Harry Mills, and quietly married him one day, while Hurok, the brains of all this mad touring, found himself in increasingly straitened circumstances back in New York; for every Pavlova touring relentlessly (and there was only one), other artists were performing in half-empty halls to indifferent audiences. He had over-reached himself, just as Gallo had suspected he would. Back in Chicago, at Christmas, Hurok had turned up unexpectedly, extracting $15,000 from the total of $20,000 that the company had managed to salt away in the hotel safe. During the earlier period, when he had been under the wing of Gallo, Hurok had toured with the company for a time; now he was conspicuously absent. With a week to go before the end of the marathon, word came through from Hurok's office in New York that he was "holding" $8,000 pending the company's finishing the tour as per the agreement.

Pavlova had agreed—against all past experience—to do one more performance in a bullring. She should have known that Mexico was not a country to change its *modus operandi* overnight. (A few days earlier she had had to deal with the police over the matter of a female dancer's leaving the theatre at night unaccompanied. An alert policeman had asked to see her "license," as it was automatically assumed that she was a prostitute.) The bullring performance on a Sunday afternoon included that strange old ritual from Maryinsky days *The Magic Flute,* complete with its faded scenery, including the little thatched house on one side of the stage. Unfortunately the audience had been allowed to buy seats around most of the circumference, and some unlucky ticket-holders found themselves beyond the line of vision. Shouts, hissing, and whistles made a discordant counterpoint to the score throughout the ballet. The dancers could do

Publicity poses for *Don Quixote*, 1924. The costumes had not arrived, and Pavlova had to use "Spanish" costumes from *The Fairy Doll*, *Danse Espagnol*, and the 1915 *Carmen* suite.

nothing but plow on. Worse was to come. *Amarilla* had scarcely begun when a violent thunderstorm broke. Much of the audience dispersed for cover before the dancers did, and the stage-hands then ambled forward to dismantle the backcloth and wing panels. The tempera paint was beginning to trickle forlornly. At this juncture, some sections of the audience who were sheltering in the lee of the stadium walls rushed forward, complaining that they were being cheated of their money's worth. So Pavlova donned her *Swan* costume, and, during a lull in the storm, bourréed out into the thunderous atmosphere to quell the vociferous minority. There was still an evening performance ahead, in the shelter of the Teatro Esperanza Iris.

As payday approached it became apparent to Harry Mills that the money that had been taken from the hotel safe was not going to make a reappearance. He spent a troubled night sitting on the steps of a church before summoning up the courage to face Pavlova with the bad news. There was only the matinee and the evening performance before the tour closed. Running expenses were singularly absent. (Gallo had paid a guaranteed $7,500 per week; Hurok's costs were fixed at $8,000 per week—hardly inflationary.) Harry blurted out his problem. "Madame, I'm in trouble." Pavlova went on applying her make-up without pause. "What?" Harry stumbled on: "This week's payroll . . . There's no money. I can't pay them. And if I don't pay them this afternoon, they won't dance this evening!" Pavlova treated it as if it were nothing more than a protruding nail in the stage. "Harry, don't worry. Mr. Hurok will pay me. I have enough money to cover the wages." Hurok went bankrupt days later.*

The tour was over. Pavlova went back to America, to continue her filming experiments in Los Angeles, and the rest of the company trekked back to Britain by way of the Caribbean. Butsova decided to stay in North America and handed in her notice. If Pavlova felt a draft of loneliness in her exposed position, she affected not to show it; the rest of the company was told to prepare for another season in Paris in the early summer.

Pavlova finally left America in the early summer of 1925. She had been laying a very mixed dish before the American public, on and off, for fifteen years, and yet at the end she was no nearer to developing an aware palate in her audience than she had been in the beginning, when they had thought *Giselle* an inferior vehicle to *Azyiade.* It was Pavlova they wanted, rather than the product she graced, and each time she attempted to introduce change and development the audience became suspicious. The pity was that she could not distance herself sufficiently to see that the ineradicable taste they had acquired for *her* was really a giant step along the path to accepting her medium of expression for its own sake. As a sign that lasting tastes could be formed, she might have taken comfort from the continuing sur-

vival of jazz music, had it not been such anathema to her. Instead she was enervated by America's endless succession of fads; from the Charleston to mahjong, these novelties won a massive response overnight. Pavlova had taken a sharp lesson in the winter of 1914-15, when she attempted to meet popular taste halfway; it was clear that Irene and Vernon Castle could do the maxixe to better effect than Pavlova could do her Pavlowana. Her role was clearly defined in the public's eye; yet it was not considered plagiarism when young girls all over the country began doing lamentable versions of *The Swan,* or *Butterfly,* for paying audiences, who seemed to display heroic tolerance. In private entertainments it was difficult to detect where frivolity ended and absurdity began. When Malvina Hoffman organized an elaborate studio party for Pavlova's birthday, the sculptress persuaded Pavlova to pose as a madonna in an ikon. The screen doors to this contrivance were flung open on the stroke of midnight to reveal the live "effigy"—who could not help breaking into a smile when Hoffman, swathed in a sari and many strings of pearls, approached with a large birthday cake. Inside the cake was a cheque for the orphans' fund. For the sake of another photograph for the society papers, Pavlova, in her madonna robes, had to shape up to a jujitsu expert on a wrestling mat. It was possibly the only time that Pavlova looked unsure of a role.

At New Year 1925, Pavlova had learned of Léon Bakst's death in Paris a few days earlier. It was the first break in the circle that had been responsible for the flowering of Russian ballet in the West, and Pavlova had a lasting and profound respect for the blazing talents of Diaghilev's team, even if she did not always see eye-to-eye with their mentor. The Ballets Russes had found the business of touring America a terrible strain in 1916 and had not been tempted to emulate Pavlova, with her amazingly brave forays year after year; nor were the members of Diaghilev's artistic brethren treated as unique or exalted beings in the States. Stravinsky made his American debut as conductor of his own music in January 1925; afterward, *Musical America* confided to its readers: "In all soberness, Igor's American visit, a rare success from the standpoint of public interest, has disclosed him to be a talented, rather grotesque composer, rather than a master who is destined to revolutionize the art." It took Bolm's restaging of *Petrushka* at the Metropolitan Opera, on March 13, to rouse enthusiasm for Stravinsky, who now became "the composer-hero of the hour." Diaghilev had first given the Fokine version of *Petrushka* in America at the Century in 1916, five years after the European premiere. This was one of the few works with a generic life of its own in the Diaghilev repertoire; other of his creations came and went, often because a key interpreter was not around to breathe life into it for more than a season or two. Pavlova kept inferior material, such as *The Fairy Doll,* running years, past all expectation. It was mistakenly assumed that she did this because she knew no better, but the exigencies of her situation compelled her to retain these war-horses in lieu of the emergence of any consis-

---

* Harry Mills later recalled that the accounts for that tour were still unbalanced at the time of Pavlova's death. During Hurok's bankruptcies of 1925 and 1926, he admitted in writing that he owed Pavlova $40,000.

At Malvina Hoffman's estate in Hartsdale, New York:
(above) with Hoffman, spring 1922; (right) October 1923: Pavlova is
sitting on the studio steps with Sam Grimson, Hoffman's husband;
behind her is Dandré, next to Nina Warburg; standing are Hoffman, on
the right, and Nina's daughter Bettina, whom Grimson later married.

BELOW May 23, 1924: A belated birthday party for Pavlova
in Hoffman's New York City studio. Pavlova is posing as a madonna
in a Russian ikon. Hoffman (seen here bearing the cake containing
a check for charity) later sculpted Pavlova in this pose.

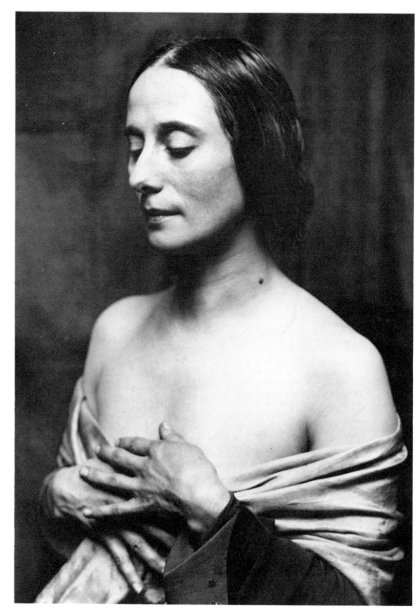

Malvina Hoffman took these photographs of Pavlova in 1924 to use as a reference for sculpture.

tently productive young choreographer. As the years went by, with the set pattern of touring and the concomitant press interviews occurring time and again, Victor Dandré's own attitudes about art tended to blur the outward view of Pavlova's actual feelings. Left to herself, she spoke calmly of the time when she would no longer be able to dance, how at that point she would teach, or continue running the company; but at other times Dandré acted as her spokesman, and then some subtle editing took place. When he later ascribed to her certain points of view which were his own beliefs, Pavlova's death had removed the risk of contradiction; however, the evidence of contemporaries gives the lie to much of the reactionary "color" spread by Dandré, who wanted Pavlova to continue touring in a pattern that was known and understood. He dreaded a change in their status quo.

It was convenient for Diaghilev to be viewed, increasingly, as the arbiter of all that was destructively avant-garde; Pavlova had been personally offended by him, but she never lost admiration for his knowledge. She could see that their current aims were divergent in many ways: she clung to the belief that the purest elements of the classical ballet vocabulary could, and should, survive, and that the old ballets from the Maryinsky era should be protected; Diaghilev, whatever his innermost beliefs, had built up the type of audience that looked continually for novelty, and there was a precarious juggling of interests between the tenets of classicism and the aims of a theatrical adventurer.

The return by Pavlova to her old European hunting grounds, in the summer of 1925, displayed something of a desire to pick up old threads, stir memories, test allegiances. She knew it would not be easy. As elsewhere, advanced schools of thought about dance abounded, with modern dancers, like Mary Wigman in Dresden, claiming critical attention and providing the basis for long and learned treatises on their aims and the methods they employed to attain them. Wigman was serious—indeed, very serious; lightness of touch was the most noticeable quality missing in her work, and also in the words used to analyze her school of training. But her sincerity earned respect, and among those who paid attention to what she was doing was Pavlova—in fact, she insisted upon members of her own company going with her to view Wigman's school. The setting at least was cheerful: the studios had bright orange walls, providing a foil for the predominant black of the students' costumes, with their tight-fitting bodices and long skirts. Wigman wore scarlet slippers—until she kicked them off to begin dancing. Against expectation, Pavlova's team quite liked what they saw. Wigman gravely offered to let Pavlova learn one of her "modern" solos. This turn of events was parried with aplomb; Pavlova accepted the idea, and then added: "Of course, it would be on the understanding that you do one of mine." The subject was not referred to again. Still, Pavlova was very impressed by Wigman and told her own dancers, "We should really stay here three years." Dandré was terrified that an enthusiasm such as this would actually result in a tour being halted.

If Germany had changed in so many respects, Pavlova's German audiences had not. Berlin's Kroll Opera House had been refurbished, but its amenities were familiar to Pavlova, and the rehearsal room still had its glassed-in verandah extension. Rain now dripped monotonously onto the panes of the roof from the overhanging branches of giant oak trees. But the auditorium had a contrasting warmth, with an eager, curious audience for Pavlova's first night. She was playing safe with her repertoire, serving up such morsels as *Coquetteries de Colombine*, which had won approval before the war. Younger dancers were tense, thinking there could be a backlash against traditional recipes; they had detected a certain agitation in Pavlova herself—something more than her usual preperformance nervousness. But all was well, and after Columbine's heartless flirtations, a great crash of applause signified that Pavlova had not lost her ability to please Berliners. German theatre was in a strange halfway house: Wigman pupils were already choreographing at the State Opera House, and yet in the waltz in *Die Fledermaus* the men's places were taken by women *en travestie*—and desperately plump ones at that, bulging out of their satin knee-breeches. At the Dresden Opera House, the corps de ballet considered that they were doing very modern things. Pavlova, in the audience, commented during an intermission, "Fokine do all this in 1910, but Imperial Theatre not permit." Other cities visited during this tour were Leipzig, Hanover, Bremen, Frankfurt, Hamburg, and Cologne. A certain apathy over advance bookings persuaded them to travel as a reduced concert troupe, with drapes instead of scenery. This meant that Pavlova was having to rely even more on her own talent at a time when she might have expected that the company would take up some of the strain.

At the time when the Pavlova Company arrived in Paris, Diaghilev had recently taken in a small group of dancers who had been touring on leave from the Soviet Union; the eldest was just twenty-two and showed a penchant for choreography. His name was Balanchivadze, which Diaghilev shortened to Balanchine. For Pavlova, Paris was a letdown. In Astruc's Théâtre des Champs-Elysées, once intended as a rival to the Opéra, the Pavlova Company found itself sharing the bill with variety artists. Applause was muted; only *The Swan* generated real enthusiasm. Pavlova did get to dance at the Opéra, at a special gala, when she presented *Autumn Leaves*. This work could strike a chord of sympathy with audiences who had been taught to discard old values but had yet to discern any great strength in newer works. In *Autumn Leaves* Pavlova made her effects gently, and with a sincerity that banished any condescension to the theme.

Pavlova was careful to keep one yardstick in the repertoire— *Giselle*, the touchstone of her Maryinsky roots, and the one big ballet in which she could draw upon an interior knowledge and emotion that carried her like a spring tide above the snags of technique and physical pain. Opening her four-week season at Covent Garden on September 28, she danced *Giselle* again, fourteen years after she had performed with Nijinsky on that same stage and in that same ballet. *The Times* assessed the effect:

In the forties *Giselle* gave to Carlotta Grisi one of her richest opportunities, and now its revival is welcome because it gives us more of Mme. Pavlova in the hour and a half that it takes to play than does any other work of its length. We may smile a little at the pale romanticism of Théophile Gautier's scenario, and scarcely trouble to let Adam's tunes take sufficient hold of us to make us whistle a bit of one of them as we go home. But the one gives us situations in which Mme. Pavlova can be lavish with her charms, the other provides measures to which her steps may really move. Perhaps the chief delight of her performance, to the musical mind, was the ease with which all her wealth of technical resource as a dancer kept its relation to the simple, almost childish, rhythm of the music. The first scene of *Giselle* allows Mme. Pavlova to exercise all her art in the expression of artlessness: the village maiden, happy with her lover, sporting with her friends, admiring the princess. Next comes disillusionment, tragedy, madness, and death. By the end of this first act the ballet would seem to have exhausted the gamut of emotions. We begin to think we have seen Mme. Pavlova in every phase, and the fall of the curtain leaves us wondering how all that elaboration of rhythmic movement could adapt itself so perfectly to such diverse emotional ends.

But the emotional resources are not exhausted. Romanticism has its advantages, for it can resuscitate Mme. Pavlova and bring her back as a peculiarly agile ghost and so provide a second act of still more coruscating pirouettes. To all this everyone else made a mere shadowy background: M. Laurent Novikoff, the devout lover, who was always ready to balance her on one toe or lift her over his head, whether as simple village maiden or as disembodied spirit; M. Clustine, whose villainy produced her mad scene; the corps de ballet of village girls in Act I, and of ill-omened spirits in Act II. All were quite efficient, and the spirit maidens had the additional usefulness of showing how big a gap there is between their conventional grace and her unique perfection.

ABOVE & OPPOSITE With Novikov in *Giselle*. Action photographs taken at Covent Garden by *The Times*, 1925.

When the Covent Garden season ended on October 24, Theodore Stier had conducted his last performance for Pavlova. Ill health was forcing him to give up the podium after a marathon of service, broken only by the seventeen months of America's involvement in the First World War. Shadowed by a heart ailment that he attributed to overwork, he went into semi-retirement and began writing a book of gentle reminiscences about his years as a wandering minstrel. He calculated that at that stage, Pavlova had traveled 350,000 miles by road, rail, and sea. Give or take 50,000 either way—she still faced voyages to the other side of the earth—the figure cloaked a saga of toil that was without historic parallel. For Pavlova the parting from Stier was sad, but her needs were unaltered; she contracted Lucien Wurmser, who had conducted for her during sporadic Continental appearances. She still had to face another English provincial tour before her adventure to the Antipodes, and she seemed fated never to spend the festival of Christmas in her own home:

the sailing date for the steamship *Armadale Castle*, bound for South Africa, was December 22. A Christmas tree was put on board with the luggage, and Pavlova decked it with presents while they were headed to their first port of call, Madeira.

The Southern Hemisphere implied adventure and unmapped territory, even if the reality was a succession of towns and cities that owed their façade and their basic sensibility to late-Victorian England. But for Pavlova the anticipation of dancing before new, untapped audiences was exhilarating. She had exploited the Northern Hemisphere exhaustively, and she had dipped below the equator into South America, performing in the most unlikely settings. She had even danced in mid-Atlantic, giving *The Swan* a flutter for first-class passengers during a concert evening on one crossing. But Africa, Australia, New Zealand—these were land masses that still carried the flavor of European pioneering, and for an émigré Russian, the sense of adventure was the more marked. No matter that South Africa deployed the worst aspects

The never-ending public duties:
ABOVE (left) accepting a twelve-foot-long key to the city of Quebec, October 1923 (the Chief of Police made
the presentation, and the Fire Department paraded in Pavlova's honor),
and (right) publicizing the Russian tea room at the "Art in Trade" exhibition at the Waldorf-Astoria Hotel,
New York, October 1923.

BELOW (left) receiving a check for her orphans' home from Mrs. Oliver Harriman, president of the
Camp Fire Girls of America, on behalf of members in China, October 1923, and (right)
a reception honoring Pavlova at the Hotel au Palace, Brussels, 1927.

of Colonial rule; there were still brief contacts with the indigenous population. Pavlova saw Kaffir dancers give a performance in Johannesburg, and it was reported that when the leader of that troupe was told that the greatest dancer in the world was coming to see him, he replied, "She hasn't seen *me* yet!" He himself was noticeably unencumbered by the overtones of foreign rule, but his "corps de ballet" were given rugby shirts and shorts to wear along with their animal plumes; only the leader was allowed to parade with a bare torso. To these Kaffirs, most of whom were mine workers, a rugby shirt was a part of their life; in some senses it was more honest than suggesting that they had all strayed in from distant horizons. Members of Pavlova's company were eager to talk to these native dancers, but a portcullis of strict, if unofficial, apartheid denied them the opportunity. It was the same in Pretoria, Kimberley, and Cape Town. Pavlova was seen, but she did not have much of an opportunity to see. Her main contacts—local managers and impresarios—were almost incestuously European; in fact, her South African representative, Leo Cherniavsky, was a Russian Jew, a former violinist who had had a protracted affair with Maud Allan before the war. It was a foregone conclusion that Pavlova's visit to Cape Town would be a success. Ladies of society strove to outdo each other in gestures of goodwill, and it was axiomatic that one of their gifts should be an ostrich feather fan, common currency in European fashion, along with the tail feathers of egrets and the skins of increasingly rare wild cats.

Pavlova had traveled 12,000 miles to Australia in order to appear in two cities on the initial leg of the journey. She won Sydney and Melbourne effortlessly. In some ways her fame had preceded her uncomfortably: *artistes* in Eastern Australia had been presenting tattered versions of *The Swan* for some time. The *Bacchanale* did not fare as well; when Pavlova presented this signature piece from earlier days, Australian audiences reacted with an embarrassed shuffling and not a whisper of applause. Apparently the scanty costumes and the overt abandon of the piece were considered risqué; Victorian England was, in many ways, still a reality in this British Dominion.

After the closing performance, Pavlova was bombarded with paper streamers, normally reserved for departing steamers. A little girl walked on stage and presented her with a boomerang bound with expensive flowers. In piping tones she said to Pavlova: "The boomerang comes back, and we hope you'll come back too." The J. C. Williamson theatre organization was already laying plans for just that eventuality, though Pavlova had the demon Tasman Sea ahead of her, and a tour down the length of New Zealand. This would take her from a mild, windy autumn in Auckland to the first gripping fingers of sleetish winter in the South Island, and there would be none of the comforts of North American central heating.

Auckland had reckoned to put its best foot forward in honor of Pavlova, and a team of workmen slaved away to prepare the stage for the great ballerina. With infinite pains they surfaced the boards with linseed oil. When a young dancer landed on the back of her head during a rehearsal, it was apparent that a lot of

With Novikov in the *Bacchanale*, Germany, c.1927.

351

Portrait in costume for *Une Soirée de Chopin*,
with added black net, New Zealand, 1926.

several New Zealand photographers which were subsequently used in many magazines and programs throughout Europe.

When Pavlova sailed from New Zealand she took with her an exotic caged bird, a present from the administrators of the Auckland Zoo. The gift reflected her continuing passion for winged creatures. She handled them with extreme sympathy, but it was a strange interest for someone who spent her life portraying an avian spirit, wild and unfettered. She had so many mortalities among the little caged birds she tried carrying from land to land that the wonder of it is that she persisted. To the long-suffering gardener back at Ivy House she wrote:

> I am once more bringing with me a beautiful collection of the most astonishing birds. I know, I know that you will chide me for having forgotten that these tiny creatures cannot possibly survive our rough climate. But isn't it possible, in heaven's name, to build something which, with the aid of central heating, will regulate the temperature so that these lovely birds can live? In my garden among the trees and bushes and the flowers I live my own life and I do not want to feel death so close at hand. We must do something. Spend as much as you like, but do something.

Paul Smikites, the gardener, did as he was bidden; a huge glass aviary was constructed in the shelter of the conservatory at Ivy House. It had elaborate ventilation as well as heating, and there were wire panels to prevent the birds from dashing themselves against the panes. But with all the care in the world, it was still inevitable that the internees would never establish much of a residency.

Paul was lord of his domain for so much of the year that Pavlova's summer visits were sometimes a time of tension. Whenever the clatter of a lawn mower broke the morning stillness, Pavlova would invariably emerge onto the verandah and call, "Paul! Do let the daisies live a little." She would rather play croquet in a hay field than fell them. Paul would retire to the gardener's lodge and subdue his temper with the aid of a bottle. He probably distrusted his mistress's whims, but much of her thinking was that of a sound plantsman. "I am going on an extended trip," she once wrote, "and I forgot to tell you that it would be very nice if the earth between the second and the third tree on the right side of the garden could be laid bare by removing the stone steps. Once this is done the soil there can breathe."

scrubbing was going to be needed before the curtain could go up. Some of the dancers took time off to see local demonstrations of dancing, including that of Maori boys at St. Stephen's College performing the native war dance, the Haka. Racial barriers were relaxed in New Zealand, and there was a lively exchange of methods, with enthusiastic Europeans learning the Maori war cries, parrot-fashion. Pavlova admired the poi-poi dances at a special presentation, at which a tattooed Maori princess told the ballerina that the dances were those of a dying race.*

While the company and their effects traveled through New Zealand on the tortuous narrow-gauge railways, Pavlova and Dandré went by motorcar, seeing spectacular scenery as a reward for nerve-racking hairpin bends on mountain roads that seemed to be fighting a losing battle with their environment. From Wellington the dancers crossed the waters to Christchurch and beyond by a reeking channel steamer that seemed determined to do a unique dance of its own. It was achingly cold in Christchurch, Timaru, and Dunedin, and the public buildings had no form of heating. Pavlova was nonplussed by the discomfort, and the creation by a hotel chef of a meringue confection named in her honor must have seemed a very fleeting recompense. More immediately lasting tributes were portraits done by

The voyage from New Zealand back to Sydney presaged a great deal of drawn-out rail travel over hundreds of miles. The message with the boomerang had worked, and Pavlova had returned. There were now bookings from Brisbane to Adelaide, with all the business of railway gauges that varied at state boundaries; and in addition to a change at Toowoomba, they encountered a derailment: a previous train had tumbled down a steep embankment, necessitating a fleet of cars to transfer passengers to a clear line farther ahead. There were very few sleeper cars, and many of the dancers were curled up on the seats of the

---

* Maori dancers had actually filled Pavlova's Palace slot in the autumn of 1911.

carriages. Though the train made few stops, wayside stations were crowded with people waiting to see the train go by; somehow they had found out that Pavlova was on board. It was akin to royalty passing through: a high spot in the year. Probably no other dancer had created such a stir in Australia since Lola Montez had visited.

The relatively shorter distances in New Zealand had allowed one-night stands, but Australia's vastness precluded them. In Australia very little heed was given to the physical limits of the dancers' endurance; the company was transported from Brisbane back down to Sydney, which took twenty-eight hours, and were then expected to hop off the train and give a matinee before entraining again that evening for Melbourne. The inevitable gauge change came at Albury at six in the morning. The scenery and costumes were slower at changing at Albury than the dancers, with the result that the latter were ready for a matinee in Melbourne while the former were conspicuously absent. The matinee drifted into an early evening performance. Afterward, who should appear backstage but Chaliapin, who was in the same city to give concerts. He had with him his younger daughter, and they posed with Pavlova for local photographers. Pavlova barely had time to exchange pleasantries with her old friend before rushing back to the railway station for the journey to Adelaide. By some miracle of interstate planning, the railway gauge remained constant between Victoria and South Australia. On board the train was a locally recruited supernumerary who was eager for all sorts of advice from the seasoned performers; they spiced up his surname, Helpman, with an extra "n" and suggested that "Bobbie" was not the best name for a boy with an ambition to have it spelled out in lights.

There was a proper season in Adelaide, surprisingly well supported, but it was as if the breathing space gave time for company members to reconsider their situations. It was virtually the end of the tour, and several dancers were ready for a cessation of the madness. Among them, Thurza Rogers had been given a fresh glimpse of her native New Zealand and elected to sign on with the J. C. Williamson organization, which operated between that country and Australia. The most serious loss was Muriel Stuart, who had accepted a proposal of marriage from a Russian violinist. Pavlova made half-hearted attempts to talk her out of the match, which involved a return to America. But Muriel was in love, and Pavlova's catalogue of the faults of Russian men fell on deaf ears. When she realized the girl's mind was made up, she put her hand on Muriel's knee and said earnestly, "Mugie, promise me one thing—that you will have a child. I never did." And with the decision taken, she mused awhile. "Tell me something—are you perhaps a little Jewish?" Muriel explained about her father's Austrian background. "Ah yes," said Pavlova, nodding. "I understand." When Muriel Stuart sailed from Adelaide, she found her cabin laid out with a veritable trousseau, all from Pavlova. In addition, there was a sum of money, the equivalent of a long-distance steamer fare, which Pavlova said was to be kept against an unforeseen emergency, when Muriel might wish to return to the fold—wherever that fold might be.

The company embarked at Adelaide for the long voyage back to Europe. After the roughness of the Great Australian Bight there was the usual brief stop at Fremantle to exchange passengers for Perth, and then the S. S. *Narkunda* headed northwest into warmer waters. The ports of call were Colombo and Aden, skipping Bombay. The heat in Aden was intolerable, bone dry and surging in waves off the rocky surfaces, like one vast bread oven. In the fourth week they reached Suez. Once through the canal and into the Mediterranean, they felt they had turned the corner. Pavlova disembarked at Marseilles, heading for her usual vacation in the Salzo-Maggiore district on the Italian-Swiss border. There was soon to be a long autumn tour of Germany. August was nearly over; they had traveled over 30,000 miles since Christmas 1925, and they knew they had to assemble again in early October. They were dealing the same pack with barely a reshuffle; but Pavlova's knee was now the joker.

At the end of her vacation, Pavlova visited Milan for a reunion with her old teacher Cecchetti. As ballet master at La Scala he was in a fever of excitement at being able to present his adored pupil to his class. Two little girls had been deputed to carry flowers to Pavlova when she arrived, and one had rehearsed a speech in French; but the sight of the famous ballerina

With Novikov in *The Fairy Doll*, New Zealand, 1926.

brought everything to a stammering halt. Pavlova patted the girl's head and kissed her; she was a little tearful herself. Cecchetti had taken the place that Petipa had once held for Pavlova: he was master and father figure, and also a link to her roots. She could be petted like a favorite daughter, and chided too. After this reunion, Cecchetti was to visit London, and Pavlova took a huge delight in entertaining him at Ivy House; to others it was plain that he himself basked in the attention. Outside the little canvas pavilion that she always had placed on the lawn for summer teas, she posed him for the camera, and then reclined at his feet in studied elegance, with an elbow on his knee. A cane lay, as if by accident, across her ankles. Her expression was enigmatic. From her humble position at the master's feet she looked like a possessive daughter. The maestro was not able to compete with such aplomb; he looked a very weary old man. But in Milan he had been the one who had sparkled with possessive pride.

If Pavlova, in her mid-forties, had any ambition to lessen the load that she carried, she seems not to have been able to find a formula that could achieve this and keep a structurally sound framework around her as well. Either she continued with the full economically balanced unit, or she became a roving guest artist, reduced to a few solo spots in someone else's program. This could not be seriously contemplated; her fame swamped that of almost anyone else of her generation, and her phenomenal energies still needed an adequate outlet. Those who saw her just as she came off stage, looking tired and at times a little bedraggled, caught only the immediate effects of her current workload. Such observers were seldom around long enough to witness the quick transformations and the resurgence of her spirit that always astonished her confederates. Her swings in mood were still evident, though by now they were mellowed by a pall of humorous wisdom that seemed to cushion her from events that would have ignited the fuse in earlier years. She had come to terms with the nature of imperfection in daily life; she did her best and hoped that others would do likewise. She was part of a world that was beginning to overreach itself with Progress; the rhythm had been dislocated by the continual speeding up of communications, and it would never again recover the old balance, when a period of "dead time" took the sting out of events and out of the reactions to those events.

In the cultural revolution of the twenties, the masses for the first time began to recognize the nature of ephemera, to accept the idea of planned obsolescence. A horse could live and work twenty years, whereas an automobile could be abandoned after four or five without the action being construed as a sin or a calamity. The middle classes acquired the caprices that had previously been the prerogative of a select few. This new attitude, the gloss of superficiality, affected everything in some measure, not least the world of the theatre, where Pavlova found herself at the mercy of a fickleness of taste that she had never before encountered. Her audience could no longer be clearly defined. Part of it followed her out of loyalty to the past, part of it was a

drifting population willing to be converted, and a certain percentage was actively looking for confirmation that the amusements of yesteryear no longer held validity. Europe was behind America in this regard, and Pavlova exploited the fact; nevertheless, she was trapped. She could push novelty and lose the majority of her audience, or play it safe and estrange the progressives. For economic reasons she played it safe, and was reduced to finding variations on previously stated themes. A ballet master with real choreographic sensibilities continued to elude her; even Diaghilev was taking huge risks with an untried youngster. Pavlova had to rely on the Clustine repertoire to a great degree, and, in 1926, on revisions by Novikov of familiar old Maryinsky works.

During October, in the little time at his disposal before the 1926-27 Continental tour, Novikov remounted some traditional dances: the *Grand Pas Hongrois* from the third act of *Raymonda*, a Pas des Bouquets from *La Fille Mal Gardée*, and a *Snowflakes* pas de trois, possibly a Novikov original. Pavlova was working on a divertissement for herself, to a Chopin mazurka. Prior to a lengthy season in Berlin at the Theater des Westens, there were appearances in Hanover, Bremen, and Magdeburg, where Pavlova tried her new solo for the first and only time. It had a melancholy air, and in the course of it Pavlova took a wreath of flowers from her head and cast it down on the stage. Someone was supposed to have suggested afterward that the action could have been interpreted as the Queen of Dance laying down her crown. Whether or not this fanciful interpretation was voiced, the dance was never repeated, though company members thought it had great charm.

The roster of dancers changed continually in these years. For the first time in the company's history, there was a German dancer, Hans Helken; he thought himself greatly superior to Novikov and could not resist saying so. There was also Alicia Vronska, who was second ballerina; her partner, Alperanoff, was very strong and managed to do all sorts of acrobatic adagio partnering while still keeping the display within the bounds of classicism. The pair brought with them their own dances, with excellent costumes and music, but it all went for nought when Vronska fell on an icy sidewalk and broke her collarbone. Pavlova had to take on extra performances, which meant that she was in almost every ballet. They tried inviting the prima ballerina from the Berlin Staatsoper to appear with the company in *The Magic Flute,* but when she arrived it became evident that her technique could not carry the ballet; she had drifted too far with modern dance trends. The company disapproved of her for other reasons: she revealed unshaven armpits, which were not at all in accord with the red wig she wore.

Nevertheless, Pavlova remained open-minded about the new German dance. She sent Algeranoff to Max Terpis, who had studied with Wigman and was now ballet master at the Staatsoper, in order that he might create a new solo for him; of all the company members, Algeranoff showed the greatest affinity for radical dance movements. Terpis asked him if the English had some sort of folklore spirit who frightened people; Algeranoff

At Ivy House, c.1926.

355

Berlin, Christmas 1926: (above) distributing presents to the girls;
(below) with Dandré and local friends.

bird family except at the height of summer. Yet another Christmas was spent abroad; in Germany in 1926 her party had to take place in the foyer of the theatre. There seemed never to be any free days except Mondays, which were crammed with rehearsals, since the programs were completely changed (with the exception of the ubiquitous *Swan*) each week. On Sundays there were two performances. All this provoked some insurrection from the dancers, and at the New Year there was something of a strike threat; the youngest dancers were militant and outspoken, while the older ones looked on with interest. Dandré was offended, but when someone pointed out that the argument was not about seven working days a week but about thirty working days a month, he took the point and began to reconstruct the schedules for the latter part of the tour, which had still to work through Poland, Austria, Hungary, Yugoslavia, and Holland—to say nothing of a subsequent Scandinavian tour for a reduced concert group.

In Vienna, after an all-night train journey, the company was confronted by the fact that copyright laws prevented the playing of Bayer's music for *The Fairy Doll* for other than the State ballet. Nor would the Volksoper permit divertissements to be given; to a snobbish élite, these smacked of variety shows. There was a sharp conflict of interest in this edict, as the Viennese wanted desperately to see *The Swan*. The company had to stitch together the format of a "ballet," named, for the occasion, *Carnival*, with jesters accompanied by a Meyerbeer galop presenting the individual sections of the entertainment—which were of course the usual divertissements. Honor was satisfied, and everyone saw his favorite dance in the course of the evening.

There were no sleeper cars for the overnight trip to Budapest, and it was a stiff and fatigued group that arrived at the Royal Opera House. One of Liszt's Hungarian Rhapsodies was placed first among the divertissements as a compliment to the city. While the rest of the company was in Budapest, Pavlova took a smaller group to Yugoslavia for a handful of performances in Belgrade. The Yugoslav ballet was in its infancy, but a *répétition générale* of *Coppélia* was staged for Pavlova. Such a distinguished onlooker was too much for the young ballerina deputed to perform the role of Swanilda; she was barely into the first waltz before she was overcome by nerves. In tears, she rushed to the footlights and called out, "Anna Pavlova, I can't! I can't!"

The company arrived in The Hague on Easter Sunday 1927 and began immediately a series of performances in various towns, using The Hague as a base for some, and Amsterdam for others. There were vast sheets of color in the bulb fields, and in Haarlem Pavlova found herself presented with one particular bouquet: it was full of a variety of huge white tulip that had been named in her honor. On their one free day the company went to Vollendam; at that time it was still a fishing port, with national dress worn as a matter of course. These glimpses of other modes and customs helped the younger dancers to understand that many of the divertissements in which they danced night after night had a basis in reality. Dandré, never one to miss the chance of an extra performance, had fitted in a return engagement in Hamburg; it

volunteered the old nursery rogue the bogeyman. A few days later Terpis turned up with the sheet music for the Scherzo from Prokofiev's *Love for Three Oranges*, and to this he devised a dance based on initial improvisations by Algeranoff. The dancer worked conscientiously for several months before risking showing it to Pavlova. He was obviously determined that her initial encouragement should be seen to have been justified.

Others might take on new images with impunity, but Pavlova was still trapped with one particular signature work, *The Swan*. In Germany, potential patrons would ask at the box office if she was dancing it at that performance; if the answer was no, they would turn away, saying that they would wait until it was on the program. The impresarios soon took the hint and pressed for its inclusion on every possible occasion. Although its physical demands were not great, Pavlova had been performing it regularly since 1907, and only some miracle of identification enabled her to dance it each time as if it were the first.

At Ivy House, the original swan had died and been replaced by an offspring, still called Jack, but Pavlova never really saw her

FASHION, 1920–1927

In her maturity, Pavlova had a relaxed confidence about the styles she wore, but even in the madness of perpetual foreign travel she would try to keep pace with European fashion dictates. Long-wearing pieces like her "tailor-made" had their hems lifted in order to extend their usefulness, and certain lengths of fur were often adapted to new uses; to this extent a vein of frugality was revealing itself. Some of her effects were contrived by dipping into the wardrobe master's boxes, though there were notable exceptions to this developing penchant for improvisation: in the early twenties Bakst designed several stunning cloaks for Pavlova. The chinchilla coat with the astrakhan panels (page 363) also verges on the starkly theatrical. Silk, which enhanced the suppleness of her body, was much favored for dresses. She did shop at the houses of famous couturiers, but she was less inclined to accept exactly what they offered. She had a tendency, now, to tamper with detail. By 1920 hats were less exuberant (page 360), and the long era of the cloche was about to begin. This denied Pavlova the extravagance of milli-nery which she had carried so effortlessly before the war, and to this extent her own natural elegance began to make more of a statement than the clothes themselves.

was convenient for the scenery and costumes for the larger ballets to be shipped from that port back to England, with the corps de ballet given leave, while a group of soloists went with Pavlova to begin the Scandinavian circuit in Stockholm. At this juncture, Pavlova was handed the news of Theodore Stier's death. Each member of the company felt it as the loss of a true friend.

Stockholm provided a sympathetic and knowledgeable audience. In Oslo Pavlova looked at Algeranoff's new bogeyman dance and told him it should go into the repertoire; he was even allowed to make his own costume without interference from the wardrobe department. The work was first seen in Copenhagen and was a success. It meant that Prokofiev was represented in the Pavlova Company's repertoire, at least in token measure. Algeranoff's bogeyman number could not compare to Prokofiev's second full-length ballet, *Le Pas d'Acier*, just being launched by Diaghilev, but even had Pavlova had the artistic ambition to present such avant-garde works, her nonstop performing schedule would have precluded it: Diaghilev's new ballet had been four years in the making.

It is quite possible that Diaghilev's efforts in promoting Olga Spessivtseva at the expense of Anna Pavlova reached Pavlova's ears even before he spoke to the French press in the fourth week of May. If not, the interview prior to the opening of *La Chatte* on May 27 would have seemed even more wounding to Pavlova. *Le Figaro* carried his artful and insidious press release:

> Tomorrow at the first performance of the Ballets Russes, a new dancer—Olga Spessiva—will be making her debut in Paris. It is true that for two seasons there danced at the Opéra a ballerina whose name was almost the same, but fate willed it, for some reason or another, that the Spessivtseva of the Opéra was not understood by the most sensitive public in the world—that of Paris. I have always believed that in one man's lifetime there is a limit to joyful experiences. So, for a whole generation there was only one Taglioni to be admired, there was only one Patti to be heard. When I saw Pavlova in her young days and mine, I was sure that she would be the "Taglioni" of my lifetime. My astonishment, then, was boundless when I met Spessiva, a creature even more rare and more refined than Pavlova. And that is saying a lot.
>
> Our great ballet master, Cecchetti, who formed Nijinsky, Karsavina, and so many others, said only last winter, during one of his lessons at La Scala in Milan: "An apple was born into the world, and it was cut in two. One half became Anna Pavlova, and the other Spessiva." I would add that, for me, Spessiva is the side that has been exposed to the sun.
>
> After having begun twenty years ago with Pavlova and Nijinsky, I come to Spessiva and Lifar. The first pair have become legendary, while the latter, very different from their predecessors, are with us, waiting their turn to become legend, and part of that splendid legend—too flattering for us—of the fame of the Ballets Russes.

At least Pavlova would also have learned that Spessivtseva did not appear at the premiere, supposedly because of an injury.

Diaghilev's article is strangely revealing. Amid the bombast for his new ballerina (who was, in any case, well enough known), his reference to the legend of "Pavlova and Nijinsky"—quite excluding Karsavina—shows the power this pairing held in his thoughts, even as late as 1927. His quoting of the apple simile, and his cruel addition to the thought, seems to stab at Pavlova in the knowledge that her company provided a strong rival for public favor. He knew there was no further hope of her adding a stellar presence to any production of his, and he can never have forgotten (even if few others knew) that he had failed to confirm the plans that would have cemented the partnership of Pavlova and Nijinsky as the stars of the Ballets Russes in 1910. And by invoking the name of Pavlova's adored Cecchetti, he was adding salt to the wound with fiendish skill. Placing Spessivtseva in the pantheon occupied by Taglioni was merely a refinement.

Pavlova never knew what it was to have nothing to do. There were always several alternatives for any minute of the day that was not already programmed. Even when she affected to take vacations, the word was a misnomer. She came nearest to relaxing when she was in the Italian Lakes area, when she broke completely with company matters, and usually banished Dandré as well. She was free then to indulge in any spur-of-the-moment pastime. She walked in the mountain meadows, took boat trips—and found friends, on whom she lavished joyous, if private, attentions; the painter Alexander Jacovlev saw much of her at these times. But these were brief interludes. In England, she was never really alone and never completely free. Vacations were the few weeks in the year when she found time for a walk around her garden, when the afternoon teas took their course and were not rushed, when the card games strayed half an hour longer into the night. There was never really a full day in which a dozen different company matters were not resolved with her active participation. Music was not listened to idly, for pleasure; it came from a pianist and was analyzed for its structure, assessed for its possibilities for dance. She was like a gyroscope that needed peak revolutions in order to remain on an even keel. Unquestionably, hers was a manic personality; she was either carried by it or fleeing from it, but certainly nobody else could compete with her concentrated energy. She was the motivation for all things. A reporter at this period of her life discovered this immediately:

> "Beg pardon, is the rehearsal today with open curtain?"
> "We do not know, sir. Madame has not arrived."
> "If you please, which programme is to be danced today?"
> "We do not know, sir. That depends on Madame."
> "How much longer may the rehearsal last?"
> "We do not know, sir. Madame must decide."

Then Pavlova emerged from the shadows and, without ceremony, began working. The reporter later recorded:

> Slight, insignificant, quiet, and yet—what tremulous elasticity, what passionate buoyancy, what wild sweetness! A small face with Slavic brow; mouth and eyes that have known much suffering. . . . Now she throws herself on the stage. Gibbering hasty Russian words, she dances—one sees that this woman is a fanatic in her art. Though the others in this rehearsal may content themselves with indications,

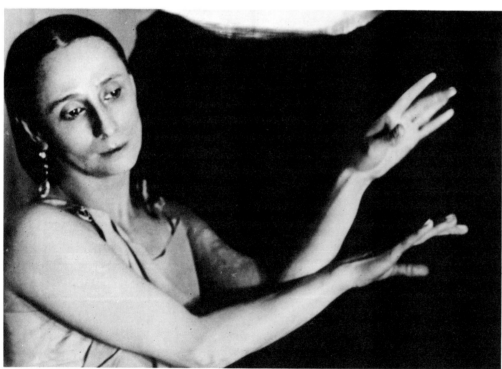

Late portraits, c.1928. By now, Pavlova was less inclined
to force cheerfulness for the camera's benefit. She may have thought
that only her hands were being photographed in the picture at left;
her expression is the one that became familiar to close colleagues.

she gives everything to the point of an abuse of humanity. Though the others may be her equal in technique (they are not, but conceivably they might be), they will never, never approach Pavlova, for here a personality—one cannot say it otherwise—is raging. . . . But of course one knows that art pushed to its utmost extremity always leads its frail life in such questionable regions.

In the summer of 1927 the burden of work was even greater than usual: prior to another Covent Garden season Pavlova and a group of soloists made lightning visits to Ostend, Wiesbaden, and Baden-Baden, fulfilling dates planned by Dandré to exploit the fact that these popular resorts were still crammed with late-summer visitors. In Germany the British Army of Occupation was still in evidence, and the Kaiser's box was crammed with British officers. Although there were no performances in Paris, the dancers went back through that city for costume fittings.

Preparations were being made for nonstop performing in England and Europe. With Edmund Russen, Dandré mapped out a pulverizing schedule for the British tour, involving appearances in over fifty towns within a span of nine weeks. Recruits were a priority. Butsova was lured back from America as second ballerina, and her husband, Harry Mills, was given the position of tour manager. Efrem Kurtz replaced Wurmser as conductor. Sometime Diaghilev dancers, concerned by the uncertainty of employment in that company, moved to Pavlova's. Max Frohman and his sister Marguerite arrived, as did Boris Romanov and Anatole Oboukhov, who had partnered Pavlova in Russia in 1914. They all brought with them various divertissements of their own, and Romanov began choreographing several new dances for Pavlova and the company. One was *Au Bal*, in which Pavlova was courted by six hussars bearing bouquets; they ended up seated on chairs in a semicircle around Pavlova as she danced a mazurka from *The Sleeping Beauty*. Other works were rehashed from old Imperial Theatres ballets: the leszhinka from *The Demon*, the tzigane from Dargomizhsky's *Roussalka*. The Frohmans contributed an old Russo-Spanish dance to Moszkowski. Pavlova watched it for a while and then turned to Algeranoff and said, "You know, Algy, I have seen so much real Spanish dancing that when I see this kind I want to laugh!" She could not change anything, because it was already the dress rehearsal.

Diaghilev had been at the Prince's Theatre with a reduced company, while Pavlova was once more confidently expected to fill the opera house at Covent Garden. Philip Page assessed the two "schools" in the *Evening Standard*:

Mme. Pavlova's season of ballet at Covent Garden (which is being very well supported even at matinees, when ballet of any type is an acquired taste), coming only a few weeks after the close of the Diaghileff troupe's visit to the Prince's Theatre, gives an opportunity for studying two opposite types of the ballet entertainment, both of which have a large following. The audiences for each overlap not at all. One does not see at Covent Garden the ecstatic youth with flowing hair who expresses his appreciation of Serge

Lifar with a mass of sibilants. The styles overlap but slightly, the Tchaikowsky music used in *Aurora's Wedding* by the Diaghileffites, and in *The Fairy Doll* by Pavlova [sic], being almost the only point of contact.

The superficial view is to declare that Diaghileff is progressive, and Pavlova, whose ballets are admittedly old-fashioned, reactionary. But this is not true, and hardly fair to the latter. Diaghileff is more of the pioneer and he admittedly creates more. That is because he has a wider conception of what ballet means, a conception which sometimes pushes him to annoying lengths, as in his production of Satie's *Mercury* and of *Parade*, which were jokes and not very good jokes. For him ballet is not merely a question of dancing or even of dancing and miming. It can go to the lengths of an anthropomorphic representation of machinery, with a little political spice thrown in. This was obviously the intention of Prokofiev's *Pas d'Acier*, the production of which I cannot imagine Pavlova even contemplating. For Pavlova, ballet means dancing, mainly in the classical ballet style, in which Diaghileff indulges only, virtually, in *Les Sylphides, Aurora's Wedding* and the middle section of *La Boutique Fantasque*.

Music is, with Pavlova, secondary, and usually second-rate; sometimes, when *Don Quixote*, composed by the late M. Minkus, is given, it is tenth-rate, and it says much for the enthusiasm of M. Efrem Kurtz, who seems to me to be an ideal ballet conductor, that he can put so much energy into his job when there are no orchestral interludes to make it interesting.

Her choreography is effective but conventional. Yet ballet owes an immense debt to Pavlova simply because she concentrates on the best dancing in the traditional style, which might otherwise be in danger of becoming choked by continuous striving after the bizarre—because it is modern; or after the ugly—because it is ugly. The technique of the Diaghileff company—though it can still number some superb dancers—is not on the whole so fine as it used to be. Pioneer work is always costly.

Page's article pinpointed the major belief that had sustained Pavlova for some twenty years: that her craft sprang from an entirely valid vocabulary, at its best impervious to fashion. She cherished the traditions of the Maryinsky, with its harboring of many diverse European developments, and in the face of Diaghilev's most extreme novelties she became alarmed and depressed; she was a *dancer* (and a unique one), and it had become clear that such as Massine, far from unique in dance technique, had employed quirkiness to cover his own limitations.

Pavlova had no real novelties to show London, though she made a delightful impression in *La Fille Mal Gardée*, which was being shown again after a long absence, and the *Grand Pas Hongrois* was fresh to London audiences. Algeranoff had been rehearsing *Bogeyman*, having been told that it was planned for the early part of the season; but when the day came, he found it missing from the program. He suspected that Dandré and Russen both disliked it, and, rather bravely, he took his problem to Pavlova, since she was the last authority for appeal. In this instance her casting vote was in favor of the strange number, but she handled the situation at one remove. "Go to Mr. Dandré and tell him I said he was to help you," she said. This buried the

Costume revisions for *Dragonfly* (above)
and *Rondino* (below).

contretemps; Dandré would never dare raise a subject once he had a clear sign of Pavlova's thinking. In matters of programming and casting he played around in strange ways until someone complained, or until Pavlova countermanded something of her own volition. If a dancer felt he was being discriminated against, he was in a tricky position, for he could never be quite sure whether it was a case of being in Dandré's bad graces or in Pavlova's.

At one point during the London season even Hilda Butsova began to feel that Dandré was nervous about her success with audiences, particularly English ones, who knew her background. When Pavlova was badly shaken in a taxi accident, Butsova covered for her in *Chopiniana,* and Dandré then went around to all the press representatives asking them not to review the performance. Pavlova had absolutely no need of this kind of protection. Butsova had come to London at the express request of Pavlova, who had often told the younger woman, "I feel safe when you are around." And this to the girl who had been given such a tearful induction into Pavlova's world in 1912. From that confused and tongue-tied beginning, she had matured into a polished performer and a sound ally for Pavlova, who was surrounded for the most part by dancers who had no knowledge of those extraordinary early years.

The first week of the provincial tour was a madcap chase around the indentations of England's south coast. Monday, October 4, saw the dancers safely arrived in Margate for an evening performance in the Winter Gardens Pavilion. The following morning they made their way to Folkestone, where there was a performance that night in the Leas Cliff Pavilion. On Wednesday morning it was Hastings, with a matinee at the White Rock Pavilion, then quickly to Brighton for an early night's rest before a matinee on Thursday afternoon at the Hippodrome. Immediately after this, a quick reverse sprint was needed, because the evening performance took place in the Devonshire Park Winter Garden, which was in Eastbourne. Friday morning saw a predawn rising for the dancers, who were already on the move by six o'clock, traveling to Portsmouth for the crossing to the Isle of Wight for a matinee at the Pier Casino. That done, they crossed the water again, back to Portsmouth, where they spent the night. When they woke up the following morning, they had to hasten along to Bournemouth for two performances; these were both in the same Winter Gardens, which may have come as a pleasant surprise. Sunday was free, inasmuch as they had the whole day to get to Leicester.

The architect of all this movement was not present to see the fruits of his planning; he was already on the Continent, perfecting plans for the winter. In Dandré's absence, Pavlova had to handle all company matters herself. Beyond the traveling there was the time needed for piling in and out of hotels and boardinghouses; there was the unpacking and packing of costumes and scenery; there were last-minute rehearsals to solve problems with curious local stages; there was an importuning public wanting autographs before and after performances; there were the performances themselves ... and there was the fact that the dancers were human and had the usual interest in eating and sleeping. There were no set classes on this tour, but many of the dancers followed Pavlova's own discipline and gave themselves a daily class as well as the usual pre-performance warm-up. These were the bare bones of any day. But Pavlova was determined to extract more. Within days of the scramble around southern England there arrived on the scene Nicolas Sergeyev, the former régisseur and part-time director of the Maryinsky—he who had espoused the establishment's cause in the unrest of 1905. The shoe was certainly on the other foot now. Sergeyev was an exile with only erratic means of support, and Pavlova was a potential employer. In her perpetual quest for dance material, she had decided that in Sergeyev lay the possibility of reconstructing something from the Petipa canon. The régisseur had carried out of Russia bound volumes containing all his notations, and in his trek around Europe he may have had moments when he felt their weight was hardly worth the carrying, but if their value was sentimental then, their contents were, in truth, pure gold.

Pavlova's personal feeling for the memory of Petipa seems to have inhibited her from too cavalier a plundering of his works. Her own two most important ballets from early days were *Giselle* and *La Bayadère,* both indelibly associated for Pavlova with the old man's careful coaching. *Giselle* she kept with her, always scrupulously maintaining the full structure . But the sprawling *La Bayadère*—that was hopelessly complex for her company to attempt. Through all her years of global wandering, Pavlova never abandoned her belief that the company's base should be strict classicism; by 1927 there must have been a dearth of sound examples. The relative failure of her attempt to present *The Sleeping Beauty* in 1916, supported by Bakst and masses of extras, had been a bitter lesson, and soon after she had been caught up in the inexorable traveling, with the economics of the entire company balanced squarely on her shoulders. Perhaps in 1927, with the prospect of reduced concert performances, a chance to use Sergeyev represented her farewell gesture to the school that sustained her. It was now or never.

Pavlova's ambition was to present part of *La Bayadère,* and it was Sergeyev's task to teach this while they traveled around England. He could speak only Russian, and the response from the company was minimal. Pavlova and Novikov worked at the pas de deux from the "white act" (the "Rajarh's Drim," as Sergeyev pronounced it). The choreography exploited Pavlova's security in balance; younger members of the company admired the way Novikov could step away from her while she was in a développé à la seconde, which she would maintain until he took her hand again. Character dancers had to be dragooned into this classical work to make up the numbers—not a popular task. "Ya charakternaya!" they shouted, to little effect. They thought the ballet hopelessly dated and stood around giggling. The fakir's dance, which introduced the main scene, looked banal in the cold light of an English provincial hall, and when eventually Pavlova saw how little progress was being made, she finally gave up. It had

ABOVE *Au Bal* BELOW *Don Quixote*

369

Olga Spessivtseva in *The Creatures of Prometheus.*

role of the toreador in *Don Quixote* on the opening night at Covent Garden, and he actually partnered Pavlova in *La Fille Mal Gardée* at a matinee. He was given very little advance warning for this, but he was a sympathetic and responsive youth, and it was fairly obvious that Pavlova already envisaged him in a leading position in the company.

She was thwarted in these plans after only two months, when Celli received a cable from La Scala offering him the leading role in a revival of *La Légende de Joseph*, with the composer conducting. Celli was tempted to accept, but he had a two-year contract with Pavlova. When he explained the situation to her, she understood the temptation, and it was tacitly agreed that he should go to Milan for the role and then return to Pavlova. When he arrived at La Scala, Celli discovered that the management there was less sanguine about his coming for just one ballet. They wanted him to commit himself for the entire season; if not, they would not grant him the role of Joseph. (Strauss was offering to bring a suitable boy from Vienna.) Celli weakened and agreed to the terms, and he wrote to Pavlova asking to be released from his contract. Pavlova was furious and declined to answer the letter. After all, it had been he who had approached her; she had not sought him out. Furthermore, she had thrust him into the limelight at the risk of offending Novikov. But Celli now had the chance of a role ideally suited to his dark, youthful good looks, and the combination of Strauss and La Scala was really irresistible. He was clever enough to ensure that his new contract stipulated that no one else could dance the role of Joseph as long as he was not in default of his contract with La Scala.

In view of Pavlova's youthful visits to Milan for schooling under Beretta, it is strange that her first stage appearance in Italy came as late as 1928, when the week at the Teatro Lirico introduced Pavlova to Italian audiences. She was very nervous, but there was tremendous applause at the end of the first evening. Later someone congratulated her and commented on the success. "I don't know," she replied. "I never judge from premiere." After one of her own performances at the Lirico, she rushed over to La Scala to see Celli in *Joseph*. Afterward she sought him out backstage and congratulated him warmly, telling him, "You made the right decision!" Cecchetti had two boxes for every performance of Pavlova's; he sat surrounded by his students, who gazed at their master's most astonishing pupil while he whispered points about the dancing.

Dandré was having an anxious time in Europe, trying to keep the company viable; he was like a track layer running ahead of a train that never slackened its pace. By the time the company reached Italy, he had the possibility of a season in Paris, though impresarios and theatre managers were all in a highly agitated state at the rate the French franc was falling, and the box-office guarantees were marked very low. Dandré hastened back to the dancers with a proposition: the prospect of work in return for a smaller salary. At the end of such a tour he cannot have been very surprised to find the idea rejected. In the event, he took the risk and confirmed the season, and found eventually that good houses carried the overheads safely.

been an extravagant hope in the context of the whirlwind schedule. Sergeyev felt that all his old mistrust of Pavlova was bitterly confirmed when she paid him his fee and suggested that he might as well return to Paris, and he departed with ill-concealed anger. The abortive attempt to restage *La Bayadère* was unfortunate, a case of the wrong time and the wrong place for the right idea.*

Although Diaghilev had used Sergeyev to coach dancers in roles from *Swan Lake* and *Giselle* and might conceivably do so again, it was never certain that money would be forthcoming for one's labors. The problem of being out of work was a painfully real one in 1927. Even the exquisite Spessivtseva took on supper party engagements in France at this time. She was supported by Vincenzo Celli, a pupil of Cecchetti, and this young Italian dancer usually negotiated the night's fee on Spessivtseva's behalf. He was walking past the Trocadero in Paris one day when a limousine stopped to let a tiny figure out. Celli recognized Pavlova and went into the theatre after her. To a dancer living precariously, Pavlova represented the one consistent source of employment, and twenty minutes later Celli had abandoned the honor and glory of dancing with Spessivtseva for the offer of a sound contract with the Pavlova Company. He was given the

---

* Sergeyev gave away the volume relating to *La Bayadère* as a wedding present, after the Second World War. At that time it seemed an unrecoverable echo of the past. In the Sergeyev Collection at Harvard there are two versions, one signed in 1930, but it is not clear that these materially revise the Maryinsky choreography as Sergeyev knew it. The fakir's dance was a distraction for Solor, before he turned to his opium pipe for consolation in his unhappiness at the loss of Nikiya. The mention of opium suggests that Sergeyev is merely following the original libretto without the excisions which took place in 1901–02 on grounds of "taste."

Cecchetti and Pavlova:
(clockwise, from upper right)
rehearsing *Amarilla* at Ivy House, 1913;
Milan, 1928; Ivy House, 1927;
St. Petersburg, c.1910.

At Ivy House during a heat wave in the late 1920s. Pavlova had the small pond
put in near the house, and it became her favorite spot for afternoon tea.

Anna Pavlova Company
1927 British Provincial Tour

Oct. 10	Leicester	De Montford Hall	mat & eve
Oct. 11	Nottingham	Empire	matinee
Oct. 12	Derby	Hippodrome	matinee
Oct. 13	Sheffield	Hippodrome	matinee
Oct. 14	Leeds	Town Hall	mat & eve
Oct. 15	Halifax	Theatre Royal	matinee
Oct. 17	Huddersfield	Town Hall	evening
Oct. 18	Bradford	King's Hall	evening
Oct. 19	Blackburn	King George's Hall	evening
Oct. 20	Llandudno	Pavilion	evening

With Novikov in *La Fille Mal Gardée*, 1927.

Oct. 21	Shrewsbury	Empire	matinee
Oct. 22	Hanley	Victoria Hall	mat & eve
Oct. 24	Manchester	Free Trade Hall	mat & eve
Oct. 27	Liverpool	Philharmonic Hall	evening
Oct. 28	Liverpool	Philharmonic Hall	mat & eve
Oct. 29	Preston	Public Hall	evening
Oct. 31–Nov. 5	Birmingham	Theatre Royal	eve's & 2 mat's
Nov. 7	Glasgow	St. Andrew's Hall	evening
Nov. 8	Glasgow	St. Andrew's Hall	mat & eve
Nov. 9	Dundee	Caird Hall	evening
Nov. 10	Aberdeen	Music Hall	evening
Nov. 11	Perth	City Hall	evening
Nov. 12	Edinburgh	Usher Hall	mat & eve
Nov. 14	Newcastle	Palace Theatre	matinee
Nov. 15	Middlesborough	Town Hall	evening
Nov. 16	West Hartlepool	Town Hall	evening
Nov. 17	Darlington	Hippodrome	matinee
Nov. 18	York	Empire	matinee
	Scarborough	Futurist Theatre	evening
Nov. 19	Hull	City Hall	mat & eve
Nov. 21	Newark	Palace Theatre	evening
Nov. 22–23	Oxford	Town Hall	evening
Nov. 24	Reading	Town Hall	evening
Nov. 25	Portsmouth	Town Hall	evening
Nov. 26	Bournemouth	Winter Garden	mat & eve
Nov. 28	Bristol	Colston Hall	mat & eve
Nov. 29	Cardiff	Empire	matinee
Nov. 30	Swansea	Empire	matinee
Dec. 1	Plymouth	Guild Hall	evening
Dec. 2	Torquay	Pavilion	mat & eve
Dec. 3	Exeter	Civic Hall	evening

Dec. 5	Bath (?)		mat & eve
Dec. 6	Cheltenham	Town Hall	evening
Dec. 7	Buxton (?)		evening
Dec. 8	Kidderminster	Opera House	evening
Dec. 9	Worcester	Public Hall	evening
Dec. 10	Rugby	Prince of Wales Theatre	evening

1927–28 Continental Tour

Dec. 12 *departure for Continental Tour; performances in Holland and Belgium*

Jan. 4–5	Bremen	Feb. 29–Mar. 1	Nuremberg
Jan. 6	Bremerhaven	Mar. 2–4	Frankfurt
Jan. 7	Bremen	Mar. 5	Mainz
Jan. 8–15	Hamburg	Mar. 6–11	Frankfurt
Jan. 16–17	Essen	Mar. 12	(travel)
Jan. 18	Duisburg	Mar. 13	Wiesbaden
Jan. 19	Hagen	Mar. 14	Karlsruhe
Jan. 20	Elberfeld	Mar. 15–17	Mannheim
Jan. 21	Dusseldorf, Palast	Mar. 18	Heidelburg
Jan. 22–23	Essen	Mar. 19	Kaiserslauten
Jan. 24	Solingen	Mar. 20	Stuttgart
Jan. 25–26	Cologne	Mar. 21	Pforzheim
Jan. 27	Dortmund	Mar. 22	Offenburg
Jan. 28	Münster	Mar. 23	(travel)
Jan. 29–30	Kassel	Mar. 24–25	Zurich
Jan. 31	Erfurt	Mar. 26	Berne
Feb. 1–3	Leipzig	Mar. 27	Lausanne
Feb. 4	Halle	Mar. 28	(travel)
Feb. 5	Magdeburg	Mar. 29–Apr. 5	Milan
Feb. 6–8	Dresden	Apr. 6	(travel)
Feb. 9	Leibnitz	Apr. 7–12	Genoa

With Vladimirov in *Grand Pas Hongrois*, 1928.

Feb. 10	Zittau	Apr. 13–17	Turin
Feb. 11	Cottbus	Apr. 18	(travel)
Feb. 12	Hirschburg	Apr. 19	Venice
Feb. 13	Gorlitz	Apr. 20	(travel)
Feb. 14	Breslau	Apr. 21–22	Trieste
Feb. 15	(free)	Apr. 23–24	Bologna
Feb. 16	Gleiwitz	Apr. 25–30	Florence
Feb. 17	Beuthen	May 1	(travel)
Feb. 18	Breslau	May 2–9	Rome
Feb. 19	Gorlitz	May 10–11	(travel)
Feb. 20	Chemnitz	May 12–17	Paris
Feb. 21–22	Bamberg	May 18–21	(free)
Feb. 23	Reichenbach	May 22	(travel to London)
Feb. 24–28	Munich		

In the spring of 1928, with the French economy collapsing, Pavlova was finding that the running of the house at St. Cloud was a constant drain on her English savings, and a decision was finally made to relinquish the home for Russian orphans. It was a blow, but in some ways it proved the validity of the original idea, for the girls were now equipped with skills that would ease their entry into the outside world.

By now Pavlova was suffering from permanent exhaustion. She could still raise her energy level for performances and suggest astonishing youth and vitality on the stage, but the general stress was beginning to leave its mark. She told Harry Mills that she wanted to stop touring with a full company and merely give concert appearances two or three times a week with a group of soloists. Mills thought it a feasible plan and began mapping out the possibilities. Hurok was back in business, Pavlova's name was still revered in America, and the main cities there would certainly sustain appearances, although it was becoming noticeable in Europe that audiences were more apathetic toward Pavlova's ballet than at any time before. There was the general economic uncertainty, and dance had splintered so quickly into different avenues of approach that it had outstripped its potential audience's capacity for adapting to each trend.

Pavlova seems not to have expressed clearly to Dandré her increasing dread of more full touring; while she was discussing with Mills all the pros and cons of the concert scheme, Dandré was quietly contracting for a return to South America, the honey pot of the war years. He presented Pavlova with a *fait accompli*. She was appalled at the prospect, but it was just too early to see the alternatives clearly enough to present them as viable. Butsova would have none of it. Faced with South America, for the second time in her long association with Pavlova she declined to renew her contract. At the end of the Paris season, Pavlova left a present for Hilda. The card that accompanied it was chillingly formal: "With my best wishes, Anna Pavlova 17 vi 28." Doubtless she felt threatened and abandoned. She had an added worry: Novikov had also had enough and announced that he was going to accept a post as ballet master in Chicago.

At the same time, in Paris, the young Balanchine was beginning to prove that Diaghilev's faith in him had not been misplaced. His *Apollon Musagète* had its premiere on June 12, and Pavlova was heartened to see that the choreography was based firmly in academic technique. If the "color" was different, still it did not violate the great principles that had nurtured them all. Pavlova understood this "neoclassicism," and she wasted no time in arranging a meeting with the young master. In view of the travel that Dandré had already committed her to, the arrangements with Balanchine were necessarily inconclusive; but it was suggested that at least two of the newly contracted dancers, Nina Kirsanova and the character dancer Thadée Slavinsky, would be in Paris long enough to learn some of Balanchine's dances.*

---

* Balanchine wanted to do a Scarlatti piece for Pavlova herself, but—as usual—Dandré thought the choice too extreme. Although she would never have admitted it, Pavlova's troublesome knee was a stronger reason for not taking on extra work at this time.

ABOVE *Invitation to the Dance*, Montevideo, 1928.
BELOW *La Fille Mal Gardée*, Montevideo, 1928.

With Vajinsky in the *Gavotte*, New Zealand, 1926.

Pavlova then took off for northern Italy, in the fond hope of some rest but also to get treatment for her troublesome knee. The diagnosis suggested a bone spur, which was at that time beyond a surgeon's guarantee. And even if she were operated on, the convalescence would extend beyond the time when Pavlova, nearing fifty, could hope to regain sufficient mobility to sustain any sort of classical technique. So instead she tried all sorts of therapies: heat, chemical, electric. Most doctors advocated rest, but she had been hearing that for years. In Chicago in 1924 Adolph Bolm had gone to see her in her dressing room; he found her depressed about her general health—and her knee. "You must take a rest," he told her solicitously. But Pavlova had shaken her head wildly. "No, no! How can I? What would become of my dancers? How can I disband my company?" She was no nearer to an answer four years later.

In the weeks of high summer, the shape of the company was pulled together once more: contracts offered, contracts signed, and replacements recruited. There was now also an additional factor: in England every foreign dancer had to have a permit from the Ministry of Labour. The paperwork was such that Dandré's desk was usually buried under hundreds of documents. A partner for Pavlova was the biggest problem; Volinine was involved with his teaching and in any event would have been astonished at the very idea of a return to South America. The best hope seemed to be Pierre Vladimiroff, who had partnered Karsavina in her New York appearances in 1924 and had been with Bolm's company thereafter. He eventually agreed to travel to Rio directly from North America. As second ballerina there was the English dancer Ruth French, and as leading character dancer there was the beautiful Elena Bekefi, whose father had been one of Pavlova's first partners at the Maryinsky. Slavinsky and Kirsanova did turn up with two Balanchine dances: *Polka Grotesque* and a lively gypsy dance using music from Rachmaninoff's *Aleko*. Then there was Boris Romanov, and his wife, Smirnova, filling in time prior to his appointment as ballet master at the Teatro Colón the following season. Smirnova reconstructed the Grand Pas from *Paquita*, which was viewed by the company as another boring old classic. Romanov tried something modern: a ballet with a sporting theme. *The Champions*, to music of Walford Hyden, turned out to have a certain *déjà vu* quality. It presented dancers as three athletes—exponents of tennis, golf, and football—each of whom plunged around in a manner suggesting the particular sport. As the tennis player, Pavlova had to wear a beret and short stockings. To follow elements of Nijinska's *Le Train Bleu* was unwise, as a taste for chic was not strong among Pavlova's audiences. The ballet was quickly retired, but it stood as a signpost of Pavlova's desire to move with the times. Even after the Rio season was under way she was still willing to take on choreographic recruits. A young Russian turned up, claiming that he had learned various dances from the Indians of Brazil; in São Paulo they rehearsed his ballet every day, but in the end it too failed. It may well have been the audiences who failed the ballet.

With Aubrey Hitchens in *Autumn Leaves*, Buenos Aires, 1928.

With Vladimirov in South America, 1928: ABOVE *Dionysus*;
BELOW (left) *The Fairy Doll*, (right) *Chopiniana*.

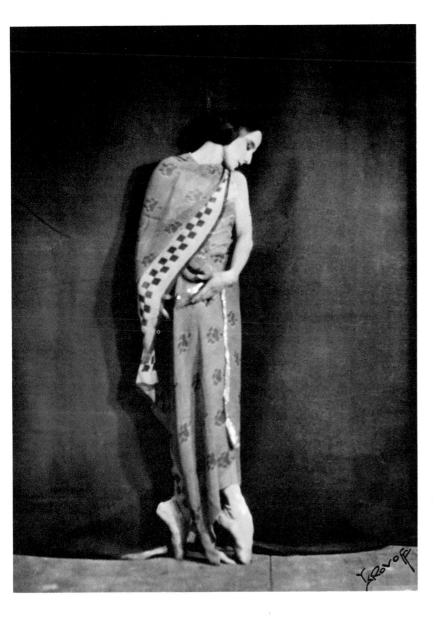

Portraits by Nicolas Yarovoff, Montevideo, 1928.

The route of this tour was Rio de Janeiro, São Paulo, and Santos, then Buenos Aires and La Plata; and finally Montevideo. In Buenos Aires, Franz van Riel photographed a series of *Autumn Leaves* studies, with Aubrey Hitchins in the role of the North Wind first done by Hubert Stowitts. Van Riel had taken lovely photographs of Pavlova on earlier tours, and she had great trust in him; at a sitting in 1919 she had remarked, "You know, this is the first time I not feel self-conscious with camera." But for *Autumn Leaves* she was more proprietorial, and she fussed about correct angles. Much to van Riel's annoyance, Pavlova had Algeranoff stationed in the studio to check the poses. There was method in this: because of the nature of the ballet, she was hoping for a greater than usual suggestion of action, and in holding extended poses she had less time for trial and error. A fellow dancer could call out instant corrections. The results were well worth the extra trouble. Although van Riel always "worked up" his prints until they looked almost like mezzotints, he retained a marvelous quality, of both mood and vitality. In Mon-

tevideo an émigré Russian named Nicolas Yarovoff took some photographs on the stage of the Teatro Urquiza, and though some of them were conventional, others were more interesting: Pavlova wrapped herself in her favorite silk scarf and stood around in starkly Byzantine shapes. The poses may have been self-consciously produced, but they were also utterly eye-catching. Pavlova was a photographer's dream.

While they were still in South America, Dandré announced the company's long-term plans. He told them that they would be traveling once more to the Orient, beginning in November. And of course it would not stop there. Already there were letters going off to Australia. That would take them through the dog days of summer once again, and then Europe would beckon conveniently, just as it had always done. There would be England, of course. And surely Spain was ready to receive Pavlova again? It would be ten years since her last visit. Time was passing; the shadow moving nearer. Cecchetti was dead. And though no one said it, Pavlova could not go on dancing forever.

Arriving in South America, 1928.

On the stage of the old Kursaal Theatre in Cairo, Pavlova, wearing her practice clothes, is seated on a chair. Around her are grouped the other members of her company, and in front of them all, in the center of the stage, one woman is dancing—or rather staggering from one pose to another, and endeavoring in the process to appear voluptuous. The impediment to any finesse in execution is a large python, which for its own safety as much as any other reason is wrapped tightly around its shifting anchorage. The performance is an audition in front of the world's most famous dancer, who happens also to be one of the world's most consistent employers of dancers. Not for this reason, but because the woman with the snake is a Russian, Pavlova sits with her face composed, politely attentive, giving the woman her due. Russian artists must be respected. Eventually there is a sign that someone has had enough. It is the snake. With a swift convulsion it empties the remains of its last meal onto the canvas floor covering. The audition is over. That night Pavlova dances as the Fairy Doll surrounded by a nauseous odor—a reminder that a desire for gainful employment, and a belief that self-expression is paramount, can lead believers down strange and tortuous paths.

London, 1927—third class for the benefit of the press.

Bremen, 1928.

In Bombay, Pavlova hears that one of her former dancers, Leon Kellaway, is appearing. With Dandré she takes a box in the theatre. Kellaway is performing an unauthorized version of her famous *Gavotte* and is appalled when suddenly he sees the occupants of the box. But Pavlova is enjoying it all immensely, and is flattered that he liked the number sufficiently to want to imitate it. Kellaway gets an invitation from Pavlova to dine on board her ship the following day.

A Burmese male dancer steps forward to perform his *pièce de résistance*: he throws a basket of broken glass onto the stage and then jumps on the glass with his bare feet. There are little shrieks of alarm from the foreign dancers in the audience who are to perform on that same stage the following night. After the performance Pavlova admires an exquisite child dancer decked in gold. "How old?" asks Pavlova of the interpreter. "Nine, Madame." "At what age begin to study?" "Start learning three years old." "Ah, how pity," says Pavlova wistfully. "I start too late."

Melbourne, 1929.

On a sticky night in Kuala Lumpur, Malaysia, Pavlova is dancing *Rondino*. Suddenly she catches sight of a camera being leveled at her by some planters who have infiltrated their way backstage. She breaks off in the middle of a measure and darts into the wings. There is a brief altercation before the abashed photographers retreat. "Very sorry to say," pronounces Pavlova coldly, "but what wrong with your country, too much whisky and soda."

In Singapore the heat is terrifying. Dandré tells the company one day that the Grand Pas from *Paquita* is to go into the program. There is a corporate groan from the company. Hidden among the grumblers, someone says, "You know why she's done this? It's because we treated Smirnova so badly in Buenos Aires, when she was trying to teach it to us."

Being met by the press in Spain.

Outside the Royal Castle in Copenhagen, 1928, after an audience with the King, during which Pavlova suggested that the Royal Danish Ballet visit Paris.

On the outskirts of Brisbane, Pavlova is being shown around the elaborate house and garden of a *nouveau riche*. The host shows her a freshly painted extension to the main house and explains that it is a bedroom suite he has had built expressly for Pavlova's use while she is in the city. Pavlova is nonplussed. A little later she turns a corner and spies a yard with poultry, and the bright plumage of a rooster. She sees her escape. "Sorry! Not possible I stay here. I work so late, and they wake me so early in the morning!"

Pavlova is rehearsing *Giselle* in Sydney. The atmosphere is electric and the cast feels emotionally drained. The orchestra cannot see the stage drama. In the mad scene Pavlova suddenly stops and goes down to the footlights. "Listen! Here is like noises in mad girl's head!"

The setting is Bombay; it is Christmas Day 1928. Pavlova stands in full view of the long sickle of sand that is Juhu Beach. She is having her fortune told by a snake charmer. Pavlova's guide for the visit is Major Sokhey, the husband of Leila Sokhey, who is destined to become known far and wide as the Indian dancer Menaka. Pavlova is interested in Leila's determination to revive Hindu dancing; she has given Algeranoff time off so that he may perform with Menaka at a concert in Bombay. (Because of the caste system, Leila has been precluded from taking lessons in India; she has already traveled to London, to Fitzroy Square, to acquire the fundamentals of Indian dance from Algeranoff—the Cockney lad recruited by Pavlova in 1921.) Later on Christmas Day, Pavlova goes to watch Leila and Algy rehearse. Algy wears a yellow Krishna dhoti (with a red swimsuit underneath) and he thinks it is the most joyous Christmas he has ever experienced.

Venice, 1928.

London in December. Lights glint in the early evening gloom. The trees around Ivy House are bare, and the sodden leaves are raked into piles. There have been two weeks of performing in London, and Pavlova is having her first Christmas at home—at last. There is a party for all those dancers who are far from their homes, including Leon Woizikovsky and Vladimiroff's wife, Felia Doubrovska, formerly of the Ballets Russes. Outside the brightly lit dining-room windows, on the verandah rail, a peacock roosts with hunched shoulders, its tail hanging like a flag at half mast in the damp air. Flying free in the warmth of the dining room is a cheerful little bird called a cadilan. Six months ago he was in Java. His two companions are already dead.

In the first week of May 1930, Pavlova arrived in Paris for performances at the Théâtre des Champs-Elysées. Since leaving Waterloo Station the morning after her first Christmas in her own home, she had done tours in England, Spain, France, Monaco, Switzerland, Germany (twice), Czechoslovakia, Sweden, and Denmark. Now she was back in France. Was there anything left to give from that outwardly frail little body? She was performing not a few short divertissements, but the full version of *Giselle*. Serge Makovsky summed up his impressions:

> Anna Pavlova—irresistible, as lithe as a flame, as light as a feather—is dancing *Giselle*. Nothing more needs to be said. Anna Pavlova never astonished one with her technique; she charmed one by her inspiration. Even in the past one never dissected her dancing (which was always full of "faults"); one only wanted to admire it, forgetting the rules of dancing in order to be further carried away by her divine talent.

Pavlova made her usual visits to various friends while she was in Paris, among them Mathilde Kchessinskaya, who had turned to teaching when the proceeds of her jewelry sales were exhausted. Mathilde faced her straitened circumstances with remarkable good humor—the very quality that had won so many audiences, and that was now winning over young pupils. Pavlova admired their evident progress and then said to Kchessinskaya, "And I thought you weren't a teacher!" Thirty years had passed since the young Anna had first stepped onto the stage where Mathilde ruled like an empress. Now Pavlova was taking the little lady flowers and gaining a new respect for her.

Pavlova also called on Trouhanova and her husband, A. A. Ignatiev; he had been present at the banquet on the evening of the 1899 graduation at the Mikhailovsky and had actually danced a mazurka with the young Pavlova after the supper. The couple were at work in their little French garden when Pavlova arrived, and at once she suggested that they let her help. Trouhanova tried to deter her. "First of all, you are too delicate to cope with a spade, and besides—you are wearing high-heeled shoes." It fell on deaf ears. "No, no! You will see! I am very strong, so strong I can dig that entire bed; and I don't care about my shoes. They are torn." A thought struck her. "I have had torn shoes all my life. It's a bad omen." The idea was banished in a flurry of activity; she set about turning over the ground of a rose bed, and she did it rapidly and capably, though at one point she stopped and looked pensively at a budding tea rose. "When that bush dies, I shall die too. This is so. I know it."

The Ignatievs were alarmed at the tired and worn appearance of their guest, and they suggested to her that a long vacation would be beneficial. Pavlova was astonished at the very idea. "What are you saying? It is utterly impossible. I *must* work the year round. The entire company depends on me. To let them go would mean paying everyone forfeit. It would take two or three months to engage another company, to rechoreograph the numbers and make new costumes, and we would lose engagements for an entire six months. Is this possible? It is unthinkable. It would cost half a million francs and destroy all that I have saved up." It was no more than the truth. Certainly she was tired, but she had the stamina of ten and did not fold up under the stress. As always, it was the company that fell apart, and Pavlova who kept going.

She had the chance of a season at Drury Lane prior to the inevitable English provincial tour. She needed a partner again. Pavlova summoned to her suite at the Plaza-Athénée the last of Diaghilev's protégés, Serge Lifar. A young man of enormous vanity, he quickly decided that the role of "Pavlova's partner" was not for him, and then began to discourse on the fact that Pavlova, in his view, was wasting her talent. At this very point he was interrupted by the arrival of Dandré. Pavlova repeated to Dandré the gist of Lifar's views, and Dandré brought the discussion to a premature conclusion. Lifar, very much on his dignity, then made a formal refusal of the job of partner; but still Pavlova kept him there, and after Dandré had left the room she discussed with Lifar the possibility of mounting a gala at the Opéra to mark the first anniversary of Diaghilev's death. By the time Lifar left the hotel, he was totally reconciled to the idea of partnering Pavlova—at least at the Opéra. Two galas were planned, but neither eventuated, and it was Volinine who was swept out of Paris on a wave of charm, to partner Pavlova in England.

In London, the stock market was trembling, and unemployment rising. Spring was late that year, but suddenly there were blossoms everywhere; at least the parks were cheerful. At Drury Lane, Pavlova once again performed *Giselle*:

> The work performed last night was seen at Covent Garden a few years ago, when there was a temporary revival of the practice of following short operas by ballets. Last night its effect was realised as never before in our day, thanks to the art of this gifted Russian dancer. . . . In the earlier portion, when Giselle dies, there was some excellent miming, and in the latter, where she rises from her tomb, she executed some entirely new and most graceful figures.

This suggests that Pavlova was shielding her knee in some way. But problem or no, her plans were already mapped out for that autumn. The announcement for a ten-week English provincial tour was printed on the back of a program for a Celebrity Concert early that summer. It caught Pavlova's eye. "Make me feel like slave," she said.

Pavlova had some time at Ivy House that summer, and she prowled around the garden restlessly. The house itself was altered. The old wooden verandah had been replaced by a brick and stucco counterpart. When photographers came to take some pictures of Pavlova by the swan pool she seemed less inclined to put on a show. She wore a light woolen dress and carried a floppy hat, and at times she let the smile slip and looked ineffably sad. She would not face the camera's eye but looked elsewhere, and her mind sometimes seemed far away. The only flash of animation was directed toward the swans, which she tried to tempt with bread and grass. But they were noticeably cautious; she was really a stranger in her own home.

For years Pavlova had wondered why England could not organize state support for ballet. In Australia she had taken up the subject: "I am strongly of the opinion that the English nation ought to endow a national school of dancing, so that it might take the sadness out of the gait and manner of the English people." By 1930 there were pockets of dance experimentation, fostered principally by former associates of Diaghilev: Marie Rambert, a Pole, was doing pioneer work, and Ninette de Valois, an Irish woman, was running an embryonic academy of dance tuition. Rambert contrived to give public performances on a very modest scale. For a charity matinee at the Scala Theatre in London that summer she presented a small ballet named *Capriol*

Suite. Pavlova was in the audience; she liked the ballet and asked about the choreographer, Frederick Ashton. She had no way of knowing that it was she who had first inspired him. He had seen her in Lima when he was twelve and had carried that initial excitement through subsequent sightings in London.

As soon as he heard that his idol had been enquiring about him, he sent a letter to Ivy House. Dandré invited him to tea. While they were talking, Ashton became aware that he was being observed through a gap above curtains that screened a glass-paneled door. Pavlova came into the room slowly, still studying him carefully. "Ah, so young!" she said. She called for tea, and Ashton was mesmerized by the ceremony of it, as Pavlova spooned varying mixtures from numerous little pots of jam into her tea. He looked at her hands and could not associate them with the exquisitely delicate gestures he had seen on stage. They were workaday hands; the left forefinger had a lumpy joint, partially concealed by two large rings.

"Well! I am just on holiday," she said, "but already I am bored." Ashton bubbled with the confidence of youth and suggested to Pavlova that she might visit the Rambert studio and see more of his choreography, but she countered this with the news that she was just about to go on tour. Pavlova was amused by Ashton's insistence that there would be time for her to make the visit before her train left; in the event, she did go to the little hall in Notting Hill Gate, and there she was shown Ashton's *Leda and the Swan.* Then she was off. (Ashton had not mentioned to her that he had auditioned for her company when she was at Covent Garden in 1925, and that Pianowski had failed him then.) After Pavlova left London, Dandré explained to Ashton that the company's prime requirement at that stage had been a strong soloist, but that when the touring commitments for 1931 were through, there would be a chance for Ashton to join the reorganized company and make ballets for its dancers.

The tour began in Southampton that September, and it was every bit as crazy as any of the others. Dandré once again stayed behind at Ivy House making plans. Pavlova was forty-nine, permanently tired, and suffering at least one chronic injury. No matter; the plans for 1931 were more epic than anything that had gone before. It would begin in Riga and Revel (now Tallinn). Riga would bring her full circle: to the young woman who had set out in 1907 with images of Marie Taglioni in her head and the simple desire to emulate that legendary figure, was it a longing to go home? It would be like creeping up to the gate. She could hardly step through: the Soviets treated her as an enemy—"the darling of the aristocrats." In the previous year, with mean-spirited self-righteousness, they had cut off Pavlova's annual financial gifts, which were usually distributed to the distressed of the former Imperial Theatres. The remaining monies had been appropriated by the "People's Government." That was not the Russia she loved and hungered for. Dandré, at least, was certain of the immediate future: the 1931 Continental tour would continue through Poland, Roumania, Serbia, Italy, France . . . and then there would be a return to America, though less taxing this time—recital-type programs for New York and seventy-five other cities. It was said that Pavlova was hoping to take with her Escudero, the Spanish dancer and former partner of La Argentina.

In Liverpool, Pavlova was working at the barre one morning when she suddenly stopped and turned to Nina Kirsanova (she seemed to be the current "favorite"). "Nina, please enquire if there is a Russian Orthodox church here. Go and pray for me. I feel so depressed. . . . I feel in the shadow of a heavy, dark cloud. I feel the sword of Damocles over my head." Nina found a church and prayed earnestly. As the tour wore on, Pavlova's knee caused her increasing pain. In the wings before going on, she would clasp Nina's hands. Once Pavlova confided to her, "It

Liverpool, November 1930, with local dance pupils.

Probably *Raymonda*.

is more difficult to conceal my state of mind from my husband, from the company." But the public was oblivious. Even critical observers were fooled: "Any brilliance that may be lacking in her feet is more than counterbalanced by the electric sparkle of her arms, the grace of her body, and the inimitable play of her face."

From Liverpool, Pavlova had to take a train to London to defend herself in a slander action in the King's Bench Division of the High Court. It seemed a trivial enough thing that had started it all, but it had snowballed to serious proportions, and now it was headline news for the whole nation. This was the man-in-the-street view of ballet and what went on behind the scenes, and it read like a parody of Somerset Maugham. (See Appendix, p. 410.)

After the court case Pavlova hurried back to the north of England to resume the tour. Her train was delayed by fog, and she arrived after the performance had begun. But when she made her entrance on cue in *Invitation to the Dance*, the audience sent up a great cheer; everyone had been following the case in the papers, and at this stage the outcome was still not known.

Dandré remained in London, trying to sort out future schedules. It had become clear that although foreign managements were still happy to employ Pavlova herself, they were less in-

clined to commit themselves to heavy guarantees for the presentation of a full ballet company. As far as Pavlova was concerned, this coincided with her own plans for a smaller concert group; but it provided a gloomy prospect for those dancers who would no longer be under her banner. After much deliberation she decided that it would be in the interests of the more junior dancers if she relinquished the stronger soloists, as these were the performers most likely to be able to secure employment elsewhere. Algeranoff was one who did not have his contract renewed for 1931.

When the company came to London at the beginning of December, the final week of the season took place at the Golders Green Hippodrome. There were two programs that week: apart from the usual divertissements, Pavlova danced *Invitation to the Dance* and *Autumn Leaves* in the first half of the week, and *Amarilla* and the Grand Pas from *Paquita* in the second. Frederick Ashton bluffed his way past the stage-door guard after a matinee and went to Pavlova's dressing room. He was determined to memorize everything about her, but he found himself staring at a small hole above her breastbone and quite forgot anything else. (Asking about it later, he was told that it was a scar from a stage dagger in *La Bayadère*.) Pavlova took Ashton's hand and said, "You will have a great future. It will come slowly, but it will come."

On Saturday night the divertissements were placed in the middle section of the program rather than at the end; Pavlova danced the *Gavotte* and *The Swan*. When Algeranoff completed his Indian solo, a member of the staff walked on stage with a huge gilded laurel wreath for the dancer. It was from Pavlova. Pavlova's last appearance was in the extract from *Paquita*, which she had first learned as a young graduate surrounded by the heady glamour of the Maryinsky. In the Hippodrome more and more flowers were carried onto the stage at the end of the evening. There was also a live parrot balancing on a trapeze bound with flowers. Pavlova laughed and put a hand to the bird; it took a nip at her fingers. In the wings two stagehands were carrying a curious tribute from an anonymous donor. It was a large circular tray with a ring of candles and hyacinths. At the center was a plaster statuette of the Madonna and Child with halos of gold stars. Dandré signaled to the men to hide the tableau from sight, but at that moment Pavlova came running into the wings. Her face clouded as she caught sight of the tray and its devotional centerpiece, but when she realized that the men were carrying it away from the stage, she stopped them and told them it should be put there with the other presents.

Pavlova had invited some of the soloists to supper at Ivy House—principally those who were having to leave the company. When they arrived they noticed the glimmer of candles in the alcove at the far end of the dining room. Normally there was a bird cage there, but the little cadilan had died while Pavlova was on the tour. In place of the cage there stood the tray with the Madonna. Pavlova saw the dancers glancing at it and quickly explained that she felt it was the wish of the sender that she should have its presence in her home, but some of the company members thought it was a prank in poor taste: it was the thirteenth day of December, and there were thirteen candles surrounding the figurine.

Before they had supper, Pavlova served *zakuski* and vodka. She was dressed in beige lace. She knew that she had to leave for the Continent early the next morning, but she tried to present a cheerful front during the dinner. Kirsanova did not brighten the mood when she noticed that there were thirteen present at the table and announced the fact. She tried to cover her blunder by saying that thirteen was her lucky number, but the party drifted to an early end. Around one o'clock they all gathered in the hall to say good-bye, and Pavlova handed out the special presents she had bought them. When Algeranoff got back to his Gower Street studio, he opened his: it was a moiré silk wallet. In it was a hundred-pound note.

Pavlova left Ivy House precipitately the following morning. It was her custom before any journey to make a tour of the house and garden, saying good-bye to all the pets and the trees and the favorite objects. On the morning of December 14 she hurried out of the house without a pause or a glance, almost running. The house had been let to some Americans for the duration of the new tour. A few of the dancers were traveling with her on the same boat train as far as Paris. Kirsanova was among them; she was one of the inner group who played cards with Pavlova. During the journey, Pavlova asked her to settle accounts for a game of rummy that had been in progress throughout the tour. Kirsanova was ahead by sixpence. Pavlova searched nervously in her bag for the correct coin. "We must finish everything in the past," she said. "We'll begin again on the new tour after the holiday."

On December 21, a thoughtful article by John Martin appeared in the New York *Herald Tribune* in which he reflected on Pavlova's impending return to America after an absence of five years.

The announcement that Anna Pavlowa is to return to America next season is of especial interest in view of the many changes that have taken place in the local scene since her last appearance here in 1925. Then she was one of a pitifully meager number of dancers whom the great theatregoing public recognized as artists; now we not only have an annual stream of distinguished visitors from Europe, but have developed as well a very considerable contingent of native dancers whose names at least are known beyond the immediate circle of those technically interested in their art.

We are, indeed, a widely different audience for dancing from the somewhat naive throngs who used to flock to Mme. Pavlowa's ballets and applaud them long and lustily in spite of the fact that in the later tours they were not always what they might have been, and that the companies which performed them were seldom even what they should have been. It was enough that there was the *Dying Swan*, even if we had to sit through a whole evening to get to it.

It was a type of audience which certainly could not have inspired Mme. Pavlowa to her finest achievements, and may even have discouraged her to the extent of the decision frequently reported

that she would not dance in America again. Perhaps it is the awakened spirit of interest in matters choreographic hereabouts that has induced her to change her mind. Certainly the announcement that her programs are to be of a type more nearly akin to the dance recital than to her former productions of ballet in traditional form would seem to imply a definite knowledge of what is going on here. . . .

The important consideration, however, is Pavlowa herself. During the last year or so intrepid critics in England and France have dared for the first time to find fault with her dancing. They have asserted that the great art of other days was fading and that the supreme star of twenty years ago was aging beyond the normal range of a dancer's useful years. Perhaps there are indications in the performances that these conclusions are well founded—one who has not seen them is in no position to say them nay—but in principle such a theory is beyond justification. If a dancer of her superb accomplishments and equipment has reached the end of her career at her years, then there is something radically wrong with dancing. . . . Perhaps she is not able to do the same acrobatic feats which made the mouths of her audience fly open with amazement, but that, after all, is not an essential part of dancing. It is scarcely more, indeed, than a compensation for youthfulness which has nothing to say and makes up for it in sensationalism.

Late version of *Paquita*.

In her dressing room, 1910–30.

It is not dancers who grow old, it is dancing. The same type and form of art that was radical twenty years ago is not only mild and unexciting today but is actually passé. . . . To be sure, the time must come for every good work of art when its full value becomes apparent with a certain agelessness; but during the middle period, between its creation and its final adjustment in the category, it frequently suffers a pitiable reversion when it is merely out of date. It is, therefore, conceivable that some of Pavlowa's repertoire may be out of date, but scarcely that Pavlowa is less an artist than she was, at a period when she should be at the very height of her potentialities. . . .

Mme. Pavlowa need not fear that we in America will still demand of her the *Swan* and its companion pieces if she does not see fit to give them; we will welcome her in her true role of artist, if she will do us the honor of playing it. If she has grown old, then she was never the artist we thought she was; if she actually was the artist we believed her to be, she has not grown old. That seems to be a reasonable statement of the case and a hospitable gesture of welcome.

Café de Paris, Monte Carlo, 1931. Seated to Pavlova's left are Felia Doubrovska, Vladimirov, and Dandré.

Pavlova spent Christmas 1930 very quietly in Cannes. Felia Doubrovska often accompanied Pavlova as she wandered around the shops, looking for clothes for the forthcoming tour. Pavlova had no really warm winter coat, and she was heading into the heart of Eastern Europe. She seldom found clothes exactly to her taste; she would snip off bits of decoration after she had bought a garment, or twist and tuck edges until the style was altered. If she found a dress she liked, she might order several. On one of their strolls, Pavlova and Doubrovska passed through the open market area in the main square. There were the usual stalls and clutter, and itinerant entertainers as well. A fortune teller beckoned to the two women; Doubrovska hung back, but Pavlova, as usual, was ready to face the future. Doubrovska waited outside the booth. When Pavlova emerged, Doubrovska was about to question her, but Pavlova wore such a stony expression that Doubrovska was suddenly abashed and said nothing. They walked on in silence.

Pavlova had ordered a white gown from Lanvin; it was an unusual departure for her—normally she did not wear white in the evening. The gown was delivered in time for the New Year's Eve party at the Casino in Cannes. During the supper the heat from the candle-lit tables became oppressive, and someone opened a window, disturbing two pigeons roosting on a gutter; a minute later the birds fluttered into the room, attracted by the light. One of the birds came down on Pavlova's right shoulder, and she turned her head away in alarm.

Soon after midnight, she excused herself and left the party. On entering the hotel Pavlova encountered Pianowski, and they sat talking in the lounge for a long time, until Pavlova expressed a desire to go for a drive in a cab. Pianowski went with her. She stopped the cab at the municipal cemetery and got out. The gates were shut, but she attracted the attention of the concierge, who finally admitted them. Pavlova wandered off. Presently she was back at the gate, complaining about the unkempt state of a Grand

Duke's grave. "Do you realize who that is?" she asked.* The concierge was unmoved. Pavlova instructed the cab driver to return to the center of town. They stopped in the market, where the first early-morning arrivals were setting up their stalls. She bought armloads of flowers, then returned to the cab and instructed that they return to the cemetery. There were too many flowers for one grave. At dawn Felia Doubrovska was awakened in the hotel by a bellboy with a big bunch of flowers. "These are from Madame Pavlova," he said. She told the boy to put the flowers in the bath, then she climbed back into bed. At 9:30 she was awakened again, this time by Victor Dandré. "Do you know where Anna is? Her bed has not been slept in."

Pavlova did not travel to Paris until January 10. The night train was south of Dijon the following morning when it was involved in a derailment and came to a violent halt. Pavlova was lying on the bunk of her sleeper, and a suitcase, dislodged from the overhead rack, struck her on the ribcage. The train had been passing through a station at the time of the accident, and passengers were able to climb down to see what had happened; Pavlova got out too. She wore only a light coat over silk pajamas, but the day was bright and sunny, and though there was snow on the ground, she walked the length of the train to see where the engine had collided with a reversing goods train. There was a long delay before the passenger carriages could be hauled back to

---

* The grave seems to have been that of Nicolas Nicolaievich, dead a little over a year. As the military commander who urged his cousin Nicolas II to accept the Witte constitution in 1905, he would have fitted Pavlova's ideal of a good royalist as well as a good radical. She may have admired him at a distance; he does not seem to have moved in the theatre set in the way that the Grand Dukes Boris and Nicolas Mikhailovich did.

a junction, to be taken by a fresh engine on a circuit back to the Paris line. During the wait, the carriages cooled rapidly.*

The train was twelve hours late getting into Paris. At the station, Pavlova was met by a group including her agent; her maid, Marguerite Letienne; and several of the dancers. Pavlova told Kirsanova that the vacation had made her stiff and that exercise would improve her circulation and ease the bruise from the suitcase. The company was using the studio of Leo Staats, ballet master at the Opéra, and it was there that Pavlova went to take class on January 12. The studio was cold and drafty; there was no heat due to a pipe having burst a few days earlier, and the big windows would not close properly. Goloshchanov, the pianist, thought Pavlova was looking quite radiant, and he noticed she had put on some weight, which suited her. "I will have to let out my *zhirok!*" she said. The following day Pavlova telephoned to enquire whether the heating had been repaired, and having been told that it had not, she went instead to the studio of Vera Trefilova. There must have been a strange comfort for Pavlova in seeing Vera—and Valerian Ivchenko, whom Vera had married. Vera and Anna, the two girls struggling in Beretta's class during a hot Italian summer. And "Svetlov"—what other turnings might Pavlova's career have taken without *him?* The world had changed so quickly. Now, here they all were, middle-aged! Indeed Valerian, with his white goatee and handlebar moustache, looked like a dumpy gnome of unfathomable age.

When Pavlova had been on her way through the city before Christmas, she had been approached in her hotel by a Russian woman carrying news of mutual friends. The woman was a representative of a fashion house on the rue du Rivoli, and at that time Pavlova had been persuaded to pay a visit. She took a liking to a fine sable coat, but Dandré counseled against it. "Annushka! It is too expensive!" Pavlova did not really like any of the alternatives, but she was persuaded that a coat of squirrel could be fashioned to her taste. Now, in January, she called once more to see if the coat was ready. The cutters had not completed the order. Pavlova chided the *vendeuse* and said, with a degree of jest, "I shall catch cold, and then I shall die, and then nobody will pay you your money."

One night that week, at a variety show, Doubrovska and Vladimiroff were taking their seats after the second intermission when they noticed Pavlova and Dandré in the circle. At the end of the performance the two dancers waited for Pavlova at the foot of the staircase. It was raining that evening, and Vladimiroff offered to hail a cab for Pavlova, but she said, "No, no. I don't want one. We'll walk." She was wearing only a light opera cloak, but Dandré dutifully took her elbow and, with a nod to the other two, conducted Pavlova down the steps. Doubrovska watched the little figure, so small beside the bulk of Dandré, disappearing into the haze of lamp-lit rain.

In the four days she had to work at Vera Trefilova's studio, Pavlova determined to lose the four pounds she had gained. She said to Ivchenko, "We working people have no time to be ill. One must take oneself in hand." He missed any import in this remark, but when Pavlova asked for the studio to be especially well heated, and placed her practice clothes on the radiators before changing, Vera began to wonder. She had never seen Pavlova warm her clothes before class. When she asked if all was well, Pavlova pointed to her chest and then put a finger to her lips. No one was to know. On the morning of January 16, the day before her departure for The Hague, she said she felt tired after her class and decided not to stay for lunch. On the doorstep she made her farewells to Vera and Valerian. "You and I, Vera, have never had a rest yet. Well, just a little longer . . . "—and she turned away, leaving the sentence hanging. Pavlova took lunch in her room at the hotel and afterward felt some discomfort, complaining of a gastric indisposition. She made an appearance at a supper party but retired early. Though she did not realize it then, she was suffering from a high fever, and during the night she collapsed while trying to reach the house telephone.

The following morning, January 17, the rest of the company was settled aboard the train for The Hague as the departure time approached. Nobody had seen Pavlova, who was usually one of the first at any station, and only as the carriage doors began slamming was Pavlova seen coming through the barrier. She was dressed in a familiar coat of red wool with a fur collar—but there the familiarity ended. Instead of the erect, self-sufficient figure that had led the way through thousands of barriers and across countless dozens of frontiers, the dancers saw a frail woman,

---

* It should be clearly understood that in Dandré's account of the train journey from Cannes in January 1931 he places himself on the train with Pavlova, and does not leave her until Paris. This does not accord with the memories of others. Details about the train accident vary, noticeably between Dandré's version and that related to other dancers in Paris by Pavlova herself. Inna Marinel (temporary secretary in 1930) suggests that Dandré had a mistress—which is entirely possible—but Marinél overloads the case when she suggests that Dandré was not on the Hague train (January 17) for that reason. Dandré, reasonably enough, claims business called him to London; however, he seems to have had time to go to the theatre with Pavlova in Paris, before leaving for London (Mme. Doubrovska's memory). According to Kirsanova, Pavlova told her about the suitcase falling and hitting her. It is surprising that Dandré makes no mention of this incident. Kirsanova would need to be an accomplished writer of fiction to invent such a telling detail. It is hard to believe that Dandré and Pavlova shared the same sleeping compartment on the train; such proximity was never a feature of their hotel life. After the accident, Dandré has it that "Pavlova woke up in a fright, but raising the blind and seeing that we were at a station and the day was beautiful and sunny, she started to dress calmly. We then came out of our carriage." Indulging in speculation, I find it hard to envisage Pavlova dressing "calmly" after a train accident, and think it much more in character that she should fling a coat on, and then go out to see what had happened. (One is reminded that Dandré always fussed over Pavlova, and would have tried to prevent her going out lightly dressed in that situation; on the other hand, in such a situation she would have ignored his requests.) My feeling is that if Dandré *was* on the train, then he did not prevent Pavlova getting out lightly clothed; and if he was dressing, he could only have followed some time later. "This incident had no effect whatever on Pavlova's health." It is an extraordinarily dogmatic statement in the light of events. It is as if he is trying to *convince* himself that it did not do so. Either he is mortified at not having been with her, or he is mortified at having had no power over her behavior. Dandré then goes on to contradict his own remarks, two paragraphs later. In the intervening paragraph he says that Dr. Zalewski was satisfied with the result of the treatment (to Pavlova's left knee) yet Dr. Zalewski, interviewed on the morning of January 23, said that he told Pavlova in Paris that he thought she might be suffering from the onset of influenza.

supported at either elbow, by her maid and her temporary secretary. These two got her into a carriage in the first-class section, where Vladimiroff, morose and unshaven, was already waiting. Pavlova was shivering, and she complained that she had not been able to obtain a hot drink. She retired to her couchette immediately. The dancers who had witnessed this late arrival were agog, and after the formalities of ticket inspection, Kirsanova made her way back through the carriages toward Pavlova's compartment. The stewards in the dining car were gossiping among themselves about the latecomer. "She must be very ill. She was talking without stopping, and sometimes sobbing. And screaming." By the time Kirsanova reached the compartment, she found Marguerite in tears outside the door. Pavlova had been given a sedative and had already fallen asleep.

She did not emerge during the stops in Belgium. There was the usual welcoming group at The Hague, and there Pavlova stepped out from the wagon-lit unaided. She had kind words for the new violinist who was waiting there, but she also told him, "I am sorry about the rehearsal tonight. We will have to postpone it. I am not well." She was scarcely aware of the bouquets that were being thrust at her, and she asked to be helped into her motorcar. As soon as she arrived at the Hotel des Indes, she was put to bed. Her suite was decorated in fashionable lilac; Pavlova's own bedroom at Ivy House had been repainted in a similar shade the year before. That evening she seemed to be in better form, and when Dandré arrived, having come through from Harwich, he found her sitting up in bed and talking with members of the company. She was eager to spend the evening with her card-playing group, and her first words to Dandré were "Just imagine! I must have been poisoned by something I ate in Paris, and the doctor, instead of treating me for that, says I have pleurisy."

Dandré, anxious for a second opinion, called in Dr. de Jong, physician to the Queen. De Jong confirmed pleurisy, and he also drew attention to a weakening of the heart action. For this he advised a little alcohol in some form, but Pavlova had recently developed an aversion to spirits and would not obey this instruction. Dandré tried having rum slipped into her tea, and wine also, but Pavlova detected the additives immediately and declared the mixtures disgusting. Dandré then asked Dr. de Jong to explain to Pavlova how crucial the treatment was, and that even after recovery great care would be needed to prevent a relapse. Pavlova brushed this aside. "But doctor, how can I possibly do all that when I have to start my season tomorrow?" She looked astonished when Dandré told her that was out of the question.

As soon as they were alone, Pavlova asked Dandré to see if Dr. Zalewski would come from Paris. Zalewski was her French physician, and she had actually consulted him while she was in Paris, at which time he had advised her that she might be coming down with influenza. Dandré's telephone call on January 18 came at a difficult time for Dr. Zalewski: another of his patients, the Grand Duke Andrei, was ill in a nursing home. The Grand Duke's wife, none other than Mathilde Kchessinskaya, was concerned at the idea of Zalewski's leaving her husband to go to Holland, and she asked that the departure be delayed. Zalewski

wavered, and in the end he put off his journey for more than forty-eight hours.

By Monday, January 19 (when the tour should have opened), Pavlova was experiencing some difficulty in breathing. She had suffered a troubled night. Marguerite coaxed her with some warm milk, which she sipped from time to time. There was a momentary sign of encouragement when she discussed, quite lucidly, company affairs with Dandré, and tried to insist that the company must not miss performances. But then she became feverish again, which made the attending doctors extremely worried. By Tuesday it was known that Pavlova's opening performance of the tour had been canceled, and the press began spreading the news of her illness, which was described at this stage as influenza.

By Wednesday morning, the hotel switchboard was jammed. In the midst of all this, Dandré displayed his remarkable capacity for making immediate assessments of the company's economic situation at any given moment; he set about trimming the outgoings, and those principal members of the company who were already established at the Hotel des Indes were asked to find cheaper accommodation. That night (Wednesday) found Schiketanz, the conductor; Bagarotti, the new first violinist; and the cellist Edmund Kurtz (brother of Efrem) all sharing one room in a very inferior lodging place. Vladimiroff left for Paris with the object of stirring Dr. Zalewski into action, and also to collect some serums which were not available in The Hague. The two men must have passed each other en route. That day, prior to Zalewski's arrival, there was increasing concern about the condition of Pavlova's left lung. Dr. de Jong discussed the possibility of resecting two ribs, but Pavlova would not hear of such an operation if it would affect her future ability to dance. She would not be saved for a living death, for by now she was obsessed by the fact that she and her company should have been dancing.

Instead of dancing in Utrecht, the company was like a form that had suddenly lost its motivating force. Every thought was centered on the bedroom in the Hotel des Indes. On Wednesday, when Nina Kirsanova arrived, she found Dandré in the outer sitting room of Pavlova's suite, with his hands clasped over his face. He begged her not to show surprise at Pavlova's altered physical appearance. Pavlova held Nina's hand and confided that she thought the end was near, that she would never leave that room alive. "Don't tell Victorushka, but find a Russian Orthodox church and go and pray for me." The distressed girl went off on her mission, and this time she knew she must pray for a miracle.

By the time Dr. Zalewski arrived in the early hours of Thursday morning, the pleurisy had already spread to the right lung. Immediately after his arrival he set about piercing the back to drain the cavity and assist breathing. The doctors had tried compresses, they had tried serums, such as were available, and Zalewski also administered a serum injection that morning. By now oxygen was being administered constantly. The heart was growing steadily weaker.

Dr. Zalewski had arrived at the hotel to discover a sort of bedlam. The foyer was crammed with a constantly shifting

№ 6 (299)
Парижъ, Суббота 31 Января 1931 г.
Цѣна отд. № 3 фр.
во Франціи.

№ 6 (299)
Samedi, 31 Janvier 1931 Paris
Prix du numéro 3 fr.
en France.

LA RUSSIE ILLUSTRÉE

ИЛЛЮСТРИРОВАННАЯ
РОССІЯ

8-я годъ изданія
Редакторъ М. П. Мироновъ
редакція и Гл. Контора
112-ter, rue Cardinet
Paris (17).
Tél.: Carnot 27-37.

8-ème année
Directeur M. MIRONOFF
Rédaction et Administration
112-ter, rue Cardinet
Paris (17).
Tél.: Carnot 27-37.

ПОСЛѢДНІЕ ДНИ
КЪ КОНЧИНѢ АННЫ ПАВЛОВОЙ

Anna
Pavlova

La célèbre danseuse est morte à la Haye dans la nuit du 24 janvier.

ВЪ УБОРКОЙ АРТИСТКИ.
Одинъ изъ послѣднихъ портретовъ знаменитой балерины, безвременно скончавшейся въ Гаагѣ, во время поѣздки по сѣверу.

The cover of *La Russie Illustrée* announcing Pavlova's death. Already the distortion of facts has begun: the caption gives the date of her death as January 24.

throng of people leaving cards and messages; others were vainly offering blood. A Dutch professor and his four daughters had placed themselves at the doctors' disposal, and with two motorcars they drove around the town all day on errands. The hotel was swamped with flowers and besieged by newspaper reporters. Telephones rang incessantly; every three hours there was a call from the Queen of the Netherlands asking for news, and there was a constant delivery of cablegrams from all over the world.

In the lilac-colored bedroom, Pavlova at one moment remembered that there was to be a performance in Brussels on Saturday, the proceeds of which were to benefit a scholarship for needy students. She was adamant that there should be no cancellation. "My company is the work of twenty years. It must outlive me." At six o'clock on the evening of Thursday, January 22, she lost consciousness. Without hope, the doctors worked on. It was near midnight that she must have sensed the imminence of her greatest, most mystical journey, and known that on this too she was irrevocably committed. She suddenly opened her eyes and tried to speak. Marguerite bent near to catch her words, and thought she heard her mistress ask for her Swan costume to be prepared. A little later, there was one more request.

"Play that last measure softly."

There was nothing more. Appalled and resigned, they waited: Marguerite, Dr. Zalewski, and Victor Dandré. The minutes carried the night to the threshold of a new day and beyond. The breathing became imperceptible, and then, at last, her spirit escaped that frail and mortal cage which could no longer keep it from a new and infinitely beckoning shore.

And after Anna Pavlova was released from that life of scarcely controlled madness, what was left? There were headlines around the world: "Idol of Prince and Pauper." Kchessinskaya told a reporter that she had been crying all morning. "It is as if a part of myself were dead. . . . In her, genius was combined with goodness. I don't think that there was ever an artist in need whom she did not help. . . ." And here Kchessinskaya burst into tears again. There were a number of people who felt almost as if their own lives had been terminated. (In Paris a boy declared there was no further reason for life, and then shot himself.) There were impresarios trembling on the brink of unexpected bankruptcy. There were mordant obituaries and a great outpouring of laudations from old colleagues: from Fokine, who was shaken by the loss of his earliest true associate and interpreter; from Mordkin, who was slumped in a haze of self-recriminatory nostalgia; from dancers, who expressed, in varying platitudes, the realization that they owed their careers entirely to a first inspirational sight of Anna Pavlova performing somewhere near their local community. There were also simpler, more immediately touching testimonies from people beyond the world of theatre who felt that something irreplaceable had passed from their lives. There were discussions about memorials, and statues, and commemorative films. There continued a stream of editorial outpourings about the passing of an era. And there remained Victor

The photograph on the cover of this issue of *La Russie Illustrée* was taken prior to the auction of Pavlova's belongings in the summer after her death.

Dandré, totally at a loss without the real motivation of his life, and faced with a desk full of unfulfilled contracts somewhere in a slumbering household that had just lost its cornerstone. A swan still fretted the water at the bottom of the garden, and pigeons still strutted the gables, but the mistress would arrive no more to command their domain.

There was, too, the grisly scramble for the life in perpetuity. Pavlova had left no will, and Dandré—it transpired—knew that he could not prove he was the legal husband of Anna Pavlova. Immediately after the company's charity performance in Brussels (when the spotlight drifted about the empty stage as a visual accompaniment to the lachrymose melody of "The Swan," and the Queen of the Belgians and the rest of the audience stood, blinking through tears), Dandré raced back to London to retrieve what securities he could from the safe at Ivy House, leaving the coffin and the mortal remains of Anna Pavlova to the mercy of others. In Dandré's absence, and in defiance of his instructions, avid harvesters of memorabilia smeared oil and plaster over the wan shell of Pavlova's face, taking one last impression of those haunted and haunting features. At an English quayside, agents and dock hands alike were frozen in the cruel flare from a lurking photographer, as the small, flower-decked coffin swayed down from the crane of a freighter in the chilly hours before dawn on January 27. To the outrage of fashionable Paris, Dandré had decided that London should be the resting place of Anna. Consumed by flames at the Golders Green Crematorium just down the hill from Ivy House: there would be the end of it. And it was an end, of sorts. But in the dank twilight of a winter's afternoon at the foot of Hampstead, where Keats had struggled to snare an image, and Constable to trap the evening light, another image now lurked. This insubstantial shape took wing, surreptitiously at first, but with ever-increasing strength. In the summer of that year, idly curious bargain hunters picked over the sale contents at Ivy House, and paid two shillings and sixpence for a pot of marguerite daisies from the conservatory of the late Madame Anna Pavlova. They were investing in a flower pot, some earth, a fleeting radiance of white bloom, and a name. And it was this last that was to prove incorruptible by time and succeeding fashion. The name became synonymous with the art it had graced. Inevitably, it was used shamelessly; the most fleeting acquaintanceship with Pavlova or her company was sufficient reputation for a school to spring up or a magazine memoir to be purveyed. Shoes continued to be sold on the reputation that Pavlova had worn the make, cosmetics on the basis of a face that hardly knew their touch, beyond the footlights.

As ballet began to increase its range, discovering different tones and resonances, Pavlova's image was sometimes at risk: just as she would herself pare away some of the photographic images of her own forceful and unique insteps and honest dancing shoes into chiseled points of idealism, so the stage imitators lapsed into pretty generalities that harvested something of the outline, but missed the kernel. Pavlova herself had confused the issue. She could flirt with a camera even in her Swan costume, giving the photographer an image that would translate readily onto a page of decorative artificiality. For the printed page the Swan could collapse harmoniously, arms gracefully draped; but under the cold blue spotlight something different happened: the head fell sideways, one arm was caught trailing backward, bereft of strength, while the other crashed open, brushing the extended knee audibly. The result was a stark shape, almost ugly, and audiences were hushed. They could never forget what they saw—because of its truthfulness, not its prettiness.

Onlookers saw in Pavlova porcelain, a reed, a feather—whatever it was she wanted them to see. She did not approach her roles with detailed psychological analyses (nor was she particularly equipped to do so), but instead she absorbed natural influences like a photographic plate, locked these impressions into her very being, and then yielded them on stage—developed, as it were, by the intensity of her own mental application. However many hundreds of times she danced a piece, she drew on the same touchstones; it seemed to be a genuinely spiritual process, employing a mental application that reached for some inner state. She knew when she had reached it, and she also knew when she had not. On those occasions she employed more will power and more basic stagecraft, of which the Maryinsky had given her an abundance. But over and above that amazingly rich and detailed schooling, there was the apparent self-hypnosis and the projecting of herself into an arena, before bodily she arrived in that space. Perhaps it was her special gift: merely to believe, with more strength and more passion than those around her, that what she was doing was the right thing for that time and that place. We cannot imagine Pavlova going on stage and saying to herself, "I will do it this way, or that." She went on stage. And she was.

From what we can infer from countless reports, Pavlova "possessed" her audiences by communicating with them openly. She risked their knowing everything she felt; there was no screen, no final refuge where some part of her lurked as an observer. Total honesty is the most difficult bridge to cross, and Anna Pavlova attempted to cross it publicly almost every day of her adult life. And she went on defying the chasm, because to step back, even momentarily, was to admit defeat. Artistry meant, for her, expressing feelings in the most open manner she could contrive. Her effect was therefore immediate and startling, beyond the framework of the viewer's normal daily experience. In Norway a little girl said, after seeing Pavlova for the first time, "It is like dreaming something that will never happen." And wherever people saw Pavlova, whether they understood the finer points of the vocabulary of ballet dancing or not, they were in no doubt about the excellence of what they were seeing, or about the truth of the expression. When she was young, and leaving St. Petersburg on one of the first of her ever-lengthening voyages, she had said good-bye to Bezobrazov with the words "The best be with you." He had shaken his head sadly and replied, "When you are taking away the best we have known?"

But she was not really taking anything away; nobody forgot what they had seen. Only she felt compelled to give elsewhere, so that more and more people would understand that dancing could be a gift as well as a creed.

REVIEWS: VIENNA 1909

Illustriertes Wiener Extrablatt May 28, 1909

An intriguing advance notice that promised a great deal gave word of the matter of the Imperial Russian Ballet of the Maryinsky Theatre in St. Petersburg. The Tsar's dancers, both male and female, are traveling through cities that are artistic centers to show the world that in Russia, besides hardworking courts-martial, zealous *agents provocateurs,* and skillful *régisseurs* of pogroms, there are also harmless people who can make use of their legs. In Berlin and Prague this ensemble was a smashing success. Yesterday it was seen for the first time in *Giselle,* a frightfully fantastic ballet by Adam that was new in the forties and even dragged along into the new opera house, although neither the public nor the critics liked it. Adam's music is like the day before yesterday's soup, dispensed in driblets. Besides, anybody who didn't have the disentangling program at hand was in no position, yesterday, to make sense of what was happening on the stage. Danced conflicts are by nature too funny for words; danced insanity is annoying; and danced jealously is cause for extreme embarrassment. I have nothing against ballerinas dying like everyone else, but it is showing them especially kind attention to bury them as they lived: in tulle and gauze. For example, the ballerina Giselle rises from her own grave after midnight—the scene is set in a sort of central graveyard for coryphées—and is so delighted to see her young man again that right away she sneaks behind him and devoutly raises one leg in the air to express her profound feelings for the beloved. The business is more simple-minded than anyone could possibly have expected, but to the Tsar's Ballet it seems important enough to be mimed like a real tragedy. Miss Anna Pavlova, the Tsar's prima ballerina, had an occasion, in the role of Giselle, to make convincing display of her great talent as a mimic artist, her grace and nimbleness, and, finally, all the bravura of the coloratura of her pointes. Unfortunately, she is neither beautiful nor does she have an especially good figure; she is thin, like the majority of her female colleagues. That does not interfere with her artistry, but it does prevent enthusiasm from becoming too audible. Ladies of the ballet must be very, very pretty if one is to believe in them. With melancholy and gratitude I thought back to the unforgettable legs that march out when our Hofoper ballet takes the field, to the blooming faces and pleasing figures that make belief in life so precious. A Tolstoyan spirit hovers over this gala ballet. Danced abstinence was expressed by Pavlova's feet and shoulders. I liked her better later in the part of a Spanish woman [in the *Raymonda* Panaderos]; then, at least, two black eyes shone with looks that must surely have been keys to the inner being of this interesting and gifted person. Besides Pavlova a Mr. Shirayev had the greatest success with his sailor's hornpipe. He manages his feet with such disdainful virtuosity that one would think they didn't

belong to him, and he even had to repeat the sailor's *pas.* The Hofoper became a *variété.* Naturally, it was sold out. The audience was entertained, with raised prices and reduced legs....

Neues Wiener Tagblatt, May 28, 1909

A small contingent of the Imperial Russian Ballet from the Maryinsky Theatre in St. Petersburg put on a guest performance in the Kroll Summer Theatre in Berlin in the last two weeks and aroused such enthusiasm in the German Imperial capital that even Director Weingartner felt called upon to take notice of the Russian artists and to invite them to Vienna to put on a two-day guest performance. Among us the mood was not so enthusiastic; they received a friendly reception, but nothing more than that. Their success in Berlin must be principally due to the fact that people there have finally had enough of the barefoot female dancers who have been appearing there like an epidemic, and perhaps also to the fact that the ballet of the Royal Hofoper is no longer at the same level of excellence as at the time of old Kaiser Wilhelm. In our court theatre the situation is different; our corps de ballet offers real perfection, and thus it is understandable that the Russian guests were a disappointment. To be sure, they are all remarkably well trained; they dance with great precision and finesse, but there was nothing special to be found in their artistry. Also there are too few of them—about ten ladies and the same number of gentlemen—to hold attention for more than a short time. Their prima ballerina, Anna Pavlova, does achieve outstanding things. A thoroughbred head with a fine profile sits above her slender figure; her movements are full of grace and yet at the same time energetic; her pirouettes show virtuosity and her gestures have a plastic quality that is quite compelling. The fantastic ballet *Giselle* has not improved since it was last performed in Vienna in 1883. Who still remembers *The Wilis? Giselle* was known by this title as early as the occasion of its premiere, which despite the brilliance of Adele Granzow was followed by only four repeat performances. It will not be long before *Giselle* is seventy years old. It is noticeable. The music is pretty in places but, considered as a whole, already antiquated and not exactly entertaining. The plot of this ballet has even less appeal; it leaves nothing to be desired in the way of nonsense. In Slavic saga the Wilis are brides who died before the wedding and find no rest in the grave; they dance in the moonlight at midnight and lure youths to their deaths. Giselle is a bride of this kind; Duke Albrecht is her victim. The final scene takes place in a graveyard. The Wilis encircle the duke in a mad whirlpool and he starts dancing his head off, but in the end he escapes death and gives his hand in marriage to a princess of his own rank. Mr. Nicolas Legat, who dances the role of the duke, is an excellent dancer who deserves at the very least to be ranked with the best toe-dancing artists of his sex. Mr. Legat doubles as ballet master, as does his colleague Alexander Shirayev, who stole the loudest applause of the evening by performing a *variété* number of which anyone ought to be ashamed. In general, the individual dances that followed *Giselle* were much better liked than the old Adam ballet. There was more life and emotion in these dances. The prima ballerina, Pavlova, and along with her the ladies called Legerova and Vil, received a great deal of applause. . . . We now think that all there is to be said has been said.

Neues Wiener Tageblatt, May 29, 1909

Tonight and last night the divertissements that were pieced together from separate dances were much more effective than the independent dance-dramas. And, once again, it was Mr. Shirayev who, with a grotesque number that he had to repeat, was given the most applause. Tchaikovsky's three-act ballet *Swan Lake* is not quite as boring as *Giselle*, but it is more brutal, and in places very vulgar, the subject being more impoverished than that of *Giselle*. Virgins are transformed into swans; they only reassume human form through the love of a youth. That's all there is to it. Tchaikovsky's music exhibits some fine twists and orchestral delicacy, such as, for example, the charming chatter of the woodwinds at the close of the first act, but apart from that it has very little appeal. A pretty waltz in the first act and a fiery mazurka in the last—that is just about all that deserves special mention. Apart from that the hand of the Russian composer, who, for his own part, probably reckoned *Swan Lake* among his weakest creations, is hardly apparent anywhere. If we didn't know Tchaikovsky from other significant works, after yesterday's rehearsal we might have had doubts about his being gifted at all. At one time there was a lot of talk about his ballet *Sleeping Beauty*. Mahler toyed with the idea of presenting it, but this never came about, because the scenery would have cost an enormous amount of money. *Swan Lake* left our belief in the creator of *Sleeping Beauty* greatly shaken. It does not appear that Tchaikovsky's ballets are of sterling quality. Miss Anna Pavlova proved herself yesterday, as customarily, to be an extraordinary artist of fine sensibilities to whom one may tip one's hat in admiration. But the other ladies are not above average. In our corps de ballet there are female soloists who dance incomparably better and who, in addition, are smartly dressed and lovely Viennese lasses. That is also the reason that—with the exception of Pavlova—people weren't persuaded to see the presentations of the Russian guests as a revelation, but instead merely accorded them the polite applause that is always given, here, to foreign artists, if they are only more or less acceptable. Critics, too, have the duty to be polite, but also the much sterner duty not to praise everything to the skies, just because it comes from abroad. Whoever approaches the, after all, respectable achievements of our Russian guests as a connoisseur of ballet as it exists here must in all truthfulness acknowledge that the former artists could learn a good deal from our people if they were to attend a ballet performance in our Hofoper. Only in one point are the Russians ahead of our people— our love of truth demands that we say this as well—they are more precise in their attack, bolder, always in the service of the rhythm. That is also the secret of their effectiveness.

Illustriertes Wiener Extrablatt, May 29, 1909

Last night the Russians danced *Swan Lake*, a fantastic ballet in three acts by Tchaikovsky. The work is new to Vienna but has made an impression here and there on German stages. The plot is that of the fairy tale. A prince celebrates his birthday and, therefore, is supposed to marry. In other words, his mother informs him by all sorts of comprehensible signs that on the following day at the court ball he is to select his future wife. At this perilous and unpleasant moment swans fly past, and this gives the prince the more pleasant idea of going hunting. But, naturally, these swans are enchanted swans. As soon as a hunter shows them attention, they are transformed into young girls and so lose their peaceful, gliding harmlessness. An evil spirit has enchanted Princess Odette and her playmates in this amusing way and, at the same time, set the condition that the young lady can only be saved if a youth finds the courage and frivolity to swear her eternal fidelity. The prince—princes *are* that way— the prince, then, makes the vow, but in the third act the evil spirit comes to the feast and brings along a girl who looks like the beloved Odette. The prince is taken in, breaks faith, and plunges the poor betrayed creature into misfortune. Tchaikovsky had a natural predisposition to the daemonic. He loved doom, the fearful aspect of every figure, in the dance as well as elsewhere. And this trait of his character may have led him to set this paltry fairy tale to music, without otherwise having recourse to the traditional ballet form. Tchaikovsky's music develops thematically, here as elsewhere, and remains in keeping with the basic coloring of the drama. The dances are by no means written with legs in mind but rather give occasion to pantomimic art, tend toward high points, and leave space for a great lyrical moment of which the violin soloist bears the burden in the pit and the female dance soloist on the stage. The solo on the stage came out much better last night than the one in the pit. Miss Pavlova danced love and longing with a truly convincing bearing. Her dancing is without the usual pauses. Her body is in restless motion; the way in which she manages transitions is distinctive of her mastery. A single flowing line accompanies the arch of the cantilena. With regard to Pavlova it is possible to speak of an art of dissolving the inner being of the melody into movement. Besides the lyrical passages already mentioned, there are also coarse and Eastern elements in Tchaikovsky's score. The great waltz comes from the same region as *Der Freischütz;* when the procession of swans goes by, Lohengrin's injunction against questions rushes past, probably unintentionally, and it returns in the third act, magnified into Fate in its full brassy radiance. There is a certain amount of Tchaikovskian charm in the sound. The dances come and go with the gestures of melancholy self-evidence. Miss Pavlova and her female ballet colleagues once again danced their way to thunderous applause. The applause was actually warmer and more genuine than it had been on the day before, but, again, it was without the enthusiasm that has been conspicuous elsewhere. The reason for this must certainly be that the ladies from St. Petersburg are not pretty. The senses have no part in the admiration their art inspires. The senses fast, while art appreciation regales itself.

Neue Freie Presse, May 29, 1909

THE BALLET OF THE TSAR by Paul Ziffere.

When we think of Russian dancing, we see before us a host of young fellows and girls in long bright-red silk jackets, wide blue velvet trousers, and high boots made of the softest leather falling into folds around the ankles. Some of them crouch on the ground, arms crossed across the chest, madly kicking up their legs before them and stamping out the rhythm of the dance with their heels. Others shrink into themselves, forming a tight little ball before springing into the air and spinning round their own axes with the speed of lightning. In addition there is the hollow clang of tambourines, a solemn chant interspersed with loud, ringing shrieks, a breathless run followed by jumping, leaping, and stamping, a violent motion of the arms, and a frenzied shriek, often resembling a fearful, despairing wail. So, we used to think, the Russians must dance, with such a superfluity of energy, as if this dance constituted a secret revolution, as if in the guttural sounds the suffering in the kingdom of the Tsars was being expressed, as if these sturdy feet wished to trample on a whole social order and stamp it into the ground with their clumping heels.

And now, all at once, we learn that there is another dance, which by order of the Tsar is taught in the Imperial Russian Ballet School. The heart of this school consists of a charming, small theatre with an elegant stage, where once a year the pupils try out their skills. Alexander III never failed to attend these performances. After the Grand Finale there was always a ceremonial dinner at which the Imperial family sat down together with the young girls, who in a gracefully studied manner picked up their knives and forks as specially taught for this occasion. The Grand Duke Vladimir made a speech and Maria Feodorovna, the Tsarina, distributed presents. It was all very festive. Then came the long joy ride in swinging Court carriages. Stately retainers gravely opened the door. "Will the gracious young lady be pleased to descend?" Anna Pavlova, the dancer, describes it all. Two black waves frame the small, Slavic forehead, a pale face with small glowing eyes (which she closes while speaking, leaving visible only two narrow slits), and thin determined lips, firmly pressed together.

The artist's parents were simple folk, and for them to take the young Anna Pavlova to the theatre was an exceptional event. There was a performance of the ballet, and when Anna Pavlova returned home she stood before the mirror on tiptoe, curved her arms, and tripped here and there as she had seen them do in the theatre. She decided to be a dancer. Her mother wrung her hands, but Anna Pavlova had once and for all made up her mind to dance on the stage in a dress of white tulle. And as she now, lost in her memories, defiantly throws back her head, one can understand how her will carried her through the hard years of training until finally, there in Krasnoye Selo, she would dance before the officers of the Imperial regiments and before the Tsar himself after his grand review of the troops, no longer as a shy and timid young girl, but as a mature and acclaimed artist. And while Anna Pavlova talks, she stretches her body to its full height as if she wishes to say: "This is a princess speaking to you." But her long, slim fingers are never for a moment still. They bend and stretch, flicker upward as if about to take a running leap, fall, stroke the air, twist, and, nimbly lifting their tips, flutter to and fro. As one watches them the whole dazzling performance takes shape before one's eyes. The march past of the regiments, the imposing officers, and the entire tripping, leaping, swaying ballet of the Tsar, whose prima ballerina is Anna Pavlovna Pavlova.

The Imperial ballet has been on tour for two nights at the Vienna Imperial Opera House. As if in some fantastic poem they whirl past us, fabulous, strange. The world of the dance is still fairyland. There are the Wilis, deserted girls who can find no rest in their graves and who at night, among the silver-grey mists, float here and there, luring young men to dance until they fall dead to the ground. There are the swan fairies, enchanted princesses who may only secretly assume human form under cover of darkness. Enchanted princesses seeking their deliverance in love. Two water sprites dwelling in the deep lakes of the Tsar's realm. At Whitsuntide the boys and girls wander about in the open air, throw colorful crowns of flowers onto the dark waters, dance, and sing, with the sole purpose of propitiating the evil spirits. The dancing here is entirely natural and unaffected, a different type of dancing, resembling the rhythmic hoofbeats of young foals racing across the steppes.

Anna Pavlova comes on stage. Just one step and it is already a dance. It seems as if with this step she is gently, caressingly stroking the earth. One is aware of a long, drawn-out ripple coursing through her supple body, right to her fingertips. Now she gestures with her hand, a tremor runs along her arm, ripples down her body through her hips, quivers in the foot, which she raises effortlessly high in the air. At first the dance is playful, jesting. It has no significance; it is but an aimless reverie. The young maidens perform circular dances, chase after one another. Suddenly they stand still and listen, bend their bodies forward, longingly stretch out their arms. But still their longing has no purpose. It is all charming inquisitiveness, delightful expectation. But now the beloved draws near. Now it is a well-dressed count, another time a prince. Sometimes it is the peasant girl Giselle, sometimes the enchanted Odette who waits for the count or the prince to deliver her. All this builds up into a delightfully surprising contrast as suddenly the dance of Giselle or Odette becomes meaningful, timidly adoring, passionate. Love lends wings to the feet of the dancer; they hardly touch the ground. Now she springs aloft, and her upstretched arms seem to say, "It is your love that makes me free, that bears me up." Her dance is a battle between the enslaving earth on which our feeble steps falter and the winged spirit floating in the free air. The dancer, in fact, becomes a special kind of creature, who seeks her home between the realms of earth and air. Every time her foot touches the ground she is a poor pining damsel, who, no sooner has she soared above it, becomes a creature of legend. But neither the peasant girl nor the fairy represents her true nature. Her essential being is a spirit perpetually swaying, swinging, balancing, bounding, flying, floating. Her essential being is the dance. All at once she stretches her body to its full extent, spreads her arms wide, the head thrown back defiantly, the eyes half-closed. Slowly she glides on her pointes, almost in slow motion, like some sumptuous flower, white and rose-red drifting along on a spring breeze. On her lips there hovers a sublime smile, which seems triumphantly to announce: "Do you now understand that I am an enchanted princess?"

So far we can follow her. We always knew in our hearts that love was a charming pas de deux. We knew that gaiety and dancing were closely connected, we knew that the thrill of an overflowing happiness caused the feet to whirl, drumming to the dance of laughter. But the dance of tears? Anna Pavlova dances pain, dances despair, dances death. Her hair flows down over her shoulders, curls like black adders round her throat, which is choked by a suppressed sob. Her steps become weak, unsteady. All her movements, following one on another so swiftly we can scarcely follow them, now falter, the rhythm broken. It is the same dance as before, only languid, disjointed, as if dragging its clipped wings. Giselle has snatched the sword from the lover whom she thought she had lost, holds it in her limp hand, lets it clang upon the floor. Her hard, exhausted face is full of grief, her form bowed down, the eyes somber. She has become again a small, helpless maiden. Already we are persuaded that the dancer is lost in Anna Pavlova the tragedienne. But all at once she recovers herself. A great harmonious wave, no longer of joy but of anguish, wells up through her body, only more solemnly, more majestically than ever. She dances, and her frivolous white tulle dress with its careless, swinging gaiety expresses far more clearly the contrast to her pain than her sobs did previously.

Then comes death, an extraordinary doll's death. Her face assumes an amazed and solemn expression. On her cheeks burn two large red spots. The arms dangle, the body becomes stiff and rigid. Suddenly she sinks to the ground, not as if thrown down, but as if someone had let her fall. One is appalled, but not by the cold shiver of death which passes by. It is rather as if some marvelous clockwork mechanism has ceased to strike, as if some old and precious Sèvres figurine were suddenly smashed.

An entirely marvelous art is the dancing of Anna Pavlova. A magic art, awakening out of a long sleep, rubbing its eyes and appearing before us in a white tulle dress like a short crinoline. When we see Pavlova dance we have the impression of leafing through some old etchings enclosed in a modern binding. The stylized eighteenth-century background is missing, the background to its garden fêtes, the setting of luxurious foliage forming arrow-straight walls, the flower-covered terraces of a palace on which Fragonard set his convivial scenes, the shaded landscapes of Watteau's pastoral romances, the shadows of the acacias under which Lancret let Camargo dance.

Pavlova's art is derived directly from Camargo, who was the first to achieve the extremely complicated "entrechat quatre," from Guimard, whose little theatre in the Chaussée d'Antin was celebrated above all others for its extravagant ballets, and from the slender Sallé, who herself was an apt pupil of Camargo. The classic art of the French style of dance lives again with Pavlova: pointe work, coupés, fleurets, contre-temps, pirouettes, and tournées. The Imperial ballet has also taken a great deal from the old Italians. One has the impression of seeing Magri, who could capriole sixteen times "sotto il corpo," and Gafarini, who in the capriole made three turns, which he called "salto tondo sotto il corpo," and Pitrot, who, as Oscar Bie relates, after a pirouette lasting two minutes with battements and tordichamps [sic] was able suddenly to stand absolutely motionless—acrobatic virtuousity. However great Pavlova's talent, one cannot help feeling that the technique of this art, the pure athleticism, plays the most important part. We allow ourselves to be stunned by the coloratura of her agile footwork, the trilling of her nimble little fingers, and when she pauses, often in the middle of a spin, one has the impression of a singer who holds a high note. It is an art adorned with a thousand scrolls and flourishes, the rococo of dancing. Where are the poised marquises, the dancing masters in white knee breeches, the charming pastoral scenes, where the thin and diffident little voice of the clavier? Is it really true then, does it live again or is it buried forever, that century of gallantry and the dance?

Once again the curtain rises. A divertissement. A filler-in, as if the ballet were far too serious, as if we required amusement and distraction. What a dismal creature man must be, to wish for dancing of even a lighter and more aimless nature. But now—what is going on all of a sudden? Trampling, whirling, the wildest stamping, dancers coiled like springs shooting upward with lightning speed. What has this clamorous performance to do with the Imperial ballet? And all at once the whole contradiction between the delicate, quiet, stylized art, summoned from France by Catherine the Great, and the brutal truth, crashing and banging, storms through the door. Two worlds here are brought face to face, as if between them there exists a dangerous hostility, like the hostility that once plunged France into the abyss. At the court people were still beating their brains out trying to decide whether the entrechat should end in the open, Italian style or in the closed, French manner, while outside in the streets they were already dancing the carmagnole. For the dance is more than an art form. It is the true mirror of an epoch, it is the alluring prospectus of a way of life, it is a *Weltanschauung*.

New York Times, March 6, 1910

"I was born in St. Petersburg—on a rainy day. You know, it almost always rains in St. Petersburg. There is a certain gloom and sadness in the atmosphere of the Russian capital, and I have breathed the air of St. Petersburg so long that I have become infected with sadness. I love the note of sadness in everything: in art, in the drama, in nature. Ah—in nature above all! I love the dreamy Russian forests, and the dream-inspiring English parks."

Anna Pavlowa, the Russian dancer who has created such a genuine sensation in New York—a slim, dark-eyed, dark-haired young woman—was seated in a rocking chair in her room at the Knickerbocker Hotel, eating candy, resting after her matinee performance, and talking as rapidly as she can dance.

"I feel much better now than on the day of my arrival in New York," she remarked.

"Do you think that your success in New York has something to do with the improvement in your health?"

"Oh no. This success cannot affect me. We have been spoiled by success everywhere, in Russia, in Germany, in France, and in England. But I feel happy, nevertheless, that our art is appreciated in this country. You see, in Europe we make a specialty of the ballet, while here I understand it is merely incidental. In Russia particularly, the ballet is a branch of art to which much attention is paid. There are theatre schools there which are supported by the government, and dancing is one of the favorite amusements of the Czar."

"Have you ever seen the Czar?"

"Have I ever seen the Czar?" repeated Mlle. Pavlova, her dark eyes half smiling, half surprised. "Why, he stroked my hair when I was a pupil—he praised me. He used to come to our school and talk to us and tell jokes and eat dinner with us—the same things we used to eat.

"I remember the performance the children gave in his honor. The ballet in Russia is a Court luxury. The masses do not pay for it there, and the immense deficit of the ballet and the opera amounts to almost four million roubles [$2 million in 1910]. In Russia we have numerous new ballets every year—about twenty different ballets. We have an enormous repertoire as compared with the ballet in France or Germany. . . .

"Yes, I believe we are on the eve of a decided revival. Until recently the ballet made no progress. In fact, it lagged behind every other form of art. While the drama and the opera kept developing new forms, the ballet created nothing. It remained on one plane. And dancing ought to make a wider appeal than the drama or the opera. In the drama, as well as the opera, there must be national characteristics, distinctions and peculiarities, while dancing is more readily understood by all.

"I have now been ten years on the stage, and I am still seeking new forms: I am working now harder than ever before. I am studying every day. I believe that the greater the artist, the more he must study, it matters not whether he or she is a painter, a writer, a musician, or a dancer. In Russia my day is crowded with work. I rise early, at nine or ten o'clock in the morning. I go out for a little walk and then go to the theatre to rehearse. Sometimes I am so busy rehearsing that I take breakfast along with me. I eat it quickly in the theatre and I rehearse until four o'clock in the afternoon. Then I go home. I glance over the newspapers and read a few pages of my favorite poet or my favorite novelist."

"Who is your favorite poet?"

"Nadson."

"And your favorite novelist?"

"Turgenev, of course."

"And of the contemporary writers?"

"I like Andreyev. But I prefer to see his dramas on the stage. When I read them in book form they make a terrible impression upon me. On the stage it is different. The characters become human and I can understand them better. I had this experience with Andreyev's *Anathema*. By the way, have you heard that the Holy Synod has forbidden the production of *Anathema* in Russia? It is strange, isn't it? The censor has approved it, the play has been given hundreds of times all over Russia, and suddenly the Synod has stopped it. Does this mean this play must not be produced here either?" she asked naively.

"Do you think that the Russian laws prevail in this country too?"

"Don't they?"

"You were telling me how you pass the day in Russia. I interrupted you."

"From five till six in the afternoon I receive. There are many artists, painters, sculptors, among my friends. But I devote only one hour to them. In the evening I sometimes have additional rehearsals. When I do not perform and have no rehearsals in the evening, I go to the theatre. I prefer the drama—the heart-stirring drama. Occasionally I go to a good concert. When some celebrated artist visits St. Petersburg, such as Nikisch, for instance, I always go to hear him, and that is a real holiday for me. I love music and I enjoy animals. I have a fine English bulldog at home. Well, what else can I say? That is all, that is my life. . . ."

"Are you interested in any of the sports?"

"I need no sports of any kind. Occasionally I go horseback riding, but that isn't very good for me. I must keep my body in a certain position for a long time when I am on horseback, and this interferes with my art. You see, I do not need any of the sports because my art combines them all. Some people use the bicycle, others play baseball or football, some people run, others take long walks, but I do not need any of these things to develop my muscles. My work, my art, is developing every muscle of my body better than any of these exercises.

"There is but one thing I love passionately, outside of my art, and that is nature. The cold, dreamy forests appeal to me, to my imagination. Tropical plants do not interest me so much. You cannot dream under palm trees. I like the melancholy note in nature, there seems to be so much poetry in it, and I forget myself, and I dream. Poetry, dreams—after all these are the only things worthwhile in life."

"Is it true that Stanislavsky, the head of the Artistic Theatre of Moscow, has made arrangements with Miss Duncan to have her instruct the new school of plastic art which he has established?" I asked.

"Stanislavsky is a great artist, and his theatre has done wonders. But Stanislavsky is not content with what he has already accomplished, and he is searching after new forms. He thinks highly of Miss Duncan's work; he respects her and is enthusiastic over her, and he wants her assistance in his experiments and efforts to perfect dramatic art. I believe that he is working in the right direction. The plastic element has been neglected in dramatic productions. I believe in progress, in going forward, forward. I believe that the ballet, for instance, should not adhere to the classical pieces only. I like to see the ballet reformed just as opera has been reformed by Wagner, who introduced live drama, live art into music."

Mlle. Pavlova helped herself to some more candy and rapidly changed the conversation, and began to speak of New York.

"I haven't seen anything here as yet. I haven't had time. You know, life here seems to be rushing at a maddening pace. It is like a crazy wheel, revolving with lightning-like rapidity. I am afraid that it would be hard for me to keep pace with it. By the way, a young woman asked me about marriage. She wanted to know whether it was true that I haven't married because I have not had the time for it. In America that must seem strange, for here I understand—one, two, three [snapping her fingers]—and you are married. There is no time to waste. And then—one, two, three—and you are divorced. In Russia such an event in a person's life is considered slowly and carefully, the couple must know each other for a long time; they must find out whether their characters are suited for each other; they reflect; they deliberate; they go through the poetic period of wooing; and then they marry. In Russia such a step is indeed an event, and it really takes up much time. Besides, I believe that artists who are really devoted to their art should not think of marriage."

Musical America March 5, 1910

RUSSIA'S POETESS OF ART IN MOTION

Anna Pavlova's Repertoire a Pandora's Box of the Terpsichorean Wiles of All Ages and Countries and When She Opens It Something Really New in Dancing Is Likely to Emerge

If New Yorkers fondly imagine that they have been regaled with every imaginable terpsichorean confection during the last two years they will during the next two months enjoy ample opportunity to ponder upon the futility of established beliefs—at least they will do all this if Anna Pavlova and the Metropolitan Opera Company's prospectus are to be trusted. To be sure, Isadora Duncan, Maud Allan and a few other apostles of the poetry of motion have of late days done wild and wonderful things, even to the extent of demonstrating that symphonies and funeral marches are danceable. But they only did it in the way the ancient Greeks would have done had they been blessed with a Beethoven or a Chopin. By the grace of the Metropolitan management and the help of a whole company of dancing Russians, Miss—or rather, Mademoiselle—Pavlova, of St. Petersburg, will show that things equally wonderful can be done after the fashion of the Russians, the French, the Bohemians, the Scandinavians, the Italians, the Spaniards, the Orientals, and, as a matter of course, the ancient Greeks and Romans.

Mlle. Pavlova—or Pavlow, Pavlouva, Pavlov, take your choice—comes to this country with the heartiest endorsement of Paris, where they know good dancing when they see it. When you meet her you do not need to know beforehand that she is a dancer, however, for the multitudinous serpentine motions and sinuous gestures with which she emphasizes her conversation would quickly apprise any one of the fact. Seated in her charming apartments at the Hotel Knickerbocker on the day after her arrival in America, she confided to a representative of *Musical America* with an alacrity that was most startling that she was over twenty-one years of age—yes, and more than that, that she was twenty-seven. She said it without hesitation, without having been asked, and with two lithe, upward flourishes of her graceful arms. On being told that she did not look it she replied that she did.

"Yes, I am twenty-seven,*" she repeated, thoughtfully, in a slightly Russianized French that was charming, "and I have been on the stage for ten years, dancing, always dancing. How did I take it into my head to become a professional dancer? Why, I don't know; I just seem to have been born to it. My parents, I know, were not inclined that way. Once,

---

* She was in fact twenty-nine.

while I was still very, very little, they took me to see a ballet performance in St. Petersburg. Well, when I came home from the theater I simply started to imitate what I had seen, and my future was decided. Did I enjoy it? Ah! *je crois bien!*

"Then I was sent to a training school—we have large and splendidly equipped schools for dancers in my country. But it was hard work, I can assure you. I had to study and practice for eight years before even starting, and to this day I have to keep at it like an athlete in training. There are a thousand and one things you must keep thinking of in dancing. The slightest motion, the least gesture must have its purpose and its meaning. You must manage your breath with more care than a singer. You must be paying attention to the position of your toes, to the motion of your arms, to the expression on your face. And all that is only a little of it. There are rehearsals and rehearsals, and still more rehearsals. And when there are no more rehearsals, there are the performances. Yes, it means work, and a good deal of it."

Mlle. Pavlova's one regret is the fact that she may not have the opportunity to show the American public how much she can do as the result of so much work.

"I think we shall be able to give some of the native Russian dances and some of the Italian and Spanish ones. I also hope to be able to do some of my ancient Greek ones. But you do not seem anxious for novelties of this kind in this country. There we are set down for *Coppélia* at our first appearance. *Coppélia!*—a thing that everybody has seen a thousand times! Of course, when you have to crowd it into forty short minutes after an opera you can't be expected to do very much. Why, look! In Europe there are ballets given that occupy an entire evening—ballets in four or five acts, just like a play or opera. In Russia we have special theaters built for them. You haven't acquired a taste for these yet, have you?"

Mlle. Pavlova seemed delighted when told of how the country had suddenly become infatuated with the Isadora Duncan dances. It confirmed her opinions that the Americans would appreciate something more than the ballet of Italian opera if some one only had the sense to break the ice.

"Ha! It is well!" she exclaimed. "But we must not stop at that. There are many other charming things besides the dances of the ancients. Frankly, I must tell you that, though I am a great admirer of that splendid artist, Isadora Duncan, her methods eventually begin to lack variety. Besides, I don't believe in dancing all of the music that she does. A Beethoven symphony is too big for such treatment. You may feel the emotions which it inspires yourself, but you don't succeed in properly conveying them to your audience. There is much music in which you will thus be handicapped in this way. It is simply too overwhelming, too grandiose to be expressed in this fashion. And if the composition is very long the repetition of the same type of gestures is bound to become somewhat tiring. I enjoy dancing Chopin, though, and I have often done the waltzes and the mazurkas. Taken altogether, I think that my work is harder than that of Isadora Duncan. You see, she never has to get up and dance on her toes, and I do."

"And Maud Allan—what do you think of her?" the dancer was asked.

"She is very highly thought of abroad, and I find much to admire in her art. One of the finest things she does is the *Hall of the Mountain King*, by Grieg. But do I like her as well as Isadora? No, I don't. She is not quite so graceful, and you can always feel that she doesn't put much of this into her work"—here Mlle. Pavlova placed her hand on her heart. "But still, she is very talented."

"What do you think of her *Salomé* dance?"

At this Mlle. Pavlova made a comically wry face, and whispered,

"No." There were to be no discussions of that sort for her.

"Have you appeared anywhere in Europe outside of Russia and Paris?"

"Yes, indeed," she answered with vivacity. "We danced before some of the nobility in England—*oh! c'était charmant!* The King and Queen were there. The King was very nice. Do you know, he complimented all of us, and said some very pleasant things to me. We were told to return soon again, and I hope we shall. In Paris, as you have already heard, we had much success all through the summer."

Asked the names of some of the dances which she and her associates might present in this city, she quickly reeled off a list of names and descriptions sufficient to stagger the memory. Folk dances, operatic dances, interpretative dances of all ages and countries seem to be at her command. If they are all she claims them to be there are some big surprises in store for the jaded theater and opera goers of this city. They promise to be something new under the sun.

"I don't know of anything more I can tell you now," she suddenly exclaimed, with some renewed circular motions of her left arm. "Come to the Metropolitan, and I hope you will enjoy yourself. You can judge better with scenery and costumes than you can from any further descriptions I could give you. Just now I am dreadfully upset. None of my trunks have come from the custom house as yet. *C'est embêtant!* An awful nuisance!"

Good Housekeeping, 1913

The ceaseless pursuit of grace is the dancer's mission. Whether it be in the gentle swaying of a lily in the wind, in, the swift flight of a swallow, or the sinuous stateliness of the swan, it must be captured, studied, reproduced. Pavlova maintains a flock of swans on her English estate. and it was from them that she derived the inspiration for one of her prettiest dances, "The Death of the Swan"

The Russian Ballet
By Anna Pavlova

SO much has been said, written, and imagined about the "historic Russian ballet" that it may come as something of a shock to most people to learn that originally it was not Russian at all. It began as German, French, and Italian by turns. We Russians did not succeed in developing any really great dancers until nearly two hundred years after the ballet's inception. Then our remarkable advance to superiority was brought about largely by the Imperial School of the Ballet, generally known as the Mariensky Institute. This school is much like

any other well-conducted school, except that it is more strict than the average. It is by no means devoted to ballet-dancing alone, although this, of course, is its main object. Every pupil who is lucky and diligent enough to complete the course receives a thorough and liberal education, quite aside from the dancing.

As is well known, the school is supported entirely at imperial expense, tuition being free for those who succeed in passing the rigid examinations. Then after the pupils have graduated into the Royal Ballet, they are paid liberal salaries, and later pensioned for life.

457

Fanny Elssler, one of the ballet's greatest glories during the thirties and forties. While in this country Mlle. Elssler danced to raise funds for the Bunker Hill Monument

The school is under the supervision of the director of fine arts, who is appointed by the Czar himself. As a rule, children are not admitted to the school before the age of ten, although some exceptions have been made. The full course, though it may be completed in six years' time, more often requires about double that period.

The real beginning of the Russian ballet came in 1670 under the Czar Alexei Michailowitsch, a deeply religious man who had heard that in other countries dancing had been found most conducive to piety. He therefore commanded one of the gentlemen of his court to collect a troupe of artists and arrange for a specimen performance. It is said that the gentleman experienced much difficulty in getting his company together; for it was generally supposed that the performers would be doomed to Siberian exile in the event of an unsuccessful exhibition. In fact, the persuasive powers of a monk, Johann Gregori, were required to carry out the undertaking. Gregori, however, proved equal to the task, and thus he became the real founder of the Russian Court Theatre.

The success of the latter was instantaneous. The lords and ladies of the court at once began to imitate the dancers, much as the country children who have seen a circus go straight to the barn and try to execute the tricks themselves. As a result of this remarkable success—for even the good Alexei was pleased—a national dramatic school was founded, with Gregori at its head and an enrollment of twenty-six pupils for the first year.

This was the beginning. By the end of the century, when Peter the Great had ascended the throne, ballet-dancing had become an established institution. If the lords and ladies did not wish to dance, it made no difference. They were forced to. Peter himself possessed considerable skill in the art. He gave lessons himself, and insisted upon a very high standard of skill. Under the Czar-

The purpose of the modern ballet is not to tell a story, but rather to make manifest its underlying emotion and set all hearts throbbing to one chord—Pavlova in her new Spanish dance

Maria Taglioni, the idol of her day. Taglioni's father, a dancing-master, had trained her from childhood for the ballet, and composed many of her chief successes. She made her début in Paris in 1827

ina Anna Ivanowna, the ballet assumed even greater importance. She it was who first thought of having dancing taught in the military college; and for this purpose she imported a German ballet-master, Lande, who filled his post with remarkable success.

And then came Catherine, the great Empress Catherine! To a woman of such whims and caprices, such temperamental impulses, dancing was food and drink. She composed many ballets herself, and made them always an essential part of the court life.

The coming of Didelot, a French ballet-master, marked an epoch in the history of the Russian ballet. The twenty-five years of his directorship under Alexander I are usually considered, with the present period excepted, of course, the golden age of dancing in Russia. It reached its climax in the careers of half a dozen really great danseuses. Not one of these, however, was of Russian birth. Foremost among them was Maria Taglioni, the Italian, a small, yellow-skinned, wrinkled woman, the last person in the world one would have picked out for a ballet-dancer. Before her first appearance in Russia, she rehearsed at the Imperial Ballet School. After she had danced, the pupils crowded about her, crying out in soft Russian accents, "Oh, you funny little wrinkled hag!"—"What a strange, shriveled-up freak you are!" But Taglioni, thinking she was being complimented, was hugely pleased, and smilingly answered, "*Merci, mes enfants!*" That evening, however, she captivated all hearts by her airy grace, and her appearance was completely forgotten in the fairy-like lightness of her step.

Then there was the incomparable Fanny Elssler! Here was a dancer who won by sheer beauty of face and form, and by the compelling force of a wonderful personality. A German by birth, she did not appear in Russia until she had

From the airy fantasies of her stage creations, Pavlova steps forth a strikingly normal, modern woman, with only the grace of her every movement to denote the dancer she is at heart

reached the age of thirty-eight, when youthful sprightliness could no longer have been hers. Yet she fascinated her audiences completely, and this in a country where ballet-dancing had by this time become the most important of all the arts. Fanny Elssler danced for three years in Russia before her final retirement from the stage, an astonishing record when one reflects that nowadays the Russian dancers are forced to retire on a a pension at the age of thirty-two. It is not too much to say that Fanny Elssler was the most popular dancer in the history of the art.

She was followed by the exquisite Carlotta Grizi, and later by Virginia Zucchi—"the divine Virginia," with the "feet of a Diana" and the "most expressive back in the world." By this time, however, the Russians had begun to assert themselves, and under Alexander II and Alexander III a number of really great ballerinas were produced from the ranks of the Ballet School itself. A series of able ballet-masters also, such as Carchetti, Kschepinski, Kiakscht, and Petipa, brought the Russian school to the proud position which it now holds.

The real greatness of the Russian ballet lies not so much in the antiquity of its traditions, nor the perfection of its technique, as in the originality of its conception of the art as a whole. The distinctive Russian dance is a ballet which follows the classical theories in the main, yet tells a very definite story with little recourse to actual pantomime. I am not thinking now of the Oriental dance-dramas, which, after all, are pantomimic plays. Nor am I thinking of the folk-dances, vastly popular in Russia. I have in mind only, the real ballet-dance, performed in the conventional short white skirt and pink fleshings, with all the traditional toe-balancing, pirouettes, fouettes, and renversées.

This style of dance was originally merely an exhibition of technical skill, possessing little if any meaning. By introducing into it a story, however, as, for instance, in the "Fille mal gardé," the ballet at once becomes a new and living art. And it is not merely the art of pantomime. It is the art of something much higher—the art of expressing the abstract in concrete form. Today it is the mission of the Russian ballet to transmit to an audience not merely the shell or outline of a story, but to make manifest its spirit and emotion. It is in the unerring interpretation of such abstract qualities that the really great dancer moves hearts.

Before beginning to study at the Imperial School, each applicant is rigidly examined as to intellectual and physical fitness. Such examinations are usually survived by about one-tenth of the applicants, for there are rarely more than eighteen vacancies. The successful candidates become probationary pupils for one year, when a second severe examination determines their fitness to continue. Those who survive this are placed under even more rigid discipline—a sort of monastic seclusion in honor of the Muse Terpsichore.

Upon the completion of this course, a boy may become danseur, danseur de caractère, or finally danseur classique. To the girls a much wider range of possibilities opens after graduation. They have any one of the following ranks, depending upon their ability, open to them: coryphee, second sujet, première sujet, première danseuse, and lastly prima ballerina absoluta. Only two or three in a generation ever attain this highest rank of prima ballerina absoluta.

Well do I remember my own entrance into the Imperial School. I was ten years old at the time, having been refused admission two years earlier because of my youth. The news that I had been actually admitted to the school was such joy to me that I scarcely thought of the hard and fast routine.

We were awakened each morning at eight o'clock by a large, solemn bell. After dressing, we had to pass before the scrutinizing glances of a teacher, who saw to it that little hands and faces were washed, teeth brushed, and hair properly dressed. Then came morning prayers in the little chapel, where a light burned always before the altar.

At nine o'clock we had a breakfast of tea, bread, and butter, followed almost immediately by the first dancing lesson. We assembled in a large, bright, airy room, furnished only with wooden benches, a piano, and a number of tall mirrors.

At noon we had luncheon, and then until four in the afternoon we were kept busy with lessons of a general nature, mathematics, history, geography, and languages. Then came dinner and a short interval of rest and recreation, followed by fencing lessons, music lessons, and special rehearsals for the dances to be presented on the stage of the

Mariensky Theater. Music was made an essential part of the course, and every pupil had to become at least an acceptable pianist.

Sometimes we visited the theater ourselves, but as a rule we had our supper at eight o'clock, and an hour later were in bed.

It was a simple and well-regulated mode of existence, though there were few breaks in the monotony. Our greatest holidays were on those occasions when the Czar visited the school. We always performed our best dances for the royal family. I recall one day when I was about twelve, the Emperor Alexander III, the Empress Marie, the Grand Duke Vladimir, and other members of the imperial family came to see us. After the ballet which we children danced in our little theater, some of us were called to the imperial family. Good, kind, simple Czar Alexander, whom all of us worshipped, took a little friend of mine up in his arms. I burst into tears. The Grand Duke and the Empress were alarmed, but both laughed when I wailed, "I want the Emperor to take me in his arms, too." Grand Duke Vladimir took me in his, but I would not be comforted. "I want the Czar to kiss me," I insisted.

Even had I never learned to dance, I should feel amply repaid for my work by the general education I acquired in the Imperial Ballet School. Great emphasis is laid there upon music, painting, and literature, for these arts are closely allied to dancing, and a dancer must be well versed in them if she would develop her powers of imagination and appreciation to their fullest extent.

After all, dancing is primarily an imaginative art. It is necessarily founded upon technique, and no dancer is ever allowed to enter the Russian Ballet without a thorough mastery of technique; yet, once the technique *is* mastered, it is better to lose sight of it altogether, and concentrate upon the imaginative phases of the art.

No movement must be mechanical, or merely conventional. Every slightest detail must have its reason; its significance in the interpretation of the music and of the imaginative idea underlying the whole dance. In creating a ballet one must constantly ask not, "Is this pretty and graceful?" but rather, "Does this exactly represent the idea intended?"

It is this superiority to technique, this soaring beyond mere pantomime, this grasping at and reproducing the *spirit* of a composition, that has made the Russian ballet unique in the history of dancing.

A shimmer of muslin skirt, a flutter of hands like two white birds, a twinkle of rhythmic feet and you have Pavlova, prima ballerina absoluta

Daily Mail, November 2, 1911

MADAME PAVLOVA MAKING FINAL PREPARATIONS FOR
HER COMING TOUR

*Venez faire des emplettes avec moi demain, je vous
en prie, j'ai tant de choses à acheter pour ma tournée
de province.*

Toujours à vous, Anna Pavlova

Who could resist the invitation? Anna Pavlova in the theatre is an unapproachable wonder. "In the life," as she expresses it herself, she is a dear little friend, as little like the typical artist as can be. A little pathetic sometimes and the least ready to assert her own wonderful individuality of any woman I have ever met. But with rehearsals for the opera and for her own tour, even apart from the performances, she is so seldom "in the life" that the chance of going shopping was seized with delight by both of us. So we set forth after many alarms and false starts two hours later than we meant to, and finally had to let the purchasing time brim over into a second day.

And how it rained!

Madame Pavlova, a quietly garbed little lady, ran from her motor-car across the wet pavement of Oxford Street, through the wide-open doors of a great shop. With the actions of a sensitive child she appealed with shy indecision to me. "Où commencerons-nous? Where do we begin? But how many people here today!" Her white-gloved hand sought to hide itself in my muff. As she disappeared into the lift not one among the crowd of buyers at the counters seemed to realise that the shyly moving figure in sensible "wet weather" boots was the greatest of all Russian dancers, the woman whose every moment is a delight, and whose charm is without equal on the stage.

Mme. Pavlova does not court notice off the stage. She wishes to be recognised only across the footlights. Her audiences she adores while she is dancing for them, but Mme. Pavlova the dancer remains at the theatre or in her studio. In her own home, with her friends, in her own hours, in what little while she has all to herself, she is Anna Pavlova, the gentle woman, shunning unnecessary publicity and intent upon passing through the crowds of people as unobtrusively as possible.

But, like a child, she enjoys to shop. Like a child she notices every detail and criticises as she goes, naively and with easy wit. Her great eyes, which have "the colour of ripe, dark-brown cherries," seem eager for fresh impressions, yet yearn wistfully for kind faces and for affection for their owner not as a dancer but as a "real" person.

A Real Fairy

The first time I saw her off the stage was in her dressing-room at the Palace Theatre. She was still dressed in the softly falling drapery she had worn in the *Valse Caprice*. The applause of the audience was still humming from the house. Those who had watched breathlessly the dance of a Grecian boy and girl, the glide and flicker of feet that never seemed to touch the floor, the supreme art of her invisible but severe technique, each footstep a note of music, wanted their idol back again. But she was upstairs, those great eyes seeming to beg sympathy from two children who had been of her audience and sought the joy of seeing her "alive." "A fairy, a real fairy," breathed one little girl—the dream of her six years come true at last. But Anna Pavlova put her arms out to the child and

bent until the waves of her dark hair touched the English flaxen curls. She kissed the rosy baby lips shyly as one child kisses another, and then, with a mother arm around her, "My little one, my little one," she said, "it is beautiful to be so young and gentle." She talked softly in French to the little ones, speaking with the pretty singing accent of the Russians and interposing Russian words of endearment. Her hands caressed the eager little faces and she received the child-love her eyes had sought. "I am glad she is not a fairy, after all," said the baby. "She is quite young, like we are."

Again I remember when some friends presented her with a dainty wrapper, a soft thing of silks and broideries. She wrapped herself in its draperies and ran about her dressing-room. "I shall never take it off, never. I shall keep it until the end of my life, it is soft and lovely. I kiss it. I—" "Madame Pavlova, please." The Russian troupe were finishing their National dance, and the *Bacchanale* was nearly due, so the wrap must go for the time with other delights—go for the joy of dancing, itself a happiness of youth. The old in heart cannot dance.

And then to be a child again, a real child, and "go shopping." To be a child with no knowledge of the value of money, but to buy dearly, or "bon marché," just what one wants. "I think," said Anna Pavlova the child, as she wrapped herself in an ermine stole and smoothed the soft whiteness of the fur with her cheek. "I think that everything is so bon marché in this London, and here in this shop so chic. I will have this for Dublin; do you like his little black tails? So, please, I would like it." She did not stop to ask the money equivalent. And the furs went down to the waiting car.

"I really am certain—and I do not say it as a compliment to you cherie, or to anyone—that the shops in London are the most agreeable in the world. There is no rush and bother. I go to buy something; it is shown to me at once, tidily from its own box or cupboard. Everything is good; even the cheapest things are worth having. I have never been shown rubbish in a London shop, as I have been in other great capitals. I like, too, the idea to let me wander about a shop—such as this house of Selfridge—without worrying me to choose all the time."

"Now, shall we dress ourselves in paletots just to find one I can wrap about me going to and from the theatre? Will you ask for me please?"

A Hypocrite in a Cloak

Now when Madame Pavlova says "Please" and throws a quick sideways glance from her dark eyes to see how I take the request, I must needs play spokeswoman for her. She pretends that English is beyond her and gazes as if deaf and dumb as long as I am by to speak for her. Presently I move away to examine a cloak more closely. When I come back the hypocrite is talking English quite quickly and well understanding the attendant's replies. She looks like a child discovered in mischief, and hastily wraps herself in a cloak of soft silk, grey-green in colour, with deep collar and cuffs of grey fox. "Is it the size for me?" she asks, as she turned this way and that in front of the long glass. "Oh do say, shall I have it? Do you not believe that such a paletot as this will be warm for me? I can wear it in the day or night. It is an economy to have such a beautiful coat. I buy it at once." But she bought another for travelling as well.

Another shopper passed while we waited for the lift. She had a tiny dog in her arms. "Oh! that little dog. I cannot have it. It is so like my dog." "Yours is a bulldog," I said. "That is a toy Pom. I see no resemblance."

"Now you laugh at me. Well, I will tease you presently. It reminds me of my dog. Left behind this time in Russia. He is ill, in character, but not wicked. I do not know what to do with him. He is badly brought up–'mal élevé'. His wife, too, is the same. It is I who will bring up their children. They will be proud parents to have such a friend for their little bulldogs, small–like that." Pavlova's hands measured an imaginary dog the size of the toy Pom.

"You are a bad friend to come shopping with," she went on. "You make us do too much talking."

"Quickly, then, what shall we buy next? Hats?"

"You think I need buy other hats? Vraiment! Well, perhaps in the country, in the train or on the boat for a tour of four months I must have several new ones. But is not this I have on charming? I found it when I came through Paris. Just grey chinchilla and little fluffy white feathers. Now do you think £26 was too much? Someone told me that it was a terrible price. But how pretty and comfortable!"

So she tried on hats one after another, turning for approval, speaking sweetly to the girls who waited on her, asking for their opinion, flitting from one glass to another, moving her head and body to try the effect of some particular chapeau in half a dozen dainty poses. Selfridge's millinery department ceased to be a shop, it became a studio, a stage on which moved the most graceful figure in Europe, and the assembled attendants composed an admiring audience, though compelled to silent applause.

Tea

"Somebody looks," whispers the shopper, timid once more. "Come away quickly, let us have our tea." We fled to the Palm Court, Anna Pavlova speeding up the stairs like thistledown in spite of the wet-weather boots, I following, feeling all arms and legs, and arriving at the top quite breathless. "Sometimes we cannot wait for the lift," she said, "these tables are taken so quickly. Let us sit behind a big tree with our backs to everyone. Smell the violets on my muff."

Over tea she told me once more that it had been the dream of her life to conquer London. And now, having conquered London, she is going to tour the provinces to conquer there, too, before her fresh triumphs in London next spring.

"You know what my dancing is to me," she said. ("Oh, do let me do the tea!") "But no one in England can know how we work at the Imperial Conservatoire in St. Petersburg. Oh, to do anything above the ordinary requires infinite patience and such hard work. I was nine [sic] at the time of my admission to the institution. For eight years the pupils are not allowed outside the walls of the buildings except during the summer holidays, and the course of studies we have to go through is as comprehensive as it can be. Yet, in spite of the hard work I am sure there is not one pupil who regrets having gone through the apprenticeship. As soon as the students show the necessary talent for music, acting and dancing they are given a place in the ballet. The next step, which comes after several years of hard work, is the chance to appear at the Opera in a solo dance. It had always been a rule that no one could be made a ballerina until she had been a soloist for seven years, and I regard it as a very great distinction that I was appointed after four years. But all the training is good and dancing is a fine art.

"After these years of probation the dancer must strike her own line. It is then, and only then, that individuality should assert itself. For my own part, I thought the old conventional ballet could be modernised to a very great extent, and made to interpret the human emotions almost as effectively as music, painting, or any other art. It was then I attempted to render by rhythmic poses and gestures such pieces as Rubinstein's waltzes, or fragments from the work of Delibes, Chopin, Tchaikovsky, Saint-Saëns, and other comparatively modern composers."

"My Own School"

"Next summer I want to found a school of dancing in London. I want to train some English children, just a few. It will be the most delightful and charming thing in my life. I will be with them and see their talent grow. We will dance together.

"It is so great a pity that there is no institution in England like our Opera House. Some of the children I have seen would have great success if they were properly trained. But you have a teacher here, another there, all on so small a scale. There would be great dancers among the English if they knew the dance. It is, of course, a question of character, of temperament, of physique. Each country has its own art, I think. An art that belongs to its people. We Russians, in Petersburg, are dancers. In Paris it is the drama, and so forth. Oh! my friend, I have a little rehearsal for the Opera in twenty minutes, and I have many more things to buy. May we come again tomorrow? I have so few opportunities to buy nice things. For me it is always la scène–the stage."

"If you are going to be pathetic," I said, "I shall leave you quite alone in the lift, and you will not be able to find your way out of the shop–"

"You are thoughtless for all those other dancers waiting for me. We will come again. Tomorrow I will be quite another lady."

And the next day Madame Pavlova was "quite another lady." We were to start from the hotel at eleven o'clock. At twenty minutes past a parcel arrived–a gown, rich black velvet with barbaric splashes of colour at throat and waist, yellow and green, and red worsted worked in a bold design. "The sun is shining. I must wear a new gown." She slipped into the elegant little frock and announced that she was ready.

Madame Anna Pavlova was gay, the sun after a long night's rest had buoyed her up.

Charm of Modern Shopping

"I did enjoy yesterday," she said as she settled herself in her automobile. "London shopping is more fascinating every time. How much we did on such a rainy day. So many things of different character and for different occasions all in one shop. In Vienna I would not have accomplished nearly so much, for I should have been in six shops instead of only one. In Paris my automobile would have been up and down the Rue de la Paix, to the Louvre, everywhere. I should only have found one thing and I should have been late for rehearsal. I should have been shown all the things I do not want, have been worried by inferior articles because they were bargains, and have finished very unhappy.

"Everything is good in England, and your shops are best. I have never done so much shopping since I came to London. All the summer at the Palace Theatre I had no time; always rehearsals for "the scene," many performances, fresh dances, as well as my favourites, my snowflake ballet of children. You remember how hard we worked all that summer weather. I could not go to shops. I used to say to a girl friend I have, "Hilda, go to buy for me, my clothes are finished. I must have something cool to wear. You are thin like I am. What fits you will fit me." She did shop so well. But this time I have been able to try on everything I have wanted to in the shop, before these long glasses, one thing after another, quickly, until I have found what I want."

All those things she could not "try on" in the shop itself she loaded onto the arms of the assistants, and we retired to the convenient little "fitting rooms," gathering more loot as we went. Dressing up is a great game, whether to children or grown women. Madame Pavlova was an example of the fact. She danced round the little room in one costume after another, suiting her mood and actions to the dress she donned. A "tailor-made" is severe and requires, if not dignified, at least quiet and sober movement; in a rest gown one may repose in graceful attitude before a long glass; and a rich evening gown for a "dinner of ceremony" should be criticised while one passes with stately grace on the arm of "my host."

It was all great fun, but withal to be taken seriously.

For the Tour

The first department we came to when we again entered Selfridge's was devoted to hosiery. Stockings, stockings, everywhere. Beautiful hose in soft silk, gold-coloured, rose-tinted, crimson as the sunset, hung on stands, and the counters were laden with piles of multi-colours. Madame Pavlova made all speed to seat herself at such a delightful place. "Now," she said, "I must buy plenty of stockings and gloves to wear in Dublin and Newcastle. Do you think they will like my dancing in Dublin? Mr. Mayer, who is organising the tour, tells me so much of the Irish audience. I am looking towards it all so much. It would astonish you if you knew how many stockings I use in the year. More for "the scene" than for "the life." All these are silk stockings. I wear silk for my dance—I must—but for my life—have you any in cotton, please, like these?"

Shoes of Gold

Madame Pavlova put out one of her wonderful feet and showed a stocking of finest lisle thread. "But, I do not know, when I think again, these are so fine, so light and how charming: the least expensive suit me best. I will have some golden silk stockings to wear with some gold shoes. We will have the shoes presently."

A few pairs of white silk daintily embroidered up the front were also chosen, but for all ordinary occasions the little lady bought lisle thread, unadorned by aught but silk clocks. She does not like openwork or "lace" stockings, for they are not becoming to the leg. She is altogether very neat and quiet in her footwear.

"Did you ever try to wear silk gloves," she asked me. "They are terrible—so—so—so scrunchy? Yes, what a good word."

I think that Madame Pavlova would have spent all the time at her disposal buying stockings if she had not looked around suddenly and discovered quite close to her—sweets and bon-bons!

So we bought, if not enough for four months, at least enough to send to all the children she knows in London, and some for friends in Russia—"that they may know English sweets," and "some for myself." And here is another fancy of Anna Pavlova, and here again she differs from every other girl or woman I ever knew. She does not like chocolates. "But," she said irrelevantly, with a look of rapture on her face, "I do like the grapes I have had in London this week. Oh! lovely big Muscats and such flavour, so splendid. We have big grapes in Petersburg, but not like those I eat here."

"I will tell you," she ran on, "something else I have liked to find here and have bought very much of. Silverware. The most beautiful things are made in silver in England, and whenever I wish to send some very nice present to my friends in Russia I send silver. When I went back at the end of the summer I took many large parcels with me. And now I cannot resist the attractions of a silversmith."

Madame Pavlova adores a good perfume like all women, but she is not extravagant in its use and chooses with much care. The English makers are the best, she thinks, and sets her faith on one particular distiller for his sweet pea perfume and another for the arum lily scent.

Before we finally left the shop of many attractions, Madame Pavlova

attempted to make a calculation of what she had purchased, used many pieces of paper, and finally gave up the idea.

"We will look at all the things at tea-time at the hotel," she finally decided.

Two Russian lady's maids worked hard all the evening arranging the purchases, two clever maids who make all the costumes the wonderful ballerina wears on the stage, working from designs. Madame Pavlova superintends all their work, examining and criticising, making vivid suggestions and being very particular over minute details.

Did ever such a charming creature of varying moods as Anna Pavlova come to London before? I doubt it.

"GRACE CURNOCK"*

Berlin, c. 1914

MY LITTLE BALLET SKIRT by Anna Pavlova, Prima Ballerina of the Imperial Russian Court Opera

. . . The "tutu"? I like it and I don't. Certainly, the short skirt is the ideal one for a dancer. In the tutu one can best show off the technique and art of the dance. The legs are free; every movement can clearly be seen. Every muscle's movement must be correct. All the movements are exact, precise—it is impossible to give way to any sudden caprice. The pattern once established must remain as it is.

The short skirt is the costume of the Classical epoch. How did it come about? Like many other types of costume, it evolved out of necessity. In the first third of the eighteenth century, at the time of the rigidly observed Classical school of ballet, the then very renowned dancer Camargo, who numbered Voltaire among her admirers, attempted to modify to suit her purposes the long ballet dress in which she had to dance. She simply cut it shorter. She made it so short that the legs could be seen and the dance technique was given its full value. That was the birth of the tutu—much to the outrage of lovers of traditional ballet. I was, incidentally, one of the first in the Russian ballet to become emancipated from the tutu. It was greatly daring of me, as until that time custom did not permit any performance of a dance to take place in anything other than the short skirt. However, in the stiff and conventional tutus I could not give the new dances the softness and whimsical flexibility required. The Greek style, for instance, which is predominant in a lot of modern dancing, can only be expressed in a flowing tunic.

In general the dress should suit the character of the dance. With the costume—often with just an accessory—the dance is stamped with its individuality. A Spanish shawl thrown across the shoulders and with which the dancer will make play builds up the whole character of the dance. And so the costume becomes a vital factor in the modern dance. In the more modern styles the dancer is freer than in the traditional skirt. She can indulge in the fancy of the moment, in a greater amount of caprice in her art; she is independent of the School. . . .

One more word about the designer, the costume, and the artist. It often occurs that the designer dreams up the most marvelous creations which, however, kill the dance stone dead, because he had only the purely artistic effect in his mind and had lost sight of the practical purpose of the costume. It is the same in all fields of creativity: one must know the purpose and dominate the material. The finest costumes that have been designed for me, and that were enchanting in the sketches,

---

* The pseudonym was the name of the writer's young daughter, who was accepted by Pavlova for tuition a year later.

would have been useless for dancing in. Frequently during fittings I have made changes, adjusted the drapery with my own hands, effected alterations. Generally speaking, however, for some time now designers have rendered the ballet an inestimable service and created scenery and costumes of a fairy-tale loveliness.

There are ballets which can only be effectively danced in the short skirt because in these lightness and a freedom from gravity are shown off to their best advantage. The tutu is like a butterfly's wing—it flaps and flutters round the body and swings harmoniously with every movement. Such ballets, which I particularly enjoy dancing, are, for instance, *The Swan, The Butterfly, The Magic Flute.* For these dances of pure illusion, the short skirt is ideally adapted. The rhythm is given its full value, and there are no tiresome folds of material to interfere with the bending and swaying. The appearance of the dancer is more ethereal, more dreamlike. Our modern ballets demand style. The short skirt is a neutral costume, to which individual, repeated movements do not lend any character. Apart from that, the individual movements are often distorted, because the eye of the spectator upon seeing the short skirt out of habit "sees" the Classical dance forms. The best known of these Classical forms is the dance on pointe. It is impossible to imagine these dances being performed in a character costume, just as one could not imagine an Egyptian or Indian dance being performed in a garment of tulle. A modern ballet endeavors to bring out the inner meaning of the ballet. I try to individualize the dances as far as possible, as well as ensuring that the outer appurtenances are suited to the content. The style of the costume must suit the style of the dance, and the dance as pure rhythmic motion—as in the Classical dances—requires the noncommittal skirt of tulle. Do I prefer the short skirt above all others? I do not know. Today there are so many kinds of dance—Egyptian, Indian, peasant dances—whose full charm is expressed by the costume. Every costume for its time, including the short skirt.

Observer, June 12, 1921

THE SADNESS OF PAVLOVA

A Talk at the Trocadero—Art and the World's Unrest

It was in the vast empty vessel of the Trocadero, the biggest hall in Paris, that Anna Pavlova told me something of her experiences and her intentions. Long black draperies on which the light would at the later performances play were being placed in position by workmen. In one corner, a muscular member of what Pavlova calls her family was going through gymnastic exercises, while in another his companion was practicing pirouettes. Two or three girls with only the remotest resemblance to a Degas picture were testing the suppleness of their limbs and executing now and again some graceful steps and gestures. The conductor of the orchestra, clad in a sweater, was addressing his final injunctions to a crowd of musicians gathered round him. On the stage a violinist was running through his repertory with a pianist, while a director was making notes on the piano as table. It was all desultory and haphazard, and the unoccupied sweep of stalls and gilded balconies looked dismal as a mausoleum. It was not easy to imagine the whole place peopled, animated, roaring delight at the little far-off figures whose movements, expressive of poetised human emotions, had wrought this miracle.

"Soon I hope to be back in London," she told me. "I am always happy to be in London, but it is difficult, very difficult, I hear just now. One cannot take a theatre for a short season, so I am going to appear at the Queen's Hall for one week after these performances in Paris. I shall be there on June 27. That will give me great pleasure, for the English people are always so appreciative. It means so much—appreciation. I do not think it is realised how hard it is for an artist to produce of the best in these days of trouble. How can one give oneself in this time of uncertainty and distress? And without that absolute giving of oneself there is no real art."

With great earnestness did she make that simple utterance, spreading her hands in the gesture of giving. After all, what better definition of art in any form than this definition of self-giving? "But, oh!" she cried sadly, "how depressed one is sometimes tempted to be in a storm-tossed world! And how fatal depression must be to those who wish to put their soul into their work!"

I asked her if she did not think that there was a greater demand than ever for the dance, precisely as the result of the tremendous and pent-up emotions of the past few years. Surely the dance, I said, highly complex in its means as it is, is the utterance of intense feelings in a simpler, directer form than the drama, since it is at once dynamic and pictorial. Was there not apparent a new enthusiasm for this quintessential, pantomimic, visualised expression?

In her admirable French, broken now and again by a word of English, she accepted and elaborated this present need for the moving expression of the dance. But she could not forget the spiritual difficulties while the material circumstances are still hard—harder than they have been, in the experience of Pavlova, at any moment except during the war.

"Not for two or three years do I expect they will really improve," she said, "and although I am grateful for the reception which is everywhere accorded me it is not yet easy to travel and to look after my large family. Certainly in some respects it was worse during the war. We were kept almost as prisoners in South America for years. It was, if you like, a triumphal tour, but, nevertheless, it lasted too long. There was no means of getting away unless we were prepared to shed members of the company in every country. The passport regulations were particularly onerous for us. There are dancers with me of many nationalities, so that it became almost impossible to move about. At any rate, we had to confine our wanderings to South America. Happily many of those obstacles have now been removed, though the passport problem is by no means solved for us yet."

Not from Pavlova, but from other sources, I have learned many authentic instances of her long-continued generosity towards those of her troop who for such reasons had to be left behind. She made herself entirely responsible for their welfare. Sometimes they had to be abandoned, and months afterwards picked up on the return of Pavlova. The stories which I have heard are of such a character that it is no wonder that these dancers, many of whom have been with her for years and years, love and reverence "Madame."

"These things," she continued, "must and do affect one's art. They make one very sad sometimes. These material difficulties and the sense of trouble and strife and sorrow that one finds everywhere are bad for the dance. But I am trying to do what I can, for I think my art is needed."

We talked about a matter of which everybody in Paris is talking—the impending departure of Isadora Duncan, that other great artist, for Moscow. She leaves at the end of this month. I repeated to Anna Pavlova, who listened eagerly, her thin pure face with the big burning eyes and the dark flattened hair parted over the broad brow bent towards me, what Isadora Duncan had said a few days before. That this American exponent of the dance—how different is her method from the method of Pavlova, and how different her majestic beauty from the sylph-like beauty of Pavlova, and yet how essentially similar their genius—should be going to her own country, now struggling in deeper adversity than any Western country, interested her greatly. Isadora Duncan complained that when she gave a spectacle at Paris the expenses and the taxes were so high that she was compelled to raise abnormally the price of places, so that her art was in reality reserved for comparatively well-to-do people. What has tempted her to go to Russia is that Lounatcharsky has offered her a *salle,* and has offered to help her to teach her pupils under the protection of the Government. She goes to Russia with the hope of founding a great popular theatre.

The sympathy of Pavlova was expressed in unmistakable terms. But the same melancholy as had tinged the whole conversation again appeared. What she doubted was whether it would, with the utmost courage, be possible, in the turbulent unhappy conditions of Russia, to keep the flame burning—that ardent flame, fed by faith in art and a consciousness of the beauty of the world, which, after all, beyond the perfection of technique, gives its inimitable quality to the dancing of these dancers. Pavlova, too, is thinking of the Russian children, and proposes to devote the proceeds of these Paris representations to the poor infants of exiled Russians, and to found a charitable fund which will, of course, bear her name.

A day or two after this conversation in the vast empty vessel of the Trocadero, I saw the crowded *salle* wild with wonderment at her ineffable aerial grace and at the exquisite though melancholy poetry of the incomparable *Mort du Cygne.*

Sunday Eagle, November 30, 1924

ANNA PAVLOWA WISHES TO PRESERVE HER ART ON THE FILMS

Anna Pavlowa would like to go into the movies. She has made her plans for less work and more play in the future. She will never tour America again, so she says, but now that she is taking the preparatory steps for her inevitable retirement, she begins to feel the need to know that her art will not die with her. She has already had screened all of her divertissements, and the films have been stored away to be released after her death.

"I should like to make ze pictures of ze ballets," she explained in her Russo-French accent, "but zat would be ver' hard, for it must be a large production in ze open air and ver' artistic. It is ver' hard to find ze right people who are artistic. I have made one picture ten years ago, but ze movies were ver' little then. Ze camera could make only so many revolutions, not good for dancing. Now you have ze slow motion camera, you have ze ver' quick camera, you have ze camera zat stops in ze midst of a movement. If one could combine ze right camera, ze right music, ze artistic people, ah, then I could dance in ze pictures, and it would be ver' beautiful and do ver' much for ze education of dancers. Mr. Griffith, now. I have seen his pictures. I admire him ver', ver' much. He ees truly artistic. I should like to think zat people will see Pavlowa dance long, long after, when I can dance no longer. For I have worked ver', ver' hard. I may come over here, dance once, twice, in New York. But tour, non, non, nevaire! I have performed my missionary—non, what you call, mission, and now I must rest."

To make this announcement of a coming rest, she gave a tea at her apartment in the McAlpin. Not one of these American, cup-of-tea-in-lap, cake-on-end-of-saucer teas. This was a Russian tea, where a table,

very substantial, but hardly too substantial for the loads of sandwiches, pastries, teas, coffees, napkins, spoons and dishes with which it was covered, occupied most of the room. We sat around this groaning board and ate, drank and smoked and talked with an easy disregard of time and space, just like the characters in a Russian novel.

Pavlowa spoke in glittering, sibilant Russian to her husband and with many graceful and delicate motions of her hands supervised the choosing of sandwiches, both cheese and chicken for herself. That done, she reverted to broken English and turned to the interviewers. On the stage, Pavlowa, more than any other dancer, seems inhuman—the ageless symbol of an ageless art. Her head is lifted high above the audience, her hair is like two wings of black velvet, her lids are lowered, and her eyes unseeing. Though she has been before the public for two decades, it is impossible to find any signs of age in her dancing. Off stage it is just as impossible to say how old she is. Her face is no longer a mask, and the black hair is pinned carelessly in the back and straggles a little about her cheeks. The face is flawless, almost too flawless, not a wrinkle, not even a hint of a line. The clear, pale complexion is well set off by a bright red flannel dress. Her throat is the throat of a young girl. She weighs one hundred and two pounds. Her manner is happy, charming and carefree. Her eyes sparkle, her hands are always moving, gracefully, expressively, as she describes her house in London, where she will now spend most of the year.

"I have bought it because of my engagement at Covent Garden. I dance there always in ze summer, and it ees, oh, so impossible that one shall live in town in London. So hot! It has ze ivy all around it, a ver' old house, with ze garden, and two swans. I call zem Jack. Both Jack. But perhaps zay have forgotten me now. Once when I have been away for so long a time touring, I came back to my house and zay have forgotten me. I have to train them all over. Ah, but now, I shall have one long rest. I shall have time to fix over my house, move everyzing, make ze kitchen into dining room, dining room into bedroom, put furniture in different places. Zat is what I like, always to move my furniture around, change, change. You know, we Russians are not so conservative, we must have movement. In my apartment in Petrograd, when I used to come back to it from my tours, I would always turn everyzing, what you call 'em, upside down. But now I cannot live in Russia, it ees impossible, ver', ver' bad time in Russia.

"You know what I would like—I would like to have a baby. But it does not go wiz my art. I would like to adopt one, bring her up to be a new Pavlowa, but that, too, is so hard. One cannot tell. Dancing must be born wiz you. One cannot train." This present rest does not mean that Pavlowa will retire from active life and work. That she will never do. "Non," emphatically, with many shakings of the head. "Nevaire! I shall always do somezing. Sometime, of course, I shall not dance. One cannot dance for ever. Then I shall supervise my company, or I shall have a school."

Schools of classic dancing are Pavlowa's particular hobby, and she is insistent that America shall have an endowed school and theater for the training of future artists. "I find your American girls," she said, "ver' capable for dancing. They have ze temperament and without temperament there is no artist. Oh, perhaps they have too much temperament for your mens, zat I do not know, but none too much for dancing. Your musical comedy dancers are ver' good, ver' amusing. I go often to ze shows for amusement, but zat kind of dancing ees a separate art. It has nozing to do with ze classic dancing. Ze girls in my company cannot do what ze music hall dancers do, and nevaire, nevaire can ze music hall dancers do what zey do. Sometimes one of my girls tries to get a job wiz a musical comedy. Zay say to her: 'Can you do ze kick? Can you do ze split?' My girl say, 'No!' Zen zay say 'Ah, zat ees a pity, you are wiz Madame Pavlowa, you are a good dancer, you are nice looking, but if you cannot do ze split, if you cannot do ze kick, you are no good for us.'

"Yet ze music halls have many more pretty, many more artistic dancers now. America improye ver', ver' much in ze arts. People give money now for music, for opera, for orchestras, for ze endowed *théâtre*, why not for ze classic dancing? You need a school. But more zan zat, you need a *théâtre* for dancing. And if your girls want to be ze great dancers, ze great artists, zay must learn zay will not make much money. Non, nevaire! I do not know if zay can learn. In America, everyone wants so much money, money, gold, gold. Many, many European countries have endowed schools—France, Italy, Spain, Germany. Why not America?"

As Pavlowa's eyes flash from one to the other of her hearers, as she emphasizes points with her hands and her body, it is easy to see why she will not think of actually retiring. What would she do with all that vitality, born with her like her genius, for she seems to make no effort to hoard it? She has no rules of health she says. She smokes a little. "It rests me, a cigarette or two, but not to excess. Zat is why ze mens smoke. Ah, ze mens, zay know what ees good." She eats everything. "But not much bread. Zat makes one heavy." She is not one of these early morning risers or cold shower fiends. She rests an hour before each performance, when she is dancing, and practices for an hour every day. She works very hard and very happily, she says. Perhaps that is why age cannot seem to stale her.

from FOUR BALLERINAS OF THE IMPERIAL THEATRE
by André Levinson (c.1912)

In our present-day theatrical scene I do not know anyone like Anna Pavlowa. It has been given to her to infuse the abstract and disciplined formulas of the classical dance with an exquisite sensitivity, refinement, and pathos, in keeping with the contemporary spirit. There is something noble and heroic in her sweeping lines, and a sort of "Japanese" clarity in her capricious pauses. The poetical flutter of her arabesques cannot be compared to anything else. The straight line from the end of the outstretched foot to the tips of her fingers gives the impression that she is taking off into space like an arrow. With Pavlova this schematically pure line turns into a wavelike ripple of inexpressible beauty, achieved by means of a marvelous turn of the lifted leg, an elegant twist of the knee, the stemlike suppleness of the body, a softening of the angles of the elbows, and a delicate movement of the hands. Taut like a tuned string, she vibrates in the air, compelling a responsive tremor in the spectator. Pavlova's line is not only decorative and extraordinarily expressive; it is symbolic. Do we not regard a Pavlova arabesque as the visible expression of something ineffable? Here the classical technique speaks in the elevated language of allegory.

Can we describe her dancing as perfection? I do not know. Thus, perhaps, the complex splendor and exquisite accuracy of *terre-à-terre* movement is not for this artist of impetuous and sudden flights, sustained and singing arabesques—impelled by the vagaries of an ephemeral breeze, yet burning with life: nor were they for Maria Taglioni, who imprinted the traditional forms with a romantic inspiration. And may not Pavlova's deliberate rejection of the rigid canons of her art in itself constitute the canon of a new kind of classical dance? A contemporary one? By virtue of a personal experience, a great tradition flowers again. If Pavlova's character dances are imbued with an ethereal but seductive eroticism, a willful, arrogant, insidious grace, and her mime with a vi-

brant storm of dramatic experience, then the classical Pavlova blossoms into pure spirit.

And yet Pavlova's dancing, individual and complex with the soaring quality of a candle flame—now and then flickering as with a gust of passion—defies any just analysis. Its exalted beauty is not to be reduced to psychological motives or any technical formula. Nor is it to be placed on the same footing as the tradition of a Taglioni, whose charm, according to all witnesses, consisted entirely of a weightless ethereality, a pure spirituality of form. "Taglioni-ism" is only one of the faces of the complex—and contemporary—art of Pavlova.

Of the many characters created by her, some are particularly unforgettable. The first movements of the Bayadère, when she inclines before the high priest in a ritual gesture of homage, is like some esoteric symbol suggestive of the spirit of Eastern mysticism. In the sharp, chiseled profile, the pure, narrow brow crowned with a priestly headband, we see the exalted and coldly stern face of an icon, until the intermittent bursts of love and passion plunge the artist into the world of mime. Their destructive consequences shatter the harmony of the soul dedicated to God: at the same time the correspondence between the movements of the ballerina and the rhythm of the musical accompaniment is destroyed. Her movements lack definition and are not even in time. She is totally subjugated by the rhythm of her internal emotions.

I am hardly aware of any other example of so powerful a display of dramatic autosuggestion. Inspired, the artist lives her role to the end. Before the eyes of the spectator the earthly spirit of the Bayadère suddenly blossoms and explodes in a series of exultant looks and gestures, then staggers and writhes under the lash of betrayal, frantically beats against invisible walls like a moth at a windowpane. The frail shoulders (magnificent when expressing fury or a challenge) and the delicate, stemlike arms submissively bear the burden of her dreadful experience. Pavlova, of course, knows nothing of laboriously acquired details of local color. But her portrayal emanates a sweet breath of exoticism. Thus, so it is said, the fragrance of Eastern spices permeates a crystal jar. In the Bayadère's death scene, her shoulders shudder with an overwhelming oppression which makes itself felt in all the conventional and symmetrical forms of the dance; there is a quickening of the tempo, a breaking up of the rhythm, culminating in a mimed scream of agony.

The concrete action of the drama is over. We enter into a misty world where the shade of the Bayadère arrives (almost transparent, no longer of the flesh) to dwell in the kingdom wherein reigns the dance. The corps de ballet parade in slow succession. Their short steps are followed by lengthy pauses, and the whole row freezes momentarily in arabesque. A dreamy atmosphere fills the stage, and the uncertain glimmer of an artificial moon throws a sad green tinge over the lily-pale tunics in the background. The leaps and feather-light runs are inaudible. The scene has shed its langor. The ballerina is dancing. From the spectral face there emanates an icy chill. Here, in this figure from the Elysian shades, all the psychological nuances are evident in every tremor of the pure, extended line.

Everything that was unusual in the drama becomes plausible in the forms of the classical dance. Here Pavlova manifests the profound symbolism of the ballet. As a result of the purifying flame of a dramatic experience, the personification of her heroine is translated into an ethereal world of incorporeal existence. And thus her delicacy and purity, insubstantial as a daydream, make her invisible to the human sight of the characters in the final scene.

Another recollection: Giselle. A simple village maiden, Giselle, gives her heart to a young man. The pair dance. The trusting girl's lover proves to be a noble engaged to the daughter of a duke. The idyll turns into catastrophe. A jealous woodsman reveals the betrayal. Giselle goes out of her mind and dies.

In this brilliantly naturalistic scene Madame Pavlova renders the librettist's intentions with inspired intuition. When she comes to herself again after the crushing, sudden revelation, fragments of memory return to her conscious mind. . . . And now, to the slow reprise of the familiar motif, she dreamily repeats the same movements of that same dance so recently partnered by her lover, repeating the steps exquisitely, hesitantly, as if listening to some far-off voice with a body suddenly become heavy. With greater power than any unrealistic rendering of a case of clinical madness, with arched back and a fixed stare, Pavlova expresses the dissolution of a winged soul, distorting the very rhythm of the dance, with unsteady, anguished, broken movements. Her rendering of madness is one of the greatest achievements of dramatic art that we have seen on the choreographic stage. . . .

One more memory. The scene is an English music hall dark with cigar smoke; on the stage are those dances which one short hour every evening, year in and year out, divert the minds of the spectators away from sporting events, or the interminable dialogues of a ventriloquist and his rocking-horse about the latest events at Epsom. These prosaic and philistine amusements act, as it were, as a fillip to the stupendous impression produced by Pavlova's dancing. It is true that the artistic material she selected for these performances was hardly compatible with her exceptional personality. A drop of water can reflect the universe, but the drop of water in which the unique genius of Pavlova was displayed in the music hall was quite inadequate.

Among these episodic creations of the artist, however, there was one unforgettable one—the Dying Swan. Posterity will award it the same glittering, legendary crown as her Giselle and Bayadère. Pavlova—the Swan—rising on both points, her arms lowered and crossed on her feathered tunic, dreamily, slowly inscribing a series of circles. With smooth motions of the arms she darts impetuously to the back of the stage, toward the imaginary horizons of paint and canvas, and, preparing for flight, she freezes for a long moment, exquisite and tense, on the brink of an airy abyss. But suddenly she arches over as if in agony, her hands pressed to her body, fluttering with little movements of pain and defiance; she moves unsteadily on legs vibrating like a violin string back toward the footlights. One leg extended before her in a marvelous arc, she sinks onto one knee in the throes of death—sustained and inexpressibly touching—and then dies. The fracturing of rhythm under the pressure of an agonizing experience here, as in the first act of *Giselle*, is, for Pavlova, a dramatic technique. Out of Saint-Saëns's pretty but rather uninspired music, and the simple, obvious symbolism of the ballet master, the ballerina has created the "white agony" of a soul crushed by the weight of the world.

Such is Pavlova's performance. Amid the chaos of the contemporary scene, she appears with the bearing of a conqueror. Her glory is unrivaled. But is it within the power of words to reveal the innermost being, the hidden springs of the dramatic transformations of the "I"?

D'ARCY v. DANDRÉ AND ANOTHER (1930)

[The following account of the lawsuit is extracted from three days of reporting in *The Times* and a general report in *News of the World*.]

In the unfamiliar atmosphere of the High Court of Justice, Madame Anna Pavlova, the celebrated dancer, had a new and entirely different part to play. With her husband, M. Victor Dandré, she was sued for alleged slander by a former young dancer in her world-travelled troupe, a Miss Elsa D'Arcy, of London. Pavlova, a striking figure in beige, and adorned with many jewels [she was also described as wearing "a simple frock of deep red, relieved by a beige scarf and big hat to match, and a long platinum chain"], sat beside her husband in the King's Bench, in a seat just in front of counsel. A gallery of fashionably-dressed women seldom took their eyes off her.

Mr. Croom-Johnson, for Miss D'Arcy, explained that she claimed damages for slander alleged to have been published by M. Dandré on behalf of both himself and his wife in the Federated Malay States. Mme. Pavlova and M. Dandré denied that M. Dandré published the words complained of. Mme. Pavlova's company arrived at Penang from Rangoon in January, 1929, and Miss D'Arcy took her part in the performance. She discovered at Ipoh, however, that without warning, she had been cut out of the programme. Miss D'Arcy went to M. Dandré to find out the reason. He told her that he had received instructions from Mme. Pavlova in which she had alleged that Miss D'Arcy had acted in an indecent and immoral manner on the steamer going to Penang. Miss D'Arcy expressed her indignation to M. Dandré, and declared there was no truth in the statement, and that nothing of any sort had happened to justify such a charge. Miss D'Arcy, still in great distress, on the following day asked M. Slavinski, who had joined the company in 1928, and with whom she had been friendly, to go to M. Dandré and see whether he could find out the trouble. M. Slavinski saw M. Dandré, and a conversation took place in Russian. M. Dandré repeated in effect, but in Russian, the statement which he had made to Miss D'Arcy. The words when translated were: *Mme. Pavlova will not allow Elsa to act owing to her immoral and indecent behaviour in the boat with you.* "There never has been a shadow of foundation for such a charge," remarked Mr. Croom-Johnson, "and these words were utterly untrue."

Counsel went on to relate that M. Slavinski, during one of the voyages, asked Miss D'Arcy to consider whether she would marry him. They were sitting side by side in two deck chairs on the deck on the journey to Penang, rather "latish" at night, and just as Mme. Pavlova, with a Mr. Pianowski, passed them, M. Slavinski, who had caught hold of Miss D'Arcy's hand, snatched a kiss from her. That was all that happened.

Cross-examined by Mr. H. Hilbery, for Mme. Pavlova and M. Dandré, Miss D'Arcy asserted that M. Slavinski and herself were merely discussing the ordinary affairs of the day. "I would hardly say that he snatched a kiss," she added. "He simply leaned over to me quickly and kissed me on the cheek. He did not even put his arm around me." M. T. Slavinski, who told counsel that he was a Pole and a professional dancer since the age of six, gave evidence that he saw M. Dandré on one occasion, and said: "I want to know the truth why Miss D'Arcy is not appearing." M. Dandré replied: "For her immoral and indecent behaviour in the boat."

Mr. Hilbery, cross-examining: "I suggest that M. Dandré never said one word about immoral or indecent conduct."

Slavinski: "Then you know more about it than I do." (Laughter.)

"M. Dandré has had a good deal of occasion to find fault with you for being drunk on the stage?"

"Never."

"At Buenos Aires did not M. Dandré himself take you off the stage because you were so drunk?"

"I do not remember such a thing." (Laughter.)

"You know what the import of the word 'immoral' is in English?"

"It means just the same as in Russian." (Laughter.)

Mrs. Violet Frances D'Arcy, mother of the plaintiff, was asked how her daughter seemed when she returned from the Eastern tour. "I thought my daughter looked thirty-two, not twenty-two," she replied.

Later Mrs. D'Arcy had an interview with M. Dandré and asked him what was the immoral and indecent conduct of which Mme. Pavlova accused her daughter. "He put his hands in his pockets and kept blinking," said Mrs. D'Arcy, "and he would not answer me." When she asked M. Dandré what Mme. Pavlova intended to do to rectify matters, he said: "I told Mme. Pavlova that she was wrong. I also think that if Elsa had gone to Mme. Pavlova they would have thrown their arms round each other's necks." M. Dandré said that Mme. Pavlova had seen Elsa in the smoking-room in a steamer, with M. Slavinski's arm round her shoulder. Mrs. D'Arcy said: "Well, there is nothing immoral in that." M. Dandré said: "You do that in your parks."

Cross-examined, Mrs. D'Arcy said that she was quite calm during the interview with M. Dandré.

Mr. Hilbery: "Did you not at the very beginning of the interview go for M. Dandré?"

"No. I consider that I was very forbearing."

"M. Dandré was quite courteous?"

"No. He did not even raise his hat when he met me."

"I suggest that, throughout the interview, M. Dandré never had a chance of getting a word in edgeways?"

"That is not true."

"Didn't you say that the whole trouble was because Mme. Pavlova was jealous of your daughter?"

"Oh, no. I would not say anything so foolish. I am one of Mme. Pavlova's greatest admirers."

"I suggest that you have worked yourself up about this interview and think that a great deal took place which did not?"

"I have a very good memory."

In evidence for the defence, M. Dandré stated that on the journey out he noticed M. Slavinski paying attention to Miss D'Arcy, and advised her not to be too friendly with him. "It was a strict thing in our company," added M. Dandré, "that the artists must regard the theatre, the steamship, and the railway station as official places, where their behaviour must be very correct."

Asked about the interview with Mrs. D'Arcy, M. Dandré said that Mrs. D'Arcy began by telling him all her grievances against Mme. Pavlova. "I could not open my mouth," added the witness, amid laughter. Mrs. D'Arcy had accused Mme. Pavlova of being jealous because Miss D'Arcy was young and beautiful and had had a big success. M. Dandré denied that he told Miss D'Arcy that Mme. Pavlova alleged she had seen her behaving in an immoral and indecent manner with M. Slavinski. Mr. Croom-Johnson, cross-examining: "Mme. Pavlova is apt to get a little upset at times?"

"Sometimes."

"If things don't go quite right does she sometimes fly into a temper?"

"Sometimes."

Finally Pavlova went into the box. At first she spoke in Russian, which had to be translated. She explained that for twenty years she had taken companies of artists on tour, and that Miss D'Arcy had been a member of her company for six years.

"Did you ever say to your husband, or to anybody else, that Miss D'Arcy had been guilty of immoral or indecent conduct?"

"Never."

"Did you always regard Miss D'Arcy as a girl of high character?"

"Yes."

"Is this case the first occasion in your life on which you have had any sort of action at law with one of your artists?"

"Yes."

Mr. Hilbery then announced that the matter between the parties had been adjusted. Defendants had carried the matter to that stage because they desired to say in public that they never desired to make any aspersions on Miss D'Arcy's character, and never had done so. Still feeling for Miss D'Arcy the highest regard engendered by six years' association with her, neither M. Dandré nor Mme. Pavlova desired that she should lose one penny in the matter. They had accordingly agreed to pay her costs and £200. It was clear also that there was no reflection on M. Slavinski in the matter.

Mr. Justice Horridge sanctioned the settlement.

Pavlova's initial retreat behind the veil of the Russian language may have been out of a modesty in exposing her idiosyncratic English to public scrutiny, but it appeared guarded. In the event, D'Arcy stood up to a lengthy cross-examination with spirit. By contrast, Dandré contributed to an implication that Pavlova was maintaining an irrational annoyance with the girl, and his denial that Mrs. D'Arcy had made any complaint concerning the alleged accusation of immoral and indecent behavior meant that one of them was telling lies in court. In effect, the case should have been about the breaking of a contract, since Pavlova had denied the girl a chance to perform again and had terminated her contract. But Pavlova countered a plea on those grounds by saying the girl had broken company rules. D'Arcy was then encouraged to press for slander.

By a strange coincidence, on the day that the *D'Arcy* v. *Dandré and Another* case opened, elsewhere in the same building another judge adjourned the further hearing of a summons taken out on behalf of Lord Inverclyde to determine whether the English court had jurisdiction to entertain the petition for the decree of nullity presented by Lady Inverclyde, or whether the jurisdiction rested in the court of the domicile, which was Scotland. Lady Inverclyde was formerly June Tripp, "Little June," the youngest of Pavlova's pupils at Ivy House before the war. June had become a star of the English stage, appearing in musicals under the stage name "June." In the summer of 1929 she had been seated one night at a gambling table in the Monte Carlo Sporting Club. Intent on the play, it was some while before she chanced to glance at the woman seated next to her. It was Pavlova. June froze with the shock of it and played on for several minutes until she had recovered herself. Then she said, "Madame, you don't remember me." Pavlova turned.

"I'm June."

"Juneshka! Little June, my darling!" Pavlova embraced her. "What are you doing?"

June tried to explain that she was in musicals by choice, but Pavlova did not seem to understand.

"*Pauvre petite*. Then you must come with me. Soon again you will dance very well!" Pavlova exclaimed, clasping June's hands assuringly.

THE SURVIVING FILM SEQUENCES OF PAVLOVA'S SOLOS

Victor Dandré's 1932 book has always caused confusion about the exact source of the dance material in the film *Immortal Swan*, assembled in various forms in 1935 and 1936. Possibly because he did not wish to offend Fairbanks, Dandré was at pains to suggest that filming done prior to the experiments at the Fairbanks studios was altogether inferior to

A rare photograph taken with a camera fast enough to show Pavlova's elevation—still exceptional in her forties. For the motion picture cameras she danced on a canvas floorcloth spread on the lawn.

that achieved by Fairbanks's technicians. Dandré carefully avoided mentioning the name of Dr. Lee de Forest, and it could have been some other experiments that Pavlova and Dandré showed to the Fairbanks, resulting in Fairbanks's suggesting that he could achieve something better However, if the Fairbanks studio ran 24-frames-per-second material on their 16-frames-per-second projector, then indeed they may well have thought to better it. It is unlikely that Dandré had studied the technicalities. Dandré's correspondence with Malvina Hoffman in 1936, at the time when he was trying to sell the memorial film about Pavlova, gives us more detail:

What your friends state—that these dances were recorded on the old basis of 16 frames to the second, whereas the present projection forces them to be done at 24 frames a second—is quite correct, but this concerns only the dances which were made in the studio of Mary Pickford; whereas the four dances made in the studio of Dr. Lee de Forest were made at the time to music, and in the exact tempo as Anna danced them. These dances are
Variation of Weber
Night by Rubinstein
Californian Poppy
and Dragonfly

The other dances which were made at Mary Pickford's studio certainly had this inconvenience and they were stretched in the laboratory of the

British International Film Co., which is considered as the best here. The Swan and the Greek Dance succeeded perfectly well, as the original tempo was slow, but the two classical variations of Fairy Doll, and Snowflakes, which Anna danced in a lively tempo, could not be stretched to the point that would have been necessary.

The Pas de Deux from *Giselle*, which was made by ourselves, is very bad as a film, and it should be entirely taken out, and this I already did when I showed the film in Paris. . . . I find that
Nuit de Rubinstein
The Swan
and Rondino in slow motion are remarkably good. . . .
California Poppy
Dragonfly
Greek Dance
are less successful, but all the same, have moments of rare beauty.

The Variations Classiques [*sic;* presumably *Snowflakes,* for which she wore the *Columbine* costume on this occasion] are certainly executed in too quick a tempo, but I must say that in London and Paris these Variations have met with very great success. . . .

Seven months later, Dandré was writing a letter of many typed pages to the lawyer Nathan Goldberger. In among this was a memorandum detailing the content of the memorial film. Dandré described the dance segments as follows:

"Rondo"—from the Grand Sonata Opus 39 (Music by Weber)
"Nuit" (Rubinstein)
"Californian Poppy" (Tchiakovsky)
Entrée and Variation from "Fairy Doll" (Bayer)
Adagio from the Ballet "Don Quixote" (Minkus)—Anna Pavlova, Pierre
    Vladimiroff, Ruth French and the Company
Fragment from Ballet "Dionysus" (Tcherepnine)
"Valse Classique" (Kadletz)
"Dragonfly" (Kreisler)
Excerpt from "Rondino" (Beethoven—Kreisler)
"The Swan" (Saint Saëns)

The mention of the title *Rondo* (as distinct from *Rondino*) suggests the item first seen in a Sunday Concert at the New York Hippodrome—though that program credited Kreisler with the music. There is an anomaly here. Nowhere does Dandré mention *Christmas*. Film footage exists of Pavlova subsiding onto an elegant sofa, discarding an evening cloak, and making rhapsodic gestures toward a rose. It has always been assumed that this constituted part of *Christmas*. Although Pavlova appears to be wearing the costume from *Christmas,* one must consider the possibility that this bit has no connection with the Tchiakovsky ballet, but that it may be a solo from the ballet done to Weber's *Invitation to the Dance* (Rondo brillante in D-flat). The *Rondino* footage has been variously assigned—to Australia, and as late as 1929. The fan that Pavlova carries supposedly dates from the 1926 visit to South Africa. Anyone who has seen the footage—particularly the slow-motion section—would agree that Pavlova's strength (and "finish"—she is, after all, dancing on a lawn) is quite exceptional. For 1929, when she was 48, it would be astonishing. A rare still photograph (illustrated here) does not provide many clues, but the combination of agapanthus and cedars in the background has a look of California, and in the footage itself there is a tiny glimpse of architectural detail in a house that looks to be Hollywood "Spanish." It is interesting to see that two cameramen filmed simultaneously. Pavlova displays unmistakable elevation, despite the difficult surface and a costume that is extraordinarily encumbering by present-day standards. From various evidence, we know that Pavlova made film experiments on the West Coast in 1924 and 1925. The background set for the Fairbanks footage suggests *Don Q. Son of Zorro,* made in 1925. Pickford, posing on the set with Pavlova, wears her costume from *Little Annie Rooney,* also of 1925. So it would seem that the Fairbanks filming (though rather primitive by comparison with Dr. de Forest's developments, registered in 1923) took place in 1925.

Of the Fairbanks material, *The Swan* has been the subject of controversy. At one point, the Estate of Michael Fokine banned its presentation on grounds of copyright infringement. The last few moments of the dance were never filmed. In the most complete version, the film seems to have run out at the crucial moment. I have seen another "take," with Pavlova dancing nearer the camera. At the end, she hurries into an improvised standing pose. It looks as if someone shouted that the film was ending; Pavlova has an amused air of complicity, a sort of "Well there you are—there's a quick ending!" Other correspondence by Dandré gives what he describes as the "exact" time taken by the different items: " 'Rondo,' 3 minutes; 'Nuit,' 3; 'California Poppy,' 4; Entree and Variation from 'Fairy Doll,' 2; Adagio from 'Don Quixote,' 3; 'Greek Dance,' 1; 'Dragonfly,' 3; Rondino,' 3; 'The Swan,' 3."

The only recording of Pavlova's voice accompanies the footage taken with the swans at Ivy House, when Pavlova calls to them, in English, and then laughs—rather despairingly—because they are not being very cooperative. This was taken after the alterations to Ivy House—not earlier than the summer of 1929.

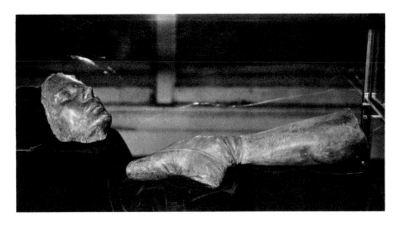

PAVLOVA'S "DEATH MASK"

There is a lack of provenance about existing masks of Pavlova's face, to be seen in various collections. One of them certainly seems to be a straightforward death mask (though the hair has apparently been bladed in at a subsequent stage); it is on the evidence of this mask that I base the mention at the end of my text, but the evidence is not quite conclusive. In 1963 Malvina Hoffman was sent a photograph of a cast purporting to be a death mask of Pavlova. Hoffman's reply reads (in part): "I have shown the picture you loaned me to Pavlova's lawyer here in New York, and he agrees with me that it certainly is not a death mask of Pavlova, and that Mr. Dandré would most certainly have informed both of us if a mask had been made." It goes without saying that once Dandré left The Hague, he would be the last person to be told of any such activity. Hoffman had seen Pavlova in Paris in January 1931, the night before the departure for The Hague, and Dandré telephoned the sculptress a few hours after Pavlova's death, asking her to meet him in London and to be with him at the time of the funeral. This she did. Her diary for these days reveals that she was prey to some unease about events taking place in The Hague: "I pray the half of what I hear is untrue."

The "mask" by Victor Frisch, which has the head turned slightly to one side (and tilted well forward on the original plinth), was exhibited by the American National Sculpture Society in 1929, so it would be tactless to suggest that it is only a cast. Frisch actually signed the bronze version. Nevertheless, his work has curious affinities with the supposed death mask: the cutoff point just behind the hairline matches precisely, and the eyes are completely closed. The neck is included in the Frisch work (though not in the other) and betrays tension—artful or otherwise. I have not been able to ascertain whether Pavlova ever allowed Frisch to take an actual cast; in the light of her hectic schedule she may have agreed to his taking one as the reference for a modeled work. If that were the case, the supposed "death" mask could be his studio original. Unless he traveled to Europe from his home in America, the latest he could have taken such a cast would have been early 1925. Hoffman never took a cast; she worked from life and from studio photographs (see p. 346).

The "death mask" seems as small as a child's face; in fact, there is a discrepancy of one inch between it and a detailed measurement recorded by Hoffman from life. This could be accounted for by shrinkage in the original cast, but the fact is disconcerting. A further mask appeared in a Diaghilev exhibition in Paris; this one differs in detail from those already mentioned. (See photograph.) The accompanying leg cast should not be confused with the Froedman-Cluzel model. It was a difficult business keeping the muscles fully flexed for the duration of the drying time required for plaster, and it is possible that this limb was first modeled and then recast with a real shoe fitted to the model.

SOURCES

Rather than pepper the text with source numerals, I have tried wherever feasible to incorporate the source into the body of the text or into an adjacent footnote. For Pavlova's early career in Russia my principal source was the Tsar's Yearbooks—the Annuals of the Imperial Theatres. I then tried to find corroborative reporting in contemporary newspapers. As well as the full series of Yearbooks, the British Library houses a particularly fine collection of the St. Petersburg paper *Novoye Vremya (New Times)* in its reserve collection at Colindale. Material thus extracted has been augmented with reviews and articles from other newspapers and journals. The New York Public Library has a marvelous collection of microfilm in its Slavonic Section and is particularly useful for Moscow papers prior to 1917. I found *Russkie vedomosti* and *Russkoye slovo* at this source. Concerning the *Petersburgskaya gazeta* (run by the opinionated balletomane Sergei Khudekov), the collection at the Château de Vincennes has suffered from fire and is thus incomplete. Books by Vera Krasovskaya published in Russia offer some quotes from issues of the *Petersburg Gazette* that I have not been able to find. Dr. Krasovskaya also supplies the *Birjevye vedomosti* review of the Trinity Street entertainment of January 18, 1902, which was not referred to by the *New Times*.

Prince Georg Kotschubei's memoir of his early encounters with Pavlova appears verbatim in Walford Hyden's 1931 book *Pavlova: The Genius of Dance*; Hyden's own contribution is more suspect, he being self-serving and careless in his approach. The other musician's look at Pavlova, Theodore Stier's *With Pavlova Round the World* (c.1927), is gentle, if haphazard, though he too causes doubts to be raised on occasions: his telling of the incident concerning Mordkin's sword is quite at odds with the details in the contemporary reports.

Victor Dandré's own book is in a rather special category by itself: essential reading, of course, but often confusingly structured, and at times deliberately misleading. Of other books by associates of Pavlova, I would put by far the greatest reliance on that by Algeranoff, which shows, I think, the rewards of keeping a diary. In relation to his period with the Pavlova Company, 1921 to 1930, he charts the general progress with great accuracy and also a refreshing absence of overcoloring.

For scholars who might conceivably wish to follow the same exhausting trail in order to arrive at their own conclusions, I can do no better than to recommend the bibliography contained in John and Roberta Lazzarini's 1980 book on Pavlova's repertoire, *Pavlova*. It seems to me they cover printed sources quite as well as anyone could. It has been instructive to see how I coincide with the Lazzarinis in the early Russian dates; usually we are not materially at odds over this period. I would beg to disagree on one or two points—as, I am sure, they would wish to disagree with some points herein. (In the Yearbooks I find no entry relating to *Midsummer Night's Dream* at the Maryinsky in 1905. Would Pavlova have played a minor role anywhere else?) I acknowledge the clue to *Giselle* in Warsaw in 1904, and only wish it could have been

more specific. Attributions and dates from, say, 1913 onward tend to be more conflicting. Wherever my own text seems assertive about a premiere, it is because of a printed program that has the year clearly printed, or because of a published review.

For the South American saga, particularly 1917–18, the scrapbooks of the conductor Alexander Smallens proved immensely useful. These are in the Dance Collection of the Lincoln Center Library of the Performing Arts in New York. Scrapbooks, if lovingly compiled, offer all sorts of riches; I found much of interest in the Theatre Collection's Robinson-Locke volumes in New York. Also of great help were the travel diary of Madge Abercrombie and the scrapbooks belonging to Muriel Stuart; her father compiled these from the moment his daughter first showed an interest in dancing.

For the record, the manuscript by Natalia Trouhanova in the Central State Archives of the Soviet Union is called "V strechi s proshlym" ("Meeting the Past"). I think the truth about Diaghilev's dealings with Pavlova is important; apart from instinct, various tenuous clues made me feel that Pavlova's first parting of the ways from Diaghilev was not the capricious whim it has been painted to be. However, it was not until I chanced upon the Pavlova-Dandré letter in papers relating to Daniel Mayer that the truth became clear. (Daniel Mayer's contracts with Anna Pavlova were given by his son Rudolph to the Royal Academy of Dancing.) The Diaghilev-Pavlova contract for 1910 was catalogued in the Lifar Collection in 1956; the Dance Collection in New York has the Brussel draft letter of January 24, 1910; the Stravinsky-Diaghilev Foundation holds the Nouvel cable of July 13, 1921. The Malvina Hoffman Estate owns the Dandré correspondence about cinematography, and the reference to the Poliakoff family (in relation to Anna Pavlova) was first published by Oleg Kerensky in 1973.

The path has been a rocky one, and even thirty-five years ago the signposts were being switched all over the place. (For instance, anything more than a cursory glance at the 1947 Magriel *Pavlova* reveals that scarcely a single picture is without some form of misinformation in the caption.) I hope we are reversing the trend nowadays. Muriel Stuart most gallantly read my final text, and was not appalled. Doubtless I shall read future volumes, by others, with renewed interest and appreciation.

INDEX

PHOTO CREDITS

425

A NOTE ON THE TYPE

The text of this book has been set in Goudy Old Style, one of the more than 100 type faces designed by Frederick William Goudy (1865-1947). Although Goudy began his career as a bookkeeper, he was so inspired by the appearance of several newly published books from the Kelmscott Press that he devoted the remainder of his life to typography in an attempt to bring a better understanding of the movement led by William Morris to the printers of the United States. Produced in 1914, Goudy Old Style reflects the absorbtion of a generation of designers with things "ancient." Its smooth, even color combined with its generous curves and ample cut marks it as one of Goudy's finest achievements.

This book was composed by New England Typographic Service, Inc., Bloomfield, Connecticut. Illustrations were prepared by Color Associates, St. Louis, Missouri. It was printed by Rae Publishing Corp., Cedar Grove, New Jersey, and bound by American Book-Stratford Press, Saddle Brook, New Jersey. The jacket was printed by Rapoport Printing Corp., New York, New York.

Typography and binding design by Dorothy Schmiderer